THE AMERICAN INFLUENCE ON INTERNATIONAL COMMERCIAL ARBITRATION

DOCTRINAL DEVELOPMENTS AND DISCOVERY METHODS

This text traces the contours of U.S. doctrinal developments concerning international commercial arbitration. It explores international commercial arbitration as a bridge that creates symmetry between what the author perceives as an anomaly arising from the disparities between the monolithic framework arising from economic globalization and a fragmented global judicial counterpart. Specifically, American common law discovery precepts are analyzed through the prism of the fundamental precepts of party-autonomy, predictability, uniformity, and transparency of spender, which the author contends to be the rudimentary tenets of both the American common law procedural rubric and the principles that international commercial arbitration seeks not only to preserve but to enhance. Therefore, as the author asserts, the discovery process endemic to American common law comports more closely with international commercial arbitration both procedurally and theoretically than with those of the "taking of evidence" methodology commonly used in international commercial arbitrations held under the auspices of arbitral institutional bodies.

Pedro J. Martinez-Fraga is a Partner and Shareholder with the Law Firm of Squire, Sanders & Dempsey L.L.P., wherein he is the coordinator for the International Dispute Resolution Practice Group for Florida and Latin America. He also serves as an Adjunct Professor of Law at the University of Miami School of Law, where he teaches transnational litigation and arbitration. Mr. Martinez-Fraga is a full Visiting Professor at the University of Navarra School of Law in Pamplona, Spain, and President of the Global Dispute Resolution Center of the Maiestas Foundation, with venues in Pamplona, Spain, and Beijing, China. Mr. Martinez-Fraga has lectured in more than a dozen non-U.S. law schools on private international law and international commercial arbitration. He has authored more than twenty peer-reviewed articles and three books on private international law. He has also served as co-editor of and contributing author to two additional texts in this field. Mr. Martinez-Fraga is on the list of counsel for victims and defendants of the International Criminal Court at the Hague.

He received his J.D. from Columbia University (Harlen Fiske Stone Scholar) and a B.A. from St. John's College, Annapolis (Highest Honors). Mr. Martinez-Fraga has been recognized as one of the "Best Lawyers in America" for commercial litigation in 2005, 2006, 2007, and 2008 and was listed as one of the "Lawdragon 3000 Leading Lawyers in America" in 2006. He has also been listed in the "highly recommended" category for dispute resolution and corporate/M&A by *PLC Which Lawyer?* (13th Edition, published by Lex Mundi) and as one of three leading individuals for dispute resolution by *PLC Which Lawyer?* (12th Edition, published by Lex Mundi). In addition, he was the recipient of the 2005 Most Effective Lawyer Award for International Law from the Daily Business Review and was a finalist for the same award in 2006. Among other distinctions, he is recognized in international directories such as Chambers and Partners. In 2001, he was named the "Lawyer of the Americas" by the University of Miami Inter-American Law Review. He has represented six countries and numerous geo-political subdivisions in international disputes, including as lead counsel in the United States for the Republic of Chile in the case against President Augusto Pinochet.

The American Influence on International Commercial Arbitration

DOCTRINAL DEVELOPMENTS AND DISCOVERY METHODS

Pedro J. Martinez-Fraga

Squire, Sanders & Dempsey, LLP

CAMBRIDGE
UNIVERSITY PRESS

CAMBRIDGE UNIVERSITY PRESS
Cambridge, New York, Melbourne, Madrid, Cape Town, Singapore, São Paulo, Delhi

Cambridge University Press
32 Avenue of the Americas, New York, NY 10013-2473, USA

www.cambridge.org
Information on this title: www.cambridge.org/9780521765886

First published 2009

Printed in the United States of America

A catalog record for this publication is available from the British Library.

Library of Congress Cataloging in Publication data

Martínez-Fraga, Pedro J.
The American influence on international commercial arbitration : doctrinal developments and discovery methods / Pedro J. Martínez-Fraga.
p. cm.
Includes bibliographical references and index.
ISBN 978-0-521-76588-6 (hardback : alk. paper)
1. Arbitration and award, International. 2. Discovery (Law) 3. Arbitration and award – United States. 4. Law – American influences. I. Title
K2400.M37 2009
347′.09–dc22 2009000342

ISBN 978-0-521-76588-6 hardback

To Ana Julieta Martínez-Fraga, who taught the meaning of courage to her siblings – Maria Eugenia and me.

"As GREGOR SAMSA awoke one morning from uneasy dreams he found himself transformed in his bed into a gigantic insect."

The Metamorphosis, Franz Kafka (1915)[1]

[1] "Als Gregor Samsa eines Morgens aus unruhigen Träumen erwachte, fand er sich in seinem Bett zu einem ungeheueren Ungeziefer verwandelt." *Die Verwandlung*, Franz Kafka (1915).

Contents

Table of Citations

CASES

STATUES

OTHER AUTHORITIES

RULES

Acknowledgments

Succinct acknowledgments are compelled. The thoughts and contributions of my students have played a decisive role in the authorship of this text. It is important, however, to add a disclaimer. Whatsoever inconsistencies or ill-witted propositions may be present are all of my doing and have nothing to do with their valuable input. Professor Michael H. Graham, Professor of Law at the University of Miami, was sufficiently gracious and generous to accept my invitation to write a foreword. The foreword, without more, justified the writing of the book. I appreciate his contribution and ubiquitous insight. My father, Pedro J. Martinez-Fraga, whose name I share, offered extremely meaningful and invaluable observations on both form and substance. Professor Dr. Rafael Domingo Oslé, former Dean of the Universidad de Navarra Law School, currently professor of law of the Universidad of Navarra and President of the Maiestas Foundation, was mercifully relentless in his review of the text and critical analysis. C. Ryan Reetz, my friend and law partner of sixteen years, significantly improved the text. John Berger, Senior Editor of Cambridge University Press, was instrumental in the text's improvement. Harout Samra, a promising lawyer and at the time of this publication an excellent law student, worked tirelessly on my less than reasonable research demands. Finally, a rosary of young colleagues at Squire, Sanders & Dempsey, starting with Raúl Mañón, Tania Cruz, Leah Storie, and Carolina Latour, were particularly helpful and unswerving in their work ethic. My secretary Ericka García certainly deserves recognition.

Foreword*

In his exceedingly thoughtful, thorough, and provocative work, Pedro J. Martinez-Fraga has drawn upon his many years as a very successful litigator and academic concentrating in international commercial dispute resolution including, but clearly not limited to, international commercial arbitration. Martinez-Fraga challenges others to see for the first time the contributions that doctrines developed in the United States, principally but not solely pretrial discovery, have had and will continue to have in the worldwide process of creating a comprehensive approach to international commercial arbitration.

The approach taken is historical, descriptive, analytical, critical, optimistic, perceptive, and, most important, realistic.

Martinez-Fraga begins with a comprehensive historical analysis clearly depicting the shift in attitude of the United States from antagonism toward commercial international arbitration to what one might call euphoric adulation. He outlines four specific factors that contributed to this change: (1) the United States Supreme Court's interpretation of "international contracts" as a normative basis for according special deference to international commercial arbitrations; (2) a perceived need for specialization akin to the creation of unique subject matter tribunals; (3) recognition that only international commercial arbitration can serve as the conceptual historical dispute resolution bridge until such time as international commercial tribunals come into existence; and (4) recognition that in an era of extensive economic globalization only international commercial arbitration today provides a methodology for dispute resolution that comports with the parties' expectations concerning the fair administration of justice as well as application of their respective judicial cultures.

Martinez-Fraga opines that it is now accepted in the United States that commercial arbitration is a flexible, reliable, transparent, uniform, and predictable methodology for resolving international disputes. Even more importantly, international commercial arbitration is presented and defended as uniquely capable of doing so while fostering party-autonomy and at the same time preserving the party's cultural and juridic expectations.

* Michael H. Graham, received a B.S.E. from the University of Pennsylvania in 1964 and a J.D. in 1967 from Columbia Law School. Professor Graham has taught evidence, civil procedure, conflict of laws, trial advocacy, and transnational litigation. He has written eleven books and numerous articles in the field of evidence, including a textbook and Nutshell for students.

Martinez-Fraga's unique perspective as an accomplished practitioner and academic fostered the development of this substantial work of compelling arguments establishing the significance of procedural changes in the conduct of international commercial arbitration with respect to the "taking and the gathering of evidence" as the concept is and more critically may be influenced in the future by the employment of American-style discovery devices. In particular, 28 U.S.C. §1782(a) is analyzed and evaluated in great depth. §1782(a) provides that a federal district court may order a resident of that district or person found therein to give testimony or statement or to produce a document or other thing for use in a proceeding in a foreign or international tribunal, which includes international commercial arbitration, upon application of any interested person. Martinez-Fraga establishes that the purpose of Congress in modifying §1782 in 1964 was to facilitate the conduct of litigation in foreign tribunals, improve international cooperation in litigation, and put the United States into *the* leadership position among world nations in this respect. Congress hoped with §1782 to encourage foreign countries to revise their procedures similarly, that is, adopt pretrial discovery of a similar nature to that provided in the Federal Rules of Civil Procedure. It is here with respect to pretrial discovery that Martinez-Fraga stresses the importance of party-autonomy. He states:

> Providing parties with the normative ability to engage in discovery pursuant to known standards and rules that have benefited from exhaustive analysis and a plethora of jurisprudence stands as paradigmatic of the practical application of the principle of party-autonomy.

Insightfully, Martinez-Fraga forcefully, unapologetically, and, I would add, correctly and bravely asserts in the face of a universe of other commentators who stress harmonization even over achieving the best result that

> [T]he perception that discovery and that the Federal Rules of Civil Procedure are doctrinally and conceptually inimical to the tenets defining arbitration and that arbitration seeks to further is simply wrong, or at least, less than clear.

Martinez-Fraga is not content to stop at this junction but instead explores the potential consequences with respect to the recognition and enforceability of arbitration awards from tribunals hostile to §1782 discovery when it comes to recognition and enforcement of international commercial arbitration awards under Article V of the New York Convention.

Finally, this work tackles two important topical issues, that is, perjury in arbitration and the apportionment of jurisdiction between arbitrators and the courts concerning the validity of a contract containing an arbitration clause as well as developments concerning the severability doctrine and the common law doctrine of manifest disregard of the law.

Party-autonomy has over the years become more and more a staple of international commercial arbitration. The common law adversary system rather than the civil law system is slowly but surely becoming the dominant approach employed. Trial type hearings are being held. Attorneys are presenting witnesses before the tribunal. These witnesses are being subjected to cross-examination by opposing counsel. Under such circumstances, Martinez-Fraga's strong support for American-style pretrial discovery in aid of the arbitration process is reasonable. His arguments in support of pretrial discovery are powerful and persuasive. The obstacle to enhanced acceptance of pretrial §1782 type discovery is not utilitarian but perspective. Discovery is a uniquely American, not a common law invention. As such, it faces resistance from others neither familiar with its workings and merits nor particularly prone to seeing something so powerful and uniquely American universally incorporated into what is of course *international* commercial arbitration, not *American* commercial arbitration. As more and more foreign attorneys and arbitrators become familiar with American-style discovery, as has already happened with the common law–style adversary system stressing party-autonomy, greater acceptance and utilization of pretrial discovery in international commercial arbitration for the good will most likely follow. At such time, Pedro J. Martinez-Fraga could say, but won't: "Told you so!!!"

Prof. Michael H. Graham
Professor of Law,
University of Miami Law School

Preface

Two separate and distinct phrases, each ascribed to a particular jurist, merit mention in a single sentence: *The law is a jealous mistress and a seamless web*. At first glance each clause on either side of the conjunctive appears unrelated to the other but for the common reference to "law." Their intimate connection, however, cannot be obviated. Because the law in its application and theoretical development (jurisprudence) purports to address some of the most delicate and difficult issues that pervade all societies, ranging from the imposition of a death penalty through the legal status of abortion, to equally important concerns in the realms of family law, international disputes, free speech, freedom of assembly, the separation of church and state, and the propriety of juridic entities and attendant liabilities of virtually every ilk (to name just a few), the law cannot help but be all-consuming and seductive because of the very nature of her transcendence subject matter. Similarly, it would be a misapprehension of the organizing principles that fashion legal subject matter to conclude that most of these issues indeed have "answers" that are certain, definitive, pristine, and universal: far from it. Hence, the "seamless web" envelops and enraptures both the practitioner and the theoretician. Like an encounter with infinity, the law has neither a beginning nor an end. It neither progresses nor degenerates but rather changes at times in fascinating ways that appear to defy man's wit. It is precisely the seductive charms of this change that best define the nature of this book.

This text does not purport to memorialize the history of arbitration. Instead, borrowing from Hegel's famous text – *The Philosophy of History* – it is really a kind of "arbitration of history" as it aspires, perhaps wrongfully and rife with flaws, to identify with precision the very essence of the different stages of *stare decisis* in the area of U.S. doctrinal developments in international commercial arbitration. At times these developments appear minute, virtually nonexistent as the imperfections of language, made even worse by flaws in reasoning and the visceral application of doctrine (often dogmatically), without engaging in the introspection and reflection that the subject matter addressed very much deserves and compels. Thus, this modest effort seeks to underscore the 180 degrees that underlie doctrinal developments that are diametrically opposite, one degree at a time. Only thus is it possible to witness the brilliance and majesty of the common law in its developmental splendor, and in so witnessing it perhaps even intuit how best to improve on what has been learned, in order to, one day, maybe, with fear and trembling, aspire to the law's perfect workings in the field of international commercial arbitration.

CHAPTER I

Introduction

In the *Museo del Prado* there hangs a masterful work by Francisco De Goya entitled "Duelo a Garrotazos," meaning "Duel with Clubs." This canvas is arresting and foreboding. Set in the context of a stark sunset, two men face one another, both buried knee high so as to preclude any hope of escape, armed with clubs that are being swung in each other's direction. Their inability to dodge blows or otherwise flee from the deadly contest is underscored by the sense of rigidity arising from being "planted." The menacing intuition in the spectator of lethal harm is eloquently spawned by the outstretched clubs that inevitably find their immovable, fixed targets. Pursuant to this methodology, the underlying dispute shall somehow be settled and the particular conflict resolved by agreement of the parties, without state intervention or furtherance of national social policies incident to otherwise dispositive judicial recourse.[1]

Domestic and international institutional arbitration in the United States, much like Goya's "alternative dispute resolution" depicted in "Duel with Clubs," was perceived by commentators, the judiciary, practitioners, and captains of industry as a blunt and imprecise methodology for dispute resolution.[2] In addition to finding

1 Francisco de Goya, *Duelo a Garrotazos*, circa. 1820–1823, mural transposed to linen, 123 × 266 cm.: donation of Emile d' Erlanger.

2 *See, e.g.*, Wilko v. Swan, et al., 346 U.S. 427 (1953) ("[I]t has enacted the Securities Act to protect the rights of investors and has forbidden a waiver of any of those rights. Recognizing the advantages that prior agreements for arbitration may provide for the solution of commercial controversies, we decide that the intention of Congress concerning the sale of securities is better carried out by holding invalid such an agreement for arbitration of issues arising under the Act."); American Safety Equipment Corp. v. J.P. Maguire & Co., Inc., 391 F.2d 821 (2d Cir. 1968) ("in some situations Congress has allowed parties to obtain the advantages of arbitration if they 'are willing to accept less certainty of legally correct adjustment' but we do not think that this is one of them. In short we conclude that antitrust claims raised here are inappropriate for arbitration."); Bernhardt v. Polygraphic Company of America, Inc., 350 U.S. 198, 203 (1956) ("for the remedy by arbitration, whatever its merits or shortcomings, substantially effects the cause of action created by the State.The nature of the tribunal where suits are tried is an important part of the parcel of rights behind a cause of action. The change from a court of law to an arbitration panel may make a radical difference in ultimate result. Arbitration carries no right to trial by jury that is guaranteed both by the Seventh Amendment and by Ch. 1, Art. 12, of the Vermont Constitution. Arbitrators do not have the benefit of judicial instruction on the law; they need not give their reasons for the results; the record of their proceedings is not as complete as it is a court trial; and judicial review of an award is more limited than judicial review of a trial."); Barrentine, et al. v. Arkansas-Best Freight System, Inc., et al., 450 U.S. 728, 744 (1981) ("because the arbitrator is required to effectuate the intent of the parties, rather than to enforce the statute, he may issue a ruling that is

arbitral proceedings bereft of the expertise and procedural safeguards endemic to judicial processes, arbitrators also were viewed as wanting in authority to award liquidated damages, costs, punitive damages, or attorneys' fees under most statutorily crafted causes of action, if not pursuant to all claims irrespective of normative foundation.[3] In the United States, however, the pendulum now has swung to maximum apogee in the opposite direction.

Four specific factors have contributed to the recognition of arbitration *in pari materia* with judicial proceedings. First, the U.S. Supreme Court has interpreted the "international contract" as a normative basis for according special deference to arbitral proceedings in an international context.[4]

Second, in poignant contrast to the orthodox view of arbitration as a blunt and imprecise instrument inimical to the equitable administration of justice in specific complex judicial disciplines, a perceived need for specialization akin to the creation of unique subject matter tribunals has spawned a plethora of uniquely tailored institutional arbitral proceedings in domestic arbitration.[5]

Third, the beginning of the new millennium highlights and emphasizes a unique phenomenon in the history of private procedural international law. The absence of civil and commercial transnational courts is glaring.[6] Parties engaged in transnational commerce may (i) submit to the jurisdiction of foreign courts, (ii) refrain

inimical to the public policies underlying the FLSA [Fair Labor Standard Act], thus depriving an employee of protected statutory rights."); McDonald v. City of West Branch, Michigan, et al., 466 U.S. 284, 291–292 (1984) ("finally, arbitral fact finding is generally not equivalent to judicial fact finding. As we explained in *Gardner-Denver*, '[t]he record of the arbitration proceedings is not as complete; the usual rules of evidence do not apply; and rights and procedures common to civil trials, such as discovery, compulsory process, cross-examination, and testimony under oath are often severely limited or unavailable [citing to 415 U.S., at 57–58]. It is apparent, therefore, that in a §1983 action, an arbitration proceeding cannot provide an adequate substitute for a judicial trial. Consequently, accordingly preclusive effect to arbitration awards in §1983 actions with severely undermined protection of federal rights that the statute is designed to provide."); *and* Alexander v. Gardner-Denver Co., 415 U.S. 36, 56–57 (1974) ("arbitral procedures, while well suited to the resolution of contractual disputes, make arbitration a comparatively inappropriate form for the final resolution of rights created by Title VII.").

3 *See, e.g.*, Steelworkers v. Enterprise Wheel and Car Corp., 363 U.S. 593, 597 (1960).

4 M/S Bremen v. Zapata Off-Shore Co., 407 U.S. 1 (1972).

5 By way of example, the American Arbitration Association has propounded no less than twelve sets of arbitration rules each specialized in a particular industry: (i) Professional Accounting and Related Services Dispute Resolution Rules, (ii) Construction Industry Arbitration Rules and Mediation Procedures (Including Procedures for Large, Complex Construction Disputes), (iii) Home Construction Arbitration Rules and Mediation Procedures, (iv) Employment Arbitration Rules and Mediation Procedures, (v) Employee Benefit Plan Claims Arbitration Rules, (vi) Resolution of Intra-Industry U.S. Reinsurance and Insurance Disputes Supplementary Procedures, (vii) Resolution of Patent Disputes Supplementary Rules, (viii) AAA Arbitration Supplementary Procedures, (ix) AAA Domain Name Dispute Supplementary Rules; these rules are a supplement to the Rules for Uniform Domain Name Dispute Resolution Policy (The rules) adopted by the United States Department of Commerce, (x) The AAA of Olympic Sport Doping Disputes Supplementary, (xi) Real Estate Industry Arbitration Rules, (xii) Securities Arbitration Supplementary Procedures, (xiii) Wills and Trusts Arbitration Rules, and (xiv) Wireless Industry Arbitration Rules of the American Arbitration Association.

6 Indeed, the American Law Institute has undertaken laudable efforts in the daunting task of developing transnational rules of civil procedure. The consultative group charged with this effort has generated very serious, coherent, and virtually viable work product. Despite these gains, however, the requisite "hybrid" and "cross fertilization" of multiple legal cultures across the entire globe remains both strategically and tactically quite distant.

from engaging in cross-border commercial activities, or (iii) avail themselves of arbitration as a preferred methodology for international dispute resolution. From a pragmatic standpoint, the first two options are unavailing. Only international arbitration may serve as the conceptual historical dispute resolution bridge until international civil and commercial tribunals come into being to administer justice equitably in transnational disputes of this ilk.

Finally, the fourth and most recent historic revolution of international transcendence is economic globalization.[7] Porous borders in the ambit of international commerce find no historical economic precedent. The international community now experiences the virtually instantaneous flow of funds as part of the ordinary course of business attendant to transnational commercial activity. The complexities incident to multiple jurisdictions, different judicial and cultural backgrounds among business persons, increasingly intricate corporate and juridic entities serving diverse functions under the banner of "expediency and economic efficacy" all militate in favor of a methodology for dispute resolution that comports with the parties' expectations concerning the fair administration of justice as well as the application of respective judicial cultures. Only arbitration is capable of satisfying both prongs.

Arbitration in the United States has experienced vertical and horizontal proliferation. The verticality resides in a unique and rather inordinate degree of specialization generated by the rigors of particular industry and professional exigencies. The horizontality has been galvanized by the practically universal acceptance in the United States of arbitration as a flexible, reliable, and predictable methodology for domestic and international dispute resolution that fosters party-autonomy, uniformity, transparency of standard, and predictability, while preserving the parties' cultural and juridic expectations. The recognition of arbitration *in pari materia* with ordinary contracts, let alone judicial proceedings, however, was a gradual and somewhat painstaking process. To be sure, it is yet to find its perfect paradigm.

This analysis thus shall be divided into nine specific sections. The first part focuses on the formation and transformation of the status of arbitration (both domestic and international) in the United States. Here, emphasis shall be placed on what will be identified as the "historically conventional view of arbitration in the United States." The second section shall consist of an exegesis of shifting paradigms bottomed on sustained analysis of the United States Supreme Court's strictures in *Wilko v. Swan*,[8] *Scherk v. Alberto-Culver*,[9] and *Mitsubishi Motors Corporation v. Soler Chrysler-Plymouth, Inc.*[10] The third section shall address significant

[7] For purposes of this analysis five "revolutions" are material. (i) the Copernican Revolution, (ii) the Agrarian Revolution, (iii) the Industrial Revolution, (iv) the Technological Information Technology Revolution, and (v) Economic Globalization.

[8] Wilko v. Swan, 346 U.S. 427 (1953), *overruled by* Rodriguez de Quijas v. Shearson/American Express, Inc., 490 U.S. 477 (1989) ("We now conclude that *Wilko* was incorrectly decided and is inconsistent with the prevailing uniform construction of other federal statutes governing arbitration agreements in the deciding of business transactions. Although we are normally and properly reluctant to overturn our decisions construing statutes, we have done so to achieve a uniform interpretation of similar statutory language and to correct a seriously erroneously interpretation of statutory language that would undermine congressional policy as expressed in other legislation [citation omitted]. Both purposes would be served here by overruling the *Wilko* decision.")

[9] Scherk v. Alberto-Culver, 417 U.S. 506 (1974).

[10] Mitsubishi Motors Corporation v. Soler Chrysler-Plymouth, Inc., 473 U.S. 614 (1985).

and novel procedural changes in the conduct of arbitral proceedings. Specifically, "the taking or gathering of evidence" shall be compared and contrasted with "common law discovery." Emphasis will be placed on the construction of a new paradigm asserting that when submitted to reasoned examination, the taking or the gathering of evidence is replete with unresolved doctrinal concerns not present in common law discovery in the context of international commercial arbitration. In fact, it will be contended that American common law discovery is configured and organized *by the very fundamental tenets* that international commercial arbitration seeks to preserve and promote.

Indeed, it will be advanced that arbitral procedural law in the context of "taking of evidence" has undergone a revolutionary transformation such that it shall require continental law practitioners to master fundamental precepts of U.S. common law discovery. The "revolutionary trilogy" beginning with the U.S. Supreme Court's directive in *Intel Corporation v. Advanced Micro Devices, Inc.*,[11] *In Re: Application of Roz Trading Ltd.*,[12] and *In Re: Patricio Clerici*,[13] will be identified in support of this novel proposition.

The fourth part of the book will focus on the role of party-autonomy in the gathering of evidence and taking of discovery in international commercial arbitration. The fifth section consists of an "unorthodox" analysis of the International Bar Association ("IBA") Rules on the Taking of Evidence in International Arbitration, the Rules of Arbitration of the International Chamber of Commerce, the Rules of the International Center for Dispute Resolution, and the Rules of the London Court of International Arbitration. This section culminates with a synthesis of international arbitration rules analyzed through the prism of party-autonomy and some of the more salient features comprising the very fabric of common law. The sixth section primarily focuses on the need for doctrinal consistency and development in the formation and application of the common law doctrine of Manifest Disregard of the Law. The seventh part explores the issue of "perjury in arbitration" and grounds for vacatur. The eighth section examines developments in the apportionment of jurisdiction between arbitrators and courts concerning the validity of a contract containing an arbitration clause as well as developments addressing the Severability Doctrine.

The ninth and final section analyzes U.S. arbitration doctrinal developments and their dialogue with the New York Convention. Four discrete issues are studied: (i) the relationship between non-signatories to arbitration agreements and their obligation to arbitrate, (ii) jurisdiction over an arbitral award debtor as a predicate to enforcement, (iii) the interjection of *forum non conveniens* in arbitral enforcement proceedings, and (iv) the tensions between rendering states and secondary enforcing states with respect to annulled international arbitration awards.

These topics were selected because of their practical importance as well as their rather extraordinary features endemic to their respective common law development. Each topic shares the need to fashion doctrinal paradigms of development that promote the fundamental principles of uniformity, predictive value, party-autonomy,

11 Intel Corporation v. Advanced Micro Devices, Inc., 542 U.S. 241 (2004).

12 In Re Application of Roz Trading Ltd., 469 F.Supp. 2d 1221 (N.D. Ga. 2006).

13 In re Clerici, 481 F.3d 1324 (11th Cir. 2007).

certainty, and transparency of standard. Each topic, it is here asserted, constitutes a part of a more comprehensive whole such that a single part cannot be modified without altering the entire construct. Scholars, judges, arbitrators, and captains of industry cannot help but detect a uniquely, or almost uniquely, American influence that doctrinal development in these discrete areas has exercised on international commercial arbitration. It is further advanced that as the anomaly between economic globalization and a fragmented global juridic framework becomes more salient, the influence of these doctrinal developments will grow to become evident and necessary.

CHAPTER 2

The Formation and Transformation of the Status of International and Domestic Arbitration in the United States

A. THE HISTORICALLY CONVENTIONAL VIEW OF ARBITRATION IN THE UNITED STATES

It is impossible to sever the U.S. judiciary's early bias against arbitration from the disdain of arbitral proceedings that pervaded English courts. A brief historical schematic is presented here.

After the 1687 enactment of the Statute of Fines and Penalties,[1] arbitration agreements were stripped of all juridic efficacy for many reasons. The primary reasons, however, were that they were not enforceable in equity, could not give rise to a cognizable cause of action, and did not constitute a viable ground for issuing a stay of a judicial proceeding based on the identical underlying cause of action between the same parties.[2] Significantly, the Act of 1854[3] vested courts with the discretion to stay a legal proceeding in deference to arbitration agreements, and such stays would be irrevocable but for leave of court. In this same vein, the Arbitration Act of 1889[4] rendered arbitration agreements irrevocable absent a court order to the contrary. Additionally, this Act provided that an arbitration agreement was endowed with the same effect as if issued by court order and bestowed courts with authority to review legal questions raised during the final arbitration hearing.[5] Notwithstanding these enactments, in the middle of the eighteenth century arbitration agreements were deemed to be against public policy for two rudimentary reasons. First, arbitration

1 Statute of Fines and Penalties, 1687, 8 and 9 Will. III c. 11, § 8 (Eng.).

2 The Statute of Fines basically provided that any action on a bond issued for purposes of guaranteeing performance of an agreement, would be limited only to the actual damages that the claimant sustained. *See e.g.* 9 C.J. 128, 129; 11 C.J.S. *Bonds* §120; William Holdsworth, 12 History of English Law 519–520 (1938). Accordingly, this legislation in effect eviscerated Coke's landmark case styled *Vynoir's Case*, 8 Coke Rep. 81B, holding that the penal bond posted to ensure enforcement of an arbitration agreement would give rise to a judgment for damages in the bond's amount, i.e. the quantum of the actual penalty. Even though in 1698 parliament enacted a statute, 9 Will. III c.15 (Eng.), that sought to remedy this problem by providing that arbitration agreement could be reduced to a court order and, therefore, a breach would be susceptible to punishment for contempt of court, the statute proved to be of little moment. Courts narrowly construed it and strictly limited its scope.

3 Act of 1854, 17 and 19 Vict. c. 125 (Eng.).

4 Arbitration Act of 1889, 52 and 53 Vict. c. 49 (Eng.).

5 *See* Paul Sayre, *Development of Commercial Arbitration Law*, 37 Yale L.J. 595, 606–7 (1928); Zechariah Chaffee, Jr. & Sidney Post Simpson, Cases and Materials on Equity (1934).

agreements were perceived as private contracts that "oust the jurisdiction" of otherwise courts of competent jurisdiction.[6]

Second, the majority view contended that, if left unsupervised by courts, arbitrations would not be welcome, and for this reason legislation providing for judicial supervision of arbitral proceedings was necessary. Remarkably, both arguments are belied by acts of the English Judiciary and Parliament. For example, it is somewhat anomalous to contend that arbitration agreements violate public policy because they "oust the jurisdiction" of courts and yet enforce arbitration awards both at law and equity. Equally asymmetrical and inconsistent is the strict enforcement of releases and covenants not to sue, both of which also arguably divest courts of otherwise competent jurisdiction. As to the perceived need to supervise judicial arbitrators, instead of devising methodologies to protect parties to arbitration agreements, the English courts consistently restricted the construction placed on numerous statutes intended to render arbitration agreements viable and legally binding.[7]

The English aversion to arbitration was largely reflected by the proclivity of U.S. courts in the nineteenth century against arbitral proceedings. In fact, the United States Supreme Court in *Hamilton v. Liverpool*[8] asserted three rudimentary precepts adverse to arbitration agreements. First, the argument said, an arbitration agreement does not constitute a sufficient basis on which to premise a stay of a judicial proceeding bottomed on the *same* causes of action arising out of or pertaining to the agreement itself. Second, specific performance is not a category of damages that can be awarded based upon an arbitration agreement, without more. Third, such an agreement would not be accorded effect as a plea at bar, "except in limited instances, i.e. in the case of an agreement expressly or impliedly making it a condition precedent to litigation that an award issue determining some preliminary questions of fact upon which any liability would be contingent."[9]

Though in the early twentieth century the Supreme Court in *dicta* fleetingly alluded to a possible new horizon that would construe arbitration agreements in a more favorable light with greater affinity toward judicial proceedings, the issue was not ripe in those few extraordinary proceedings.[10] The Supreme Court, however, in *Marine Transit Corp. v. Dreyfus*,[11] observed that, at least theoretically, the Federal Arbitration Act (the "Act") was crafted with the intent to substantially

[6] This phrase was turned into a term of art in the case of *Kill v. Hollister*, 1 Wils. 129 (1746). It has found some foundation because jurists sought analytical support for it by referring to *Coke on Littleton*, 53 v; "if a man make a lease for life, and by deed grant that if any waste or destruction be done, that it shall be redressed by neighbors, and not by sought or plea," nevertheless an "action of waste shall lye, for the place wasted cannot be recovered without a plea." See Creswell & Campbell, *Critical Comments*, *in* Scott *v. Avery*, 5 H.C.L. 811, 837, 853 (1855).

[7] *See* Chaffee & Simpson, *supra* note 18, at n.520; Tobey v. County of Bristol, 23 F. Cas. 1313 (C.C.D. Mass. 1845) (No. 14,065) (Story, J.); 2 J. Story, Equity Jurisprudence § 670.

[8] Hamilton v. Liverpool, London & Globe Ins. Co., 136 U.S. 242 (1890).

[9] *Id.*

[10] *See, e.g.*, The Atlanten, 252 U.S. 313, 315 (1920); Red Cross Line v. Atlantic Fruit Co., 264 U.S. 109, 123–4 (1924).

[11] Marine Transit Corp. v. Dreyfus, 284 U.S. 263 (1932).

and meaningfully alter the prevailing judicial penchant against arbitration.[12] Even though some of the 1925 language in the Congressional Archives is more than a shade anachronistic, it is emblematic because it constitutes the first formal and most forceful congressional pronouncement evincing that Congress rejected the judicial branch's derision of arbitration. Also, the Act marked a trend encouraging institutional arbitration. By way of example, the Federal Prison Industries Act of 1930 included an arbitration provision.[13] Another example is The Norris-La Guardia Act, which proscribed petitions for injunctive relief where a party had failed to meet the predicate of undertaking "a reasonable effort" to settle a labor dispute pursuant to arbitration.[14] Likewise, elaborate provisions providing for arbitration form part of the Railway Labor Act of 1926.[15]

B. HOMEGROWN SKEPTICISM OF ARBITRAL PROCEEDINGS

Engrafting upon a rich English common law tradition the fundamental premises accounting for the derisive attitude of U.S. courts towards arbitration would fall short of a complete and intellectually honest account. Indeed, the proposition that (i) arbitration agreements violate public policy because they divest courts of their otherwise competent jurisdiction, and (ii) arbitrators cannot be trusted to administer justice equitably absent a judicial tribunal do find their genesis in the English history of juridic development of arbitral proceedings.[16] The most pernicious tenets

[12] *See* H.R. Rep. No. 96 (1924):

> Arbitration agreements are purely matters of contract, and the effect of the bill is simply to make the contracting party live up to his agreement. He can no longer refuse to perform his contract when it becomes disadvantageous to him. An arbitration agreement is placed upon the same footing as other contracts, where it belongs.... the need for the law arises from the anachronism of our American law. Some centuries ago, because of the jealousy of the English courts for their own jurisdiction, they refused to enforce specific agreements to arbitrate upon the ground that the courts were thereby ousted from their jurisdiction. This jealousy survived for so long a period that the principle became firmly embedded in the English common law and was adopted with it by the American courts. The courts have felt that the precedent was too strongly fixed to be overturned without legislative enactment, although they have frequently criticized the rule and recognized its illogical nature and the injustice which results from it. The bill declares simply that such agreements for arbitration shall be enforced, and provides a procedure in the Federal courts for their enforcement.... it is particularly appropriate that the action should be taken at this time where there is so much agitation against the costliness and delays of litigation. These matters can be largely eliminated by agreements for arbitration, if arbitration agreements are made valid and enforceable.

[13] 18 U.S.C. § 744(g) (1930).

[14] 29 U.S.C. § 108 (1932).

[15] 45 U.S.C. § 157–159 (1926).

[16] The early history of English jurisprudence with respect to the recognition and enforcement of arbitration agreements remain mysterious and somewhat opaque. While it is somewhat established that medieval guilds and some very early maritime transactions availed themselves of arbitration as a dispute resolution methodology choice, substantial scholarship is now of a single voice in contending that its roots are formally embedded in Greek law. *See, e.g.*, Pedro J. Martinez-Fraga, The New Role of Comity in Private Procedural International Law 120 n.160 (2007), *citing to* Sheila Ager, Interstate Arbitration in Greece (1996); Thucydides, History of the Peloponnesian War, Chapter XXVIII, Lines 2 to 3; Sturges & Murphy, *Some Confusing Matters Relating To Arbitration Under the United States Arbitration Act*, 17 Law and Contemp. Probs. 580 (1952). *See also* Paul Sayre, *Development of Commercial Arbitration Law*, 37 Yale L.J. 595, 597 (1927); Jones, *Development of Commercial Arbitration*, 21 Minn. L. Rev. 240, 243–244 (1927); Baum & Pressman, *The Enforcement of Commercial Arbitration*, 8 N.Y.U. L. Rev. 238, 239–249 (1930); *and* Bucklan, Textbook of Roman Law 527–528 (1921); Radin, Handbook of Roman Law 308 (1927).

of U.S. jurisprudence against arbitration, however, were cultivated in the petri dish of national legal culture and not imported from the other side of the Atlantic. These two propositions dominated judicial thinking and lawmaking (common law) until 1985. First, it was asserted that arbitration was confected to resolve simple contractual disputes between parties and not for the adjudication of complex commercial domestic or international disputes. Second, the majority view held that statutory causes of action aimed at providing a specific protected class of consumers or prospective plaintiffs with a remedy such that, unlike other claims resting upon legislatively created rights, prospective plaintiffs would serve as "private attorney-general[s] who protect the public interest."[17]

The Second Circuit Court of Appeals' analysis and holding in the seminal case *American Safety Equipment Corp. v. JT Maguire & Co., Inc*, is a paradigm illustrating these two propositions.[18]

Despite the procedural morass underlying *American Safety Equipment*, the facts are simple and didactically helpful. The licensee plaintiff, American Safety Equipment Corp. ("ASE"), filed an action in federal district court against defendant Hickok Manufacturing Co., Inc. ("Hickok") seeking declaratory relief and asserting that the license agreement entered into between the parties "was illegal and void *ab initio* and that no royalty obligations had or would accrue under it."[19] In addition, the complaint averred that the operative agreements "violated the Sherman Act because they unlawfully extended Hickok's trademark monopoly and unreasonably restricted ASE's business."[20]

Significantly, the license agreement upon which the complaint, in part, was premised[21] contained an arbitration clause.[22] Invoking this clause twelve days after the filing of the main action, defendant's assignee J.P. Maguire & Company, Inc. ("Maguire") invoked the arbitration clause seeking to arbitrate a claim for approximately $321,000 of purported royalties allegedly due under the license agreement. At that juncture, however, ASE filed a second declaratory judgment action, this time directed at Maguire, incorporating the identical claims averred against the defendant and adding a count seeking to enjoin Maguire's request for arbitration.[23] Maguire responded by petitioning the court for a stay of the declaratory judgment proceeding pursuant to the Federal Arbitration Act, 9 U.S.C. §§2–4, 6, pending complete adjudication of all arbitral issues. An identical stay was also filed as to

[17] *See, e.g.*, Waldron v. Cities Service Co., 351 F.2d 671, 673 (2d Cir. 1966). The rationale underlying this proposition is that specific statutes are tailor made to serve both private and public interests and, therefore, provide private rights for the general public that may be susceptible to certain earmarked statutory torts that transcend damages to just a single individual.

[18] *American Safety Equipment*, 391 F.2d at 821.

[19] *Id.* at 823.

[20] *Id.*

[21] *American Safety Equipment* also predicated claims on a Manufacturing Agreement entered into between the parties, which had extended their business relationship for seven years, from 1959 until 1966. *Id.* at 823.

[22] The arbitration clause in pertinent part reads:

> All controversies, disputes and claims of whatsoever nature and description arising out of, or relating to, this Agreement and the performance or breach thereof, shall be settled by arbitration. *Id.* at 823.

[23] The complaint averred that: (i) the License Agreement was illegal because of the purported antitrust violations, (ii) the district court had exclusive jurisdiction to adjudicate the alleged illegality, and (iii) Maguire's request for arbitration was not viable if premised on the License Agreement because defendant's (Hickok) assignment was invalid. *Id.* at 823.

ASE's initial underlying cause against the defendant.[24] Upon formally abandoning all rights to enforce the challenged provisions of the license agreement, the defendant demanded that plaintiff arbitrate all issues pertaining to the license agreement and also moved to stay the plaintiff's declaratory relief proceeding pending the end of all arbitral labor in that arbitration. Not to be outdone, the plaintiff filed an additional motion seeking preliminary injunctive relief against this second arbitral demand as well.[25]

The district court held that the arbitration clause was broad enough to encompass all claims. It also found and ruled that arbitration of the antitrust causes of action did not violate public policy. Thus, "the judge stayed [plaintiff's] two declaratory judgment actions pending arbitration, and directed arbitration with respect to 'all claims, disputes and controversies between the parties relating to the License Agreement, including the issue as to the validity thereof.'"[26] On appeal the Second Circuit succinctly enunciated the issue before it as "whether the district court erred in staying ASE's actions and ordering arbitration of ASE's antitrust allegations."[27] The circuit court further crystallized the issue, adding a foreboding single-sentence observation after the query: "[t]he question before us is whether the statutory right ASE seeks to enforce is of a character inappropriate for enforcement by arbitration. This is a difficult issue, not often litigated."[28]

In reversing the district court's ruling and holding "that the antitrust claims raised here are inappropriate for arbitration," the Circuit Court rested its analysis on four fundamental observations.

First, it underscored that there was substantial and meaningful authority for the proposition that arbitration should not be stayed in deference to a judicial proceeding.[29] Second, the Second Circuit Court of Appeals highlighted that contrary to this plethora of authority, the case before it was distinguishable in fundamental ways. By way of example, the case at bar raised the issue of whether a claim predicated on a contract is void and, therefore, legally unsustainable because of a federal statute. Consequently, the case brought into high relief "the conflict between federal statutory protection of a large segment of the public, frequently in an inferior

[24] *Id.*

[25] *Id.*

[26] *Id.* at 823–824.

[27] *Id.* at 824.

[28] *Id.* Here the Second Circuit quoted the then seminal case *Wilko, supra* note 2. The *Wilko v. Swan* decision, which reached the Supreme Court from the Second Circuit (Wilko v. Swan, 201 F.2d 439 (2d Cir. 1953)), shall be analyzed in the next section of this analysis.

[29] Specifically, the Court underscored five cases: Fallick v. Kehr, 369 F.2d 899 (2d Cir. 1966) (holding that discharge and bankruptcy did not stay claims asserting misappropriation of partnership funds then invoked arbitration); Greenstein v. National Skirt and Sportswear Ass'n., 178 F.Supp. 681 (S.D.N.Y. 1959), appeal dismissed, 274 F.2d 430 (2d Cir. 1960) (holding that stay of arbitration proceeding pursuant to a collective bargaining agreement even where plaintiff averred that the agreement violated the Sherman Act); United States for Use and Benefit of Capolino Sons, Inc. v. Electronic and Missile Facilities, Inc., 364 F.2d 705 (2d Cir. 1966), dismissed under Rule 60, 385 U.S. 924 (1966) (holding that arbitration was appropriate in contention concerning Miller Act claim); Evans v. Hudson Cole Co., 165 F.2d 970 (3rd Cir. 1948) (approving arbitration of a claim predicated on the Fair Labor Standards Act); *and* Prima Paint Corp. v. Flood & Conklin Manufacturing Co., 388 U.S. 395 (1967) (holding that despite averment that contract and painting arbitration clause was void *ab initio* based upon allegation of fraud in the inducement, the gravamen issue of whether the contact actually was the product of fraudulent inducement was within the ambit of an arbitration proceeding).

bargaining position, and encouragement of arbitration as a 'prompt, economical and adequately solution of controversies.'"[30]

Third, the stale and homegrown prejudice concerning arbitrability of specific statutory rights was raised as a salient analytical principle. "A claim under the antitrust laws is not merely a private matter. The Sherman Act is designed to promote the national interest in a competitive economy; thus, the plaintiff asserting his rights under the Act has been likened to a private Attorney General who protects the public's interest . . . We do not believe that Congress intended such claims to be resolved elsewhere than in the courts. We do not suggest that all antitrust litigations attain these swollen proportions; the courts, no less than the public, are thankful that they do not. But in fashioning a rule to govern the arbitrability of antitrust claims, we must consider the rule's potential effect."[31] Although related to the second point, this third tenet draws a finer distinction, perhaps suggesting that in crafting an appropriate rule in the context of antitrust statutory rubric, a distinction should be observed where the legislation at issue is less likely to affect the national economy or a lesser number of prospective claimants.[32]

The fourth and final pillar of the court's reasoning reposes on the twin national principles that diminish arbitration as a viable alternative dispute resolution methodology when compared to judicial recourse; namely, that arbitration is best tailored for simple contractual disputes entailing *de minimus* complexities and little, if any, public policies. There is no substitute for the opinion's own language:

> On the other hand, the claim here is that the agreement itself was an instrument of illegality; in addition, the issues in antitrust cases are *prone to be complicated*, and the evidence extensive and diverse, far better suited to judicial than to arbitration procedures. Moreover, it is the business community generally that is regulated by the antitrust clause. Since commercial arbitrators are frequently men drawn for their business expertise, it hardly seems proper for them to determine these issues of great public interest. As Judge Clark said concerning the analogous situation in *Wilko v. Swan*, 201 F.2d at 445 (dissenting opinion):
>
> Adjudicating by such arbitrators may, indeed, provide a business solution to the problem if that is the real desire; but it is surely not a way of assuring the customer that objective and sympathetic consideration of his claim, which is envisaged by the Securities Act.[33]

The Second Circuit's virtually mechanical recitation, and even more egregious, its reflexive application of the twin propositions on which the judiciary generally

[30] *American Safety Equipment*, 391 F.2d at 826 (citing *Wilko*, 346 U.S. at 438) (emphasizing that "[i]n that case, the Supreme Court frankly recognized a similar collision of public policies and faced up to it; we must do no less here.").

[31] *Id.* at 827.

[32] There appears that with respect to this point the court itself stresses the issue as being one of first impressions, without so stating. In this connection, it is worth noting that it found no conceptual distinction between a statute that spawns a policy of ascribing rights to large segments of the population having an inferior bargaining position, and an adhesion contract. "For the same reason, it is also proper to ask whether contracts of adhesion between alleged monopolies and their customers should determine the forum for trying antitrust violations," adding that "Congress would hardly have intended that." *Id.*

[33] *Id.* at 827.

bases its antagonism toward arbitration (inapplicability of statutory causes of action providing private rights to a class of individuals with inferior bargaining postures and arbitration as wanting in ability to adjudicate and process complex technical matters with possible public policy ramifications) is both disconcerting and disappointing. Put simply, these twin tenets are treated as sacrosanct first principles. Therefore, we never find a court questioning, analyzing, or otherwise scrutinizing the guiding precepts upon which it premises adjudication, which presumably affects public policy, the protected class at issue, congressional intent, and the practicing bar and bench. The lack of sustained analysis and rigor to which these two principles were submitted is equaled only by the less than clear *dicta* presumably vesting the opinion with conceptual symmetry.

By way of example, the court speculated that the averred antitrust violations do not constitute a defense to Maguire's claim for royalties. "[T]he arbitrator might promptly proceed within the fine limits, leaving it to the arbitrators to decide what goods were so sold. However, the district court, rather than ruling on these several contentions, held that they should all be decided by arbitrators. In that it erred; the antitrust claims pressed by appellant may not be submitted to arbitration. The district court should have, in the first instance and with appropriate expedition, determined so much of this case as may be necessary in order that in the arbitration, if there is one, of the claims under the License Agreement, the arbitrators will not be called upon to determine antitrust issues."[34]

Even though the extent to which the issue was before the appellate tribunal in the first instance is unclear, the court still addressed the issue of arbitrability where a non-party to the subject arbitration agreement may be involved, as would be the case with Maguire's claim. Oddly, after identifying the argument from the perspective of the adverse parties, the Second Circuit delegated the issue to the district court. "Whether Maguire can compel ASE to arbitrate is an issue to be decided by the courts."[35] In furtherance of this latter proposition, the Second Circuit attempted, without actually referencing the "severability doctrine," to distinguish its holding from Supreme Court and Second Circuit precedent,[36] where the arbitration clause in an agreement allegedly entered into pursuant to fraud in the inducement was severed from the entire contract and the case referred to arbitration. The Court dismissed applicability of this authority and of the severability doctrine without any reasoned examination or significant inquiry. Disappointingly, it merely stated the vacuous proposition that the "approach is not available here; it accomplishes nothing to treat the arbitration clause separately if Maguire is not a party to it."[37]

The fraud in inducement cases directly applies to this case. The gravamen of the claim is that the substance of the contract is void as a result of the purported fraud. Here the issue is whether the entire contract or those aspects of it concerning antitrust claims are illicit because of public policy favoring the protection of certain classes having less than arms-length bargaining posture. A second issue is whether this outweighs the parties' explicit intent to arbitrate. Maguire's standing to arbitrate

[34] *Id.* at 828 (citation omitted).

[35] *Id.* at 829 (citations omitted).

[36] *See* Prima Paint Corp. v. Flood & Conklin Mfg. Co., 388 U.S. 395 (1967); Robert Lawrence Co. v. Devonshire Fabrics, Inc., 271 F.2d 402 (2d Cir. 1959), *cert. granted*, 362 U.S. 909, *appeal dismissed*, 364 U.S. 801 (1960).

[37] *American Safety Equipment*, 391 F.2d at 829.

is an issue within the ambit of classical arbitrability. If indeed he is not a party to the license agreement *and* could not be an assignee but for ASE's approval, which was never forthcoming, then that claim falls within the scope of arbitration as much as fraud in the inducement claim where the severability doctrine dictates arbitrability because the asserted fraudulent inducement is directed at the subject matter of the contract generally and not the arbitration clause specifically.

The court's parceling of issues and instructions to the district court on remand do not present a useful analysis either doctrinally or *in praxis*.

The weight and influence of the twin precepts galvanizing judicial hostility against arbitration were far reaching and decisive. The judiciary, however, was less than of a single voice on the issue. Consequently, even in cases where antitrust claims in "notice pleading" jurisdictions were averred, the Seventh Circuit, by way of illustration, attempted to diminish the weight of statutory causes of action in favor of staying all judicial proceedings and referring the case to arbitration. The analysis in *University Life Insurance Company of America v. Unimarc Ltd.* is eloquent and illustrative on this point.[38]

In that case the Seventh Circuit affirmed a district court ruling that compelled arbitration despite the defendant's subsequent filing of a judicial proceeding that the district court stayed upon holding an evidentiary hearing.[39]

After canvassing authority holding that statutory antitrust claims are not arbitrable (including the Second Circuit's pronouncement in *American Safety Equipment Corp.*), the Seventh Circuit engaged in an analysis that sought to enforce arbitration over formal technical arguments entailing the mechanical application of categorical rules. In this very same spirit it observed that "[e]ven if there were an iron clad rule that arbitration must be stayed when antitrust issues permeate the issues to be arbitrated, the rule would not be activated by mere allegations of an antitrust violation."[40] The argument was amplified to highlight that "[o]therwise a party to an arbitration agreement who wanted to delay arbitration so long as possible could achieve this end simply by filing a frivolous antitrust suit – which seems to be what happened here."[41] The court was impelled to address the technical pleading issue endemic to "a regime of notice pleading." Hence, it reiterated that even though the allegations at issue may survive a Fed.R.Civ.P. 12(b)(6) motion to dismiss, the issue would be one for the California district court and not the appellate tribunal to decide. Also, were the plaintiff's antitrust claims dismissed, they would still be allowed to file a second amended complaint. The pleading before the court, however, (the first amended complaint) raised antitrust averments that were "insubstantial and thus provide no basis for refusing to order arbitration."[42]

The Seventh Circuit's salubrious attitude toward arbitration and against a formulaic approach to adjudicating the propriety of a motion to stay an arbitral proceeding in favor of a judicial action, despite the parties' explicit intent to have all claims submitted to arbitration, is artfully summarized in its recognition that "'there's a special providence in the fall of a sparrow,' *Hamlet, Act V, Sc. II, Line 232*, is not the contemporary philosophy of antitrust."[43] Even though the Seventh Circuit's analytical

38 University Life Insurance Company of America v. Unimarc Ltd., 699 F.2d 846 (7th Cir. 1983).

39 *Id.* at 848.

40 *Id.* at 851 (citation omitted).

41 *Id.*

42 *Id.* at 853.

43 *Id.*

fulcrum is ostensibly the insufficiency of the antitrust averments advanced in the first amended complaint, the studious reader cannot help but posit whether the court in fact used technical arguments to rightfully exalt substance over form in configuring the proposition that an enforceable arbitration clause gives rise to an alternative dispute resolution methodology *in pari materia* with judicial recourse. Conspicuously present because of its absence is any reference in the opinion, even fleetingly and in passing, to any of the four badges and vestiges of conceptual prejudice upon which judicial hostility directed toward arbitration was premised: (i) the ousting of jurisdiction from courts of otherwise competent jurisdiction, (ii) the view that an arbitration proceeding requires judicial supervision, (iii) the conviction that arbitration was not well-suited for administering complex domestic or international cases, and (iv) the idea that arbitration is not the appropriate dispute resolution methodology to administer certain types of statutory claims that provide defendants with rights in situations where they lacked equal bargaining fiat.

Thus, without departing from settled jurisprudence and precedent, the Seventh Circuit crafted an analytical framework pursuant to which the purportedly non-arbitral claims are scrutinized for "substantiality" despite lax rigors of a "notice pleading" federal standard, for purposes of enforcing a valid arbitration clause. *University Life Insurance Company of America* stands as an emblematic case where strict procedural analysis allowed for the triumph of substance over form in the context of a hostile judicial environment favoring the converse with respect to the subject matter at issue: arbitration.

In addition to the four precepts of prejudice that galvanized judicial antagonism against arbitration, the development of a judicial consciousness and awareness that would recognize arbitration as equal to a judicial proceeding was contingent on a more modest proposition. An arbitration agreement had to be recognized as equal to any other contract consonant with the goals of the Federal Arbitration Act. Even though the Federal Arbitration Act is rooted in Congressional authority to enact substantive rules under the Commerce Clause, it was not until 1967, forty-two years after the Act's enactment, that the Supreme Court held that "it is clear beyond dispute that the Federal Arbitration Statute is premised upon and confined to the uncontestable federal foundations of 'control over interstate commerce and over admiralty.'"[44]

After overcoming obstacles that hindered the construction of arbitration agreements as equal to other legally binding and enforceable contracts, the fundamental predicate had been placed for the doctrinal development of arbitration as an alternative dispute resolution methodology to reach its natural and intended purpose: equal status with judicial proceedings.

[44] Prima Paint Corporation v. Flood & Conklin Mfg. Co., 388 U.S. 395, 405 (1967) (citing H.R. Rep. No. 96 (1924); *and* S. Rep. No. 536 (1924)).

CHAPTER 3

Wilko v. Swan, *Scherk v. Alberto-Culver*, and *Mitsubishi v. Soler:* Crafting a Level Playing Field

A. *WILKO v. SWAN*

Despite increasing juridic consciousness concerning virtues endemic to arbitral proceedings, the twin domestic badges of doctrinal hostility[1] against arbitration were not readily dispelled and thus required a case controversy that would appropriately frame an issue that may prove to be determinative. Nothing short of a direct analysis of whether a statutory right is appropriate for arbitration would suffice if the analytical rubric was to be materially reconfigured. This very question was raised and thoroughly addressed by the Supreme Court in the paradigm-setting case of *Wilko v. Swan*.[2] Indeed, *Wilko*'s prominent place in the Supreme Court's development of arbitration law is confirmed by even a cursory glance at the interest it has garnered in the academe.[3]

The facts in *Wilko* seem tailor made for a re-examination of arbitral proceedings that would place alternative dispute resolution on a level playing field with judicial recourse. The plaintiff securities purchaser brought an action against a securities brokerage firm to recover damages pursuant to Section 12(2) of the Securities Act of 1933.[4] The complaint alleged that plaintiff had been defrauded by the brokerage

1 (a) The conviction that certain classes of statutory rights are not arbitrable, and (b) the belief that arbitration is ill-suited for complex domestic or cross border controversies.

2 *Wilko, supra* note 2. *Wilko* would endure as historically and judicially relevant despite its eventual reversal because of the Court's fashioning the origins of the doctrine of manifest disregard of the law as one of just a handful of common law defenses against confirmation, recognition, and enforcement of an arbitral award and as a foundation for vacatur.

3 *See, for example*, James M. Gaitis, *Unraveling the Mystery of Wilko v. Swan: American Arbitration Vacatur Law and the Accidental Demise of Party Autonomy*, 7 Pepp. Disp. Resol. L.J. 1 (2007); Larry J. Pittman, *The Federal Arbitration Act: The Supreme Court's Erroneous Statutory Interpretation, Stare Decisis, and a Proposal for Change*, 53 Ala. L. Rev. 789 (2002); and F. Chet Taylor, *The Arbitrability of Federal Securities Claims: Wilko's Swan Song*, 42 U. Miami L. Rev. 203 (1987).

4 48 Stat. 74, 15 U.S.C. §77a et seq., 15 U.S.C.A. §77a et seq., s. 12(2), 48 Stat. 84, 15 U.S.C. §771(2), 15 U.S.C.A. §771(2), reads "any person who – paragraph 2 sells a security (whether or not exempted by the provisions of s. 77c of this title, other than paragraph (2) of subsection (a) of s. 77c of this title), by the use of any means or instrument of transportation or communication in interstate commerce or of the mails, by means of a prospectus or oral communication, which includes an untrue statement of a material fact or omits to state the material facts necessary in order to make the statements, in the light of the circumstances under which they were made, not misleading (the purchaser not knowing of such untruth or omission) and who shall not sustain the burden of proof that he did not know, and in the exercise of reasonable care could not have

firm through the instrumentalities of interstate commerce into purchasing 1,600 shares of the common stock of Air Associates, Inc. based upon false representations. Specifically, the complaint averred that the defendant had represented that "pursuant to a merger contract with the Borg Warner Corporation, Air Associates' stock would be valued at $6.00 per share over the then-current market price, and that financial interests were buying up the stock for the speculative profit."[5] Plaintiff further averred that a codefendant to the underlying action and a director of and counsel for Air Associates was simultaneously divesting himself of his own Air Associates' stock, which included all or some of the securities that plaintiff purchased. Finally, scarcely two weeks after acquiring the securities, plaintiff sold the stock at a loss that was ascribed to the brokerage firm's misrepresentations and forbearances of material information.

The brokerage firm did not even answer the complaint and instead filed a motion to stay the judicial proceeding pursuant to Section 3 of the United States Arbitration Act. The motion was accompanied by an affidavit asserting that the parties' relationship was governed by the terms of identical market agreements and underscoring that plaintiff had failed to pursue arbitration as agreed upon.[6]

The district court mechanically held that the arbitration agreement in effect violated public policy because it wrested from plaintiff the benefits and advantages of judicial recourse as a remedy provided for by the Securities Act, and thus denied a stay.[7] A divided Second Circuit Court of Appeals[8] reversed the district court and held that the Securities Act did not proscribe arbitration in lieu of a judicial proceeding where agreed upon by the parties. The Supreme Court exercised certiorari jurisdiction upon finding that the case presented an "important and novel federal question affecting both the Securities Act and the United States Arbitration Act."[9]

The court aptly framed the issue before it as "whether an agreement to arbitrate a future controversy is a 'condition, stipulation, or provision binding any person acquiring any security to waive compliance with any provision' of the Securities Act which s. 14 declares 'void.'"[10] At issue, however, was the *perceived* need to reconcile two policies that *appeared* irreconcilable but only upon the most surface and literal analysis. First, it is established, as the court itself observed, that "[t]he reports of both Houses on that Act [the Federal Arbitration Act] stressed the need for avoiding the delays and expenses of litigation,[11] and practice under its terms raises hope for its usefulness both in controversies based on statutes[12] or on

known, of such untruth or omission, shall be liable to the person purchasing such a security from him, who may sue either at law or in equity in any course of competent jurisdiction, to recover the consideration paid for such security with interest thereon, less the amount of any income received thereon, upon the tender of such security, or for damages if he no longer owns the securities."

5 *Wilko*, 346 U.S. at 429.

6 *Id.*

7 *See* Wilko v. Swan, 107 F.Supp. 75 (D.N.Y. 1952).

8 Wilko v. Swan, 201 F.2d 439 (2d Cir. 1953).

9 *Wilko*, 346 U.S. at 430 (citation omitted).

10 *Id.*

11 Citing H.R. Rep. No. 96 (1924); *and* S. Rep. No. 536 (1924). *See* Marine Transit Corp. v. Dreyfus, 284 U.S. 263 (1932).

12 Citing Agostini Bros. Bldg. Corp. v. United States, 142 F.2d 854 (4th Cir. 1944); Watkins v. Hudson Coal Co., 151 F.2d 311 (3rd Cir. 1945); Donahue v. Susquehanna Collieries Co., 138 F.2d 3 (3rd Cir. 1943); Donahue v. Susquehanna Collieries Co., 160 F.2d 661 (3rd Cir. 1947); *and* Evans v. Hudson Coal Co., 165 F.2d 970 (3d Cir. 1948).

standards otherwise created."[13] The second policy at odds with Congressional intent to promote arbitral proceedings is the rights that Congress accorded to investors pursuant to the Securities Act proscribing waiver of any of these statutorily created rights. Significantly, the Court only accorded scant and passing reference to these two policies, characterizing them as being in conflict and, therefore in need of reconciliation. This very characterization assumes an inconsistency where, beyond a plain language analysis, there simply is none.[14]

In reversing the Second Circuit and holding that "the intention of Congress concerning the sale of securities is better carried out by holding invalid such an agreement for arbitration of issues arising under the Act [the Securities Act],"[15] the Supreme Court reduced an arms-length negotiated arbitration agreement to the status of a "stipulation" within the meaning of 15 U.S.C.A. s. 77 and Section 14.[16] The diminishment of arbitration and subordination of the Act to the Securities Act of 1933 so as to create a semblance of conflict based upon a claim needing analysis is premised on no less than eight insufficient and defective propositions upon which the Court bottomed its opinion.

First, it is assumed that because the case before the Court "requires subjective findings on the purpose and knowledge of an alleged violator of the Act," these findings must be "applied by the arbitrators without judicial instruction on the law."[17] This extraordinary observation is blind adhesion to juridic prejudice asserting that the arbitral process is somehow ill-equipped or otherwise disadvantaged when faced with complex factual or legal analyses, let alone the intricate application of law to fact. The proposition is articulated without any analysis whatsoever.

Second, it is observed that arbitral awards "may be made without explanation of their reasons," and hence a person seeking relief under the Securities Act of 1933 would likely be prejudiced.[18] The character and nature of an arbitral award is here misapprehended, as is the arbitration procedure altogether. Unlike appellate opinions, arbitration awards are not binding and do not purport to have *stare decisis* effect on subsequent arbitrations concerning identical legal issues and similar factual patterns. Consequently, arbitrators are not charged with crafting a ruling, as would an appellate tribunal, because they are resolving a particular dispute between individuals rather than creating binding legal precedent as part of a state's or a geopolitical subdivision's exercise of its sovereignty. To infer from the formal and substantive differences between an appellate judicial opinion and an arbitral award that a claimant pursuing a legislatively enacted right would be disadvantaged if forced to honor its agreement to arbitrate instead of seeking judicial recourse is to misapprehend the nature and characters of both arbitration and judicial proceedings.

[13] Citing Marine Transit Corp. v. Dreyfus, 284 U.S. 263 (1932); Kentucky River Mills v. Jackson, 206 F.2d 111 (6th Cir. 1953); Campbell v. American Fabrics Co., 168 F.2d 959 (2d Cir. 1948); Columbian Fuel Corp. v. United Field Gas Co., 72 F.Supp. 843 (D.C.W.Va. 1947), *affirmed*, 165 F.2d 746 (4th Cir. 1948); Matter of Springs Cotton Mills v. Buster Boy Suit Co., 88 N.Y.S. 2d 295 (App. Div. 1949), *affirmed*, 300 N.Y. 586 (1949); White Star Mining Co. v. Hultberg, 220 Ill. 578 (1906); Oregon-Washington R. & N. Co. v. Spokane, P. & S.R. Co., 83 Or. 528 (1917); STURGES, COMMERCIAL ARBITRATIONS & AWARDS 502, 793–798 (1930).

[14] *See Wilko*, 346 U.S. at 438.

[15] *Id.*

[16] 15 U.S.C.A. §77. §14 reads:

> "Any condition, *stipulation*, or provision binding any person acquiring any security to waive compliance with any provision of this subchapter or of the rules and regulations of the Commission shall be void." (emphasis supplied).

[17] *Wilko*, 346 U.S. at 436.

[18] *Id.*

Third, in this same spirit, the Court notes that arbitrations lack a "complete record of their proceedings," and, therefore, presumably here too a claimant would be prejudiced. As with the second proposition, this premise assumes that a record of the proceedings identical to a judicial action is a *sine qua non* to the equitable administration of justice. It, however, turns a blind eye on the practical likelihood of an arbitral process keeping meticulous records of evidence and testimony, not to mention that the multiple federal and state judicial jurisdictions lack uniformity with respect to dispositive rules of judicial administration.

Fourth, it is assumed that "the arbitrator's conception of the legal meaning of such statutory requirements as 'burden of proof,' 'reasonable care,' or 'material fact' cannot be examined."[19] The Court's novel exegesis of the juridic conceptual categories attendant to arbitrators finds no foundation, and quite remarkably the Court does not purport to craft any such pretext. This extraordinarily bold generalization is merely advanced as yet another ground on which to create an analytical framework that would limit the arbitrability of specific statutorily created rights.

Fifth, the assertion is made that the judicial basis on which "to vacate an award is limited."[20] The parties' desire to seek finality is a fundamental tenet of both arbitral and judicial proceedings. This salient element, elevated as a principal feature of arbitration, constitutes one of the critical bargained-for elements that parties simply cannot engraft onto a judicial proceeding, but it is kept well within the parameters of control by accepting arbitration as an alternative dispute resolution methodology. The desire for finality in dispute resolution is inextricably bound to the valued precept of party-autonomy underlying both arbitration and judicial proceedings. The Court's generalization and oversimplification completely ignores the most distinctive principle of the common law system itself, the tenet of party-autonomy that supplies a normative imperative rendering an "adversarial system" possible in the first instance.

Sixth, the rosary of predicates justifying the non-arbitrability of specifically created statutory rights includes the blanket assertion that "the interpretations of the law by the arbitrators in contrast to manifest disregard are not subject, in the federal courts, to judicial review for error in interpretation."[21] Again, here too the precept of party-autonomy plays a critical role that the Court entirely undermines. Narrowing the scope of judicial review is precisely a hallmark of the parties' exercise of autonomy in alternative dispute resolution that cannot be disavowed without doing violence to the integrity of the law of contracts as well.

Seventh, the Court embarks on what is perhaps the most opaque premise to support its holding. This proposition has two parts. At the outset, the Court declares that "[t]he United States Arbitration Act contains no provision for judicial determination of legal issues such as is found in the English law."[22] Quite surprisingly, support for this contention is premised on the United Kingdom Arbitration Act of 1950[23] and Halsbury's Statutes of England.[24] In this initial assertion the Court infers

[19] *Id.* (citation omitted). [20] *Id.*

[21] *Id.* at 437. It is critical to underscore that in the context of international arbitration "manifest disregard for the law" is a legally cognizable basis on which to vacate an award that is unique to the United States because it is not one of the basis for vacating an award contained in the New York Convention.

[22] *Id.*

[23] United Kingdom Arbitration Act of 1950, Act14 Geo. VI, C.27, §21.

[24] 29 Halsbury's Statutes of England II at 106.

that "the protected provisions of the Securities Act require the exercise of judicial discretion to fairly assure their effectiveness,"[25] and, consequently, "Congress must have intended s. 14 to apply to waiver of judicial trials and review."[26] The relevance of the 1950 U.K. Arbitration Act and of Halsbury's Statutes of England is devoid of precedent or conceptual import. It is suspect even when viewed under the kindest and most generous light. As to the conclusion that statutory "protective provisions" compel a proscription of waiver of a judicial proceeding in favor of agreed to arbitration finds no analytical or logical normative grounding.

Eighth and lastly, it is asserted that "[w]hile the Securities Act does not require petitioner to sue, a waiver in advance of a controversy stands upon a different footing."[27] When stripped of the observation concerning lack of symmetry, this proposition is a restatement of the second part of the seventh ground and subject to critique on an identical basis.

The dissent, authored by Justice Frankfurter and joined by Justice Minton, presents a paragon of lucid legal reasoning. Plainly put, the dissent observes that there are no facts of record susceptible to judicial notice from which it may be inferred that "the arbitral system as practiced in the City of New York, and as enforceable under supervisory authority of the District Court for the Southern District of New York, would not afford the plaintiff rights to which he is entitled."[28] In addition, "the tortuous course of litigation, especially in the City of New York,"[29] is placed in sharp relief with "[t]he impelling considerations that led to the enactment of the Federal Arbitration Act."[30] The gravamen of the majority opinion, that arbitrators somehow are not bound to adhere to the rule of law, is significantly and meaningfully challenged in the dissent, which explicitly references Section 10 of the Federal Arbitration Act.[31]

Even though the term party-autonomy is not specifically referenced, Justice Frankfurter concludes his analysis with a meticulous and common sense review of the record and underscores that it *does not* demonstrate "that the plaintiff in opening an account had no choice but to accept the arbitration stipulation, thereby making the stipulation an unconscionable and unenforceable provision in a

25 *Wilko*, 346 U.S. at 437.

26 *Id.* (citation omitted).

27 *Id.* at 438.

28 *Id.* at 439.

29 *Id.* at 440.

30 *Id.* at 439.

31 §10 of the Act provides:

§10. Same; Vacation; grounds; rehearing.

(a) In any of the following cases the United States court in and for the district wherein the award was made may make an order vacating the award upon the application of any party to the arbitration –

(1) Where the award was procured by corruption, fraud, or undue means;

(2) Where there was evidence partiality or corruption in the arbitrators, or either of them;

(3) Where the arbitrators were guilty of misconduct in refusing to postpone the hearing, upon sufficient cause shown, or in refusing to hear evidence pertinent and material to the controversy; or any other misbehavior by which the rights of any party have been prejudiced; or

(4) Where the arbitrators exceed their powers, or so imperfectly execute them that a mutual, final, and definite award upon the subject matter submitted was not made.

(5) Redesignated (b)

(b) If an award is vacated in the time within which the agreement required the award to be made has not expired, the court may, in its discretion, direct a rehearing by the arbitrators.

(c) The United States District Court for the district wherein an award was made that was issued pursuant to section 580 of title 5 may make an order vacating the award upon the application of a person, other than a party to the arbitration, who is adversely affected or aggrieved by the award, if the use of arbitration for the award is clearly inconsistent with the factors set forth in section 572 of title 5.

business transaction . . . it is one thing to make out a case of overreaching as between parties bargaining not at arms-length. It is quite a different thing to find in the anti-waiver provision of the Securities Act a general limitation on the Federal Arbitration Act."[32] Unlike the majority opinion, Justice Frankfurter emphasizes the parties' equal bargaining power in selecting arbitration as the preferred methodology for dispute resolution despite the "benefits" that the Securities Act accords to prospective claimants and the strictures of the anti-waiver provision.[33]

Read with care and brought to its logical conclusion, the dissent demonstrates that the appearance of a conflict suggested by a simple, plain meaning analysis of the pertinent statutory provisions and "apparently" competing public policies is but an appearance of a conflict and an attendant need for reconciliation. In effect the "special rights" that §12(2) of the Securities Act confers on prospective plaintiffs[34] are preserved and furthered where the parties have selected arbitration as a dispute resolution methodology. Indeed, no right conferred by the Securities Act to purchasers would be adversely compromised in an arbitral proceeding. Thus, the phenomenology of conflict and need for reconciliation is reduced precisely to just a phenomenon when the eight premises upon which the opinion reposes are challenged, the actual rights conferred by the Securities Act are analyzed in the context of an arbitration regime, and the concept of party-autonomy is seen as the most defining common law feature and an element endemic to arbitration.

B. *SCHERK v. ALBERTO-CULVER:* A NON-REVERSAL REVERSAL AND A LOOK AT *M/S THE BREMEN v. ZAPATA*

The marked transformation that was to place arbitration agreements "on equal footing with other contracts" and *in pari materia* with judicial proceedings occurred in small conceptual increments.[35] The Supreme Court's command in *Wilko v. Swan*

[32] *Id.* at 440.

[33] Congressman Graham of Pennsylvania from the committee on the judiciary expressly addressed the binding effect of a party's agreement to arbitrate in the Report that he submitted to the company H.R. 646. His remarks on this point merit consideration and reconsideration:

> The Bill declares simply that such agreements for arbitration shall be enforced, and provides a procedure in the Federal courts for their enforcement. The procedure is very simple, following the lines of ordinary motion procedure, we do see technicality, delay, and expense to a minimum and at the same time safeguarding the rights of the parties. There is provided a method for the summary trial of any claim that no arbitration agreement ever was made, and there is also provided a hearing if the defeated party contends that the award was secured by fraud or other corruption or undue influence, or that some evident mistake not affecting the merits exists in the award. ***If the parties to the arbitration are willing to proceed under it, they need resort to the courts at all. If one party is recalcitrant he can no longer escape his agreement, but his rights are amply protected. At the same time the party willing to perform his contract for arbitration the delay in cost of litigation*** machinery is provided for the prompt determination of his claim for arbitration and the arbitration proceeds without interference by the Court. Report accompanying H.R. 646, 68th Cong., No. 95.

[34] These special rights can be summarized as (i) the right to recover for misrepresentation where the seller is made to assume the burden of proving lack of *scienter;* (ii) the enforceability of the special rights in any court of competent jurisdiction federal or state; (iii) a wide choice of venue accorded to the purchaser; (iv) the privilege of nation-wide service of process, and (v) no diversity jurisdiction amount requirement.

[35] *See* C. Edward Fletcher, *Learning to Live with the Federal Arbitration Act: Securities Litigation in a Post-McMahon World*, 37 Emory L.J. 99 (1988); *and* Stephen L. Hayford, *Commercial Arbitration in the Supreme Court 1983–1995: A Sea Change*, 31 Wake Forest L. Rev. 1 (1996).

merely reinforced and further entrenched the legacy of prejudices that the Federal Arbitration Act sought to eviscerate. It took twenty-three years for the virtually identical issue to reach the Supreme Court anew, but this time in a different world that ascribed normative features to international commerce and transnational contracts in particular. Technically, however, the Court sought to "square the circle" and in many ways succeeded where Leibniz failed. Specifically, it is clear that the Court realized an imperative need to distance itself from its seminal *Wilko v. Swan* ruling by literally reaching the converse result but without expressly reversing itself. By highlighting and emphasizing the principles of certainty, predictability, transparency of standard, party-autonomy, and unjustified hostility against international contracts and arbitral proceedings, yet under the guise of identifying six salient distinguishing factors from *Wilko v. Swan*, the Supreme Court in *Scherk v. Alberto-Culver*[36] crafted a conceptual link that made possible the judicial transformation from its command in *Wilko v. Swan* to the decisive and noteworthy ruling in *Soler v. Mitsubishi*.[37] The Court's opinion in *Sckerk v. Alberto-Culver*, in turn, was premised on one of the very first judicial acknowledgments of economic globalization. Though that term does not appear in the opinion, it has a normative basis that would materially contribute to the development of arbitration to a level together with judicial proceedings. Accordingly, any discussion of *Wilko v. Swan* would be wholly inaccurate and incomplete without taking seriously the Supreme Court's unprecedented analysis in *M/S The Bremen v. Zapata Off Shore Co.*[38]

That seminal ruling is decisively bottomed on a novel perception of an economic horizon of unprecedented international consequence. Indeed, in *The Bremen* the Supreme Court placed in high relief the global character of commercial transactions in which the United States is a protagonist. Moreover, the Court underscores the juridic need to develop a corresponding judicial rubric that comports with global or transnational commercial transactions. Thirty years *before* the reality of economic globalization, *The Bremen* articulated the mandate to fashion rules that would accommodate a new world economic order.[39] A brief recitation of the operative facts underlying this case is compelled.

The issue before the Court was whether a forum selection clause in a contract stating that "[a]ny dispute arising must be treated before the London Court of Justice" is controlling when the U.S. party to the contract files an action against another party to the agreement (a German corporation) in a federal district court in the United States.[40]

In November 1977, plaintiff Zapata Off-Shore Company ("Zapata"), a corporation headquartered in Houston, Texas, signed a contract with defendant Unterweser, a German corporation, with the business purpose of transporting an oceanic oil drill belonging to Zapata christened "Chaparral" from Louisiana to a port on the

36 Scherk v. Alberto Culver Co., 417 U.S. 506 (1934). *See* Jennifer M. Eck, *Turning Back the Clock: A Judicial Return to Caveat Emptor for U.S. Investors in Foreign Markets*, 19 N.C. J. Int'l L. & Com. Reg. 313 (1994).

37 Soler v. Mitsubishi, 473 U.S. 614 (1985).

38 M/S The Bremen v. Zapata Off Shore Co., 407 U.S. 1 (1972).

39 Jason Webb Yackee, *Choice of Law Considerations in the Validity & Enforcement of International Forum Selection Agreements: Whose Law Applies?*, 9 UCLA J. Int'l L. & For. Aff. 43 (2004).

40 *The Bremen*, 407 U.S. at 1.

outskirts of Ravenna, Italy, in the Adriatic Sea. Specifically, Zapata had contracted to drill earmarked oil reserves. The transportation contract that the parties executed contained two relevant clauses. First, both parties had agreed that any dispute arising from the contract had to be adjudicated before the London Court of Justice. Second, two additional interactive clauses having the effect of indemnifying Unterweser concerning any contractual liability or tort regarding the execution of the terms of the agreement also were agreed to as part of the contract.[41] Relying on precedent from the Fifth Circuit Court of Appeals,[42] the district court held that defendant Unterweser had to comply with equitable principles and abstain from prosecuting parallel litigation that had been filed before the London Court of Justice. The district court also found that it had subject matter and *in personum* jurisdiction.

The Fifth Circuit Court of Appeals affirmed the district court's decision based upon the *Carbon Black* precedent, observing that the case "at the very least" stood for the proposition that a forum selection clause "will not be enforced unless the selected state would provide a more convenient forum than the state in which the suit is brought."[43] Based on this premise the Fifth Circuit also held that irrespective of the forum selection clause, the district court limited the exercise of its jurisdiction by dismissing the case on the grounds of *forum non conveniens*.[44] The majority of the Panel of the Fifth Circuit[45] approved the district court's ruling, which was premised on five dispositive observations:

41 On January 5, 1968 Unterweser's deep water tug called *The Bremen* left Venice, Louisiana with the *Chaparral* being towed towards Italy. When *The Bremen* and the *Chaparal* reached international waters in the Gulf of Mexico and were severely affected by a storm. During the tempest the *Chaparral* lost one of its elevator legs that had be raised for the journey. In addition, the drilling platform also was seriously damaged. The crisis led Zapata to instruct *The Bremen* to tug the *Chaparral* to Tampa, Florida which was the nearest port of possible refuge. *Id.* at 1910. In stark defiance of the form selection clause providing that "any dispute arising must be treated before the London Court of Justice" Zapata filed a claim before the Federal District Court in Tampa averring U.S. $3.5 million in damages against Unterweser and against *The Bremen, in rem* according to allegations of negligence and breach of contract. *Id.*

42 *See* Carbon Black Export, Inc. v. The Monrosa, 254 F.2d 297, 300–301 (5th Cir. 1958), *Cert. dismissed*, 359 US 180 (1959) (holding that forum selection clauses are not binding as being against public policy because their objective is to wrest jurisdiction from Courts that otherwise would have exercised it.).

43 *Id.* at 1912.

44 The doctrine of forum non-conveniens, in part, provides a Court with discretion to dismiss a case in favor of a more convenient forum so long as such ruling advances the equitable principles of justice by minimizing costs and maximizing access to evidence. The Doctrine was first articulated in the venerable chestnut Gulf Oil v. Gilbert, 330 U.S. 501 (1947) in a brilliant opinion authored by Justice Jackson. The Doctrine was later developed within the context of international litigation in *Piper Aircraft Co. v. Reyno*, 454 U.S. 235 (1981). In *Piper Aircraft Co.* the Supreme Court reversed the Third Circuit which had denied a petition to dismiss on the grounds of *forum non-conveniens* merely because the Court found Scottish Law to be less favorable to plaintiff than the law of the forum. The Supreme Court applied an analysis pursuant to which a Court must first consider certain private and public interests so as to determine whether plaintiff's choice of forum poses an undue burden on the defendant or the Court. In accordance with this analysis the public interest component includes both the interests of the forum as well as those of the alternate forum. For a succinct but quite informative account of the development and contemporary status of the Doctrine of Forum Non-Conveniens, *see* GARY BORN, INTERNATIONAL LITIGATION AND ARBITRATION 341–366 (3rd ed. 1996).

45 The Fifth Circuit's original opinion issued from a Panel that was divided two to one, in fact, defendant filed a motion for reconsideration and hearing *on banc* before all fourteen judges of

1. The flotilla never left the Fifth Circuit's *mare nostum*, and the accident took place in the district court's vicinity.
2. A considerable number of prospective witnesses, including the entire crew of the Zapata, resided in the area close to the Gulf of Mexico.
3. All prevoyage preparation work, including inspection and repairs, was undertaken in the vicinity of the Gulf.
4. The testimony of *The Bremen's* crew was readily available by deposition.
5. Other than the forum selection clause, England had no interest in any issue configuring the case, contacts with the parties, or any other possible connecting factor.[46]

In *The Bremen*, the Fifth Circuit also observed that Zapata was a U.S. corporation and therefore the trial court's judgment to dismiss the case in favor of a foreign forum, particularly where it was likely that English courts would recognize as binding the contract's exculpatory clauses, was problematic.[47] A majority of the Fifth Circuit opined that such clauses were against public policy and thus unenforceable based on long-settled Supreme Court precedent.[48]

The Supreme Court exercised *certiorari* jurisdiction arising from a direct and explicit conflict among the circuits on the specific question concerning the extent to which parties to a contract have autonomy to select a foreign forum, independently of the situs where the alleged breach of contract or negligence occurred. The Supreme Court reversed the Fifth Circuit and founded its analysis on eight fundamental tenets.

First, the Court underscored that for at least two decades there had been a significant and material expansion in global commerce and transnational commercial activities by firms based in the United States.[49] In this context, it emphasized that the barriers of distance that once limited commercial transactions now comprised a "modest territory" and had practically disappeared.

the Fifth Circuit. Six of the fourteen judges dissented with a "majority" opinion of eight judges affirming the district court.

[46] *The Bremen*, 407 U.S. 1.

[47] Christine L. Davitz, *U.S. Supreme Court Subordinates Enforcement of Regulatory Statutes to Enforcement of Arbitration Agreements: From The Bremen's License to the Sky Reefer's Edict*, 30 VAND. J. TRANSNAT'L L. 59 (1997).

[48] The Fifth Circuit explicitly found analytic support for this proposition in *Bisso v. Inland Waterways Corp.*, 349 U.S. 85 (1955), and *Dixilyn Drilling Corp. v. Crescent Towing and Salvage Co.*, 373 U.S. 697 (1963).

The Court's public records contained affidavits by British lawyers opining that exculpatory clauses in contracts under English law were deemed "*prima facie* valid and binding" against Zapata because of an illegal action filed in England in which Zapata averred that Unterwesser's breach of contract or negligence caused damages to the *Chaparal*.

[49] *Id.* at 8. Here the Court referenced the two decades between 1953 and 1973. This argument is of greater significance and relevance today in the context of a socioeconomic policy of economic globalization, the fragmentation and dissolution of the former Soviet Union, the economic integration of China with one-third of the global population and a growing economy that between 1985 through 2006 has expanded at an unprecedented rate of eight percent *per annum* (the highest sustained growth of any economic model in economic history) and the renaissance of a Europe without borders that finds itself negotiating nearly logistics toward the implementation of a European constitution that will recognize multiple membership categories. *See, e.g.*, JEFFREY D. SACHS, THE END OF POVERTY: ECONOMIC POSSIBILITIES FOR OUR TIME (PENGUIN 2005).

Second, there were numerous U.S. companies specializing in transporting heavy equipment and machinery across thousands of nautical miles and oceans that constitute a fundamental part of everyday international commerce.[50]

Third, as a general policy, U.S. industries shall be disadvantaged and stifled in their expansion and development if, "notwithstanding solemn contracts, we insist on a parochial concept that all disputes must be resolved under our laws and in our courts."[51]

Fourth, the analysis enunciated by the Fifth Circuit in *Carbon Black* is inapplicable in the context of international commerce: "[w]e cannot have trade and commerce in world markets and international waters exclusively on our terms governed by our laws and resolved in our courts."[52]

Fifth, eight years earlier, in *National Equipment Rental, Ltd.*,[53] the Court held that a party to a federal district court proceeding may be susceptible to service of process in a district where the party otherwise could not be served pursuant to the parties' voluntary designation of an agent for purposes of accepting service of process in that jurisdiction. The Court noted that:

> [It] is settled, as the courts below recognized that parties to a contract may agree in advance to submit to the jurisdiction of a given court, to permit notice to be served by the opposing party, or even to waive notice altogether.[54]

The Supreme Court stated that the *sub judice* merely constituted the other side of the very same proverbial coin. Put simply, forum selection clauses, pursuant to which any contractual dispute for civil obligation in the context of an international transaction is to be adjudicated in a foreign venue, must be absolutely binding upon the parties. Indeed, the only exception to the ironclad pronouncement is when adherence to the particular clause at issue inevitably leads to an "irrational" result under the facts and circumstance of a specific case.[55]

Sixth, in the case before the Court, the subject forum selection clause was negotiated at arms-length and in a commercially reasonable manner by sophisticated and experienced persons. Accordingly, but for a finding of fraud, other similarly compelling circumstances or valid grounds establishing that the negotiation process was materially asymmetrical and, therefore, inherently unfair, the clauses negotiated by the parties shall be binding.[56]

[50] *The Bremen*, 407 U.S. at 9. [51] *Id.*

[52] *Id.*

[53] National Equipment Rental, Ltd. v. Szukhent, 375 U.S. 311 (1964).

[54] *Id.* at 315–316. [55] *The Bremen*, 407 U.S. at 10.

[56] *Id.* at 12. Significantly, the Court rejected the proposition asserting that forum selection clauses are but illegal methodologies used to wrest and divest courts of jurisdiction to administer justice equitably. Shunning this long standing vestige of prejudice developed by English courts and adopted mechanically and without reflection by the U.S. judiciary to the extent of constituting an integral part of our jurisprudential culture, constituted a major doctrinal development in the elevation of arbitration to the status of a dispute resolution methodology at that same level as judicial proceedings. The Supreme Court artfully and with commendable intellectual integrity articulated that such propositions are rooted in a historical legacy that caused Courts to resist "any attempt to reduce the power and business of a particular court and has little place in an era when all courts are overloaded and when businesses once essentially local, now operate in world markets." The Court further asserted that "[n]o one seriously contends in this case that the forum selection clause 'ousted' the district court of jurisdiction over Zapata's action. The threshold

Seventh, the record overwhelmingly demonstrated that the forum selection clause had been "a vital part of the agreement, and it would be unrealistic to think that the parties did not conduct their negotiations, including fixing the monetary terms, with the consequences of the forum clause figuring prominently in their calculations."[57]

Finally, notwithstanding the inconveniences inherent in filing and prosecuting a cause in a remote and extensively inconvenient forum (one that maximizes expenditure of resources and minimizes access to proof and other evidence), the Court underscored that the party opposing the forum selection clause must meet a high and difficult burden of proof. Adherence to a forum selection clause is particularly unnecessary in cases concerning international commerce and in cases that do not entail merely domestic parties seeking the adjudication of a local (national) controversy.[58]

The appropriate construction to be placed on the clause, according to the Court, is one where full force and effect is accorded to the clause unless the party challenging the forum demonstrates with clarity and specificity that enforcement of the clause would be irrational and unjust or that the clause is null and void on grounds of fraud or material disparity in the parties' ability to negotiate the subject matter in question.[59]

Significantly, the Supreme Court does not mention arbitration, an arbitration clause, nor does it undertake the requisite leap into a brave new doctrinal world where an arbitration clause is treated no differently than a forum selection clause. However, the Court does undertake two important conceptual developments that would prove decisive in transforming arbitration into a dispute resolution methodology *in pari materia* with judicial proceedings. Notably, the nature and character of an "international contract," analyzed through the prism of a new economic order that contemplates porous trade borders and cross-border transactions as common commercial dealings, was exalted in a manner that finds little or no precedent in Supreme Court jurisprudence. Indeed, the Court *de facto* appears to have engrafted normative properties to "international contracts." The creation of this new "normative precept" would certainly redound to the benefit of both domestic and international arbitral proceedings.

question is whether the Court should have exercised its jurisdiction to do more than give effect to the legitimate expectations of the parties, manifested in their freely negotiated agreement, by specifically enforcing the forum selection clause." *Id.*

57 *Id.* at 14.

58 *Id.* at 17–19. ("We are not here dealing with an agreement between two Americans to resolve their essentially local disputes in a remote alien forum. In such a case, the serious inconvenience of the contractual forum to one or both of the parties might carry greater weight in determining the reasonableness of the forum clause. This case, however, involves a freely negotiated international commercial transaction between a German and an American corporation for towage of a vessel from the Gulf of Mexico to the Adriatic Sea. As noted, the selection of a London forum was clearly a reasonable effort to bring vital certainty to this international transaction and to provide a neutral forum experienced and capable in the resolution of admiralty litigation.")

59 *Id.* at 18–19. *See also* Howard W. Schreiber, *Appealability of a District Court's Denial of a Forum-Selection Clause Dismissal Motion: An Argument Against "Cancelling Out"* The Bremen, 57 FORDHAM L. REV. 463 (1988).

Conceptually it is critical to note that in highlighting the importance of an international contract,[60] the Court implicitly embarks on a shift that places greater weight on the virtually abandoned principle of party-autonomy. This very doctrinal development, irrespective of intent to use this cornerstone, allows the Court the flexibility to stress the material significance of a forum selection clause. According material weight to, and taking seriously, forum selection clauses contained in international contracts constitutes the second major development the Court articulates in *The Bremen*.[61]

The judicial deference ascribed to forum selection clauses, presumably to further the very principles that arbitration seeks to foster (reliability, uniformity, predictability, and certainty), shall also prove to be decisive in placing arbitration on a level playing field with judicial proceedings. A synthesis that would equate forum selection clauses and arbitration clauses, particularly but not necessarily in an international context, would constitute the final premise necessary to eviscerate the badges of prejudice that, as of the adjudication of *The Bremen*, still stifled the elevation of arbitration as a dispute resolution methodology enjoying the same prestige as judicial proceedings.[62]

The holding in *The Bremen*, like Socrates' legendary cloak said to have been riddled with holes that vastly diminished the visible presence of any fabric, reveals more than it conceals. Indeed, it has provided a reasonable basis for scholars to launch significant scholarly analysis.[63] Despite an elaborate emphasis on the "sanctity of contractual obligations," the analysis is framed by emphasis on the presence of international commerce and the proliferation of United States multinationals that principally conduct transnational business. It is with keen regard for these two factors that the Court engrafted considerable weight on the parties' autonomy and to the legitimacy of the foreign forum selection clause. The principle of party-autonomy could have been articulated more comprehensively and coherently to diminish the importance placed on the nature of international contracts and transactions.[64]

60 It should be noted that the Supreme Court construes as synonymous the terms "international contract" and "dispute or international controversy".

61 Jane VanLare, *From Protection to Favoritism? The Federal Policy Toward Arbitration Vis-a-Vis Competing State Policies*, 11 HARV. NEGOTIATION L. REV. 473 (2006).

62 Graydon S. Staring, *Forgotten Equity: The Enforcement of Forum Clauses*, 30 J. MAR. L. & COM. 405 (1999), *and* David Marcus, *The Perils of Contract Procedure: A Revised History of Forum Selection Clauses in the Federal Courts*, 82 TUL. L. REV. 973 (2008).

63 *See* Richard L. Barnes, *Rediscovering Subjectivity in Contracts: Adhesion and Unconscionability*, 66 LA. L. REV. 123 (2005), Leandra Lederman, *Viva Zapata!: Toward a Rational System of Forum-Selection Clause Enforcement in Diversity Cases*, 66 N.Y.U.L. REV. 422 (1991), Lee Goldman, *My Way and the Highway: The Law and Economics of Choice of Forum Clauses in Consumer Form Contracts*, 86 NW. U.L. REV. 700 (1992), Michael Mousa Karayanni, *The Public Policy Exception to the Enforcement of Forum Selection Clauses*, 34 DUQ. L. REV. 1009 (1996), Richard D. Freer, *Erie's Mid-Life Crisis*, 63 TUL. L. REV. 1087 (1989), *and* Robert A. de By, *Forum Selection Clauses: Substantive or Procedural for Erie Purposes*, 89 COLUM. L. REV. 1068 (1989).

64 Significantly, the Supreme Court in *The Bremen* speaks of "international contracts" in the most generic of terms. It fails to distinguish among international construction contracts, international distribution agreements, international agency agreements, international franchise agreements, and international asset purchase agreements, to cite only a handful of the more salient cross-border contracts. Even the most cursory analysis reflects that each of these contracts comprises materially distinct allocations of risks that pervade every aspect of contractual formation through actual tactical execution and performance. The normative value that the Supreme Court in very general

It is armed with the normative resonance now ascribed to international contracts and the juridic integrity engrafted upon forum selection clauses that the principle of party-autonomy was finally poised to serve a decisive role in the development of arbitral proceedings in the United States. In fact, only one year after issuing the opinion in *The Bremen* the Supreme Court was able to muster sufficient jurisprudential analysis that allowed it to distance itself from *Wilko v. Swan* without overruling it and contribute to the development of arbitral proceedings.

In *Scherk v. Alberto-Culver Co.*,[65] the Supreme Court exercised *certiorari* jurisdiction "[b]ecause of the importance of the question presented."[66] The specific question the court addressed was whether its holding in *Wilko v. Swan* that "an agreement to arbitrate could not preclude a buyer of a security from seeking a judicial remedy under the Securities Act of 1933, in view of the language of §14 of that Act, barring '[a]ny condition, stipulation, or provision binding any person acquiring any security to waive compliance with any provision of this subchapter. . . .'"[67]

This narrow issue reached the Court after the Seventh Circuit disavowed an arbitration clause contained in a contract between a U.S. plaintiff and a German defendant residing in Switzerland, where the contract at issue was executed in Austria with respect to three corporations organized under the laws of Germany and Liechtenstein.[68]

In reversing the Seventh Circuit's pronouncement, the Court observed that the arbitration agreement at issue was binding, dispositive, and controlling with respect to any dispute relating to the subject of international commercial transaction, irrespective of the mandate of §14 of the Securities Act, proscribing all stipulations such as those concerning arbitration that would conflict with this provision.[69] The Supreme Court meticulously enunciated that (i) the plaintiff was a U.S. corporation conducting most of its business activities in the United States; (ii) defendant was a German national whose companies were organized under the laws of Germany and Liechtenstein; (iii) negotiations led to the execution of the contract at issue in Austria and the closing of a transaction in Switzerland, the United States, England, and Germany; and (iv) the subject matter of the contract principally concerned the sale-purchase of companies that organized under the laws of European countries and that conducted business mostly, if not exclusively, directed at European markets.[70] Clearly, the international character of the facts framing the issues before the Court materially distinguished the case from the Court's prior ruling in *Wilko v. Swan*, where all of the parties were U.S. entities.

Moreover, in holding that "the provisions of the Arbitration Act [Federal Arbitration Act] cannot be ignored in this case,"[71] the Court walked a delicate line ostensibly drawn for the purpose of crafting a new rule of law that would distance

terms placed on the genetic concept of an "international contract," without more, not taking into consideration at all the meaningful differences among international agreements, is somewhat disconcerting and unavailing to both bench and bar. Put simply, the polestar summarized in the term "international contract" without due emphasis on and juridic development as to the precept of *party-autonomy* limits the otherwise extraordinary character of the Court's analysis in *The Bremen*.

65 Scherk v. Alberto Culver Co., 417 U.S. 506 (1934).

66 *Id.* at 510.

67 *Id.*

68 *Id.*

69 *Id.* at 513.

70 *Id.*

71 *Id.*

it from its ruling of twenty-three years earlier, *Wilko v. Swan*, while not technically reversing itself.

Painstakingly, no less than six purportedly material, distinguishing, factual and/or legal predicates were identified. First, the Court noted that "*Wilko* concerned a suit brought under §12(2) of the Securities Act of 1933, which provides a defrauded purchaser with the 'special right' of a private remedy for civil liability. There is no statutory counterpart of §12(2) in the Securities Exchange Act of 1934, and neither §10(b) of that Act nor Rule 10b-5 speaks of a private remedy to redress violations of the kind alleged here, while federal case law has established that §10(b) and Rule 10b-5 create an implied private cause of action, the Act itself does not establish the 'special right' that the Court in *Wilko* found significant."[72] Second, the Court observed that while "both the Securities Act of 1933 and the Securities Exchange Act of 1934 contain sections barring waiver of compliance with any 'provision' of the respective acts, certain of the 'provisions' of the 1933 Act that the Court held could not be waived by *Wilko's* agreement to arbitrate find no counterpart in the 1934 Act."[73] In this connection, it was emphasized that "the Court in *Wilko* noted that the jurisdictional provision of the 1933 Act allowed a plaintiff to bring suit 'in any court of competent jurisdiction–federal or state–and removal from a state court is prohibited.' The analogous provision of the 1934 Act, by contrast, provides for suit only in the federal district courts that have 'exclusive jurisdiction,' thus significantly restricting the plaintiff's choice of forum."[74] Fourth, while the Supreme Court accepted the premise that for all practical purposes the respective waiver provisions of the 1933 Act and the 1934 Act are materially identical, despite different wordings of no moment, it highlighted that "respondent's reliance on *Wilko* in this case ignores the significant and, we find, crucial difference between the agreement involved in *Wilko* and the one signed by the parties here. *Alberto-Culver's* contract to purchase the business entities belonging to *Scherk* was truly an international agreement."[75] The Court, confident with its ruling in just the immediately preceding term, in *M/S Bremen v. Zapata Off-Shore Co.*,[76] elevated the status of an "international contract," practically ascribing to it normative foundation:

> Such a contract involves considerations and policies significantly different from those found controlling in *Wilko*. In *Wilko*, quite apart from the arbitration provision, there was no question but that the laws of the United States generally, and the federal securities laws in particular, would govern disputes arising out of the stock-purchase agreement. The parties, the negotiations, and the subject matter of the contract were all situated in this country, and no credible claims that have been entertained that any international conflict-of-laws problems would arise. In this case, by contrast, in the absence of the arbitration provision considerable uncertainty existed at the time of the agreement, and still exists, concerning the law applicable to the resolution of disputes arising out of the contract.
>
> Such uncertainty will almost inevitably exist with respect to any contract touching two or more countries, each with its own substantive laws and conflict-of-laws rules. *A contractual provision specifying in advance the form in which*

72 *Id.* at 514 (citations omitted).
73 *Id.*
74 *Id.* (citations omitted).
75 *Id.* at 515.
76 M/S Bremen v. Zapata Off-Shore Co., 407 U.S. 1 (1972).

> *disputes shall be litigated and the applicable law to be applied is, therefore, an almost indispensable precondition to achievement of the orderliness and predictability essential to any international business transaction. Furthermore, such a provision obviates the danger that a dispute under the agreement might be submitted to a forum hostile to the interests of one of the parties or unfamiliar with the problem area involved.*[77]

The Supreme Court's concern with increasingly prevalent international transactions and the need for certainty, predictability, and uniformity caused it not only to accord a weight and significance to an international contract that had not been ascribed to such agreements prior to *Bremen v. Zapata*, but also to the six factors used to distinguish *Alberto-Culver* from *Wilko.* This juridic construct at first seems to be a logical classification of a contractual provision. When submitted to reasoned examination, however, its extraordinary character is rendered plain. Specifically, the Court observed that "[a]n agreement to arbitrate before a specified tribunal is, in effect, a specialized kind of forum selection clause that posits not only the situs of the suit but also the procedure to be used in resolving the dispute."[78]

By stating that an agreement to arbitrate is "a specialized kind of forum selection clause," the Court implicitly placed arbitration on an equal footing with judicial recourse. Even though a forum selection clause suggests that parties shall avail themselves of a specific judicial system that consists, in particular, of (i) rules of evidence, (ii) rules of civil procedure, (iii) norms for judicial administration, (iv) specific order of proof, (v) appellate recourse, (vi) a rubric of damages unique to that jurisdiction, and (vii) considerations of national policies in the construction and application of law to fact pursuant to the equitable administration of justice, none form part of arbitration proceedings. The Court's analysis inherently disavows these features as conceptual obstacles to treating litigation and arbitration equally.[79]

Lastly, conceptual distance is placed between *Wilko* and *Alberto-Culver* based upon the analytical support the Court found in *The Bremen.*[80] Once having crossed the doctrinal threshold in holding that an arbitration clause is a specialized kind of forum selection clause, then it necessarily follows that the jurisprudence governing forum selection clauses must be applied *equally* to arbitration clauses. Indeed, the Court liberally so proceeds:

> In *The Bremen* we noted that forum selection clauses 'should be given full effect' when 'a freely negotiated private international agreement [is] unaffected by fraud. This qualification does not mean that any time a dispute arising out of a transaction is based upon an allegation of fraud, as in this case, the clause is unenforceable. Rather, it means that an arbitration or forum selection clause in a contract is not enforceable *if the inclusion of that clause in the contract was the product of fraud or coercion.*[81]

77 *Scherk*, 417 U.S. at 516. (emphasis supplied) 78 *Id.* at 519.

79 Indeed, arbitration clauses, choice of law clauses, and choice of courts or choice of forum clauses, are distinct rather than specialized iterations of each other as they serve different purposes and are selected based upon materially diverse underlying policies considerations. For an excellent analysis that touches upon this issue. *See* Georgios Petrochilos, Procedural Law in International Arbitration (2004).

80 *Scherk*, 417 U.S. at 519 n.14. 81 *Id.* (citation omitted) (emphasis supplied).

Accordingly, the determination, by way of example, of an averment of fraud in the inducement into entering a contract now shall be adjudicated by an arbitral panel and not a court where the agreement at issue contains an arbitration clause. Certainly the Court undertook meticulous steps and applied extraordinary rigor in refraining from reversing its earlier decision in *Wilko* while preserving and advancing the integrity of an arbitration agreement within the context of a legal issue nearly identical to one raised in its earlier holding. Indeed, the Court managed successfully to square the circle even though it did not openly confront the badges of prejudice that historically justified judicial hostility against arbitration and rule that arbitration stands on the same level playing field as a judicial proceeding. It did, however, provide the necessary rubric for the subsequent landmark case, *Mitsubishi Motors Corporation v. Soler Chrysler-Plymouth, Inc.*[82]

C. *MITSUBISHI v. SOLER CHRYSLER-PLYMOUTH:* THE FINAL DECISIVE PARADIGM

Decided eleven years after *Alberto-Culver*, the Supreme Court in *Mitsubishi v. Soler* addressed what is conceptually a virtually indistinguishable legal issue from those considered in *Wilko* and *Scherk*.[83] As framed by the Court:

> The principal question presented by these cases is the arbitrability, pursuant to the Federal Arbitration Act, [citation omitted] and the Convention on the Recognition and Enforcement of Foreign Arbitral Awards ("Convention") of claims arising under the Sherman Act, and encompassed within a valid arbitration clause in an agreement embodying an international commercial transaction.[84]

82 Mitsubishi Motors Corp. v. Soler Chrysler-Plymouth, Inc., 473 U.S. 614 (1985).

83 For extensive discussion of *Mitsubishi v. Soler*, see Lisa Sopata, *Mitsubishi Motors Corp. v. Soler Chrysler-Plymouth, Inc.: International Arbitration and Antitrust Claims*, 7 NW. J. INT'L L. & BUS. 595 (1986); Eric A. Posner, *Arbitration and the Harmonization of International Commercial Law: A Defense of* Mitsubishi, 39 VA. J. INT'L L. 647 (1999); Monroe Leigh, *Federal Arbitration Act – Convention on the Recognition and Enforcement of Foreign Arbitral Awards – arbitrability of antitrust claims arising from an international transaction*, 80 A.J.I.L. 168 (1986).

84 *Id.* at 616 (citation omitted).

A brief thumbnail sketch of the Convention's history provides helpful context. In 1958, approximately twenty-six of the forty-five members of the United Nations adopted the United Nations Convention on the Recognition and Enforcement of Foreign Arbitral Awards (the "Convention:" or "New York Convention"), *opened for signature* June 10, 1958, 330 U.N.T.S. 38. The League of Nations (predecessor to the United Nations) had adopted two multilateral treaties, (i) the Geneva Protocol on Arbitration Clauses, *open for signature* September 24, 1923, 27 L.N.T.S. 157, and (ii) the Geneva Convention on the Execution of Foreign Arbitration Awards, *open for signature* September 26, 1927, 92 L.N.T.S. 301.

The Convention's fundamental organizing principle is to liberalize procedures for the enforcement of *foreign* arbitral awards. Significantly, the 1927 Geneva Convention had placed the burden of proof *on the party actually seeking enforcement of an arbitral award*. In addition, the 1927 Geneva Convention did not place any restrictions or limitations on the party seeking vacatur and opposing enforcement. The consequences of this regime were clear, and now with the benefit of hindsight, are even clearer. Arbitration awards were far from ambulatory for enforcement purposes. The scheme did not provide for a framework that encouraged the growth of transnational commerce because of the uncertainty attendant to the resolution that would issue from tribunals foreign to a claimant. Likewise, arbitration awards were susceptible to multiple challenges on virtually every conceivable ground within a context that placed the burden on the party seeking enforcement.

The Convention turned this standard and its underlying policy on its head. It shifted the burden of proof in an enforcement proceeding to the party opposing enforcement and severely and materially narrowed its defenses to the now familiar set of seven detailed in Article V.

In fact, the Court found it expedient to narrow the issue even further:

> We granted certiorari primarily to consider whether an American court should enforce an agreement to resolve antitrust claims by arbitration when that agreement arises from an international transaction.[85]

Significantly, the federal district court ordered Mitsubishi (plaintiff) and Soler (defendant/counterclaimant) "to arbitrate each of the issues raised in the complaint and in all the counterclaims, save two and a portion of a third. With regard to federal antitrust issues, it recognized that the courts of appeals, following *American Safety Equipment Corp. v. J.P. Maguire & Co.*, uniformly had held that the rights conferred by antitrust laws were 'of a character inappropriate for enforcement by arbitration.'"[86] The district court, however, following the directive in *Alberto-Culver*, held that the international component of the claims required adherence to the arbitration agreement even with respect to the antitrust claims.[87]

The First Circuit Court of Appeals, finding analytical foundation in the doctrine enunciated in *American Safety*, held that antitrust claims are not susceptible to adjudication pursuant to arbitration proceedings and that "neither [the Supreme Court's] decision in *Scherk* nor the Convention required abandonment of that doctrine in the face of an international transaction."[88]

For the first time, the Supreme Court placed arbitration on a level playing field with judicial proceedings when it reversed the First Circuit on this part of its ruling and actually challenged and refuted the long-standing badges of prejudice that had nourished judicial hostility against arbitration. The majority's opinion surgically focused on the six rudimentary precepts that had sustained this derisive and diminishing preconception of arbitral processes. Numerous scholars have written extensively on the applicability of *Mitsubishi* to varying areas of law and what it represented going forward.[89]

First, the Court observed that "[t]he mere appearance of an antitrust dispute does not alone warrant invalidation of the selected forum *on the undemonstrated*

It was not until 1970 that the United States ratified the Convention 3 U.S.T. 2517, T.I.A.S. No. 6997. Congress subsequently enacted Chapter 2 to Title 9, the United States Code, 9 U.S.C. §§201–208 for purposes of implementing U.S. obligations pursuant to the Convention. Also, the provisions of Chapter 1 of Title 9, the United States Arbitration Act, 9 U.S.C. §1 *et seq.*, were rendered applicable to Chapter 2 to the extent that they did not conflict with the Convention. 9 U.S.C. §208.

85 *Id.* at 624 (citation omitted). The facts in *Mitsubishi* are simple and only command cursory recitation. Plaintiff, an automobile manufacturer filed an action against an automobile dealer alleging, among other claims, nonpayment of stored vehicles, contractual storage penalties, damage to manufacturer's warranties and goodwill, and expiration of distributorship. The dealer filed a counterclaim asserting violations of the Sherman Act, the Automobile Dealers' Day in Court Act, Puerto Rico Dealers' Act, and Puerto Rico Antitrust and Unfair Competition Statutes.

86 *Id.* at 620.

87 *Id.* at 621 (citation omitted).

88 *Id.* at 623.

89 Jill A. Pietrowski, *Enforcing International Commercial Arbitration Agreements Post-Mitsubishi v. Soler*, 36 Am. U.L. Rev. 57 (1986); David Westin, *Foreign Plaintiffs in Products Liability Actions: The Defense of Forum Non Conveniens*, 83 A.J.I.L. 438 (1989); Charles H. Brower, *EMERGING DILEMMAS IN INTERNATIONAL ECONOMIC ARBITRATION: Mitsubishi, Investor-State Arbitration, and the Law of State Immunity*, 20 Am. U. Int'l L. Rev. 907 (2005); Joseph T. McLaughlin, *CHOICE-OF-LAW PROBLEMS IN INTERNATIONAL COMMERCIAL ARBITRATION. By Horacio A. Grigera Naon*, 16 Fordham Int'l L.J. 946 (1993).

assumption that the arbitration clause is tainted. A party resisting arbitration of course may attack directly the validity of the agreement to arbitrate."[90]

It is clear that the parochial and archaic misconception that had been decisive in prior decisions holding that a prospective claimant pursuant to a specially enacted statutory cause of action would be prejudiced by the want of recourse to challenge a wrongfully issued arbitration award had now been stripped of all legitimacy. Implicit, if not explicit, in the Court's ruling on this critical point is the conviction that arbitration gives parties ample opportunity to correct wrongs despite the narrow grounds available for such reconsiderations.

Second, the perennial objection to the perceived ill-suited nature of arbitration to process complex commercial disputes is directly questioned and disavowed by the Court's analysis. The Court specifically observed that the "potential complexity should not suffice to ward off arbitration. We might well have some doubt that even the courts following *American Safety* subscribe fully to the view that antitrust matters are inherently insusceptible to resolution by arbitration . . . in sum, the factor of potential complexity alone does not persuade us that an arbitral tribunal could not properly handle an antitrust matter."[91] This proposition was endorsed and supported by arbitration's hallmark of being able to secure experts even in the most intricate legal fields to participate in the presentation and elucidation of sophisticated factual, economic, and legal issues. Identification of this feature, endemic to the arbitration procedure, was without precedent in Supreme Court jurisprudence.

Third, it was underscored that it is important to reject "the proposition that an arbitration panel will pose too great a danger of innate hostility to the constraints on business conduct that antitrust law imposes. International arbitrators frequently are drawn from the legal as well as the business community where the dispute has an important legal component, the parties and the arbitral body with whose assistance they have agreed to settle their dispute can be expected to select arbitrators accordingly."[92]

Fourth, when presented with the premise that parties to an arbitration proceeding are somehow inherently incapable of securing able and competent arbitrators who subscribe to standard ethical norms in the performance of their task, the Court noted that it would not "indulge the presumption that the parties and arbitral body conducting a proceeding will be unable or unwilling to retain competent, conscientious and impartial arbitrators."[93]

Fifth, the argument that the Sherman Act promotes national interests, and therefore the treble-damages component to rights accorded to private litigants was not susceptible to adjudication in an arbitral context, was emphatically rejected. Here, for the first time, the Court announced that such remedies are remedial in nature despite also playing an important role in penalizing wrongdoers and thus creating a chilling effect with respect to prospective tortfeasors.[94]

Lastly, the Court highlighted the need for national courts "to shake off the old judicial hostility to arbitration, and also their customary and understandable unwillingness to cede jurisdiction of a claim arising under domestic law to a foreign

[90] *Id.* at 632 (emphasis added).
[91] *Id.* at 633–634.
[92] *Id.* at 634.
[93] *Id.*
[94] *Id.* at 635. (The Court specifically found that "[t]he importance of the private damages remedy, however, does not compel the conclusion that it may not be sought outside an American court.")

or transnational tribunal. To this extent, at least, it will be necessary for national courts to subordinate domestic notions of arbitrability to the international policy favoring commercial arbitration."[95]

Accordingly, the First Circuit's ruling was reversed to the extent that it held that statutorily created antitrust claims are not arbitrable. More importantly, however, the Supreme Court disrobed the cloak of legitimacy that had vested the four fundamental badges of judicial hostility against arbitration as grounds for subordinating arbitral proceedings to a role inferior to that of judicial recourse in both domestic and international arbitration. This seminal ruling spawned meaningful institutional arbitration (both domestically and internationally) in the United States. Today, claims based upon (i) unfair and deceptive trade practice statutory causes of action,[96] (ii) age discrimination,[97] (iii) sports-related claims arising from punishments adjudicated against athletes for violations of collective bargaining agreement,[98] (iv) Racketeer Influenced and Corrupt Organizations (RICO) statutory causes of action,[99] (v) The Civil Rights Act of 1991,[100] (vi) The Labor Management Relations Act, 1947,[101] (vii) seeking the award of punitive damages,[102] and (viii) class actions,[103] to mention just a few, are susceptible to arbitration without material judicial interdiction of any sort.

D. THE REVERSAL OF *WILKO v. SWAN*: TIME FOR A NEW PARADIGM

Significantly, scarcely four years from its decision in *Mitsubishi*, the Court in *Rodriquez de Quijas v. Shearson/American Express* revisited the question of "whether a predispute agreement to arbitrate claims under the Securities Act of 1933 is enforceable, requiring resolution of the claims only in a judicial forum."[104] The resulting opinion triggered a lively debate about the Supreme Court's development of arbitration doctrine.[105] Petitioners had invested approximately $400,000 in securities

95 *Id.* at 638–639 (citation omitted).

96 *See, e.g.*, JLM Industries, Inc. v. Stolt-Nielson, 387 F.3d 163 (2d Cir. 2004).

97 *See, e.g.*, Gilmer v. Interstate/Johnson Lane Corp., 500 U.S. 20 (1991).

98 *See, e.g.*, Sprewell v. Golden State Warriors, 266 F.3d 979 (9th Cir. 2001).

99 *See, e.g.*, Shearson/American Express, Inc. v. McMahon, 482 U.S. 220 (1987).

100 *See, e.g.*, Maye v. Smith Barney, Inc., 897 F.Supp. 100 (S.D.N.Y. 1995).

101 *See, e.g.*, Stroehmann Bakeries, Inc. v. Local 776, International Brotherhood of Teamsters, 969 F.2d 1436 (3rd Cir. 1992).

102 *See, e.g.*, Mastrobuono v. Shearson Lehman Hutton, Inc., 514 U.S. 52 (1995)

103 *See, e.g.*, Green Tree Financial Corp. v. Bazzle, 539 U.S. 444 (2003).

104 Rodriguez de Quijas v. American Express, Inc., 490 U.S. at 478.

105 *See, for example*, Michael A. Scodro, *Arbitrating Novel Legal Questions: A Recommendation for Reform*, 105 YALE L.J. 1927 (1996); J. R. Sever, *Rodriguez de Quijas V. Shearson/American Express, Inc.: A Green Light to Arbitration, a Yellow Light to Investors*, 64 TUL. L. REV. 1312 (1990); R. DOUGLAS CAMPBELL, *RESOLUTION OF DISPUTES IN THE NEW MILLENNIUM: PERCEPTIONS, MYTHS AND THE LAW: COMMENT ALTERNATIVE DISPUTE RESOLUTION: "WAIVER OF TRIAL" CLAUSE MANDATING ARBITRATION OF SECURITIES DISPUTES SHOULD REQUIRE THE APPLICATION OF STATE LAW*, 31 ST. MARY'S L. J. 1039 (2000); J. Kirkland Grant, *Securities Arbitration: Is Required Arbitration Fair to Investors?*, 24 NEW ENG.L. REV. 389 (1989); Leslie William Moore, Rodriguez de Quijas v. Shearson/American Express, Inc.: *Is Securities Arbitration Finally Above Suspicion?*, 78 KY. L.J. 839 (1990); William C. Hermann, *Arbitration of Securities Disputes: Rodriguez and New Arbitration Rules Leave Investors Holding a Mixed Bag*, 65 IND. L.J. 697 (1990); LAURIE F. HUMPHREY, *RODRIGUEZ DE*

pursuant to an executed standard customer agreement with a broker. That agreement included an arbitration clause providing that "the parties agreed to settle any controversies 'relating to [the] account' through binding arbitration that complies with specified procedures."[106] The investments did not yield profits, prompting the petitioner to sue respondent and its broker-agent in charge of the accounts. That action averred that petitioner's funds were lost "in unauthorized and fraudulent transactions."[107] Moreover, petitioners further averred in their pleading violations of federal and state law, including claims arising from Section 12(2) of the Securities Act of 1933 (15 U.S.C. §77/(2), together with claims bottomed on three sections of the Securities Exchange Act of 1934.[108]

Borrowing analytic support from *Wilko v. Swan*, the district court entered an order compelling the submission of all claims to arbitration but for those raised pursuant to Section 12(2) of the Securities Act. Upon respondents' motion for reconsideration, the district court not only reaffirmed its ruling but also entered a default judgment against the broker.[109]

The Fifth Circuit Court of Appeals reversed, holding that the arbitration agreement was "enforceable because this Court's subsequent decisions have reduced *Wilko* to 'obsolescence.'"[110] *Certiorari* jurisdiction ensued.

Remarkably, the Court observed "that *Wilko* was not obviously correct, 'for the language prohibiting waiver of compliance with any of the provisions of this title could easily have been read to relate to substantive provisions of the Act without including the remedy provisions.'"[111] In addition, the Court acknowledged that it had not read the language in *Wilko* and advanced two reasons for this construction. Even a surface analysis renders plain that both grounds upon which the erroneous ruling was predicated had a foundation in two of the four badges of prejudice responsible for the doctrinal stagnation of arbitration. The Court noted that "[f]irst, [it had] rejected the argument that 'arbitration is merely a forum of trial to be used in lieu of a trial at law.'"[112] The Court further stressed that this proposition was premised on the view that "Section 14 does not permit waiver of 'the right to select the judicial' in favor of arbitration, [citation omitted] because 'arbitration lacks the certainty of a suit at law under the Act to enforce [the buyers'] rights.'"[113] In tandem, the following argument was identified as also supporting the misguided *Wilko* opinion. Second, the Court concluded that the Securities Act was intended to protect buyers of securities, who often do not deal at arm's length with sellers by offering them "a wider choice of courts and venue than is enjoyed by participants in other business transactions, making 'the right to select a judicial forum' a particularly valuable feature of the Securities Act."[114]

QUIJAS V. SHEARSON/AMERICAN EXPRESS, INC. AND LAMPF, PLEVA, LIPKIND, PRUPIS & PETIGROW V. GILBERTSON: BLURRING THE DISTINCTIONS BETWEEN THE SECURITIES ACTS AND AMONG SECURITIES CLAIMS, 42 Case W. Res. 659 (1992).

106 Rodriguez de Quijas v. American Express, Inc., 490 U.S. at 478.

107 *Id.*

108 *Id* at 479.

109 *Id.*

110 *Id.*

111 *Id.* at 480 (citing Alberto-CulverCo. v. Scherk, 484 F.2d 611, 618 n.7 (7th Cir. 1973) (Stevens, J. dissenting), *rev'd*, 417 U.S. 506 (1974)).

112 *Id.* (citation omitted)

113 *Id.* (citation omitted)

114 *Id.* (citation omitted).

With penetrating lucidity, the Court premised its affirmance on four critical insights. First, it enunciated that the Court's characterization of arbitration in *Wilko* was governed "by what Judge Jerome Frank called 'the old judicial hostility to arbitration.'"[115] Indeed, it identified an erosion over time "beginning in the lower courts."[116] In fact, it emphasized that "questions of arbitrability must be addressed with a healthy regard for the federal policy favoring arbitration."[117] This salubrious and explicit reference to federal policy favoring arbitration, particularly in the context of determining the arbitrability of a federally created right directed at a particular universe of possible and, therefore, prospective claimants, constitutes a stark indictment against the historical prejudices that stunted the development of arbitration and cultivated judicial prejudice against arbitral proceedings both as (i) an alternative dispute resolution methodology on the same level playing field as judicial proceedings, and (ii) a contract equal to any other legally cognizable contractual agreement.[118]

Second, significant analytical support was drawn from its prior ruling in *Mitsubishi*. The "shift in the court's view on arbitration away from those adopted in *Wilko*" was forcefully asserted and is shown by the flat statement in *Mitsubishi*:

> By agreeing to arbitrate a statutory claim, a party does not forgo the substantive rights afforded by the statute; it only submits to the resolution in an arbitral, rather than a judicial, forum.[119]

Wilko's fundamental tenet asserting that arbitral proceedings do not and cannot accord special classes of prospective claimants protected by federal legislation protection akin to that found pursuant to judicial recourse was resoundingly rejected as a legacy of prejudice pervading U.S. judicial culture. Nowhere in *Wilko*, nor in other cases preceding *Wilko*, do scholars encounter any series of arguments, contentions, premises, or propositions arising from sustained analysis that corroborate,

115 *Id.* (citing Kulukundis Shipping Co. v. Amtorg Trading Corp., 126 F.2d 978, 985 (2d Cir. 1942)).

116 *Id.* (citing *Scherk*, 484 F.2d. at 616 (Stevens, J. dissenting) (citing cases), Sherson/American Express, Inc. v. McMahan, 482 U.S. 220 (1987); Mitsubishi Motors Corp. v. Solar, 473 U.S. 614 (1985), *and* Moses H. Cone Memorial Hospital v. Mercury Construction Corp, 103 S. Ct. 927 (1983)).

117 *Rodriguez de Quijas*, 490 U.S. at 481 (quoting Moses H. Cone Memorial Hospital v. Mercury Construction Corp., 460 U.S. 1, 24 (1983)).

118 Although not referenced in the case nor addressed by the parties at any stage in the proceedings culminating with the Supreme Court's review of this cause, ultimately the doctrine of severability pursuant to which an arbitration clause embodied in a contract would be construed as a free standing contract having the identical juridic dignity as the more general contract embodying it. Even though the origins and genesis of the doctrine of severability can be traced to the FAA, 9 U.S.C. §§1–16, the doctrinal development was a product of jurisprudence, i.e. caselaw. As discussed supra., the trilogy of Supreme Court opinions commencing with *Prima Paint Corporation v. Flood & Conklin Mfg. Co.*, 388 U.S. 395 (1967); *Southland Corp. v. Keating*, 465 U.S. 1 (1984); and the interesting and somewhat polemical seminal case of *Buckeye Check Cashing, Inc. v. Cardgna*, 546 U.S. 440 (2006). The critical premise embodied in the FAA that spawn this jurisprudence is the clear directive contained in 9 U.S.C. §2, which indeed codifies to some extent the federal policy promoting and embracing arbitration and places arbitration agreements in *pari materia* with all other contracts. This section in pertinent part provides:

> A written provision in . . . a contract . . . to settle by arbitration a controversy thereafter arising out of such contract . . . or any agreement in writing to submit to arbitration an existing controversy arising out of such a contract . . . shall be valid, irrevocable, and enforceable, save upon such grounds as exist at law or in equity for the revocation of a contract.

119 *Rodriguez de Quijas*, 490 U.S. at 481 (citing *Mitsubishi*, 473 U.S. at 628).

pursuant to any objective criteria, this long-standing badge of prejudice against arbitral proceedings.[120]

Third, the paucity of any recorded evidence in the case from which it may be inferred that the contract at issue was an adhesion contract provided a firm premise from which to infer that Section 2 of the FAA "allows the courts to give relief where the party opposing arbitration presents 'well-supported claims that the agreement to arbitrate resulted from the sort of fraud or overwhelming economic power that would provide grounds for revocation of any contract.'"[121] Specifically, the methodology for relief provided by Section 2 of the FAA certainly comports with the Securities Act's public policy to protect buyers from the disadvantages foisted upon them by sellers in the marketplace. This public policy concern constituted a recurring theme in *Wilko v. Swan*.[122]

Fourth, inevitably the Supreme Court addressed the irreconcilable antinomy between the analyses and holdings in *Wilko* and *McMahon*. The conceptual inconsistencies arising from these two cases in particular were inimical to the universally accepted canon of statutory construction that the 1933 and 1934 acts must be construed harmoniously as they "constitute interrelated components of the federal regulatory scheme governing transactions and securities."[123] The Court also observed that in addition to resolving the inconsistent construction applied to two interrelated federal statutes within a common statutory rubric, the resolution of this antinomy also serves "to discourage litigants from manipulating their allegations merely to cast their claims under one of the securities laws rather than the other."[124] Consequently, the only viable methodology for addressing this inconsistency in statutory construction would be to overrule *Wilko*.[125]

Finally, the Court rejected petitioner's last argument asserting that should the Supreme Court reverse its decision in *Wilko*, the new decision would not be binding on the parties because it would be akin to ruling retroactively on the operative facts of the case. Two propositions were instrumental in rejecting this contention. At the outset, there is significant authority holding that the law announced by the Supreme Court governs the case at bar.[126] Secondly, the very reasonable and commonsense premise was advanced asserting that "[a]lthough our decision to overrule *Wilko*

[120] In support of this premise, the Supreme Court observed:

> To the extent that *Wilko* rested on suspicion of arbitration as a method of weakening the protections afforded in the substantive law to would-be complainants, *it has fallen far out of step with our current strong endorsement of the federal statutes favoring this method of resolving disputes.*
>
> *Once the outmoded presumption of disfavoring arbitration proceedings is set to one side, it becomes clear that the right to select a judicial forum and the wider choice of courts are not such essential features of the Securities Act that §14 is properly construed to bar any waiver of those provisions. Nor are they so critical that they cannot be waived under the rationale that the Securities Act was intended to place buyers of securities on an equal footing with sellers. Wilko identified two different kinds of provisions in the Securities Act that would advance this objective. . . .*
>
> *These measures, moreover, are present in other federal statutes which have not been interpreted to prohibit enforcement of predispute agreements to arbitrate.* Citing as examples to *Shearson/American Express, Inc. v. McMahon* (construing the Securities Exchange Act of 1934; *see* 15 U.S.C. §78aa); *id.* (construing the RICO statutes; *see* 18 U.S.C. §1965); Mitsubishi Motors Corp. v. Soler Chrysler-Plymouth, Inc., supra (construing the antitrust laws; *see* 15 U.S.C. §15). *Id.* at 481–82.

[121] *Id.* at 483–84.

[122] *See, e.g.*, *Wilko*, 346 U.S. at 435.

[123] Ernst & Ernst v. Hochfelder, 425 U.S. 185, 206 (1976).

[124] *Rodriguez de* Quijas, 490 U.S. at 485.

[125] *Id.*

[126] In this connection, the Court cited to *St. Francis College v. Al-Khazraji*, 481 U.S. 604, 608 (1987); *and United States v. Schooner Peggy*, 5 U.S. (1 Cranch) 103, 109 (1801).

establishes a new principle of law for arbitration agreements under the Securities Act, this ruling furthers the purposes and effect of the Arbitration Act without undermining those of the Securities Act."[127]

The dissent does not discuss any of the precedents exemplifying a doctrinal development in the law governing U.S. arbitral proceedings seeking to place arbitration on an equal footing with judicial actions. This glaring omission, to a large extent, weakens what was already a flawed analysis, shifting the issues from "whether a predispute agreement to arbitrate claims under the Securities Act of 1933 is unenforceable, requiring resolution of the claims only in a judicial forum."[128] The following two themes in the case are particularly disconcerting: (1) The dissent's explicit reference to an analogy between the Court of Appeals' "judicial activism" in concluding that the arbitration agreement is enforceable and the Supreme Court's subsequent decisions reducing *Wilko* to "obsolescence," and (2) the majority's holding as indefensible actions that modify the construction of a statutory provision that Congress had not amended in three and a half decades, as want of respect for work-product.[129]

Equally unsatisfactory from an analytical and juridic perspective is the dissent's bewildering assertion that "a justice's vote in a case like this depends more on his or her views about the respective lawmaking responsibilities of Congress and this Court than on conflicting policy interests." The Court goes on to state that "judges who have confidence in their own ability to fashion public policy are less hesitant than those of us who are inclined to give wide latitude to the views of the voters' representatives on non-constitutional matters."[130] It is challenging to draw a meaningful connection between the issue causing the Court to exercise its *certiorari* jurisdiction and the contention that the adjudication of a dispute arising from a federally enacted statutory right by means of arbitration somehow gives rise to an issue concerning the separation of powers. The Court in the first place overruled a precedent that rested on a flawed proposition that no longer has doctrinal nor conceptual compatibility with Supreme Court and federal appellate court rulings. Not surprisingly, the dissent's *tour de force* reconfiguration of the dispositive issues undergoes practically no analysis, and its authors provide only conclusions.

The overruling of *Wilko* constitutes a landmark contribution both to arbitration and judicial proceedings.

[127] *Rodriguez de* Quijas, 490 U.S. at 485.
[128] *Id.* at 478.
[129] *Id.* at 486.
[130] *Id.* at 487.

CHAPTER 4

Procedural Change and 28 U.S.C. §1782: The Taking of Evidence v. Common Law Discovery

A. SECTION 1782 AND ITS ELEMENTS

The fundamental propositions governing Section 1782 can be succinctly summarized by citing the statute:

> (a) The district court of the district in which a person resides or is found may order him to give his testimony or statement or to produce a document or other thing for use in a proceeding in a *foreign* or *international tribunal*, including criminal *investigations* conducted *before* formal accusation. The order may be made . . . upon the application of *any interested person* and may direct that the testimony or statement be given, or the document or thing be produced, before a person appointed by the Court (emphasis supplied).

The current iteration of Section 1782 was modified in 1964. Courts have observed that Section 1782 was amended "to facilitate the conduct of litigation in foreign tribunals, improve international cooperation in litigation, and put the United States into the leadership position among world nations in this respect."[1] According to the Senate Report that accompanied the final version of the draft that eventually became the current iteration of Section 1782, "Congress hoped to encourage foreign countries to revise their judicial procedures similarly."[2]

Analysis of the opinions federal courts have issued construing Section 1782 establishes that the jurisprudence is of a single voice in holding that this provision aspires to the "twin goals" of (i) providing an efficient means for the assistance of *interested persons* engaged in international disputes to provide them with direct access to federal district courts, and (ii) encouraging foreign courts to provide comparable means of foreign assistance to those litigants in U.S. courts seeking the production of documents and information in foreign jurisdictions.[3] The Eleventh Circuit Court

[1] *See* In Re: Bayer A.G., 146 F.3d 188, 191–92 (3d Cir. 1998).

[2] *See In Re: Application of Asta Médica, S.A.*, 981 F.2d 1, 5 (1st Cir. 1992) (citing to S. Rep. No. 88-1850 (1964), *as reprinted in* 1964 U.S. C. C. A.N. 372, 3788).

[3] *See* Schmidtz v. Bernstein, Libhard and Lifhsitz, LLP, 376 F.3d 79, 84 (2d Cir. 2004). (The Second Circuit Court of Appeals emphatically has underscored that the twin goals of §1782 can be synthesized and stated as "providing efficient means of assistance to participants in international litigation in our federal courts and encouraging foreign countries by example to provide similar means of assistance to our courts.") *See also* Lancaster Factory Co., Ltd. v. Mangone, 90 F.3d 38, 41 (2d Cir. 1996) (citing F.Rep.No. 1580, 88th Cong., 2d Session. 2 (1964), *reprinted in* 1964 U.S.C.C.A.N. 3782, 3783); In Re:Gianoli Aldunte, 3 F.3d. 54, 58 (2d Cir. 1993) (same proposition); In Re: Ishihara Chemical Co., 251 F.3d 120, 124 (2d Cir. 2001) (citing the twin goals

of Appeals has recognized that the "legislative history shows that the purpose behind the proposed [1964 amendments to §1782] was to encourage other nations to follow the lead of the United States and to adjust their procedures in order to improve practices of international cooperation in litigation."[4]

In tracing the legislative intent underlying §1782, the Eleventh Circuit in *Trinidad and Tobago* asserted that Congress deliberately amplified the statute's scope to (i) include not only depositions and written interrogatories but also the discretion to secure documents and other tangible evidence, (ii) permit federal district courts to assist proceedings in "foreign tribunals" without limiting the meaning of "foreign tribunals" within the statute to courts or exclusively judicial fora, (iii) permit "interested persons" (and not just foreign tribunals as is the case in less efficient proceedings pursuant to Hague Convention strictures) directly to petition a federal district court for judicial assistance, and (iv) eliminate the requirement that the discovery process used be applicable only while there is a "pending proceeding" and that the documents and information produced only be used by a foreign tribunal.[5] The passage of the Act of March 3, 1863, however, soon restricted this

of §1782 as (i) providing efficient means of assistance to participants in international litigation pursuant to our federal courts and (ii) encouraging foreign countries by dint of this example to promote similar or analogous assistance to U.S. litigants); In Re Edelman, 295 F.3d 171, 175 (2d Cir. 2002) ("at bottom, this statute affords access to discovery of evidence in the United States for use in foreign proceedings."); In Re: Letter Rogatory from the Nedens District Court, Norway, 216 F.R.D. 277, 279 (S.D.N.Y. 2003) ("therefore, granting a motion to compel [party] to provide a blood sample would efficiently assist a request made by the Norwegian Court and would encourage Norway to provide similar assistance to our courts."); In Re Application of Grupo Gamma, S.A. de C.V., 2005 W.L. 937486, *1 (S.D.N.Y. 2005); In Re: Request of Oric, 2004 W.L. 2980648 (N.D.Ill. 2004); In Re: Application of Servicio Panamericano de Protección, S.A., 354 F.Supp. 2d 269, 273–74 (S.D.N.Y. 2004); In the Matter of the Application of Procter & Gamble Co., 334 F. Supp.2d 1112, 1113 (E.D.Wis. 2004); *and* In Re: Application of Guy, 2004 W.L. 1857580 (S.D.N.Y. 2004).

See also Anonymous, Extra-Statutory Discovery Requirements: Violating the Twin Purposes of 28 U.S.C. Section 1782, 29 VAND. J. TRANSNAT'L L. 117 (1996); Jeffrey A. Wortman, *In Search of Discovery: The Split Between the Circuits Surrounding a Threshold Discoverability Requirement to Provide Assistance Under 28 U.S.C. 1782*, 30 TEX. INT'L L.J. 583 (1995); Timothy M. Zabbo, *EVIDENCE – NO EXTRA STATUTORY BARRIERS TO OBTAINING DISCOVERY UNDER 28 U.S.C. §1782*, 29 SUFFOLK TRANSNAT'L L. REV. 147 (2005); Mousa Zalta, *RECENT INTERPRETATION OF 28 U.S.C. 1782(A) BY THE SUPREME COURT IN INTEL CORP. V. ADVANCED MICRO DEVICES, INC.: THE EFFECTS ON FEDERAL DISTRICT COURTS, DOMESTIC LITIGANTS, AND FOREIGN TRIBUNALS AND LITIGANTS*, 17 PACE INT'L L. REV. 413 (2005); Richard D. Haygood, *Euromepa v. Esmerian: The Scope of the Inquiry Into Foreign Law When Evaluating Discovery Requests Under 28 U.S.C. sec. 1782*, 21 N.C.J. INT'L L. & COM. REG. 491 (1996); Nathan Reierson, *OUT OF BOUNDS? APPLICABILITY OF FEDERAL DISCOVERY ORDERS UNDER 28 U.S.C. SECTION 1782 BY INTERNATIONAL ATHLETIC GOVERNING BODIES FOR USE IN INTERNAL DISPUTE RESOLUTION PROCEDURES*, 19 LOY. L.A. ENT. L.J. 631 (1999); Peter Metis, *INTERNATIONAL JUDICIAL ASSISTANCE: DOES 28 U.S.C. 1782 CONTAIN AN IMPLICIT DISCOVERABILITY REQUIREMENT?*, 18 FORDHAM INT'L L.J. 332 (1994); Anna Conley, *A NEW WORLD OF DISCOVERY: THE RAMIFICATIONS OF TWO RECENT FEDERAL COURTS' DECISIONS GRANTING JUDICIAL ASSISTANCE TO ARBITRAL TRIBUNALS PURSUANT TO 28 U.S.C. §1782*, 17 AM. REV. INT'L ARB. 45 (2006).

4 *See* In Re: Request for Assistance from Ministry of Legal Affairs of Trinidad and Tobago, 848 F.2d. 1151 (11th Cir. 1988).

5 In *Trinidad and Tobago*, the Court analyzed with extraordinary scholastic skill §1782's legislative history. Here the Court in painstaking detail observed that "the Act of March 2, 1855 first

first statute. The 1863 Act allowed U.S. courts to obtain testimony to assist foreign courts only if such testimony was for use in suits (i) that pertained to the recovery of money or property, (ii) that were pending in a foreign country with which the United States was at peace, and (iii) in which the government of the foreign country was a party or had an interest. This 1863 statute, with its limitations, remained relatively intact until 1948.

Beginning in 1948 Congress enacted several amendments that broadened the scope of the statute. Both changed the limitation that the "suit [be] for the recovery of money or property" and eventually only required that the action be a "judicial proceeding."[6] During this time, however, Congress retained the requirement that the judicial proceeding be pending in a foreign country with which the United States was at peace.

In 1964, Congress enacted the most recent amendment to §1782. These modifications marked a significant departure from Congress' cautious approach to international judicial assistance.[7] Congress adopted, without objection, a set of proposals submitted by the Commission on International Rules of Judicial Procedure that revised §1782. The legislative history demonstrates unambiguously that the purpose underlying the proposals was to encourage other nations to follow the lead of the United States and to adjust their procedures in order to improve practices of international cooperation in litigation.[8]

It is critical to note that 28 U.S.C. §1782 petitions are subject to the absolute discretion of federal district courts.[9] Hence, even where all of the statutory elements are met, only upon an affirmative showing that the trial court engaged in abuse of discretion shall a ruling be reversed.

Even though it is less than clear from the jurisprudence, courts tend to limit grants of 28 U.S.C. §1782 petitions only to those cases where a showing that the information or documents sought also *would be* discoverable in the foreign jurisdiction initiating the petition ("the requesting forum").[10] This fundamental tenet categorically was rejected by the Second Circuit Court of Appeals. The Court in *In The Matter of the Application of Euromepa, S.A. v. Esmerian, Inc.*,[11] elucidates this premise as well as the concept of symmetrical reciprocity in the production of documents and information pursuant to a §1782 petition.

In that case the Second Circuit reversed a trial court ruling that denied a §1782 petition. The reversal was predicated on a finding of "abuse of discretion."[12] The

authorized federal courts to assist foreign tribunals. This statute granted federal courts the power to compel the testimony of witnesses in order to assist foreign courts. In Re: Letter Rogatory from the Justice Court, District of Montreal, Canada, 523 F.2d 562, 564 (6th Cir. 1975). *Trinidad and Tobago*, 848 F.2d at 1153–1154.

6 *See Act of May 24, 1949*, Ch. 139, §93, 63 Stat. 103 (1949).

7 *Letter Rogatory from Montreal, Canada*, 523 F.2d at 656.

8 *See Trinidad and Tobago*, 848 F.2d at 1153–1154.

9 *See, e.g.*, United Kingdom v. United States, 238 F.3d 1312, 1318–19 (11th Cir. 2001); *and* Lo Ka Chun v. Lo To, 858 F.2d 1564, 1565–66 (11th Cir. 1988) (holding that Congress has granted federal district courts like discretion under §1782).

10 *See, e.g.*, In Re: Application of Asta Médica, S.A., 981 F.2d 1, 7 (1st Cir. 1992); *and* Lo Ka Chun v. Lo To, 858 F.2d 1564, 1566 (11th Cir. 1988).

11 In the Matter of the Application of Euromepa, S.A. v. Esmerian, Inc., 51 F.3d 1095 (2d Cir. 1995).

12 *Id.* at 1097.

Court observed that "to say that a district court may or may not, in its discretion, order discovery, does not mean that it is free to do so on inappropriate grounds. In this case, we conclude that the district court misapplied our guiding precedence, and misperceived the extent to which it should construe foreign law in deciding whether to order discovery."[13] In fashioning its holding the Second Circuit dispensed with four premises that purported to constitute the dispositive standard in adjudicating a §1782 petition. As an analytical point of departure the Court highlighted that in enacting §1782, Congress crafted "a one way street."[14] Otherwise stated, the legislation "grants wide assistance to others but demands nothing in return."[15]

Appellate courts, for a considerable time, were in disarray as to the issue of whether the exhaustion of remedies in the petitioning foreign jurisdiction constituted a predicate to the filing of a §1782 petition. The Second Circuit underscored that it had already rejected "any implicit requirement that any evidence sought in the United States be discoverable under the laws of a foreign country."[16] Consequently, the Second Circuit suggested that the *discoverability* of the documents or information sought in the "petitioning foreign jurisdiction" is but *a factor* to consider in adjudicating such a request.

Finally, the Court sweepingly removed any doubt concerning the extent to which a district court must first research the procedural or substantive law of the petitioning foreign jurisdiction as a predicate to the adjudication of a §1782 petition. Precedent from other circuits holds that discovery would be proscribed where such gathering of evidence would offend the laws of the relevant foreign jurisdiction. Here the Court highlighted that it is neither necessary nor desirable to engage in an exhaustive analysis of foreign law for the purpose of somehow divining the attitudes of foreign nations with respect to efforts seeking judicial assistance in the production of documents or information in the United States.[17] This precept does not purport to state that a district court should disregard in its totality consideration of foreign law and the attitude of foreign countries with respect to the particular issues that may be raised in a §1782 petition. Engaging in explicit reference to the legislative history as it relates to the "nature and attitudes of the government of the

13 *Id.*

14 *Id.*

15 *Id.* (citing In Re: Malev Hungarian Airlines, 964 F.2d 97, 99 (2d Cir.), *cert. denied*, 506 U.S. 861 (1992)). *See also* John Deere Ltd. v. Sperry Corp., 754 F.2d 132, 135 (3d Cir. 1985) (holding that §1782 "does not require reciprocity as a predicate to the grant of a discovery order.")

16 *Id.* at 1098 (citing In Re: Application of Aldunate, 3 F.3d 54, 59 (2d Cir.) ("if Congress had intended to impose such a sweeping restriction on the district court's discretion, at a time when it was enacting liberalizing amendments to the statute, it would have included the statutory language to that effect.")), *cert. denied*, 510 U.S. 965 (1993).

17 The conclusion concerning this critical precept rested on the commentaries of one of the principal architects of the current version of §1782:

> [The statute's] drafters realized that making the extension of American assistance dependent on foreign law would open a veritable pandora's box. They definitely did not want to have a request for cooperation turn into an unduly expensive and time-consuming fight about foreign law. That would be quite contrary to what they sought to be achieved. They also realized that, although civil law countries do not have discovery rules similar to those of common law countries, they often do have quite different procedures for discovering information that would not properly be evaluated without a rather broad understanding of the subtleties of the applicable foreign system. It would, they judged, be wholly inappropriate for an American district court to try to obtain this understanding for the purpose of honoring a simple request for assistance.
>
> Hans Smit, *Recent Developments in International Litigation*, 35 S.Tex. L.J. 215, 235 (1994).

country from which the [discovery] request emanates," the Third Circuit Court of Appeals interpreted the drafters' language and intent with respect to this issue as "authoriz[ing] district courts to scrutinize the underlying fairness of the foreign proceedings to ensure that they comply with notions of due process."[18]

In *Euromepa*, the Second Circuit adopted the Third Circuit's exegesis on this point and concluded that "it is unwise – as well as intention with the aims of §1782 – for district judges to try to glean the accepted practices and attitudes of other nations from what are likely to be conflicting and, perhaps, biased interpretations of foreign law."[19]

Euromepa established four principles as a dispositive standard in adjudicating a Section 1782 petition but remained in direct and express conflict with the First Circuit Court of Appeals' pronouncement three years earlier in the matter of *In Re: Application of Asta Médica, S.A., et al.*[20]

In that case the First Circuit reversed the trial court's ruling in favor of a petition that sought from a person residing within the district court's own jurisdiction documents and deposition testimony. The Court premised its analysis on the opinions entered by (i) the Tenth Circuit, (ii) the Third Circuit, (iii) the Second Circuit, and (iv) the Federal District Court for the Eastern District of Pennsylvania, all of which interpreted the dispositive standard as requiring consideration of the issue of whether the discovery sought in the United States would be discoverable and permissible in the country of origin.[21] The conflict between the holding in *Asta Médica, S.A.*, and *Euromepa* was decisively and exhaustively addressed by the Supreme Court in *Intel Corporation v. Advanced Micro Devices, Inc.*[22]

B. *INTEL CORP. v. ADVANCED MICRO DEVICES*: DISCOVERY IS ENGRAFTED UPON ARBITRATION AND CHANGE RESHAPES THE HORIZON

Unbeknownst to the divided Circuit Courts of Appeals, the resolution of the conflict between them would spawn nothing short of a revolutionary development in the procedural rules applicable to arbitrations, particularly in an international context.

18 *Euromepa*, 51 F.3d at 1099.

19 *Id.*

20 In Re: Application of Asta Médica, S.A., 981 F.2d 1 (1st Cir. 1992).

21 *See id.* at 6 (citing *In Re: Request for Assistance from Ministry of Legal Affairs of Trinidad and Tobago*, 848 F.2d 1151, 1156 (11th Cir. 1988) ("the district court must decide whether the evidence would be discoverable in the foreign country before granting assistance"); *Lo Ka Chun*, 858 F.2d at 1566 (reversing the trial court with instruction for the district court to determine whether the evidence sought in the United States is discoverable in the country of origin [Hong Kong 1988]); John Deere, Ltd. v. Sperry, 754 F.2d 132, 136 (3d Cir. 1985); In Re: Court of the Commissioner of Patents for the Republic of South Africa, 88 F.R.D. 75, 77 (E.D.Pa. 1980) ("few actions could more significantly impede the development of international cooperation among courts than if the courts of the United States operated to give litigants in foreign cases processes of law to which they were not entitled in the appropriate foreign tribunals."). *See also Malev Hungarian Airlines*, 964 F.2d 97 (2d Cir. 1992) (holding that trial court abused its discretion in ruling that a party filing a §1782 petition first must attempt to secure a ruling from a Hungarian court in a case where the information sought under the petition would be readily discoverable in conformance with Hungarian rules.")

22 *Intel*, 542 U.S. 241 (2004).

In this same vein, the original drafters of the 1863 iteration of Section 1782, the drafters of the 1948 amendments to that statute, and finally, the authors of the 1964 amendments to the statute certainly would have been surprised to learn that their work-product soon would form and transform the principles governing and organizing one of the most critical procedural components of an arbitral proceeding: the gathering of evidence or *the taking of discovery*.

The doctrinal quagmire that obscured the dispositive standard to be followed in the adjudication of Section 1782 petitions was considerably addressed in 2004 in the now seminal Supreme Court case of *Intel Corp. v. Advanced Micro Devices* ("AMD").[23] This ruling fashioned clear and flexible standards for the consideration of Section 1782 applications. Of equal import, however, it paved the path for the virtually unbridled incorporation of discovery into foreign arbitral proceedings where witnesses and information presumably reside in the United States.

In exercising its jurisdiction,[24] the Supreme Court identified the issue before it as one "concern[ing] the authority of federal district courts to assist in the production of evidence for use in a foreign international tribunal."[25] After a detailed review of the action's procedural history, the Court noted that pursuant to the Ninth Circuit Court of Appeals' pronouncement, a claimant before the Director-General for Competition of the Commission of the European Communities ("European Commission" or "Commission") qualified as an "interested person" for purposes of Section 1782. Additionally, the Supreme Court observed that the Commission "is a tribunal" when acting in the capacity of a "first-instance decision-maker." Likewise, the Court held that the "discovery . . . sought under Section 1782(a) must be in reasonable contemplation, but need not be 'pending' or 'imminent'" (emphasis in original). Finally, the Supreme Court reasoned that "Section 1782(a) contains no threshold requirement that evidence sought from a federal district court would be discoverable under the law governing the foreign proceeding."[26]

Because petitioner, in part, as alternative relief asked the Court to exercise "supervisory authority to adopt rules barring Section 1782(a) discovery here,"[27] a factual analysis of the case is compelled.

[23] *See* Kandy L. Parson, *A remedy fashioned by an arbitrator is within the scope of the arbitrator's authority if the remedy is rationally related to the contract and to the breach, as interpreted by the arbitrator: Advanced Micro Devices, Inc. v. Intel Corp.*, 23 Pepp. L. Rev. 243 (1995); Jessica T. Martin, *Advanced Micro Devices v. Intel Corp. and Judicial Review of Commercial Arbitration Awards: When Does a Remedy "Exceed" Arbitral Powers?*, 46 Hastings L.J. 1907 (1995); E. Morgan Boeing, *MAJORITY AND DISSENT IN INTEL: APPROACHES TO LIMITING INTERNATIONAL JUDICIAL ASSISTANCE*, 29 Hastings Int'l & Comp. L. Rev. 381 (2006); Daniel A. Lock, *SECTION 1782(A) AFTER INTEL: RECONCILING POLICY CONSIDERATIONS AND A PROPOSED FRAMEWORK TO EXTEND JUDICIAL ASSISTANCE TO INTERNATIONAL ARBITRAL TRIBUNALS*, 27 Cardozo L. Rev. 1035 (2005).

[24] The Court exercised *certiorari* jurisdiction "in view of the division among the circuits on the question of whether §1782 (a) contains a foreign discoverability requirement." The Court also granted review on two other questions. First, does §1782 (a) make discovery available to complainants . . . , who do not have the status of private "litigants" and are not sovereign agents? [citation omitted]. Second, must a "proceeding" before a foreign "tribunal" be "pending" or at least "imminent" for an applicant to invoke §1782(a) successfully?" *Id.* at 252.

[25] *Id.* at 246.

[26] *Id.* at 246–7.

[27] *Id.* at 264.

C. INTEL CORP.: A CLOSER LOOK

AMD (respondent) and Intel (petitioner) are global competitors in the microprocessor industry. In October 2000, AMD filed an antitrust complaint with the Directorate-General for Competition of the Commission ("DG-Competition").[28] The Commission is the executive and administrative organ of the European Communities and is charged with responsibility for a gamut of subject matters encompassed by the European Union treaty, including treaty provisions and regulations governing commercial competition.[29] Indeed, the DG-Competition, which functions under the Commission's auspices, constitutes the European Union's principal antitrust law enforcement agency.[30]

Significantly, AMD's complaint averred counts for violations of European competition law concerning (i) *Intel*'s purported abuse of its dominant position in the European market pursuant to loyalty rebates, (ii) *Intel's* exercise of exclusive purchasing agreements with manufacturers and retailers, (iii) purported price discrimination, and (iv) standard-setting cartels.[31] In this regard, AMD recommended that the DG-Competition seek discovery of documents Intel had produced in a private antitrust suit filed in a federal district court in Alabama.[32]

It should be observed that the DG-Competition "declined" to pursue judicial assistance in the United States.[33] This refusal precipitated AMD's filing of a Section 1782(a) petition with the Federal District Court for the Northern District of California, where both Intel and AMD have their respective headquarters, seeking an order compelling Intel to produce documents discovered in the *Intergraph* litigation together with materials filed with the Federal District Court in Alabama. In this connection, AMD averred "that it sought the materials in connection with the complaint it had filed with the European Commission."[34]

As a predicate to its ruling on the meaning of a "foreign tribunal" within Section 1782(a), the Court underscored that despite wanting in the formal status of a "party" or "litigant" in Commission proceedings, an entity filing a complaint is accorded "significant procedural rights" and "may submit to the DG-Competition information in support of its allegations, and may seek judicial review of the Commission's disposition of a complaint."[35] The Court further emphasized that a complainant appearing before the Commission (i) is empowered to initiate an investigation, (ii) is vested with the right to provide the DG-Competition with information for its consideration, and (iii) may elect to seek judicial recourse should the Commission either discontinue the investigation or dismiss the complaint.[36] Thus, a complainant's rights in a proceeding before the Commission provide a compelling and attractive factual basis from which to infer that it has "a reasonable interest in obtaining [judicial] assistance and therefore 'qualifies as an interested person' within any fair construction of that term."[37]

28 *Id.* at 250.

29 *Id.*

30 *Id.*

31 *Id.*

32 *Id.*

33 This seemingly innocuous fact will prove to be quite material in the analysis evaluating possible methodologies for avoidance of §1782 application.

34 *Intel*, 542 U.S. at 250.

35 *Id.* [citations omitted]

36 *Id.* at 256.

37 *Id.*

Indeed it was precisely based upon meticulous scrutiny of the rights accorded to complainants before the Commission that the Court bottomed its rejection of petitioner Intel's first of five propositions upon which it had based its appeal that AMD was not an "interested person" within the meaning of Section 1782(a). Here, Intel had averred that Section 1782(a) only included "'litigants, foreign sovereigns, and the designated agents of those sovereigns' and excludes AMD, a mere complainant before the Commission accorded only 'limited rights.'"[38]

In considering whether the assistance sought by an "interested person" comports with the requisite predicate of "youth in a foreign or international tribunal," the Court premised its analysis on what has now become the guide post standard for determining "foreign or international tribunal" status for purposes of Section 1782(a). Specifically, the Supreme Court stressed that "both the Court of first instance and the European Court of Justice, qualify as tribunals. But those courts are not proof-taking instances. Their review is limited to the record before the Commission. . . . hence, AMD [respondent] could 'use' evidence in the reviewing courts *only* by submitting it to the Commission in the current, investigative stages."[39] Put simply, the two "appellate" tribunals to which the Commission is accountable are limited to review and analysis of *only* the evidence that a complainant submits in a proceeding before the Commission, thereby underscoring both (i) the importance of the Commission as an adjudicative body, and (ii) the material significance of "evidence gathering" at the Commission level.

Part of the conceptual rubric developed to determine whether a tribunal is "an international or a foreign tribunal" for purposes of Section 1782(a) was fashioned by seeking analytical support from the records of the Commission on International Rules of Judicial Procedure ("Rules Commission").[40] Upon consultation it became clear that 1958 Congress instructed the Rules Commission to serve in an advisory capacity to recommend procedural revisions "'for the rendering of assistance to foreign courts *and quasi-judicial agencies*.'"[41] The Commission responded by replacing the original term "any judicial proceeding" with the phrase "a proceeding in a foreign or international tribunal."[42] The Rules Commission's draft that Congress adopted incorporating this change was construed by Congress to "provid[e] the possibility of U.S. judicial assistance in connection with [administrative and quasi-judicial proceedings]."[43] The Supreme Court also cited academic commentary, asserting that "[t]he term 'tribunal'. . . . includes investigating magistrates, administrative and ***arbitral tribunals***, and quasi-judicial agencies, as well as conventional civil, commercial, criminal, and administrative courts" (emphasis supplied). It is in this specific reference that any form of the word "arbitration" appears at all in the opinion. Although the Court clearly identifies an arbitral tribunal as susceptible to meeting the Section 1782(a) "foreign or international tribunal" standard, the fleeting reference is clearly *dicta* and, therefore, of persuasive but certainly nonbinding effect. This allusion to arbitration, however, constitutes a major and material doctrinal step

38 *Id.*

39 *Id.* at 258.

40 *Id.*

41 *Id.*, citing to §2, 72 Stat. 1743, with emphasis added by the Court.

42 *Id.* at 258.

43 *Id.* (citing to S.Rep. No. 1580, at 7–8, U.S. Code Cong. & Admin. News 1964, pp. 3782, 3788).

toward a jurisprudentially binding proposition holding that in fact arbitral tribunals, under appropriate circumstances, are flatly within Section 1782(a)'s purview.

In fashioning the operative standard for the definition of a "foreign or international tribunal" within the meaning of 28 U.S.C. §1782(a), the Supreme Court stressed the indicia suggesting that the tribunal at issue acts or otherwise serves as a first instance decision-maker.[44] Hence, (i) the processing of a complaint, (ii) evaluation of evidence, (iii) the nature and extent of a tribunal's accountability to reviewing courts, (iv) the procedural rules governing the analysis, revision, and introduction of evidence of the reviewing courts, and (v) the extent to which the tribunal's recommendations or findings are binding, appear to be the salient dispositive talisman for determining "foreign or international tribunal" status within the ambit of Section 1782(a).

Petitioner's second material challenge to the Ninth Circuit's ruling was in the form of the proposition that AMD's complaint had not flourished or progressed beyond the investigative phase of the Commission's proceeding. Thus, the argument says, the embryonic procedural posture was far from reaching an adjudicative juncture within the Commission's agenda.[45]

After reviewing the 1964 amendments to Section 1782,[46] the majority opinion fashioned a "within reasonable contemplation" test that obviates the need to have a "pending proceeding" requirement.[47]

Intel raised the "foreign discoverability rule" as a doctrinal obstacle proscribing grants of the Section 1782(a) petitions. This objection was predicated on two policy precepts. First, petitioner asserted that Section 1782(a) petitions must be limited to avoid offending foreign governments. Second, Intel argued that only by placing limitations on Section 1782(a) petitions can parity between litigants be maintained.[48] Both propositions were soundly rejected.

To be sure, the Court observed that while "there is no reason to assume that because a country has not adopted a particular discovery procedure it would take offense at its use."[49] In this same vein, the Court dismissed concerns addressing parity among parties in contentious proceedings by advancing the commonsense proposition that "[w]hen information is sought by an 'interested person,' a district court could condition relief upon that person's reciprocal exchange of information" and hence ensure a level playing field among litigants.[50] In furtherance

44 *Id.*

45 *Id.*

46 The Supreme Court enunciated that:

> The legislative history of the 1964 revision is in sync; it reflects Congress' recognition that judicial assistance would be available 'whether the foreign or international proceeding or *investigation* is of a criminal, civil, administrative or other nature.'
>
> Citing to S.Rep. No. 1580, at 9, U.S. Code Cong. & Admin. News 1964, pp. 3782, 3789 (emphasis supplied by court).

47 Specifically, the Court rejected "the view expressed in *In Re: Ishihara Chemical Co.*, that §1782 comes into play only when adjudicative proceedings are 'pending' or 'imminent', *See* 251 F.3d, at 125 (proceeding must be 'imminent-very likely to occur and very soon to occur'). *Instead, we hold that §1782(a) requires only that a dispositive ruling by the Commission, reviewable by the European Courts, be within reasonable contemplation.*" (emphasis supplied) (citing *Crown Prosecution Serv. of United Kingdom*, 870 F.2d, at 691; *Trinidad and Tobago*, 848 F.2d at 1155 n. 9 (C.A. 11 1988); HANS SMIT, INTERNATIONAL LITIGATION 1026 ("it is not necessary . . . for the [adjudicative] proceeding to be pending at the time the evidence is sought, but only that the evidence is eventually to be used in such a proceeding.").

48 *Intel*, 542 U.S. at 261.

49 *Id.*

50 *Id.*

of this tenet, the Court enunciated that "the foreign tribunal can place conditions on its acceptance of the information to maintain whatever measure of parity it concludes is appropriate."[51]

Petitioner's fourth fundamental basis for challenging the Ninth Circuit's opinion advanced that it is necessary for a Section 1782(a) petitioner to show that under U.S. law discovery in domestic litigation analogous to the foreign proceeding would be viable and permissible.[52] This proposition too was rejected on the ground that comparisons among and between legal systems are often difficult if not altogether impossible. By way of example, in the United States there is no governmental body equivalent to the European Commission regime, pursuant to which AMD would not be free to file its own case at the equivalent of a trial court level or the European Court of Justice but rather participate "only as complainant, and 'interested person' in Commission-steered proceedings."[53]

Finally, the Court rejected petitioner's assertion that, in the alternative, it should assume a supervisory role with respect to compliance with a Section 1782(a) petition. In dispensing with this proposition, the Supreme Court appeared to have advanced two propositions that would prove to be critical to parties to an arbitration where one party seeks to oppose the filing of a Section 1782 petition on the ground that the arbitration clause at issue proscribes this specific discovery methodology based upon the plain language of such a clause.

First, the Court emphasized that the European Commission does not desire federal district court supervision.[54] Second, it was less than clear whether the European Commission meant to assert that it "never" or "hardly ever" would turn to judicial assistance from U.S. tribunals.[55]

This ruling simplifies and makes clear the applicable standard in adjudicating a Section 1782 petition. It may be synthesized to a formula where only three requirements are necessary for purposes of meeting this test: (i) The person or entity from whom information is sought must be present within the jurisdiction of the federal district court where the petition is filed; (ii) the intent underlying the use of the information elicited pursuant to the petition must be limited to providing assistance to a foreign tribunal; and (iii) the juridic entity or person must be an "interested person," within the meaning of Section 1782.[56] This holding represents a succinct and readily applicable restatement of the legislative elements comprising the statute and now constituting binding judicial precedent, or, in the terminology of analytical jurisprudence, a binding individual norm.[57]

Beyond the three-prong test that the Court enunciated as a predicate to grant a Section 1782 application, a second precept based on the very principles that

[51] *Id.* (citing *Euromepa*, 51 F.3d, at 1101). Moreover, at fn. 14 the Court states that:

> A civil law court, furthermore, might attend to litigant-parity concerns in its merits determination: 'in civil law countries, documentary evidence is generally submitted as an attachment to the pleadings or as part of a report by an expert. . . . a civil law court generally rules upon the question of whether particular documentary evidence may be relied upon only in its decision on the merits.'" (Citing Hans Smit, *Recent Developments in International Litigation*, 35 S. Tex. L. Rev. 215 (1994)).

[52] *Intel*, 542 U.S. at 261.

[53] *Id.*

[54] *Id.* at 264–6.

[55] *Id.* at 266.

[56] This rubric comports with the Second Circuit's holding in *In Re Application of Aldunate*, 3 F.3d 54 (2d Cir. 1993), *cert. denied sub nom.* Foden v. Aldunate, 114 S.Ct. 443 (1993).

[57] *See* In Re: Bayer, 146 F.3d at 193; In Re: Application of Esses, 101 F.3d 873, 875 (2d Cir. 1996); *and* In Re: Letter Rogatory from the First Court of First Instance in Civil Matters, 42 F.3d 308, 310 (5th Cir. 1995).

Congress sought to develop in enacting Section 1782 also was articulated. Upon a finding by a district court that the three-prong standard has been met, a court must then exercise its discretion in adjudicating the merits of the petition. As briefly noted, a district court is not compelled to grant a petition "merely" because the dispositive standard has been met.[58] The Supreme Court undertook great pains to emphasize the dispositive factors to be considered by federal district courts in the exercise of their discretion in adjudicating Section 1782 petitions. These elements include (i) an evaluation of whether the "person"[59] or "entity" who is the target of the petition for production of documents and disclosure of information is a party to the foreign proceeding (if the answer to this simple inquiry is in the affirmative, the need to provide judicial assistance generally will not be as apparent as when evidence is sought from a person or entity who is not a party to the proceeding at issue); (ii) "the nature of the foreign tribunal, the character of the proceedings under way abroad, and the receptivity of the foreign government or the Court or agency abroad to U.S. federal court judicial assistance;" and (iii) whether the petition has been confected to circumvent extant foreign restrictions concerning the gathering of evidence or other public policies of the foreign state or the United States, or the information elicited is "unduly intrusive or burdensome [and] may be rejected or trimmed."[60]

The Supreme Court's opinion not only elucidates the statute's elements and the manner in which they have been interpreted by federal courts, such as the term "interested parties,"[61] the nature and character of a "proceeding" before a "foreign tribunal," it also amplifies the dispositive standard by observing that pursuant to Section 1782, federal district courts may adjudicate such petitions more liberally and with fewer restrictions in applying the Federal Rules of Civil Procedure. The very definition of the term "tribunal" as used by the Court in the first prong of

58 *Intel Corp.*, 542 U.S. at 264.

59 The legislation commonly referred to as the "*The Dictionary Act*" contains definitions that govern the meaning of terms and words codified in Congressional enactments (federal legislation). This statute provides that "unless the context indicates otherwise – "the word "*person*" includes "corporations, companies, associations, firms, partnerships, societies, and joint stock companies, as well as individuals" 1 U.S.C. §1.

60 *Intel Corp.*, 542 U.S. at 264.

61 *See* Ishihara Chemico Co. Ltd. v. Shipley Co., et al., 251 F.3d 120, 124 (2d Cir. 2001) (observing that §1782 provides sufficient meanings for assistance to parties involved in international litigation before federal courts); Lancaster Factoring Co. v. Mangone, 90 F.3d 38, 42 (2d Cir. 1996) (holding that the agent of a trustee appointed by the Court to protect the interests of a foreign debtor is an "*interested person*" within the meaning of §1782; "the legislative history to §1782 makes plain that 'interested person' includes 'a party to the foreign . . . litigation.' Senate Report at 8, 1964 U.S.C.C.A.N. at 3789"); *Esses*, 101 F.3d at 875–876 (holding that the sibling of a person who died without a testament in a foreign state is "an *interested person*" for purposes of the statute; §1782); In Re: Letter of Request from the Crown Prosecution Service of the United Kingdom, 870 F.2d 686 (D.C. Cir. 1989) (adjudicating that a foreign minister of legal affairs, a general prosecutor, or other prosecutor have been recognized on numerous occasions as persons or entities within the ambit of §1782 as "*interested persons*"; federal courts unanimously have indicated that a party in interest to the foreign proceeding may serve as a petitioner or "*interested person*" within §1782's purview without need of first securing an order from the foreign tribunal of origin authorizing the prosecution of documents or disclosure of information); *Malev*, 964 F.2d at 101 ("we believe it was improper for the district court to predicate its denial of an application for discovery under 28 U.S.C. §1782 on the absence of a request for assistance from the Hungarian court").

the standard that it promulgated demonstrates that it had interpreted Congressional intent in crafting Section 1782 in conformance with a literal reading of the statute's terms. Both a plain-meaning construction of the terms embodied in Section 1782 and that statute's legislative intent suggest a liberal and not a restrictive application.

Justice Breyer's dissent is neither clairvoyant (i.e., containing any predictive value as to material future developments that the majority opinion inevitably shall spawn) nor particularly novel and insightful. Shining because of its absence is any reference, let alone sustained analysis, of Professor Smit's work and commentaries concerning Section 1782, upon which Justice Ginsburg, writing for the majority, rested significant parts of the opinion, particularly when addressing the meaning of a "foreign or international tribunal" within Section 1782's ambit. Likewise, the effect that the opinion inevitably would have on international arbitral proceedings is nowhere referenced, despite the majority's explicit dicta incorporating Professor Smit's analysis concluding that "[t]he term 'tribunal' . . . includes . . . administrative and arbitral tribunals."[62] This dissent overlooked the valuable and sustained scholarship concerning the genesis and exploration of the contours of Section 1782.[63]

Instead, Justice Breyer's dissent focuses on the costs and delays of U.S. style discovery and an exigent need for a categorical limitation on the discretion accorded to federal district courts in adjudicating Section 1782 petitions. With respect to the economic and temporal byproducts of the discovery process, the dissent emphasizes the study authored by the Brookings Institution, which found that "60% of litigation costs in a typical federal case are attributable to discovery and agreed that high litigation costs are often attributable to abuse of the discovery process."[64] The categorical limitation that the dissent articulated has two proposed prongs. The suggested categorical standard, however, is hardly novel or a departure from pre-*Intel* jurisprudence.

The first prong suggests that "when a foreign entity possesses few tribunal-like characteristics, so that the applicability of the statute's word 'tribunal' is in serious doubt, then a court should pay close attention to the foreign entity's own view of its tribunal – like or non tribunal – like status. By paying particular attention to the views of the very foreign nations that Congress sought to help, courts would better achieve Congress' basic cooperative objectives in enacting the statute."[65]

The second prong is divided into two premises. Where both premises are true, the argument says, discovery should be proscribed. Consequently, the district court

62 *Intel*, 542 U.S. at 258.

63 Professor Hans Smit's scholarship concerning international arbitration generally and §1782 in particular constitutes leading authority in the field of international jurisprudence. Hence, it is virtually expected that in issuing any pronouncement on the salient features of §1782 the Supreme Court would seek analytical support in this opus. In addition, Professor Smit's professorship at Columbia Law School coincided with Justice Ginsberg's tenure at the law school as a student. The Justice received her LLB from Columbia University in 1959. As the author of the majority opinion it stands to reason that her acquaintance with Professor Smit's works would be underscored by her personal academic training.

64 *Id.* at 268. *See* The Brookings Institution, Justice for All: Reducing Costs and Delay in Civil Litigation, Report of a Task Force 6–7 (1989); T. Willging, J. Shapard, D. Steinstra & D. Miletich, Discovery and Disclosure Practice, Problems, and Proposals for Change 1–2, 4, 8, 14–16 (Tables 3–5) (Federal Judicial Center, 1997) (consults for a study outlining the contours of discovery costs).

65 *Id.* at 270.

should exercise its discretion in denying a Section 1782 petition where (i) "a private person seeking discovery would not be entitled to that discovery under foreign law, and (ii) the discovery would not be available under domestic law in analogous circumstances."[66]

Painfully absent from Justice Breyer's analysis is any attempt to detail long-term consequences arising from the majority opinion's liberal construction of Section 1782(a). The dissent shies from purporting to comment on important dicta or otherwise identifying specific tribunals that would be encompassed within Section 1782's rubric. The Court's *dicta* referencing investigating magistrates, administrative tribunals, arbitral tribunals, quasi-judicial agencies, and conventional civil, commercial, criminal, and administrative fora is not at all referenced by the dissent. Instead, the dissent appears to rest on the implicit premise that, at least in an international context, the character and nature of a tribunal is not susceptible to immediate translation into its U.S. or common law equivalent. Having subscribed to this quite limiting proposition, Justice Breyer is left with no doctrinal alternative but to attempt to fashion some sort of standard that would facilitate this "translation" effort.

The *Intel* holding and incident analysis has rendered it doctrinally possible to revolutionize arbitral procedural law in the specific context of "the taking of evidence" or "discovery." The majority opinion's analysis provides a rich academic harvest to be reaped by lower tribunals faced with the need to adjudicate Section 1782 petitions in the context of international arbitrations where the petitioner seeks to elicit a ruling holding that an arbitral tribunal constitutes a "foreign or international tribunal" within Section 1782's purview. Post *Intel* the cross-fertilization of legal cultures in the domain comprising the taking of evidence and discovery is now inevitable, requiring both bench and bar in the United States and abroad to focus on the nuances arising from the proliferation of the Federal Rules of Civil Procedure governing discovery in the context of transnational arbitration.

[66] *Id.*

CHAPTER 5

The Gathering of Evidence v. Common Law Discovery

The Second and Fifth Circuits' pre-*Intel* rulings in *Nat'l Board Co., Inc. v. Bear Stearns & Co., Inc.*[1] and *Republic of Kazakhstan v. Biedermann*,[2] respectively, were challenged and submitted to sustained critical analysis by the United States District Court for the Northern District of Georgia in *In Re: Application of Roz Trading Ltd.*[3]

A. *IN RE: ROZ TRADING LTD.*

In this important recent case, petitioner Roz Trading Ltd. ("Roz Trading") successfully secured an order pursuant to 28 U.S.C. Section 1782(a) directing respondent the Coca-Cola Company ("Coca-Cola") to produce documents for use in foreign arbitral proceedings involving Roz Trading and the government of Uzbekistan.[4] The facts are succinct.

Petitioner Coca-Cola Export Company (a subsidiary of Coca-Cola) and the government of Uzbekistan executed a Joint Venture Agreement entered into among these entities. Roz Trading, however, averred that the government of Uzbekistan without justification and through violent means confiscated its interest in the joint venture.[5] In this regard, petitioner further alleged that its employees had no recourse but to flee Uzbekistan because they rightfully feared for their lives.[6] Because of the haste under which Roz Trading's employees left Uzbekistan and the disconcerting circumstances surrounding their departure, documents were left behind and petitioner's employees were unable to retrieve them from Uzbekistan. Roz Trading further asserts that the Coca-Cola Export Company and the government of Uzbekistan, together with Coca-Cola, conspired to eliminate Roz Trading from the joint venture.[7]

Roz Trading sought recourse by filing a Request for Arbitration before an arbitral panel of the International Arbitral Centre of the Austrian Federal Economic

[1] Nat'l Board Co., Inc. v. Bear Stearns & Co., Inc., 165 F.3d 184 (2d Cir. 1999).

[2] Republic of Kazakhstan v. Biedermann, 168 F.3d 880 (5th Cir. 1999).

[3] In Re: Application of Roz Trading Ltd., 469 F.Supp. 2d 1221 (N.D.Ga. 2006). Significantly, *National Board Company, Inc. v. Bear Stearns & Co., Inc.*, and *The Republic of Kazakhstan v. Biedermann*, were decided five years prior to the Supreme Court's command in *Intel*, and stand for the proposition that only governmental bodies constitute "tribunals" within the meaning of §1782(a).

[4] *See* Peter Ashford, DOCUMENTARY DISCOVERY AND INTERNATIONAL COMMERCIAL ARBITRATION, 17 Am. Rev. Int'l Arb. 89 (2006).

[5] *Id.* at 1223.

[6] *Id.*

[7] *Id.*

Chamber in Vienna (the "Centre") pursuant to the Joint Venture Agreement. Furthermore, Roz Trading petitioned the Court to compel respondent (Coca-Cola) to produce documents for the proceedings held at the Centre initiated by petitioner. The district court identified as concerns the following two issues: (i) "whether the Court has the authority to entertain the application, specifically, whether the scope of 28 U.S.C. Section 1782(a) includes proceedings before an arbitral panel of the Centre; and (ii) whether the factors listed in *Intel Corp.* favor granting the application."[8] Both questions were answered in the affirmative.

After considerable analysis of the Supreme Court's statutory construction of Section 1782's language and its references to Congressional intent in crafting and amending the statute, the Court held that "[a] finding that an arbitral panel of the Centre is a 'tribunal' within the meaning of Section 1782 is consistent with the ruling in *Intel*."[9] Significantly, the Court stressed that "*Intel* did not expressly hold arbitral bodies to be 'tribunals.'" It quoted approvingly language that included "arbitral tribunals" within the term's meaning in §1782(a). The Supreme Court also determined the D.G.-Competition to constitute a "tribunal" when it acted as a first instance decision-maker in a proceeding "that leads to a dispositive ruling, i.e. a final administrative action both responsive to the complaint and reviewable in Court."[10]

Notably, the analysis leading to the landmark holding juridically bringing an arbitral tribunal within Section 1782's ambit was bottomed on four fundamental precepts. First, based upon the Supreme Court's holding in *Scherk v. Alberto Culver Co.*, and *Mitsubishi Motors Corp. v. Solar Chrysler-Plymouth, Inc.*, the Court concluded that both "common usage" and "widely accepted definition" of "tribunals" encompassed arbitral fora.[11] Inquiry into the philological configuration of the word "tribunal" did not merely stop with common or widely accepted usage as mentioned in the referenced cases but also included analysis of secondary sources.[12]

Second, a detailed reading of the 1964 amendment to the statute was undertaken. Here, the Court concluded that when Congress deleted the phrase "judicial proceeding" and replaced it with "international or foreign tribunal," it intended to amplify the statute's scope to include proceedings not strictly judicial in nature and character.[13] Thus, it enunciated that "[t]here is no clearly expressed legislative intent that the term 'tribunal' does not include arbitral panels such as those convened by the Centre or that the term should be construed other than as it is commonly defined."[14] Indeed, the Court went further and flatly stated that "it would be improper for [it] to consider legislative history or impose its own limitations upon the meaning of the statute's terms."[15]

Third, a careful exegesis and reading of *National Board Company* and *Biedermann*, the Court argued, misconstrues Section 1782's legislative history, in part because neither the Second Circuit nor the Fifth Circuit in deciding these cases five years

[8] *Id.*

[9] *Id.* at 1224–25 (emphasis in original).

[10] *Id.* (citing *Intel*, 542 U.S. at 255).

[11] *Id.*

[12] In what is clearly an effort destined to be as comprehensive as possible, the district court sought analytical support in (i) Professor Smit's work, *International Litigation*, (ii) *Black's Law Dictionary* (8th Ed. 2004), (iii) *William Blackstone, Three Commentaries* 17 (London, Strahan, Cadell & Prince 1787) (10th Ed.), and (iv) *Joseph Story, Commentaries on Equity Jurisprudence* (Boston, Little Brown & Co. 1866) (9th Ed.).

[13] *Roz Trading*, 469 F.Supp. 2d at 1226.

[14] *Id.*

[15] *Id.* (citing *Turkette*, 452 U.S. at 587).

prior to *Intel* had the benefit of the Supreme Court's analysis. The district court's reasoning went deeper than just mere deference to the Supreme Court's analysis of the relevant legislative history. Specifically, it underscored that the Second Circuit erroneously relied on the use of the term "international tribunal" in 22 U.S.C. §§270–270g. Reliance on this statutory framework was fatally flawed as it was the very statute replaced by Section 1782. Indeed, 22 U.S.C. §§270–270g applied only to intergovernmental tribunals.[16] The district court observed that Section 270, as relied upon by the Second Circuit, read:

[16] 22 U.S.C. §§270–270g (1958) reads as follows:

§270 *International tribunals; administration of oaths; perjury*: Whenever any claim in which the United States or any of its nationals is interested is pending before an international tribunal or commission, established pursuant to an agreement between the United States and any foreign government or governments, each member of such tribunal or commission, or the clerk or a secretary thereof, shall have authority to administer oaths in all proceedings before the tribunal or commission; and every person knowingly and willfully swearing or affirming falsely in any such proceedings, whether held within or outside the United States, its territories or possessions, shall be deemed guilty of perjury and shall, upon conviction, suffer the punishment provided by the laws of the United States for that offense, when committed in its courts of justice.

§270 (a) *Same; testimony of witnesses; documentary evidence; subpoenas*: Any such international tribunal or commission shall have power to require by subpoena the attendance and the testimony of witnesses and the production of documentary evidence relating to any matter pending before it. Any member of the tribunal or commission may sign subpoenas.

§270 (b) *Same; contempts*: Any failure to attend as a witness or to testify as a witness or to produce documentary evidence in an appropriate case may be regarded as a contempt of the authority of the tribunal or commission and shall be punishable in any court of the United States in the same manner as is provided by the laws of the United States for that offense when committed in its courts of justice.

§270 (c) *Same; commissioners to take evidence; procedure*: To afford such international tribunal or commission needed facilities for the disposition of cases pending therein said tribunal or commission is authorized and empowered to appoint competent persons, to be named as commissioners, who shall attend the taking of or take evidence in cases that may be assigned to them severally by the tribunal or commission and make report of the findings in the case to the tribunal or commission. Any such commissioner shall proceed under such rules and regulations as may be promulgated by the tribunal or commission and such orders as the tribunal or commission may make in the particular case and may have and perform the general duties that pertain to special masters in suits in equity. He may fix the times for hearings, administer oaths, examine witnesses, and receive evidence. Either party to the proceeding before the tribunal or commission may appear before the commissioner by attorney, produce evidence, and examine witnesses. Subpoenas for witnesses or for the production of testimony before the commissioner may issue out of the tribunal or commission by the clerk thereof and shall be served by a United States marshal in any judicial district in which they are directed. Subpoenas issued by such tribunal or commission requiring the attendance of witnesses in order to be examined before any person commissioned to take testimony therein shall have the same force as if issued from a district court and compliance therewith shall be compelled under such rules and orders as the tribunal or commission shall establish. Any person appointed as commissioner may be removed at the pleasure of the tribunal or commission by which he is appointed.

§270 (d) *Same; subpoenas; applications by agent to United States district court*: The agent of the United States before any international tribunal or commission, whether previously or hereafter established, in which the United States participates as a party whenever he desires to obtain testimony or the production of books and papers by witnesses may apply to the United States district court for the district in which such witness or witnesses reside or may be found, for the issuance of subpoenas to require their attendance and testimony before the United States district court for that district and the production therein of books and papers, relating to any matter or claim in which the United States on its own behalf or on behalf of any of its nationals is concerned as a party claimant or respondent before such international tribunal or commission.

§270 (e) *Same; issuance of subpoenas by United States district court; proceedings thereon; notice to foreign governments; filing transcripts of testimony with agent of United States:* Any United States district court to which such application shall be made shall have authority to issue or cause to be issued such subpoenas upon the same terms as are applicable to the issuance of subpoenas in suits pending in the United States district court, and the clerk thereof shall have authority to administer oaths respecting testimony given therein, and the marshal thereof shall serve such subpoenas upon the person or persons to whom they are directed. The hearing of witnesses and taking of their testimony and the production of books and papers pursuant to such subpoenas shall be before the United States district court for that district or before

> Whenever any claim in which the United States or any of its nationals is interested is pending before an international tribunal or commission, established pursuant to an agreement between the United States and any foreign government or governments.[17]

The district court not too subtly announced that the Second Circuit had "failed to note that the statutory language was *expressly* so limited [intergovernmental tribunals]."[18] Because, the Court additionally reasoned, "Congress included the express limitation 'established pursuant to an agreement between the United States and any foreign government or governments' indicates that when Congress wants to limit a statute to apply only to governmental bodies, it is capable of doing so. The Second Circuit's interpretation of §§270–270g renders this express limitation meaningless in violation of the 'long-standing general principle that courts must not interpret one provision of a statute to render another provision meaningless.'"[19]

Consonant with this analysis, the district court disregarded the Fifth Circuit's holding in *Biedermann* under the theory that the holding rested on a false premise. Simply stated, the Fifth Circuit's point of departure in *Biedermann* is the proposition that the term "tribunal" is "ambiguous," a tenet that the district court found to be untenable based on its prior analysis of the term based upon the *Intel* construction of legislative history, a plain language analysis, and the very amendments to the statute.[20]

Fourth, the structure and purpose of the Centre was closely reviewed. Two salient features in the Centre's constitution were deemed virtually dispositive in classifying it as a "tribunal" for Section 1782(a) purposes. The Centre is an "international" forum in nature. "It must rely on the aid of courts beyond its jurisdiction – such as United States District Courts acting pursuant to Section 1782(a) – to enforce its demands and to aid its inquiries, both within and without Austria."[21] In fact, Article 1 of the Centre's Rules of Arbitration states that its purpose is "to make arrangements for the settlement by arbitration of disputes in which ***not all contracting parties*** had their place of business or other normal residence in Austria."[22]

a commissioner or referee appointed by it for the taking of such testimony, and the examination may be oral or upon written interrogatories and may be conducted by the agent of the United States or his representative. Reasonable notice thereof shall be given to the agent or agents of the opposing government or governments concerned in such proceedings who shall have the right to be present in person or by representative and to examine or cross-examine such witness at such hearing. A certified transcript of such testimony and any proceedings arising out of the issuance of such subpoenas shall be forwarded by the clerk of the district court to the agent of the United States and also to the agent or agents of the opposing government or governments, without cost.

§270 (f) *Same; perjury; contempts; penalties*: Every person knowingly or willfully swearing or affirming falsely in any testimony taken in response to such subpoenas shall be deemed guilty of perjury, and shall, upon conviction thereof, suffer the penalty provided by the laws of the United States for that offense when committed in its courts of justice. Any failure to attend and testify as a witness or to produce any book or paper which is in the possession or control of such witness, pursuant to such subpoena, may be regarded as a contempt of the court and shall be punishable as a contempt by the United States district court in the same manner as is provided by the laws of the United States for that offense in any other proceedings in its courts of justice.

§270 (g) District Court of the United States for the District of Columbia a district court of United States

17 *Roz Trading*, 469 F.Supp. 2d at 1226. (citing 22 U.S.C 270 at App. A).

18 *Id.*

19 *Id.* (citing *Burlison*, 455 F.3d at 1247).

20 *Id.* at 1228.

21 *Id.* at 1229.

22 *Id.* (citing to Article 1 of the Centre's Rules of Arbitration).

In addition, Article 589 of the Centre's Rules of Civil Procedure contemplates recourse to judicial fora when necessary to facilitate its equitable administration of justice.[23]

The effect that *In Re: Roz Ltd.* shall have in the doctrinal development of jurisprudence prescribing the use of Section 1782(a) in arbitral proceedings is less than settled.[24] To date, there is no authority at the district court or appellate court levels either following or rejecting the holding or analysis in *In Re: Roz Ltd.* Somewhat surprisingly, the scholarship analyzing this extraordinary holding is scant at best.[25] Irrespective, however, of the paucity of authority and scholarship currently developed on this most meaningful procedural doctrine, it is undisputed that the issue shall spawn considerable attention as it revolutionizes the procedural configuration of evidence gathering in the context of international arbitration.

B. THE ORTHODOX MISCONCEPTION OF COMMON LAW DISCOVERY IN INTERNATIONAL ARBITRATION

From an orthodox perspective international arbitration typically does not contemplate discovery as governed by the standard enunciated in Fed.R.Civ.P. 26. The rulings in *Intel* and *In Re: Roz Trading Ltd.* have caused two distinct and material modifications in the conduct of international arbitration. First, "discovery" has been introduced as sharing the same doctrinal space as "the taking of evidence." Second, scholars and practitioners now have been forced to re-examine the very concept of "taking of evidence" traditionally used in arbitration. As suggested, the "taking of evidence" in its current theoretical and pragmatic status is in many respects vague, lacking in predictive value, and inimical to the time-honored and venerable concept of party-autonomy, which is the fulcrum of ***both*** the theoretical underpinnings of the Federal Rules of Civil Procedure governing discovery ***and*** the configuration of arbitration as an alternative dispute resolution methodology. These material changes have been broadened in scope to apply even to discovery in aid of execution in an arbitration proceeding.

23 *Id.* The Court also observed that "[t]he Centre's rules embrace discovery sought through such mechanisms such as §1782(a)."

24 The public records reflect that Respondent's appeal to the Eleventh Circuit Court of Appeals was dismissed for lack of jurisdiction on March 28, 2007. An order entered by the Eleventh Circuit on that date read:

> This appeal is DISMISSED FOR LACK OF JURISDICTION. The December 19, 2006 Order, directing production of documents for use in a proceeding before a foreign tribunal pursuant to 28 U.S.C. §1782, is not final or immediately appealable because it contemplates further substantive proceedings concerning the scope of production. *See* 28 U.S.C. §1291, In Re: Commissioner's Subpoenas, 325 F.3d 1287, 1292 (11th Cir. 2003); Pitney Bowes, Inc. v. Mestre, 701 F.2d 1365, 1368 (11th Cir. 1983); Broussard v. Lippman, 643 F.2d 1131, 1133 (5th Cir. 1981).

25 *See, e.g.*, Pedro J. Martinez-Fraga, *El Arbitraje y El Proceso Global, La Justicia Norteamericana Abre Las Puertas A Los Tribunales Extranjeros*, LA GACETA, May 21, 2007; Pedro J. Martinez-Fraga, *Globalización Procesal y Arbitraje Internacional*, DIARIO LA LEY, No. 6758, July 18, 2007; Eric Schwartz and Alan Howard, *International Arbitration Discovery Applications to Rise?*, NEW YORK LAW JOURNAL, Volume 237, May 4, 2007; Daon Zupanec, *Discovery For Use in Foreign Proceeding – "Foreign or International Tribunal" – Arbitral Body*, FEDERAL LITIGATOR (March 2007); Douglas H. Yarn and Gregory Todd Jones, *Chapter 9: Arbitration, B. Prehearing Issues, Alternative Dispute Resolution: Practice and Procedure in Georgia* (2007); American Law Institute, *Recent Developments in Domestic and International Arbitration Involving Issues of Arbitrability, Consolidation of Claims and Discovery of Non-Parties*, ALI ABA Course of Study (March 7–9, 2007).

Intel's progeny, at least as may be gleaned from the Eleventh Circuit's opinion in *In Re: Patrizio Clerici*,[26] provides for the use of Section 1782(a) for aid in execution of a judgment. The conceptual step necessary to expand this holding to apply to arbitral awards is virtually nonexistent.

C. DISCOVERY IN AID OF EXECUTION OF A NON-U.S. ARBITRAL AWARD: NO LONGER AN OUTLANDISH PROPOSITION

In *In Re: Patrizio Clerici* a Panamanian court issued a letter rogatory to take evidence from an alleged judgment-debtor who had relocated to Florida. The United States filed an *ex parte* Section 1782 application in the United States District Court for the Southern District of Florida seeking the appointment of an assistant United States attorney as a commissioner charged with securing the requested discovery. The district court denied respondent Patrizio Clerici's Motion to Vacate the Court's previous order granting the Section 1782 application and appointing a commissioner but stayed the proceeding pending disposition of the appeal that ensued to the Eleventh Circuit. The underlying facts are illustrative.

Respondent Patrizio Clerici is a U.S. citizen residing in Miami, Florida. In 1998 Patrizio Clerici initiated an action in Panama against the judgment-creditor, a Panamanian corporation called No-Name Corporation ("No-Name"). The proceeding was filed with the Second Court of the Circuit of Colon, Civil Branch, Republic of Panama (the "Panamanian Court").[27] Incident to this proceeding, Patrizio Clerici pursued the attachment of certain assets (property) purportedly belonging to No-Name. The attachment was perfected. No-Name filed papers seeking dismissal of the lawsuit for want of prosecution and to vacate the attachment. That motion was granted in its entirety and No-Name proceeded to file an incidental action before Panamanian tribunals alleging damages arising from Patrizio Clerici's lawsuit and attendant attachment proceeding. No Name bottomed its complaint on the averment that it was a start up entity in the process of growth and development when Patrizio Clerici's lawsuit "changed the commercial image of the company" and "negatively impacted No-Name's credit with various banks and its image in the community, resulted in the denial of its request for an increase in credit, and led to lost sales and profits."[28] The Panamanian court issued Judicial Decree No. 1166, pursuant to which Patrizio Clerici was compelled to pay in balboas[29] \$1,996,598.00 in compensatory damages and \$294,589.70 in costs. The Eleventh Circuit observed "that No-Name's foreign judgment against Clerici has not been domesticated and is not currently enforceable in Florida. While No-Name filed a domestication action, No-Name never pursued it."[30]

No-Name filed a postjudgment petition in the same Panamanian court where No-Name had secured the underlying judgment. This petition was entitled "Ordinary Proceeding Involving More Than a Certain Amount (Incident of Damages) Petition (Complementary Execution)."[31]

26 In re Clerici, 481 F.3d 1324 (11th Cir. 2007).

27 *Id.* at 1327.

28 *Id.*

29 A balboa is the equivalent of one U.S. dollar.

30 *Id.* at 1327–8.

31 *Id.* at 1328. Significantly, No Name's petition sought for the Panamanian court to "begin the procedure complementary to the execution" of its judgment "pursuant to the provisions of

Upon noting that Patrizio Clerici did not dispute the first and fourth requirements for grant of a Section 1782 petition,[32] the Eleventh Circuit stressed the second requirement that Patrizio Clerici's contention asserting the petition does not seek evidence but rather attempts to enforce a foreign judgment was meritless. In particular the Court contended that "the Panamanian Court asked for assistance in obtaining only Clerici's sworn answers to questions regarding his assets and other financial matters." Furthermore, the Eleventh Circuit highlighted that "[t]he district court recognized this key distinction and properly concluded that the request for assistance was limited to seeking evidence from Clerici, and therefore, was proper under Section 1782."[33]

The Court likewise dismissed Patrizio Clerici's assertion that the third statutory requirement (for use in a foreign or international proceeding) was not met. Here the Eleventh Circuit assumed the posture that indeed a proceeding was pending in Panama and that consonant with this Panamanian proceeding Clerici was asked to answer questions under oath. This contention was buttressed with the hypothetical that "[h]ad Clerici been residing in Panama, No-Name or the Panamanian Court would have been able to interrogate Clerici directly with the questions proposed by No-Name."[34]

Article 1049 and 1050 of the Judicial Code of Panama." The petition identified the following questions to be asked to Clerici regarding his assets and other financial matters 'In the Republic of Panama ***or in any other part of the world***' (emphasis supplied):

1. What properties (real or personal), credits, sustenance means or any other source of income did he [have] on April 27, 2001 in the Republic of Panama or in any other part of the world?
2. What properties (real or personal), credits, sustenance means or any other source of income did he [have] on September 27, 2002 in the Republic of Panama or in any other part of the world?
3. What transfers, conveyances or donations has he made after April 27, 2001 and September 27, 2002 in the Republic of Panama or in any other part of the world? Please explain the reasons for these conveyances.
4. What is the amount of your patrimony to the date of this proceeding?
5. How and by what means are you going to fulfill the obligations acquired by means of Resolution No. 1166 of September 27, 2002, announced by the Second Court of the Civil Circuit of Colon (Republic of Panama), where you are condemned to pay an amount greater than TWO MILLION BALBOAS (B/2,000,000.00) (legal currency of the Republic of Panama) to the corporation NONAME CORP.?
6. Are you in bankruptcy? Please explain the reasons.
7. How many nationalities or citizenships do you have up to date?
8. In what countries do you file income-tax returns?
9. With what financial entities (banks, investment houses, to mention some) in the world have you had or have business relations or a relation as a client?

[32] The four requirements were clearly and forcefully identified by the Supreme Court in *Intel* as follows:

(i) The request must be made by 'foreign or international tribunal' or by 'any interested person';
(ii) The request must seek evidence, whether it be the 'testimony or statement' of a person or the production of 'a document or other thing';
(iii) The evidence must be 'for use in a proceeding in a foreign or international tribunal'; and
(iv) The person from whom discovery is sought must reside or be found in the district of the district court ruling on the application for assistance. *Intel*, 542 U.S. at 255.

Additionally, "a district court's compliance with a §1782 request is not mandatory." *United Kingdom v. United States*, 238 F.3d 1312, 1319 (11th Cir. 2001).

[33] *Id.* at 1332.

[34] *Id.* at 1332–3.

Lastly, the Eleventh Circuit further sought to bolster its holding on the premise that "the Supreme Court has recognized the 'broad range of discovery' authorized under Section 1782 and has held that Section 1782 is not limited to proceedings that are pending or imminent."[35]

The Eleventh Circuit's analysis and holding in *In Re: Patrizio Clerici* are disconcerting in the context of the specific litigation referenced in that case and would be equally troubling within the framework of a transnational arbitral proceeding. There are three propositions that appear to render the Eleventh Circuit's opinion at odds with the Supreme Court's command in *Intel* as well as with settled jurisprudence from other circuit courts of appeals.

D. THE PITFALLS IN *IN RE: PATRICIO CLERICI*: DISCOVERY IN AID OF A NON-U.S. ARBITRAL AWARD

First, in permitting the Panamanian Court – a foreign tribunal – to obtain financial information for a purported judgment creditor, the Eleventh Circuit not only extended Section 1782 far beyond its intended purpose, but it also rendered a ruling inconsistent with the Supreme Court's construction of Section 1782. Indeed, in *Intel* the Supreme Court placed considerable emphasis on the premise that the proceeding "for which discovery is sought under Section 1782(a) *must be in reasonable contemplation*, but need not be pending or imminent."[36] Even upon surface consideration it is evident that the requirement of a pending or contemplated proceeding necessarily means that a proceeding for which discovery is sought under Section 1782 *cannot be a proceeding that already has concluded with no possibility of any future adjudication on the merits.* Simply stated, the Eleventh Circuit ignored and carved out this element of the *Intel* holding in ruling that a "proceeding" need *not* be adjudicative.[37]

Moreover, the Eleventh Circuit overlooked that at the time of enacting the modern iteration of Section 1782, Congress admonished that the district courts' discretion in applying Section 1782 should be guided by the "character" and "nature" of the foreign proceedings.[38] The *form* the foreign tribunal takes – be it administrative or quasi-judicial – is generally irrelevant, so long as the evidence is in connection with an ongoing adjudication of some sort.[39] For example, the relevant Senate Report explains the following:

> [I]t is intended that the Court have discretion to grant assistance when proceedings are pending before investigating magistrates in foreign countries.[40]

Nowhere is it suggested that Congress intended to extend the statute to cover proceedings not adjudicative in nature. Hence, the Eleventh Circuit's novel analysis comports neither with the *Intel* mandate nor Congressional intent.

Second, the Eleventh Circuit's holding expressly and directly conflicts with settled jurisprudence standing for the proposition that discovery pursuant to Section

[35] *Id.* at 1333.

[36] *Intel*, 542 U.S. at 259 (emphasis supplied).

[37] *Clerici*, 481 F.3d at 1333.

[38] *See S.Rep. No. 88–1580 §9* (1964), *as reprinted in* 1964 U.S.C.C.A.N. 3782, 3788.

[39] *Id.*

[40] 1964 U.S.C.C.A.N. 3782, at 3788.

1782 is proscribed where the discovery sought, such as in *In Re: Patrizio Clerici*, is not for use in a foreign proceeding. Sustained analysis is necessary. In providing postjudgment asset-discovery assistance to foreign creditors pursuant to Section 1782, the Court promotes a conflict with decisions of other courts of appeals. Postjudgment discovery in aid of execution is precluded by the express language of Section 1782, which provides that the government will honor a foreign court's discovery request only to the extent that it is "for use in a proceeding in a foreign tribunal."[41] In *Euromepa*, the Second Circuit held that an analogous request failed the "for use in a proceeding" requirement of Section 1782. There a French trial court requested that federal courts take evidence from the trial-plaintiff regarding the ownership of, and insurance coverage for, stolen jewels.[42] The district court rejected the request because the case was no longer pending before the French evidence-collecting courts – their trial and intermediate appellate-level courts – and therefore it was unnecessary to compel the discovery of new evidence.[43]

The proponent of the evidence appealed, arguing that because there was a pending bankruptcy proceeding where it was trying to avoid paying the French judgment, evidence exonerating it from any obligation in the underlying action would be highly relevant. The Second Circuit rejected this argument, concluding that because "[t]he *merits* of the dispute between [the resident-debtor] and [the evidence proponent] have already been *adjudicated* and will not be considered in the French Bankruptcy Proceeding," the discovery sought was not for use in a proceeding before a foreign tribunal, which is a prerequisite to a Section 1782 order.[44] Put simply, nothing was left to adjudicate; all that remained was merely to enforce the extant judgment.[45] Accordingly, there was no "proceeding" to take evidence to where a Section 1782 order would apply.

Significantly, in *Intel* the Supreme Court left unaffected the *Euromepa* decision as to the nature of the foreign proceeding. The Eleventh Circuit, however, observed that *Euromepa* was unpersuasive for the proposition that the foreign proceeding must be adjudicative in nature.[46] For purposes of its analysis, the Eleventh Circuit acknowledged that the discovery being sought by the United States government was for use in postjudgment execution proceedings before the Panamanian tribunal.[47] As in *Euromepa*, nothing else was reasonably contemplated before the Panamanian proceeding in *In Re: Patrizio Clerici*, and thus the Court's decision creates a stark departure from an explicit conflict with the Second Circuit on the narrow issue of whether the "proceeding" before a foreign tribunal must (i) be adjudicative and (ii) not have been resolved on the merits.

Third and finally, it is the purpose of discovery under Section 1782 to assist "foreign and international tribunals" and the litigants in *adjudicative* proceedings abroad. Congress did not provide *any* indication that it intended to authorize discovery by foreign tribunals for use in postjudgment execution proceedings. Neither *Intel*, Section 1782, nor any other federal statute authorizes a federal court to enforce a foreign

[41] *See* 28 U.S.C. §1782(a).

[42] *Euromepa*, 154 F.3d at 26.

[43] *Id.*

[44] *Id.* at 28 (emphasis supplied).

[45] *Id.*

[46] *Clerici*, 481 F.3d at 1333 n. 10.

[47] *Id.* at 1333.

judgment pursuant to a letter rogatory.[48] Such a normative command is nowhere to be found. Nevertheless, the Court's decision invites foreign litigants to circumvent basic policies requiring the domestication and recognition of foreign judgments in accordance with state law before authorizing discovery in aid of execution of such judgments.

In federal courts, discovery in aid of execution on a judgment is permitted by operation by the Federal Rule of Civil Procedure 69(a), which provides, in relevant part:

> In aid of the judgment or execution, the judgment creditor or a successor in interest when that interest appears of record, may obtain discovery from any person, including the judgment debtor, in the manner provided in these rules or in the manner provided by the practice of the state in which the district court is held.[49]

Stated otherwise, a judgment creditor may use any of the discovery rules (Rules 26 to 37) or any discovery tool authorized by the state in which the district court sits to find a judgment-debtor's assets and execute them. Undertaking this expedition is what petitioner in *In Re: Patrizio Clerici* was attempting to accomplish on the Panamanian tribunal's behalf.

The Eleventh Circuit ignored the idea that a valid and enforceable judgment is necessary before a purported creditor is entitled to discovery in aid of execution pursuant to Rule 69(a).[50]

In *In Re: Patrizio Clerici*, there is no valid judgment anywhere in the United States. No-Name attempted to domesticate the judgment in Florida but did not do so. Pursuant to Florida law, until all objections have been disposed of by the state court, no foreign judgment will be recognized and enforced.[51]

Reference to federal law leads to the same results. Rule 69(a) further provides that in federal courts, "[t]he procedure on execution shall be in accordance with the practice and procedure of the state in which the district court is held."[52]

The Eleventh Circuit overlooked that the petitioner in *In Re: Patrizio Clerici* (i.e., the U.S. government) was attempting to request evidence on behalf of the Panamanian tribunal for which there is no right to discovery under the Rules of Procedure until the judgment has been domesticated pursuant to state law. Without a valid judgment in the United States, it is difficult to fathom how there would be any basis for discovery of information that everyone (including the foreign tribunal and the U.S. government) has admitted is for the purpose of, and complementary

48 *See In Re: Letter Rogatory*, No. 01-MC-212(JC), 2002 WL 257822, at *1 (E.D.N.Y. Feb. 6, 2002); *Tacul, S.A. v. Hartford Nat'l Bank & Trust Co.*, 693 F.Supp. 1399, 1400 (D.Conn. 1988); *In Re Civil Rogatory Letters*, 640 F.Supp. 243, 244 (S.D. Tex. 1986).

49 FED.R.CIV.P. 69(a).

50 *See, e.g.*, Sanderson v. Winner, 507 F.2d 477, 480 (10th Cir. 1974) ("defendant will have ample opportunity for discovery under Rule 69, F.R.Civ.P. *if it obtains judgment.*" (emphasis added)); United States v. Kulukundis, 329 F.2d 197, 199 (2d Cir. 1964) (Rule 69(a) discovery "available only after judgment is rendered"); Fuddruckers, Inc. v. KCOB I, LLC, 31 F.Supp. 2d 1274, 1278 (D.Kan. 1998) ("by its terms, . . . Rule 69(a)'s federal or state law 'option' related *only to postjudgment* discovery." (emphasis added)); *accord* 13 Moore's Federal Practice §69.04[1] ("there can be no discovery [under Rule 69(a)] before the judgment is entered").

51 *See* FLA. STAT. §55.604 (2005).

52 *See* FED.R.CIV.P. 69(a).

to, executing a judgment. The Court, however, authorizes the taking of evidence in aid of execution before the foreign judgment has been recognized in the United States.

Doubtless, *In Re: Patrizio Clerici* vastly expands the type of proceedings where Section 1782 discovery is obtainable, effectively rewriting the statute in a manner never contemplated by Congress. The decision opens the door to the taking of postjudgment discovery by litigants unwilling to assume the burdens and obligations associated with domesticating and recognizing a foreign judgment in the United States. The prognosis is no different with respect to arbitral proceedings. Parties to an arbitration where an arbitral award is rendered outside the United States may now seek discovery in aid of execution of the arbitral award before recognition and enforcement of the award pursuant to the New York Convention is secured before a federal district court. It exposes U.S. individuals and businesses to costly discovery requests to collect on foreign judgments or arbitral awards that may be wholly insufficient to meet recognition and domestication requirements.

CHAPTER 6

What Has Really Happened? The Effects of a Trilogy Examined

The trilogy: *Intel, In Re: Roz Trading Ltd.*, and *In Re: Patrizio Clerici,* engraft upon arbitration the very issues endemic to the policies underlying Section 1782(a); namely, the viability of the statute's twin objectives. Whether Section 1782(a) furthers the objective of proliferating among the community of nations the Federal Rules of Civil Procedure and promotes U.S. style discovery internationally, and (b) by so doing champions reciprocity in the field of judicial assistance among nations, certainly remains to be seen. A handful of commentators have observed that the use of Section 1782 empowers foreign litigants, and now parties to international arbitral proceedings, at the expense of U.S. citizens and businesses. Indeed, there is little evidence that Section 1782, in any context, has spawned an acceptance of U.S. common law discovery precepts or has in any way improved judicial cooperation among nations.

One inevitable question is whether the doctrinal development of incorporating *discovery* into arbitration proceedings constitutes progress or a stark defiance of the very principles that arbitration, at least theoretically, purports to further? The interminable and daunting nature of the intelligent and coherent contrasting points of view this question spawns should not detract from efforts to address it and, in so doing, look beyond the more readily apparent responses to the inquiry.

A. REDISCOVERING DISCOVERY IN INTERNATIONAL ARBITRAL PROCEEDINGS AND THE PRINCIPLE OF PARTY-AUTONOMY

If it is assumed that a defining precept of arbitration is the principle of party-autonomy, and more generically so, the principles of *predictive value, transparency of standard, uniformity*, and *certainty*, then it is less than clear that the incorporation of U.S. common law-style discovery into arbitration proceedings consonant with the Section 1782 rubric and the Fed.R.Civ.P. 26 standard undermines the policy objectives that arbitration fervently seeks to promote.

Ironically, party-autonomy is perhaps the most overlooked and undervalued principle in what is essentially–literally according to its very essence–an adversarial system theoretically predicated on individual initiative and a salubrious dose of judicial *laissez-faire.*[1] With respect to U.S. common law, nowhere is the precept

[1] Several scholars, however, have weighed the issues surrounding party autonomy. For examples, see Sam Blay, PARTY AUTONOMY IN CHINESE INTERNATIONAL ARBITRATION: A COMMENT ON RECENT DEVELOPMENTS, 8 AM. REV. INT'L ARB. 331 (1997);

of party-autonomy more prevalent than in the Federal Rules of Civil Procedure generally and those rules of civil procedure governing discovery in particular.

Giving parties the normative ability to engage in discovery pursuant to known standards and rules that have benefited from exhaustive analysis and a plethora of jurisprudence stands as paradigmatic of the practical application of the principle of party-autonomy. The cornerstone standard enunciated in Fed.R.Civ.P. 26[2] may at first appear exceedingly liberal and broad to civil law practitioners engaged in arbitration until the rule is actually studied, let alone contrasted with the "taking or gathering of evidence" counterpart (if indeed intellectual honesty allows for such characterization as a "counterpart"). Not all information or documents "reasonably calculated to lead to the discovery of admissible evidence" are discoverable under Fed.R.Civ.P. 26. The scope of discoverable subject matter is limited by a relevance tenet applicable to the parties' claim or defense. This limitation is material and meaningful. It is the term "relevant" that is further defined as that which is "reasonably calculated to lead to the discovery of admissible evidence." Consequently, while nonadmissible evidence may be discoverable subject to privilege and doctrinal (i.e., work product) limitations, the subject matter of discoverable information must fall within the ambit of applicable claims and defenses. This limiting element eviscerates "fishing expedition" platitudes often cited by common law and civil law practitioners and experienced jurists who elect to overlook the standard's true rigor.

Perhaps most emblematic of the pervasiveness of the principle of party-autonomy in the Federal Rules of Civil Procedure is Rule 27 concerning depositions before action or pending appeal, which is commonly also overlooked and certainly less frequently invoked than those rules governing depositions, interrogatories, request for production of documents, requests for admission, and subpoenas that may be served for purposes of engaging in non-party production of documents. Rule 27 provides a *prospective* plaintiff with a legal basis for perpetuating testimony through deposition examination *before* the filing of an action. The simplicity of the rule obscures its extraordinary character.

Paul Michell, *ARBITRAL & JUDICIAL DECISION: PARTY AUTONOMY AND IMPLIED CHOICE IN INTERNATIONAL COMMERCIAL ARBITRATION*, 14 AM. REV. INT'L ARB. 571 (2003); Anoosha Boralessa, *THE LIMITATIONS OF PARTY AUTONOMY IN ICSID ARBITRATION*, 15 AM. REV. INT'L ARB. 253 (2004); LOUISE ELLEN TEITZ, *The Hague Choice of Court Convention: Validating Party Autonomy and Providing an Alternative to Arbitration*, 53 AM. J. COMP. L. 543 (2005); Mo Zhang, *Contractual Choice of Law in Contracts of Adhesion and Party Autonomy*, 41 AKRON L. REV. 123 (2008).

2 Often commentators, practitioners, and courts misapprehend what most deem to be the most commonly known civil common law procedural tenet. It is not rare to consult a legal text or analyze an appellate opinion only to find that the standard for discovery pursuant to Fed.R.Civ.P. 26 is cited as rendering discoverable that which is "reasonably calculated to lead to the discovery of admissible evidence." This reading, or more precisely misreading, of the rule is only part of the operative talisman.

Fed.R.Civ.P. 26(b)(1) reads:

(b) **Discovery Scope and Limits.** Unless otherwise limited by order of the court in accordance with these rules, the scope of discovery is as follows:

(1) ***In General.*** Parties may obtain discovery regarding any matter, not privileged, ***that is relevant to the claim or defense of any party***, including the existence, description, nature, custody, condition, and location of any books, documents, or other tangible things and the identity and location of persons having knowledge of any discoverable matter. . . . ***relevant information need not be admissible at the trial if the discovery appears reasonably calculated to lead to the discovery of admissible evidence***. . . .

Context is necessary to underscore the pervasive nature of the precept of party-autonomy in the Federal Rules of Civil Procedure generally and specifically with respect to those rules controlling discovery, as Rule 27 exemplifies. By way of example, Fed.R.Civ.P. 3 is a single-sentence rule stating that "[a] civil action is *commenced* by filing a complaint with the court." Although at first innocuous in appearance, the rule sets the tone for the fundamental precept of party-autonomy that defines the structure of the very common law system, far beyond just the Federal Rules of Civil Procedure. Note that the commencement of an action is governed by the party filing the complaint and not a court doctrinally issuing a formal order after undertaking independent consultation and inquiry to determine the viability and sustainability of a claim. This procedure stands in sharp relief with the civil code or continental system, pursuant to which a civil action is commenced upon the Court's actual "acceptance" of the action. Significantly, civil proceedings within the rubric of a civil code system are not automatically or perfunctorily "accepted." The judge or judges first undertake an independent inquiry and evaluation to determine whether sustainable claims have been averred as well as evaluate the procedural propriety of the action itself.

Rule 27 contemplates the taking of a deposition (i) without an underlying pending action, (ii) at the initiative of a private party, and (iii) actually executed by private parties with respect to the taking of the deposition (actual examination) and its defense.[3] The virtual absence of judicial intervention in the process, as highlighted by the lack of need for even an underlying cause of action, is extraordinary when compared to and contrasted with the civil code system. In the majority of civil code or continental jurisdictions a judge or judges conduct the actual examination of witnesses. Party participation is limited, at most and only under certain specific circumstances, to providing the court with written questions to be posed to the witness. The party seeking to examine the witness through the court exercises little or no influence on the manner, form, or style (as in direct, cross-examination, and redirect in the common law system) with respect to framing the actual question. Moreover, the court is free to exercise its unbridled discretion in selecting which questions are to be asked of the witness. Three propositions here need to be emphasized.

First, rarely, if ever, shall a court in a civil code or continental jurisdiction examine a witness *before* the commencement of an action.[4] Second, the commencement

[3] Fed.R.Civ.P. 27(a)(1) reads:

Rule 27. Depositions Before Action or Pending Appeal

(a) Before Action.

(1) Petition. A person who desires to perpetuate testimony regarding any matter that may be cognizable in any court of the United States may file a verified petition in the United States district court in the district of the residence *of any expected adverse party*. The petition shall be entitled in the name of the petitioner and shall show: 1, that the petitioner *expects* to be a party to an action cognizable in a court of the United States *but is presently unable to bring it or cause it to be brought,* 2, the subject matter of the expected action and the petitioner's interest, 3, the facts which the petitioner desires to establish by the proposed testimony and the reasons for desiring to perpetuate it, 4, the names or description of the persons the petitioner *expects* will be adverse parties and their addresses so far as known, and 5, the names and addresses of the persons to be examined and the substance of the testimony which the petitioner *expects* to elicit from each, and shall ask for an order authorizing the petitioner to take the depositions of the persons to be examined named in the petition, for the purpose of perpetuating their testimony. (emphasis supplied)

[4] *See, e.g.,* Oscar Chase, *American "Exceptionalism" and Comparative Procedure*, 50 Am. J. Comp. L. 277, 294 (2002); *and* Mirjan Damaska, *The Uncertain Fate of Evidentiary Transplants: Anglo-American and Continental Experiments*, 45 Am. J. Comp. L. 839, 844 (1997).

of the very action is *unilaterally determined by the court* and not the parties. Third, in most civil code or continental jurisdictions the *commencement of an action* is procedurally indistinguishable from the start of the actual trial itself. Unlike common law jurisdictions where filing a complaint initiates an action that automatically triggers a proceeding encompassing a pretrial phase, which is configured by the taking of discovery and proactive motion practice, in civil code or continental system jurisdictions there simply is no *pretrial* phase. The merits of the case in the civil code system are evaluated, challenged, bolstered, and critically tested once the very action is "accepted."

Federal Rule of Civil Procedure 27, while standing poles apart from the fundamental framework of civil code or continental system jurisdictions because of the rule's reliance on the precept of party-autonomy, is close to the tenets that both define the essence of arbitration and distinguish arbitral proceedings from judicial processes that arbitration seeks to promote: principally party-autonomy, predictability, party initiative, and *de minimus* judicial intervention.[5] Indeed, judicial intervention in a Rule 27 effort to memorialize and perpetuate testimony is limited to the court's evaluation of a filed verified petition to determine whether it (the court) is "satisfied that the perpetuation of the testimony may prevent a failure or delay justice."[6]

Rules 3 and 27 of the Federal Rules of Civil Procedure are helpful didactic instruments or paradigms that, contrary to visceral reactions or common perception, demonstrate a close conceptual and doctrinal affinity with many salient precepts that form and transform arbitration, providing arbitral proceedings with distinct characteristics and features from those constituting judicial procedures. To be sure, as seen in the early to mid-twentieth century philosophical school of phenomenology, exemplified by the works of Edmund Husserl and Maurice Merleau-Ponty (to reference only two protagonists who developed theories initially advanced by Hegel primarily in *The Phenomenology of the Spirit*), criteria based on mere perception, without more, is often dangerous and misleading. Piercing through what is perceived and identifying the dissonance between *perception* and *essence* is the satisfying terrible task that has consumed and drained the energies of Western jurists and philosophers alike. Were we to seek conceptual foundations on perception without applying synthetic and analytic reason, it would only be correct to subscribe to the propositions that the world is flat and that the sun revolves around the Earth while traveling from east to west across the sky every day.

The perception that discovery and the Federal Rules of Civil Procedure are doctrinally and conceptually inimical to the tenets defining arbitration and that arbitration seeks to further is simply wrong, or at least less than clear.

5 At least from one perspective, it can be advanced with considerable intellectual rigor and credibility that arbitration (whether domestic or international, these characterizations are of no moment to this analysis) cannot exist without some judicial intervention. At issue, however, is the nature and character of such interdiction. It is here suggested that judicial intervention in arbitral proceedings should be subordinated to the arbitration itself such that courts act as "facilitators" for purposes of executing the will of the parties and those rulings or panel pronouncements that necessitate judicial involvement, such as the compulsion of party and non-party witnesses, and compliance with non-final arbitral panel rulings. Naturally, the recognition and enforcement of arbitral awards necessitate judicial intervention for limited purposes as does the narrow grounds that may give rise to viable appeals from arbitral awards.

6 *See* FED.R.CIV.P. 27(a)(3).

In fact, this prejudice is arguably as pernicious and damaging to arbitration (both domestic and international) as were the four badges of prejudice that delegitimized arbitral proceedings and prolonged the *perception* that arbitration should always be subordinate to judicial proceedings: (i) the view that arbitration agreements or arbitral clauses embedded in commercial contracts wrongfully wrest jurisdiction from courts that otherwise may exercise competent jurisdiction over parties and the subject matter at issue; (ii) the perception that specific statutory causes of action are not susceptible to adjudication pursuant to arbitration; (iii) the conviction that arbitration proceedings must be conducted under the auspices of courts; and (iv) the perception that arbitration and arbitrators are ill-equipped to adjudicate complex technical disputes.

CHAPTER 7

The New Unorthodox Conception of Common Law Discovery in International Arbitration

The phenomenology commands adjustment to bridge the gap between *essence* and *phenomenon*, what *is* and what is *seen*. Careful analysis establishes that *discovery* and the underlying tenets configuring the system commonly referred to as the Federal Rules of Civil Procedure, while conceptually and doctrinally distant from the civil code and the continental system, are close to arbitration and the underlying policies that sustain and define it as distinct from judicial proceedings because of its foundation rooted in party-autonomy. The "classical conception" of the civil code or continental system, however, is materially and significantly distant conceptually and doctrinally from arbitration generally and the precept of party-autonomy that is so endemic to the configuration of arbitration and arbitral proceedings. Accordingly, discovery as framed, formed, and defined by the Federal Rules of Civil Procedure clearly comports with the nature of arbitration, and it is only because of the misperception arising from want of familiarity on the part of practitioners from other non-common law jurisdictions, and adherence to platitudes of discovery abuses by common law practitioners, judges, and commentators, that the affinity between discovery and arbitration has been obscured.

Before having engaged in a schematic and rather skeletal analysis of Fed.R.Civ.P. 3 and 27, with reference to the discovery standard enunciated in Fed.R.Civ.P. 26 so as to dispel notions of "unbridled scope" and a boundless license to engage in a fishing expedition, the following proposition was posed: If it is assumed that a defining precept of arbitration is the principle of party-autonomy, and more generally so, the principles of predictive value, transparency of standard, and certainty, then it is less than clear that the incorporation of U.S. common law style discovery into arbitration proceedings consonant with the Section 1782 rubric and Fed.R.Civ.P. 26, undermines the policy objectives that arbitration fervently seeks to promote. Upon careful consideration that takes seriously the principles that configure and underlie U.S. common law discovery, it becomes apparent that there is a compelling argument to be made in favor of the conceptual and doctrinal affinity between discovery and arbitration.

Remarkably, common perception promotes the proposition that "the taking of evidence," so often referenced in the context of arbitration proceedings and juxtaposed to discovery to highlight the virtuosity of this methodology, perhaps in itself is also the victim of mere unchallenged perception and, therefore, actual misperception.

Despite its obvious nature, the question must be asked: Is there such a thing as "the taking of evidence in international commercial arbitration"? Perhaps the visceral "yes" answer deserves closer attention.

A. THE IBA RULES ON THE TAKING OF EVIDENCE IN INTERNATIONAL COMMERCIAL ARBITRATION

On June 1, 1999, the International Bar Association ("IBA") Council by resolution adopted the rules entitled "IBA Rules on the Taking of Evidence in International Commercial Arbitration" (the "Rules"). The foreword to this laudable effort in part identifies the purpose of these Rules "as a resource to parties and to arbitrators in order to enable them to conduct the evidence phase of international arbitration proceedings in an efficient and economical manner. The Rules provide mechanisms for the presentation of documents, witnesses of fact, expert witnesses, and inspection, as well as for the conduct of evidentiary hearings."[1] Moreover, the Foreword to the Rules further suggests that the effort is the product of an attempt to harmonize a confluence of distinct juridic cultures and traditions.[2] The Rules indeed comprise a hybrid compromise largely workable and helpful in the context of international commercial arbitration proceedings. It shall be suggested, however, that they are conceptually and doctrinally further removed from the principles that configure arbitration proceedings and that arbitration purports to promote – party-autonomy, predictive value, uniformity, transparency, certainty, and transparency of standard – than U.S. common law discovery. In fact, the proposition will be asserted contending that "the taking of evidence" in international commercial arbitration actually disavows these precepts while, as already has been suggested, U.S. common law discovery within the rubric of 28 U.S.C. Section 1782 promotes them.

Even though the word "evidence" is mentioned exactly fifteen times in the Foreword and Preamble to the Rules,[3] *Article* 1 of the Rules entitled "**Definitions**" nowhere defines the critical term "evidence." To be sure, for example, the term "*Evidentiary Hearing*" is defined as "any hearing, whether or not held on consecutive days, at which the Arbitral Tribunal receives oral evidence."[4] While this entry is

1 *See* International Bar Association, IBA Rules on the Taking of Evidence in International Commercial Arbitration (1999).

2 The Foreword to the Rules specify that they "reflect procedures in use in many different legal systems, and they may be particularly useful when the parties come from different legal cultures." *See* International Bar Association, IBA Rules on the Taking of Evidence in International Commercial Arbitration, Foreword (1999).

Also, the Preamble to the Rules stresses that the Rules are intended "to govern in an efficient and economical manner the taking of evidence in international commercial arbitrations, particularly those between Parties from different legal traditions."

3 The word "evidence" appears ten times in the Foreword and is repeated on five occasions in the Preamble.

4 *See* International Bar Association, IBA Rules on the Taking of Evidence in International Commercial Arbitration, Article 1, Definitions (1999).

By way of contrast, if not also comparison, FED.R.CIV.P. 26(b)(1) speaks to the ability of parties to "obtain discovery *regarding any matter*. . . . " (emphasis supplied). This subsection of the rule further qualifies – without limitation – "any matter to include 'the existence, description, nature, custody, condition, and location of any books, documents, or other tangible things and the identity and location of persons having knowledge of any discoverable matter.'"

clear on the meaning of an "evidentiary hearing" within the terms of the Rules, there is no significant predicate from which to infer the significance of the term "evidence" as referenced in the Rules. The gravity of this omission is compounded and made worse because of the Rules' very noble and practical aspiration to fashion a set of norms that would provide practitioners from diverse legal cultures with the comfort level that arises from the recognition of considerable conceptual familiarity framed by the Rules. Regrettably, this goal is measurably frustrated in the context of international arbitration because virtually every legal system has its own rubric and definition of "evidence."[5]

Equally wanting from the Rules' Article 1 Definition section is *any* definition of the term "relevance," without which it is hardly possible to have any conceptually consistent system for the "presentation of evidence." The Foreword to the Rules, nonetheless, in pertinent part states that "[t]hese IBA Rules of Evidence replace the IBA Supplementary Rules governing the presentation and reception of evidence in International Commercial Arbitration, originally issued in 1983. The IBA Rules of Evidence reflect procedures in use in many different legal systems, and they may be particularly useful when the parties come from different legal cultures."[6] These two critical omissions – definitions of "evidence" and "relevance" – are disconcerting and certainly do not further the aims promoted by the principles of predictive value, transparency of standard, certainty, and even party expectation.

The same debilities are hardly present in the Federal Rules of Civil Procedure, even though these rules do not purport to reconcile the competing conceptual and equitable norms of different legal cultures. It is imperative to underscore that what the Federal Rules of Civil Procedure lack in cross-fertilization of varying and often irreconcilable legal principles pertaining to foreign jurisdictions, they to some extent compensate for because of the Federal Rules' adherence to the precepts of party-autonomy,[7] predictive value,[8] transparency of standard,[9] and certainty.[10]

While Article 2, entitled "Scope of Application" of the Rules, indeed provides some guidelines for the interaction between the Rules and the General Rules,[11]

5 Kevin M. Clermont & Emily Sherwin, *A Comparative View of Standards of Proof*, 50 AM. J. COMP. L. 243 (Spring 2002); and Michele Taruffo, *Rethinking the Standards of Proof*, 51 AM. J. COMP. L. 659 (Summer 2003).

6 International Bar Association, IBA Rules on the Taking of Evidence in International Commercial Arbitration, Foreword (1999).

7 See the examples here detailed by analyzing, albeit superficially, FED.R.CIV.P. 3 and 27.

8 This precept is present where FED.R.CIV.P. 26(b)(1) enunciates with considerable rigor and detail the subject matter of discovery.

9 FED.R.CIV.P. 26(b)(1) defines "relevant information as well as the parameters within which such information must be contained (i.e. "relevant to the claim or defense of any party"), in addition to being limited by the law governing privileges.

10 While it would be inaccurate and unavailing to ascribe to the principle of "certainty" the unrealistic proposition that expectations as to likely outcome would be fostered, "certainty" from a private procedural international standpoint, and within the context of *discovery* or the taking of evidence in international commercial arbitration, is applicable to the parties' expectation that a uniform standard or criteria, far beyond the mere individual experiences of a panel of arbitrators, which standard is the beneficiary of exhaustive scholarly writings, draftors' annotation, and jurisprudence, shall be applied to petitions concerning "evidence" or "discoverable matters."

11 The General Rules are defined in *Article 1*, Definitions of the Rules as meaning "the institutional or *ad hoc* rules according to which the Parties are conducting their arbitration."

the "scope of application" of the Rules is of no moment in placing limitations on "evidence" (whatever may be meant by evidence within this framework) and devoid of any standard for the "taking of evidence." In fact, the principles of party-autonomy, certainty, predictive value, and transparency of standard are significantly undermined in paragraphs 3 and 4 of Article 2.

Paragraph 3 of Article 2 of the Rules reads:

> In the event of any dispute regarding the meaning of the IBA Rules of Evidence, the Arbitral Tribunal shall interpret them according to their purpose and in the manner most appropriate for the particular arbitration.[12]

Notably, instead of citing an objective standard or test to which the tribunal must make reference and apply when faced with a dispute of this ilk, the Rules merely delegate the resolution of this problem to the panel's whim. Because arbitral panels in international commercial arbitrations tend to comprise representatives from distinct and often quite different legal traditions and cultures, the absence of a "known standard" to be applied in interpreting the meaning of the Rules wrests from the parties the ability to decide *a priori* on a more uniform and "objective" methodology for the resolution of such disputes.[13]

In this same spirit, paragraph 4 of Article 2 of the Rules provides:

> Insofar as the IBA Rules of Evidence and the General Rules are silent on any matter concerning the taking of evidence and the Parties have not agreed otherwise, *the Arbitral Tribunal may conduct the taking of evidence as it deems appropriate, in accordance with the general principles of the IBA Rules of Evidence.*[14]

At the outset the general term "taking of evidence" is not defined. As such, it is unclear what is meant by "conduct the taking of evidence." This term of art is nowhere identified in the Rules' definitions. Furthermore, the absence of any definition of the term "evidence" merely complicates matters. Here too the fundamental precepts of party-autonomy, predictive value, uniformity, transparency of standard, and certainty certainly are not followed, let alone enhanced. In fact, they are directly undermined. Paragraph 4 engrafts virtually unbridled authority to the arbitral tribunal. Reposing the "conduct [of] the taking of evidence as it deems appropriate" to the arbitral tribunal subordinates the parties' will and thus the precept of party-autonomy to a system more closely identified with an inquisitorial

12 *See* International Bar Association, IBA Rules on the Taking of Evidence in International Commercial Arbitration, Article 2, Scope of Application (1999).

13 Within the framework of the Federal Rules of Civil Procedure, the meaning of specific and potentially dispositive terms may be gleaned from many sources including (i) jurisprudence governing the construction of terms of art and other legal terms, (ii) advisory notes drafted by the committee members charged with drafting and revising the rules, (iii) a well-developed body of jurisprudence interpreting the rules, and (iv) scholastic materials authored by academicians and practitioners that comment extensively on most of the salient and material elements of the rules. To date, the IBA Rules on the Taking of Evidence in International Commercial Arbitration lack the benefit of any single one of these sources, let alone the advantages arising from having the ability to consult all or some in unison as to a specific conflict.

14 International Bar Association, IBA Rules on the Taking of Evidence in International Commercial Arbitration, Article 2, Scope of Application (1999) (emphasis supplied).

approach than with one deeply rooted in party-autonomy.[15] Article 2 does yield, to some extent, to party-autonomy in advising the following:

> Whenever the Parties have agreed to the Arbitral Tribunal has determined to apply the IBA Rules of Evidence, the Rules shall govern the taking of evidence, *except to the extent that any specific provision of them may be found to be in conflict with many mandatory provision of law determined to be applicable to the case by the parties* or by the Arbitral Tribunal.[16]

The second part of the disjunctive places the parties' will *in pari materia* with a determination by the Arbitral Tribunal.

Just as the concept of "relevance" and the meaning of "evidence" remain obscure, nowhere in the Rules is "materiality" defined. The absence of any standard for "materiality" further causes confusion when adjudicating an evidentiary dispute between parties from disparate legal systems and cultures. Yet, three factors are essential configuring "documents" that purportedly may be deemed "evidence" within the meaning of the Rules.

First, the production of documents pursuant to the Rules is bottomed on a showing of "reliance." In this connection, parties seeking the production of documents must state the reason(s) why the documents sought "are relevant and material to the outcome of the case."[17]

The "reliance" requirement is susceptible to the critique of being unduly limiting and tactically prejudicial. In stark contrast with the Fed.R.Civ.P. 26 relevance rubric commanding a relationship to the claims and defenses and detailing the meaning of "relevance," here the party seeking the production of documents must disclose its mental impressions concerning the strategy of the case that presumably would be furthered were the document requested produced. Disclosure of a party's

[15] For completeness' sake, it must be underscored that paragraph 4 does explicitly reference a scenario where "the parties have not agreed otherwise." This language notwithstanding, however, the absence of a reference to potentially dispositive norms or other criteria is again disconcerting. In addition to any specific reference to a body of law or doctrine that may comport with elements of the parties' will as expressed in the dispositive arbitration clause, such as the selection of a specific substantive law, paragraph 4's mention of "accordance with the general principles of the IBA Rules of Evidence," also is less than immediately intuitive. The Rules' definition section does not identify *any* "general principles." In fact, the Rules are completely bereft of any section or appendix purporting to enunciate underlying or governing general principles. Thus, it necessarily must be inferred that whatsoever "general principles of the IBA Rules of Evidence" may be referenced, should be somehow extrapolated from the totality of the Rules themselves. This task certainly requires greater guidance and more comprehensive analysis so that it may be of significant practical assistance to arbitrators and parties alike.

[16] *See* International Bar Association, IBA Rules on the Taking of Evidence in International Commercial Arbitration, Article 2 (1999) (emphasis supplied).

[17] Article 3, paragraph 1 embodies the "reliance" predicate:

> 1. Within the time ordered by the tribunal, each party shall submit to the Arbitral Tribunal and to the other Parties *all documents available to it on which it relies*, including public documents and those in the public domain, except for any documents that have already been submitted by another Party. International Bar Association, IBA Rules on the Taking of Evidence in International Commercial Arbitration (1999) (emphasis supplied).

Paragraph 3(b) of *Article* 3 first enunciates the "relevance" and "materiality" requirements. The complete subsection provides:

> (b) A description of how the documents requested are *relevant* and *material* to the outcome of the case. (emphasis supplied).

work-product rarely promotes the equitable administration of justice, particularly when evidence is sought for impeachment or credibility purposes. In addition, divulging the manner in which propositions are to be proved flatly disadvantages the moving party. Pursuant to this rubric, parties must now engage in a predicate analysis before submitting a formal document request to determine whether the benefits arising from the documents requested outweigh the partial or complete disclosure of the party's arbitration strategy. It must be stressed that, unlike the common law system, the Rules are a product of clear compromise. Thus, they provide the arbitrators with sufficient latitude to question and interrogate witnesses and parties as would a judge presiding in a civil code or continental jurisdiction. Consequently, a party engaged in this preliminary analysis must assume that disclosure of its work product shall be broader than the premises that the party advances because of the high likelihood of questions from the panel.

Second, the concept of "relevance" needs to be defined if indeed the production process is to foster predictability, uniformity, certainty, and objective transparency pursuant to a known standard to be applied to particular points of contention. Certainly, the incorporation of the Federal Rules of Civil Procedure to international commercial arbitration where parties seek to avail themselves of the 28 U.S.C. Section 1782 framework allays this concern through explicit reference to Fed.R.Civ.P. 26(b)(1). In the context of "evidence" within the U.S. common law system the substantive Rules of Evidence for United States Courts and Magistrates (the "Rules of Evidence") would apply in a dispositive manner.[18] The Rules are completely devoid of any scholarship, commentary, guidepost, or other effort to provide this critical term of art with substantive content.

Third, the precept of "materiality" is nowhere defined by the Rules. Moreover, the Rules lack reference to any system of "statutory construction" that may otherwise facilitate the definition of this key term within the Rules' framework. Also, when viewed in their totality, it is virtually impossible conceptually to glean from the use of the word "material" in the Rules a specific and workable meaning that would appease and meet the expectations of parties from different legal cultures and traditions. While "materiality" from an evidentiary perspective does not form part of the Federal Rules of Civil Procedure, nor is there a need for the term to be incorporated into the Federal Rules of Civil Procedure, it is amply addressed by the Rules of Evidence.[19]

[18] FED. R. EVID. 401 reads:

> **Rule 401**. Definition of "Relevant Evidence."
>
> 'Relevant Evidence' means evidence having any tendency to make the existence of any fact that is of consequence to the determination of the action more probable or less probable than it would be without the evidence.

FED. R. EVID. 402 also would be availing:

> **Rule 402. Relevant Evidence Genetally Admissible; Irrelevant Evidence Inadmissible.**
>
> All relevant evidence is admissible, except as otherwise provided by the Constitute of the United States, by act of Congress, by these Rules, or by other rules proscribed by the Supreme Court pursuant to statutory authority. Evidence which is not relevant is not admissible.

For a sense of the scholarship and jurisprudence defining the contours of Rules 401 and 402, *see, e.g.*, GRAHAM, HANDBOOK OF FEDERAL EVIDENCE (West, 6th ed. 2001).

[19] *See, e.g.*, MICHAEL GRAHAM, HANDBOOK OF FEDERAL EVIDENCE (2001); CHRISTOPHER MUELLER & LAIRD KIRKPATRICK, EVIDENCE UNDER THE RULES: TEXT, CASES, AND PROBLEMS (2004); and ARTHUR BEST, WIGMORE ON EVIDENCE (1995).

The absence of any definition, methodology of construction, or authority clarifying the meaning of such important terms as (i) evidence, (ii) relevance, and (iii) material within a framework that requires that the party propounding a document request as a predicate disclose the reasons why from that party's perspective the documents sought are relevant and material to the outcome of the case, diminish the pervasiveness of the principle of party-autonomy throughout the Rules generally and Article 3 in particular.

Hence, discovery must be conducted through the arbitral panel upon a showing that the documents elicited are somehow "relevant" and "material" to the outcome of the case. Upon submission of such information, the panel, typically composed of members of different legal traditions and cultures, unilaterally decides on the scope, extent, and propriety of the request. Likewise, the production of documents also must be shared in its totality with the panel.[20] In this same spirit, the parties themselves are not empowered to review original documents deemed subject to production without first securing the panel's *imprimatur.*[21]

The authority accorded to the panel pursuant to the Rules further evinces the diminished role bestowed to the principles of party-autonomy, predictive value, uniformity, and party expectation pursuant to the transparency of governing standards. To be sure, the Rules are rife with examples. Six salient observations, however, are particularly illustrative.

At the outset, and by way of example, the panel is empowered to admit as "evidence" a witness statement produced by a witness who, without justification or a valid reason, elects not to appear at an Evidentiary Hearing, as defined by Article 1 of the Rules.[22] The Rules' text does not offer any guidance as to what type of "exceptional circumstances" would warrant the admission of such evidence. In the context of judicial assistance sought pursuant to Section 1782 for use in an international commercial arbitration, the parties would have the benefit of academic commentary and incident jurisprudence.

Second, the Arbitral Tribunal is vested with authority to exercise its discretion in allowing a party to take evidence from a recalcitrant witness who elects not to appear to testify at the proceeding where the panel decides that the recalcitrant witness' testimony "would be relevant and material."[23]

20 *See, e.g.*, International Bar Association, IBA Rules on the Taking of Evidence in International Commercial Arbitration, Article 3 (1999).

21 *See, e.g.*, International Bar Association, IBA Rules on the Taking of Evidence in International Commercial Arbitration, Article 3 (1999).

22 *See, e.g.*, International Bar Association, IBA Rules on the Taking of Evidence in International Commercial Arbitration, Article 4 (1999), which reads:

> 8. If a witness who has submitted a Witness Statement does not appear without a valid reason for testimony at an Evidentiary Hearing, except by agreement of the Parties, the Arbitral Tribunal shall disregard that Witness Statement *unless, an exceptional circumstances, the Arbitral Tribunal determines otherwise. (emphasis added).*

23 *See, e.g.*, International Bar Association, IBA Rules on the Taking of Evidence in International Commercial Arbitration, Article 4 (1999), which states:

> 10. If a party which is to present evidence from a person who will not appear voluntarily at its request, the Party may, within the time ordered by the Arbitral Tribunal, ask it to take whatever steps are legally available to obtain the testimony of that person. The party shall identify the intended witness, shall describe the subjects on which the witness's testimony is sought and shall state why such subject are relevant and material to the outcome of the case. *The Arbitral Tribunal shall decide on this request and shall take the necessary steps if in its discretion it determines that the testimony of that witness would be relevant and material. (emphasis supplied).*

Third, the Rules authorize the panel to appoint experts to seek counsel on specific issues. The Rules further vest the panel with the normative right to establish terms of reference for any panel-appointed expert report. Such a report would automatically be sent to *both* the panel and the parties.[24] Hence, the panel controls the extent and quality of expert testimony, irrespective of the parties' volition. Also, the Rules are silent concerning the extent to which a party or parties have any standing and normative claim to preclude the introduction of this evidence. Although purely within the realm of speculation, it is reasonable to infer that the absence of any reference to party objection may be construed as parties not having a right to preclude the introduction of such evidence.[25]

Fourth, the panel may *sua sponte* engage in the inspection of evidence, including real and personal property. Also, the panel, again on its own initiative, may order a panel-appointed expert to conduct inspections of this ilk.[26] This discretion is inapposite to fundamental common law discovery rules because of the extent to which it empowers the panel to be *judge*, *jury*, and *party* to the proceeding. This rule grants the panel the initiative to explore evidence not contemplated by the parties and that does not constitute any part of the parties' order of proof. In effect, it wrests the proceeding from the parties themselves, providing them with a mere right to attend the subject inspection. Certainly, party-autonomy, predictive value, transparency of standard, and certainty are undermined pursuant to the application of this norm.

Fifth, the rules proscribe "unreasonably leading" questions, and in this context, also reference "direct and redirect testimony." This command, however, is not meaningful even as to form. Significantly, the rules do not provide for any methodology of interrogation or examination of parties. Additionally, the panel is accorded unbridled discretion to limit or exclude questions posed to witnesses, evidence presented, and even the appearance of fact and expert witnesses.[27] This authority in the

[24] *See, e.g.*, International Bar Association, IBA Rules on the Taking of Evidence in International Commercial Arbitration, Article 6 (1999), which reads:

> 1. The Arbitral Tribunal, after having consulted with the Parties, may appoint one or more independent Tribunal-Appointed Experts to report to it on specific issues designated by the Arbitral Tribunal. The Arbitral Tribunal shall establish the terms of reference for any Tribunal-Appointed Expert report after having consulted with the Parties. A copy of the final terms of reference shall be sent by the Arbitral Tribunal to the Parties.

[25] Significantly, the Rules contemplate a framework that actually allows a party unilaterally to stop the production of documents by raising an objection (*See, e.g.*, International Bar Association, IBA Rules on the Taking of Evidence in International Commercial Arbitration, Article 3 (1999)). Consequently, the logical construction would suggest that party objections would not be considered in this context, even though there is not explicit authority within the Rules supporting this proposition.

[26] International Bar Association, IBA Rules on the Taking of Evidence in International Commercial Arbitration, Article 7 (1999), which reads:

> Subject to the provisions of Article 9.2, the Arbitral Tribunal may, at the request of a Party or on its own motion, inspect or request the inspection by a Tribunal Appointed Expert of any site, property, machinery or any other goods or process, or documents, as it deems appropriate. The Arbitral Tribunal shall, in consultation with the Parties, determine the timing and arrangement for the inspection. The Parties and their representatives shall have the right to attend any such inspection.

[27] International Bar Association, IBA Rules on the Taking of Evidence in International Commercial Arbitration, Article 8 (1999), stating that:

> 1. The Arbitral Tribunal shall at all times have complete control over the Evidentiary Hearing. The Arbitral Tribunal may limit or exclude any question to, answer by or appearance of a witness (which term includes, for the purpose of this Article, witnesses of fact and any Experts), if it considers such question, answer or

absence of a governing standard, test, or criteria is less than helpful and wanting in predictive value as it concentrates the decision-making process on the panel's individual and collective legal training and experience. It is likely that in an international commercial arbitration the diverse experience of the arbitral tribunal would add a layer of complexity that can only undermine the very precepts that arbitration seeks to promote.

Sixth, the panel is empowered to request the introduction of evidence into the proceeding, independent of party initiative, by requiring witnesses to provide testimony consonant with the panel's own examination of such witnesses.[28] Here too, the absence of any reference to the parties' ability to limit the panel's inquiry, together with the lack of rigorous defining precepts that should be ascribed to the key terms of "evidence," "relevance," and "material," renders any unilateral inquiry by the panel potentially inimical to party expectation, uniformity, and certainty. Also, it deprives the parties of the strategic and tactical advantages arising from controlling the order of proof in a proceeding.

The IBA Rules on the Taking of Evidence of International Commercial Arbitration are a wonderful contribution and an invaluable assistance to international commercial arbitration. This effort certainly has provided some guidance where before there was no pole star whatsoever. It certainly constitutes a framework on which to build a rubric of norms that shall facilitate the gathering of information, its presentation, and the assessment of the evidentiary value of such data in the field of international commercial arbitration. It also must be recalled that the Rules were "designed to supplement the legal provisions and the institutional or *ad hoc* rules according to which the Parties are conducting their arbitration."[29] Therefore, the Rules must be understood, to avoid being misunderstood, as supplementary in nature.

The Rules' virtuosity, however, should not detract from the debilities that cry for improvement and that may actually undermine the extent to which the Rules may be incompatible with norms promulgated by institutional arbitral centers selected by the parties. Also, the Rules' very legitimacy considerably suffers when party expectations are not met as a result of want of definitional rigor and the uncertainties inevitably spawned by reposing too much discretion coupled with unbridled latitude on the panel.

The "taking of evidence" promulgated by the Rules is certainly true to the proposition advanced in the Foreword advising that they "reflect procedures in use in many different legal systems, and they may be particularly useful when the parties come from different legal cultures."[30] Regrettably, to some extent the

appearance to be irrelevant, immaterial, burdensome, duplicative or covered by a reason or objection set forth in Article 9.2. Questions to a witness during direct and redirect testimony may not be unreasonably leading.

28 International Bar Association, IBA Rules on the Taking of Evidence in International Commercial Arbitration, Article 8 (1999), states:

> 4. Subject to the provisions of Article 9.2, the Arbitral Tribunal may request any person to give oral or written evidence on any issue that the Arbitral Tribunal considers to be relevant and material. Any witness called and questioned by the Arbitral Tribunal may also be questioned by the Parties.

29 International Bar Association, IBA Rules on the Taking of Evidence in International Commercial Arbitration, Preamble (1999).

30 International Bar Association, IBA Rules on the Taking of Evidence in International Commercial Arbitration, Foreword (1999).

philosophy of jurisprudence appears to have been abandoned in the fashioning of the Rules. Analytical jurisprudence is concerned with the procedural development of conceptual categories such that the incorporation of seemingly diverse premises and propositions can be reconciled to form a separate, distinct, and independent precept that draws normative legitimacy from the integrity of its unique constitution as a whole and not from vestiges of its parts. Analytical jurisprudence cannot and should not substitute the development of novel conceptual categories by engaging in procedural bargaining akin to a commercial transaction.

The Rules are the product of compromise and not the fruits of jurisprudence. Not even traces of the most pragmatic manifestation of legal realism may be gleaned from them. Instead, they constitute a collection of Rules rather than the embodiment of a code. Despite the banal nature of the metaphor, it is difficult to resist the temptation of characterizing them as the classic image represented by the popular adage that "a horse by committee is a camel."

Reasoned analysis arguably demonstrates that the incorporation of Section 1782, meaning the introduction of the Federal Rules of Civil Procedure, into international commercial arbitration is certainly not as foreign to the principles underlying arbitral proceedings as may first appear. To the contrary, as exemplified through analysis of Fed.R.Civ.P. 3, 26, and 27, used for illustrative purposes, the doctrinal development holding that an arbitration tribunal is a foreign or international tribunal within the ambit of Section 1782(a) conceptually comports with the most fundamental tenets that define arbitration and, in turn, that arbitration explicitly promotes. These principles have been here defined as (i) party-autonomy, (ii) predictive value, (iii) transparency of standard, and (iv) certainty.

This doctrinal development has enriched arbitral proceedings also with respect to the policies traditionally associated with arbitration, such as expediency, finality, and the economical and efficient administration of justice. Such policies are ultimately predicated upon the referenced principles. If it is less than axiomatic that "history repeats itself," then it may be perhaps true that "history repeats itself but not exactly in the same way every time." Such appears to be the case with the perception, or misperception, viscerally precipitated by the mere reference to "discovery" in the context of arbitration. Like the four badges of prejudice,[31] the proposition that discovery is repugnant to arbitration is intrinsically flawed and does not resist strict analytical scrutiny. In fact, sustained reflection demonstrates the converse to be true.

"The taking of evidence" also compels an ocular adjustment, but in a diametrically opposite direction. Deemed at only an intuitive and mechanically reflexive level to provide parties with a hybrid rubric for the production of documents and information to be administered by the arbitral tribunal and not the parties that thus comport with the expectations of parties from diverse legal traditions, at least under one analysis, quite the opposite is the case. There is no set of rules that even sets

[31] These have been identified as the proclivity of arbitral proceedings (i) to oust jurisdiction from courts otherwise enjoying competent jurisdiction, (ii) subscribing to the proposition that arbitration is inadequate for the adjudication of certain categories of statutorily created causes of action, (iii) arbitration can best, and perhaps only, take place under the auspices of courts, and (iv) arbitrators and the arbitral process are not competent to administer proceedings entailing complex and highly technical issues.

out to define "evidence," "relevance," "material," and "methodology" for the production or exchange of documents, or a standard pursuant to which the production or exchange of documents and information is to be governed. Remarkably, the Rules, purporting to be supplementary to *ad hoc* proceedings or institutional rules, represent the most comprehensive exemplar on the production of documents and information.

B. A REVIEW OF THE RULES OF ARBITRATION OF THE INTERNATIONAL CHAMBER OF COMMERCE

The Rules of Arbitration of the International Chamber of Commerce (the "ICC Rules") do not even reference the phrase "taking of evidence," let alone define a governing standard for the production of documents and information. Moreover, the precept of party-autonomy is substantially tempered by allocating considerable authority to the Arbitral Tribunal. Some provisions, however, merit observation.[32]

By way of example, the Arbitral Tribunal is empowered to "deliberate at any location it considers appropriate."[33] The Arbitral Tribunal also is vested with normative authority to decide on the application of rules of procedure incident to a national law, where the ICC rules and the parties are silent on this issue.[34] Where the parties have not specified the language or languages to be used during the arbitral proceeding – presumably in the arbitration agreement – the Arbitral Tribunal is charged with arriving at this decision. Thus, under the ICC Rules the parties are not privileged to agree beyond the confines of the Arbitration Agreement on

[32] The ICC Rules' definitions Article is scant containing only three defined terms:

> Article 2
> Definitions
> In these Rules:
> (i) "Arbitral Tribunal" includes one or more arbitrators.
> (ii) "Claimant" includes one or more claimants and "Respondent" includes one or more respondents.
> (iii) "Award" includes, *inter alia*, an interim, partial or final Award.

There is no reference to procedural strictures of whatsoever ilk, let alone specific procedural provisions governing the taking and use of evidence.

[33] *See* International Chamber of Commerce, Rules of Arbitration, Article 14 (1998), *available at* http://www.iccwbo.org/court/arbitration/id4093/index.html. It should be noted, however, that paragraph 2 of this very article does reference that "after consultation with the parties," the Arbitral Tribunal may conduct hearings and meetings "at any location it considers appropriate unless otherwise agreed by the parties."

[34] *See* International Chamber of Commerce, Rules of Arbitration, Article 15 (1998), *available at* http://www.iccwbo.org/court/arbitration/id4093/index.html, reads:

> Article 15
> Rules Governing the Proceedings
> 1. The proceedings before the Arbitral Tribunal shall be governed by these rules and, where these rules are silent, by any rules which the parties or, failing them the Arbitral Tribunal may settle on, whether or not reference is thereby made to the Rules of Procedure of a national law to be applied to the arbitration.

The wide latitude accorded to the Arbitral Tribunal is the subject matter of very helpful commentary by Yves Derains and Eric A. Schwartz who observe that:

> Article 15(1) allows the parties *and the arbitrators* the greatest possible freedom in structuring the proceedings before the Arbitral Tribunal, subject only to the Rules themselves and any provisions of law that may apply mandatorily. In this regard, it establishes the following hierarchy among the governing rules. First, the Rules themselves; second, where no provisions of the Rules apply, any rules that the parties may agree upon; and third, *any rules the arbitrators may settle*. YVES DERAINS AND ERIC A. SCHWARTZ, A GUIDE TO THE ICC RULES OF ARBITRATION 230 (Kluwer, 2nd Ed. 2005).

the operative language for the proceeding.[35] Moreover, even though the Arbitral Tribunal is empowered to determine the rule of law to be applied to the proceeding only if the parties fail to reach agreement on this issue, the ICC rules provide that "[i]n all cases the Arbitral Tribunal shall take account of the provisions of the contract and the relevant trade usages," presumably in (i) applying the rules of law selected by the parties, (ii) supplementing the rules of law selected by the Arbitral Tribunal, or (iii) in modifying either of the two foregoing propositions.[36]

In crafting the Terms of Reference, the Arbitral Tribunal is responsible for arriving at operative timetables.[37] In stark contrast with U.S. common law discovery or

[35] International Chamber of Commerce, Rules of Arbitration, Article 14 (1998), *available at* http://www.iccwbo.org/court/arbitration/id4093/index.html, reads:

> Language of the Arbitration
> Article 16
> In the absence of an agreement by the parties, the Arbitral Tribunal shall determine the language or languages of the arbitration, due regard being given to all relevant circumstances, including the language of the contract.

Even though this article does not explicitly state that an agreement by the parties beyond the scope of the subject arbitration clause shall be subordinated to the Arbitral Tribunal's ruling on the issue, the reference to "all relevant circumstances, including the language of the contract," may be construed as precisely divesting the parties of this authority, even though an equally plausible construction suggesting that the parties merely cannot agree on the language to govern the proceeding and recourse to the Arbitral Tribunal is necessary, is entirely plausible.

Derains and Schwartz reconfirm the primacy of the Arbitral Tribunal and the rather general principles by which it is bound, in determining the language of the arbitration. They note that:

> In determining the language or languages of the arbitration, the Arbitral Tribunal is required, under Article 16, to give due regard to all relevant circumstances. These are stated to 'include' the language of the contract, but unlike certain other arbitration rules the ICC rules do not treat the language of the contract as a default language for the arbitration. [citing as contrast AAA International Arbitration Rules, Article 14; LCIA Rules, Article 17; WIPO Arbitration Rules Article 40(a)]. YVES DERAINS AND ERIC A. SCHWARTZ, A GUIDE TO THE ICC RULES OF ARBITRATION 232–3 (Kluwer, 2nd Ed. 2005).

[36] International Chamber of Commerce, Rules of Arbitration, Article 17 (1998), *available at* http://www.iccwbo.org/court/arbitration/id4093/index.html, reads:

> Article 17
> Applicable Rules of Law
> 1. The parties shall be free to agree upon the rules of law to be applied by the Arbitral Tribunal to the merits of the dispute. In the absence of any such agreement, the Arbitral Tribunal shall apply the rules of law which it determines to be appropriate.
> 2. *In all cases the Arbitral Tribunal shall take account of the provisions of the contract and the relevant trade usages.* (emphasis supplied).

Here too Derains and Schwartz, in the context of commenting on a shift in international thinking that no longer suggests recourse to the rule of conflict of a particular jurisdiction, note:

> Nothing in the alteration of the former text, an Arbitral Tribunal nevertheless remains free to apply a rule of conflict if it considers this appropriate, whether that rule originates in a national legal system, an international convention or general principles of international private law. Indeed, the arbitrators may devise their own rules of conflict. However, whatever method is employed, the arbitrators must provide a reasoned explanation for their choice in accordance with the legitimate expectations of the parties. YVES DERAINS AND ERIC A. SCHWARTZ, A GUIDE TO THE ICC RULES OF ARBITRATION 242 (Kluwer, 2nd Ed. 2005).

Despite the limitation articulated in the last sentence of the commentary, it is clear that "the alteration of the former text" bestows on the Arbitral Tribunal significantly greater flexibility in deciding the applicable substantive law. In addition, one must confess that such standards as compliance with "the legitimate expectations of the parties" and "a reasoned explanation" are far from iron-clad conceptual limitations on the Arbitral Tribunal's mission to apply the applicable law to the arbitration.

[37] Pursuant to the Federal Rules of Civil Procedure, only where the parties cannot reach agreement on a scheduling report is judicial intervention triggered. *See* FED.R.CIV.P. 26 (f). Paragraph 4 of ICC Rules Article 18 does state that "after having consulted with the parties," is the Arbitral Tribunal to proceed in fashioning the governing timetable. International Chamber of Commerce,

even standard pretrial proceedings, the Arbitral Tribunal, at its unbridled discretion and thus without reference to any pre-existing objective criteria communicated to the parties, is empowered to hear witness testimony – both expert and lay witnesses – and may do so outside the parties' presence. This ICC rule is bereft of any procedural methodology to be used in having a witness testify. The taking of testimony of expert or fact witnesses beyond the parties' presence raises due process concerns, such as the right to cross-examine or present rebuttal evidence, that are wholly lacking from the Federal Rules of Civil Procedure.[38] The Arbitral Tribunal is privileged to decide *sua sponte* and without party consultation to summon a party for purposes of eliciting additional evidence.[39]

The authority vested in the Arbitral Tribunal in the conduct of hearings is broad and entirely discretionary. To be sure, the parties' strategic and tactical intent with respect to so critical an issue as the order of proof may be completely altered by the Arbitral Tribunal.[40] In this connection, the Arbitral Tribunal is authorized to

Rules of Arbitration, Article 18 (1998), *available at* http://www.iccwbo.org/court/arbitration/id4093/index.html, provides:

Article 18
Terms of Reference: Procedural Timetable
4. When drawing up the Terms of Reference, or as soon as possible thereafter, the Arbitral Tribunal, after having consulted the parties, shall establish in a separate document a provisional timetable that it intends to follow for the conduct of the arbitration and shall communicate it to the Court and the parties. Any subsequent modifications of the provisional timetable shall be communicated to the Court and the parties.

38 International Chamber of Commerce, Rules of Arbitration, Article 20 (1998), *available at* http://www.iccwbo.org/court/arbitration/id4093/index.html, states:

Article 20
Establishing the Facts of the Case
3. The Arbitral Tribunal may decide to hear witnesses, experts appointed by the parties or any other person, in the presence of the parties, or in their absence provided they have been duly summoned.

Derains and Schwartz observe that the Arbitral Tribunal is invested with the authority to preclude witness testimony:

> Indeed, that an ICC Arbitral Tribunal may, depending on the circumstances, refuse to hear witnesses without denying a party due process has been confirmed by courts in both France [citing to *Societe Soubaigne c/ societe Limmareds Akogar, Cour d'appel de Paris* (March 15, 1984), *Rev. arb.* (1985), p. 285; *Honeywell Bull S.A. c/Computacion Bull de Venezuela CA, Cour d'appel de Paris* (June 21, 1990), *Rev. arb.* (1991), p. 96; *see also Fouchard Gaillard and Goldman,* p. 698] and England, where the High Court (Kerr, J.) held, in connection with an application for refusing the enforcement of an ICC Award made in Geneva, that the ICC arbitrator had not breached natural justice in refusing to hear oral testimony because such testimony was 'completely unnecessary' in the circumstances of that case. [citing *to Dalmia Dairy Industries, Ltd. v. National Bank of Pakistan* (1978) 2 Lloyd's Rep. 223, 269.] YVES DERAINS AND ERIC A. SCHWARTZ, A GUIDE TO THE ICC RULES OF ARBITRATION 276 (Kluwer, 2nd ed. 2005).

39 International Chamber of Commerce, Rules of Arbitration, Article 20, paragraph 5 (1998), *available at* http://www.iccwbo.org/court/arbitration/id4093/index.html. This single sentence paragraph reads:

Article 20
Establishing the Facts of the Case
5. At any time during the proceedings, the Arbitral Tribunal may summon any party to provide additional evidence.
In this connection, Derains and Schwartz note that "[i]t is, thus, left to the Arbitral Tribunal to decide on a case-by-case basis how much, if any, discovery should be allowed, taking account of the specific circumstances of each case, absent a contrary agreement of the parties." YVES DERAINS AND ERIC A. SCHWARTZ, A GUIDE TO THE ICC RULES OF ARBITRATION 281 (Kluwer, 2nd ed. 2005).

40 International Chamber of Commerce, Rules of Arbitration, Article 21, paragraph 1 (1998), *available at* http://www.iccwbo.org/court/arbitration/id4093/index.html, provides:

Article 21
Hearings
1. When a hearing is to be held, the Arbitral Tribunal, giving reasonable notice, shall summon the parties to appear before it on the day and at the place fixed by it.

continue a hearing despite the absence of a party or witness summoned to present testimony at that particular hearing. Also, the ICC rules make clear that "[t]he Arbitral Tribunal shall be in full charge of the hearings."[41]

The want of any guidelines for the production of documents and information in the ICC Rules highlights and underscores the subordination of the principle of party-autonomy to the Arbitral Tribunal's authority. Reposing the gamut of issues attendant to this procedural concern on the Arbitral Tribunal's virtually unbridled discretion certainly does not further the principles of party-autonomy, predictive value, transparency of standard, and certainty. In the context of an international commercial arbitration where a party has sought to avail itself of the Federal Rules of Civil Procedure by filing a 28 U.S.C. Section 1782 petition, these four important precepts would be present to facilitate the proceeding. Supplementing the ICC Rules with the Rules (IBA Rules on the Taking of Evidence in International Commercial Arbitration) does little, if anything, to promote these principles. Hence, the perception that the ICC Rules, together with the Rules, more closely comport with the precepts underlying arbitration than the U.S. Federal Rules of Civil Procedure is, at best, debatable and suspect. Here too, the dissonance between essence and phenomenon is eloquently revealing.

C. REVISITING THE RULES OF THE INTERNATIONAL CENTRE FOR DISPUTE RESOLUTION

The ICDR Rules governing international arbitration (International Centre for Dispute Resolution) fare no better in promoting party-autonomy, predictive value, transparency of standard, uniformity, and certainty. Seven provisions illustrate this point.

At the very outset, a party during an arbitral proceeding governed by the ICDR Rules may be proscribed from amending or supplementing its claim, counterclaim, or defense at the tribunal's complete discretion. The ICDR Rules do not provide any guidance or standard to be consulted in reaching such a determination. These Rules also do not state whether the amendment or supplementing process is to be liberally construed. The Rules are equally silent on whether proximity to the final hearing may constitute a basis for limiting or altogether denying a party its right to amend or supplement claims or defenses. Indeed, the ICDR Rule merely references in very general terms prejudice arising from delay and possible issues concerning scope.[42] Where an arbitrator is removed pursuant to ICDR Article 10 in a three-arbitrator tribunal configuration, the two remaining arbitrators at their sole and unbridled discretion may decide to continue the proceeding and render decisions, rulings, and an award, should they deem fit.[43] Significantly, Article 11 paragraph 1

[41] *See* International Chamber of Commerce, Rules of Arbitration, Article 21, paragraph 2 and 3 (1998), *available at* http://www.iccwbo.org/court/arbitration/id4093/index.html.

[42] International Centre for Dispute Resolution, International Arbitration Rules, Article 4 (2007), *available at* http://www.adr.org/sp.asp?id=28144, states:

> During the arbitral proceedings, any party may amend or supplement its claim, counterclaim or defenses, unless the tribunal considers it inappropriate to allow such amendment or supplement a claim or counterclaim if the amendment or supplement would fall outside the scope of the agreement to arbitrate.

[43] *See* International Centre for Dispute Resolution, International Arbitration Rules, Article 11, paragraph 1 (2007), *available at* http://www.adr.org/sp.asp?id=28144:

> 1. If an arbitrator on a three person tribunal fails to participate in the arbitration for reasons other than those identified in Article 10 [a successful challenge or death], the two other arbitrators *shall have the power*

references three factors to be considered by the two remaining arbitrators in their deliberation concerning any ruling or issuance of an award: (i) where present the reasons expressed by the third arbitrator for non-participation, (ii) the stage of the arbitration, and (iii) "other matters as they consider appropriate." Even though the third precept is a general "catch all clause," absent from the recitation is *any* reference to the party's will, which presumably contracted for a three-person tribunal in the first instance. In addition, "[i]f a substitute arbitrator is appointed under either Article 10 or Article 11, the Tribunal shall determine at its sole discretion whether all or any prior hearing shall be repeated."[44]

The tribunal is charged with holding "conferences or hear[ing] witnesses or inspect[ing] property or documents at any place it deems appropriate. The parties shall be given sufficient written notice to enable them to be present at any such proceedings."[45] This scant and rather ephemeral reference to "evidence" or documents and information to be used as evidence is hardly availing in the context of a proceeding with exigent needs for vigorous document and information exchange arising from complex facts and the application of law to fact.

The apogee, however, of authority reposed on the tribunal is found in Article 16, paragraphs 1 and 3 of the ICDR rubric. According to these strictures, the tribunal is provided with absolute authority as to the conduct of the arbitration, with the only limiting factor being the very general proposition that the parties are to be treated fairly and granted an opportunity to present their respective cases. Furthermore, the tribunal directly and explicitly may fashion the order of proof to be used throughout the proceeding.[46] Pursuant to Article 22 of the ICDR Rules, "[t]he Tribunal may appoint one or more independent experts to report to it, in writing, on specific issues *designated by the Tribunal* and communicated to the parties."[47] Finally, pursuant

at their sole discretion to continue the arbitration and to make any decision, ruling or award, notwithstanding the failure of the third arbitrator to participate. In determining whether to continue the arbitration or render any decision, ruling or award without the participation of an arbitrator, the two arbitrators shall take into account the stage of the arbitration, the reason, if any expressed by the third arbitrator for such non-participation and such other matters as they consider appropriate in the circumstances of the case. In the event that the two other arbitrators determine not to continue the arbitration without the participation of the third arbitrator, the administrator on proof satisfactory to it shall declare the office vacant, and a substitute arbitrator shall be appointed pursuant to the provisions of Article 6, unless the parties otherwise agree. (emphasis supplied)

44 International Centre for Dispute Resolution, International Arbitration Rules, Article 11, paragraph 2 (2007), *available at* http://www.adr.org/sp.asp?id=28144.

45 *See* International Centre for Dispute Resolution, International Arbitration Rules, Article 13, paragraph 2 (2007), *available at* http://www.adr.org/sp.asp?id=28144

46 International Centre for Dispute Resolution, International Arbitration Rules, Article 16, paragraphs 1 and 3 (2007), *available at* http://www.adr.org/sp.asp?id=28144, state:

1. Subject to these rules, the tribunal may conduct the arbitration *in whatever manner it considers appropriate*, provided that the parties are treated with equality and that each party has the right to be heard and is given a fair opportunity to present its case.

3. The tribunal *may in its discretion direct the order of proof* bifurcate proceedings, exclude cumulative or irrelevant testimony or other evidence, and direct the parties to focus their presentations on issues the decision of which could dispose of all or part of the case.

Thus, in addition to controlling the order of proof, an extremely important strategy typically reserved for parties as they should be privileged to decide on the coherence and thematic effect of the presentation of the evidence in their case, the tribunal also substitutes its judgment for that of the parties' in directing the parties on how best to present issues and also in identifying which issues may be deemed in whole or in part case dispositive.

47 International Centre for Dispute Resolution, International Arbitration Rules, Article 22, paragraph 1 (2007), *available at* http://www.adr.org/sp.asp?id=28144 (emphasis supplied).

to its own discretion, the tribunal "may reopen the hearings at any time before the award is made."[48]

As with the ICC Rules, the ICDR rubric is devoid of any procedural methodology addressing the gathering of documents or information. Indeed, the words "evidence," "relevance," and "taking of evidence" appear nowhere in the text. Also, as with the ICC Rules, the ICDR Rules hardly stand to benefit by being supplemented with the IBA Rules on the Taking of Evidence in International Commercial Arbitration. The ICDR uses the tribunal as the conceptual fulcrum for its rules. Indeed, no standard or test is identified for the conduct of document and information production and exchange. The parties are affirmatively deprived of the right to engage in such fundamental decision making as fashioning the order of proof in a manner that from their perspective most lucidly and persuasively presents their respective cases.

Here too the comparison between "the taking of evidence" and "discovery" sharply turns into contrast.

D. THE RULES OF THE LONDON COURT OF INTERNATIONAL ARBITRATION

The Rules of the London Court of International Arbitration (the "LCIA Rules") are wanting in any procedural methodology in governing the conduct of document and information production. Neither doctrinally nor conceptually do they materially and significantly differ from the ICC Rules or the ICDR Rules as to this narrow and specific issue.[49] The LCIA Rules confer on a three-member Arbitral Tribunal the authority to continue the arbitration process, undertake deliberations, issue rulings, and even enter an award where one of the members of the Arbitral Tribunal fails to participate in the proceeding.[50] Here too, Article 12, paragraph 12.2, of the LCIA Rules, consonant with its ICDR counterpart (ICDR Article 11, paragraph 1), identifies three fundamental tenets to be considered by the two remaining arbitrators in determining whether to continue the arbitration: (i) the stage of the arbitration, (ii) any explanation advanced by the third arbitrator concerning nonparticipation,

[48] International Centre for Dispute Resolution, International Arbitration Rules, Article 24, paragraph 2 (2007), *available at* http://www.adr.org/sp.asp?id=28144.

[49] It is not here suggested that the ICC, ICDR, and LCIA Rules governing arbitral proceedings are doctrinally and conceptually alike. Indeed, a comparative study of the three frameworks, which is not the objective of this work, would establish demonstrable and meaningful disparities among them. The focus in this effort fundamentally centers on the very narrow issues of *party-autonomy* and the extent to which the Rules provide for a viable methodology governing the production of documents and information.

[50] London Court of International Arbitration, LCIA Arbitration Rules, Article 12, paragraphs 12.1 and 12.2 (1998), *available at* http://www.lcia-arbitration.com. These paragraphs, respectively, state:

> **Article 12. Majority Power to Continue Proceedings**
>
> 12.1 If any arbitrator on a three-member Arbitral Tribunal refuses or persistently fails to participate in its deliberations, the two other arbitrators shall have the power, upon the written notice of such refusal or failure to the LCIA Court, the parties and the third arbitrator, to continue the arbitration (including the making of any decision, ruling or award), notwithstanding the absence of the third arbitrator.
>
> 12.2 In determining whether to continue the arbitration, the two other arbitrators shall take into account the stage of the arbitration, any explanation made by the third arbitrator for his non-participation and such other matters as they consider appropriate in the circumstances of the case. The reasons for such determination shall be stated in any award, order or other decision made by the two arbitrators without the participation of the third arbitrator.

and (iii) a general "catch all clause" referencing other matter that may be of importance within the context of the particular case. Again, *nowhere* is there any mention of the will of the parties or of the somewhat important proposition that the parties at the very outset presumably first agreed in the subject arbitration agreement to a three-person Arbitral Tribunal.

The LCIA Rules also vest the Arbitral Tribunal with broad discretion in discharging its duties in accordance with "such law(s) or rules of law as (it) may determine to be applicable."[51] In conformance with this stricture, the Arbitral Tribunal also is accorded broad discretion to modify the submission schedule set forth in Article 15 of the LCIA Rules irrespective of the parties' volition.[52] The Arbitral Tribunal may, in its absolute discretion, schedule and hold hearings at any geographical situs that it may deem convenient and appropriate.[53]

While the LCIA Rules do not define "relevance," "evidence," or materials that are the subject matter of production and exchange between the parties, they do provide the Arbitral Tribunal with authority to compel the appearance of witnesses and also to limit and even proscribe the appearance of witnesses. The Arbitral Tribunal also may "require any party to give notice of the identity of each witness that party wishes to call (including rebuttal witnesses), as well as the subject matter of that witness's testimony, its content and its relevance to the issues in the arbitration."[54] Also consonant with its ICC and ICDR counterparts, the LCIA Rules provide the Arbitral Tribunal with a normative foundation, allowing it to appoint experts independent of the parties. The experts may subsequently be submitted, at the Arbitral Tribunal's discretion pursuant to a "necessary" standard, to examination by the parties.[55]

[51] *See* London Court of International Arbitration, LCIA Arbitration Rules, Article 14, paragraph 14.2 (1998), *available at* http://www.lcia-arbitration.com.

[52] *See* London Court of International Arbitration, LCIA Arbitration Rules, Article 15, paragraph 15.1 (1998), *available at* http://www.lcia-arbitration.com, stating that:

> Unless the parties have agreed otherwise under Article 14.1 *or* the Arbitral Tribunal should determine differently, the written stage of the proceedings shall be as set out below. (emphasis supplied).

[53] *See* London Court of International Arbitration, LCIA Arbitration Rules, Article 16, paragraph 16.2 (1998), *available at* http://www.lcia-arbitration.com, which provides:

> The Arbitral Tribunal may hold hearings, meetings and deliberations at any convenient geographical place *in its discretion*; and if elsewhere than the seat of the arbitration, the arbitration shall be treated as an arbitration conducted at the seat of the arbitration and any award as an award made at the seat of the arbitration for all purposes. (emphasis supplied).

See also, e.g., London Court of International Arbitration, LCIA Arbitration Rules, Article 19, paragraph 19.5 (1998), *available at* http://www.lcia-arbitration.com, providing that:

> The Arbitral Tribunal *shall have the fullest authority* to establish time limits for meetings and hearings, or for any parts thereof. (emphasis added).

[54] London Court of International Arbitration, LCIA Arbitration Rules, Article 20, paragraph 20.1 (1998), *available at* http://www.lcia-arbitration.com.

[55] London Court of International Arbitration, LCIA Arbitration Rules, Article 21, paragraph 21.1 subsections (a) and (b) (1998), *available at* http://www.lcia-arbitration.com, read:

> 21.1 Unless otherwise agreed by the parties in writing, the Arbitral Tribunal:
>
> (a) may appoint one or more experts to report to the Arbitral Tribunal on specific issues, who shall remain impartial and independent of the parties throughout the arbitration proceedings, and
>
> (b) may require a party to give any such expert any relevant information or to provide access to any relevant documents, goods, samples, property or site for inspection by the expert.

See also London Court of International Arbitration, LCIA Arbitration Rules, Article 21.2 (1998), *available at* http://www.lcia-arbitration.com.:

> 21.2 unless otherwise agreed by the parties in writing, if a party so requests or *if the Arbitral Tribunal considers it necessary*, the expert shall, after delivery of his written or oral report to the Arbitral Tribunal and the

Unique to the LCIA Rules is Article 22, entitled *Additional Powers of the Arbitral Tribunal.* The broad latitude conferred upon the Arbitral Tribunal on a vast multiplicity of issues compels citation of this article in its entirety.[56] This extraordinary provision is to some extent unexampled in the degree to which it reposes authority on the Arbitral Tribunal, arguably in some instances, to the detriment of party-autonomy, which is so critical to the integrity of arbitral proceedings and the conceptual structure of arbitration generally as a product of the parties' will. Stated as succinctly as possible, the provision encompasses seven general categories where the arbitrators are vested with the broadest of discretion:

1. the ability to provide for the amendment of claims, counterclaims, defenses, and replies,
2. the identification and introduction of issues into the arbitral proceeding even though the parties *did not* raise such issues,
3. the authority to serve as inspectors of property and things "related" to the arbitration's subject matter,
4. authority to compel the production of documents and information,
5. discretion on the application of Rules of Evidence in the conduct of the proceeding,
6. authority to correct, with some limitations, "any" contract between the parties including the arbitration agreement, and
7. control over third-party and nonparty joinder practice.

parties, participate in one or more hearings at which the parties shall have the opportunity to question the expert on his report and to present expert witnesses in order to testify on the points at issue. (emphasis supplied).

56 Article 22 Additional Powers of the Arbitral Tribunal

22.1 Unless the parties at any time agree otherwise in writing, the Arbitral Tribunal shall have the power, on the application of any party or of its own motion, but in either case only after giving the parties a reasonable opportunity to state their views:

(a) to allow any party, upon such terms (as to costs and otherwise) as it shall determine, to amend any claim, counterclaim, defence and reply;

(b) to extend or abbreviate any time-limit provided by the Arbitration Agreement or these Rules for the conduct of the arbitration or by the Arbitral Tribunal's own orders;

(c) to conduct such inquiries as may appear to the Arbitral Tribunal to be necessary or expedient, including whether and to what extent the Arbitral Tribunal should itself take the initiative in identifying the issues and ascertaining the relevant facts and the law(s) or rules of law applicable to the arbitration, the merits of the parties' dispute and the Arbitration Agreement;

(d) to order any party to make any property, site or thing under its control and relating to the subject matter of the arbitration available for inspection by the Arbitral Tribunal, or any other party, its expert or any expert to the Arbitral Tribunal;

(e) to order any party to produce to the Arbitral Tribunal, and to the other parties for inspection, and to supply copies of, any documents or classes of documents in their possession, custody or power which the Arbitral Tribunal determines to be relevant;

(f) to decide whether or not to apply any strict rules of evidence (or any other rules) as to the admissibility relevance or weight of any material tendered by a party on any matter of fact or expert opinion; and to determine the time, manner and form in which such material should be exchanged between the parties and presented to the Arbitral Tribunal;

(g) to order the correction of any contract between the parties or the Arbitration Agreement, but only to the extent required to rectify any mistake which the Arbitral Tribunal determines to be common to the parties and then only if and to the extent to which the law(s) or rules of law applicable to the contract or Arbitration Agreement permit such correction; and

(h) to allow, only upon the application of a party, one or more third persons to be joined in the arbitration as a party provided any such third person and the applicant party have consented thereto in writing, and thereafter to make a single final award, or separate awards, in respect of all parties so implicated in the arbitration.

E. SYNTHESIS OF INSTITUTIONAL ARBITRATION RULES AND PARTY-AUTONOMY

Even the most surface analysis of the major institutional rules independently and in conjunction with each other, together with the IBA Rules on the Taking of Evidence in International Commercial Arbitration, suggests that significant doctrinal development in the realm of document and information production is necessary if arbitration is to serve as a forum responsive to the needs of economic globalization. Greater cross-fertilization between legal cultures and traditions, particularly between U.S. common law and civil code systems, is no longer a theoretical luxury but rather a practical necessity. Such confluence of legal systems is required if complex transnational disputes are to be aired and processed in accordance with party expectations and in an environment where party-autonomy remains possibly the single most important defining character of commercial arbitration, which is a paradigmatic creature of contract and, therefore, the parties' will.

The *Intel, In Re: Roz Trading Ltd.*, and *In Re: Patrizio Clerici* cases have precipitated visiting and revisiting, reading and rereading the orthodox view concerning the taking of evidence, which many commentators, jurists, practitioners, and captains of industry quite complacently accepted as apposite with the underlying tenets that define and distinguish commercial arbitration from other dispute resolution methodologies, including judicial recourse. Under at least one analysis, however, it is possible to take seriously the proposition that the "taking of evidence," as promoted by the major arbitral institutions and the very IBA Rules on the subject, actually place greater conceptual weight on the precept of arbitral tribunal discretion as opposed to party-autonomy. The consequences are clear. At least with respect to the production of documents and information, the time-honored precepts of predictive value, transparency of standard, uniformity, and certainty are best served pursuant to a procedural rubric centered on party-autonomy and with clearly delineated standards and norms. All the better, such a rubric was accompanied by a plethora of judicial opinions, academic commentaries, and rules of construction to give rise to more than just a compilation of rules and to develop the status of a code where the relationship between norms is governed by known and transparent principles.

The Federal Rules of Civil Procedure governing discovery certainly approximate this description. It would be less than rigorous and even akin to sinking to the level of intellectual dishonesty to hold fast to the cultural prejudice asserting that from the perspective of analytical jurisprudence U.S. common law discovery is inimical to commercial arbitration while the "taking of evidence," as embodied by institutional norms and the IBA Rules on the subject are but logical extensions of the very precepts governing the most salient features of arbitral proceedings.

CHAPTER 8

And Now How Do We Avoid 28 U.S.C. Section 1782 in International Commercial Arbitration?

Adherence to Section 1782(a) in the context of international commercial arbitration reconfigures the procedural law applicable to arbitration with respect to the gathering of documents and information by parties, and even the very commencement of the proceeding. Post *Intel* and progeny, an "interested person" may prosecute a Section 1782(a) petition with the federal district court in the United States *prior to* actually filing and serving a request for arbitration so long as the filing of such arbitral proceeding is "reasonably imminent."[1] Thus, the arbitration, which now as a matter of law constitutes a "foreign or international tribunal," need not even be pending before prospective respondents find themselves with a binding normative legal obligation to respond to discovery pursuant to the Federal Rules of Civil Procedure. *Intel* and progeny divest prospective institutional arbitral centers from engaging in the most rudimentary arbitration case management exercises. Similarly, this extraordinary doctrinal development in U.S. arbitration – as in private procedural international law – also divests arbitral tribunals[2] of all authority concerning the applicable standard, the conduct, the admissibility, and the nature and character of the disclosure and exchange of documents and information between parties to the arbitral proceeding.

Irrespective of whether Section 1782 is deemed a positive doctrinal development in both U.S. and international arbitral proceedings, there are numerous paradigms pursuant to which risk assessment models would suggest that a party to a transaction would be decisively and materially disadvantaged should a dispute arise precipitating the invocation of an arbitration clause and, consequently, the possible filing of Section 1782 petitions by the adverse party. The most common scenario where a party to an arbitral proceeding would be disadvantaged were Section 1782 applications to be filed with U.S. federal district court is the common case pursuant to which the seat of arbitration is located outside the United States and its territories, and the party

1 It is less than clear, however, whether as a matter of law a federal district court may exercise its discretion in favor of granting a §1782 petition prior to the filing of a request for arbitration where, despite the imminence of the proceeding, there is a finding of record that the petition was filed and prosecuted for purposes of perfecting or rendering possible the actual claim as opposed to gathering documents and information for use presumably with respect to the adjudication of the merits. This issue is one of first impressions yet to be decided.

2 This "wresting of authority" certainly is in pace with respect to most major arbitration institutions. Already we have examined in considerable detail the extent to which the ICC, the LCIA, and the ICDR accord the arbitral tribunal virtually unbridled discretion in the (i) conduct, (ii) fashioning of the applicable standard, (iii) admissibility of document and information disclosure.

captioned as a "respondent" to a Section 1782 petition has headquarters, affiliates, assets, agents, representatives, bank accounts, or past transactions falling within the ambit of Fed.R.Civ.P. 26 in the United States, while the "petitioner" is a non-U.S. entity with no ties whatsoever to the United States other than the transaction at issue, giving rise to the arbitral proceeding now characterized as a proceeding in a "foreign or international tribunal." Pursuant to this scenario, respondent is meaningfully exposed in sharp relief to the petition whose assets and contacts are beyond the jurisdiction of federal district courts.

Intel and progeny to date have yet to address these novel issues. Two methodologies, both strategically and tactically to be executed at the stage of negotiating the arbitration clause, do suggest themselves as possible defenses in the effort to preclude application of Section 1782 discovery to an arbitral proceeding.

A. THE FIRST PARADIGM

First, a return to first principles is necessary. Because arbitration itself, and hence the Arbitral Tribunal, are creatures of contract, in both theory and praxis, the parties' intent must be paramount in the construction of the terms of the arbitration clause. Where the parties in advance agree to foreclose recourse to Section 1782, the Arbitral Tribunal presumably would honor the agreement and shy from supporting a Section 1782 application. In fact, the tribunal theoretically is empowered to issue an order proscribing any such application. The possible practical difficulty arises with the ubiquitous issue of enforcement.

Assuming that the movant seeking to prosecute a Section 1782 petition unilaterally does so under the theory that, *inter alia*, such petitioner meets the statute's strictures, which are independent of and parallel to the Arbitral Tribunal's ambit, it is certainly conceivable that a federal district court may find the argument persuasive despite the plain meaning of the language in the arbitration clause. Consequently, although advisable and potentially dispositive, it is far from certain that inclusion of language proscribing recourse to a Section 1782 petition in an arbitration clause would indeed limit the parties or otherwise foreclose them from availing themselves of the Federal Rules of Civil Procedure pursuant to this framework. Also, one would be hard pressed to conclude that a federal district court *necessarily* would defer to an Arbitral Tribunal's interlocutory ruling. Close scrutiny of the *Intel* opinion to some extent suggests that even if the Arbitral Tribunal conclusively and indisputably ruled that it did not wish for Section 1782 discovery to prosper, the vast discretion vested in federal district courts certainly may be exercised, notwithstanding the Arbitral Tribunal's volition. Specifically, in *Intel* the discovery sought was granted as a matter of law even though, quite significantly, the EU competition commission had refused to seek it. The narrow issue is whether the court addressing a Section 1782 application would enforce the parties' prior agreement not to file any such request.

A related issue arises pursuant to the scenario where the movant unilaterally prosecuting a Section 1782 petition successfully secures documents and information and upon attempting to introduce these materials into evidence during the arbitration is precluded from so proceeding by the Arbitral Tribunal. Would a categorical denial by the Arbitral Tribunal of consideration of evidence secured pursuant to Section 1782 contrary to the explicit language of the governing arbitral agreement prescribing such discovery place in jeopardy the integrity of the final award rendered in such a proceeding? Greater analysis is necessary.

(i) The Consequences of Refusal and Manifest Disregard of the Law

Refusal to consider materials lawfully secured pursuant to established jurisprudence construing a federal statute is susceptible to the characterization, at least under one of many analyses, of precluding a party from presenting its case. If so, such a ruling by the Arbitral Tribunal may directly and explicitly trigger application of Article V of the New York Convention.[3] Article V I(*b*) proscribes recognition and enforcement of an arbitral award where a party was "unable to present his case." Certainly, the petitioner to the Section 1782 application may have a built in appellate recourse insurance ground capable of providing it with a substantial and measurable basis for setting aside the award should it determine the award to be contrary to its interests. Therefore, an Arbitral Tribunal's blanket foreclosure of materials secured in accordance with Section 1782 runs the immediate and material risk of rendering any prospective award unenforceable.

Further analytic and legal support for this interpretation may be found in 9 U.S.C. Section 10(a)(3) of the Federal Arbitration Act ("FAA").[4] In *praxis*, this

[3] Article V of the New York Convention governing the recognition and enforcement of arbitral awards and so central to the universal success of international commercial arbitrations compels citation in its entirety:

Article V

1. Recognition and enforcement of the award may be refused, at the request of the party against whom it is invoked, only if that party furnishes to the competent authority where the recognition and enforcement is sought, prove that:

(a) The parties to the agreement referred to in article II were, under the law applicable to them, under some incapacity, or the set agreement is not valid under the law to which the parties have subjected it or, failing any indication thereon, under the law of the country where the award was made; or

(b) the party against whom the award is invoked was not given proper notice of the appointment of the arbitrator or of the arbitration proceedings or was otherwise unable to present his case; or

(c) the award deals with a difference not contemplated by or not falling within the terms of the submission to arbitration, or it contains decisions on matters beyond the scope of the submission to arbitration, provided that, if the decisions on matters submitted to arbitration can be separated from those not submitted, that part of the award which contains decisions on matters submitted to arbitration may be recognized and enforced; or

(d) the composition of the arbitral authority or the arbitral procedure was not in accordance with the agreement of the parties, or, failing such agreement, was not in accordance with the law of the country where the arbitration took place; or

(e) the award has not yet become binding on the parties, or has been set aside or suspended by competent authority of the country in which, or under the law of which, that award was made.

2. Recognition and enforcement of an arbitral award may also be refused if the competent authority in the country where recognition and enforcement is sought finds that:

(a) the subject matter of the difference is not capable of settlement by arbitration under the law of that country; or

(b) the recognition or enforcement of the award would be contrary to the public policy of that country. (emphasis supplied)

[4] 9 U.S.C. §10(a)(3) of the FAA provides:

§10. Same; Vacation; Grounds; Rehearing.

(a) In any of the following cases the United States court in and for the district wherein the award was made may make an order vacating the award upon the application of any party to the arbitration

(3) where the arbitrators were guilty of misconduct in refusing to postpone the hearing, upon sufficient cause shown, or in refusing to hear evidence pertinent and material to the controversy; or of any other misbehavior by which the rights of any party have been prejudiced.

provision constitutes a codification and interpretation of Article V(*b*) of the New York Convention. It seeks to underscore the need for fundamental due process as a predicate to recognition and enforcement of a foreign arbitral award by identifying as a ground for vacating an award any instance where (i) the arbitrators "refus[ed] to hear evidence pertinent and material to the controversy;" or in cases where "any other misbehavior by which the rights of any party have been prejudiced." A blanket preclusion by the Arbitral Tribunal of any consideration of documents or other information elicited pursuant to Section 1782 may quite conceivably fall within *both* of the referenced categories: (i) denial of an opportunity to present a case, and (ii) misbehavior by an arbitrator adversely compromising the rights of a party.

Indeed, multiple countries had different views on what elements actually rendered an arbitral award "international" or "foreign" for purposes of the Convention. Not surprisingly, the conceptual differences were between common law and civil law doctrinal views on the subject rooted in their respective legal and cultural traditions. These divergent views were carefully canvassed by the Second Circuit Court of Appeals in *Bergesen v. Joseph Muller Corp.*[5]

In that case the plaintiff, a Norwegian owner of three cargo vessels, filed an action against the charterer of the ships for the recognition and enforcement of a judgment arising from an arbitral award rendered in New York in favor of the plaintiff owner and against the defendant charterer. The underlying arbitration arose from clauses contained in the charter parties. The district court entered judgment recognizing and enforcing the arbitration award and an appeal ensued to the Second Circuit, which affirmed the district court's ruling. The Second Circuit identified the issue to be considered as "whether the 1958 Convention on the Recognition and Enforcement of Foreign Arbitral Awards, 21 UST 2517, TIAS No. 6997, 330 UNTS 38, is applicable to an award arising from an arbitration held in New York between two foreign entities."[6]

After a recitation of the operative facts and reference to the commercial reasons underlying the Convention as, in part, attributable to "the rapid expansion of international trade following World War II," and the penchant and proclivity of international merchants for "arbitration over litigation because it is faster, less expensive and more flexible,"[7] the Second Circuit premised its affirmance on a painstaking analysis of the different propositions asserted for purposes of defining a "foreign" or "international" award within the *draft* Convention's then aspirational objectives.

5 Bergesen v. Joseph Muller Corp., 710 F.2d 928, 931 (2d Cir. 1983). *See also* Albert Jan van den Berg, *When is an Arbitral Award Nondomestic Under the New York Convention of 1958?* 6 PACE L.REV. 25, 32–38 (1985).

6 *Id.*

7 *Id.* The court also noted that in 1958 a convention was held to address the inefficacy of international agreements in securing enforcement of arbitral awards even when such arbitration proceedings were had under the auspices of the ICC or the LCIA. In this same vein, the Second Circuit observed that "[t]he United States attended and participated in the conference but did not sign the Convention. Ten years later, in 1968, the Senate gave its consent, but at session was delayed until 1970 in order for Congress to enact the necessary implementing legislation [citing to McMahon, *Implementation of the United Nations Convention on Foreign Arbitral Awards in the United States*, 2 J.MAR. L. COM. 735, 737 (1971)]. There was no opposition to the proposed legislation, H.R. Rep. No. 91–1181, 91st Cong., 2d Sess. 2, *reprinted in* 1970 U.S. Code Cong. & Ad. News. 3601, 3602, which became 9 U.S.C. §s 201–208 (1976)." *Id.*

The nations from Western Europe, it was advanced, and their counterparts from common law jurisdictions were at a doctrinal and conceptual stalemate.[8] By way of example, France, Italy, and then West Germany found the proposal unacceptable because, in their view, a territorial criterion was ill-suited as a litmus test to determine the character of an award as foreign or domestic. Instead, these nations subscribed to a three-prong test that considered (i) the nationality of a party, (ii) the subject of the dispute, and (iii) the rules of arbitral procedure, as the most material factors to be analyzed in determining the character and nature of an award as foreign or domestic.[9] West Germany and France were of a single voice in asserting that the nationality of an award must be determined *by the law governing the proceeding.*

To advance a viable alternative to the territorial doctrine, eight European nations proposed that the Convention "apply to the recognition and enforcement of arbitral awards other than those considered as domestic in the country in which they are relied upon."[10] The Court further noted that "[e]ight other countries, including the United States, objected to this proposal, arguing that common law nations would not understand the distinction between foreign and domestic awards. These latter countries urged the delegates to adopt only the territorial criteria."[11] Having delineated the two doctrinal camps and the resolution synthesizing a compromise formula, the Second Circuit surgically addressed the six propositions upon which the appellant charterer bottomed its appeal.

First, appellant asserted that "the award may not be considered as a foreign award within the purview of the second sentence of Article I (1) because it fails to qualify as an award 'not considered as domestic.'"[12] In this connection, appellant further averred that "the purpose of the 'not considered as domestic' test was to provide for the enforcement of what it terms 'stateless awards,' i.e. those rendered in the territory where enforcement is sought but considered unenforceable because of some foreign component."[13] This argument was flatly rejected on the ground that "some countries favoring the provision desired it so as to preclude the enforcement of certain awards rendered abroad, not to enhance enforcement of awards rendered domestically."[14]

Second, appellant urged a narrow construction of the Convention concerning the omission of any definition of nondomestic awards to conclude that eligible awards were very few in both theory and practice. Here, the Second Circuit stressed that "[t]he Convention did not define domestic awards. The definition appears to have been deliberately left out in order to cover as wide a variety of eligible awards

8 *Id.* at 931.

9 *See* G. Haight, Convention on the Recognition and Enforcement of Foreign Arbitral Awards 1 at 2 (1958).

10 *Bergesen* at 931 [citing to *Haight* at 2].

11 *Id.* The Second Circuit further underscored that:

> A working party composed of representatives from ten states to which the matter was referred recommended that both criteria be included. Thus, the Convention was to apply to awards made in a country other than the state where enforcement was sought as well as to awards not considered domestic in that state. The members of the Working Party representing the western European group agreed to this recommendation, provided that each nation would be allowed to exclude certain categories of awards rendered abroad. At the conclusion of the conference this exclusion was omitted, so that the text originally proposed by the Working Party was adopted as Article I of the Convention. *Id.*

12 *Id.* at 932.

13 *Id.*

14 *Id.*

as possible, while permitting the enforcing authority to supply its own definition of 'non-domestic' in conformity with its own national law." In fact, this omission, as the Court aptly grasped, rendered it more palatable for states promoting the territorial doctrine to ratify the Convention while simultaneously making the Convention more appetizing to "those states which espoused the view that the nationality of the award was to be determined by the law governing the arbitral procedure."[15] Consequently, the view was adopted by the Court that awards "not considered as domestic" refer to awards falling within the Convention's purview "not because made abroad, but because made within the legal framework of another country, e.g., pronounced in accordance with foreign law or involving parties domiciled or having their principal place of business outside the enforcing jurisdiction."[16] To be sure, the construction that the Court adopted best comports with the Convention's principal objective of rendering international arbitration awards enforceable transnationally irrespective of divergent, and often conceptually irreconcilable, doctrinal differences embedded at the very heart of different legal cultures and traditions.

Third, the Court rejected the proposition that the Convention must be narrowly construed because of the two accession reservations that the United States adopted pursuant to Article I (3).[17] The contention was rejected on the ground that "the United States acceded to the Convention with a declaration of reservations provides little reason for [the Court] to construe the accession in narrow terms." The Court further added that "[h]ad the United States exceeded to the Convention without these two reservations, the scope of the Convention doubtless would have wider impact. . . . nonetheless, the treaty language should be interpreted broadly to effectuate its recognition and enforcement purposes."[18] Succinctly stated, the norms governing the construction of treaties is not subordinated to instances that may be drawn from the two Article I (3) reservations that the United States secured as a predicate to accession.

Fourth, it was advanced that the implementing statute "was not intended to cover awards rendered within the United States."[19] In support of this premise, reference was made to Section 202 of Title 9 of the United States Code entitled "Agreement or Award Falling Under the Convention," which in pertinent part reads:

> An agreement or award arising out of such a relationship which is entirely between citizens of the United States shall be deemed not to fall under the Convention unless that relationship involves property located abroad, envisages performance or enforcement abroad, or has some other reasonable relation with one or more foreign states.[20]

[15] *Id.*

[16] *Id.* (citations omitted).

[17] *Id.* at 932. This contention was predicated on a Presidential Proclamation dated September 1, 1970, 21 UST 2517, TIAS No. 6997.

[18] *Id.* at 933 [citing Comment, *International Commercial Arbitration Under the United Nations Convention and the Amended Federal Arbitration Statute*, 47 Wash. L.R. 441 (1972), and *Scherk*, 417 U.S. at 520 n. 15 (identifying the Convention's objective as an effort "to encourage the recognition and enforcement of commercial arbitration agreements in international contracts")].

[19] *Id.* [citing H.R. Rep. No. 91–1181, 91st Cong., 2d Sess. 2, *reprinted* in 1970 U.S. Code Cong. & Ad. News 3601, 3602].

[20] *Id.* [citing §202 of Title 9 of the United States code entitled "Agreement or Award Falling Under the Convention"].

This statutory rubric's legislative history, however, demonstrates that it was intended to guarantee that "an agreement or award arising out of a legal relationship exclusively between citizens of the United States is not enforceable under the Convention in [United States] courts unless it has a reasonable relation with a foreign state."[21] The Court reasoned that "[h]ad Congress desired to exclude arbitral awards involving two foreign parties rendered within the United States from enforcement by our courts it could readily have done so. It did not."[22]

Moreover, additional analytical support for the premise that arbitral awards issued in the United States constitute the appropriate subject matter for enforcement pursuant to the Convention was found in the remaining sections of the implementing statute. In fact, the Court observed that while "Section 204 supplies venue for such an action and Section 206 states that '[a] Court having jurisdiction under this chapter may direct that arbitration be held . . . at any place therein provided for, *whether that place is within or without the United States*'."[23] This construction was further supported by what in effect would be an analysis premised on a *reductio ad absurdem*. Specifically, the Court underscored that "[i]t would be anomalous to hold that a district court could direct two aliens to arbitration within the United States under the statute, but that it could not enforce the resulting award under legislation which, in large part, was entrusted for just that purpose."[24]

Appellant's fifth and penultimate assertion stated that Congress could not have intended to apply the Convention to a transaction akin to the one at bar "because it would remove too broad a class of awards from enforcement of the Federal Arbitration Act, 9 U.S.C. Sections 1–13."[25] This proposition was discarded on the simple ground that there was no basis from which to conclude "that Congress did not intend to provide overlapping coverage between the Convention and the Federal Arbitration Act."[26]

Sixth, the final proposition upon which the appeal was predicated asserted that the petition itself was technically insufficient and, therefore, "did not meet the requirements of the Convention."[27] In particular, appellant placed a rather novel construction on Article IV(1) of the Convention[28] by suggesting that either (1) a duly authenticated original or a certified copy of a duly authenticated original is

[21] *Id.*

[22] *Id.* [citing Sumitomo Corp. v. Parakopi Compania Maritima, 477 F.Supp. 737, 741 (S.D.N.Y. 1979), *aff'd*, 620 F.2d 286 (2d Cir. 1980)]; Gerald Aksen, *American Arbitration Accession Arrives in the Age of Aquarius: United States Implements United Nations Convention on the Recognition and Enforcement of Foreign Arbitral Awards*, 3 Sw. U. L. Rev. 1, 16 (1971) (Under implementing legislation Convention should apply when foreign contacts are substantial, i.e. "where a foreign person or corporation is a party to an agreement involving foreign performance, or where the business deal has some other 'reasonable relation with one or more foreign states.'"); *see also McMahon* at 740–43 (questioning whether section 202 covers awards similar to that in the present case).

[23] *Id.* (citation supplied by the Second Circuit Court of Appeals).

[24] *Id.*

[25] *Id.* at 934.

[26] *Id.*

[27] *Id.*

[28] Article IV(1) of the Convention provides:

1. To obtain the recognition and enforcement mentioned in the preceding article, the party applying for recognition and enforcement shall, at the time of the application, supply:
(*a*) The duly authenticated original award or a duly certified copy thereof;
(*b*) the original agreement referred to in article II or a duly certified copy thereof.

required pursuant to Article IV(1). Here, the Court observed that "[c]opies of the award and the agreement which have been certified by a member of the Arbitration Panel provide a sufficient basis upon which to enforce the award and such were supplied in this case."[29]

As exemplified in *Bergesen v. Joseph Muller Corporation*, the very fundamental issue of what constitutes an "international" or "foreign" tribunal has been the subject matter of considerable debate and controversy among practitioners, judges, and scholars from civil code and common law traditions. The hybrid and flexible resolution of this fascinating clash of juridic cultures and doctrines provides sufficient conceptual grounds from which to argue forcefully and persuasively, based upon the particular facts configuring a case, that under such circumstances an international arbitration having the arbitral seat in the United States certainly may constitute a "foreign or international tribunal" for purposes of a Section 1782 application. Thus, the incorporation of language in an arbitration clause selecting the United States or any of its territories as the arbitral seat far from ensures preclusion of a Section 1782 application.

In addition to triggering issues concerning Article V of the Convention that may adversely compromise the integrity of a prospective final award because of the failure to accord a party an opportunity to present its case, an Arbitral Tribunal's blanket rejection of Section 1782 discovery may be construed as manifest disregard of the law.

Pursuant to 9 U.S.C §10(a) an arbitration award may be vacated only where the arbitrators (i) engaged in misconduct, (ii) "exceeded their powers, or so imperfectly executed them that a mutual, final and definite award upon the subject matter submitted was not made."[30] Significantly, unlike the strictures set forth in Article V of the Convention for setting aside an award, a meaningful departure in the jurisprudence governing the vacation of an award sought to be enforced in a U.S. district court recognizes vacating an award where there is a determination that the award arose from the arbitral tribunal's manifest disregard of the law. To command reversal under this precept, the award "must fly in the face of clearly established

[29] *Id.*

[30] *See* 9 U.S.C. §10(a)(4). Indeed the grounds for vacating an award for rehearing are quite narrow and all set forth in §10(a)–(b), which reads:

§10. Same; vacation; grounds; rehearing

(a) In any of the following cases the United States Court in and for the District wherein the award was made may make an order vacating the award upon the application of any party to the arbitration.

(1) Where the award was procured by corruption, fraud, or undue means.

(2) Where there was evident partiality or corruption in the arbitrators, or either of them.

(3) Where the arbitrators were guilty of misconduct refusing to postpone the hearing, upon sufficient cause shown, or in refusing to hear evidence pertinent and material to the controversy; or of any of other misbehavior by which the rights of any party have been prejudiced.

(4) Where the arbitrators exceeded their powers or so imperfectly executed them that a mutual, final, and definite award upon the subject matter submitted was not made.

(5) Where an award is vacated the time within which the agreement required the award to be made has not expired, the court may, in its discretion, direct a rehearing by the arbitrators.

(6) The United States district court for the district wherein an award was made that was issued pursuant to section 580 of Title 5 may make an order vacating the award upon the application of a person, other than a party to the arbitration, whose adversely affected or aggrieved by the award, if the use of arbitration or the award is clearly inconsistent with the factors set forth in section 572 of Title 5.

legal precedent."[31] Manifest disregard shall be found where "(1) the applicable legal principle is clearly defined in that subject to reasonable debate; and (2) the arbitrators refused to heed that legal principle."[32]

By way of example in *Jacada (Europe) v. International Marketing Strategies* the plaintiff British software developer filed state court action to vacate an arbitral award that had been rendered in favor of the defendant distributor. The distributor, however, conversely filed an action in federal court to enforce the arbitral award issued in its favor. Upon removal of the state court proceeding, transfer, and consolidation of the actions, the federal district court entered a judgment in favor of the distributor who sought enforcement. The Sixth Circuit Court of Appeals affirmed the district court's ruling and rejected the appellant developer's contention that the arbitrator's decision displayed manifest disregard of the law.

There vacatur of the award was premised on the proposition that the arbitral tribunal had purposely and intentionally omitted to consider and accord any weight to a limitation of damages provision. This fact was not contested and, indeed, the arbitrators observed that "'the potential effect of the limitation of damages provision is to . . . exclude damages for a large breach of the Agreement while permitting damages for a small breach of the contract.'"[33] Therefore, the Sixth Circuit reasoned that because the limited liability provision rendered the distributor's right "meaningless" as the distribution agreement, the arbitrators "disregarded the provision to effectuate a core purpose of the contract [distributor's] right to distribute [developer's] software package throughout Europe, the Middle East, and Africa."[34]

The command in *Jacada (Europe)* is clear. Where an arbitral tribunal construes a contract to further the underlying goals and purpose of that agreement, manifest disregard of the law shall not ensue even where such contractual construction intentionally and deliberately obviates a contractual provision negotiated at arm's-length between the parties. The Sixth Circuit's analysis in *Jacada (Europe)* and its recitation of the elements defining manifest disregard of the law may shed some light on the issue of whether an arbitral tribunal's foreclosure of Section 1782 discovery or its decision to strictly construe language in an arbitration clause proscribing recourse to Section 1782 may constitute manifest disregard of law for purposes of vacating an award. Arguably, the first prong of the manifest disregard of law standard is met where the tribunal disregards Section 1782 as the applicable procedural legal principle, which is both *clearly defined and not subject to reasonable debate*. The blanket refusal to consider *any* of the Section 1782 discovery comports with the second prong.

This proposition would be analytically enhanced where it is undisputed that consideration of such discovery would further the subject contract's objectives. As in *Jacada (Europe)*, in this hypothetical the arbitral tribunal would be reading out of the contract a provision presumably to further the equitable administration of justice and the goal of the arbitration agreement, if such a goal is in part defined as a consideration of all potentially relevant and material documents and information

[31] *See* Jacada (Europe), Ltd. v. International Marketing Strategies, 401 F.3d 701, 713 (6th Cir. 2005) (citing Merrill Lynch v. Jaros, 70 F.3d 418, 421 (6th Cir. 1995)).

[32] *See* Nationwide Mut. Ins. Co. v. Home Ins. Co., 330 F.3d 843, 847 (6th Cir. 2003) (citing Dawahare v. Spencer, 210 F.3d 666, 669 (6th Cir. 2000)).

[33] *Jacada*, 401 F.3d at 713.

[34] *Id.*

leading to a comprehensively transparent airing of the issues in controversy. Here, the agreement shall be deemed to be the arbitration clause itself. The converse analysis may be equally engaging.

Again, following the *Jacada (Europe)* analysis, would manifest disregard of the law attach where an arbitral tribunal exercises its discretion to foreclose consideration of all documents and information arising from Section 1782 application, particularly considering an arbitration clause that does not mention Section 1782 at all? Under this hypothetical the arbitrators are not asked to read out of or otherwise deliberately ignore a bargained-for contractual provision, unlike in *Jacada (Europe)* and the first hypothetical. Here, however, the arbitral tribunal is being asked to disregard arguably applicable procedural law governing the gathering of evidence. Can the disregard of a procedural law not arising from the seat of the arbitration rise to the level of manifest disregard of law? The analogy with *Jacada (Europe)* rapidly collapses. In addition to not addressing the intentional omission of a legal provision in a contract (be it the actual contract or the arbitration clause construed under the severability doctrine as a free-standing contract), the federal law of the United States – a jurisdiction foreign to the arbitral seat – is being applied. The problem becomes exquisitely more complex because in this hypothetical, unlike the test enunciated in *Jacada (Europe)* pursuant to which the arbitrators' decision yields an award that "must fly in the face of clearly established legal precedent," in this paradigm there is no "precedent." Also distinct from *Jacada (Europe)*, at issue in this hypothetical is the alleged disregard for *procedural* and not *substantive* law.

While the construction of hypotheticals illustrates to some extent the many dormant issues that remain for adjudication and scholarship to create, if not binding precedent, a body of commentary that may serve to facilitate arbitrators, courts, practitioners, and captains of industry in addressing this issue, it also provides a clear understanding of the rather mercurial and elusive nature of the "manifest disregard of the law" standard unique to U.S. enforcement proceedings and finds no doctrinal basis in Article V of the Convention. Indeed, the jurisprudence in this area commands greater rigor in its doctrinal development.

Certainly, general fundamental elements of the manifest disregard of the law doctrine are clear and beyond cavil. By way of example, it is undisputed that an arbitral award may be vacated if the manifest disregard of the law is plainly evident from the arbitration record.[35] It is less than clear, however, the nature and character of the record that arbitral proceedings keep. Thus, the complete absence of any meaningful guidance to the configuration of a record, as verbatim transcripts are not a requirement in arbitration proceedings, may indeed conceivably hamper the review of the systematic misapplication of law during the actual proceeding. It is also settled that a reviewing court must accord an arbitral panel's decision "great deference." Indeed, "[a] party petitioning a federal court to vacate an arbitral award bears the heavy burden of showing that the award falls within the very narrow set of circumstances delineated by statute and caselaw."[36] Beyond these very rudimentary precepts it appears to be hardly discernible from a conceptual standpoint an objective test that would suggest categorically when the doctrine actually attaches.

35 *See, e.g.*, Goldman v. Architectural Iron Co., 306 F.3d 1214, 1216 (2d Cir. 2002).

36 Duferco Int'l Steel Trading v. T. Klaveness Shipping A/S, 333 F.3d 383 (2d Cir. 2003).

The doctrine's origins can be traced in *dicta* contained in *Wilko v. Swan*.[37] There the Supreme Court observed that "the interpretations of the law by the arbitrators *in contrast to manifest disregard* are not subject, in the federal courts, to judicial review for error in interpretation."[38] Notably, the doctrine finds its genesis in five words that scarcely constitute a subordinate clause within a single sentence. The Supreme Court did not offer any guidance or otherwise elaborate on what would be an example of a manifest disregard of the law warranting vacatur of an arbitration award, let alone a standard for the practicing bench and bar. It is from this "modest" statement, without more, that jurisprudence has developed, in effect amending the very narrow grounds for vacating an award embodied in the FAA.[39]

B. THE *DUFERCO* ANALYSIS

As numerous scholars have aptly noted, the Second Circuit in *Duferco* undertook a meaningful analysis of some cases within the sparse universe of authority where manifest disregard for the law was found by federal appellate courts.[40] After stating that Second Circuit had first enunciated the "severely limited" and "highly deferential" arbitral award standard in 1960,[41] the Court observed that as of June 24, 2003, it had vacated "some or all of an arbitral award for manifest disregard in the following four out of the last *forty-eight* cases where [it] applied the standard."[42] But for the

[37] Wilko v. Swan, 346 U.S. 427 (1953), *overruled on other grounds*, Rodriguez de Quijas v. Shearson/Am. Express, Inc., 490 U.S. 477, 485 (1989).

[38] *Wilko*, 346 U.S. at 436–37 (emphasis supplied).

[39] *Duferco Int'l Steel*, 333 F.3d at 388.

[40] *See* Mary A. Bedikian, *Alternative Dispute Resoluton*, 53 WAYNE L. REV. 73 (2007); Joshua Ratner and Christian Turner, *Second Circuit Survey: Origin, Scope, and Irrevocability of the Manifest Disregard of the Law Doctrine*, 24 QUINNIPIAC L. REV. 795 (2006); Jennifer J. Johnson, *WALL STREET MEETS THE WILD WEST: BRINGING LAW AND ORDER TO SECURITIES ARBITRATION*, 84 N.C.L. REV. 123 (2005); Jeffrey W. Stempel, *Keeping Arbitrations from Becoming Kangaroo Courts*, 8 NEV. L.J. 251 (2007); JEFFREY R. BABBIN, ERIKA L. AMARANTE, VICTOR A. BOLDEN, GATES GARRITY-ROKOUS, *Developments in the Second Circuit: 2002–2003*, 36 CONN. L. REV. 1187 (2004); Hans Smit, *MANIFEST DISREGARD OF THE LAW IN THE NEW YORK SUPREME COURT, APPELLATE DIVISION, FIRST DEPARTMENT*, 15 AM. REV. INT'L ARB. 111 (2004); Christopher R. Drahozal, *New Experiences of International Arbitration in the United States*, 54 AM. J. COMP. L. 233 (2006).

[41] That standard was articulated by the Second Circuit in *Amicizia Societa Navegazione v. Chilean Nitrate and Iodine Sales Corp.*, 274 F.2d 805, 808 (2d Cir.), *cert. denied*, 363 U.S. 843 (1960).

[42] *Duferco Int'l Steel*, 333 F.3d at 389. The Court identified these cases as the following four: (a) *Halligan v. Piper Jaffray, Inc.*, 148 F.3d 197, 204 (2d Cir. 1998) (holding that "[i]n view of the strong evidence that Halligan was fired because of his age and the agreement of the parties that the arbitrators were correctly advised of the applicable legal principles, we are inclined to hold that they ignored the law or the evidence or both."); (b) *New York Telephone Co. v. Communication Workers of America*, 256 F.3d 89, 92–93 (2d Cir. 2001) (*per curiam*) ("holding that opinions relied on by the arbitrators were not the law of the circuit and "it was therefore 'manifest disregard of the law' for the arbitrator to reject *Seatrain* and apply another rule."); (c) *Fahnestock & Co., Inc. v. Waltman*, 935 F.2d 512, 519 (2d Cir. 1991) (holding that "this is an appropriate case under the provisions of §10(d) of the FAA for vacatur of the punitive damages award."); (d) *Perma-Line Corp. of America v. Sign Pictorial and Display Union*, 639 F.2d 890, 894–96 (2d Cir. 1981) (remanding arbitration award based upon public policy arising from an illegal contractual provision, with possibility of confirmation if arbitrators could justify illegal provision.).

For authority, in *dicta* observing a punitive damage award by an arbitral panel would support vacatur, *See Sapic v. Government of Turkmenistan*, 345 F.3d 347, 365 (5th Cir. 2003) (stating: "thus,

decision in *Halligan*, the remaining three cases concerned review of arbitral awards that exceeded the arbitrator's authority. Accordingly, the Second Circuit contends that in those cases "it is arguable that manifest disregard need not have been the basis for vacating the award, since vacatur would have been warranted under the FAA."[43] Also, the Second Circuit aptly defined the standard for application of the doctrine in the negative. Despite the apparent want of doctrinal development, the Court's "guidepost" is of meaningful assistance. It explained that its "reluctance over the years to find manifest disregard is a reflection of the fact that it is a doctrine of last resort – its use is limited only to those exceedingly rare instances where some egregious impropriety on the part of the arbitrators is apparent, but where none of the provisions of the FAA apply."[44] Thus, three elements are discernible in this standard. First, the doctrine is one of "last resort." It may only be used upon exhausting all other grounds upon which vacatur would be appropriate. In addition, the "last resort" prong would only apply to the most extreme and egregious circumstances. Lastly, the doctrine may attach only where the provisions of the FAA simply do not apply.

This three-prong test is applied in the context of the long-standing arbitration precept that contends that the objective of arbitral proceedings is to resolve a very discreet dispute between parties independent of judicial intervention or the influence of doctrines embodied in legislative enactments or case law that reflect the public policy of the state far beyond the particular dispute at issue or industry considerations. In this connection, the Second Circuit stressed the need to refrain from interfering with a process to avert frustrating "the intent of the parties, and thwart the usefulness of arbitration, making it 'the commencement, not the end, of litigation.'"[45]

Quite remarkably, despite articulating the historical test, its own exegesis of a practical standard for application of the doctrine, and briefly tracing the doctrine's historical genesis, the Second Circuit admitted that the rare and infrequent application of the doctrine has generated a paucity of jurisprudence. Consequently, says the Second Circuit, the doctrine's "precise boundaries are ill-defined, although its rough contours are well known."[46] Therefore, in addition to constituting (i) a doctrine of last resort, (ii) to be applied only in the most extreme and egregious circumstances, (iii) where no provision of the FAA is applicable, and (iv) in the very limited context of industry standards and the issues framed by the very specific contours of the dispute between the parties, a three-inquiry standard was fashioned to attempt to define with greater clarity and precision the doctrine's triggering standard.

if punitive damages were indeed awarded in this case, it would be incumbent upon us to vacate such an award, in spite of the discretion typically granted to arbitral decisions.")

43 *Duferco Int'l Steel*, 333 F.3d at 389.

44 *Id.*

45 *Id.* (citations omitted).

46 *Id.* The Court also noted that a predicate for the doctrine's application must be "more than a simple error in law or a failure by the arbitrators to understand or apply it; and, it is more than an erroneous interpretation of the law." *Id.* Indeed, the Court appears to have carved a special space beyond both mere misunderstanding in the application of law to fact or the construction of law and an error in the interpretation of the law. The degree of error in the interpretation of the law or application of law to fact encompasses an element of *intent*. Accordingly, the movant seeking vacatur must establish "that the arbitrators were fully aware of the existence of a clearly defined governing legal principle, but refused to apply it, in effect, ignoring it." *Id.*, citing *Merrill Lynch v. Bobker*, 808 F.2d 930, 933 (2d Cir. 1986); and *Greenberg v. Bear, Stearns & Co.*, 220 F.3d 22, 28 (2d Cir. 2000), *cert. denied*, 531 U.S. 1075, 121 S.Ct. 770, 148 L.Ed. 2d 669 (2001).

First, a court must determine whether the authority ignored in itself was not vague or ambiguous, that is, clear,[47] and also applicable to the issues before the tribunal. Therefore, the law must be clear and clearly applicable.

Second, assuming that the first inquiry is answered in the affirmative, a court must find "that the law was in fact improperly applied, leading to an erroneous outcome."[48] Emphasis here is placed on the final outcome having a direct causal nexus with the improper application to obviate a scenario where irrespective of the propriety of the application of law to facts, the result would still have been the same. Put simply, the doctrine is irrelevant if the erroneous result would have followed from a correct application of the law. Also, should the arbitral award be susceptible to multiple reasonable readings, the doctrine shall be deemed inapplicable if even one such reading renders a legally sustainable justification for the outcome.[49]

Third, upon satisfaction of the first two inquiries, the "intent" component is analyzed. This subjective analysis purports to determine, to some extent, the arbitrators' knowledge of the law, because it is plain and obvious that only that which is known can be *intentionally* disregarded. For purposes of fulfilling this inquiry, the Second Circuit identifies two factors to be considered. At the outset, only the law that the parties communicated to the arbitrators will be analyzed for purposes of arriving at a conclusion concerning the arbitrators' knowledge of the law that presumably was intentionally disregarded. Second, the presumption of knowledge and intent to disregard shall be engrafted upon the arbitrators for purposes of this analysis where it has been determined that the parties did not educate the arbitrators as to the legal tenets at issue, but that the nature and character of the error was so blatant and obvious that it would be an affront to reason not to acknowledge it as capable of being recognized by the average person qualified to serve on an arbitral panel.[50]

Since the Second Circuit's ruling in *Duferco v. Int'l Steel Trading v. T. Klaveness Shipping A/S*, that Court to date[51] has reviewed a total of *twelve cases* concerning petitions to vacate arbitral awards (excluding *Duferco*) based upon the manifest disregard of the law doctrine.[52] Where *Duferco* is included, then of the total of *thirteen*

[47] *Duferco Int'l Steel*, 333 F.3d at 390 (citing Westerbeke Corp. v. Daihatsu Motor Co. Ltd., 304 F.3d 200, 209 (2d Cir. 2000)); *Merrill Lynch*, 808 F.2d at 934.

[48] *Duferco Int'l Steel*, 333 F.3d at 390.

[49] *See e.g.*, Willemijn Houdstermaatshaepij, B.V. v. Standard Microsystems Corp., 103 F.3d 9, 13 (2d Cir. 1997) (citing Matter of Andros Compania Maritima, S.A. of Kissavos, 579 F.2d 691, 704 (2d Cir. 1978)).

[50] *Id.*

[51] August 17, 2007.

[52] *See* Bernhard Porzig v. Dresdner, Kleinwort, et al., 2007 U.S. App. LEXIS 18674 (2d Cir. 2007); IMC Maritime Group, Inc., et al. v. Russian Farm Community Project, 2006 U.S. App. LEXIS 4088 (2d Cir. 2006); Alicia Nicholls v. Brookdale University Hospital & Medical Center, et al., 2006 U.S. App. LEXIS 26152 (2d Cir. 2006); Bear, Stearns & Co., et al. v. 1109580 Ontario, Inc., 409 F.3d 87 (2d Cir. 2005); Nutrition 21, Inc. v. Andrew Werthhim, 2005 U.S. App. LEXIS 22223 (2d Cir. 2005); Warren Hardy v. Walsh Manning Securities, LLC, 341 F.3d 126 (2d Cir. 2003); IBAR Limited, et al. v. American Bureau of Shipping, 2004 U.S. App. LEXIS 4273 (2d Cir. 2004); Michael E. Wallace, et al. v. DALJIT Buttar, et al., 378 F.3d 182 (2d Cir. 2004); Ralph Tobjy v. Citicorp, 2004 U.S. App. LEXIS 22324 (2d Cir. 2004); Richard Hoeft, et al. v. MVL Group, Inc., et al., 343 F.3d 57 (2d Cir. 2003); Banco de Seguros del Estado v. Mutual Marine Office, Inc., et al., 344 F.3d 255 (2d Cir. 2003); *and* Douglas Carpenter v. John E. Potter, 2003 U.S. App. LEXIS 20947 (2d Cir. 2003).

cases exactly *eleven awards* have been affirmed despite the manifest disregard of the law challenge.[53] *One* case was remanded,[54] and the award was vacated on the ground of manifest disregard of the law in one other action.[55] *Two* cases appear to be of particular interest: *Wallace v. Buttar* and *Hardy v. Walsh*.

In *Wallace v. Buttar*, the Court framed the issue as a case that "raises questions regarding the scope of federal court review of a decision issued by an arbitral panel."[56] Quite remarkably, the Second Circuit observes that the case is resolved pursuant to "application of the familiar principle that the scope of such review is highly constrained." The Court further adds that "[t]his is especially true with regard to an arbitral panel's assessment of whether the documentary and testimonial evidence presented to it is sufficient to satisfy a particular legal claim."[57] The Court then advanced the extraordinary observation that "[f]ederal district judges are, of course, highly skilled in matters of weighing evidence. As illustrated by the result we reach here, however, *district judges must put these skills aside when faced with the question of whether a decision issued by an arbitral panel should be confirmed*."[58]

The procedural history and the district court's findings cry for reasoned examination. Petitioner, the Buttars, instituted an arbitration proceeding with the National Association of Securities Dealers, Inc. ("NASD"), naming Montrose and Winston as respondents. The statement of claim was premised of averments asserting false representations concerning a particular investment opportunity that included an allegedly fraudulent representation of guaranteed returns within a two-month period as a result of investing in the company at issue. An amended claim statement was filed with the NASD containing factual averments identical to those asserted in the initial statement of claim, but naming Michael Wallace, David Jacaruso, and Joseph Scotti as respondents, in addition to the original respondents, Montrose and Winston.[59] The arbitral panel conducted a three-day hearing on the Buttars' claim even though all parties to the arbitration were represented *by counsel*, Winston Jacaruso, and Scotti personally did not appear at the final arbitral hearing.[60] The Buttars supplied the panel with a posthearing memorandum that purported to set forth the rudimentary precepts of "control person liability" under North Carolina *and* federal law. Wallace and Jacaruso, through counsel, also submitted posthearing memorandum, but the

53 *See, e.g.*, Alicia Nicholls v. Brookdale University Hospital & Medical Center, 2006 U.S. App. LEXIS 26152 (2d Cir. 2006); IMC Maritime Group, Inc. v. Russian Farm Community Project, 2006 U.S. App. LEXIS 4088 (2d Cir. 2006); Nutrition 21, Inc. v. Andrew Wortheim, 2005 U.S. App. LEXIS 22223 (2d Cir. 2005); Bear, Stearns & Co. v. 1109580 Ontario, Inc., 409 F.3d 87 (2d Cir. 2005); Ralph Tobjy v. Citicorp., 2004 U.S. App. LEXIS 22324 (2d Cir. 2004); Michael Wallace, et al. v. Daljit Buttar, et al., 378 F.3d 182 (2d Cir. 2004); IBAR Ltd., et al. v. American Bureau of Shipping, 2004 U.S. App. LEXIS 4273 (2d Cir. 2004); Duferco Int'l Steel Trading v. Klaveness Shipping, 333 F.2d 383 (2d Cir. 2003); Richard Hoeft, et al. v. MVL Group, Inc., et al., 343 F.3d 57 (2d Cir. 2003); Banco de Seguros del Estado v. Mutual Marine Office, Inc., et al., 344 F.3d 255 (2d Cir. 2003); *and* Douglas Carpenter v. John Potter, 2003 U.S. App. LEXIS 20947 (2d Cir. 2003).

54 *See* Warren Hardy v. Walsh Manning Securities, LLC, 341 F.3d 126 (2d Cir. 2003).

55 Bernhard Porzig v. Dresdner, Kleinwort, et al., 2007 U.S. App. LEXIS 18674 (2d Cir. 2007).

56 *Wallace*, 378 F.3d at 378.

57 *Id.*

58 *Id.* (emphasis supplied).

59 *Id.* at 185.

60 Wallace also was represented by counsel and testified by telephone. *Id.*

submission was virtually bereft of legal analysis of whatsoever type, even though the Second Circuit observed that it was "notable for its use of invective."[61]

The panel considered evidence characterized as "neither non-existent nor overwhelming" concerning the status of Wallace, Jacaruso, and Scotti as "control persons,"[62] together with testimony from a stockbroker who testified that upon being employed at Montrose, Winston urged him to invest in securities pertaining to the company at issue. The broker further testified regarding his increasing concern that brokers at Montrose "'were being forced [by Winston] to buy . . . securities that they didn't want to buy for their customers.'"[63]

The NASD served all parties with the arbitral award, which, in part, asserted that the panel "'made no determination with respect to the claims asserted against' Montrose, but that the stay[64] 'does not apply to respondents Winston, Wallace, Scotti, and Jacaruso.'"[65]

The Buttars filed an action in the U.S. District Court for the Eastern District of North Carolina seeking confirmation of the award. Four days later, Wallace, Jacaruso, and Scotti filed actions to vacate the award in the U.S. District Court for the Southern District of New York. The Buttars voluntarily dismissed their confirmation action in North Carolina and cross-moved for confirmation of the award in the New York proceeding.[66] The district court granted the motions to vacate the award and denied the cross-motion to confirm the award.[67] The district court understood it to be "'undisputed that Winston, a broker employed by Montrose, committed a primary violation of the securities laws, that Jacaruso and Scotti were directors and shareholders of Montrose and Wallace was its president.'"[68] Consequently, the only remaining issue was whether the panel could have properly found Wallace, Jacaruso, or Scotti liable for Winston's acts and omissions.

With respect to this issue the district court held that the panel could not have held Wallace, Jacaruso, or Scotti liable for Buttars' losses without engaging in both (i) manifest disregard of the law, and (ii) manifest disregard of the facts. Indeed, the district court found that there was no evidence ever presented before the panel from which it may be inferred that Wallace, Jacaruso, or Scotti had the requisite intent to commit fraud as coparticipants in Winston's scheme.[69] A review of the district court opinion reveals how the court succinctly yet eloquently addresses this issue:

> The totality of the evidence . . . overwhelmingly indicates that Wallace never dealt with the Buttars, lacked awareness of all wrongdoing in respondents' account [and] had no duty nor reason to educate himself of the activity in the Buttars' account. . . .

61 *Id.*

62 *Id.* at 186.

63 *Id.*

64 On December 7, 2001, the U.S. District Court for the Southern District of New York had issued a stay of all legal proceedings against Montrose pursuant to §362(a) of the Bankruptcy Code, 11 U.S.C. §362(a).

65 *Id.* at 187.

66 Winston neither filed an action to vacate the award nor any papers in opposition to the Buttars' cross-motion to confirm the award.

67 *See* Wallace v. Buttar, 239 F.Supp. 2d 388 (S.D.N.Y. 2003).

68 *Id.* at 188.

69 *Id.*

> There was no evidence of any action taken by Jacaruso and Scotti in connection with the transactions in which Winston defrauded the Buttars.
>
> Clearly the arbitrators could not have found that Wallace, Jacaruso, and Scotti possessed the requisite intention to defraud the Buttars without manifestly disregarding this evidence, or lack of evidence.[70]

Lastly, the district court found that the panel had manifestly disregarded the law in concluding that Wallace, Jacaruso, and Scotti were liable as control persons.[71] After engaging in a sustained and reasoned analysis on authority addressing manifest disregard of the law and manifest disregard of the evidence, the Second Circuit reversed and remanded the conceptual talisman that appears as a recurring theme in the Second Circuit's analysis and can be reduced to two words: "colorable evidence." Significantly, the Court stressed that the district court had placed considerable weight on Ninth Circuit authority[72] applying a "manifest disregard of the facts" doctrinal analysis, yet in a decision issued post *Wallace v. Buttar* (the district court action) the very Ninth Circuit uncontrovertedly asserted that "manifest disregard of the facts is not an independent ground for vacatur in this circuit."[73] Additionally, in *Coutee* the Ninth Circuit also underscored that "it does not appear that any other circuit has adopted a manifest disregard of the facts standard," and that the Second Circuit has recently clarified that *Halligan*[74] is, in fact, based on the orthodox standard of manifest disregard of the law.[75] In this regard, the Second Circuit further amplified and explained the *dicta* and holding in *Halligan* by stating that in that case the Arbitral Tribunal simply offered no explanation for the rejection of the claim, which had been established with "overwhelming evidence" and material admissions from a party opponent. Thus, the Second Circuit in *Halligan* "held that the district court had erred in confirming the award caused the evidence in the claimant's favor was so strong as to engender *the firm belief that the arbitrators here manifestly disregarded the*

70 *Wallace*, 239 F.Supp. 2d at 394–95.

71 *Id.* at 396.

72 American Postal Workers Union AFL-CIO v. U.S. Postal Service, 682 F.2d 1280 (9th Cir. 1982); Pacific Reinsurance Management Corp. v. Ohio Reinsurance Corp., 935 F.2d 1019 (9th Cir. 1991).

73 Coutee v. Barington Capital Group, LP, 336 F.3d 1128, 1133 (9th Cir. 2003).

74 Halligan v. Piper Jaffray, Inc., 148 F.3d 197, 202, 204 (2d Cir. 1998) (appeared to stand for the proposition that an arbitral award may be vacated on the ground of "manifest disregard of the facts" when the award "runs contrary to 'strong evidence' favoring the party bringing the motion to vacate." Cited by the district court at *Wallace*, 239 F.Supp. 2d at 392).

75 *Coutee*, 336 F.3d at 1133. Indeed, the Second Circuit in *Wallace* announced that authority adopting the construction in *Halligan* that manifest disregard of the facts constitutes a separate and distinct basis for vacatur is misplaced, citing to the following authority as having misapprehended the rule in *Halligan*:

> *See, e.g.*, Hakula v. Deutsche Bank AG, 2004 U.S. Dist. LEXIS 8297, No. 01 Civ. 3366, 2004 WL 1057788 at *6 [*192] (S.D.N.Y. May 11, 2004); Gwynn v. Clubine, 302 F.Supp. 2d 151, 167–68 (W.D.N.Y. 2004); Ono Pharmaceutical Co. Ltd. v. Cortech, Inc., 2003 U.S. Dist. LEXIS 19556, No. 03 Civ. 5840, 2003 WL 22481379 at *2 (S.D.N.Y. Nov. 3, 2003); Tripi v. Prudential Securities, Inc., 303 F.Supp. 2d 349, No. 02 Civ. 6225, 2003 WL 22208351 at *3 (S.D.N.Y. Sept. 23, 2003); Raiola v. Union Bank of Switzerland LLC, 230 F.Supp. 2d 355, 357 (S.D.N.Y. 2002); GFI Sec. LLC v. Labandeira, 2002 U.S. Dist. LEXIS 4932, No. 01 Civ. 00793, 2002 WL 460059 [**26] at *4 (S.D.N.Y. March 26, 2002); McDaniel v. Bear Stearns & Co., Inc., 196 F.Supp. 2d 343, 351 (S.D.N.Y. 2002).

law or the evidence or both."[76] Therefore, the district court's reliance on the Ninth Circuit's adoption of the manifest disregard of the evidence language considerably undermines the ruling's normative basis.

In addition, the Second Circuit reasoned that there was a "colorable basis" under North Carolina law pursuant to which control person liability may attach. Similarly, the Court concluded that the award in its entirety was, "at least *colorably*, based upon the facts and the law as presented to the Panel."[77]

Wallace v. Buttar stands as an emblematic post *Duferco* case that clarifies the manifest disregard of the law doctrine, at least to the extent of emphasizing the need to find almost universally intuitively cognizable wrongdoing in the application of law to fact by an arbitral tribunal and, in effect, explaining that there is no such doctrine as the "manifest disregard of the facts" precept.

A second post *Duferco* case worthy of note is *Hardy v. Walsh Manning Securities, LLC*. Without engaging in any analysis of the facts configuring the case, it is worth emphasizing the procedural oddity that attached to the Second Circuit's affirmance in part and remand in part. Curiously, the court had determined that the arbitration award sought to be confirmed in that case was not susceptible to enforcement as written. The query became, from a judicial perspective, "what should be done?" The award at issue, according to the Court, (i) did not contain any legal reasoning, (ii) advanced an explicit legal conclusion susceptible to only one plausible reading, and (iii) does not rest on a colorable interpretation of the law.[78] Consequently, the Court found itself "reluctant to announce that the Award is void outright as written [i.e. hesitant to conclude that the arbitral panel manifestly disregarded the law]."[79]

The Court answered its query by seeking clarification of the award but not from the district court. To be sure, the actual language used merits citation. "Although certainly not the normal course of things, we do have the authority to remand to the Panel for purposes broader than a clarification of the terms of a specific remedy. That is, we have the authority to seek a clarification of whether an arbitration panel's intent in making an award 'evidence(s) a manifest disregard of the law.'"[80]

C. ORDER OUT OF CHAOS: THE NEED FOR A UNIFORM STANDARD FOR "MANIFEST DISREGARD OF THE LAW" BEYOND MERE INTUITION

Since 1980 through August 2007 exactly *twenty-four* cases vacated arbitration awards based upon the doctrine of manifest disregard of the law.[81] Analysis of this authority

[76] *Id.* at 192 (citing *Halligan*, 148 F.3d at 204).
[77] *Id.* at 196.
[78] *Id.* at 133.
[79] *Id.* at 133–34.
[80] *Id.* at 134 (citing Americas Ins. Co. v. Seagull Compañia Naviera, S.A., 774 F.2d 64, 67 (2d Cir. 1985)).
[81] *See:*

(a) **First Circuit Court of Appeals:** S.D. Warren Co. v. United Paperworkers' Int'l. Union, 815 F.2d 178 (1st Cir. 1987);
(b) **Second Circuit Court of Appeals:** Perma-Line Corp. of America v. Sign Pictorial and Display Union, 639 F.2d 890 (2d Cir. 1981); Halligan v. Piper Jaffray, et al, 148 F.3d 197 (2d Cir. 1998); New York Telephone Co. v. Communications Workers of America, 256 F.3d 89 (2d Cir. 2001); Wallace v. Buttar, 378 F.3d 182 (2d Cir. 2004); Bernhard Porzig v. Dresdner, Kleinwort, et al., 2007 US App. LEXIS 18674 (2d Cir. 2007);

reflects fourteen fundamental principles that appear to be shared by all, if not most, of the cases. First, the authority appears to be of a single voice in holding that a district court reviewing an arbitration award where vacatur is sought must engage in a *de novo* proceeding. Second, the grounds upon which vacatur may be predicated are extremely narrow and limited to those set forth in the FAA 9 U.S.C. Section 10(a). Third, arbitrators by operation of law need not provide reasons justifying their conclusions or to keep a record of the proceedings either simultaneously or sequentially. Fourth, a district court's finding of legal error on behalf of the arbitral tribunal, without more, does not constitute a legally binding ground for vacatur. Fifth, while it is clear in virtually every circuit that the conduct warranting vacatur must be "egregious" in nature and character, there is some uncertainty inherent in the term that flows over to the attendant legal analyses. Sixth, an arbitration tribunal's interpretation of an ambiguous clause in a contract or an ambiguous construction of an otherwise unambiguous clause in the operative agreement shall not give rise to vacatur. In fact, reviewing tribunals are charged with construing any ambiguity in the arbitral tribunal's interpretation of the contract at issue in favor of sustainability of the award. Also, to the extent that the arbitral tribunal's interpretation of a contractual provision may comport with even a modicum of "reasonableness," such award shall be upheld and defy vacatur challenges. Seventh, a common occurrence present among some circuits is a blurring of the distinction between the foregrounds for vacatur set forth in the FAA 9 USC Section 10(a) and the common law doctrine of manifest disregard of the law. Eighth, in the context of domestic arbitral proceedings, greater impartiality in the resolution of disputes has been identified when arbitrators are appointed from lists pertaining to independent

(c) **Third Circuit Court of Appeals:** United States Steel and Carnegie Pension Fund, et al. v. John McSkimming, 759 F.2d 269 (3d Cir. 1985); Exxon Shipping Co. v. Exxon Seaman's Union, 993 F.2d 357 (3d Cir. 1993); Roadway Package System, Inc. v. Scott Kayser, 257 F.3d 287 (3d Cir. 2001); Pennsylvania Power Co. v. Local Union No. 272 of the Int'l Brotherhood of Electrical Workers, 276 F.3d 174 (3d Cir. 2001); Citgo Asphalt Refining Co. v. The Paper, Allied-Industrial, Chemical and Energy Workers Int'l Union Local No. 2–991, 385 F.3d 809 (3d Cir. 2004); Merck & Co., Inc. v. Paper Allied-Industrial, Chemical and Energy Workers Int'l, Union, Local 2–86, 2007 U.S. App. LEXIS 13986 (3d Cir. 2007);

(d) **Fourth Circuit Court of Appeals:** Patten v. Signator Ins. Agency, et al., 441 F.3d 230 (4th Cir. 2006);

(e) **Fifth Circuit Court of Appeals:** Hughes Training, Inc., et al. v. Gracie Cook, et al., 254 F.3d 588 (5th Cir. 2001);

(f) **Sixth Circuit Court of Appeals:** NCR Corp. v. Sack-Co., Inc., 43 F.3d 1076 (1995); Nationwide Mutual Ins. Co. v Home Ins. Co., 330 F.3d 843 (6th Cir. 2003);

(g) **Seventh Circuit Court of Appeals:** Young Radiator Co. v. Int'l Union, United Automobile, Aerospace and Agricultural Implement Workers of America, 734 F.3d 321 (7th Cir. 1984);

(h) **Eighth Circuit Court of Appeals:** Missouri River Services, Inc. v. Omaha Tribe of Nebraska, 267 F.3d 848 (8th Cir. 2001); Boise Cascade Corp. v. Paper Allied-Industrial, Chemical and Energy Workers (PACE), Local 7–0159, 309 F.3d 1075 (8th Cir. 2002); Gas Aggression Services, Inc. v. Howard Avista Energy LLC., et al., 319 F.3d 1060 (8th Cir. 2003);

(i) **Ninth Circuit Court of Appeals:** American Postal Workers Union AFL-CIO v. United States Postal Service, 682 F.2d 1280 (9th Cir. 1982); Coast Trading Co., Inc. v. Pacific Molasses Co., 681 F.2d 1195 (9th Cir. 1982); Stead Motors of Walnut Creek v. Automotive Machinists Lodge No. 1173, 843 F.2d 357 (9th Cir. 1988);

(j) **Eleventh Circuit Court of Appeals:** Montes v. Shearson Lehman Bros., Inc., 128 F.3d 1456 (11th Cir. 1997).

arbitration agencies as opposed to self-regulating organizations or SROs. Ninth, courts in unison hold that parties are free to structure arbitration clauses as they see fit. Tenth, arbitration agreements (clauses) may amplify judicial review of an arbitration award beyond the scope of the FAA.[82] Eleventh a reviewing court may remand an award back to the arbitral tribunal in cases where an arbitration award is found to be ambiguous.[83] Twelfth, the burden of proving that the arbitrators exceeded their authority is a significant one not readily met.[84] Thirteenth, and finally, an arbitral tribunal is bereft of any discretion to render an award containing a remedy not provided for in the underlying contract containing the arbitration clause.[85]

Despite these shared elements, the authority defining the factors to be considered in vacating an award on the common law ground of manifest disregard of the law is far from uniform. Indeed, even a surface review of some of the more salient cases from the different circuits demonstrates substantially different standards and, in some instances, the test is confused with the four basis for vacatur codified in 9 U.S.C. Section 10(a). This latter confusion is particularly prevalent where vacatur rests on a finding that an arbitral tribunal exceeded the scope of its authority.[86] The disparate and often contradictory standards applied in cases of vacatur based upon manifest disregard of the law contribute to the creation of an ill-conceived conceptual category practically based upon intuition, bringing to mind Justice Stewart's criteria for a finding of pornography in violation of the First Amendment: "But I know it when I see it."[87] Keen as this observation undoubtedly may be, subjective intuition should play no role in analytical jurisprudence and, therefore, in the doctrinal development of the fundamental elements of arbitration.

D. *HALLIGAN v. PIPER JAFFRAY*

Six cases are emblematic of the problem, and, to some extent, suggestive of a practical and theoretically consistent resolution.[88] *Halligan v. Piper Jaffray,*

[82] Gateway Tech., Inc. v. MCI, 64 F.3d 993, 997 (5th Cir. 1995) (holding that "[i]n this case, however, the parties contractually agreed to permit expanded review of the arbitration award by the federal courts. Specifically, their contract details that '[t]he arbitration decision shall be final and binding on both parties, except that errors of law shall be subject to appeal.' Such a contractual modification is acceptable because, as the Supreme Court has emphasized, arbitration is a creature of contract and the FAA's pro-arbitration policy does not operate without regard to the wishes of the contracting parties. . . .").

[83] Cleveland Paper Handlers and Sheet Straighteners Union No. 11 v. E.W. Scripps Co., 681 F.2d 457 (6th Cir. 1982).

[84] Federated Department Stores, Inc. v. JVB Industries, Inc., 894 F.2d 862, 866 (6th Cir. 1990) ("given the strong federal policy in favor of enforcing arbitration agreements, [citations omitted] the burden of proving that the arbitrators exceeded their powers is very great.").

[85] Coast Trading Co. v. Pac. Molasses Co., 681 F.2d 1195, 1198 (9th Cir. 1982 (vacating "arbitration award as being contrary to remedies provided in the contract" and rejecting proposition that post-dispute submission modified contractual terms.).

[86] *See* 9 U.S.C. §10(a)(4).

[87] Jacobellis v. State of Ohio, 378 U.S. 184, 197 (1964).

[88] At the very outset the jurisprudence addressing this concern must determine whether a reviewing judicial tribunal may actually hold an evidentiary hearing, beyond just the examination of an award and the "arbitration procedure's record" in applying this common law doctrine. This question is particularly relevant because of the very lax requirements concerning any legal obligation on the part of the arbitral tribunal (i) to craft an opinion setting forth the rationale for its findings, and (ii) to keep *any* record whatsoever. It is here suggested that some, if not most,

Inc.,[89] is quite helpful.[90] There, Irene Halligan (Mrs. Halligan), serving as executrix for the estate of Theodore Halligan (Halligan), appealed two orders entered by the United States District Court for the Southern District of New York. The orders, respectively, refused vacatur and confirmed an arbitration award entered in favor of defendants (collectively Piper). Halligan had alleged that defendants terminated his employment in violation of the Age Discrimination in Employment Act (ADEA), 29 U.S.C. Section 621 et seq. The second order entered dismissed Mrs. Halligan's federal court action on the ground of *res judicata* because it arose from the same facts as those underlying the ADEA claim in arbitration. Mrs. Halligan bottomed her appeal on the doctrine of manifest disregard of the law.[91]

Specifically, Halligan submitted an ADEA claim, together with other averments, to arbitration before an NASD panel of arbitrators. The record suggests that "[b]efore he could complete his own re-direct testimony, however, his health deteriorated and in early 1995 the arbitrators were advised that Halligan was unable to testify further."[92] Pursuant to stipulation his redirect testimony was stricken from the record, but the direct testimony had been subject to cross-examination. Upon his passing the arbitration continued.

Even though the record was rife with compelling evidence suggestive of age discrimination, ten evidentiary facts were particularly central to the Second Circuit's analysis:

1. Defendant conceded in the form of a party admission throughout the proceeding that Halligan was "basically qualified."
2. Halligan ranked fifth out of twenty-five institutional salesmen.
3. He held a number one ranking from 1987 through 1991.
4. The record established that he "had consistently been among [defendant's] top salesmen."
5. He testified to recurring discriminatory statements published by defendants.
6. Halligan had contemporaneous writings concerning relevant conversations.
7. During the arbitration several witnesses testified having heard Halligan say that he was "being fired."
8. Numerous witnesses testified on Halligan's behalf that defendant's personnel had expressed their intention to terminate Halligan because of his age.

of the standards adopted by the various circuit courts cannot be ***meaningfully*** applied without an evidentiary hearing providing for the actual examination of the arbitral panel itself. For example, is "awareness" of the applicable law that was not applied to be construed the same as "knowledge" of the relevant authority? Is the non-application of case dispositive authority contained in written submissions sufficient to trigger application of the doctrine? Can knowledge or awareness be inferred as a matter of law from such circumstances? Is non-application of case dispositive authority contained in written submissions to be construed as a matter of law as "intentionally" non-applying governing jurisprudence or statutory law? These questions find no definitive answers in the twenty-four post 1980 through August 2007 cases vacating arbitration awards based upon manifest disregard of the law.

89 Halligan v. Piper Jaffray, Inc., 148 F.3d 197 (2d Cir. 1998).

90 For an interesting analysis of *Halligan*, see Mark B. Rees, *HALLIGAN v. PIPER JAFFRAY: THE COLLISION BETWEEN ARBITRAL AUTONOMY AND JUDICIAL REVIEW*, 8 Am. Rev. Int'l Arb. 347 (1997).

91 *Halligan*, 148 F.3d at 198.

92 *Id.*

9. Even though defendant's personnel denied having made discriminatory statements, "their testimony was occasionally inconsistent or ambiguous."
10. Halligan presented testimony from current and former clients who consistently testified that he was among the best in his field.[93]

The arbitral tribunal rendered an award that identified the parties' respective claims and defenses, denying Halligan any relief. "The award did not contain any explanation or rationale for the result."[94] Mrs. Halligan petitioned the district court for vacatur pursuant to Section 10(a) of the FAA asserting, *inter alia*, that both the compelling evidence and clear standard commanded a finding of manifest disregard of the law on the arbitrators' part. The district court predicated its denial of the petition for vacatur and corollary order confirming upon a finding that "the determination of what constitutes 'direct evidence' [of discrimination] . . . is a difficult one to make."[95]

Upon observing that federal courts have experienced an increase in the scrutiny and controversy attendant to the use of predispute arbitration agreements for purposes of adjudicating statutory claims of employment discrimination, such as here, the Second Circuit enunciated what it opined to be the standard for application of the doctrine of manifest disregard of the law. In this connection, it articulated that it "clearly means more than error or misunderstanding with respect to the law."[96] The Court additionally enunciated a two-prong predicate standard for application of the doctrine: "A court must find both that (1) the arbitrator knew of a governing legal principle yet refused to apply it or ignored it altogether, and (2) the law ignored by the arbitrators was well defined, explicit, and clearly applicable to the case."[97] The difficulties with the application of this standard are compounded and multiplied in the context of mandatory binding arbitration of employment discrimination disputes as a condition of employment. Perhaps not surprisingly, "[t]he major independent arbitration agencies have formulated due process standards for the adjudication of these disputes". Yet, "[i]ndustry self-regulatory organizations (SROs) like the [National Association of Securities Dealers] NASD have been singled out for criticism because, among other reasons, the role they play in determining the pool of available arbitrators and selecting the arbitrator who will hear a particular discrimination claim against a member firm of the SRO calls into question the impartiality."[98] The clear implication of likely impartiality may, in part, account for scant recordkeeping and little more than conclusions memorialized in awards.

93 *Id.* at 198–99.

94 *Id.* at 200.

95 The Second Circuit's opinion emphasizes the recitation of the district court's principal rationale:

> In addition, the record . . . does not indicate the Panel's awareness, prior to its determinations, of the standards for burdens of proof . . . the Panel was faced with the task of evaluating conflicting witness testimony, and where it did not issue a written opinion, I [Judge Kimba Wood] cannot conclude that the Panel did in fact disregard the parties' burden of proof . . . *crediting one witness over another does not constitute manifest disregard of the law* [and] this Court's role is not to second-guess the fact-finding done by the Panel. *Because there is factual as well as legal support for the Panel's ultimate conclusion, I determine that the Panel did not manifestly disregard the law . . . internal citations and footnote omitted. Id.* at 200. (emphasis supplied)

96 *Id.* at 202 (citations and internal quotations omitted).

97 *Id.* (citing DiRussa v. Dean Witter Reynolds, Inc., 121 F.3d 818, 821 (2d. Cir. 1997), *cert. denied*, 118 S.Ct. 695 (1998)).

98 *Id.*

Accordingly, a reviewing tribunal would face a daunting task in trying to marshal applicable evidence to evaluate the doctrine's applicability.[99]

In applying the standard and reversing the district court, the Second Circuit, in addition to the ten salient evidentiary issues identified here, underscored two observations. First, the record was conclusive in establishing "that counsel for both parties generally agreed on the applicable law (and still do on appeal). Second, the dispositive law was explained to the arbitrators.[100] The Second Circuit's specific and carefully crafted holding merits close scrutiny. The Court specifically held that "[i]n view of the strong evidence that Halligan was fired because of his age and the agreement of the parties that the arbitrators were correctly advised on the applicable legal principles, we are inclined to hold that they ignored the law, the evidence or both."[101]

The language of the Court in what is unclear to be *dicta* or the actual holding, despite the Second Circuit's subsequent effort to clarify this issue, although at first innocuous, is particularly disconcerting. Three actual possibilities are contained in the single sentence pronouncement. The Court finds that it is inclined to vacate the award on the basis of the doctrine of manifest disregard of the law because the arbitrators "ignored the law."[102] The analysis does not stop here. The Court additionally states that the arbitrators also could have just ignored the evidence.[103] A third scenario is suggested. The arbitrators conceivably could have ignored both law and evidence. It was this tripartite pronouncement, it shall be recalled, that led numerous courts to adopt – quite wrongfully – a "manifest disregard of the facts" standard in addition to the "manifest disregard of the law" doctrine. As earlier referenced,[104] it was not until six years later in *Wallace v. Buttar* that the Second Circuit classified this language as *dicta* and disavowed "manifest disregard of the facts" as a common law doctrine compelling vacatur.

The opinion's debilities are subtle but with palpable contours. The two-prong test is too abbreviated to find universal application to standard fact-intensive

99 To be sure, federal courts have expressed considerable concern over this issue. *See, e.g.*, Cole v. Burns Int'l SEC. Serve, 105 F.3d 1465, 1479 (D.C. Cir. 1997) ("Despite the Supreme Court's recent endorsement of arbitration of statutory claims, however, concerns remain regarding arbitration's ability to live up to the Court's expectations, particularly in cases involving mandatory arbitration of statutory claims which is imposed as a condition of employment. In fact, the Equal Employment Opportunity Commission has taken the position that such agreements are unenforceable in a number of cases being litigated around the country."); *and* Prudential Ins. Co. of Am. v. Lai, 42 F.3d 1299, 1305 (9th Cir. 1994) (holding that "appellants were not bound by any valid agreement to arbitrate those employment disputes, because they did not knowingly contract to forego their statutory remedies in favor of arbitration").

100 *Halligan*, 148 F.3d at 204 (citing De Gaetano v. Smith Barney, Inc., 983 F.Supp. 459, 563 (S.D.N.Y. 1997)) (It was emphasized that "even under a strict construction of the meaning of manifest disregard, it is [doubtful that] it is necessary for arbitrators to state that they are deliberately ignoring the law. Indeed, it is a true challenge to the imagination to conceive of a scenario where an arbitral tribunal would admit to ignoring deliberately the applicable legal precepts. In the realm of arbitral disputes, however, little is impossible.).

101 *Id.* Quite curiously, even though arbitral tribunals are not invested with the obligation to keep records or fashion awards explaining the basis for the findings (factual or legal), the court did state that "[a]t least in the circumstances here, we believe that when a reviewing court is inclined to hold that an arbitration panel manifestly disregarded the law, the failure of the arbitrators to explain the award can be taken into account."

102 *Id.* 103 *Id.*

104 *See, supra*, n. 444 (explaining *Wallace*, 378 F.3d 182).

arbitration proceedings. While the first prong speaks to whether arbitrators "knew of a governing legal principle yet refused to apply it," it takes for granted the meaning of the word "know" as an essential element of the test. Is "knowing" the applicable law for purposes of vacatur under this standard present where the parties in fact have briefed the dispositive jurisprudence? Can knowledge be inferred from the briefing of the parties alone as a matter of law? Again, is "awareness" the same as "knowledge" in the context of application of this regime?

The second part of the first prong is equally bewildering. This pronouncement references two concepts in the disjunctive: *refusal* or *ignorance*. "Refusal" suggests an *intentional* disregard of the law. "Ignorance" or "ignoring" the law is closer to a *negligence* or nonintentional recklessness standard. Thus, at least with respect to this first prong, it stands to reason that the first part of the test shall be satisfied upon a threshold finding that the arbitral tribunal somehow knew the law but failed to apply it by inexplicably not according it *any* weight. This standard is dramatically more relaxed and less exacting than its disjunctive counterpart – *refusal* – that compellingly suggests a deliberate intent not to use that which is known.

The first and second prongs must be met in the conjunctive. The second prong just uses the word "ignored." This construction would lend support to an interpretation of the standard as met where the arbitrators merely acted "negligently" or "carelessly" in not applying the governing legal principles. The second prong, however, goes on to require that the dispositive legal principle must be "well defined, explicit, and clearly applicable to the case." These exigencies virtually raise the applicability of the governing legal principles to the status of a science. It would not be unreasonable to posit that rarely are the "governing principles" applicable to any proceeding (i) well-defined, (ii) explicit, and let alone (iii) "clearly applicable to the case." Indeed, particularly in the context of the common law tradition, the exercise of distinguishing cases as well as analogizing them to the fact pattern at issue is rarely clear or explicit. The question of "governing authority" also raises more concerns than it addresses. Again, especially in the common law rubric, often authority is found from jurisdictions other than the one selected by the parties. Here, where only persuasive authority exists, can the two-prong standard be applied at all?

E. *NEW YORK TELEPHONE CO. v. COMMUNICATIONS WORKERS OF AMERICA*

The Second Circuit itself addressed this issue in *New York Telephone Co. v. Communications Workers of America Local 1100, AFL-CIO District 1.*[105] There, the Court affirmed a judgment of the District Court for the Southern District of New York vacating a labor arbitration agreement entered against the *New York Telephone Co.* ("NY Tel") and denying NY Tel's cross-motion for summary judgment seeking confirmation. After engaging in a virtually boilerplate recitation of the deference accorded to arbitration awards and the *de novo* standard of review charged to reviewing tribunals, the Court stressed that "[t]he arbitrator expressly disregarded [the Second Circuit's

[105] New York Telephone Co. v. Communications Workers of America Local 1100, AFL-CIO District 1, 256 F.3d 89 (2d Cir. 2001).

holding] in *International Longshoreman's Ass'n v. Seatrain Lines, Inc.*,[106] [citation omitted]." Instead, the Second Circuit observed, the arbitrator elected to rely "on two (more recent) opinions from outside this Circuit."[107] Therefore, the Second Circuit held that vacatur was warranted because "[t]hese opinions are not the law of [the Second Circuit] it was therefore 'manifest disregard of the law' for the arbitrator to reject *Seatrain* and apply another rule."[108]

It is noteworthy that nowhere in the opinion is there any reference or citation to the two-prong test enunciated in *Halligan*. The Court limited its manifest disregard of the law affirmance to the narrow ground that the arbitrator relied on – albeit more modern authority than that arguably on point from the Second Circuit – authority from a different circuit that can only be persuasive in nature. Here the elements of "knowledge," "intentional," nonapplication of authority, or reckless or negligent "ignoring" of governing authority simply played no role in the analysis. Application of persuasive authority only where binding legal principles exist significantly and meaningfully relaxes the standard for application of the doctrine. The application of persuasive authority, without more, tends to suggest legal error rather than a deliberate undertaking. Yet all circuits are in unison in holding that legal error alone shall not trigger application of the doctrine.

F. *UNITED STATES STEEL & CARNEGIE PENSION FUND v. JOHN McSKIMMING*

Greater clarity even within the same sophisticated appellate tribunals is absolutely imperative.

The Third Circuit in *United States Steel & Carnegie Pension Fund, et al. v. John McSkimming*[109] reversed a district court judgment affirming an arbitration award concerning a statutory labor dispute under the enforcement provision of the Employee Retirement and Income Security Act ("ERISA"), 29 U.S.C. Section 1132 (1982). In reversing the judgment and vacating the award at issue based on the doctrine of manifest disregard of the law, we encounter yet a third standard of review.

In this cause the Court identified the applicable standard as one requiring that an arbitrator's award be upheld:

> If the interpretation can in any rational way be derived from the agreement, viewed in the light of its language, its context, and any other indicia of the parties' intention; only where there is a manifest disregard of the agreement,

[106] *See, e.g.*, International Longshoreman's Ass'n v. Seatrain Lines, Inc., 326 F.2d 916 (2d Cir. 1964), *and New York Telephone*, 256 F.3d at 91.

[107] *New York Telephone*, 256 F.3d at 93 (citing Washington Post v. Washington-Baltimore Newspaper Guild, Local 35, 787 F.2d 604 (D.C. Cir. 1986); United Steelworkers of America v. United States Gypsum Co., 492 F.2d 713. These cases were decided twenty-two years and ten years, respectively, after *Seatrain*.).

[108] *Id.* (citing *Halligan*, 148 F.3d at 202). Notably, *Halligan* nowhere addresses the issue of whether persuasive authority from another jurisdiction where legal principles governing the dispute are present in the jurisdiction at issue, constitutes manifest disregard of the law.

[109] United States Steel & Carnegie Pension Fund, et al. v. John McSkimming, 759 F.2d 269 (3d Cir. 1985).

> totally unsupported by principles of contract construction and the law of the shop, may a reviewing court disturb the award.[110]

Remarkably, even though the Third Circuit amply adopts this standard, it inexplicably applies it together with yet *another* standard, which may have absolutely nothing to do with the doctrine of manifest disregard of the law, everything to do with 9 U.S.C. Section 10(4), but one that the court certainly does treat as central to its reasoning and holding. In particular, it underscored that "[i]f an arbitral decision is based 'solely upon the arbitrator's view of the requirements of enacted legislation,' rather than on the [contract], the arbitrator has 'exceeded the scope of the submission,' and the award will not be enforced."[111]

Both standards enunciated by the Third Circuit Court of Appeals merit closer attention. In the first standard a "reasonableness" test is adopted such that only if whatsoever connection between the award and the labor contract at issue can only be construed as *irrational* can vacatur attach. Otherwise restated, this standard appears to stand for the proposition that an arbitration award shall be affirmed unless it cannot be sustained under any rational legal hypothesis. The standard is so exacting that it certainly stands in sharp relief when compared to the two Second Circuit Court of Appeals pronouncements here analyzed in *Halligan* and *NY Tel.*

The second standard that the Third Circuit articulates is poles apart from the first and somewhat difficult to classify as it is not altogether clear that it falls within the ambit of either manifest disregard of the law or 9 U.S.C. Section 10. Issuance of vacatur on the finding that an arbitrator premised an award on her interpretation of enacted legislation rather than the text of the operative agreement is difficult to reconcile as a test with any of the preceding three standards already reviewed. The question becomes whether legal error in methodology applied constitutes manifest disregard of the law. Would the vacatur ensue on the same doctrinal ground were an arbitrator to reach the right result but based on the wrong analysis?

The want of analysis in the articulation of standards, use of precedent, and inartfully advanced assumptions is conducive to mere subjective relativism in the doctrine's application.

G. YET ANOTHER PARADIGM: *PATTON v. SIGNATURE INS. AGENCY*

In *Patton v. Signature Ins. Agency*,[112] the Fourth Circuit Court of Appeals identifies yet a fifth standard for the application of manifest disregard of the law. There the Court stated that the doctrine attaches and vacatur shall issue where the arbitration award "fail[s] to draw its essence from the governing arbitration agreement."[113] Distinguishing between "misapplication of contractual interpretation" or "erroneous interpretation," where neither ground suffices for vacating an award,[114] the

110 *Id.* at 270–71 (citing Ludwig Honold Mfg. Co. v. Fletcher, 405 F.2d 1123, 1128 (3d Cir. 1969); United Food & Commercial Workers, Local 590 v. Great Atlantic and Pacific Tea Company, 734 F.2d 455, 457 (3d Cir. 1984); Sun Petroleum Prods. Co. v. Oil, Chemical and Atomic Workers, Local 8–901, 681 F.2d 924, 928 (3d Cir. 1982)).

111 *Id.* at 271.

112 Patton v. Signature Ins. Agency, 441 F.3d 230 (4th Cir. 2006).

113 *Id.* at 237.

114 Apex Plumbing Supply, Inc. v. U.S. Supply Co., 142 F.3d 188, 194 (4th Cir. 1998).

Court carved a category triggering application of the doctrine where an arbitrator "amended or altered the agreement" and thereby "acted without authority."[115] By altering the agreement, so says the argument, the "essence of the agreement" is frustrated and thus a "scope" or "authority" arbitrator issue arises but with a common law and not a 9 U.S.C. Section 10, normative foundation.[116]

The "essence of the agreement" foundation for manifest disregard of the law is a factually intensive and quite subjective standard. First, it assumes that there is such a thing as a *single* "essence" of an agreement. It is not unusual for contracts to create multiple binding obligations and incident objectives. In addition, it is often unusual, if not altogether impossible, to distinguish between disavowing the "essence of an agreement" and simply misconstruing as a matter of contractual interpretation primary or secondary contract objectives. Also of significance is the Fourth Circuit's want of any suggestion in articulating the applicable manifest disregard of the law standard any need for arbitrators to engage in irrational or extreme conduct in executing her obligation in construing the operative agreement. The need for the doctrinal development of this test is immediately obvious. Its conceptual growth, however, can be readily nurtured by the various other paradigms examined. Amplification of the five tests[117] already canvassed is testimony to something of a loosely constructed but rich framework on which to build and engraft upon "the essence of the agreement" standard greater rigor, universality, and elements that may enhance the predictive value of its application.

Since its genesis and inception in *Wilko v. Swan*, the doctrine of manifest disregard of the law purporting to address the enforceability of arbitration agreements and

115 *Patton*, 441 F.3d at 236.

116 Citing to *Apex Plumbing Supply, Inc. v. U.S. Supply Co.*, the opinion explained that:

> While the 'essence of the agreement' standard was first articulated by courts reviewing labor arbitration awards, the courts have generally acknowledged that it applies to other arbitration proceedings as well. *Id.* at 235.

117 Intentionally we have refrained from engaging in analysis of the vacatur of arbitration awards premised on "public policy" ground. It is, however, critical to observe that courts have disagreed, certainly in the context of employment disputes, on whether an arbitration award reinstating a discharged employee violates public policy. *See e.g. American Postal Workers Union v. United States Postal Serv.*, 789 F.2d 1, 8 (D.C. Cir. 1986) (holding that "[t]he arbitrator's award was not itself unlawful, for there is no legal proscription against the reinstatement of a person as the grievant. And the award did not otherwise have the effect of mandating any illegal conduct."); *Northwest Airlines, Inc. v. Airline Pilots Ass'n Intern.*, 808 F.2d 76, 84 (D.C. Cir. 1987) (holding that "so long as the Board acts within its jurisdiction and its awards draw their essence from the collective bargaining agreement, and neither contravene established law nor require an unlawful act, [citation omitted] and like precedent under the RLA compel that such awards be enforced."); *C/F* Opinions holding that arbitration awards reinstating employees are susceptible to vacatur when the awards are found to be "inconsistent with some significant public policy." E.I. Dupont de Nemours v. Grasselli Emp. Ass'n, 790 F.2d 611, 616 (7th Cir.) (quoting Robert A. Gorman, Labor Law Unionization and Collective Bargaining at 597 (1976)), *cert. denied*, 479 U.S. 853 (1986); Iowa Elec. Light & Power Co. v. Local Union 204 of the International Brotherhood of Electrical Workers, 834 F.2d at 1427 n. 2 (8th Cir. 1987) (incorporating the same test); *see also* Board of County Commissioners v. L. Robert Kimball & Associates, 860 F.2d 683, 686 (6th Cir. 1988) (holding that the standard is "whether arbitrator's interpretation of the contract jeopardizes . . . public policy"), *cert denied*, 494 U.S. 1030 (1990); United States Postal Service v. American Postal Workers Union, 736 F.2d 822, 824 (1st Cir. 1984) (rejecting standard requiring that the award and issue violate statutory rule). For a comprehensive analysis of this split among the circuits, *see* Exxon Shipping Co. v. Exxon Seaman's Union, 993 F.2d 357, 363 (3d Cir. 1993).

the permissible scope of judicial review of arbitration awards has received the greatest amount of doctrinal and conceptual scrutiny in the context of disputes arising from collective bargaining agreements. Though many such cases misapprehend FAA strictures for vacatur with the common law doctrine of manifest disregard of the law, there has been some effort to tailor the doctrine to meet the specific underlying facts comprising the agreement at issue. More specifically, and by way of example, in the case of individual employment disputes courts have deemed it both desirable and logical to emphasize the strict enforcement of the arbitration agreement while promoting a *de minimus* review of arbitration awards. The jurisprudence suggests that in the context of noncollective bargaining agreements where individuals pursue statutory rights that have been congressionally enacted, arbitration appears to be viewed as merely a substitute for litigation. Thus, the doctrine of manifest disregard of the law, when applied to such cases, appears to be subject to a standard having greater proclivity for vacatur and enhancing judicial intervention in the arbitral process.

H. *MONTES v. SHEARSON LEHMAN BROS., INC.*: A LITERAL PARADIGM

An example of a scenario where judicial intervention in the form of a reviewing tribunal scrutinizing an arbitration award concerning a private individual's efforts to prosecute its rights arising from federally enacted legislation, that is, outside a collective bargaining context, minimizing an arbitration award's binding effect while maximizing judicial fiat in applying the manifest disregard of the law doctrine is eloquently detailed in the Eleventh Circuit's pronouncement in *Montes v. Shearson Lehman Bros., Inc.*[118] In addition, this opinion underscores the need to develop a transparent standard, universally applicable, for the manifest disregard of the law doctrine. As demonstrated in considerable detail after tracing the borders of a line of jurisprudence applying the doctrine, the Eleventh Circuit in effect circles back to the most fundamental principles in its effort to distill the meaning and, therefore, the applicability of the doctrine.

In *Montes*, plaintiff Delfina Montes ("Montes") was employed with Shearson Lehman Bros., Inc. ("Shearson Lehman"), where in addition to a forty-hour weekly work description requirement, she exceeded the forty-hour threshold with the expectation of receiving overtime pay. Interestingly, Shearson Lehman asserted that "although Montes worked more than forty hours weekly that she recorded on her time cards, she was exempt from the [Fair Labor Standards Act], 29 U.S.C. Section 201 et seq., FLSA's overtime payment requirements because she had either an 'administrative' or 'executive' position."[119] Upon leaving Shearson Lehman, Montes filed an action seeking overtime pay based upon the FLSA. Shearson Lehman removed the action to the Federal District Court for the Southern District of Florida. The district court referred the case to arbitration and the arbitration board issued an award denying Montes any relief and in favor of Shearson Lehman. After petitioning the district court to vacate the Board's decision without any success, Montes appealed to the Eleventh Circuit.[120]

[118] Montes v. Shearson Lehman Bros., Inc., 128 F.3d 1456 (11th Cir. 1997).

[119] *Id.* at 1456.

[120] *Id.*

Even though on appeal Montes raised numerous grounds for reversal of the district court's ruling and issuance of an order vacating the Board's decision, the gravamen of her appeal rested on the contention that "Shearson's attorney improperly urged the arbitration board specifically to disregard the FLSA to find in Shearson's favor and that the Board apparently did so."[121]

Upon a preliminary recitation of the governing *de novo* standard of review together with the presumptions accorded to arbitration awards,[122] the Court, finding analytical support in *Wilko v. Swan*, enunciated that arbitrators cannot be reversed for errors or misrepresentations of law.[123] In this connection the opinion provides that "every other circuit except the Fifth (which has declined to adopt any non-statutory grounds for vacating arbitration awards),[124] has expressly recognized that 'manifest disregard of the law' is an appropriate reason to review and vacate an arbitration panel's decision."[125] It is upon this explicit acknowledgment of the doctrine that the Eleventh Circuit struggles to distill from all authority the applicable governing standard for the doctrine.

Indeed, this opinion is emblematic of the patent want of a polestar setting forth the doctrine's elements in a consistent and uniform manner. The Court's recourse to such fundamental authority as *Black's Law Dictionary* and the *American Heritage Dictionary of the English Language* is testimony to this conceptual void. An effort to extrapolate a legal standard governing the doctrine by engaging in a superficial philological analysis of the doctrine's *name* is indeed somewhat arresting. Even though the Court premises this analysis with the caveat that there is a need to "give meaning to the distinction made by the Supreme Court in *Wilko* between an erroneous interpretation of the law and a manifest disregard of it," it still sallies to glean this critical distinction, quite remarkably, by reviewing the plain lexicological meaning of the term. The analysis merits citation in its entirety.

The Eleventh Circuit begins at the beginning by noting that "'[m]anifest' means 'evident to the senses, especially to the sight, obvious to the understanding, evident to the mind, not obscure or hidden, and is synonymous with open, clear, visible, unmistakable, indubitable, indisputable, evident, and self-evident.' *Black's*

121 *Id.* Montes also had bottomed her appeal on the averments that the Board's decision was "arbitrary, capricious, and violative of public policy." Also, she challenged the district court's referral of the case to arbitration. On this ground the Eleventh Circuit did affirm the district court's ruling. *Id.*

122 The Court referred to its ruling of four years earlier in *Brown v. Rauscher Pierce Refsnes, Inc.*, 994 F.2d 1175 (11th Cir. 1993), in an effort to delineate "the general circumstances in which arbitration awards can be vacated:

> Our review of commercial arbitration awards is controlled by the Federal Arbitration Act ("FAA"). *See* 9 U.S.C.A. §§1–16. Judicial review of arbitration awards under the FAA is very limited. *Booth v. Hume Publishing, Inc.*, 902 F.2d 925, 932 (11th Cir. 1990). *The FAA presumes that arbitration awards will be confirmed*, 9 U.S.C.A. §9, and enumerates only four narrow basis for vacatur, none of which are applicable in this case. In addition to these four statutory grounds for vacatur, we have recognized two additional non-statutory basis upon which an arbitration award may be vacated. First, an arbitration award may be vacated if it is arbitrary and capricious [citations omitted]. Second, an arbitration award may be vacated if enforcement of the award is contrary to public policy. (citations omitted) (emphasis supplied)

123 *Montes*, 128 F.3d at 1460.

124 Because the Eleventh Circuit opinion in *Montes v. Shearson Lehman* was rendered in 1997, it obviously could not have taken note of *Hughes Training, Inc., et al. v. Gracie Cook*, 254 F.3d, 588, 592 (stating that "[a]n arbitration agreement may therefore expand judicial review of an arbitration award beyond the scope of the Federal Arbitration Act.").

125 *Montes*, 128 F.3d at 1460.

Law Dictionary, 962 (6th Ed. 1990). *See also American Heritage Dictionary of the English Language*, 794 (New College Ed. 1981) ('Clearly apparent to the sight or understanding; obvious.')."[126] In this same vein, the Court treats the word "disregard." Here too it borrows from *Black's Law Dictionary* and *The American Heritage Dictionary of the English Language* for guidance:

> 'Disregard,' in turn, means 'to treat as unworthy of regard or notice; to take no notice of; to leave out of consideration; to ignore; to overlook; to fail to observe,' [citations omitted] ('To pay no attention or heed to; fail to consider; ignore.'). An arbitration board that incorrectly interprets the law has not manifestly disregarded it. It has simply made a legal mistake. To manifestly disregard the law, *one must be conscious of the law* and *deliberately ignore it.*[127]

Armed with this "standard," the Eleventh Circuit concludes that because the arbitrators in the award's summary of argument identifies the parties' plea, together with a complete absence of evidence in the record or elsewhere "to indicate that they did not heed this plea," it concludes that the doctrine attaches and thus vacates the award in reversing the district court's ruling.[128]

A careful reading of the opinion in its totality compellingly suggests that the Eleventh Circuit reached the right result but based upon questionable doctrinal grounds. Helpful as consultations to basic dictionaries may be, it is hardly a suggested methodology for identifying the conceptual difference between a *legal mistake* and the common law doctrine of *manifest disregard of the law*. To be sure, a more careful, jurisprudential, and helpful analysis that would create *stare decisis* to assist the practicing bar, the bench, captains of industry, prospective claimants, and arbitrators, entails a careful reading of precedent in the purest pursuit of the common law tradition to distill and extrapolate from that authority the various legal tests that have triggered application of the doctrine. Despite explicit reference to the adoption of the doctrine by practically all circuits, thus emphasizing its very juridic universality, the Court abandons rather starkly this methodology and proceeds to consult dictionaries. Moreover, the weight accorded to the absence of any evidence of record or elsewhere directed to the twin issues of *knowledge* and *intent* is even more puzzling. Positive affirmations from negative premises have hardly played a role in either the common law or civil law traditions in the formation and transformation of legal precepts. To the contrary, such inferences have been historically criticized, if not altogether disavowed.[129]

The analysis nowhere purports to reconcile any of the six standards here reviewed from the Second, Third, and Fourth Circuit Courts of Appeals with yet its new seventh paradigm based upon a plain-meaning analysis of the doctrine's nomenclature together with references to single-sentence citations of cases where the issue of manifest disregard of the law was addressed.

126 *Id.*

127 *Id.* (emphasis supplied).

128 *Id.* at 1461–62.

129 *See, e.g.*, David Fontana, *Refined Comparativism in Constitutional Law*, 49 UCLA L. Rev. 539 (2001). For completeness' sake, academic integrity compels emphasizing that the Eleventh Circuit did comb the record comprising witness examination for purposes of determining that Montes was correct in asserting that "because she lacked supervisory authority, she . . . does not fit within the 'exclusive' exemption from the FLSA" [citation omitted]. *See Montes*, 128 F.3d at 1463–1464.

The fundamental policies governing international commercial arbitration and domestic arbitration make clear that arbitral proceedings:

1. primarily, if not exclusively, concern the resolution of particular disputes among private parties,
2. do not entail the application of law to fact to effectuate the equitable administration of justice in the context of underlying public policies enacted by a sovereign in the exercise of its sovereignty through the different branches of government, especially the judicial and the legislative branches,
3. do not constitute binding or even persuasive precedent,
4. contemplate "appellate review" only on the narrowest of grounds,
5. are not bound by rules of judicial administration, evidence, and only to a limited extent, civil procedure,
6. do not adjudicate issues of great political importance, such as constitutional concerns, *per se*, but if at all only incidentally and without social transcendence,
7. contemplate the role of an arbitrator as materially distinct from that of a judge,
8. secure jurisdiction on contractual and not legislative ground,
9. enjoy equal hierarchy with judicial proceedings, and
10. establish a unique relationship with the judiciary pursuant to which courts presumably assume a subordinate role designed to facilitate the arbitral tribunal's resolution of specific disputes rather than intervene in the arbitral proceeding to influence substantively and materially the resolution of the dispute at issue.

The very nature of judicial processes, however, compels courts to seek consistent normative grounding and foundation on established precedent clearly elucidating accepted legal norms. With respect to the common law doctrine of manifest disregard of the law this imperative is yet to be fulfilled. While there is no doubt that the brilliance and majesty inherent in the common law process is identifiable once an effort is undertaken to trace the conceptual development of the doctrine from the rather abbreviated subordinate clause giving rise to it in *Wilko v. Swan*, through the twenty-four cases since 1980 through August 2007 that have vacated arbitration awards based on application of the doctrine, greater doctrinal development is necessary for purposes of reaching a single standard that integrates the seven discernible tests asserted in the corpus of this jurisprudence.[130]

[130] The seven tests command recitation:

First, the Second Circuit announced a two-prong test to be applied in the conjunctive. Pursuant to that paradigm, the manifest disregard of the law doctrine attaches where (i) a court finds that the arbitrator knew of a governing legal principle yet refused to apply it or ignored it all together, and (ii) the law ignored by the arbitrators was well defined, explicit, and clearly applicable to the case.

Second, the Second Circuit also fashioned a standard in accordance with which application of the doctrine would be warranted if instead of applying the substantive law of the governing jurisdiction, persuasive authority from other jurisdictions, irrespective of the recent nature of that jurisprudence, is applied. Put simply, only positive law or jurisprudence consonant with the substantive law contained in the arbitration clause may preclude the doctrine's attachment. Significantly, there is no reported authority as of August 2007 speaking to the issue of whether "persuasive authority" from a jurisdiction other than that identified in the arbitration clause would give rise to attachment of the doctrine in a scenario where the substantive law of the jurisdiction selected by the parties and memorialized beyond cavil in the arbitration clause is not on point or otherwise cannot fully dispose of a genuine material issue constituting a predicate to the equitable administration of justice in the arbitral proceeding.

I. THE SECOND PARADIGM: AVOIDING SECTION 1782

Neither the due process argument embedded in Article V of the Convention and in Section 10(a)(3) of the FAA arising from the averment that the arbitral tribunal foreclosed a party from presenting its case by not at all considering that party's evidence nor the possible contention that refusing to acknowledge language in an arbitral clause addressing proscription of the use of Section 1782 have been addressed by courts or commentators as of the publication date of this test.

Likewise, even in the absence of any reference to Section 1782 in the arbitration clause at issue, exercise of the arbitral tribunal's discretion in favor of foreclosing all consideration of discovery secured by a party pursuant to Section 1782 where the seat of the arbitration is outside the jurisdiction of the United States and its territories also constitutes a case of first impressions. While the construction of hypothetical paradigms may somewhat facilitate analysis of viable doctrinal developments that may in turn foster party-autonomy, predictive value, transparency of standard, and certainty, the necessity for the sustained analysis of developed jurisprudence is simply indispensable.

The second methodology for attempting to circumvent the use of Section 1782 in an international commercial arbitration also is best addressed at the formation stage of the arbitration clause. By agreeing to have the seat of the arbitral proceeding in the United States or its territories, the "use in a foreign or international tribunal" element of Section 1782 by definition cannot be met as a "foreign or international

Third, the Third Circuit articulated a paradigm bottomed on "reasonableness" or "a reasonable relationship" standard. Specifically, the Court attempted to enunciate the test as follows:

> If the interpretation can in any rational way be derived from the agreement, viewed in the light of its language, its context, and any other indicia of the parties' intention; only where there is manifest disregard of the agreement, totally unsupported by principles of contract construction and the law of the shop, may a reviewing court disturb the award.

This test can be succinctly summarized as holding that an arbitral award may not be vacated pursuant to the doctrine if the language of the operative agreement can be sustained as rational and coherent under any reasonable hypothesis of law, logic, or interpretive construction precepts.

Fourth, the doctrine shall attach upon a showing that an award issued based *only* on the arbitrators' view of the requirements of legislation rather than on the plain meaning of the operative contract.

Fifth, the "Essence of the Contract" test is recurring throughout the case law. The Fourth Circuit, however, explained that the doctrine attaches and vacatur shall issue where the arbitration award fails to draw its essence from the governing arbitration agreement. Here courts have carved a juridic space between "*misapplication of contractual interpretation*" and "*erroneous interpretation*", neither of which sufficed for nullification purposes, where vacatur is warranted in the presence of an interpretation that completely undermines the factual and juridic tenets underlying the contract at issue.

Sixth, in the context of a adjudicating confirmation petitions concerning collective bargaining contracts versus individual labor contracts where individual parties seek enforcement of statutory rights, the Fourth Circuit too has announced that there shall be a greater emphasis placed on the roll of a judicial tribunal reviewing the award's propriety and lesser weight accorded to the presumptions of correctness attaching to an arbitration award and *party-autonomy* in fashioning the underlying contract. The converse would hold true in the context of collective bargaining agreements. The different proclivities for vacatur rise to the level of a new standard in reviewing a petition seeking confirmation of an arbitration award.

Seventh, the Eleventh Circuit introduced a rudimentary but novel lexicographic analysis based upon the doctrine's very nomenclature.

tribunal" within the meaning of the statute refers to a non-U.S. jurisdiction. This technique is also susceptible to significant challenges. Most notably, the party seeking to prosecute a Section 1782 petition may credibly and meaningfully assert that despite the arbitration's seat in the United States or its territories, the proceeding is still "international" in nature and character and therefore within the statute's clearly contemplated purview.

Juridic support for this proposition may be found in the extraordinarily broad definition of "international" contained in Chapter 2 of the FAA.[131] That provision provides that an arbitration agreement falls within the Convention [Chapter 2-Convention on the Recognition and Enforcement of Foreign Arbitral Awards, 9 U.S.C. Sections 201–208] where the agreement at issue concerns (i) property located outside the United States, (ii) contemplates either performance or enforcement abroad, or (iii) has a "reasonable relation" with a foreign state.[132] Consequently, having both language proscribing recourse to Section 1782 in an arbitration agreement *and* a provision in the arbitration agreement identifying the United States or its territories as the arbitral seat far from ensures that a Section 1782 application shall not ensue as an important component of the procedural law governing the conduct of the arbitration.

With respect to this methodology, the complete absence of any jurisprudence or even commentaries addressing the issue only highlights our need to consider patience as a necessary virtue as we await the development of juridic and academic authority.

[131] When Congress ratified the Convention in 1970 it also enacted implementing legislation: 9 U.S.C. §s 201–208. Within this framework, only §202 offers a definition of whether an award is non-domestic. §201 simply implements the Convention. §203 provides for Federal Jurisdiction over all cases within the Convention's purview. §204 determines the venue in which those cases can be filed.

§205 provides for removal of all cases falling within the Convention. §206 provides a Federal district court adjudicating a proceeding arising from the Convention to order or compel arbitration. §207 in effect serves as a three year statute of limitations within which time frame a party may seek an enforcement order. §208 simply states that the FAA applies to proceeding brought under the Convention with the provisal that the statute not conflict with the Convention or the implementing legislation codified at §s 202–207.

[132] Chapter 2 of the FAA, 9 U.S.C. §202, reads:

§202. Agreement or award falling under the Convention.

An agreement or arbitral award arising out of a legal relationship, whether contractual or not, which is considered as commercial, including a transaction, contract, or agreement described in §2 of this title, fall under the Convention. An agreement or award arising out of such a relationship which is entirely between citizens of the United States shall be deemed not to fall under the Convention *unless the relationship involves property located abroad, envisages performance or enforcement abroad, or has some other reasonable relation with one or more foreign states.* For the purpose of this section a corporation is a citizen of the United States if it is incorporated or has its principal place of business in the United States.

CHAPTER 9

Perjury & Arbitration: The Honor System Where the Arbitrators Have the Honor and the Parties Have the System

Because there is no such thing as a *lex arbitrai* comparable to a *lex fori*, in part because of the ten premises already identified,[1] perjury in arbitration has not received the attention that the subject actually commands. Indeed, unlike judicial proceedings, witnesses in an arbitration rarely testify under oath. In fact, it is even unclear what effect, if any, the taking of such an oath may have from a legal perspective. Testifying under oath upon penalty of perjury in a judicial proceeding is conceptually coherent because the proceeding itself is but a sovereign's exercise of sovereignty through the judiciary. Naturally, no such exercise exists in the context of the resolution of a private dispute that is the creature of contract providing jurisdiction to "decision makers" labeled "arbitrators" exclusively on the basis of the parties' agreement and where the judiciary is subordinate to the role of facilitating the arbitral tribunal's pronouncements in discharging its responsibilities. It would be somewhat simplistic and a disfavor to the practicing bar, bench, arbitrators, parties, and captains of industry merely to ignore the need for doctrinal development and underscore whatsoever jurisprudence has been generated by this concern on such rudimentary political grounds alone.

The paucity of authority even touching upon this issue is alarming yet eloquent. What cases do exist, however, are invaluable points of departure for greater development and analysis. Moreover, it shall be suggested, some of the premises contained in this modest handful of authority support the proposition that the Federal Arbitration Act's (FAA's) most essential policies concerning vacatur of an award find the identical foundation in the Federal Rules of Civil Procedure. Therefore, the connection between those precepts that not only underlie but define arbitration itself as an alternative dispute resolution methodology, such as *party-autonomy*, uniformity, predictive value, certainty, and transparency of standard, and the Federal Rules of Civil Procedure governing discovery, finds a parallel with the conceptual nexus between Federal Rule of Civil Procedure 60(b) and 9 U.S.C. §10(a)(1). The deeper the inquiry into the tenets fundamental to the Federal Rules of Civil Procedure, the closer many of these rules appear to be with respect to those propositions that arbitration – both domestic and international – not only purports to preserve but also promotes.

In addition to the connection between Fed.R.Civ.P. 60(b) and Section 10(a)(1) of the FAA, the question of perjury in the context of arbitration exclusively cannot

[1] *See, supra*, at Chapter 8.

be set aside, if at all, on the theoretical basis already referenced if it is accepted that arbitration proceedings can never be completely severed from judicial intervention, even where such intervention is limited to facilitating the arbitral tribunal's management of the arbitration process and adjudicating issues concerning confirmation, recognition, and execution of arbitration awards. While it is not being suggested that either domestic or international arbitration regimes be modified to somehow invest sovereigns with normative authority to punish witnesses with criminal sanctions upon a finding of perjury regarding testimony rendered in an arbitral proceeding, truthful testimony likely to form part of a record that may be examined for execution purposes by a judicial tribunal somehow deserves to be encouraged. In this same vein, perjured testimony should and must be sanctioned and emphatically discouraged. Thus, more than just propositions resting on principles of symmetry suggest that both arbitration processes and judicial proceedings may best find their perfect workings where both systems are able to sanction perjured testimony and develop standards that may assist a reviewing tribunal in according such testimony due weight.

Fortunately, the issue addressing the extent to which perjured testimony may constitute grounds for vacatur was first reviewed by the Second Circuit Court of Appeals at the very apogee of its historical moment when it boasted many of the greatest legal talents in its distinguished history. Indeed, this issue finds as a point of departure a wonderful and little known chestnut authored by Judge Augustus Hand.

In *Karppinen, et al. v. Karl Kiefer Machine Co.*,[2] the Court reviewed a district court ruling affirming a petitioner's request for confirmation of an arbitral award. The Second Circuit affirmed the district court's decision. The facts of the case are simple and compel recitation. Allegedly, the appellant seller sold to the appellee purchaser a machine for "filling jams, jellies, preserves and marmalade into containers." The record also indicates that the actual purchase price of $7,950 was tendered and the machine timely delivered.[3] The purchaser appellee, however, averred that the machine was not fit for the purpose for which it was purportedly intended to be used and, therefore, sought to rescind the agreement. Predictably, the seller appellant denied this averment and the controversy was submitted to an *ad hoc* arbitration. The arbitral tribunal entered an award granting rescission and the purchaser immediately filed a motion for confirmation. The seller, however, sought vacatur and, in support of its cross-motion, asserted that the award had been induced by perjured testimony.[4] Upon issuance of a ruling in favor of the purchaser, an appeal to the Second Circuit ensued.

Remarkably, and perhaps not too surprisingly when viewed in the context of perhaps the Second Circuit's finest moment, as early as 1951, thirty-four years before the Supreme Court's seminal holding in *Mitsubishi*, Judge Hand emphasized

2 Karppinen, et al. v. Karl Kiefer Machine Co., 182 F.2d 32 (2d Cir. 1951).

3 *Id.*

4 *Id.* Also, "[a]n affidavit by the president of [the seller] stated that his company had contended during the arbitration proceedings that the complaints against its machine had been made in bad faith and that the buyers were seeking to rescind because they wished to buy a cheaper machine of a lower productive capacity." Moreover, the seller further asserted that the purchaser "had rebutted this contention by falsely testifying before the arbitrators that his company had purchased at a higher price-$8,150.00-another machine with even greater capacity."

that "[i]t goes without saying that there should be great hesitation in upsetting an arbitration award. The award here must stand unless it is abundantly clear that it was obtained through 'corruption, fraud, or undue means.'"[5] Furthermore, the Court observed that it would assume, as did the district court "that an arbitration award may be set aside in a case of material perjured evidence furnished the arbitrators by a prevailing party." Judge Hand, nonetheless, underscored that the Court would "not decide the somewhat disputed question whether the word 'fraud' in Section 10(a) of the Arbitration Act [FAA] has a broader scope than that word has when applied to permit a collateral attack on a judgment rendered upon perjured testimony."[6] It did state in *dicta* that to the extent that "perjury is 'fraud' within the meaning of the statute [9 U.S.C. §10(a)(1)], then, since it necessarily raises issue of credibility which has already been before the arbitrators once, the party relying on it must first show that he could not have discovered it during the arbitration, else he should have invoked it as a defense at that time."[7]

While the Second Circuit aptly refrained from adjudicating the related but unripe issue concerning whether the meaning of "fraud" within the FAA has a broader scope than its Federal Rule of Civil Procedure counterpart for vacating a judgment, it clearly crafted a test that would prove to be helpful in determining the extent to which federal district courts could exercise authority to review factual issues either passed upon by arbitrators or that otherwise should have been raised at the arbitration proceeding as the appropriate fact-finding tribunal of first instance. The reasoning is crisp and clear. *If* perjury is fraud within the meaning of the FAA, then it follows that it raises issues of *credibility*. Thus, the argument says, such issues already should have been determined during the arbitral process, and the movant must be charged with the burden of establishing that she could not have discovered this deception during the arbitration.

The fourth observation upon which the Court predicated its affirmance focused on the "materiality" of the alleged misrepresentation. Here the analysis was surgical and succinct; "[b]ut even on the assumption that an award may be vacated for perjury as to material evidence the judgment below must be affirmed."[8] Specifically, the Second Circuit noted that the question of the price that seller paid to a third party for a replacement machine was, to a large extent, extraneous to the issues arbitrated. The parties had duly identified those issues as limited to (i) the fitness of the machine to perform the work that it purportedly was sold to do, (ii) determining fault if indeed it was established that the machine was defective, and (iii) adjudication on whether the thirty-day limit in the guarantee had been waived. Consequently, the question of truthfulness concerning testimony addressing the narrow issue of replacement value is of no moment.

Having asserted this premise, it was rather axiomatic for the Court to conclude that extensive, or even any, oral advocacy on the question of replacement value had any bearing on the case. The specific language merits citation:

> It would be a surprising innovation if every party objecting to an arbitration award could recall all the witnesses in order to vacate the award on the basis of some evidence alleged to be untruthful which had but a remote and speculative bearing on the issues before the arbitrators. It is unnecessary for us to lay down

[5] *Id.* at 34.
[6] *Id.*
[7] *Id.* at 35.
[8] *Id.*

> any general rule as to when or how far oral hearings on questions of alleged perjured testimony before arbitrators should be allowed.[9]

The remoteness of the allegedly perjured testimony accorded the Court the opportunity prudently to exercise its discretion in not having to adjudicate two complex questions. First, does *perjury* constitute *fraud* within the FAA vacatur regime? Second, is the scope of *fraud* within the meaning of 9 U.S.C. §10(a)(1) broader than its Federal Rules of Civil Procedure counterpart directed at vacating a judgment? Three other queries of significant importance in the doctrinal development of the effects of perjury on vacating an arbitral award, and even on the conduct of an arbitration proceeding, were addressed. The Second Circuit conclusively ruled that only with "reluctance" should evidentiary hearings be held by a reviewing judicial tribunal to determine the extent to which perjured testimony supports a petition for vacatur. Also, the Court introduced considerations of "materiality" into any analysis entailing perjured testimony as a ground for nullification of an arbitration award. Although at first this inquiry has the semblance of ease of execution and analytical simplicity, upon reflection quite the opposite is true. Questions of materiality are often fact intensive and require laborious review of evidentiary or factual submissions. Moreover, a complete command of the operative dispositive legal issues is a predicate to any meaningful pronouncement on the subject. Finally, the Court adroitly crafted a test appropriately placing the burden on the movant to demonstrate that she could not have learned of the misrepresentation of the issue during the arbitration.

When appreciated through the prism of historical doctrinal development, the opinion is extraordinary at many levels. Foremost, rendered in 1951, it does not mention any of the badges of prejudice that nourished judicial skepticism of and disdain for arbitration. To the contrary, it stresses the need to proceed cautiously and with trepidation whenever reviewing an arbitration award. Consonant with this approach, which mirrors the FAA's fundamental policies and congressional intent, the Court purposefully limited the scope of its inquiry, albeit not articulated, in deference to arbitral proceedings and the new developing relationship between judiciary and arbitration. Lastly, in fashioning a test placing a considerable burden on a movant seeking vacatur on grounds of perjury to demonstrate that she could not have learned of the deception during the arbitral proceeding, the Court again is bestowing primacy on the arbitral tribunal's factual findings and exercise of judgment in assessing credibility.

It was not until sixteen years after the ruling in *Karppinen, et al. v. Karl Kiefer Machine Co.* that the issue of perjury as grounds for vacating an arbitration award resurfaced. On this occasion, the concern was raised as a secondary ground for vacatur and, not surprisingly, treated as such by the Court in *Kirschner v. West Company.*[10] Borrowing from Judge Hand's cornerstone premise in *Karppinen*, the district court remarked as to the secondary argument for nullification concerning perjury that:

> [S]ince it [perjury] necessarily raises issues of credibility which have already been before the arbitrators once, the party relying on it must first show that he

9 *Id.*
10 Kirschner v. West Company. 247 F.Supp. 550 (E.D.P.A. 1965).

> could not have discovered it during the arbitration, lest he should have invoked it as a defense at that time.[11]

The opinion, regrettably, did not touch upon any of the issues that Judge Hand identified but did not address. Moreover, it likewise shied from amplifying on those tenets that the *Karppinen* opinion raised for the first time in the history of U.S. jurisprudence. Instead, the analysis limited itself to the following four observations, none of which meaningfully contributed to any conceptual or doctrinal development in this very narrow area.

First, the district court granted considerable weight to the record finding that plaintiffs had refrained from producing "any after discovered evidence to establish that defendant's witnesses testified falsely." Second, the court noted that plaintiffs instead limited their reliance only to that evidence that had been introduced at the arbitration proceeding. Third, it was underscored that if "the perjury of defendant's witnesses [were] as patent as is now claimed, it should have been made apparent to the arbitrator in the proceedings beforehand."[12] Fourth, the district court opined that plaintiff's efforts to seek vacatur based upon perjury were presented in such a manner that it hardly constituted anything other than asking the district court judge to substitute his judgment for that of the arbitral tribunal.[13] It was on these bases that the award was confirmed.

The limited analysis in *Kirschner* merely stresses the need to find definitive answers to the questions raised but intentionally not addressed in *Karppinen*. Even though these issues are far from being exhausted, the analysis in *Biotronik Mess v. Medford Medical Instrument Co.*,[14] marks a significant doctrinal development. Most importantly, the district court in *Medford* understood with significant rigor the close conceptual connection between Fed.R.Civ.P. 60 and 9 U.S.C. Section 10(a)(1). Neither the analysis nor the holding, however, amplify on the inevitable theoretical consequences of finding a conceptual link between these two strictures, one fashioned for purposes of vacating judgments arising from a judicial proceeding and a second directed at the nullification of arbitration awards by a reviewing tribunal.[15] It should be appreciated that the opinion is extraordinary in its internal organization, dividing the issue of fraud quite skillfully into "Parts I and II." We shall only analyze *Part I*.

[11] *Id.* at 553 (citing Karppinen v. Karl Kiefer Mach. Co., 187 F.2d 32, 35 (2d. Cir. 1951)).

[12] *Id.* at 553. This argument is but a modest permutation of Judge Hand's stricture that the movement seeking vacatur on the ground of perjury must establish that the subject misrepresentation could not have been discovered at the time of the arbitration.

[13] *Id.*

[14] Biotronik Mess v. Medford Medical Instrument Co., 415 F.Supp. 133 (D.C.N.Y. 1976).

[15] 9 U.S.C. §10(a) of the FAA applies not only to domestic awards, but also to actions brought under the Convention. *See e.g.* 9 U.S.C. §208 (applying Chapter 1 (9 U.S.C. §§1–16) to actions and proceedings brought under Chapter 2 (9 U.S.C. §§201–208) to the extent that Chapter 1 does not conflict with Chapter 2); Indocomex Fibres Pte Ltd. v. Cotton Co. Int'l, 916 F.Supp. 721, 727–728 (N.D.Ill. 1996) (finding fraud defense under §10(a) within the "contrary to public policy" defense under the Convention). The Court in *Indocomex Fibres Pte.* further reasoned that fraud under §10(a) "requires a showing of bad faith during the arbitration proceedings, such as bribery, undisclosed bias of the arbitrator, or willfully destroying evidence, and further requires that such evidence of fraud was unavailable to the arbitrator during the course of the proceeding." *Indocomex*, 916 F.Supp. at 728 (discussing cases).

That action arises from a petition seeking enforcement of an arbitration award entered by the International Chamber of Commerce Court of Arbitration at Berne, Switzerland. Petitioner, Biotronik Mess-Und Therapiegeraete GmbH & Co., ("Biotronik") was a West German manufacturer of implantable cardiac pacemakers and accessories. Respondent Medford Medical Instruments Co. ("Medford") was a New Jersey corporation having its principal place of business in Medford, New Jersey. Critical to the dispute was Medford's legal relationship to Biotronik as Biotronik's American distributor for approximately three years.[16]

The dispute centers around three agreements where only the third plays a decisive role in generating an issue of "first impression."[17] In the first agreement, Biotronik allegedly provided Medford the exclusive right to market its products in the United States (the "First Exclusivity"). A second exclusive distributorship was negotiated providing for a twelve-month duration period ("Second Exclusivity"). Upon the running of the twelve-month time frame in the Second Exclusivity, Biotronik appointed a different firm to serve as its new American distributor.[18] Six months into the post Second Exclusivity twelve-month time frame a dispute arose between the parties concerning shipments of products that Biotronik purportedly had tendered to Medford prior to expiration of the Second Exclusivity. It was for these products delivered and allegedly not paid that Biotronik demanded payment. While Medford did not deny an obligation for the shipments, it did assert that any such liability must be treated together with liability running against Biotronik purportedly arising from a Third Agreement entered into by the parties that allegedly, among other claims, renewed Medford's distributorship. Consequently, Medford proposed that both parties resolve their differences by not asserting claims otherwise held.[19] An arbitration initiated by Biotronik ensued and an order was entered in Biotronik's favor.

Understandably, Biotronik petitioned the Federal District Court for the District of New Jersey, the jurisdiction encompassing Medford's principal place of business, for enforcement of the award. Medford principally opposed the award on the theory that the Third Agreement, executed only "one day prior to the termination of Medford's distributorship,"[20] entitled Medford to significant royalties incident to Biotronik's sale of pacemakers in the United States during a two-year time frame. Thus, reasoned Medford, it had no obligation in favor of Biotronik. Moreover,

16 *Biotronik*, 415 F. Supp. 133.

17 *Id.* at 138, n. 15 (stating that "[a]lthough cases under 9 U.S.C. §10(a) are persuasive, no case seems to have considered the precise question presented here. However, further confirmation in the caselaw that the instant facts do not constitute fraud may be obtained from cases arising under Federal Rule of Civil Procedure 60(b)).

18 *Id.* at 135.

19 *Id.* at 136. Significantly, the Second Exclusivity contained the following arbitration clause:

> 13. In the event of any controversy or claim arising out of or related to any provision of this agreement, or the breach thereof, the parties shall attempt to reach an amicable settlement. If they fail to agree, the dispute shall be settled under the Rules of Conciliation and Arbitration of the International Chamber of Commerce, Paris, France, by three arbitrators appointed in accordance with the laws then prevailing. The arbitration shall take place in Berne, Switzerland. German material law (Materielles Recht) and German law of Procedure (Prozessrecht) must be applied. The award shall be final and binding and may be entered in any court having jurisdiction or application may be made to any court for judicial acceptance of the award or an order for enforcement, as the case may be.

20 *Id.*

Medford alleges that enforcement should be denied, in part because "Biotronik's failure to disclose the Third Agreement to the arbitral tribunal triggers application of 9 U.S.C. Section 10(a), providing that any award 'procured by . . . fraud' within the meaning of Section 10(a) of the FAA (9 U.S.C. Section 10(a)), n. 11 and that 'fraud', even though not one of the defenses enumerated in Article V of the Convention, became a defense through the incorporation provision of 9 U.S.C. Section 208."[21]

In finding that the award entered in favor of Biotronik is eminently enforceable, the Court found analytical support for its holding in two distinct lines of authority. First, it noted that "[m]ost courts have held that an arbitration award is not fraudulently obtained within the meaning of Section 10(a) of the United States Arbitration Act when the protesting party had an opportunity to rebut his opponent's claims at the arbitration hearing."[22] Here the rules fashioned in *Karppinen* and later applied in *Kirschner* were followed as helpful analogous scenarios concerning alleged misrepresentations or omissions comprising part of an arbitral proceeding. Thus, the district court correctly noted that while Medford asserts that the arbitral tribunal was defrauded because of Biotronik's omission in referencing the Third Agreement, the issue is more accurately recast as whether Biotronik in the first instance was invested with the normative obligation of presenting evidence to the arbitral tribunal that favors Medford's claims and defenses.

Second, the district court keenly observed that there is a *functional* connection between Fed.R.Civ.P. 60(b)[23] and 9 U.S.C. Section 10(a), as both strictures concern vacating a final judgment or order. Significantly, the Court outright *assumed* that "fraud" within the meaning of Fed.R.Civ.P. 60(b) is the same as that pursuant to Section 10(a)(1). This conceptual leap is significant. The Second Circuit in *Karppinen* explicitly reserved adjudication on the very narrow and specific issue of whether "the word 'fraud' in *Section 10(a)* of the Arbitration Act has a broader scope than that word has when applied so as to permit a collateral attack on a judgment rendered upon perjured testimony."[24] The district court's analysis that there is no meaningful distinction between the meanings of "fraud" within Fed.R.Civ.P. 60 and 9 U.S.C. Section 10(a)(1) does not rest on review of *any* authority. In addition, it completely omits to identify the "scope" issue that Judge Hand felt impelled to raise as a possible concern.

[21] Medford also asserts that should fraud not constitute a defense pursuant to the §208 incorporation provision, it should be cognizable as a defense within the "public policy" stricture contained in Article V(2)(b) of the Convention, n. 12. *Id.*

[22] *Id.* at 137.

[23] Fed.R.Civ.P. 60(b) in pertinent part reads:

> (b) **Mistakes; Inadvertence; Excusable Neglect; Newly Discovered Evidence; Fraud, etc.** On motion and upon such terms as are just, the court may relieve a party or a party's legal representative from a final judgment, order, or proceeding for the following reasons: (1) mistake, inadvertence, surprise, or excusable neglect; (2) *newly discovered evidence which by due diligence could not have been discovered in time to move for a new trial under Rule 59(b);* (3) *fraud (whether heretofore denominated intrinsic or extrinsic), misrepresentation, or other misconduct of an adverse party*; (4) the judgment is void; (5) the judgment has been satisfied, released, or discharged, or a prior judgment upon which it is based has been reversed or otherwise vacated, or it is no longer equitable that the judgment should have prospective application; or (6) *any other reason justifying relief from the operation of the judgment.* The motion shall be made within a reasonable time, and for reasons (1), (2), and (3) not more than one year after the judgment, order, or proceeding was entered or taken. (emphasis supplied)

[24] *Karppinen*, 187 F.2d at 34. Judge Hand in *Karppinen* also reserved judgment on the question of whether perjury was fraud for purposes of 9 U.S.C. §10(a)(1).

The district court did state that a "comparison between Section 10(a) and Rule 60(b) is sound, since, just as Section 10(a) counteracts a strong policy favoring the finality of arbitration awards [citations omitted], so Rule 60(b) opposes the strong policy favoring the finality of judgments [citation omitted]."[25] The command in Rule 60(b) is clear and benefits from extensive jurisprudence interpreting this provision. Indeed, "in order to justify setting aside a final judgment on the grounds of fraud 'it must appear that such fraud charged really prevented the party complaining from making a full and fair defense [citations omitted].'"[26]

In addition to borrowing support from authority suggesting that a mere omission, without more, shall not rise to the level of fraud justifying nullification of a final judgment, the Court rested on Third District authority that in turn relied on *Karppinen,* enunciating that just because an arbitration award *may* be vacated upon a showing of fraud:

> Does not obliterate the hesitation with which courts should view efforts to re-examine awards [citing *Karppinen.*] To do otherwise would defeat the primary advantages of speed and finality which led to the development of arbitration in business disputes [citations omitted].[27]

Medford's contentions certainly did not fall within the purview of Fed.R.Civ.P. 60(b) and, therefore, according to the district court's reasoning, nor can it be construed as within the ambit of Section 10(a)(1). If the premise that fraud under Fed.R.Civ.P. 60(b) is the same as fraud within the meaning of Section 10(a)(1), then the Court's holding in favor of enforcement and rejecting Medford's claims bottomed on omission appears proper and well-reasoned. The holding is further bolstered by "considerations of international reciprocity [that] furnish an additional reason to construe defenses narrowly."[28] Because the district court held that the arbitral award was not procured through fraud within the meaning of Section 10(a)(1), it never reached the issue of whether "the defense of fraud with a 9 U.S.C. Section 10(a) may be asserted in an enforcement action under the Convention by reason of 9 U.S.C. Section 208."[29]

It is less than clear whether *Medford* truly may stand for the proposition that fraud in the context of Fed.R.Civ.P. 60(b) has the same legal significance as fraud within the ambit of Section 10(a)(1). As noted, other than the general observation that both norms provide parties with an opportunity to challenge considerable presumptions

[25] *Biotronik*, 415 F.Supp. at 138.

[26] *Id.* Borrowing support from United States v. International Telephone & Telegraph Corp., 349 F.Supp. 22, 29 (D. Conn. 1972), the Court elaborated on the nature and character of conduct warranting vacatur of a final judgment or order:

> Only the most egregious conduct, such as bribery of a judge or member of a jury, or the fabrication of evidence by a party in which an attorney is implicated, will constitute fraud on the court [citations omitted]. Less egregious misconduct, *such as non-disclosure to the court of facts allegedly pertinent to the matter before it, will not ordinarily rise to the level of fraud on the court.* Citing *Kupferman v. Consolidated Research and Manufacturing Co.*, 459 F.2d 1072 (2d Cir. 1972) (emphasis supplied).

[27] *Biotronik*, 415 F.Supp. at 139.

[28] *Id.* at 139. The Second Circuit has stated:

> [C]onsiderations of reciprocity – considerations given express recognition in the Convention itself – counsel courts to invoke the public policy defense with caution lest foreign courts frequently accept it as a defense to enforcement of arbitral awards rendered in the United States. Parsons & Whittemore Overseas Co. v. Societe Generale de L'Industrie Du Papier (RAKTA), 508 F.2d 969, 973–74 (2d Cir. 1974).).

[29] *Id.*

of finality accorded to final judgments or other decrees, it shied from any effort to develop other premises that would further support this proposition, which was all but assumed in the opinion. Application of Fed.R.Civ.P. 60(b)jurisprudence, policy underpinnings, and analysis to determine whether the omission of a potentially material fact from an arbitral tribunal constitutes grounds for declining enforcement appears to be novel, and perhaps even helpful, because it raises more questions than are answered by the analysis.

What are the doctrinal tenets that would support application of a Fed.R.Civ.P. 60(b) analysis to a Section 10(a)(1) defense to an enforcement proceeding? Is "fraud" within the meaning of Fed.R.Civ.P. 60(b) the same as within the ambit of 9 U.S.C. Section 10(a)(1)? Does 9 U.S.C. Section 10(a)(1) have a broader scope for fraud than that applied to collateral attacks on judgments entered in judicial proceedings? Is "perjury" the equivalent of "fraud" for a 9 U.S.C. Section 10(a)(1) analysis, or even more generally within the FAA? Is it possible to infer the extent to which a material omission may have fraudulently procured an arbitral award without examining the arbitrators? More recent decisions addressing the specific issue of misleading or false statements communicated to the arbitral panel as the ground for opposing enforcement of an arbitration award and seeking vacatur have not seen occasion to address these issues.[30]

To date the jurisprudence does not address these questions. As an initial approach to finding possible answers, it is here suggested that courts and commentators alike have to distill those principles underlying arbitral and judicial proceedings that find common ground. A second step would entail the extent to which those principles may best or only function within a regime created by a sovereign's exercise of sovereignty through a judiciary or legislature. Where functional common ground between judicial and arbitration norms, such as with the operation of Fed.R.Civ.P. 60(b)and 9 U.S.C. Section 10(a)(1) in challenging the meaningful presumption accorded to final judgments, decrees, or awards, can be distilled without having to consider underlying issues concerning public policy objectives in the implementation of norms because of having their origins in a sovereign's exercise of sovereignty (judiciary, legislative, or executive), then a workable framework can certainly be gleaned as helpful. We already have analyzed a concrete example. Best to revisit it.

The similitude between Fed.R.Civ.P. 60(b)and 9 U.S.C. Section 10(a)(1) is a primary example of a situation where a federal norm arising from the exercise of sovereignty (Fed.R.Civ.P. 60(b)) while functionally connected in its objective to an arbitration norm (Section 10(a)(1)), may not necessarily be used as an analytical tool for fashioning application methodologies for its arbitration "counterpart."

Without purporting to set forth a test, but rather only suggesting a workable and practical guide, the predicate inquiry concerning whether a judicially or legislatively enacted norm may serve as a paradigm for the doctrinal development of an arbitral

[30] *See, e.g.*, Dandong Shuguang Axel Corp. Ltd. v. Brilliance Machinery Co., 2001 U.S. Dist. LEXIS 7493 at *19 (N.D.Ca. 2001) ("stating that fraud under §10(a) requires a showing of bad faith during the arbitration proceedings, such as bribery, undisclosed bias of the arbitrator, or willfully destroying evidence, and further requires that such evidence of fraud was unavailable to the arbitrator during the course of the proceeding. Thus, when one party knowingly makes false statements to or conceals evidence from the arbitration panel, a court may set aside the award.") (internal citations and quotations omitted).

precept should contemplate reasoned examination of four preliminary questions. First, is the implementation of the judicial or legislative norm dependent upon other judicial or legislative norms for its efficacy? Second, is the judicial or legislative norm being used as a paradigm primarily or just incidentally furthering a general juridic or legislative policy? Third, assuming that such a norm in fact is furthering a juridic or legislative policy, does such a policy comport with its arbitration "counterpart?" Fourth, is the legislative or juridic norm at issue a "functional" equivalent (or semiequivalent) to its arbitration "counterpart?" The answer to these four inquiries, together with a balancing test, should suffice for providing an initial orientation on the extent to which such a paradigm may be applicable to a reasoned examination of the meaning and construction of an arbitral precept or norm.

Following through with the Fed.R.Civ.P. 60(b)and Section 10(a)(1) analysis, it appears that the answer to the first inquiry (the extent to which the rule is dependent on other rules within a specific framework) is in the affirmative, or arguably so. Specifically, a Fed.R.Civ.P. 60(b) challenge assumes an adversarial system where the parties *were* and *are* at liberty to conduct discovery as contemplated by the Federal Rules of Civil Procedure. The same generally does not hold true for the "counterpart" arbitral parties seeking to oppose enforcement and impose vacatur pursuant to 9 U.S.C. Section 10(a)(1). It therefore follows that on this single ground the scope of or standard for vacatur pursuant to Section 10(a)(1) should be broader when premised on grounds of perjury or fraud because the parties would have been less likely to discover the misrepresentation and raise it during the arbitral tribunal where the parties are vastly limited when compared to parties litigating under the Federal Rules of Civil Procedure in their ability to conduct extensive discovery or discovery at all.

The second (whether the judicial or legislative norm is primarily or incidentally intended to further a sovereign's policy) and third (if so, does such a policy comport with the arbitration norm's policy objective) inquiries seem to suggest an answer in the affirmative. The unquestioned goal of both Fed.R.Civ.P. 60(b)and Section 10(a)(1) is identical. Both rules are concerned with providing nonprevailing parties with a viable and legitimate methodology for challenging a meaningful presumption accorded to final judgments, decrees, orders, and awards entered as the end product of contentious proceedings. In particular, arbitration awards and final judgments are presumed final and binding. Moreover, the burden is placed on the movant to demonstrate, in accordance with the issue here discussed, that the award was procured by fraud perpetrated on the tribunal pursuant to false statements (perjury) The twin policies of finality and correctness engrafted upon final judgments and awards, and the precept that a nonprevailing party should not be foreclosed under narrow and limited circumstances from challenging such judgments and awards, are not materially different with respect to Fed.R.Civ.P. 60(b) and Section 10(a)(1).

The fourth inquiry (whether the legislative or juridic norm is the *functional* equivalent of its arbitration "counterpart"), also appears to be answered in the affirmative based upon the two immediately preceding inquiries.

After applying this test, it is only appropriate for the analysis to benefit from a balancing examination that would help in determining whether, if any, answers in the affirmative are outweighed by negatives. Here, the question of perjury or an underlying misrepresentation on the court may or may not be so factually intensive as to command the panoply of discovery devices available to parties to a federal judicial proceeding. One additional consideration is that direct, cross, and redirect examination techniques common to judicial proceedings also are severely constrained in arbitration processes. Irrespective of the merits of these limitations, the result is overwhelmingly suggestive of greater restrictions placed upon parties to an arbitration with respect to their ability to ferret out perjured testimony or fraud. Reason does seem to dictate that despite the presumption of correctness and the public policy in favor of finality attaching to arbitration awards, the issue of award procurement resulting from misleading the arbitral tribunal through perjury certainly argues in favor of a more narrow scope for fraud within Section 10(a)(1) than required under a Fed.R.Civ.P. 60(b)analysis.

The gravity of the question of perjury in arbitration is not exemplified by the paucity of authority addressing this issue. As the authority now stands, the need for a rubric that would first discourage perjury by imposing sanctions, albeit not the criminal penalties that a state or geopolitical subdivision may prescribe, merits serious consideration. Perjury in arbitration technically may still be defined as lying under oath on issues material to the case or outcome dispositive punishable by the forfeiture of claims or defenses in the case of parties, or the discretion to draw an opposite and negative inference from the testimony against the party on whose behalf it is being proffered, in the case of non-parties.

Further, it is not enough merely to limit a 9 U.S.C. Section 10(a)(1) analysis to the very general test crafted by the few courts that have grappled with this issue. The proposition is that if perjury is fraud, the fraud thus raises an issue of credibility. It then follows that the issue necessarily must have been raised, overtly or tacitly, before the tribunal of first instance and already assessed by the factfinders. This is simply too general and circular an argument. Under this rationale, there is no need for a reviewing tribunal ever to consider vacatur of an arbitration award on the ground of perjury directed at the arbitral tribunal because, at the conclusion of the analysis, the alleged misrepresentation can always be reduced to or characterized as a credibility issue. Accordingly, the four-prong "orientation test" here suggested, together with a balancing of negatives and affirmatives analysis, should be adopted in considering such issues as the extent to which a legislative or juridic norm, benefiting from extensive commentary and case law, should serve as a paradigm in the construction and application of its arbitration "counterpart." In the case of perjury in arbitration, the need is clear.

Lastly, though it is likely to sound like heresy of the rankest ilk, witnesses to an arbitration proceeding, including parties, should be compelled to take an oath consonant with a framework akin to the one suggested here. Only thus will the allocation of honor in an honor system achieve the desired objective of efficacy in the resolution of particular and individual disputes. Who knows? Occasionally, perhaps even *truth* may result from such a process.

CHAPTER 10

Developments in the Apportionment of Jurisdiction Between Arbitrators and Courts Concerning the Validity of a Contract Containing an Arbitration Clause, and Transformations Regarding the Severability Doctrine

The doctrinal development of arbitration in the United States in large measure constitutes the rediscovery and renaissance of the venerable principle of party-autonomy.[1] This precept, in turn, certainly cannot be conceptually severed from the juridic dignity accorded to contractual agreements. It followed from the four historical propositions that deemed arbitration to be a second-tier dispute resolution methodology;[2] that an arbitration clause was (i) neither a "free standing" contract separate and distinct from the underlying agreement embodying it, nor (ii) an agreement enjoying equal dignity with commercial contracts of whatsoever ilk.

The doctrinal development of arbitration in the United States in large measure has sought to place arbitration at the same level as judicial proceedings. As referenced, this effort, however, has been undertaken parallel with the transformation of arbitration agreements from the status of a secondary genre of a "binding"[3] contract to one equal in all respects to enforceable commercial contracts. This transformation required sustained analysis of four rudimentary questions.

1 For purposes of this analysis it is assumed that the "demise" of judicial intervention in arbitral proceedings is tantamount to *party-autonomy* in conformance with basic premises upon which the adversarial system rests. In fact, in tracing the borders of this development, it becomes clear that "intervention" itself is transformed into "assistance" and "cooperation." Such that instead of assuming a protagonist's role in arbitration proceedings, courts shall assume the more modest subordinated task of supporting arbitration proceedings with respect to such issues as the compulsory process of witnesses and the recognition and enforcement of arbitral awards.

2 These badges of prejudice have been identified as: (i) the contention that arbitration ousts jurisdiction of otherwise courts having competent jurisdiction over parties and subject matter, (ii) the proposition that arbitration is ill-suited as a dispute resolution methodology for certain classes of federally enacted statutory causes of action aimed at protecting specific classes of prospective victims, (iii) the assertion that arbitration must be conducted under the auspices of courts, and (iv) the perception that arbitrators lack the requisite training and skill set to adjudicate justice equitably with respect to complex and specialized subject matters.

3 The many exceptions to which arbitration agreements were submitted by judicial fiat by dint of the four propositions identified in the immediately preceding footnote alone, rendered it a euphemism to use the word "binding" in an arbitral context as it is used when discussing commercial contracts or judicial decrees. Because of the historical legacies of prejudice that nourished judicial skepticism for and rejection of arbitration as an alternative dispute resolution methodology, irrespective of any finding of wrongdoing or illicit activity attendant to an arbitration agreement, a court may simply render the arbitration clause unenforceable as a matter of "policy" without more. This status identifies a quite unique space that provided judges with virtually unbridled discretion in adjudicating the propriety of an arbitration clause. Mere recourse to any of the four referenced propositions generated by historical prejudice and ignorance would have sufficed for voiding an otherwise perfectly enforceable arbitration contract.

First, as a matter of substantive federal arbitration law, is an arbitration provision severable from the remaining contract? Second, is a challenge to a contract containing an arbitration clause to be adjudicated by a judge or an arbitrator? Third, is there a federal substantive law created by the Federal Arbitration Act (FAA)? Fourth, is such a law applicable in state as well as federal courts? These four inquiries found final resolution on February 21, 2006,[4] but only after first having been identified, albeit embryonically, on June 12, 1967.[5]

Their answers will in turn resolve the issue of whether a court or an arbitrator should consider the claim that a contract containing an arbitration provision is void for illegality. It is only after resolving this final issue that the answers to these four questions shall find their perfect working. Moreover, in addition to addressing systematically these four questions, the precepts of party-autonomy implicitly, if not explicitly, had to play an important role if the doctrinal development is to be internally consistent as well as harmonious with the common law framework predicated on an individualistic adversarial party paradigm. In this same vein, party-autonomy would best be integrated into any analysis, in part, by minimizing or redefining the role of judicial intervention in arbitral proceedings.

With respect to this last proposition, it has been assumed that without some degree of judicial *cooperation* or *assistance*, in contrast with "intervention," arbitration proceedings simply could not be viable, that is, they would not exist. Accordingly, any doctrinal development of meaningful consequence to the elevation of arbitration to the same level as judicial proceedings and, consequently, of the rediscovery and reintroduction of the principle of party-autonomy as to the law and jurisprudence governing, configuring, and defining arbitration, would be conceptually necessary. Revisiting *Prima Paint v. Flood & Conklin Mfg. Co.* is an indispensable predicate to any analysis seeking to identify the doctrinal development that engrafts upon arbitration clauses – arbitration contracts – the same status as commercial contracts as a matter of law.

A. WHO DECIDES THE VALIDITY OF A CONTRACT HAVING AN ARBITRATION CLAUSE: JUDGE OR ARBITRATOR?

The exact issue before the Court in *Prima Paint* was "whether the federal courts or an arbitrator is to resolve a claim of 'fraud in the inducement,' under a contract governed by the United States Arbitration Act of 1925, where there is no evidence that the contracting parties intended to withhold that issue from arbitration."[6] The facts giving rise to this query are eloquent enough. Plaintiff, Prima Paint Co., filed an action in federal district court premised on a purchase agreement and a consulting agreement arising from its acquisition of defendant's business and retention of defendant's chairman in an advisory capacity. The complaint alleged, among other things, that defendant had "fraudulently represented that it was solvent and able to perform its contractual obligations, whereas it was in fact insolvent and

[4] On this date the Supreme Court issued its landmark opinion in *Buckeye Check Cashing, Inc. v. Cardegna*, 545 U.S. 440 (2006).

[5] On this date the Supreme Court issued its opinion in *Prima Paint Corp. v. Flood & Conklin Mfg. Co.*, 388 U.S. 395 (1967).

[6] *Prima Paint*, 388 U.S. at 396.

intended to file a petition under Chapter XI of the Bankruptcy Act, 52 Stat. 905, 11 U.S.C. s. 701 et seq., shortly after execution of the consulting agreement."[7]

Simultaneously with the filing of its complaint, Prima Paint Co. moved the Court for issuance of an order enjoining defendant from proceeding with arbitration. Defendant cross-moved to stay the district court action pending conclusion of all arbitral labor under the theory that the issue presented, whether there was fraud in the inducement of the consulting agreement, was a question for the arbitrators and not the district court.[8] Defendant's motion to stay the legal proceeding pending arbitration was granted, and the Court held "that a charge of fraud in the inducement of a contract containing an arbitration clause as broad as this one[9] was a question for the arbitrators and not for the court."[10] An appeal ensued to the Second Circuit, which dismissed Prima Paint's petition, holding that "the contract in question evidenced a transaction involving interstate commerce; that under the controlling *Robert Lawrence Co.* decision a claim of fraud in the inducement of the contract generally – as opposed to the arbitration clause itself – is for the arbitrators and not for the courts; and that this rule – one of 'national substantive law' – governs even in the face of a contrary rule."[11] The Supreme Court affirmed the Second Circuit's ruling.

At the outset of a three-prong analysis, the Supreme Court held that the consulting agreement between plaintiff, Prima Paint Co., and defendant squarely fell within the realm of contracts specified in Sections 1 and 2 of the FAA and, therefore, provided a legal foundation for invoking the stay provision of Section 3.[12] The

[7] *Id.* at 398.

[8] *Id.* at 399.

[9] The clause at issue read:

> any controversy or claim arising out of or relating to this Agreement, or the breach thereof, shall be settled by arbitration in the City of New York, in accordance with the rules then obtaining of the American Arbitration Association. . . . *Id.* at 398.

[10] *Id.* at 399. The district court found analytical support for this proposition in *Robert Lawrence Co. v. Devonshire Fabrics, Inc.*, 271 F.2d 402 (2d Cir. 1959), *cert. granted,* 362 U.S. 909, *appeal dismissed*, 364 U.S. 801 (1960).

[11] *Id.* at 400.

[12] *Id.* at 401. 9 U.S.C. §§1–3 read:

> Chapter 1 – General Provisions [9 U.S.C. §§1–3]
>
> §1. "Maritime transactions" and "Commerce" defined; exceptions to operation of title "Maritime transactions," as herein defined, means charter parties, bills of lading of water carriers, agreements relating to wharfage, supplies furnished vessels or repairs to vessels, collisions, or any other matter in foreign commerce which, if the subject of controversy, would be embraced within admiralty jurisdiction; "commerce," as herein defined means commerce among the several States or with foreign nations, or in any Territory of the United States or in the District of Columbia, or between any such Territory and another, or between any Territory and any State or foreign nation, or between the District of Columbia and any State or Territory or foreign nation, but nothing herein contained shall apply to contracts of employment of seamen, railroad employees, or any other class of workers engaged in foreign or interstate commerce.
>
> §2. Validity, Irrevocability, and Enforcement of Agreements to Arbitrate.
>
> A written provision in any maritime transaction or a contract evidencing a transaction involving commerce to settle by arbitration a controversy thereafter arising out of such contract or transaction, or the refusal to perform the whole or any part thereof, or an agreement in writing to submit to arbitration an existing controversy arising out of such a contract, transaction, or refusal, shall be valid, irrevocable, and enforceable, save upon such grounds as exist at law or in equity for the revocation of any contract.
>
> §3. Stay of Proceedings Where Issue Therein Referrable to Arbitration.
>
> If any suit or proceeding be brought in any of the Courts of the United States upon any issue referrable to arbitration under an agreement in writing for such arbitration, the Court in which such suit is pending,

Court further underscored that plaintiff had "acquired a New Jersey paint business serving at least 175 wholesale clients in a number of states, and secured [defendant's] assistance in arranging the transfer of manufacturing and selling operations from New Jersey to Maryland."[13] Thus, it concluded that "[t]here could not be a clearer case of a contract evidencing a transaction in interstate commerce."[14]

Second, the Court resolved a split of authority among the circuits on the narrow and specific question of whether a claim of fraud in the inducement of a contract containing an arbitration clause is to be adjudicated by a federal court or referred to arbitration.[15]

Even though the Supreme Court observed and stressed that, pursuant to a plain language analysis, the FAA's statutory language does not expressly and necessarily provide federal courts with authority to adjudicate fraud in the inducement claims, Section 4 plainly does not relate to or contemplate scenarios where a stay of a federal proceeding is petitioned in deference to an arbitral proceeding.[16] The Court,

> upon being satisfied that the issue involved in such suit or proceeding is referrable to arbitration under such an agreement, shall on application of one of the parties stay the trial of the action until such arbitration has been had in accordance with the terms of the agreement, providing the applicant for the stay is not in default in proceeding with such arbitration.

13 *Id.* 14 *Id.*

15 On this issue the Second Circuit Court of Appeals holds that pursuant to federal law arbitration clauses are "separable" from the contract of which they form a part and, consequently, absent a claim that the fraud at issue was specifically directed to the arbitration clause itself, a broad arbitration clause shall be found to encompass arbitration of the averment that the contract itself was induced by fraud. *See, e.g.*, Robert Lawrence Co. v. Devonshire Fabrics, Inc., 271 F.2d 402 (2d Cir. 1959); In Re Kinoshita & Co., 287 F.2d 951 (2d Cir. 1961). In stark contrast, the First Circuit Court of Appeals had repeatedly held that the issue of "severability" must be governed by state law. The argument thus says that where a state deems such a clause as inseparable from the corpus of the contract, a claim for fraud in the inducement *must* be adjudicated by court of competent jurisdiction. *See, e.g.*, Lummus Co. v. Commonwealth Oil Ref. Co., 280 F.2d 915, 923–924 (1st Cir.), *cert. denied,* 364 U.S. 911 (1960). Accordingly, the issue of arbitration in federal court or, stated otherwise, the standing of an arbitration agreement with respect to any other enforceable contract, remained less than clear.

16 9 U.S.C. §4 provides:

> §4. Failure to Arbitrate Under Agreement; Petition to United States Court Having Jurisdiction For Order to Compel Arbitration; Notice and Service Thereof; Hearing and Determination.
>
> A party aggrieved by the alleged failure, neglect, or refusal of another to arbitrate under a written agreement for arbitration may petition any United States District Court which, save for such agreement, would have jurisdiction under Title 28, in a civil action or in admiralty of the subject matter of a suit arising out of the controversy between the parties, for an order directing that such arbitration proceed in the manner provided for in such agreement.
>
> Five days' notice in writing of such application shall be served upon the party in default. Service thereof shall be made in the manner provided by the Federal Rules of Civil Procedure. The Court shall hear the parties, and upon being satisfied that the making of the agreement for arbitration or the failure to comply therewith is not in issue, the Court shall make an order directing the parties to proceed to arbitration in accordance with the terms of the agreement. The hearing and proceedings, under such agreement, shall be within the district in which the parties for an order directing such arbitration is filed. If the making of the arbitration agreement or the failure, neglect, or refusal to perform the same be in issue, the Court shall proceed summarily to the trial thereof. If no jury trial be demanded by the party alleged to be in default, or if the matter in dispute is within admiralty jurisdiction, the Court shall hear and determine such issue. Where such an issue is raised, the party alleged to be in default may, except in cases of admiralty, on or before the return day of the notice of application, demand a jury trial of such issue, and upon such demand the Court shall make an order referring the issue or issues to a jury in the manner provided by the Federal Rules of Civil Procedure, or may specially call a jury for that purpose. If the jury finds that no agreement in writing for arbitration was made or that there is no default in proceeding thereunder, the proceeding shall be dismissed. If the jury find that an agreement for arbitration was made in writing and that there

however, enunciated that it would be "inconceivable that Congress intended the rule to differ depending upon which party to the arbitration agreement first invokes the assistance of a federal court. We hold, therefore, that in passing upon a Section 3 application for a stay while the parties arbitrate, a federal court may consider only issues relating to the making and performance of the agreement to arbitrate, in so concluding, we not only honor the plain meaning of the statute but also the unmistakably clear congressional purpose that the arbitration procedure, when selected by the parties to the contract, be speedy and not subject to delay and obstruction in the courts."[17]

The fourth and final tenet upon which the decision rests relates to the question of whether a federal court's issuance of a stay in deference of an arbitral proceeding, notwithstanding a contrary state rule, is constitutional. This inquiry was answered in the affirmative.[18] After reviewing the mandate in venerable chestnuts such as *Erie R. Co. v. Thompkins*[19] and *Guaranty Trust Co. of New York v. York*,[20] the Court predicated its affirmance of the rule's constitutionality on a thoughtful and eloquent exegesis of the legislative intent and jurisprudence construing the Act.[21]

> is a default in proceeding thereunder, the Court shall make an order summarily directing the parties to proceed with the arbitration in accordance with the terms thereof.

17 *Id.* at 404. §4 in pertinent part reads:

> The court shall hear the parties, and upon being satisfied that the making of the argument for arbitration for the failure to comply therewith is not an issue, the court shall make an order directing the parties to proceed to arbitration in accordance with the terms of the agreement. If the making of the arbitration agreement or the failure, neglect, or refusal to perform the same be an issue, the court shall proceed summarily to the trial thereof.

18 *Id.* at 405.

19 Erie R. Co. v. Thompkins, 304 U.S. 64 (1938).

20 Guaranty Trust Co. of New York v. York, 326 U.S. 99 (1945).

21 This jurisprudential analysis compels citation in its entirety:

> It is true that the Arbitration Act was passed thirteen years before this Court's decision in *Erie R. Co. v. Thomkins*, *supra*, brought to an end the regime of *Swift v. Tyson*, 16 Pet. 1, 10 L.Ed. 865 (1842), and that at the time of enactment Congress had reason to believe that it still had power to create federal rules to govern questions of 'general law' arising in simple diversity cases – at least, absent any state statute to the contrary. If Congress relied at all on this 'oft challenged' power, *see Erie R. Co.*, 304 U.S., at 69, 58 S.Ct., at 818, it was only supplementary to the admiralty and commerce powers, which formed the principal basis of the legislation. Indeed, Congressman Graham, the bill's sponsor in the House, told his colleagues that it 'only affects contracts relating to interstate subjects and contracts in admiralty.' 65 Cong. Rec. 1931 (1924). The Senate Report on this legislation similarly indicated that the bill "[relates] to maritime transactions and to contracts in interstate and foreign commerce.' S.Rep. No. 536, 68th Cong., 1st Sess., 3 (1924).
>
> Non-congressional sponsors of the legislation agreed. As Mr. Charles L. Bernheimer, chairman of the Arbitration Committee of the New York Chamber of Commerce, told the Senate subcommittee, the proposed legislation 'follows the lines of the New York Arbitration Law, applying it to the field wherein there is Federal jurisdiction. These fields are in admiralty and in foreign and interstate commerce.' Hearing on S.4213 and S.4214, before the Subcommittee of the Senate Committee on the Judiciary, 67th Cong., 4th Sess., 2 (1923). In the joint House and Senate hearings, Mr. Bernheimer answered 'Yes; entirely' to the statement of the Chairman, Senator Sterling, that 'what you have in mind is that this proposed legislation relates to contracts arising in interstate commerce.' Joint hearings on S.1005 and H.R.646 before the Subcommittees of the Committees on the Judiciary, 68th Cong., 1st Sess., 7 (1924). Mr. Julius Henry Cohen, draftsman for the American Bar Association of the proposed bill, said the sponsor's goals were: '[F]irst. . . . to get a State statute, and then to get a federal law to cover interstate and Foreign commerce and admiralty, and, third, to get a treaty with Foreign countries.' Joint Hearings, supra, at 16 (emphasis added). *See also* Joint Hearings, supra, at 27–28 (statement of Mr. Alexander Rose). Mr. Cohen did submit a brief to the Subcommittee urging a jurisdictional base broader than the commerce and admiralty powers, Joint Hearings, supra, at 37–38, but there is no indication in the statute or in the legislative history that this invitation to go beyond those powers was accepted, and his own testimony took a much narrower path. *Id.* at 405.

While *Prima Paint* stands, in part, for the unquestioned proposition that the FAA finds its genesis and normative foundation in the Commerce Clause, the opinion only suggests that the substantive rules of the FAA are to apply in state as well as in federal proceedings. Consequently, despite implicitly asserting the extraordinary proposition that the FAA gives rise to a *corpus* of federal substantive law applicable in state and federal fora, this doctrinal development did not attain "explicit status" until 1983, pursuant to the Supreme Court's command in *Moses H. Cone Memorial Hospital v. Mercury Construction Corporation.*[22]

The procedural configuration in *Moses H. Cone* is now eminently predictable. The district court stayed the proceeding pending resolution of a concurrent state court case pursuant to an order to compel arbitration, which initiated the entire proceeding. The Supreme Court held that the lower court indeed had abused its discretion because there were no indicia of exceptional circumstances warranting issuance of a stay. In furtherance of its ruling, the Court observed that "the presence of federal-law issues" pursuant to the FAA was "a major consideration weighing against surrender [of federal jurisdiction]."[23] Consequently it construed the underlying issue of arbitrability as an inquiry of substantive federal law; "federal law in the terms of the Arbitration Act governs that issue in either state or federal court."[24]

Both *Prima Paint* and *Moses H. Cone* illustrate a material doctrinal development often undermined, if not altogether ignored, by the broader issue concerning the elevation of arbitration to a state of equal status with judicial proceedings and the issue of arbitrability within federal purview. This predicate and essential transformation of arbitration agreements entails their theoretical development such that they may enjoy equal hierarchy with other forms of binding and enforceable contractual arrangements in the pantheon of U.S. jurisprudence. Hence, *Moses H. Cone*, decided sixteen years after *Prima Paint*, renders explicit what was contained only implicitly in the Court's earlier mandate, that is, irrespective of state law considerations, a federal court is empowered to issue a stay in favor of having matters adjudicated pursuant to arbitration and not in the context of court proceedings because the FAA governs the question of arbitrability in either state or federal fora.

To be sure, while the legislative history is far from being opaque, it is also less than clear on the issue of rendering arbitration agreements enforceable beyond just the federal arena. The House Report may be suggestive of more universal objectives:

> The purpose of this bill is to make valid and enforceable agreements for arbitration contained in contracts involving interstate commerce or within the jurisdiction or admiralty, or which may be the subject of litigation in the federal courts.[25]

The Supreme Court itself has recognized that "[t]his broader purpose can also be inferred from the reality that Congress would be less likely to address a problem whose impact was confined to federal courts than a problem of large significance in the field of commerce. The Arbitration Act sought to 'overcome the rule of

[22] Moses H. Cone Memorial Hospital v. Mercury Construction Corporation, 460 U.S. 1 (1983).
[23] *Id.* at 26. [24] *Id.* at 24.
[25] H.R. Rep. No. 96 (1924).

equity, that equity will not specifically enforce any arbitration agreement.'"[26] It is demonstrable that by 1984[27] it was finally meaningfully identified in the jurisprudence that part of the FAA's goal was to ensure parties to an arbitration agreement touching upon interstate commerce that neither federal courts, state courts, nor legislatures would frustrate their expectations. In addition, it also was rendered plain that Congress had been struggling with three rudimentary and, therefore, obstinate problems in fostering the development of arbitration. First, the prejudicial historical legacy of English courts requiring that arbitration proceedings be conducted under the auspices of courts and that arbitration generally, as a conceptual matter, was somehow against public policy because it "ousted" jurisdiction from courts that otherwise enjoyed competent jurisdiction and weighed heavily on the national collective judicial consciousness. Historical baggage, like old habits, apparently is proverbially hard to break.

Second, nationally grown prejudices directed at arbitral proceedings were no less pernicious. The unchallenged precepts that arbitration was ill-suited for the administration of justice arising from certain statutorily created rights as well as the view that arbitrators (together with the arbitral process itself) lacked competence to process complex commercial disputes of a domestic or international nature certainly hampered legislative efforts to accord arbitration its rightful place as an alternative dispute resolution methodology.

Third, Congress had to identify and then confront the problem arising from state arbitration statutes that fail to mandate enforcement of arbitral agreements. The result of these three sectors of influence was a restricted and restrictive reading of the Act that necessarily would limit the Act's scope to arbitrations only sought to be enforced in federal tribunals. Such a reading "would frustrate Congressional intent."

While *Prima Paint* does resolve the inquiry as to whether a federal court or an arbitrator is to adjudicate a claim of fraud in the inducement directed at a contract governed by the FAA absent evidence that the contracting parties intended to segregate that issue from arbitration, it leaves open the question of whether the FAA pre-empts state legislation that directly and explicitly conflicts with FAA strictures by directing parties to pursue the statutory causes of action in state court. The resolution of this federal pre-emption issue is an essential condition precedent to the juridic elevation of arbitration agreements to the same level as that enjoyed by commercial contracts. In addition, the resolution of this issue in favor of federal pre-emption highlights and underscores anew the critical role of the precept of party autonomy, even though this principle is not explicitly referenced in *any* of the Supreme Court authority that ultimately answers the four questions[28]

[26] *See* Southland Corporation v. Keating, et al., 465 U.S. 1, 13 (1984) (citing *Hearing on S.4214 Before a Subcomm. of the Senate Comm. on the Judiciary*, 67th Cong. (1923) ("Senate Hearing") (remarks of Sen. Walsh). The Court went on to cite the House Report attendant to the bill that stated:

> [t]he need for the law arises from.... the jealousy of the English courts for their own jurisdiction.... this jealousy survived for so lon[g] a period that the principle became firmly embedded in the English common law and was adopted with it by the American courts. The courts have felt that the precedent was too strongly fixed to be overturned without legislative enactment.... *Id.* (citing H.R. REP. No. 96 (1924)).

[27] *Southland Corporation*, 465 U.S. at 14.

[28] The four questions are the following: (i) as a matter of substantive federal arbitration law, is an arbitration provision severable from the remaining contract? (ii) is a challenge to a contract

addressed by the *Prima Paint*, *Southland Corporation*, and *Buckeye Check Cashing, Inc.*, trilogy.

The FAA's pre-emption over state legislation rendering it judicially impossible for parties to an arbitration agreement to arbitrate state statutory claims where the statute at issue proscribes judicial resolution to disputes based on the specific statutory rubric was addressed by the Supreme Court in *Southland Corporation v. Keating*.[29]

There the Supreme Court observed that it had "probable jurisdiction to consider (a) whether the California Franchise Investment Law, which invalidates certain arbitration agreements covered by the FAA violates the Supremacy Clause, and (b) whether arbitration under the Federal Act is impaired when a class action structure is imposed on the process by the state courts."[30] The case reached the Court pursuant to a ruling from the California Supreme Court by a vote of 4–2 that reversed a holding that claims asserted under the Franchise Investment Law are indeed arbitrable. The California Supreme Court construed the Franchise Investment Law as requiring "judicial consideration of claims brought under that statute and concluded that the California statute did not contravene the Federal Act."[31] The Supreme Court held that Section 31512 of the California Franchise Investment Law violates the Supremacy Clause.[32] Moreover, it also held that "[t]he judgment of the California Supreme Court denying enforcement of the arbitration agreement is reversed."[33] The reversal was predicated on four fundamental propositions.

First, it was observed that the California Court's judgment had the plain effect of nullifying a valid and enforceable contract requiring arbitration. Therefore, the ruling explicitly conflicts with the FAA providing the opportunity for "parties to an arbitrable dispute [to move] out of court and into arbitration as quickly and easily as possible."[34] In this regard, it was emphasized that "[c]ontracts to arbitrate are not to be avoided by allowing one party to ignore the contract and resort to the courts." Further adding that "[s]uch a course could lead to prolonged litigation, one of the very risks the parties, by contracting for arbitration, sought to eliminate."[35] Significantly, analytical support for this rationale is plainly grounded on the precept of party-autonomy. The parties' will in electing to resolve disputes pursuant to an arbitral proceeding as clearly embodied in an arbitration clause negotiated at arm's-length is particularly highlighted in the Court's analysis. In fact, direct reference is made to the *Bremen v. Zapata* analysis where, as discussed, the Court observed "that [a] contract fixing a particular forum for resolution of all disputes 'was made in an arm's-length negotiation by experienced and sophisticated businessmen, and absent some compelling and countervailing reason it should be honored by the

containing an arbitration clause to be adjudicated by a judge or an arbitrator? (iii) is there a federal substantive law created by the FAA? (iv) is such a law applicable in state as well as federal courts?

29 *Southland Corporation*, 465 U.S. 1.

30 *Id.* at 3.

31 *Id.* at 3–4.

32 *Id.* at 9.

33 *Id.*

34 *Id.* at 5–6 (citing Moses H. Cone Memorial Hospital v. Mercury Construction Corp., 103 S.Ct. 927, 940 (1983)).

35 *Id.*

parties and enforced by the Courts.'"[36] The emphasis on party initiative and the de-emphasized role of courts in an arbitral context marks an analytical turning point.

Second, the California Supreme Court's construction of the Franchise Investment Law[37] placed that legislation in direct and explicit conflict with Section 2 of the FAA. Thus, the Court found that the Franchise Investment Law "violate[d] the supremacy clause."[38] After asserting that in enacting Section 2 of the FAA Congress was instituting a national policy favoring arbitration and divesting states from legislatively requiring dispute resolution pursuant to judicial proceedings,[39]

36 *Id.* (citing *The Bremen,* 407 U.S. at 14). Here the Supreme Court also stressed that in *Zapata* it had deemed an arbitration clause to be a special kind of forum selection clause. While this proposition is plagued with conceptual difficulties that distort the nature of both arbitration and judicial proceedings, these issues do not detract from the Court's explicit, although not articulated, return to *party-autonomy* as a conceptual fulcrum to be used in according arbitration the same hierarchy as judicial proceedings and arbitration contracts the same judicial integrity as commercial contracts. It is also important to note that by 1984, one year before its seminal decision in *Mitsubishi*, the Court no longer finds it necessary to engage in a protracted recitation of the four badges of prejudice that nourished judicial contempt for arbitration, even though it does refer to the "old common law hostility toward arbitration." *Id.* at 860.

37 The California Franchise Investment Law states:

> Any condition, stipulation or provision purporting to bind any person acquiring any franchise to waive compliance with any provision of this law or any rule or order hereunder is void. Cal. Corp. Code §31512 (West 1977).

38 *Southland Corporation*, 465 U.S. at 10.

39 This proposition has elicited as much controversy as Justice Burger's majority opinion holding that the FAA was intended to apply to state court proceedings as well as federal cases. Justices Thomas and O'Connor have vigorously criticized the opinion and perhaps it is precise to state that most scholars agree that the FAA's legislative history does not contain any explicit language supporting this proposition. In fact, some scholars argue that "[t]he structure of the [FAA] reveals an unquestionably integrated, unitary statute, consisting of core provisions and provisions supplementing them." Ian R. Macneil, American Arbitration Law: Reformation, Nationalization, Internationalization 105–06 (1992). Professor Macneil also asserts that the FAA was designed to apply only to federal courts, i.e. one jurisdiction, based upon his own exegesis drawn from the historical fact that the FAA was patterned after the New York arbitration law. In a very thoughtful article by Christopher R. Drahozal entitled *In Defense of Southland: Reexamining the Legislative History of the Federal Arbitration Act*, Mr. Drahozal disagrees with Professor Macneil's conclusion that "[a]ny reading of the.... [FAA] leading to substantive and procedural parts with different applicability creates a monstrosity found nowhere else in the world of American arbitration." Ian R. Macneil, American Arbitration Law: Reformation, Nationalization, Internationalization 107 (1992). Mr. Drahozal argues that:

> As the above description of the FAA demonstrates, the language of the Act supports construing §2 to apply more broadly than the rest of the Act. §2 alone by its terms applies to maritime transactions and transactions in interstate commerce, which could cover proceedings in federal and state court. The rest of the Act creates procedures applicable only in federal court. I do not suggest that the language of the Act requires this interpretation, but it certainly is a pausible one.
>
> Moreover, the fact that the FAA is based on New York arbitration law – which does not bind courts other than New York courts – does not show that the FAA likewise applies only in a single jurisdiction. Macneil disregards a key distinction between the New York arbitration law and the FAA: the draftors of the FAA inserted the phrase "maritime transactions and contracts evidencing a transaction involving commerce" into §2. Obviously, no jurisdictional nexus was present in the original New York law. Plainly, the draftors of the FAA knew that they were drafting a statute for a federal system, in which federal law is supreme over state law. Their use of the New York model does not demonstrate that §2 is limited to a single jurisdiction, i.e. federal court. Finally, it is not surprising that there is no similar statute elsewhere in American arbitration law, since the FAA was designed to be enacted by the national government in a

the Court discerned only two limitations governing the enforceability of arbitration pursuant to the Federal Arbitration Act. First, the provisions of the FAA "must be part of a written maritime contract or a contract 'evidencing a transaction involving commerce.'"[40] Second, such a clause only may be revoked upon "grounds as exist at law or in equity for the revocation of any contract."[41] Obviously, neither limitation proscribes applicability to state courts, or so the argument says.

Third, borrowing from its *Prima Paint* opinion entered seventeen years earlier – 1967 – the Court observed that its prior construction of the FAA's legislative history led it to conclude that the statute "is based upon. . . . the incontestable federal foundations of 'control over interstate commerce and over admiralty.'"[42] Thus, the Court amplifies its reasoning by observing that Congressional authority as to the commerce clause has a long-standing juridic history of having been deemed plenary.[43] Having established, at least to its satisfaction, this minor premise, the majority concludes that it follows that because the Arbitration Act "was an exercise of the Commerce Clause power clearly implied that the substantive rules of the Act were to apply in state as well as federal courts."[44]

Thus at this juncture, in reversing the California Supreme Court's ruling, the Court has construed the FAA (i) as having substantive *and* procedural provisions,[45] (ii) where the substantive provisions apply to *both* federal and state courts, and (iii) with only two limitations on the enforceability provisions: (a) The provision must be part of a written maritime contract or a contract concerning a transaction that touches and concerns commerce; and (b) the clause would be susceptible to revocation based on extant legal principles or equitable principles applicable to all contracts.

The opinion candidly acknowledges that "[a]lthough the legislative history is not without ambiguities, there are strong indications that Congress had in mind something more than making arbitration agreements enforceable only in the federal courts. The House Report plainly suggests the more comprehensive objectives:

> The purpose of this bill is to make valid and enforceable agreements for arbitration contained in *contracts involving interstate commerce* or within the jurisdiction or admiralty, *or* which may be the subject of litigation in the federal courts.[46]

federal system, while other arbitration laws are enacted by the states. Christopher Drahozal, *In Defense of Southland: Reexamining the Legislative History of the Federal Arbitration Act*, 78 NOTRE DAME L. REV. 101, 112 (2002).

40 *Southland Corporation*, 465 U.S. at 10.

41 *Id.*

42 *Id.* (citing Prima Paint Corp. v. Flood & Conklin Mfg. Corp., 87 S.Ct. at 1806 (quoting H.R. Rep. No. 96, 68th Cong., 1st Sess. 1 (1924))).

43 *Id.* at 12 (referencing Chief Justice Marshall in Gibbons v. Ogden, 22 U.S. 1 (1824)).

44 *Id.*

45 Indeed, it is based on this analysis that federal courts, for example, on the issue of punitive damages, hold that an arbitral tribunal's award granting punitive damages preempts state law or policy otherwise proscribing such awards. *See, e.g.,* Mastrobuono v. Shearson Lehman Hutton, Inc., 514 U.S. 52 (1995); Raytheon Co. v. Automated Business Systems, Inc., 882 F.2d 6 (1st Cir. 1989) (holding that arbitration award entered pursuant to AAA rules allowing for punitive damages was proper); Todd Shipyards Corp. v. Cunard Line, Ltd., 943 F.2d 1056, 1062 (9th Cir. 1991) (same).

46 *Id.* at 12 (citing H.R. Rep. No. 96, 68th Cong., 1st Sess. 1 (1924)) (emphasis supplied).

Critical to the majority opinion is the ability to broaden the Act's scope and purpose, which it derives from the proposition "that Congress would be less likely to address a problem whose impact was confined to federal courts than a problem of large significance in the field of commerce."[47] Thus, the Court added that "[t]he Arbitration Act sought to overcome the rule of equity, that equity will not specifically enforce any arbitration agreement."[48] The struggle to find a predicate on which to ground Congressional intent justifying a broader scope and purpose for application of the Act is certainly a debility that pervades the opinion and that has spawned the referenced criticism. The majority, however, is not persuasive in its analysis but devastatingly so in its conclusion.[49] Put simply, the "broader purpose" of the Act that the majority gleans from the legislative history and statutory constructions that lead to greater coherence and uniformity in both analysis and application merits serious consideration.[50]

Fifth, Justice O'Connor's viable contention that Congress understood the FAA "as a procedural statute applicable only in federal courts,"[51] is frontally addressed by referencing the opinion's ever present battle horse, contracts "involving commerce," as an express limitation to be read together with the limitation that would arise had Congress called on the Commerce Clause to evidence the Act's state court application but then find itself limited only to transactions involving interstate commerce.[52]

The Court reasoned that the anomaly in Justice O'Connor's construction of the Act causing claims brought pursuant to the California Franchise Investment Law in state court to be nonarbitrable cannot be reconciled with the proposition that were such a claim brought in a federal district court with subject matter premised on

47 *Id.*

48 *Id.* (citing Hearing on S.4214 before a Sub Comm. of the Senate Comm. on the Judiciary, 67th Cong., 4th Sess. 6 (1923) ("Senate Hearing") (remarks of Sen. Walsh)). Also citing to the House Reporting accompanying the Bill:

> '[T]he need for the law arises from. . . . the jealousy of the English courts for their own jurisdiction. . . . this jealousy survived for so lon[g] a period that the principle became firmly embedded in the English common law and was adopted with it by the American courts. The courts have felt that the precedent was too strongly fixed to be overturned without legislative enactment. . . . ' H.R. Rep. No. 96, *supra*, 1–2 (1924).

49 This opinion is well articulated by Mr. Drahozal. He eloquently states:

> I agree that the Chief Justice's opinion failed persuasively to make the case that the FAA applies in state court. But the Chief Justice nonetheless reached the correct conclusion. . . . a reexamination of the FAA's legislative history reveals that while the 'primary purpose' of the FAA was to make arbitration agreements enforceable in federal court, a secondary purpose was to make arbitration agreements enforceable in state court [citation omitted]. A contemporaneous commentator, overlooked by the critics, sums it up well: '[t]he Act is broad enough to apply to actions commenced in state courts as well as to those instituted in federal courts, and it was so intended by those who drafted it.' [citation omitted]. While ambiguities in the legislative history remain, this interpretation of the legislative history results in fewer ambiguities than the prevailing interpretation. Christopher R. Drahozal, *In Defense of Southland. Reexamining the Legislative History of the Federal Arbitration Act*, 78 Notre Dame Law Review 33 (2002).

Even though it far from clarifies any ambiguity in the legislative history, there is merit in the Court's observation that Congress faced two problems: "the old common law hostility toward arbitration, and the failure of state arbitration statutes to mandate enforcement of arbitration agreements." *Southland Corporation*, 465 U.S. at 14.

50 It is worth underscoring again that only fleetingly and on two occasions does the Court reference the legacy of prejudice originating in the English courts. *See, e.g., id.*

51 *Id.*

52 *Id.*

diversity jurisdiction, under such scenario, "the arbitration clause would have been enforceable."[53]

Perhaps most persuasive is the proposition that it would be odd, if not altogether ill-conceived, to ascribe to Congress "the intent, in drawing on the comprehensive powers of the Commerce Clause, to create a right to enforce an arbitration contract and yet make the right dependent for its enforcement on the particular forum in which it is asserted."[54] This argument is bolstered, particularly when considering the Act's presumably broader scope, by the perplexing statistics establishing that the overwhelming number of civil litigation cases filed in the United States rest in state courts. Here the Court, naturally limited to the date on which the opinion issued in 1984, identifies rather astonishing statistics. Only 2 percent of all civil litigation in the United States is filed in federal courts.[55] Two hundred and six thousand filings were recorded in federal district courts during a twelve-month window ending on June 30, 1982, excluding bankruptcy filings. During a comparable period, however, an impressive 13,600,000 civil filings, excluding traffic cases, were reported in state courts.[56]

The most salient single proposition in *Southland* is the assertion that in fashioning substantive provisions forming part of the FAA, these provisions are applicable both to state and federal courts, and therefore wrest from state legislatures the ability to undermine or otherwise circumvent the FAA. While even today the debates arising from the Act's legislative history remain as relevant as ever and similarly as never-ending rich material for scholastic analysis, the conclusion is powerful and compelling. It is a tortured reading of the FAA to limit it only to the realm of federal jurisdiction. Such a construction surely would carve out from the Act its effectiveness, particularly in light of the staggering state court filings when compared to federal court proceedings initiated during a comparable time frame. It would also, as the Court to some extent articulated or tried to articulate, condition a right on the forum on which it is filed. Lastly, the hypothetical that the majority opinion crafted concerning a federal court sitting in diversity where the parties have executed an arbitration agreement that constitutes the subject matter of the federal court filing is certainly illustrative and presents an aberration to the precepts that Justice O'Connor proposed.

Prima Paint and *Southland Corp.* answer the four questions posed. First, as a matter of substantive federal arbitration law an arbitration provision is severable from the remaining contract. Second, a challenge to a contract containing an arbitration clause at first instance is to be adjudicated by an arbitrator so long as the challenge is not directed at the arbitration clause itself. Third, the FAA does create a substantive federal law having a normative basis in the Commerce Clause. Fourth, the substantive law provisions of the FAA are applicable to both state and federal fora.

53 *Id.* The Court found the arbitration clause to encompass claims under the California Franchise Investment Law. The clause, in pertinent part, reads:

> Any controversy or claim arising out of or relating to this Agreement or the breach hereof," appears broad and general enough to include the statutory cause of action.

54 *Id.*

55 *Id.* at 16, n. 8 (citing to Administrative Office of the United States Court, Annual Report of the Director 3 (1982)).

56 *Id.*

Incident to this time frame was virtually a vertical increase in international commercial arbitration.[57] Thus, the stage was set for the Court to sharpen and amplify the doctrinal development it had initiated with *Prima Paint* and continued in *Southland Corporation*. An important permutation of the issues addressed in those two cases is "whether a court or an arbitrator should consider the claim that a contract containing an arbitration provision is void for illegality."[58] The Court's analysis and opinion highlights a conceptual refinement of the issues first addressed in *Prima Paint* and redefines the role of judicial intervention in arbitral proceedings as well as the meaningful return to party-autonomy as a guiding principle in common law jurisprudence as well as the law of arbitration. *Buckeye Check Cashing Inc. v. Cardegna* has drawn praise and criticism from judges, practitioners, and commentators.

Buckeye Check Cashing is a procedural rosary of reversals. Here respondent (plaintiff) filed a putative class action in Florida circuit court averring that petitioner (defendant) "charged usurious interest rates and, that the Agreement violated various Florida lending and consumer-protection laws, rendering it criminal on its face."[59] The trial court denied petitioner's subsequent motion to stay or dismiss the state court proceeding in favor of arbitration.[60] In denying petitioner's motion, the court held that a judicial tribunal rather than an arbitration panel as a matter of law should adjudicate the specific and narrow issue of whether the contract is illegal and void *ab initio*.

Florida's Fourth District Court of Appeals reversed the trial court ruling on the theory that respondents failed to challenge the arbitration provision itself at the trial court level and instead elected to aver that the contract in its entirety was void, the agreement to arbitrate was enforceable, and the issue concerning the contract's legal viability should be determined by an arbitrator.[61]

On appeal the Florida Supreme Court, which reversed the Fourth District Court of Appeal, embraced the premise that enforcement of an arbitral agreement in a contract challenged as unlawful "could breathe life into a contract that not only violates state law, but also is criminal in nature. . . ."[62]

The two reversals (the Fourth District Court of Appeals reversing the trial court and the Florida Supreme Court reversing the Fourth District Court of Appeals) were followed by the Supreme Court's reversal of the Florida Supreme Court on the narrow question of "whether a court or an arbitrator should consider the

[57] Catherine A. Rogers, *Emerging Dilemmas in International Economic Arbitration: The Vocation of the International Arbitrator*, 20 AM. U. INT'L L. REV. 957, 965 (2005).

[58] Cardegna v. Buckeye Check Cashing, Inc., 546 U.S. 440 (2006).

[59] *Id* at 443.

[60] The contract at issue contained an arbitration clause providing that:

> 2. *Arbitration Provisions.* Any plain, dispute, or controversy . . . arising from or relating to this Agreement . . . or the validity, enforceability, or scope of this Arbitration Provisions or the entire Agreement (collectively "Claim"), shall be resolved, upon the election of you or us or said third-parties, by binding arbitration. . . . this arbitration Agreement is made pursuant to a transaction involving intrastate commerce, and shall be governed by the Federal Arbitration Act ("F.A.A.") 9 U.S.C. §1–16. The arbitrator shall apply applicable substantive law consistent [*sic*] with the F.A.A. and applicable statu[t]es of limitations and shall honor claims of privilege recognized by law. . . . " *Id.*

[61] *Id.*

[62] *Buckeye Check Cashing*, 894 So.2d at 862 (quoting Party Yards v. Templeton, 751 So.2d 121, 123 (Fla. App. 2000)."

claim and that a contract containing an arbitration provision is void for illegality."[63]

Providing an arbitration agreement, that is, an arbitration clause, with the same juridic hierarchy as a commercial contract is a predicate for discerning between two different challenges requiring disparate analyses and attendant conclusions. First, the Court adjudicated a challenge to the validity of the arbitration clause or the agreement to arbitrate, as was the case in *Southland Corp.*[64] The second challenge concerns testing the legality of the underlying contract memorializing the commercial transaction and issue that also contains an arbitration clause. Here, the argument says, the entire agreement would be rendered unenforceable because, by way of example, it could have been fraudulently induced, the agreement may be illegal because it seeks to realize an objective that is against public policy, or the very illegality of one of the contract's clauses may render the whole contract invalid.[65] Upon review of the complaint, the Court underscored that it is the second, i.e., a challenge to the contract as a whole and not specifically to the arbitration clause, that brings before it the issue concerning whether court or arbitrator should adjudicate the validity of the contract.

Four critical premises were analyzed in highlighting the primacy of the arbitral process, the precept of party-autonomy, and the new rule of judicial intervention in arbitral proceedings. First, the Florida Supreme Court had placed considerable weight on the distinction arising between "void" and "voidable" contracts. Indeed, it asserted that "Florida public policy and contract law" permit "no severable, or salvageable, parts of a contract found illegal and void under Florida Law."[66] The Court rejected this proposition based upon its understanding of *Prima Paint*. Specifically, the Supreme Court observed how "[t]hat case rejected application of state severability rules to the arbitration agreement *without discussing* whether the challenge at issue would have rendered the contract void or voidable."[67] In addition, further analytic support was drawn from *Southland Corp.* where the Court deliberately and explicitly elected *not* to consider whether the legal and factual averments in the underlying complaint rendered the contract at issue either void or voidable. Instead, it rejected the assertion that the enforceability of an arbitration agreement is contingent upon a state legislature's determination as to the applicable forum for enforcement of a state law statutory cause of action.[68] Likewise, the Court held that it "cannot accept the Florida Supreme Court's conclusion that the enforceability of the arbitration agreement should turn on 'Florida public policy and contract law.'"[69]

63 *Id* at 442.

64 The Supreme Court characterized the issue in *Southland Corp.* as "challenging the agreement to arbitrate as void under California law and so far as it purported to cover claims brought under the State Franchise Investment Law." *Id.* at 444.

65 *Id.* The opinion emphasizes that because "[t]he issue of the contract's validity is different from the issue of whether any agreement between the alleged obligor and obligee was ever concluded, [o]ur opinion today addresses only the former, and does not speak to the issue decided in the case cited by respondents (and by the Florida Supreme Court), which hold that it is for courts to decide whether the alleged obligor ever signed the contract [citations omitted]."

66 *Buckeye Check Cashing*, 894 So.2d at 864.

67 *Id.* at 446 (citing to *Prima Paint,* 388 U.S. at 400–404).

68 *Id.*

69 *Id.* (citing *Buckeye Check Cashing*, 894 So.2d at 864).

Second, the FAA's "substantive" command in Section 2 was emphasized in the context of the Court's prior ruling in *Prima Paint.* Not surprisingly, respondents had argued that *Prima Paint's* stricture only was predicated on Sections 3 and 4 of the FAA's "Procedural" provisions further asserting that both of these sections exclusively applied to the Federal Court, while Section 2 is the only provision that the Supreme Court had applied to state court. This contention was rejected in what is, in effect, a scholarly critique of the Court's own analysis in *Prima Paint.* Specifically, the Supreme Court observed that while "Section 4, in particular, had much to do with *Prima Paint's* understanding of the Rule of Severability [citation omitted]," the Court explained that the severability doctrine has its genesis in Section 2 of the FAA. Therefore, "[r]espondent's reading of the *Prima Paint* as establishing nothing more than a Federal-Court rule of procedure *also* runs contrary to *Southland's* understanding of that case."[70] Not to place epicycles upon epicycles in a Ptolemaic effort "to save the appearances," *Southland's* own application of Section 2 is a state court proceeding explicitly predicated on *Prima Paint's* "reli[ance] for [its holding] on Congress' broad power to fashion substantive rules under the Commerce clause."[71]

Consequently, the Court in *Buckeye* holds that the Severability Doctrine is applicable to the case at bar because of an exegesis finding that the 1967 ruling in *Prima Paint* addressing Sections 3 and 4 of the FAA, and thus developing the Severability Doctrine from the 1953 single-sentence ruling in *Wilko*, is applicable to state court proceedings and found to be such in *Southland* in 1984 because of the Doctrine's foundation on Section 2 of the FAA, which in turn rests on judicial acknowledgment of Congress' broad powers to craft substantive rules pursuant to the Commerce Clause. The normative sequence is the following:

1. *Prima Paint*, in deciding whether a federal court or arbitrator is to adjudicate fraud in the inducement and misrepresentation claims directed at the underlying contract containing the arbitration clause, crafts the Severability Doctrine but only in the context of interpreting Sections 3 and 4 of the FAA;
2. *Southland* applies Section 2 of the FAA to a state court proceeding concerning the prosecution of state legislation (the California Franchise Investment Law) based upon its reading of *Prima Paint* as resting on Congressional authority to fashion substantive rules pursuant to the Commerce Clause;
3. The Supreme Court in *Southland* concludes that Section 2 of the FAA is the substantive provision based upon the Commerce Clause upon which *Prima Paint's* analysis of Sections 3 and 4 of the FAA can only ultimately be predicated;
4. Thus, the Supreme Court in *Buckeye* finds a normative basis in rejecting the Florida Supreme Court's public policy contention that enforceability of the contract should rest on Florida public policy and contract law.

70 *Id.* at 447. It is worth reiterating for completeness' and clarity's sake that the "substantive directive of §2 of the FAA is that arbitration agreements are to be accorded the same juridic hierarchy as any other contract.

71 *Id.* (citing *Southland*, 465 U.S., at 11, *and Prima Paint* 388 U.S. at 407 (Black, J., dissenting) ("[t]he Court here holds that the [FAA] as a matter of *Federal Substantive Law*. . . . ") (emphasis added)). In this connection, the Court stressed that in *Southland* it had refused to "believe Congress intended to limit the Arbitration Act to disputes subject only to *Federal-Court* jurisdiction." *Id.* (citing to 465 U.S. at 15).

Third, respondents advanced the remarkably circular pronouncement that because the underlying contract containing the arbitration agreement was void *ab initio* under Florida law, and Section 2 of the FAA only applies to contacts that are "valid, irrevocable and enforceable," there is no conceivable contract or agreement to which Section 2 can possibly apply.[72] The Supreme Court analyzed this issue by scrutinizing Section 2 of the FAA to glean a broader understanding of the word "contract" within the meaning of Section 2.[73]

Finally, even though under the *Prima Paint* rubric a court and not an arbitrator conceivably may enforce an arbitration clause that an arbitrator later finds to be void, as respondents suggest, "it is equally true that respondents' approach permits a court to deny effect to an arbitration provision in a contract that the Court later finds to be perfectly enforceable."[74] This *apparent* anomaly is reconciled by the *Prima Paint* doctrine providing for separate enforcement of the underlying contract and the arbitration agreement, that is, the Severability Doctrine.

In addition to refining the doctrinal framework established in *Prima Paint* and *Southland Corp.*, which answered the four queries identified here, *Buckeye* serves as a guide to interpreting both *Prima Paint* and *Southland* together as part of a doctrinal and conceptual development seeking to emphasize

1. the FAA's federal pre-emption to render conceptually possible the proposition,
2. the FAA has substantive provisions,
3. these substantive provisions apply both to federal and state fora,
4. that Section 2 is the basis for the FAA's substantive directives, and
5. the substantive command contained in Section 2, which pervades Sections 3 and 4, is ultimately grounded on Congress' broad powers to craft substantive rules based upon the Commerce Clause.

Certainly, as Justice Thomas' abbreviated dissent seeks to emphasize, concerns have not been dispelled or otherwise allayed with respect to the fundamental issue of whether the FAA applies to state courts. The Act's legislative history is ambiguous and difficult to construe in any definitive manner. As already referenced, Justice Burger's analysis in *Prima Paint* on the issue is far from overwhelmingly compelling. *Prima Paint*, *Southland Corp.*, and *Buckeye* constitute an important trilogy that enriches the doctrinal development of arbitration in the United States. All three cases, decided during a thirty-nine-year time frame, seek to place arbitration contracts at the same juridic level as commercial contracts. The trilogy also bolsters arbitration's juridic integrity and standing by redefining the relationship between arbitration and judicial proceedings.

The Supreme Court further refined and underscored the integrity of commercial arbitration as standing *in pari materia* with judicial proceedings and thus also

[72] *Id.* at 447.

[73] The Court stated:

> We do not read "contract" so narrowly, the word appears four times in §2. Its last appearance is in the final clause which allows a challenge to an arbitration provision 'upon such grounds as exists at law or in equity for the revocation of any *contract*'." (Emphasis added). There can be no doubt that "contract" as used this last time must include contracts that later prove to be void. Otherwise, the grounds for revocation would be limited to those that rendered an contract voidable-which would mean (implausibly) that an arbitration agreement could be challenged as voidable but not as void. *Id.* at 448.

[74] *Id.*

highlighted the precept of party-autonomy scarcely two years after its pronouncement in *Buckeye*. To be sure, in *Preston v. Ferrer*,[75] the Court addressed the narrow and solitary question of whether "the FAA overrides not only state statutes that referred certain state-law controversies initially to a judicial forum, but also state statutes that referred certain disputes initially to an administrative agency?"[76] As a predicate to analyzing the Court's affirmative holding on this narrow inquiry, the procedural history in *Preston* commands some attention.

The familiar fact pattern giving rise to jurisprudence apportioning jurisdiction between judicial and *quasi-judicial* (administrative) proceedings and an arbitral tribunal is present here except for a quite notable development. Significantly, petitioner Preston's effort to enforce an arbitration clause precipitated respondent's submission of a petition to the California Labor Commissioner "charging that the contract was invalid and unenforceable under the California Talent Agencies Act (TAA)."[77] In this connection, respondent averred that petitioner was in stark violation of the TAA because he acted as a talent agent but lacked the requisite license that the TAA's statutory rubric prescribed. Consequently, so the argument went, "petitioner's unlicensed status rendered the entire contract void."[78]

Upon the labor commissioner's issuance of an order holding that the labor commissioner lacked authority to grant respondent's motion to stay arbitration, respondent filed an action in the Los Angeles Superior Court applying for a declaration that the subject arbitration clause is not arbitrable and for issuance of injunctive relief proscribing petitioner from prosecuting claims in an arbitration. Not surprisingly, petitioner in turn filed papers moving to compel arbitration. The Superior Court denied petitioner's motion and further enjoined petitioner from pursuing relief consonant with the arbitration clause "'unless and until the Labor Commissioner determines that. . . . she is without jurisdiction over the dispute between [petitioner] and [respondent].'"[79] The noteworthy juridic *deus ex machina* occurred during the pendency of petitioner's appeal from the Superior Court's adverse ruling. It was at this time that the U.S. Supreme Court issued its opinion in *Buckeye* holding that challenges to the validity of a contract providing for arbitration ordinarily "be considered by an arbitrator, not a court."[80] Despite this development, however, the California Court of Appeals affirmed the Superior Court's judgment and reiterated that the operative provisions of the TAA vests "exclusive original jurisdiction" over the contention before the labor commissioner.[81] Instead of adopting the clear command in *Buckeye*, the California Court of Appeals engaged in an exercise aspiring to draw a material distinction that was wholly unavailing. Notably, the Court addressed *Buckeye* by fleetingly labeling the Supreme Court's mandate in that case as "inapposite" because *Buckeye* "did not involve an administrative agency with exclusive jurisdiction over a disputed issue."[82] The California Supreme Court denied petitioner's papers seeking review.

75 *Preston v. Ferrer*, 128 S.Ct. 978 (2008).
76 *Id*. at 981.
77 *Id*. at 982.
78 *Id*.
79 *Id* at 924.
80 *Buckeye*, 546 U.S. at 446.
81 *Preston*, *supra* note 590, at 924.
82 145 Cal. at Pp.4th, at 447, 51 Cal. Reptr. 3d. at 634. Significantly, the dissenting judge viewed *Buckeye* as dispositive under the theory that the FAA ("the Act") compelled expedited confirmation, recognition, and enforcement of the arbitral agreement and the Act itself did not give rise

In reversing the California Court of Appeals, the Court enhanced the independence and integrity of arbitral proceedings while furthering the fundamental precept of party-autonomy already embodied in its directive in *Buckeye*. Whether judicial or administrative, remedies for dispute resolution set in legislative pronouncement shall not pre-empt enforcement of an arbitration clause. Moreover, the statutorily enacted tenet prescribing exhaustion of dispute resolution remedies as a predicate to enforcement to an arbitration clause is of no consequence where the parties have executed a binding arbitration agreement. Analytical support for this principle was predicated on seven specific propositions.

First, borrowing from its pronouncement in *Southland Corp.*, the Court reiterated the application of the national policy favoring arbitration as applying "'in state as well as federal courts and forclose[s] state legislative attempts to undercut the enforceability of arbitration agreements.'"[83] Accordingly, emphasis was placed on the FAA's displacement of conflicting state law.[84]

Second, absent specific allegations directed at the arbitration clause at issue, there are no grounds at equity or law that may invalidate an arbitration agreement. Here the court aptly rested on its holding in *Prima Paint*.[85]

Third, the applicability and holding in *Buckeye* was significantly clarified. Because the contract between petitioner and respondent involved *commerce*, the Court underscored that Section 2 of the FAA was triggered.[86] Significantly, respondent never (i) placed at issue whether the subject arbitration clause properly fell within the ambit of §2, (ii) sought to invalidate the entire contract, or (iii) failed to preserve, if attempted at all, any specific challenge to the validity of the arbitration clause.[87] It thus followed that from a pleading perspective the record was ripe for application of the rule in *Buckeye* mandating that an arbitrator *and not a judge* must first determine the validity of a contract averred to be invalid in its entirety.

Fourth, respondent advanced the novel proposition that "the TAA merely requires exhaustion of administrative remedies *before* the parties proceed to arbitration."[88] Here the Court observed that where the TAA's procedural provisions conflict with the FAA's dispute resolution rubric, as in that case, by granting "the Labor Commissioner Exclusive Jurisdiction to decide an issue that the parties agreed to arbitrate" and by imposing "pre-requisites to enforcement of an arbitration agreement, that are not applicable to contracts generally," the policy favoring arbitration in furtherance of the FAA's directive shall take precedent.[89]

to any independent normative basis for recourse to a state administrative agency from prior resort to a state court. *Id at 450–451, 51 Cal. Reptr. 3d, at 636–637 (Vogel, J., Dissenting).*

83 *Id.* at 925.

84 *Id. Citing Allied-Bruce Terminix Cos. v. Dobson*, 513 U.S. 265, 272 (1995). *See also, Buckeye*, 546 U.S. at 445–446; *Doctor's Associates*, Inc., v. Casarotto, 517 U.S. 681, 684–685 (1996); *Terry v. Thomas*, 482 U.S. 483, 489 (1987).

85 *Id.* at 925.

86 Section 2 of the FAA reads:

> A written provision in any . . . contract evidencing a transaction involving commerce to settle by arbitration a controversy thereafter arising out of such contract or transaction . . . shall be valid, irrevocable, and enforceable, saved upon such grounds as exist at law or at equity for the revocation of any contract. 9 U.S.C. §2.

87 *Preston, supra* note 590, at 926.

88 *Id.* at 984 (emphasis supplied).

89 *Id.* at 985.

Fifth, as already enunciated in *Gilmer* v. *Interstate/Johnson Lane Corp.*,[90] "[t]he 'mere involvement of an administrative agency in the enforcement of a statute,' we held, does not limit private parties' obligation to comply with their arbitration agreement."[91] This tenet was emphatically amplified by noting that the court "disapprove[d] the distinction between judicial and administrative proceedings drawn by [respondent] and adopted by the appeals court."[92] In addition the majority underscored that "[w]hen parties agree to arbitrate all questions arising under a contract, the FAA supersedes state laws lodging primary jurisdiction in another forum, whether judicial or administrative."[93]

In a rare analysis, analytical support was predicated on the arbitral institution's procedural rules. Indeed, explicit reference was made to the incorporation of the FAA rules, and Rule 7(b) in particular, in part providing that "[t]he arbitrator shall have the power to determine the existence or validity of a contract which an arbitration clause forms a part."[94] The Court's careful and adroit use of the arbitral institution's rules to highlight the primacy accorded to an arbitration agreement is but a reaffirmation of the significance of the doctrine of party-autonomy as a fundamental pillar of arbitral proceedings.[95]

The Supreme Court's analysis in *Buckeye* and *Preston* in furthering the precept that party-autonomy (even though these words never appear in either opinion) directly contributes to a framework helpful in defining the apportionment of jurisdiction between courts and arbitral tribunals. Again, although not explicitly stated, if courts and arbitral tribunals are deemed to be of equal stature and status, it follows that judicial intervention in arbitral proceedings must be redefined so that it may be limited merely to providing arbitral tribunals with logistical and ministerial support that does not "touch or concern" the underlying merits of the cause.[96]

90 *Gilmore v. Interstate/Johnson Lane Corp.*, 500 U.S. 20 (1991).

91 *Id.* at 28–29.

92 *Preston, supra* note 590, at 929.

93 *Id.*

94 *Id.* at 931.

95 Throughout this book emphasis has been placed on the all too often overlooked principle of *party-autonomy*. Here we seek to elevate anew this tenet's standing in the academic discussions concerning the integration of legal precepts from diverse legal and national/ethnic cultures into an international commercial arbitration rubric that would facilitate the equitable administration of justice, in part, by aspiring to comport with the expectation of parties from diverse legal cultures participating in an international contention. The principle of *party-autonomy* is a fundamental tenet endemic to cross-border l dispute resolution methodologies. Indeed, no other principle is better suited or sufficiently flexible to purport even to command the construction of a framework aspiring to meet the expectation of parties from disparate legal cultures and ethnic traditions. Here it has been advanced, by way of example, that when the "taking of evidence" or "gathering of evidence" as these terms are used and reference by the procedural rules of the LCIA, ICDR, ICC, and IBA, and later compared and contrasted with a meticulous and detailed analysis of the Federal Rules of Civil Procedure governing *discovery*, it becomes patently and starkly evident that U.S. style discovery, although foreign to the majority of legal traditions beyond the common law, when duly understood beyond surface analyses predicated on generalizations and "sloganized" premises, most aptly comports with the principle of *party-autonomy* in contrast with the "gathering of evidence" or "taking of evidence," as defined by the procedural rules of arbitral institutions, which fail to define "evidence" and wrest from the parties even a resemblance of *party-autonomy*.

96 The issue of the rule of courts in arbitral proceedings in the context of developing a *lex arbitrai akin a lex fori* defined as subservient to the arbitral tribunal and charged only with the task of furthering the will of the party and of the arbitrators, was very thoroughly and thoughtfully addressed by Georgios Petrochilos in his work *Procedural Law in International Arbitration*, Oxford private International Law Series (2004).

It is recognized and acknowledged that arbitration can no more completely disengage itself from judicial recourse and judicial proceedings than a private citizen may be able to sever her ties to the state. This proposition is patent and inalterable. It should not, however, obscure the more prevalent and salient issue. The pre-emptive nature of the Federal Arbitration Act, the principle of party-autonomy, and, more importantly, the dispute resolution integrity of arbitral proceeding, should not and cannot be subordinated to judicial recourse. Moreover, if arbitration is to fill the void that economic globalization created by giving rise to a both parallel and intercepting "juridic globalization" pursuant to which the cross fertilization of procedural laws from multiple legal cultures are adopted to maximize party-autonomy, uniformity, predictive value, transparency, and party expectation, discernable criteria must be crafted to render glaring the boundaries and contours of judicial and arbitral processes.

The precept of party-autonomy, so essential to the common law and its "adversarial system," cries for incorporation into the anatomy and procedural structure of international commercial arbitration. Indeed, to the extent that arbitration contracts have been construed to stand on *pari materia* with judicial precedent because of the policy according prominence to the parties' will in the shifting of dispute resolution proceeding from the state to private individuals, we have identified this public policy as a juridic renaissance of the precept of party-autonomy. Additionally, even where it may seem, as shall be demonstrated below in the context of the Supreme Court's most recent pronouncement of the apportionment of jurisdiction between courts and arbitral tribunals as of the date of this writing, it may appear that party-autonomy is being sacrificed for the greater good of curtailing judicial intervention at *any* adjudicative level of arbitral processes. Close scrutiny compels the conclusion that the ostensible diminution of the precept for a greater overarching good is but the preservation and even enhancement of the very principle at first glance thought to have been diminished. Put simply, endemic to most forms of arbitral proceeding is the highest expression of party-autonomy.

On March 25, 2008, the United States Supreme Court fashioned an exquisitely reasoned opinion that addressed the narrow and solitary issue of "whether statutory grounds for prompt vacatur and modification [of an arbitral award] may be supplemented by contract."[97] The Court in *Hall Street Associates, LLC v. Mattel* answered the query in the affirmative. A brief review of the somewhat complex and inordinate procedural predicates giving rise to the analysis merits consideration.

Here, a simple dispute acquired a most exceptional juridic life of its own. Plaintiff Hall Street filed an action contesting the defendant-tenant (Mattel) issuance of a notice of intent to terminate a lease of real property. After a bench trial, the district court found for Mattel on the discrete issue of propriety of termination, causing the parties to agree to arbitrate a remaining indemnity claim that presumably ran in favor of the plaintiff-landlord, Hall Street.[98] The arbitration agreement, however, contained a rather exceptional feature that provided the parties with a determinative appellate review standard where (i) "the arbitrator's findings of facts are

[97] Hall Street Associates, LLC v. Mattel, Inc., 170 L.ED 2d 254, 259 (2008).
[98] *Id.* at 260.

not supported by substantial evidence, or (ii) . . . the arbitrator's conclusions of law are erroneous."[99]

After issuance of an arbitral award in favor of Mattel on the indemnity question, plaintiff filed a motion with the district court seeking vacatur or modification of the arbitral award on the ground that the award misapprehended as a matter of law an applicable state environmental act. The District Court agreed, vacated the award, and remanded the matter for further consideration to the arbitrator.[100] Significantly, "[t]he court expressly invoked the standard of review chosen by the parties in the arbitration agreement, which included review for legal error, and cited *LaPine Techonology Corp. v. Kyocera Corp., 130 F.3d 884, 889 (CA9 1997)* for the proposition that the FAA leaves parties 'free . . . to draft a contract that sets rules for arbitration and dictates an alternative standard of review.'"[101]

To satisfy the arbitrator's adherence to the District Court's instructions concerning applicability of a state court act at issue, each party sought modification again at the District Court level based upon the stipulated standard of review for legal error. Both parties subsequently appealed to the Ninth Circuit, where the defendant for the first time advanced the proposition that the Ninth Circuit's recent *en banc* action overruling *LaPine* in *Kyocera Corp., The Prudential-Bache Trade Servs, Inc.* 341 F.3d 987, 1000 (2003), *rendered the arbitration agreements provision for judicial review bottomed on legal error wholly unenforceable as a matte of law.*[102] The Ninth Circuit found residence in Mattel's contention and held that "[u]nder *Kyocera* the terms of the arbitration agreement controlling the mode of judicial review are unenforceable and severable."

In affirming the Ninth Circuit's pronouncement, the Supreme Court disavowed two propositions that petitioner Hall Street advanced that ultimately reconciled a split between the circuits.[103] First, the Court observed that the proposition of judicial review arising from its decision in *Wilko v. Swan*[104] expanded and amplified the grounds for appellate review codified in Sections 10 and 11 of the FAA by recognizing "manifest disregard of the law" as an additional ground for vacatur not included in Section 10. In this connection, the Court underscored that "[q]uite apart from its leap from a supposed judicial expansion by interpretation to a private expansion by contract, Hall Street overlooks the fact that the statement it relies on expressly rejects just what Hall Street asks for here, general review for an arbitrator's legal errors."[105]

99 *Id.*

100 *Id.*

101 *Id*

102 *Id.* at 261.

103 The Ninth and Tenth Circuits have held that parties may not contract for expanded judicial review. [**15] See *Kyocera Corp. v. Prudential-Bache Trade Servs., Inc.*, 341 F.3d 987, 1000 (CA9 2003); *Bowen v. Amoco Pipeline Co.*, 254 F.3d 925, 936 (CA10 2001). The First, Third, Fifth, and Sixth Circuits, meanwhile, have held that parties may so contract. See *Puerto Rico Tel. Co. v. U.S. Phone Mfg. Corp.*, 427 F.3d 21, 31 (CA1 2005); *Jacada (Europe), Ltd. v. International Marketing Strategies, Inc.*, 401 F.3d 701, 710 (CA6 2005); *Roadway Package System, Inc., v. Kayser*, 257 F.3d 287, 288 (CA3 2001); *Gateway Technologies, Inc., v. MCI Telecommunications Corp.*, 64 F.3d 993, 997 (CA5 1995). The Fourth Circuit has taken the latter side of the split in an unpublished opinion, see *Syncor Int'l Corp. v. McLeland*, 120 F.3d 262 (1997), while the Eight Circuit has expressed agreement with the former side in dicta, see *UHC Management Co. v, Computer Sciences Corp.*, 148 F.3d 992–998 (1998).

104 *Wilko v. Swan*, 246 U.S. 427, 74 S.Ct. 182, 98 L.Ed. 1698 (1963).

105 *Id.* at 262.

Second, the Supreme Court noted that Hall Street's emphasis on Congressional intent promoting enforceability of private agreements to arbitrate does violence to FAA "textual features at odds with enforcing a contract to expand judicial review following the arbitration."[106] Moreover, further analytic support was found in the plain meaning of language embodied in Section 9 of the FAA commanding that regarding an application for an order confirming an award, a court "must grant" the order "unless the award is vacate, modified, or corrected as prescribed in Sections 10 and 11 for that."[107]

The Supreme Court command in Hall Street represents a stark analytical departure from primary reliance on the precept of party-autonomy to a more tempered analysis favoring *predictability, uniformity, and transparency* to enhance a seemingly overriding principle that when developed to its logical conclusion necessarily harkens back to party-autonomy as an unavoidable and unnecessary conclusion: the protection of arbitral proceedings from judicial intervention. To be sure, where parties accorded autonomy to engraft judicial intervention into arbitral proceedings to reconfigure and redefine the rule or courts and judiciary with respect to arbitration are concerned, the very principle party-autonomy ultimately would fail. If arbitration is to stand *in pari materia* with judicial processes, then courts must assume the role of facilitators charged with assisting arbitral tribunals and not the tasks and responsibility of benignly intervening in arbitrations and in adjudicative capacity. The *Hall Street* decision preserves and enhances this delicate balance between court and arbitral tribunal, judge and arbitrator, seemingly, but only seemingly, at the expense of party-autonomy, only to rescue this very concept in the overarching goal of securing the dignity of arbitration.

These judicial efforts are susceptible to meaningful and material critique with respect to technical matters of statutory construction and *tour de force* arguments that bring to mind the proliferation of epicycles within Ptolemy's *Almagest* to reconcile recurring discrepancies that challenged a rubric that sought to "save appearances" where the underlying premise was predicated on the proposition that the sun revolved around the earth. Irrespective of the intellectual and conceptual debilities that rendered the Severability Doctrine possible, judicial tenets rendering Section 2 of the FAA a substantive and not a procedural provision, and providing for the FAA's application to state courts, the importance of the principle of party-autonomy and the doctrine of limited judicial intervention in arbitral proceedings were significantly advanced. This development simultaneously enhanced arbitration's standing while diminishing even further the last vestiges of historical prejudices that fueled judicial contempt and skepticism for arbitration.

106 *Id.* at 264.

107 *Id.*

CHAPTER 11

U.S. Arbitration Law and Its Dialogue with the New York Convention: The Development of Four Issues

U.S. common law developments in the field of international commercial arbitration are practically too numerous and vast in scope to articulate, let alone analyze within a paradigm that seeks to discern doctrinal development. This task is rendered even more daunting when the proposition that "development equals progress" is challenged as a tenet that lacks inherent universality, and therefore is only true depending on the particularity of circumstances without in itself embodying apodictic features. Therefore, the developments analyzed here have been limited only to four salient principles having one common denominator; the extent to which they may justify amending the New York Convention to further the principles of uniformity, predictive value, certainty, party-autonomy, and transparency of standard in the Convention's application.

Together with the creation of the International Criminal Court (the "Rome Statute") and the European Union, the New York Convention is likely the most successful international juridic accomplishment of the past century. As of this writing, the Convention enjoys 142 signatory nations. It can be asserted with confidence that the entire international commercial community of nations has signed the Convention. The absence of transnational courts of civil procedure vested with jurisdiction to adjudicate international private disputes has created a void that international commercial arbitration is filling in a manner universally acclaimed as effective and essential to the success of international commerce, particularly in a climate of economic globalization. The myopic effect of commenting on contemporary historical developments creates the expected distortion that erroneously reconfigures historical perspective. International commercial arbitration today serves as a historical temporal bridge until transnational courts of civil procedure with jurisdiction to adjudicate private commercial disputes become a functional reality rather than an aspirational academic exercise. Doubtless the *eidos* on the blackboard shall become a viable reality. The global institutionalization of these tribunals is still decades from coming into being. The New York Convention has rendered global alternative dispute resolution possible. Accordingly, it has spared entrepreneurs, captains of industry, and merchants engaged in cross border transactions from having to submit to the perils and uncertainties endemic to litigation pursued in foreign jurisdictions against persons or entities residing in those jurisdictions and serving political and economic functions that redound to the benefit of political systems that do not necessarily value the virtues of an independent judiciary.

It is in this context of virtually unprecedented judicial success that U.S. doctrinal developments in arbitration in the following four narrow areas shall be analyzed: (i) nonsignatories to agreement to arbitrate, (ii) jurisdiction to enforce, (iii) *Forum Non Conveniens*, and (iv) annulled awards. The paradox raised by this analysis is simple enough. Are the developments to be considered suggestive of ambiguities and less than perfect drafting, evinced by the Convention's plain language, that cry out for correction through amendment? Is the Convention's success so daunting and spectacular as to elevate the somewhat trite and banal adage that "if it is not broken, why fix it" to the level of an axiom to be observed? Perhaps a different perspective to be considered is whether the developments to be examined constitute "progress" or just mere "change" that are but indifferent in nature and character, that is, a change of inconsequential juridic moment?

A. NONSIGNATORIES TO AGREEMENTS TO ARBITRATE

There is U.S. authority for the proposition that nonparties to an arbitration agreement may be forced to participate in a specific arbitration proceeding. This premise has been developing for some time and has itself spawned disparate nuances and conflict among the circuits. Its existence and development are not novel. They do, however, stand in stark contrast with the language contained in Article II of the Convention, which in pertinent part reads that states shall recognize "an agreement in writing under which the parties undertake to submit to arbitration."[1] Remarkably, however, the Convention does not contain *any* reference to the application of arbitration clauses (i.e., arbitration agreements) to nonparties. Case law on this issue highlights and emphasizes different scenarios and the triggering of long recognized and established legal tenets that may justify what at the surface appears to be contrary to, and certainly beyond the ambit of, the Convention's plain language, if not altogether inimical to it. Sustained analysis is warranted.

The orthodox grounds for binding nonsignatories to an arbitration agreement are configured by multiple legal theories. By way of example, the Second Circuit Court of Appeals has stated that these "theories arise out of common law principles of contract and agency law."[2] Indeed, the Court acknowledged that "five theories for binding non-signatories to arbitration agreements [have been amply recognized]: (1) incorporation by reference, (2) assumption, (3) agency, (4) veil-piercing/alter ego, and (5) estoppel."[3]

[1] *Article II* of the Convention states:

1. Each Contracting State shall recognize an Agreement in writing under which the parties undertake to submit to arbitration all or any differences which have arisen or which may arise between them in respect of a defined legal relationship, whether contractual or not concerning a subject matter capable of settlement by arbitration.
2. The term "agreement in writing" shall include an arbitration clause and a contract or an arbitration agreement, signed by the parties or contained in an exchange of letters or telegrams.
3. The Court of a Contracting State, when seized of an action in a matter in respect of which the parties have made an agreement within the meaning of this article, shall, at the request of one of the parties refer the parties to arbitration, unless it finds that the said agreement is null and void, inoperative or incapable of being performed.

[2] Thomson-CFS, S.A. v. American Arbitration Association, 64 F.3d 773, 776 (2d Cir. 1995).

[3] *Id.*

In that case, *Thomson-CSF, S.A. v. American Arbitration Association*, a corporate parent that had recently acquired a subsidiary, filed an action in the District Court for the Southern District of New York against the subsidiary's supplier petitioning for a declaration stating that it, the corporate parent, was not bound by the arbitration clause contained in the agreement between the subsidiary and the supplier. Moreover, the corporate parent sought injunctive relief seeking to proscribe any additional proceedings against it under the general agreement and the arbitration clause. The defendant/supplier predictably cross-moved, seeking an order compelling the corporate parent to arbitrate any of its claims if it elected to proceed as such. The district court denied the parent corporation's request for relief and granted the supplier's motion seeking to compel the corporate parent to arbitration.

The Second Circuit reversed the district court's ruling holding that "[t]he district court below improperly extended the limited theories upon which this Court is willing to enforce an arbitration agreement against a nonsignatory. The district court's hybrid approach dilutes the safeguards afforded to a nonsignatory by the "ordinary principles of contract and agency and fails to adequately protect parent companies, the subsidiaries of which have entered into arbitration agreements."[4] This holding was predicated on analysis of six rudimentary grounds. First, while the record on appeal demonstrated that the parent corporation (*Thomson*) was aware that the operative agreement containing the arbitration clause at issue sought to bind it as an affiliate of its subsidiary (*Rediffusion*), the record was equally illustrative in demonstrating that "Thomson explicitly disavowed any obligations arising out of the [agreement at issue] and filed [an] action seeking a declaration of non-liability under the Agreement."[5] Thus, it was based on this record evidence that the Second Circuit concluded that *Thomson* did not *assume* to be bound by the agreement. Certainly, this phase of the analysis is fact-intensive and susceptible to the deference ascribed to factual inferences and to the application of legal principles to such "factual findings."

Second, despite the hornbook precepts prescribing that under theories of agency law a nonsignatory to an arbitration agreement may be bound by the agreement,[6] the Court focused on the timing reflecting that *Thomson* in fact had acquired its subsidiary *after* the subject agreement had been executed by Rediffusion and the supplier (E & S). Consequently, the Court aptly reasoned that "*Thomson* could not possibly be bound under an agency theory."[7]

Third, the Court engaged in the requisite fact-intensive analysis attendant to a piercing of a corporate veil or alter ego determination effort. Without engaging in the tedious and well-recognized recitation of the virtually universal piercing of the corporate veil standard, the Second Circuit exercised its judgment in placing little if any weight on the district court's finding that "[c]ounsel for E & S now asserts that an alter-ego relationship between *Thomson* and Rediffusion may exist."[8] The Court further acknowledged that "[w]hile E & S concedes that it can make no showing of fraud [a primary element, without more, justifying piercing of the corporate veil], it

4 *Id.* at 780.

5 *Id.* at 777.

6 *See, e.g.*, Interbras Cayman Co. v. Orient Victory Shipping Co., S.A., 663 F.2d 4, 6–7 (2d Cir. 1981); A/S Custodia v. Lessin Int'l, Inc., 503 F.2d 318, 320 (2d Cir. 1993).

7 *Thomson*, 64 F.3d. at 777.

8 *Id.*

argues that Thomson sufficiently dominated Rediffusion as to justify veil piercing."[9] However, after enunciating the traditional litany of facts that typically give rise to an inference that piercing the corporate veil is necessary and appropriate,[10] the Second Circuit, after canvassing the borders of the piercing of the corporate veil doctrine together with the record evidence, concluded that "E & S (the subsidiary) has not demonstrated that Thomson exerted the degree of *control* over Rediffusion necessary to justify piercing the corporate veil." The Court continued its observation, noting that while the district court "found that 'Thomson has common ownership with [R]ediffusion; that Thomson actually controls [R]ediffusion; . . . [a]nd Thomson incorporated Rediffusion] into its own organizational and decision-making structure, '*the district court did not find an abandonment of the corporate structure.*'"[11] Based upon a totality of circumstances analysis, the Second Circuit drew diametrically opposite factual inferences from those that the district court crafted in determining the separate juridic integrity between Thomson and Rediffusion. Therefore, the piercing of the corporate veil/alter ego theories was deemed inconsequential for purposes of engrafting upon *Thomson* the obligation to arbitrate under the agreement.

Fourth, the theory of *estoppel* was discarded, despite the command to arbitrate premised on an *estoppel* theory in *Deloitte Noraudit A/S v. Deloitte Haskins and Cells.*[12] Even though the trial court had not analyzed the case based upon an *estoppel* theory, it had engrafted onto Thomson knowledge of the subject agreement, prior to the completion of Thomson's acquisition of Rediffusion.[13] Despite the visceral appeal of this *estoppel* argument, "*Thomson* . . . never acquired, nor sought to acquire, imaging equipment from E & S. Rather, E & S asserts a theory of benefit under the [agreement] which in essence amounts to an anti-trust violation-according to E & S."[14] Because the nature of the benefit that inured to Thomson's gain was *indirect* rather than *direct, estoppel* was rejected on appellate review as inapplicable and beyond the ambit of *Deloitte's* command.

Fifth, a second permutation of the *estoppel* theory was equally deemed inapplicable. Arbitration between a nonsignatory and a signatory shall ensue where

9 *Id.*

10 Specifically the Court noted that piercing the corporate veil is warranted where (i) no bank accounts, (ii) offices, (iii) stationary, (iv) transactions, and other activities were undertaken in the name of the subsidiary. (Citing Cart Blanche (Singapore)Pte., Ltd. v. Dinners Club Int'l, Inc., 2 F.3d 24, 29 (2d Cir. 1993)). Also, there was reference to circumstances where the parent and subsidiary share (i) common office and staff, (ii) common officers, (iii) bank accounts where funds are intermingled,(iv) a relationship that is not arms length in nature, and (v) an accounting system pursuant to which they are not deemed separate profit centers. (Citing Walter E. Heller& Co. v. Video Innovations, Inc, 730 F.2d 50, 53 (2d Cir. 1984)).

11 *Id.* at 778. In particular, the Second Circuit reached a quite different conclusion based on the facts of record that of the district court noting that corporate formalities between *Thomson* and Rediffusion were followed as well as a complete absence of any *intermingling of corporate finances and directorship. Id.*

12 Deloitte Noraudit A/S v. Deloitte Haskins and Cells, 9 F.3d 1060, 1064 (2d Cir. 1993).

13 The district court found that:

> *Thomson* had notice of the Working Agreement prior to . . . completing the purchase of Rediffusion, that E & S expressed the intension to bind *Thomson* to the Agreement prior to the completion of the purchase of Rediffusion, that *Thomson* incorporated [Rediffusion] into its own organizational and decision-making structure, and that *Thomson* benefited from that incorporation. *Thomson*, 64 F.3d. at 778 (omitting district court citation).

14 *Noraudit*, 9 F.3d at 1064.

the nonsignatory is successful in establishing a close nexus and relationship between (i) the parties involved, and (ii) the operative occurrence or transaction.[15] Because this version of *estoppel* has been crafted to estop a *signatory* from attempting to circumvent its obligation pursuant to a contract that it executed and promised to honor, it is apposite to the fact pattern presented in *Thomson* where the *signatory* (E & S) seeks to compel a *nonsignatory* to arbitrate. Accordingly, this doctrine too was found to be inapplicable.

Sixth and finally, the district court's reliance on *Deloitte* and *McAllister*[16] was found to be unavailing. This conclusion was based on a "hybrid" analysis of these two cases. Significantly, in both *Deloitte* and *McAllister* the Second Circuit remanded to the district court with instruction to conduct evidentiary hearings applying basic principles of contract and agency law. Here, however, the Second Circuit observed that the district court found a nonsignatory to be bound to an arbitration agreement "with a less than full showing of some articulable theory under contract or agency law."[17]

Thomson is of considerable didactic importance both for its substantive affirmations and because of its glaring omissions. The opinion illustrates the fundamental contractual and commercial legal precepts applicable to arbitration agreements where the participation of a nonsignatory is at issue. Considered under a clinical light, that such basic precepts as (i) assumption, (ii) agency, (iii) corporate veil/alter ego, and (iv) estoppel can be applied, in effect, to circumvent the time-honored and presumably (only presumably) proposition that a nonparty to an agreement may be deemed a party for liability and not beneficiary reasons, is truly astounding and extraordinary. The use of traditional doctrines to avert a most orthodox principle is testimony to the doctrinal-positive development of U.S. arbitration. Where before courts struggled first to justify arbitration's subordinate role with respect to judicial proceedings and lesser judicial status as a contract than that enjoyed by commercial contracts, now the exceptional character and nature of an arbitration agreement compels the reconfiguration of the application of even the most orthodox and fundamental precepts of contractual law, contract interpretation, and corporate law to exempt arbitration agreements from judicial limitations engrafted upon commercial contracts.

This development often is overlooked, as it indeed has a proclivity to be undermined if not examined in the context of a fluid-developing doctrinal rubric. Also, the rules governing arbitration contracts must reflect sufficient flexibility to comport

[15] *See, e.g.*, Sunkist Soft Drinks, Inc. v. Sunkist Growers, Inc., 10 F.3d 753, 757–58 (11th Cir. 1993) (stating that "[t]herefore, the focus of our inquiry should be on the nature of the underlying claims asserted . . . to determine whether those claims fall within the scope of the arbitration clause contained in the license agreement") Cert. denied., 513 U.S. 869, 115 S.Ct. 190, 130 Lawyers Ed. 2d 123(1994); J. J. Ryan & Sons, Inc. v. Rhone Poulenc Textile, S.A., 863 F.2d 315, 320–21 (4th Cir. 1988) (stating that "[w]hen the charges against a parent company and its subsidiary are based on the same facts and inherently inseparable, a court may refer claims against the parent to arbitration even though the parent is not formally a party to the arbitration agreement."); McBro Planning & Dev. Co. v. Triangle Elec. Constr. Co., 741 F.2d 342, 344 (7th Cir. 1984) (citing authority for the proposition that because the operative claims are "intimately founded in and intertwined with the underlying contract obligations," referral to arbitration of non-signatory is appropriate).

[16] McAllister Bros., Inc. v. A & S Transp. Co., 621 F.2d 519 (2d Cir. 1980).

[17] *Thomson*, 64 F.3d. at 780.

with the development of increasingly complex corporate configurations operating in an arena of equally complicated transnational transactions.

The omissions in the *Thomson* opinion are equally exceptional. At the outset, *nowhere* in the opinion is there *any* reference to the New York Convention and the implications of nonsignatory participation in an arbitration proceeding for purposes of execution of a prospective arbitral award. In this same vein, there is no mention, let alone a sustained effort, to reconcile or explain the apparent antinomy between the possible issuance of an order compelling a nonsignatory to an arbitration agreement or its underlying agreement to participate in the arbitration process, and in the plain language contained in Article II of the New York Convention, in part, contracting states should only recognize "an agreement in writing under which the parties undertake to submit to arbitration."[18]

Also absent from the opinion is any true analysis of the FAA. The reader only finds a passing boiler plate recitation that hardly expounds upon the issue of the Act's substantive provisions and a question of federal preemption that would be particularly helpful because contract law is typically governed by state law.[19] This discussion would have been especially appropriate because the subsidiary, Rediffusion, was a British company and the supplier (E & S) was a U.S. corporation located in Salt Lake City, Utah, where the agreement at issue was negotiated and executed.

The Second Circuit's holding in *Thomson* stands in stark contrast with the Fourth Circuit's ruling in *International Paper Company v. Schwabedissen Maschinen & Anlagen*[20] In *International Paper* the signatory successfully secured an arbitration award against a non-signatory to the operative contract containing the arbitration clause at issue based upon an estoppel theory and where the non-signatory also attempted to raise a Convention Article II defense precisely by asserting that only a party to a written contract would be subject to execution of such an arbitral award.

In affirming the district court's ruling and rejecting the non-signatory's contentions, the Fourth Circuit stated that "[a] non signatory is estopped from refusing to comply with an arbitration clause 'when it receives a *direct benefit* from a contract containing an arbitration clause.'"[21] Critical to the affirmance was the Court's finding that the contract between the distributor (Wood) and the manufacturer (Schwabedissen) provided "part of the factual foundation for every claim asserted by the purchaser non-signatory (Paper) against the manufacturer.[22] Specifically the purchaser averred that seller "failed to honor the warranties in the contract between the manufacturer and the distributor (Wood – Schwabedissen) and as part of the allegations sought damages, revocation, and rejection consonant with the Wood-Schwabedissen contract.[23] Accordingly, because the totality of the purchaser's case

18 *See* New York Convention, Article II, paragraph 2.

19 Early in the discussion the opinion, borrowing from *International Bank*, 282 F.2d 231, 233 (2d Cir. 1960), decided nearly one-half century earlier, enunciated that "[i]t does not follow, however, that under the [Federal Arbitration] Act an obligation to arbitrate attaches only to one who has personally signed the written arbitration provision." *Thomson*, 64 F.3d. at 776.

The Supreme Court has directed circuit courts to "apply ordinary state law principles that govern the formation of contracts," First Options of Chicago, Inc. v. Kaplan, 514 U.S. 938, 944 (1995).

20 International Paper Company v. Schwabedissen Maschinen & Anlagen, 206 F.3d 411 (4th Cir. 2000).

21 *Id* at 418.

22 *Id.*

23 *Id.*

rested upon the rights it alleged to have under the operative contract, the Fourth Circuit rightfully concluded that "it cannot seek to enforce those contractual rights and avoid the contract's requirement that 'any dispute arising out of' the contract be arbitrated."[24]

In addition, the Court rejected the purchaser's assertion that the Convention precludes recognition and enforcement of the arbitral award "because it requires United States Courts to enforce international arbitration agreements only against parties to 'an agreement in writing.'"[25] Here the Court cited authority standing for the proposition that "the estoppel doctrine also applies to non-signatories to arbitration agreements governed by the Convention."[26]

In *International Paper*, the very procedural oddity of the case provided a fertile ground for the issues raised as well as the Court's adjudication of these concerns. Curiously, it was the purchaser (Paper) who first filed a request for arbitration before the International Court of Arbitration in Geneva.[27] It was in that proceeding that the purchaser lost on the ground that it had failed to assert any basis for recovery against the manufacturer because the arbitral panel concluded that no contract existed between manufacturer and Westinghouse (purchaser's predecessor-in-interest.) Moreover, the distributor was not an agent for the manufacturer and purchaser's predecessor-in-interest was not a third-party beneficiary to the contract between the distributor and the manufacturer. This finding and factual configuration caused purchaser to face an arbitral award assessing costs against it in addition to a ruling in the manufacturer's favor. It was upon issuance of this award that purchaser refused compliance and sought leave to file a second amended complaint petitioning to aver a breach of both an implied warranty of workmanlike service and an oral contract to repair.[28] Ironically, it was the party who first sought arbitral recourse that subsequently attempted to aver any connection with an arbitration agreement between the manufacturer and the distributor, specifically in grounds of not being a signatory, while in the initial arbitration that it had commenced the arbitral tribunal found that there was no contract whatsoever between purchaser's predecessor-in-interest and the manufacturer.

International Paper, particularly when considered together with *Thomson*, provides for a more comprehensive view of the jurisprudence supporting a non-signatory's participation in an arbitration proceeding and the enforceability of the prospective arbitral award against such a "party" despite the plain language of Article II of the Convention. In this case, although only treated in the context of a footnote, the primacy of the Convention, which forms part of the FAA, and, therefore, may give rise to federal preemption, articulates with considerable coherence the relationship between state law rules of contractual interpretation, highlights the primacy now accorded to arbitration agreements, which not only enjoy the same juridic hierarchy as other contracts, but also command exceptional conceptual treatment to the extent that venerable contract principles are circumvented so as to bolster the tactical execution of arbitration agreements. In this single and limited respect it can be persuasively

[24] *Id.*

[25] *Id.* (citing to Article II, paragraph 1 of the Convention).

[26] *Id.* (citation omitted).

[27] *Id.*

[28] *Id.*

asserted that arbitration agreements actually enjoy a more privileged position than do other forms of contracts.

Upon review of the leading case law addressing the extent to which non-signatories to an arbitration agreement may be judicially compelled to participate in the arbitral process, three propositions are clearly discernable in what is a morass of analyses that all share a proclivity for being factually intensive. First, there is no ostensible standard that is uniformly and universally applicable. Second, some cases tend to apply a "proximity" or "relationship" test. Pursuant to this paradigm, the analysis focuses on the extent to which the parties, the transaction, and the occurrences at issue between and among the non-signatory, the signatories, and the subject matter of the underlying contract, are in fact intertwined. This test is extremely factually intensive. As may be gleaned from the opinions in *Thomson* and *International Paper*, it is not rare, indeed common, for courts-district courts and the reviewing appellate court- to draw different inferences and conclusions upon analysis of the identical factual record.[29] The second test that is readily discernable concentrates on fundamental tenets of contract and corporate law. Analyses of such precepts as agency, beneficiary status, estoppel, corporate governance, and corporate veil queries, all seem to be applied indiscriminately in what appears to be a "contract-corporate" paragon or test. Third, courts at times apply a hybrid of these two analyses. These cases can best be described as applying a "totality of circumstances" test. Indeed, in some instances the "contract-corporate" test itself is treated as multiple individual free standing standards, fulfillment of any one of which would suffice to render a non-signatory bound to an arbitration proceeding. Furthermore, the direct and indirect beneficiary theories are also deemed to be independent on and distinct from the "contract-corporation" test.[30]

Accordingly, there is a need for integrating the five "theories" enunciated in *Thomson* into a comprehensive standard to be uniformly applied in determining the arbitrability of non-signatories to a contract containing an arbitration clause. Also, the role of the Convention and the FAA in creating a conceptual link between the compulsion of non-signatories to participate in an arbitration proceeding where a state court order constitutes the basis of compelling participation and the enforceability of an arbitration award entered against the non-signatory, commands more rigorous conceptual and doctrinal development.

In turn, the three analyses are bound by one common feature; they are all fact intensive and, to that extent, lacking in rigor with respect to predictive value. In addition, many of the cases fail to underscore or even mention the surface inconsistencies apparent between the joinder of a non-signatory to an arbitration process and the plain language of Article II of the Convention, or otherwise reference the FAA and the extent to which federal policy and preemption principles pervade this jurisprudence, even if silently so. In this same spirit, many cases omit the more long term analysis concerning enforceability of a prospective adverse

[29] Because most cases concerning the issue of a non-signatory's joinder to an arbitral proceeding only entails scrutiny of factual issues that rarely command evaluation of character or credibility, the often reference objection asserting that a district court (i.e. the trial court) is "closer to the facts" than the reviewing second instance tribunal, certainly finds little if any foundation in this body of jurisprudence.

[30] *See, e.g.*, Bridas S.A.P.I.C. v. Government of Turkmenistan, 345 F.3d 347 (5th Cir. 2003).

arbitral award pursuant to Article V of the Convention against a non-prevailing non-signatory.[31]

Finally, the question must be raised. Is this doctrinal development evinced by the case law governing the extent to which a non-signatory to an arbitration agreement subject to compulsion to participate in the arbitration proceeding arising from such an agreement, a line of jurisprudence that calls for amending the New York Convention? Would it be of greater service to transnational commerce, not to mention the juridic principles of party-autonomy, uniformity, predictability, certainty, and transparency of standard, to amend the Convention so as to eliminate completely any perceived ambiguity or vagueness? Are practitioners, courts, arbitrators, and commerce better served by abstaining from any amendment effort-irrespective of whether such effort seeks to establish beyond cavil either the complete exclusion or qualified inclusion of non-signatories to an arbitration agreement-or merely cultivate the aspirational objective that this authority will find its perfect workings with the development of a unified standard? Even so, is the United States hurting itself to the extent that this jurisprudence represents an aberration when compared to the majority of the Convention's signatories? Certainly these questions raise numerous complexities that cannot be adequately identified, let alone addressed, without spilling the amount of ink contained in the tomes of a very well stocked library. The identification here, however, of these limited issues does suggest that there are practical options for eliminating ambiguities and promoting the referenced principles, albeit with the difficulties incident to all endeavors worth undertaking.

[31] For some of the more salient appellate court decisions addressing the joinder of non-signatories to an arbitration agreement and, therefore, to an arbitral process, *See, e.g.*, Denney v. BDO Seidman, LLP, 412 F.3d 58, 70 (2d Cir. 2005) (Remanding case "to the district court to enable it to consider the merits of the estoppel claim asserted by the . . . defendants, and, specifically, whether the issues the Deutsche Bank defendants seek to arbitrate are indeed intertwined with the [operative] agreements", and also holding that non-signatory plaintiffs may be compelled to arbitrate pursuant to the same "proximity or relationship" test.); Contec Corp. v. Remote Solution, Co., 398 F.3d 205, 209 (2d Cir. 2005) ("A useful benchmark for rational sufficiency can be found in our estoppel decision in *Choctaw* . . . where we held that the signatory to an arbitration agreement is estopped from avoiding arbitration with a non-signatory when the issues the non-signatory is seeking to resolve in arbitration are intertwined with the agreement that the estopped party has signed.") (Internal quotation marks and citation omitted); Trippe Manufacturing Company v. Niles Audio Corporation, 401 F.3d 529, 532 (3d Cir. 2005) (Articulating that "[t]here are five theories for binding non-signatories to arbitration agreements. (1) incorporation by reference, (2) assumption, (3) agency, (4) veil-piercing/alter ego, and (5) estoppel."); Bridas S.A.I.C. v. Government of Turkmenistan, 345 F.3d 347, 361 (5th Cir. 2003) (Holding that the district court abused its discretion in applying the "intertwined claims theory of equitable estoppel to this case", and also rejecting "the direct beneficiary" theory for binding a non-signatory); Javitch v. First Union Securities, 315 F.3d 619, 629 (6th Cir. 2003) (Holding that "It is only a signatory that may be estopped from avoiding arbitration with a non signatory when the issues the non-signatory is seeking to resolve in arbitration are intertwined with the underlying contract", and applying the "contract-corporate" test articulated in Thomson); Employers Ins. of Wausau v. Bright Meadow Specialties, Inc., 251 F.3d 1316, 1322 (11th Cir. 2001) (Acknowledging that "[c]ourts, however, have recognized a number of theories under which non-signatories may be bound to the arbitration agreements of others."); *and* In Re: The Matter of Arbitration between Judy Lee v. Chica, 983 F.2d 883, 887 (8th Cir. 1993) (Holding that party "can be compelled to arbitrate [claimant's] claims against him as the disclose agent of [party], arising out of customer agreement, even though he did not sign the customer agreement.").

B. JURISDICTION TO ENFORCE

The New York Convention's universal success can be measured in multiple ways. The one hundred and forty-two signatories is certainly emblematic of the Convention's universal acceptance, which can only be translated into a meaningful measure of success. An additional badge of success is exemplified by the extent to which the Convention has contributed to according international commercial arbitration universal legitimacy and credibility. In turn, this status, which has defied and surpassed orthodox views that nourished judicial skepticism and disdain for arbitration, provided international commercial arbitration with the necessary normative foundation to serve as a substitute for transnational court of civil procedure invested with jurisdiction to adjudicate private civil disputes, until such time as these courts become a viable reality. The Convention's laudable contributions in the field of international commercial arbitration in both theory and *praxis* are substantial. This success, however, does rest on the fragile premise holding that signatory nations shall exercise best efforts and good faith in adhering to the recognition and enforcement strictures embodied in Article V.

Congress implemented the Convention by enacting Chapter II of the FAA. Section 203 specifically reads:

> An action or proceeding falling under the Convention shall be deemed to arise under the laws and treaties of the United States. The district courts of the United States (including the courts enumerated in Section 460 of Title 28) shall have original jurisdiction over such an action or proceeding, regardless of the amount in controversy.

Notably, nowhere in the FAA do we find language concerning exercise of personal jurisdiction over the party against whom enforcement of an arbitration award is sought as a predicate to the recognition and enforcement of an otherwise legally viable award. Likewise, nowhere in Article V of the Convention, or anywhere else in this treaty, is the issue of jurisdiction over an "arbitral award debtor" a condition precedent to recognition and enforcement.

The development of U.S. jurisprudence, all of the single voice (albeit with some dissonant notes that shall inevitably compel analysis) requiring the exercise of such jurisdiction over an "arbitral award debtor" poses critical questions having constitutional consequences that may not be able to find reconciliation with the general policies in favor of universal enforcement that underlie the Convention. If indeed the constitutional concerns cannot be harmonized with the Convention's enforcement policy, which policy is shared by the overwhelming majority of the signatory nations, what doctrinal developments should the United States judiciary, and possibly legislature, undertake to foster reciprocity among signatory nations in the recognition and enforcement of foreign arbitral award to mitigate or altogether eliminate disparate and unfavorable treatment directed at U.S. "arbitral award creditors" seeking enforcement pursuant to Article V in foreign jurisdictions?

Despite what is now a developed corpus of jurisprudence on the issue governing and enforcing U.S. courts' personal jurisdiction over a prospective "arbitral award debtor," the Ninth Circuit Court of Appeals' opinion in *Glencore Grain Rotterdam*

B.V. v. Shivnath Rai Harnarain Co.[32] is perhaps uniquely eloquent. The facts merit recitation. That case is predicated on eleven international sale/purchase contracts between Green, a Netherlands corporation having its principal place of business in Rotterdam, and Shivnath Rai, a manufacturer and exporter of rice with its place of incorporation in India and principal place of business in New Delhi.[33] The parties had contracted for the purchase of approximately 300 tons of rice that Shivnath Rai was to supply to Glencore Grain. Additionally, delivery was destined to take place at the Port of Kandla, India. An arbitration clause was contained in each of the operative agreements.[34]

Issues concerning delivery precipitated Glencore Grain's filing of a request for arbitration before the London Rice Brokers Association ("LRBA"). The LRBA entered an award in favor of Glencore Grain in the approximate amount of US$6.5 million, including interest, which placed the award at a figure in excess of US$7 million. Shivnath Rai failed to challenge the decision "*in England, where the award became final and remains enforceable, nor did Shivnath pay up.*"[35]

Glencore sought enforcement of the award by filing suit in the High Court of Delhi at New Delhi, India, where the award remained pending. Glencore Grain then filed an application in the Federal District Court for the Northern District of California, seeking recognition and enforcement of the award pursuant to the Convention.[36] A motion to dismiss asserting six separate and independent grounds, including want of personal jurisdiction, ensued.[37]

The district court denied Glencore Grain's petition seeking confirmation of the award. The Ninth Circuit affirmed the district court's ruling, premising its affirmance on seven grounds, each of which merits consideration. First, Glencore Grain's contention that the Convention and the FAA "do *not* say: (1) neither the Convention nor its implementing legislation expressly requires personal jurisdiction over the party against whom confirmation is sought; and (2) lack of personal jurisdiction over the defendant in the state where enforcement is sought is not among the Convention's seven defenses to recognition and enforcement of a foreign arbitration award."[38] This proposition was rejected in its entirety.

Specifically, while the Court recited the hornbook doctrine that a statute cannot engraft or grant personal jurisdiction contrary to the Constitution where it is indeed

32 Glencore Green Rotterdam B.V. v. Shivnath Rai Harnarain Co., 284 F. 3d 1114 (9th Cir. 2002).

33 *Id.*

34 The arbitration clause provide:

> Any dispute arising on this Contract shall be referred for settlement to the Arbitration by two Members of [the London Rice Brokers'] Association's Panel of Arbitrators or their Umpire, being also a member of this Panel. Each party to appoint one Arbitrator in having the right to reject one nominee. . . . the parties to the arbitration shall have the right of appealing against any Award (except on questions of law) within thirty days from the date of Award to the London Rice Brokers' Association, whose decision shall be final. Any payments arising out of the Award are due to be made within thirty days of the date thereof. *Id.*

35 *Rotterdam*, 284 F. 3d at 1118.

36 June 10, 1958, 21 U.S.T. 2517, TIAS 6997, 330 UNTS 38, reprinted following 9 U.S.C.A. §201 (West 1999).

37 *Rotterdam*, 284 F. 3d at 1119.

38 *Id.* at 1121 (citing to Convention, art. V, 21 U.S.T. 2517).

The Ninth Circuit offered a turgid three word sentence to this analysis as a transitional sentence stating; "We do not." The meaning of this rather succinct statement is that it (the Ninth Circuit) did not find any significance comparable to that accorded to the proposition by Glencore Grain.

constitutionally proscribed,[39] it did enunciate that Article III, Section 2, Clause 1 of the Constitution does outline the "'character of the controversies over which federal judicial authority may extend,' the lower federal courts rely on Congress to confer this authority through statutory grants of jurisdiction."[40] In sharp relief to the subject matter jurisdiction finding its normative genesis in Article III of the Constitution, the Court further asserts that personal jurisdiction is a product of the Due Process Clause "and represents a restriction on judicial power not as a matter of sovereignty but as a matter of personal liberty."[41] It is from this premise, together with the test governing general and specific personal jurisdiction announced in *International Shoe Co. v. Washington*[42] and progeny, that the Ninth Circuit reasoned that "[t]hus, it is not significant in the least that the legislation implementing the Convention lacks language requiring personal jurisdiction over the litigants." Indeed, it was on this very rationale that the Court went on to "hold that neither the Convention nor its implementing legislation removed the district courts' obligation to find jurisdiction over the defendant in suits to confirm arbitration awards."[43]

Second, characterizing its holding as "so unexceptional"[44] that for this reason it likely explains the paucity of authority on point, the Court appears to glean juridic support and corroboration for its holding in the Restatement (Third) of Foreign Relations Law, Sections 487, cmt. c (1987). There the Court borrowed language from the Restatement stating that "[a]n arbitral award is ordinarily enforced by confirmation in a judgment. . . . as in respect to judgments . . . an action to enforce a foreign arbitral award requires jurisdiction over the award debtor or his property."[45] The Restatement's analysis on this point is limited and far from persuasive as it fails to place its findings in the context of the practice undertaken by the community of nations identified as signatories to the Convention. Also, it is wanting in analysis of the Convention as well as the FAA.

Third, the Ninth Circuit sought to draw additional analytical support from a federal district court case addressing the purported jurisdictional requirement under the Convention. There, the Court expressly analyzed the holding and attendant rationale in *Transatlantic Bulk Shipping Ltd. v. Saudi Chartering S.A.*[46] Even though the district court in fact held that the FAA's grant of original subject matter jurisdiction to federal district courts did not necessarily extend to an endowment of plenary

39 Citing Gilson v. Republic of Ir., 682 F.2d. 1022, 1028 (D.C. Cir. 1982).

40 *Id.* (citation omitted).

41 *Rotterdam*, 284 F. 3d at 1121 (internal citations omitted).

42 International Shoe Co. v. Washington, 326 U.S. 310 (1945).

43 *Id.*

44 *Id.*

45 *Id.* The Ninth Circuit's characterization of the Restatement as "authority" is disconcerting, particularly when addressing an issue to paramount to the relationship among the U.S. judiciary and the judiciaries of the remaining one hundred and forty-one signatories to the Convention. While the Restatement is a wonderful and illustrative resource, it is hardly binding authority. Furthermore, its "authority", which is solely of a "persuasive" nature and character, stems from the academic undertaking eloquently reflected by its very name: "Restatement." Put simply, the *Restatement*'s goal is to canvass and study caselaw in a particular field addressing specific issues and to "re-state" the law based upon that academic and scholastic exercise. The theory underlying this task is that by restating jurisprudence ambiguities in language, *dicta*, and holding shall be removed and the actual juridic significance of a case distilled as embodied by the *Restatement* itself. Where, as here, there is but a handful of decisions on point, the normative basis of the *Restatement* is significantly weakened, even as persuasive authority.

46 Transatlantic Bulk Shipping Ltd. v. Saudi Chartering S.A., 622 F.Supp. 25 (S.D.N.Y. 1985).

personal jurisdiction over "arbitral award debtors" from all over the world that are unable to demonstrate residence, conduct, consent, property, or other facts tending to establish a nexus with the enforcing jurisdiction, that is, the United States.

The district court, however, failed to consider the underlying spirit and general policy pervading the Convention in isolation and, more importantly, in the context of the community of signatory nations and their collective and respective practices when confronting reciprocal scenarios, that is, U.S. "arbitral award creditors" seeking confirmation, recognition, and enforcement of an arbitration award in a foreign jurisdiction. Also, the district court, as did the Ninth Circuit here, refrained from engaging in any attempt to reconcile the due process concerns identified with the mechanics and policies configuring the Convention.

Fourth, the Ninth Circuit additionally relied on three cases adopting the reasoning and holding in *Bulk Shipping*'s: *Italtrade Int'l U.S.A., LLC v. Sri Lanka Cement Corp.*,[47] *Dardana Ltd. v. Yuganskneftegaz*,[48] and *CME Media Enters. B.V. v. Zelezny*.[49] Somewhat remarkably, the Ninth Circuit engaged in no analysis whatsoever of the opinions and holdings in *Italtrade Int'l U.S.A.* and *Dardana Ltd.* It limited its analysis to the opinion in *Zelezny* and first qualified its exegesis of that case by characterizing that *Zelezny* had followed *Bulk Shipping* "in spirit, if not in letter."[50] The district court in *Zelezny*, however, even under the Ninth Circuit's own reading of the case, confirmed the arbitration award and *did not* exercise personal jurisdiction over the "arbitral award debtor." Instead, it appeared to have exercised *quasi in rem* jurisdiction over certain property.[51]

Consequently, it is difficult to extrapolate from the authority upon which the Ninth Circuit relied any conceptual or doctrinal development that reconciles the purported need for exercise of personal jurisdiction over the "arbitral award debtor" as a predicate to confirmation, recognition, or enforcement of an otherwise judicially sound arbitration award in compliance with the Convention.

The Court's reference to and implicit reliance on the Second Circuit's opinion in *Dardana* is somewhat disconcerting. In *Dardana* the Second Circuit explicitly announced:

> This Court has not expressly ruled on the question of whether a party seeking to enforce a foreign arbitral award under the Convention must establish a basis for exercising personal jurisdiction over the other party, or the property of that party, against whom enforcement is sought. . . .
>
> It may not be necessary to reach this difficult issue in this case as *Dardana* has suggested several alternative theories of jurisdiction.[52]

As a technical matter, pursuant to the Second Circuit's holding, the case is inconclusive if used in support of the proposition that exercise of personal jurisdiction

47 Italtrade Int'l U.S.A., LLC v. Sri Lanka Cement Corp., 2002 W.L. 59399, at *2 2002 U.S. Dist. LEXIS 1322, at *5 (E.D.La. 2002).

48 Dardana Ltd. v. Yuganskneftegaz, No. 00 Civ. 4633, 2001 W.L. 1131987, at *1 2001 U.S. Dist. LEXIS 16078, at *4 (S.D.N.Y. 2001).

49 CME Media Enters. B.V. v. Zelezny, No. 01 Civ. 1733, 2001 W.L. 1035138, 2001 U.S. Dist. LEXIS 13888 (S.D.N.Y. 2001).

50 *Rotterdam*, 284 F. 3d at 1122.

51 *Id.* (citing *Zelezny*, 2001 U.S. Dist. LEXIS 13888, at *8).

52 *Dardana* at 206–207.

over the "arbitral award debtor" is a requisite predicate to confirmation of an award pursuant to the Convention.[53]

Fifth, albeit in a footnote, the Ninth Circuit seems to rely on the decision in *CSEE Transport Wiking Trader v. Navimpex Centrala Navala.*[54] Here again, no analysis of *CSEE Transport* is offered other than to qualify its reference to this authority by observing that the Second Circuit "has not expressly adopted the *Bulk Shipping* position."[55]

Sixth, perhaps the most noteworthy premise in the Ninth Circuit's opinion is the tension that it identified between placing a gloss over the FAA that would dispense with the predicate of having jurisdiction over "an arbitral award debtor" and constitutional Due Process concerns. In this connection the Court did contemplate the need to "avoid such constitutionally questionable constructions whenever fairly possible."[56] After reviewing the seminal authority governing the satisfaction of due process requirements in the context of personal jurisdiction,[57] both specific and general personal jurisdiction were found wanting with respect to *Shivnath Rai*. Thus, neither *Shivnath Rai*'s quantitative systematic activities with the forum, independent of the underlying averments forming part of the arbitral proceeding and giving rise to the award sought to be enforced, nor *any* qualitative nexus between the merits and underlying facts that spawned the arbitral award against *Shivnath Rai* were found sufficient to meet fundamental due process concerns. This issue certainly will command greater attention and analysis that was omitted by the Ninth Circuit in its opinion.

As a final premise in support of its affirmance of the district court's ruling, the Court applied a "reasonableness" test also at the essence of personal jurisdiction analyses. In particular, seven factors were scrutinized:[58]

1. the degree to which a defendant intentionally and purposely interjected itself into the affairs of the foreign state;
2. analysis and consideration of the likely burdens that a defendant may face if forced to litigate in the foreign forum;

[53] In the interest of academic integrity and for completeness' sake, it must be mentioned that the Court in *Dardana* does identify *Base Metal Trading, Ltd. v. OJSC "Novokuznetsky Aluminum Factory*, 283 F.2d 208, 212-13 (4th Cir.) (requiring petitioner to establish personal jurisdiction and finding that "the presence of property alone will not support jurisdiction"), *cert. denied*, 537 U.S. 822, 123 S.Ct. 101, 154 L.Ed. 30 (2002), and also cites *Bulk Shipping*, and *Zelezny*. *Dardana* at 206.

[54] CSEE Transport Wiking Trader v. Navimpex Centrala Navala, 989 F.2d 572, 580 (2d Cir. 1993).

[55] *Rotterdam*, 284 F. 3d at 1121, fn 4.

[56] *Id.* at 1122 (citing United States v. Buckland, 277 F.3d 1173, 1179 (9th Cir. 2002) (*en banc*)).

[57] The Court canvassed in considerable detail the analyses in Milliken v. Meyer, 311 U.S. 457, 463, (1940); International Shoe Co. v. Washington, 326 U.S. 310 (1945); Hanson v. Denckla, 357 U.S. 235, 251 (1958); *and* Helicopteros Nacionales de Colombia, S.A. v. Hall, 466 U.S. 408, 415 n. 9 (1984).

We place emphasis on this analysis because, as later discussed, the tension between the plain language contained in Article V of the Convention, the decision of whether to amend the Convention or pursue caselaw doctrinal development, to a large extent should depend on the conceptual universality of the U.S. doctrine of Due Process. This authority provides a rich reservoir from which to analyze the applicability of Due Process in the context of the exercise of personal jurisdiction over a non-resident or "foreign" defendant.

[58] This test was carefully crafted by the Supreme Court in Burger King Corp. v. Rudzewicz, 471 U.S. 462 (1985).

3. whether the exercise of jurisdiction would cause conflict with the sovereignty of the defendant's home state;
4. consideration of the universe of interests that the foreign state may have in adjudicating the dispute;
5. analysis of a resolution of the controversy at issue that is most efficient;
6. the extent to which the forum meets and comports with plaintiff's interests in conveniently and efficiently seeking relief; and
7. the existence of an adequate alternative forum.[59]

We circle to the beginning of the inquiry. Even though Article V of the Convention is bereft of any language from which it may be inferred that jurisdiction over an arbitral award debtor is a predicate to enforcement or, stated otherwise, lack of jurisdiction in the forum where the arbitral award is sought to be enforced proscribes enforcement, the Ninth Circuit's compelling analysis on specific and general jurisdiction with emphasis on Due Process requirements commands particular consideration. While five of the seven propositions upon which the Ninth Circuit bottoms its affirmance are arguably technical in nature and mostly concerned with the interpretation issues, if not altogether the actual formation, of normative grounds upon which it may premise its ruling, both the Due Process and closely related "reasonableness" test stand on different footing.

Certainly the Convention should not be subordinated to the idiosyncrasies endemic to different legal systems, even where such particularities enjoy constitutional status. A theory of universal relativism is not being espoused in endorsing and promoting the proposition that exercise of personal jurisdiction over an "arbitral award debtor" is a condition precedent to enforcement in the forum where the award is sought to be enforced, To the contrary, it is universal doctrinal acceptance, not necessarily limited to the community of signatory nations, that is being advanced.

Due Process, as embedded in the Fifth and Fourteenth Amendments of the United States Constitution, is hardly an idiosyncratic and parochial constitutional norm. The authority relied upon by the Ninth Circuit in its analysis of general and specific personal jurisdiction is uniquely eloquent in expressing the fundamental fairness embodied in the concept of due process by carefully framing it within a framework of quantitative and qualitative contacts that in turn cannot be severed from notions of fairness, notice, and party expectation. These precepts, although here explored in the context of federal jurisprudence, belong to and are shared by the community of civilized nations. While the cultural, historical, and geographical limitations present in finding a universal definition for a concept such as "fundamental fairness" may engraft upon what may be intuitively known to all cultures a sense of vagueness and material differences contingent upon the jurisdictional prism through which it is examined, such is not the case with the concept of due process.

[59] *Rotterdam*, 284 F. 3d at 1125. With the exception of paragraph 1, the "*reasonableness*" test is certainly very similar to a classic *forum non conveniens* analysis as articulated in the venerable chestnut *Gulf Oil v. Gilbert*, 330 U.S. 501, 67 S.Ct. 839, 91 L.Ed. 1055 (1947) by Justice Jackson, and *Gilbert v. Gulf Oil's* progeny. The similitude between the "reasonableness test" and a classic *forum non conveniens* analysis is particularly clear with respect to the *public factor* component of a *forum non conveniens* inquiry.

The laudable policies embedded in the New York Convention seeking to render universal the enforcement of arbitral awards simply cannot and should not blindly override so universal and universally accepted a doctrine as due process.

Moreover, in the context of a proposition holding that an enforcing Court must exercise personal jurisdiction over an "arbitral award debtor" against whom an award is sought to be enforced, this comports with the universally accepted premise that "jurisdiction," as that word's Latin etymology suggests, is the ability "to speak or pronounce the law." This basic requirement can only be ignored upon penalty of reconfiguring in an unprecedented manner universal rules of civil procedure. Despite the vast and profound differences in the manner in which the exercise of jurisdiction by courts is determined and understood between civil law and common law practitioners, both systems are of a single voice in holding that *jurisdiction* over the person must be present as a conceptual requirement to adjudication of whatsoever kind.

Rather than lead to universal relativism that subordinates the Convention to the particularities, nuances, and idiosyncrasies contained in the organic law and jurisprudence of different sovereigns, at a constitutional level incorporation of due process as expressed by Supreme Court cases addressing a forum's exercise of personal jurisdiction over a nonresident defendant and the incident need to meet, depending on the case, the due process requirements of either the Fifth or the Fourteenth Amendment to the U.S. Constitution. This actually enriches the Convention's framework. It bestows upon it the legitimacy, and therefore the normative feature that arises from the very concept of Due Process itself.

Here it appears that amending Article V to reflect jurisdictional requirement on the part of the enforcing court consonant with Due Process strictures would be in the best interest of commerce, signatory nations, prospective signatory nations, and the very goals and objectives that the Convention seeks not only to preserve but also to further.

C. *FORUM NON CONVENIENS*: A NIGHTMARE OF UNPREDICTABILITY?

Nonenforcement of arbitration awards beyond the four corners and language of Article V of the Convention has not been limited to the enforcing court's lack of personal jurisdiction over the "arbitral award debtor." At least one U.S. court has sought to dismiss efforts seeking to enforce an otherwise perfectly enforceable arbitration award rendered in a foreign jurisdiction on the ground of *forum non conveniens*.[60] This decision stands in sharp contrast with the due process considerations enunciated in *Glencore Grain Rotterdam B.V. v. Shivnath Rai Harnarain Co.*

[60] For completeness' sake, it should be observed that the District Court for the District of Columbia in *TermoRio S.A. E.S.P. v. Electrificadora Del Atlantico S.A. E.S.P.*, 421 F.Supp.2d 87 (D.D.C. 2006), dismissed an action seeking confirmance of a foreign arbitral award that had been vacated by a competent tribunal of the primary state (rendering state), in part, on grounds of forum non conveniens. On appeal, however, in affirming the district court's rulings, the Court of Appeals for the District of Columbia observed that "because we hold that the district court properly dismissed appellant's enforcement action under Article V(1)(e) of the New York Convention, we find it unnecessary to determine whether the case might have been dismissed on the ground of forum non conveniens, the alternative basis announced by the district court. TermoRio S.A. E.S.P. v. Electranta S.P., 487 F.3d 928, 933 (C.A.D.C., 2007).

Here it shall be suggested that application of the doctrine is without jurisprudential foundation, constitutes the subordination of the Convention to an idiosyncrasy of a jurisdiction that does not even rise to a constitutional level, and creates uncertainty because it carves out from the Article V enforcement process all predictive value.

In *In the Matter of the Arbitration between Monegasque de Reassurances (Monde Re) and Nak Naftogaz of Ukraine and State of Ukraine*,[61] a Monaco-based reinsurer (Monde Re) serving as subrogee to a Russian insurer (Sogaz) filed an action with the Federal District Court for the Southern District of Florida seeking enforcement of a foreign arbitral award against Ukraine and a Ukrainian company (Naftogaz, a merger-surviving entity arising from the merger between Ukragazprom and several other Ukrainian companies) seeking confirmation of an award in the amount of $88,374,401.49 entered by the International Commercial Court of Arbitration in Moscow. Naftogaz's efforts to annul the ICCA award were rejected.[62]

Respondents Ukraine and Naftogaz moved to dismiss the petition based upon multiple grounds, including *forum non conveniens.* After observing that the Foreign Sovereign Immunities Act ("FSIA") does not affect a "federal judiciary's inherent power to decline jurisdiction over complex and inconvenient lawsuits brought in the United States that implicate foreign parties only; require the application of foreign law; and entail no contacts with the interests of the United States," the district court granted Ukraine's motion, which in turn rendered Naftogaz's motion moot.

Remarkably, the Court sought to find jurisprudential justification for its dismissal in Article III of the Convention.[63] Specifically, great reliance was placed on the subordinated clause contained in Article III stating that signatory states shall recognize arbitral awards "'in accordance with the rules of procedure of the territory where the award is relied upon.'"[64] Thus, the Court reasoned, "[b]ecause *forum non conveniens* is more procedural than substantive in nature, the Convention cannot be read as affecting the discretion of federal courts to decline jurisdiction where judicial economy, convenience, and justice so compel."[65]

The district court cherry-picked a subordinate clause from Article III of the Convention without providing its opinion with the analytical rigor that would inevitably ensue from citation of the entire language in the sentence from which only a part was underscored. The entire sentence, *which does not end where the Court placed a period*, provides as follows:

> Each Contracting State shall recognize arbitral awards as binding and enforce them in accordance with the rules of procedure of the territory where the award is relied upon, *under the conditions laid down in the following articles.*

[61] In the Matter of the Arbitration between Monegasque de Reassurances (Monde Re) and Nak Naftogaz of Urkraine and State of Urkaine, 158 F.Supp.2d 377 (S.D.Fla. 2001).

[62] *Monegasque*, 158 F.Supp.2d at 379–80.

[63] *Id.* at 383. Article III of the Convention in its entirety reads:

Article III

Each Contracting State shall recognize arbitral awards as binding and enforce them in accordance with the rules of procedure of the territory where the award is relied upon, *under the conditions laid down in the following articles*. There shall not be imposed substantially more onerous conditions or higher fees or charges on the recognition or enforcement of arbitral awards to which this Convention applies than are imposed on the recognition or enforcement of domestic arbitral awards.

[64] *Id.*

[65] *Id.*

The stricture in Article III, based on its very own plain language, must be read together with other related provisions of the Convention: notably Article V. Nowhere, however, in Article V is there *any* reference to the rules of procedure governing the court or forum where enforcement is sought. In fact, the word "procedure," or any permutation of that word, appears only once in Article V.[66] Its reference is in connection with the procedural propriety of the conduct of the arbitration and the extent to which it comported with the parties' agreement. Put simply, there is no authority or support in Articles III and V of the Convention when read together and in their entirety for the proposition that the doctrine of *forum non conveniens* can be applied by the court where confirmation of an arbitral award is sought, on the ground that the doctrine is *procedural* and not *substantive* in nature.

The district court also sought to premise its holding on three cases it cited as being "actions arising under the Convention itself may be dismissed on the ground of *forum non conveniens*."[67] The three cases cited are: *Jain v. de Mere*,[68] *CNA Reinsurance v. Trustmark Ins. Co.*,[69] and *Oil Basins Ltd. v. Broken Hill Proprietary Co. Ltd.*[70] None of these three cases supports the district court's ruling. Also, they do not stand for the proposition for which they are cited.

At the very outset, none of the cases relied upon by the Court concern a dismissal on the ground of *forum non conveniens* of a petition seeking confirmation or recognition and enforcement of a foreign arbitral award, as was the case in *Monegasque*. By way of example, in *Jain v. de Mere*, the doctrine of *forum non conveniens* merely was discussed in the context of other authority applying the doctrine for purposes of dismissing a case so that an *arbitration* may take place in a different forum. Specifically, the Court in *Jain v. de Mere* recognized that respondent de Mere had not "moved for dismissal on grounds of *forum non conveniens*."[71] Moreover, the doctrine of *forum non conveniens* played absolutely no role in the adjudication of the issues underlying the case. These issues were succinctly enunciated as follows:

> This case presents an issue of first impression: whether federal courts have power to compel arbitration between two foreign nationals where their arbitration agreement fails to specify a location for the arbitration or a method for choosing arbitrators. We hold that federal courts have this power and therefore reverse the decision of the district court.[72]

Under no reasonable analysis can it be inferred from the facts in *Jain v. de Mere*, the single issue presented to the Court, or the holding of the case, that the Seventh Circuit somehow provided a doctrinal basis for supporting the proposition that the doctrine of *forum non conveniens* attaches to a petitioner seeking confirmation of a foreign arbitral award in a U.S. forum. Quite simply, the issue was never discussed.

66 *See* Article V1(d) stating:

> (d) the composition of the arbitral authority or the arbitral *procedure* was not in accordance with the agreement of the parties, or, failing such agreement, was not in accordance with the law of the country where the arbitration took place." (emphasis supplied)

67 *Monegasque*, 158 F.Supp.2d at 383.

68 Jain v. de Mere, 51 F.3d 686 (7th Cir. 1995).

69 CNA Reinsurance v. Trustmark Ins. Co., 2001 WL 648948 (N.D. Ill. 2001).

70 Oil Basins Ltd. v. Broken Hill Proprietary Co. Ltd., 613 F.Supp. 483 (S.D.N.Y. 1985).

71 *Jain*, 51 F.3d at 692.

72 *Id.* at 688.

The reference to *CNA Reinsurance v. Trustmark Ins. Co.* is equally puzzling and bewildering. There petitioner filed a petition to compel arbitration in the Northern District of Illinois pursuant to Section 4 of the FAA, 9 U.S.C. Section 4. The respondent cross-moved to compel arbitration in London and for dismissal of the petition on a number of grounds, including *forum non conveniens.* The *forum non conveniens* basis for dismissal, however, was to *secure a forum for arbitration and not* for purposes of opposing a confirmation of an arbitration award rendered in a foreign jurisdiction. Indeed, it was observed that the parties, "as evidenced by their competing motions to compel arbitration in their preferred forums, they are unanimous in their opinion that the dispute falls within the scope of the arbitration clause."[73] As with *Jain v. de Mere*, this opinion lends no analytical support to the holding in *Monegasque.* Again, the issues decided in *Monegasque* bear absolutely no rational relationship to the concerns adjudicated by the district court in *CNA Reinsurance v. Trustmark Ins. Co.*

The analysis is no different with respect to the Southern District of New York's opinion in *Oil Basins Ltd. v. The Broken Hill Proprietary Co. Ltd.* There too "[b]oth parties acknowledge that the issue before the Court is governed by [a]n arbitration clause. The only dispute concerns the location in which arbitration should take place."[74] At no point was the doctrine of *forum non conveniens* triggered other than in a discussion concerning the appropriate forum in which to conduct an arbitral proceeding, which did not at all concern confirmation, recognition, or enforcement of an arbitration award rendered in a foreign jurisdiction that was filed with the Southern District of New York. Not even in *dicta* is this issue addressed. Likewise, neither is the relationship between the doctrine of *forum non conveniens* as a procedural tenet and its applicability to issues arising from the Convention nor its adoption in the form of the FAA part of the subject matter of the analysis.

The doctrine of *forum non conveniens* is exclusive to common law systems. There is no comparable procedural tenet in any other body of organic law and jurisprudence. Unlike due process, which, irrespective of the nomenclature used, has been the subject matter of universal scholarship and application in evaluating the propriety of both arbitral and judicial proceedings, *forum non conveniens* finds no universal appeal and actually has encountered substantial and measurable resistance when used by the United Kingdom within the European Union's judicial system. While due process, so the argument says, may be implicitly embodied in the Convention's general framework, for example in Article VI(b) of the Convention where recognition and enforcement of an arbitral award may be refused where a party has been deprived of the ability "to present his case," this presents an emblematic case where due process is central to the non-recognition and non-enforcement of an arbitration award.

The doctrinal development seeking to engraft upon Article V enforcement proceedings the possibility of a *forum non conveniens* defense lacks conceptual foundation and practical justification. A thorough and contextual reading of Article III together with Article V render the proposition untenable. In addition, because of the "idiosyncratic" and non-universal nature of this *procedural* doctrine, it would be inimical to the very narrow grounds contained in Article V on which to decline confirmation, recognition, and enforcement of an arbitration award. Application of

[73] *CNA Reinsurance*, at *6.

[74] *Oil Basins*, 613 F.Supp. at 486.

the doctrine would also foist lack of predictability and uniformity unto Article V confirmation petitions.

D. ANNULLED AWARDS AND THE *IN RE: CHROMALLOY, BAKER MARINE*, AND *TermoRio* TRIO

The doctrinal development of U.S. arbitration placing arbitral proceedings in *pari materia* with judicial proceedings certainly promoted a national policy favoring arbitration to minimize the long-standing historical prejudices that had nourished judicial and academic skepticism toward arbitral proceedings generally. The confirmation of arbitral awards, however, has spawned a tension between two policies. First, the national policy supporting confirmation of foreign arbitral awards is certainly a requisite predicate to the preservation and enhancement of the very principles that international commercial arbitration seeks to further: international commerce, uniformity, transparency of standard, predictability, and party-autonomy. The second policy consideration, of equal standing with the first, is the deference to be accorded to a tribunal of competent jurisdiction in the primary state that vacates an arbitration award rendered in that jurisdiction on the ground that it is inimical to the substantive law of the rendering state. This tension, to some extent, is embodied in the plain language of Articles V and VII of the New York Convention. Specifically, Article V(i)(e) reads:

> Recognition and enforcement of the award *may* be refused, at the request of the party against whom it is invoked, only if that party furnishes to the competent authority where the recognition and enforcement is sought, proof that:
>
> > (e) The award has not yet become binding on the parties, or has been set aside or suspended by a competent authority of the country in which, or under the law of which, that award was made. (emphasis supplied)

Significant ink has been spilled over the use of the permissive *may* as according the secondary state where enforcement is sought discretion in refusing confirmation of the foreign arbitration award vacated or otherwise suspended by a competent tribunal in that jurisdiction. The problem is simple. Does the Convention's regime contemplate having a court in the secondary state sit in judgment of a tribunal in the primary state to determine whether the tribunal in the primary state properly applied its own substantive law in vacating or otherwise suspending an arbitration award, the rendition of which, by the arbitral tribunal, comports with the substantive law of the secondary state? Is this philological normative basis to be taken seriously, and if so, how? Are tribunals in the secondary state where enforcement is sought best placed to sit in judgment of the legal analysis underlying the vacatur of an arbitration award by the primary state? Would investing secondary states with the ability to sit in judgment of vacatur proceedings undertaken by the primary state provide the nonprevailing party with an incentive to apply to multiple secondary signatory states for confirmation of the award vacated in the primary state?

Clearly, a rubric must be developed such that signatory nations seeking to confirm an arbitration award vacated by a competent tribunal of the primary state may proceed in a manner consonant with rudimentary precepts of comity and due deference and recognition for the judiciary of the primary state. The answers to these queries must be harmonized with the strictures asserted in Article VII (1) of the Convention:

> 1. The provisions of the present Convention shall not affect the validity of multilateral or bilateral agreements concerning the recognition and enforcement of arbitral awards entered into by the Contracting States nor deprive any interested party of any right he may have to avail himself of an arbitral award in the manner and to the extent allowed by the law or the treaties of the country where such award is sought to be relied upon.

Certainly, the precepts of party-autonomy, uniformity, transparency of standard, and predictability would be undermined should courts fail to fashion a conceptual underpinning reconciling the permissive *may* enunciated in Article V(1)(e) with the mandatory language asserted in Article VII(1). The jurisprudence directly addressing this issue suggests a development favoring deference afforded to any vacatur entered by the primary state. Although the three principal opinions on this issue are very well-reasoned analyses, they do fail to craft a universal construct that would decisively provide a polestar for arbitrators, practitioners, courts, and captains of industry who seek to confirm an arbitration award in a secondary state while fearing the parochialism that may be endemic to judicial review of the arbitration award by a competent tribunal in the primary state. Even though the Convention's framework certainly contemplates a party's right to seek vacatur of an award before a tribunal within the jurisdiction of the rendering state (Article V(1)(e)) the breadth of grounds upon which a primary state may vacate an award, in contrast with the substantially more narrow principles upon which a secondary state may premise vacatur, may certainly detract from the prevalence of the principle of party-autonomy to the extent that it emphasizes judicial intervention pursuant to a broad scope of review at the conclusion of an arbitration proceeding that the parties envisioned as bringing finality to a dispute and susceptible to appellate review only on the most narrow grounds and under the gloss of strong presumptions in favor of the arbitral tribunal's decision.

The District Court for the District of Columbia addressed whether a judicial ruling issued by a competent tribunal of the rendering state vacating an arbitration award should be disturbed. The case lacked precedent and the Court quite aptly identified it as one of "first impression."[75] There the Court observed that "[w]hile Article V provides a discretionary standard, Article VII of the Convention *requires* that, 'The provisions of the present Convention *shall not* . . . deprive any interested party of any right he may have to avail himself of an arbitral award in the manner and to the extent allowed by the law . . . of the count[r]y where such award is sought to be relied upon.' (internal citations omitted). In other words, under the Convention, [petitioner] maintains all rights to the enforcement of this Arbitral Award that it

[75] In the matter of Chromalloy Aero Services and The Arab Republic of Egypt, 939 F.Supp. 907, 908 (D.D.C. 1996). In addition, deeper into the opinion, the court reiterated that as it had "stated earlier, this is a case of first impression. There are no reported cases in which a case of the United States has faced a situation, under the Convention, in which the court of a foreign nation has nullified an otherwise valid arbitral award." *Id.* at 911.

would have in the absence of the Convention."[76] The facts of the case provide much necessary perspective for any analysis of the Court's reasoning and holding.

Petitioner Chromalloy had entered into a contract with the Republic of Egypt and the Air Force of the Arab Republic of Egypt (collectively referred to as "Egypt") for the provision, maintenance, and repair of helicopters belonging to the Egyptian Air Force. Within approximately two-and-one-half years of executing the agreement, Egypt unilaterally notified Chromalloy that it was canceling the agreement.[77] Chromalloy, however, advised Egypt that it "rejected the cancellation of the contract" and commenced arbitration proceedings on the basis of the arbitration clause contained in Article XII and Appendix E of the Contract.'"[78] The record suggests that Egypt drew down Chromalloy letters of guaranty by approximately $11,475,968.00.

After a protracted arbitration proceeding the arbitral panel ordered Egypt to pay to Chromalloy $272,900.00 plus 5 percent interest, and $16,940,958.00 plus 5 percent interest. Additionally, the panel also instructed Chromalloy to pay to Egypt 606,920 pounds sterling, in addition to 5 percent interest from a date certain.[79] Chromalloy applied to the district court for enforcement of the award and virtually two weeks later Egypt filed an appeal with the Egyptian Court of Appeal, petitioning for nullification of the award. Egypt also filed a motion with the district court to stay Chromalloy's petition to enforce the award.

Significantly, the Egyptian Court of Appeal "suspended the award" causing Egypt to file with the district court a Motion to Dismiss Chromalloy's petition. Finally, Egypt's Court of Appeal at Cairo entered an order nullifying the award.[80]

Upon observing that it had original jurisdiction pursuant to the Foreign Sovereign Immunities Act, 28 U.S.C. §1330,[81] three critical premises meaningfully contributed to confirmation of the award irrespective of the collateral estoppel/*res*

[76] *Id.* at 910.
[77] *Id.* at 908.
[78] *Id.*
[79] *Id.*
[80] *Id.*
[81] 28 U.S.C. § 1330. Actions against foreign states, reads:

(a) The district courts shall have original jurisdiction without regard to amount in controversy of any nonjury civil action against a foreign state as defined in section 1603(a) of this title as to any claim for relief in personam with respect to which the foreign state is not entitled to immunity either under sections 1605-1607 of this title or under any applicable international agreement.
(b) Personal jurisdiction over a foreign state shall exist as to every claim for relief over which the district courts have jurisdiction under subsection (a) where service has been made under section 1608 of this title.
(c) For purposes of subsection (b), an appearance by a foreign state does not confer personal jurisdiction with respect to any claim for relief not arising out of any transaction or occurrence enumerated in sections 1605-1607 of this title.

28 U.S.C. section 1605 provides seven exceptions to sovereign immunity that codifies what has become known as the "Restrictive Theory of Sovereign Immunity". They may be summarized as follows:

(a) "A foreign state shall not be immune from the jurisdiction of the United States or of the states in any case"
    (i) when the foreign sovereignty "has waived its immunity either explicitly or by implication, notwithstanding any withdrawal of the waiver which the foreign state may purport to effect except in accordance with the terms of the waiver"
    (ii) in which the action is based upon a **commercial activity** carried on in the United States by the foreign state; or upon an act performed in the United States in connection with a **commercial activity** in a foreign state elsewhere; or upon an act outside the

judicata issues pervading the analysis. First, the arbitral tribunal decided, based on the allegations, to reject Egypt's argument that the contract at issue should be governed by Egyptian administrative law. Instead, the "panel held that it did not matter which substantive law they applied – civil or administrative." Therefore, the district court

territory of the United States in connection with a **commercial activity** of the foreign state elsewhere and that state causes a **direct effect** in the United States [§ 1605(a)(2)];

(iii) in which the rights and property taken in violation of international law are at issue and that property or any property exchanged for such property is present in the United States in connection with a **commercial activity** carried on in the United States by a foreign state; or that property or any property exchanged for that property is owned or operated by an agency or instrumentality of a foreign state and that agency or instrumentality is engaged in a **commercial activity** in the United States [§1605(a)(3)];

(iv) in which rights and property in the United States acquired by succession or gift or rights in immovable property situated in the United States are at issue [§1605(a)(4)];

(v) not otherwise encompassed in paragraph (2) above, in which money damages, are sought against a foreign state for personal injury or death, or damage to or loss of property, occurring in the United States and caused by the tortuous act or omission of that foreign state or of any official or employee of that foreign state while acting within the scope of his office or employment, except this paragraph shall not apply to [§1605(a)(5)];

(A) any claim based upon the exercise or performance or the failure to exercise or perform a discretionary function regardless of whether the discretion be based, or

(B) any claim arising out of malicious prosecution, abuse of process, libel, slander, misrepresentation, deceipt, or interference with contract rights;

(vi) **in which the action is brought, either to enforce an agreement made by the foreign state with or for the benefit of a private party to submit to arbitration all or any differences which have arisen or which may arise between the parties with respect to a defined legal relationship, whether contractual or not, concerning a subject matter capable of settlement by arbitration under the laws of the United States, or to confirm an award made pursuant to such an agreement to arbitration, if (A) the arbitration takes place or is intended to take place in the United States, (B) the agreement or award is or may be governed by a treaty or other international agreement in force for the United States calling for the recognition and enforcement of arbitral awards, (C) the underlying claim, save for the agreement to arbitrate, could have been brought in a United States court under this section or section 1607, or (D)(i) of this subsection is otherwise applicable [§1605(a)(6)1]**,

(vii) not otherwise covered by paragraph (2), in which money damages are sought against a foreign state for personal injury or death that was caused by an act of torture, extrajudicial killing, aircraft, sabotage, hostage taking, or the provision of material support or resources (as defined in section 2339A of title 18) for such an act if such act or provision of material support is engaged in by an official, employee, or agent of such foreign state while acting within the scope of his or her office, employment, or agency, except that the court shall decline to hear a claim under this paragraph. [§1605(a)(7)].

This seventh exception is qualified by two provisions providing that a court shall not have jurisdiction to prosecute a cause against a foreign nation where the foreign state

(a) "was not designated as a state sponsor of terrorism under §6(j) of the Export Administration Act of 1979 (citation omitted) or §620A of the Foreign Assistance Act of 1961 (citation omitted) at the time the act occurred, unless later so designated as a result of such act or the act is related to Case Number 1:00CV03110(E.G.S.) in the United States District Court for the District of Columbia; and

(b) even where the foreign state at issue is designated as a sponsor of terrorism, the act in question occurred within the national territory of a foreign state and that state was not accorded an opportunity to arbitrate pursuant to international law or "neither the claimant nor the victim was a national of the United States [citation omitted] when the act upon which the claim is based occurred."

Conditions under which an action in admiralty may be brought are also set forth in the subsections to section 7.

concluded that this decision, at most, rose to the level of a "mistake of law" but certainly does not provide a premise for vacatur of the arbitration award. Together with this observation, the Court reasoned that the Egyptian court's rendition of the arbitration award as null under Egyptian law is but a reflection of the skeptical view of arbitration that predated the Supreme Court's command in *Mitsubishi*. The opinion underscored that:

> In Egypt, however, it is established that arbitration is an exceptional means for resolving disputes, requiring departure from the normal means of litigation before the courts, and the guarantees they afford. Egypt's complaint that, the Arbitration Award is null under Arbitration Law, . . . because it is not properly grounded under Egyptian law, reflects this suspicious view of arbitration, and is precisely the type of technical argument that U.S. courts are not to entertain when reviewing an arbitral award."[82]

Thus, critical to the adjudicative process was the strong policy favoring arbitration, minimizing judicial intervention into arbitral proceedings, and the very exigent and universally cognizable flaws that must be gleaned, beyond just "mere" technical mishaps, for the nonconfirmation, recognition, or enforcement of an arbitral award on the part of the secondary state.[83] The question becomes whether this very compelling policy that was the product of decades of doctrinal development should be invested with such weight to engulf other policy considerations of equal standing arising from the organizing principles governing the relationship between and among the judiciaries of different sovereigns. Two propositions seem critically important for purposes of uniformity and harmonization. At the outset, a policy cannot be adopted that ignores the Convention's vision that the rendering state's vacatur of an arbitration award simply cannot be ignored in favor of the secondary state's command to confirm, recognize, and enforce foreign arbitral awards but for those falling within the narrow purview of the Convention's Article V, where the exercise of judicial discretion is to be applied in the context of a strong presumption favoring confirmation of an award. Similarly, despite the explicit language of Article V(I)(e), a primary state's refusal, suspension, or nullification of an arbitration award should not mechanically, without more, suffice to render an award void by the secondary state without engaging in an inquiry that satisfies the command in Article VII.

Second, although the district court explicitly references *Scherk v. Alberto-Culver*,[84] the proposition contending that an arbitration agreement is but a type of form selection clause upon which the Court heavily relies is really first articulated and developed with the Supreme Court in *The Bremen v. Zapata*. This observation notwithstanding, confirmation of the arbitration award despite the Egyptian tribunal's nullification found measurable analytical support this tenet. The Court recognized that "[a]n agreement to arbitrate before a specified tribunal is, in effect,

82 *Id.* at 911 (omitting internal citations and references to case law and authority).

83 The Court in Chromalloy, quite significantly, does not use the terms "primary state" or "secondary state". Likewise, the Convention also is bereft of any reference to "primary state" or "secondary state". As shall be examined, the terms appear to be the product of jurisprudence and is significantly developed in Termorio v. Electranta, 487 F.3d 928 (C.A.D.C. 2007).

84 *Chromalloy*, 939 F.Supp. at 911.

a specialized kind of forum-selection clause. . . . the invalidation of such an agreement . . . would not only allow the respondent to repudiate its solemn promise but would, as well, reflect a parochial concept that all disputes must be resolved under our laws and in our courts."[85]

The deference ascribed to the parties' decision to arbitrate all disputes arising out of or pertaining to the contract at issue in Egypt is testimony to the primacy provided to the precept of party-autonomy. In effect, the Court views its role as an enforcing or confirming tribunal as practically performing a ministerial function in confirming awards in the context of a national policy favoring the confirmation of awards by signatory nations except for extreme scenarios where Article V is triggered. Moreover, Article V(1)(e) is not a mechanical formulistic ground for vacatur, certainly in the Court's analysis, when read together with the prescription embodied in Article VII. Simply stated, because a court in the rendering state nullifies an arbitral award, triggering an Article V(1)(e) issue for possible refusal of confirmation, dismissal of the petition seeking confirmation, recognition, or enforcement does not *automatically* attach.

Third, the facts of record underscore debilities in Egypt's effort to have the U.S. court render *res judicata* effect to the Egyptian tribunal's vacatur. In particular, the record established that the arbitration agreement at issue between Egypt and Chromalloy precluded any appeal to Egyptian courts.[86] Even though the Court does not particularly stress this very important condition of the arbitration agreement in its *res judicata* analysis, it is an element that should be conceded meaningful significance. Egypt directly, expressly, unilaterally, and with full knowledge breached a material term of the arbitration agreement by seeking appellate recourse in the Egyptian judiciary, a course of action that the parties explicitly excluded in their agreement, perhaps for fear of the very prospect of having the judiciary of a sovereign adjudicate the legal viability of an arbitration award entered against the sovereign itself and its instrumentality, in this case the Egyptian Air Force. This fact alone likely precluded the Circuit Court of Appeals for the District of Columbia from rendering any pronouncement concerning the propriety of the district court's ruling in *Chromalloy*.

Instead, the *res judicata* argument is grounded on the "strong public policy behind judicial enforcement of binding arbitration clauses. A decision of this Court to recognize the decision of the Egyptian court would violate this clear U.S. public policy."[87]

This application of public policy should not be understood in a vacuum that reads out of the opinion Egypt's stark and uncontroverted breach of the arbitration agreement by pursuing appellate recourse within the Egyptian judicial system. While it appears violative of the Convention's framework simply to have this most

[85] *Id.*

[86] Appendix E to the contract defines the "Applicable Law Court of Arbitration." The clause in pertinent part provides:

It is . . . understood that both parties have irrevocably agreed to apply Egypt (sic) Laws and to choose Cairo as seat of the court of arbitration.

* * * * * *

The decision of said court shall be final and binding and cannot be made subject to any appeal or other recourse. (Appendix E to the Contract). *Id.* at 912.

[87] *Id.* at 913 (omitting citations and internal quotations).

important but less than all-encompassing consideration eliminate the pronouncements of a primary state's vacatur of an arbitration award, a responsible reading of the *Chromalloy* opinion compels engrafting upon Article V's permissive "*may*" the conceptual category of judicial temperament and reasoning that proactively should scrutinize primary state awards in the context of the terms and conditions of the governing arbitration agreement. This standard is consonant with the narrow grounds enunciated in Article V and simultaneously does not wrest from the judiciary in the primary state the panoply of premise embodied in its substantive law that may give rise to the nullification of an award rendered within its jurisdiction.

Put simply, *Chromalloy* must be read within the parameters of the stark and uncontroverted disregard for the parties' agreement that the Egyptian tribunal exercised. The discretion that Article V vests in secondary state tribunals that conceivably shall have to be exercised, under certain circumstances, as disregarding the ruling of a tribunal in the rendering state must be grounded in objective and universal disregard of commonly held juridic precepts. The issue in *Chromalloy* with respect to the normative ground on which the Court elected to disregard the Egyptian tribunal's vacatur is not one of policy as it is a proposition of law.

Scarcely three years following the district court's analysis and holding in *Chromalloy*, the Second Circuit in *Baker Marine v. Chevron Nigeria Ltd.*[88] affirmed the district court's ruling denying petitions to enforce awards rendered in a foreign jurisdiction, in large part based upon the vacatur entered by a court in the rendering state. Here too, close scrutiny of the procedural and factual configuration commands attention.

Baker Marine centers on a contract that it and Danos and Curole Marine Contractors, Inc. ("Danos") executed with Chevron Corporation ("Chevron") pursuant to which Baker Marine would provide local support while Danos supplied management and technical equipment for the barge services rendered in favor of Chevron.[89]

The operative agreement contained in the arbitration clause identifying Nigeria as the seat of arbitration also provided for the application of Nigerian substantive law. In addition, the parties agreed that any judgment entered upon the award would issue in whatsoever court had jurisdiction over the matter.[90] Baker Marine averred that both Danos and Chevron violated the contracts and proceeded to prosecute claims in accordance with the arbitration agreement in Lagos, Nigeria. Two awards were entered in Baker Marine's favor for $2.23 million in damages against Danos, and a second award was issued by a different panel against Chevron in Baker Marine's favor for $750,000.[91] Predictably, Baker Marine sought immediate enforcement of both

88 Baker Marine Nigeria Ltd. v. Chevron Nigeria Ltd., 191 F.3d 194 (2nd Cir. 1999).

89 *Id.* at 195.

90 The arbitration clause in pertinent part stated:

> Any dispute, controversy or claim arising out of this Contract, or the breach, termination or validity thereof, shall be finally and conclusively settled by arbitration in accordance with the Arbitration Rules of the United Nations Commission on International Trade Law (UNCITRAL).

Separate clauses specified that the arbitration "procedure (insofar as not governed by said UNCITRAL rules . . .) shall be governed by the substantive laws of the Federal Republic of Nigeria" and moreover, the clause stated that the contracts "shall be interpreted in accordance with the laws of the Federal Republic of Nigeria." In this connection, the agreements asserted that "judgment upon the award of the arbitrators may be entered in any court having jurisdiction thereof," and that the agreement and any award arising from it "shall be governed by the 1958 United Nations Convention on Recognition and Enforcement of Foreign Arbitration Awards." Nigeria is a party to the New York Convention.

91 *Id.* at 195–96.

awards before the Nigerian Federal High Court. Respondents Danos and Chevron also sought recourse to the same court filing papers to vacate the award based upon multiple grounds. The Nigerian Federal High Court vacated both awards. The grounds for vacatur were succinct. Four fundamental and principal premises were articulated. First, the court held that the arbitrators wrongfully awarded punitive damages. Second, it concluded that the arbitral tribunal exceeded the scope of the submissions. Third, it was observed that parole evidence was wrongfully admitted. Finally, the court acknowledged that the awards were inconsistent.[92]

Baker Marine filed claims with the Federal District Court for the Northern District of New York petitioning confirmation of the awards pursuant to the FAA, implementing the Convention. The petitions were denied based upon principles of comity and Convention strictures. Specifically, the district court noted that "'it would not be proper to enforce a foreign arbitral award under the Convention when such an award has been set aside by the Nigerian courts.'"[93]

Very much like the district court in *Chromalloy*, Baker Marine first placed considerable emphasis on Article VII, forcing the Second Circuit to revisit the very tension that the district court in *Chromalloy* identified between Article VI(e) and Article VII. Also, it now had to accord some part of its analysis to distinguishing the case at bar from *Chromalloy*. Because Baker Marine had argued that "the district court's ruling failed to give effect to Article VII of the Convention, which provides that the Convention shall not "'deprive any interested party of any right he may have to avail himself of an arbitral award in the manner and to the extent allowed by the law or the treaties of the count[r]y where such award it sought to be relied upon,'" the Second Circuit simply asserted that it "[was] sufficient answer that the parties contracted in Nigeria that their disputes would be arbitrated under the law of Nigeria."[94]

Central to the Second Circuit's holding were two simple but virtually case dispositive findings. First, "[t]he governing agreements make no reference whatever to United States law." Second, "[n]othing suggests that the parties intended United States arbitral law to govern their disputes."[95]

It is in addressing Baker Marine's contention that Article V(1)(e)'s use of the now very familiar permissive "may," that the Second Circuit deems it necessary to distinguish *Baker Marine* from *Chromalloy*. With surgical precision, the Court honed in on the solitary but material factual predicate that rendered the Egyptian tribunal's vacatur of no juridic moment for purposes of a confirmation, recognition, and enforcement of award analysis. The Court highlighted and underscored, albeit in a footnote, that "[a]fter the arbitrator entered an award in favor of the

[92] *Id.* at 196. The Second Circuit's opinion states that these grounds were advanced as basis for vacatur, "among other things." By way of example, the Nigerian High Court found that the award entered against Danos "was unsupported by the evidence." *Id.*

[93] *Id.*

[94] *Id.* at 196–97

[95] *Id.* Additionally, the court observed:

> Furthermore, as a practical matter, mechanical application of domestic arbitral law to foreign awards under the Convention would seriously undermine finality and regularly produce conflicting judgments. If a party whose arbitration award has been vacated at the site of the award can automatically obtain enforcement of the awards under the domestic laws of other nations, a losing party will have every reason to pursue its adversary 'with enforcement actions from country to country until a court is found, if any, which grants the enforcement.' *Id.* (citing to ALBERT JAN VAN DEN BERG, THE NEW ARBITRATION CONVENTION OF 1958: TOWARDS A UNIFORM JUDICIAL INTERPRETATION 355 (1981)).

American Company, the American Company applied to the United States courts for confirmation of the award, the Egyptian government appealed *to its own courts*, which set aside the award the district court concluded that Egypt was seeking 'to repudiate its solemn promise to abide by the results of the arbitration,' and that recognizing the Egyptian judgment would be contrary to the United States policy favoring arbitration."[96]

The Second Circuit's studious word selection should not be overlooked. The observation that the Egyptian government "appealed to its own court's" cannot be underestimated. Egypt not only disavowed a material term of the arbitration agreement but proceeded to engage in the very activity that this particular clause sought to proscribe. This difference, without more, warrants a different result from *Chromalloy* that does not necessarily give rise to a disparate legal analysis. The Court also distinguished itself from *Chromalloy* by stressing that Baker Marine "is not a United States citizen, and it did not initially seek confirmation of the award in the United States. Furthermore, Chevron and Danos did not violate any promise in appealing the arbitration award within Nigeria. Recognition of the Nigerian judgment ***in this case*** does not conflict with United States public policy."[97] Accordingly, affirmance was deemed consonant with (i) comity considerations, (ii) the strictures of both Article V(1)(e) and Article VII(1), without doing violence to the command asserted in either article, (iii) U.S. public policy, and (iv) the analysis and diametrically opposite holding in *Chromalloy*.

The reference to the words "in this case" and to "United States public policy" deserve attention. Despite denial of the petition seeking confirmation, the Second Circuit's careful crafting of language to reflect that the holding is appropriate "in this case" suggests that Articles V and VII are not to be applied mechanically as a practically perfunctory task when faced with a petition seeking confirmance of an arbitral award vacated by competent tribunals in the rendering state. The particularities of the case at issue form and transform the applicable analysis. Stated otherwise, *Chromalloy* and *Baker Marine* are perfectly reconcilable opinions, and under one view, standing for this same doctrinal principle for the following two reasons; (i) *Chromalloy* does not stand for the proposition that a secondary state is obligated to affirm an arbitration award that has been nullified by a competent tribunal in the primary state or rendering state; (ii) *Baker Marine* does not stand for the proposition that a secondary state must dismiss a petition seeking confirmation of a award rendered in the primary state and nullified by a competent tribunal of the primary state. To the contrary, both opinions acknowledge, admittedly with less clarity than would be desired, the tribunal in the secondary state, while not standing in judgment of the acts, omissions, and analysis of the competent tribunal of the primary state nullifying the arbitration award entered in that jurisdiction, engages in a reasoned analysis of whether party-autonomy was violated by the reviewing tribunal of the rendering state.

There is no question that the term party-autonomy appears nowhere in either the *Chromalloy* or the *Baker Marine* opinions. As also referenced, it is equally beyond dispute that the holdings in both cases are indeed diametrically opposed. What

96 *Id.* (citing *Baker Marine*, 191 F.3d at 912, 913) (emphasis supplied).

97 *Id.*

remains the same, however, is an analysis that does not purport to question the primary state's construction or application of its own substantive law but rather whether in applying its substantive organic law and jurisprudence the competent tribunal of the rendering state did violence to the plain language of the arbitration agreement, that is, the will of the parties, or stated doctrinally through the prism applied here for analysis the principle of party-autonomy.

Instead of "deconstructing" its analysis to reflect the actual principle or principles around which the opinion is organized, both courts elect to articulate the more abbreviated but less helpful "rationale" that says that somehow the actions of the competent tribunal in the rendering state in *Chromalloy* offend U.S. public policy while the Nigerian court's vacatur comports with U.S. public policy. Thus, "U.S. public policy," nowhere defined in either opinion, is transformed into a conceptual "catch-all" clause that is a phrase substituting the reasoned activity of judging whether the competent tribunal in the primary state disregarded party-autonomy or the plain language of the arbitration clause at issue, in applying its substantive law leading to the nullification of an arbitration award. The "public policy" referenced in both opinions is not the "public policy" enunciated in Article V(2)(b).[98] Therefore, without complete awareness but with keen analysis, the courts carefully crafted an implicit test with the nomenclature "public policy" that in effect constitutes a judicial standard consisting of a determination of whether the competent court in the rendering state vacated an award in such a manner as to disavow a material term of the arbitration clause.[99]

An important doctrinal development on how best to address whether a secondary state indeed may decline a petition seeking confirmation, recognition, and

[98] In fact neither opinion rests any part of its rationale or holding on Article V(2)(b). This section is simply not even referenced.

[99] For completeness' sake, in *Hilmarton v. Omniun de Traitenent et de Valorisation-OTV*, 20 Y.B. Com' Arb. 663 (1994), the French Court de Cassation held that Article VII affords those parties seeking enforcement of foreign arbitration awards the right to take advantage of domestic law more favorable to enforcement than Article V. The parties had agreed to ICC arbitration in Geneva, where Swiss law would govern any dispute. After a controversy arose between the parties the arbitrator denied the claim holding that the contract violated Swiss public law. A Swiss Court annulled the award on the single ground that the arbitrator had misconstrued Swiss public policy. Despite the annulment, OTV sought to enforce the award in France under the New York Convention. Hilmarton asserted that the award had been vacated in Switzerland, the rendering state. The Court de Cassation disagreed and relied on Article 1502 of the French New Code of Civil Procedure, pursuant to which the annullment in the primary state does not constitute the ground for rejecting enforcement. The Court thus held that domestic French law favored OTV's application to enforce the annulled award.

To resolve the issues raised by the reference authority, a respected commentator had suggested that the New York Convention should be amended to eliminate the country of origin's power to vacate and arbitral award. *See* Kenneth R. Davis, *Unconventional Wisdom: A New Look at Articles V and VII of the Convention on the Recognition and Enforcement of Foreign Arbitral Awards*, 37 Tx. Int'l L.J. 43, 85–87 (2002) in this commentator's opinion, the country whose laws were applied to the controversy should be the only sovereign state with authority to vacate an award. This proposed solution, however, does not address the issue of the country of enforcements discretion to enforce arbitration awards according to its domestic law. This discretion is contrary to the tenet of *uniformity* and causes potential conflicting decisions where one country vacates the award and another enforces it, without truly providing for any guidance for the resolution of such inevitable conflicts.

enforcement of an arbitration award vacated in the rendering state by a competent tribunal was advanced by the DC Circuit in 2007. In *TermoRio S.A. v. Electranta S.P.*,[100] appellant TermoRio entered into a contract with Electraificadora del Atlántico S.A. E.S.P. ("Electranta"), a state-owned power utility, pursuant to which TermoRio would generate energy for Electranta's purchase. Electranta, however, allegedly failed to meet its obligations under the contract, and the dispute was submitted to an arbitration tribunal in Colombia consonant with the power purchase agreement. The tribunal ruled in favor of TermoRio, entering an award in excess of $60 million.[101] Upon issuance of the award, Electranta filed an extraordinary writ in a court in Colombia seeking to vacate the award. Colombia's highest ranking administrative court, the Consejo de Estado ("Counsel of State") vacated the award "on the ground that the arbitration clause contained in the parties' Agreement violated Colombian law."[102]

TermoRio filed an action in the district court against Electranta and the Republic of Colombia petitioning enforcement of the arbitral award. The district court dismissed the petition on multiple grounds but most notably upon the finding that "there is nothing in the record here indicating that the proceedings before the Consejo de Estado were tainted or that the judgment of the Court is other than authentic, the district court was, as it held, obliged to respect it."[103] The Circuit Court affirmed the judgment, "holding that, because the arbitration award was lawfully nullified by the country in which the award was made, appellants have no cause of action in the United States to seek enforcement of the award under the FAA or the New York Convention."[104]

The opinion is comprehensive and particularly impressive because of the manner in which it fully integrates into what may be synthesized as an analysis resting on eleven fundamental premises and no fewer than seven policy considerations. Foremost as a point of departure the Court revisited the vibrant national policy favoring alternative dispute resolution by arbitration. In this regard, it also placed considerable emphasis on the close connection between the need to have global enforceability of awards purporting to bring finality to private disputes in the area

[100] Termorio S.A. v. Electranta, S.P 487 F.3rd 928 (C.A.D.C. 2007).

[101] *Id.* at 929.

[102] *Id.*

[103] *Id.* The translated iteration of the arbitration clause at issue reads:

> Any dispute or controversy arising between the Parties in connection to the execution, interpretation, performance or liquidation of the Contract shall be settled through mechanisms of conciliation, amiable composition or settlement, within a term no longer than three weeks. If no agreement is reached, either party may have recourse to an arbitral tribunal that shall *be governed from in accordance with the Rules of Conciliation and Arbitration of the International Chamber of Commerce.* The tribunal shall be made up of three (3) members appointed by the Chamber, and shall be seated in the city of Barranquilla [Colombia]. The award, which shall be binding on the parties, must be rendered within a maximum term of three months. *Id.*

[104] *Id.* The Circuit Court clarified that it neither would adjudicate whether the doctrine of forum *non conveniens* may be applied by a district court to dismiss a petition seeking confirmation, recognition and enforcement award. Likewise, the Court declined to decide whether 9 U.S.C. section 302 incorporates the New York Convention instead of other legal provisions related to the New York Convention. Here the Court explains that because the "Panama Convention and the New York Convention are substantively identical for purposes of this case and neither party challenges the district court's analysis. We therefore resolve this matter with reference to and using the language of the New York Convention. *Id.* at 933.

of private international law and a climate of economic globalization. Without necessarily articulating it in such terms, the Court appreciates the contribution of the concept of party-autonomy to dispute resolution in a climate of proliferating transnational commerce. It observed that "[a]s international trade has expanded in recent decades, so too has the use of international arbitration to resolve disputes arising in the course of that trade. The Convention's purpose was to encourage the recognition and enforcement of commercial arbitration agreements in international contracts and to unify the standards by which agreements to arbitrate are enforced in signatory countries." Moreover, the Court proceeded to note that "the utility of the New York Convention in promoting the process of international commercial arbitration depends upon the willingness of national courts to let go of matters they would normally think of as their own."[105]

Third, the Court, quite adroitly, examined how the Convention is a structured framework providing for different regimes of analyses attaching to a competent court in the primary state and a court of first instance in a secondary forum adjudicating a petition seeking confirmation of an award.[106] While certainly this observation is corroborated by the language contained in Article V(1)(e) (ostensibly according to the primary state all the latitude for vacating an award endemic to its national substantive law) and Article V as it pertains to the secondary state where confirmation, recognition, and enforcement is sought, the analysis substantively shies from crafting a standard or methodology that would provide uniformity and predictability to an enforcing court's exercise of discretion when adjudicating a petition seeking confirmation of an award that was vacated in the primary state. Indeed, the recitation of the dual standard applicable to rendering competent tribunals and secondary state courts adjudicating petitions for confirmation is helpful in identifying the general subject matter to be examined. The analysis, however, falls disappointingly short of drawing a distinction between the conceptual difference inherent in (1) granting a petition for confirmation despite a vacatur entered by a competent tribunal of the primary state because it misapprehends a fundamental term in the arbitration clause, and (2) a tribunal in a secondary state confirming an arbitral award, despite the nullification of such an award by a competent court of the primary state based upon the proposition that the award is contrary to the substantive law of that jurisdiction.

The identification of two regimes contained in the Convention for purposes of vacatur attaching to the primary state and the secondary state is certainly accurate, as represented in the opinion. Doubtless the primary state has the greater latitude accorded to it by the substantive law of its jurisdiction, while the secondary state is "limited" to those grounds enunciated in Article V of the Convention. The disappointment in the opinion is the want of a synthetic extrapolation based upon

[105] *Id.* at 933–34 (citing *Scherk v. Alberto-Culver Co.* and *Mitsubishi*), (citations and internal quotations and brackets omitted).

[106] The Circuit Court annunciated that:

> [T]he Convention mandates very different regimes for the review of arbitral awards (1) in the state in which, or under the law of which the award was made, and (2) the other states where recognition and enforcement are sought. The Convention specifically contemplates that the state in which, or under the law of which, the award is made, will be free to set aside or modify an award in accordance with its domestic arbitral law and its full panoply of express and implied grounds for relief. [citation omitted]. However, the Convention it equally clear that when an action for enforcement is brought in a foreign state, the state may refuse to enforce to award only on the ground explicitly in Article V of the Convention. *Id.* at 935.

Chromalloy, Baker Marine, and the very fact pattern underlying *TermoRio*. The analysis would be quite simple. Without impairing the rights accorded to parties arbitrating in the primary state; that is to say, respecting the primary state's jurisdiction over an award for review and nullification purposes, a secondary state would be invested with a normative ground for nullification where the primary state disregarded a material term in the arbitration clause. This single analysis, which is succinct and quite readily applicable where warranted, would reconcile the "tension" between the primary state and the secondary state concerning nullification and confirmation issues. Also, such analysis would harmonize any ostensible or surface inconsistencies between the "infamous" permissive "*may*" contained in Article V and the strictures enunciated in Article VII concerning rights of enforcement. Despite distinguishing *Baker Marine* from *Chromalloy* on this ground, the Court of Appeals was hesitant to fashion a test or "rule of law" that would generate uniformity, predictability, certainty, party-autonomy, and transparency of applicable standard.

The identification of the primary state entails, upon reading the opinion, a more complex analysis than merely identifying the arbitral seat, which usually defines the rendering state or jurisdiction. The *indicia* defining a primary state entails

1. identification of the parties' nationality,
2. place of performance,
3. arbitral seat,
4. place of transaction or occurrence, and
5. an analysis of the totality of circumstances, including party expectation.[107]

Moreover, as to the secondary state, the Court of Appeals commented on the public policy reasoning clearly articulated in *Baker Marine*. It pronounced that "[t]he Court [the Second Circuit] also remarked on the undesirable consequences that would likely follow from adoption of *Baker Marine's* argument: as a practical matter, mechanical application of domestic arbitral award to foreign awards under the Convention would seriously undermine finality and regularly produce conflicting judgments. If a party whose arbitration award has been vacated at the site of the award can automatically obtain enforcement of the awards under the domestic laws of the other nations, a losing party will have every reason to pursue its adversary with enforcement actions from country to country until a court is found, if any, which grants the enforcement."[108] Accordingly, the Court of Appeals reasoned that adoption of appellants' argument would undermine the very principles that the Convention precisely seeks to preserve and promote; "an arbitration award does not exist to be enforced in other Contracting States if it has been lawfully 'set aside' by competent authority in the State in which the award was made. *This principle controls the disposition of this case.*"[109]

Again, this very important policy consideration certainly deserves to be highlighted and stressed, but it cannot be elevated to the level of a binding norm or controlling judicial construct. A policy argument is precisely that, a proposition that

[107] *Id.* at 935.

[108] *Id.* at 936 (citing *Baker Marine*, 191 F.3d at 197 n.2 (quoting ALBERT JAN VAN DEN BERG, THE NEW YORK ARBITRATION CONVENTION OF 1958: TOWARDS A UNIFORM JUDICIAL INTERPRETATION 355 (1981))).

[109] *Id.*

has consequences beyond an immediate case and that therefore must be considered in any adjudicative process, irrespective of the facts or the particular controversy. Hardly, however, should such policy be case dispositive or otherwise deemed so overwhelming in character and nature to engulf any other consideration. In addition, a policy attendant to a rule of law is too general and thus lends itself to the pernicious practice of mechanical application rather than the reasoned analysis incident to the application of a legal precept to a fact pattern.

The battle of underlying policies between Article V(1)e and Article VII was deftly addressed. The Court itself identified the dangers endemic to engrafting upon a policy consideration normative judicial character. In the context of distinguishing *Chromalloy*,[110] it noted that "appellants are simply mistaken in suggesting that the Convention policy in favor of enforcement of arbitration awards effectively swallows the command of Article V(1)(e). A judgment whether to recognize or enforce an award that has not been set aside in the State in which it was made is quite different from a judgment whether to disregard the action of a court of competent authority in another state."[111]

The question ultimately did not rest, as examined by the Circuit Court, on the issue of disregard for a foreign tribunal's modification or nullification of an arbitral award rendered within its jurisdiction. Instead, considerable weight is placed on the need to recognize that a court in a secondary state, or more specifically U.S. courts, are neither invested with unfettered authority to confirm an award in direct defiance of a judgment nullifying that very award nor privileged to "go behind an award" in the *absence of extraordinary circumstances*.[112] Accordingly, the analysis in determining confirmation where a competent court of the rendering state nullified an award rests on a finding of "extraordinary circumstances" that the court did not find present.

The analysis, however, did not limit itself merely to considerations pertaining to the confirming court in the secondary state. To be sure, the Court of Appeals went so far as to articulate the borders of the test of public policy arising from Article V(2)(b). In this regard the Court understood that such a standard "cannot be simply whether the courts of a secondary state would set aside an arbitration award if the award had been made and enforcement sought within its jurisdiction. . . . [T]he Convention contemplates that different Contracting States may have different grounds for setting aside arbitration awards."[113] Thus, the Court concluded, "it is unsurprising that the courts have carefully limited the occasions when a foreign judgment is ignored on grounds of public policy.[114]

110 On this point the Court noted:

> We need not decide whether the holding in *Chromalloy* is correct, because, as appellees point out, 'the present case is plainly distinguishable from *Chromalloy* where an express contract provision was violated by pursuing an appeal to vacate the award. Here, Electranta preserved its objection that the panel was not proper or authorized by law, promptly raised it in the Colombian courts, and received a definitive ruling by the highest court on this question of law.'" *Id.* at 937.

111 *Id.* at 937; *see also* Yusuf Ahmed Alghanim & Sons v. Toys R Us, Inc., 126 F.3d 15, 23 (2d Cir 1997) (holding that "[t]he Convention specifically contemplates that the state in which, or under the law of which, the award is made, will be free to set aside or modify an award in accordance with its domestic arbitral law and its full panoply of express and implied grounds for relief.")

112 *Termorio*, 487 F.3rd at 938. 113 *Id.* at 938.

114 *Id.* The public policy ground for determining whether to credit the judgment of a court in the primary state vacating an arbitration award has been the subject matter of extensive commentary.

The eighth premise upon which the Court predicated affirmance arose from the Convention's history emphasizing that parties are empowered to seek to vacate or modify an award in the rendering state pursuant to the law of that jurisdiction. According to the Court's analysis, "the language and history of the Convention make it clear that such a motion is to be governed by domestic law of the rendering state."[115]

Ninth and finally, a classical analysis of the elements defining "primary state status" was undertaken. No less than six factors were considered:

1. the matter was deemed "a peculiarly Colombian affair" because it concerned Colombian parties,
2. a service contract with Colombia as a place of performance,
3. the contract spawned an arbitration in Colombia,
4. the Colombian arbitration decision led to litigation in Colombia,
5. the parties agreed to be bound by the laws of Colombia, and
6. the Consejo de Estado is the highest ranking expositor of Colombian law.

When these factors are considered in their totality, together with a complete absence of any wrongful or aberrant treatment of the terms of the arbitration clause at issue, the Court of Appeals found additional support for its affirmation of the district court's ruling.

Certainly the *TermoRio v. Electranta* opinion suggests a specific doctrinal development that superficially appears to favor allocating a competent tribunal in a primary statewide and almost unfettered nonreviewable discretion, absent the most extreme and egregious conduct, to determine the validity of an arbitration award rendered in its jurisdiction and applying the substantive law of the primary state. The corollary to this proposition is that the secondary state is extraordinarily limited in confirming an award that had been previously vacated by a competent tribunal in the rendering state. The trend, however, is much deeper and complex.

It is significant to note that *Chromalloy* and *Baker Marine* remain binding jurisprudence. Moreover, the Court of Appeals in *TermoRio* certainly did not reverse or even criticize *Chromalloy*. The opinion limited its treatment of *Chromalloy* simply to distinguishing it from the case before it. In this same vein, the reasoning in *Baker Marine* was not exalted over that embodied in the *Chromalloy* opinion. The Court of Appeals correctly gleaned that *Baker Marine* was procedurally and factually closer to the *TermoRio* facts and juridic development than *Chromalloy*. While indeed the Court of Appeals characterizes its holding as standing for the proposition that the district court did not err in dismissing appellants' claim to enforce the disputed arbitration award,[116] its analysis does provide for fertile ground meriting further examination.

The Court of Appeals quite judiciously articulated the standard and cited some of the better known comments on the subject:

> A judgment is unenforceable as against public policy to the extent that it is repugnant to fundamental notions of what is decent and just in the state where enforcement is sought. [citations and internal quotations omitted]. The standard is high and infrequently met. As one court wrote, '[o]nly in clear-cut cases ought it to avail defendant.' [citation omitted]. In the classic formulation, a judgment that 'tends clearly' to undermine the public interest, the public confidence in the administration of the law, or security for individual rights of personal liberty or of private property is against public policy.

115 *Id.* at 939.

116 *Id.* at 933.

Despite the Convention's sophisticated framework contemplating different regimes for the review of arbitration awards in primary and secondary states, neither the Convention's language nor the analysis in *TermoRio* set forth a transparent standard to be applied by the courts in secondary states reviewing awards vacated or modified by competent tribunals of the primary state, although *TermoRio's* treatment of *Chromalloy* may implicitly have done so, as already has been suggested. By neither criticizing nor reversing *Chromalloy*, the appellate court implicitly, if not altogether explicitly, crafted a standard of review for courts in secondary states that does not place these tribunals in the awkward and inadequate position of sitting in judgment of a foreign court's interpretation, construction, and application of its own substantive law, which presumably is foreign to the courts in the secondary states.

The test is simple. Where a competent tribunal in the rendering state vacates an arbitral award and in so doing disregards a material term in the arbitration clause that would have directly affected the adjudication of vacatur, a court in a secondary state where confirmation of the award was vacated in the primary state should be rightfully empowered to grant the petition seeking confirmation despite the competent tribunal's vacatur or modification in the rendering state. No doubt the test is far from perfect, but it does have the virtues of simplicity, ease of application, and does not place the courts in secondary states in the virtually untenable posture of rendering judgment as to the manner in which a foreign tribunal interpreted and applied its own substantive law. Moreover, the proclivity or penchant that parties whose awards have been vacated by competent tribunals in the rendering state may have in attempting to secure recognition, confirmation, and enforcement of a vacated award by applying to multiple courts *in seriatum* in the hope of reversing the rendering state's court pronouncement is significantly mitigated, if not altogether dispelled from a practical perspective.

Queries certainly do remain with respect to what, for example, may constitute a material term in an arbitration clause? Similarly, it is conceivable that the concept of "harmless error" may apply to a vacatur issued by a competent tribunal in the rendering state with respect to some provision in the applicable arbitration clause. Still, some may view this paradigm as an unwarranted limitation foisted upon a tribunal by a foreign tribunal (that of the secondary state reviewing a petition for confirmation). Under this view, any formal amendment to the Convention or the development of jurisprudence promoting this test would be construed a violation of international law in that it may be understood to constitute an undue interference with a sovereign's exercise of sovereignty through the judicial system. These issues cannot find immediate formulistic resolution.

A competent tribunal of the rendering state should not be accorded unbridled discretion in applying the substantive law of its jurisdiction pursuant to papers seeking vacatur of an arbitration award without accountability where material provisions of the arbitration clause have been ignored or violated to justify nullification. A return to fundamental doctrine is important in analyzing this issue. Even though it is here recognized that neither domestic nor international commercial arbitration can exist without judicial intervention of some kind, it is essential to the integrity of arbitration as an alternative dispute resolution methodology for judicial intervention to be *minimized*. By *minimized* it is suggested that the role of the judiciary be circumscribed to that of a facilitator subordinate to the arbitral process. Because arbitration is governed by the precept of party-autonomy, even in its very jurisdictional genesis as a creature of contract, and its goal is but the specific resolution of disputes between parties and not the equitable administration of justice through the implementation of statutory and case law in furtherance of social policies that transcend the particular dispute at issue, bestowing upon a competent tribunal in the rendering state unbridled appellate review certainly does violence to the most important principles underlying arbitration as an alternative dispute resolution methodology. Thus, "minimize" as used here connotes a *qualitative* (not quantitative) change in the relationship between courts and arbitral proceedings such that courts are "limited" to facilitating the implementation of the arbitral tribunal's rulings, as, for example, with the compulsion of hostile or otherwise recalcitrant witnesses. It does not connote or denote a mere "lessening" of judicial intervention.

The *TermoRio* opinion is fundamentally positive in that it appears to have reached the right result. Its reliance on public policy appears to engraft upon such concerns the appearance of normative value. Instead, the legal community would have been better served were greater emphasis placed on developing the conceptual categories that a court in a secondary state adjudicating a petition seeking confirmation, recognition, and enforcement of an arbitration award otherwise vacated, nullified, or modified by a competent tribunal in a primary state, should use as a guidepost. Lastly, the Court's trepidation in seeking to harmonize the surface tensions in the language contained in Article V (providing a court with authority to refuse recognition of an arbitration award) and Article VII (granting parties the right to avail themselves of any right they may possess to enforce an arbitral award in a jurisdiction where such an award is expected to be relied on) is inextricably intertwined with the lack of doctrinal development applicable to the principles governing the relationship between rendering state tribunals and secondary state courts.

Under any analysis, the *Chromalloy, Baker Marine*, and *TermoRio* trio must be understood as a significant *first* step toward development of a comprehensive regime that will redefine the role of courts:

1. in rendering states reviewing arbitration awards,
2. with respect to the nature of their intervention in arbitral proceedings,
3. as between competent tribunals in rendering states and tribunals in secondary states called to reach diametrically opposite results, and
4. such that the fundamental precepts of party-autonomy, uniformity, predictive value, and transparency of standard are furthered.

Reasoned examination does suggest that the *Chromalloy, Baker Marine*, and *TermoRio* trio indeed answer, at least at a preliminary level that excludes application of analytical jurisprudence, the four inquiries that began this section. First, does the Convention's regime contemplate having a court in a secondary state sit in judgment of a tribunal in the primary state to determine whether the tribunal in that state properly applied its own substantive law in vacating or otherwise suspending an arbitration award, the rendition of which, by the arbitral tribunal, comports with the substantive law of the secondary state? Second, is this philological normative basis to be taken seriously, and if so how? Third, are tribunals in the secondary state where enforcement is sought best placed, or competent at all, to sit in judgment of the legal analysis underlying the vacatur of an arbitration award by the primary state? Fourth, would investing secondary states with the ability to sit in judgment of vacatur proceedings undertaken by the primary state provide the nonprevailing party with an incentive to apply to multiple secondary signatory states for confirmation of the award vacated in the primary state?

What remains are not answers to questions but methodologies to be developed to best arrive at these answers in a manner consonant with the fundamental precepts that form and transform arbitration.

Conclusion

Eliminating the badges of judicial prejudice and hostility against arbitration has been a gradual doctrinal development, but certainly one that reached fruition with the Supreme Court's mandate in *Mitsubishi*. The acceptance of arbitration as an alternative dispute resolution methodology in domestic and international contexts by the judiciary, scholars, captains of industry, and practitioners has advanced the cause of fashioning a dispute resolution framework that comports with contemporary economic globalization. It has mitigated the fissure between an economic order characterized by economic globalization and a fragmented transnational judicial rubric. Indeed, it has served to create a temporal bridge in dispute resolution until such time as transnational courts of civil procedure competent to adjudicate private commercial disputes become a viable reality. This success, however, has spawned new issues that must be addressed if the cross-fertilization of legal systems is to be incorporated into international commercial arbitrations and parties from different juridic and cultural backgrounds are to have their expectations fulfilled when engaging in alternative dispute resolution of this kind. By way of example, such fundamental developments as the incorporation of U.S. common law discovery in certain international commercial arbitral contexts compels judges, practitioners, commentators, and arbitrators to discard old prejudices and consider new paradigms that actually underscore debilities endemic to orthodox preconceptions and views governing this issue and best comport with contemporary developments. These changes, however, are far from settled and require sustained analysis if they are to be tempered in accordance with the very principles that define international commercial arbitration and its underlying policies and aspirations. In this same vein, the questions of Manifest Disregard of the Law, the issue of perjury in arbitration, and a coherent paradigm organizing the nature and character of interactions between courts and arbitral proceedings all have developed substantially and measurably in the last twenty-five years, but the need for more elaborate and comprehensive paradigms promoting uniformity, *party-autonomy*, certainty, predictive value, and transparency of standard remains an exigency if indeed international commercial arbitration is to continue to fill the void of future transnational courts of civil procedure with jurisdiction to engage in the equitable administration of justice with respect to civil and commercial private disputes.

The dialogue between U.S. doctrinal developments in international commercial arbitration and the plain language as well as underlying policies of the New York Convention also has experienced measurable and quite significant growth. Two examples merit a brief revisit. The question of jurisdiction over an arbitral award debtor as a predicate to enforcement certainly, as discussed, finds no textual foundation in the New York Convention. Such a jurisdictional requirement, however, is fundamentally premised on the principle of *due process.* This precept in turn does not suffer from the possible classification of a parochial idiosyncratic nature despite its constitutional status. Accordingly, the question of universal acceptance of jurisdiction as a predicate to enforcement within the context of signatory nations perhaps commands amendment to the Convention. Standing in sharp relief is the doctrine of *forum non conveniens.* Neither constitutional nor substantive in nature, this procedural doctrine is unique to common law systems. Arguably, it suffers from parochialism and an idiosyncratic constitution if measured by the talisman of universal acceptance. Even though the doctrinal development of jurisprudence is not and cannot be based upon "development by plebiscite," the universality of a juridic construct is fundamental to any serious analysis contemplating the possible application of the doctrine within the context of an international matrix primarily concerned with the free ambulatory recognition, confirmation, and execution of an arbitral award within the strictures of a specific paradigm. It is rather patent that the doctrine of *forum non conveniens,* despite its many virtues, cannot command a modification in the Convention. The identification of these issues and their submission to sustained reasoned analysis, without more, is a step – although a very modest one – in a productive relationship that promotes international commercial arbitration and a coherent and unified relationship between the judiciaries of the community of nations.

The new paradigms are helpful and their poignantly suggestive natures are equally availing. They are in flux, formation, and transformation such that the very nature of international commercial arbitration is at stake with respect to its future configuration and efficacy. There is an inherent contradiction between change and constancy. This tension, however, is susceptible to compromise and reconciliation. Lest that in a climate of economic globalization we wake up one day after experiencing uneasy dreams to discover that arbitration has turned into an alternative dispute resolution methodology that defies recognition. Here Franz Kafka's tale is certainly helpful. The guarded analysis of the common law's virtually imperceptible but material transformations is an imperative. These changes, and prospective suggested changes, must not lead to a paradigm that mutilates the fundamental configuration, purpose, and spirit of international commercial arbitration.

The challenge is certainly daunting. Yet, under any analysis, is it not one worth having?

APPENDIX A

Duelo a Garrotazos

APPENDIX B

Selected Cases

List of Selected Cases (chronologically, by Court)

1 Wilko v. Swan, 346 U.S. 427 (1953)
2 Prima Paint Corp. v. Flood & Conklin Mfg., 388 U.S. 395 (1967)
3 The Bremen et al. v. Zapata Off Shore Co., 407, U.S. 1 (1972)
4 Scherk v. Alberto-Culver Co., 417 U.S. 506 (1974)
5 Cone Memorial Hospital v. Mercury Construction Corp., 460 U.S. 1 (1983)
6 Southland Corp. et al. v. Keating et al., 465 U.S. 1 (1984)
7 Mitsubishi Motors Corp. v. Soler Chrysler-Plymouth, Inc., 473 U.S. 614 (1985)
8 Rodriguez de Quijas et al. v. Shearson/American Express, Inc., 490 U.S. 477 (1989)
9 Intel Corporation v. Advanced Micro Devices, Inc., 542 U.S. 241 (2004)
10 Buckeye Check Cashing v. John Cardegna et al., 546 U.S. 440 (2006)
11 Thomson-CSF, S.A. v. American Arbitration Association, 64 F.3d 773 (2d Cir. 1995)
12 Baker Marine (Nig.) Ltd. v. Chevron (Nig.) Ltd., 191 F.3d 194 (2d Cir. 1998)
13 Duferco International Steel v. Klaveness Shipping, 333 F.3d 383 (2d Cir. 2002)
14 In Re: Patricio Clerici, 481 F.3d 1324 (11th Cir. 2007)
15 Termorio S.A. v. Electranta S.P. et al., 487 F.3d 928 (D.C. Cir. 2007)
16 In the Matter of the Arbitration of Certain Controversies between Chromalloy Aeroservices and the Arab Republic of Egypt, 939 F. Supp. 90 (D.D.C. 1996)
17 In Re Application of: Roz Trading, 469 F. Supp. 2d 1221 (N.D.Ga. 2006)

WILKO v. SWAN ET AL., DOING BUSINESS AS HAYDEN, STONE & CO.

SUPREME COURT OF THE UNITED STATES

346 U.S. 427

October 21, 1953, Argued
December 7, 1953, Decided

MR. JUSTICE REED delivered the opinion of the Court.

This action by petitioner, a customer, against respondents, partners in a securities brokerage firm, was brought in the United States District Court for the Southern

District of New York, to recover damages under §12 (2) of the Securities Act of 1933. The complaint alleged that on or about January 17, 1951, through the instrumentalities of interstate commerce, petitioner was induced by Hayden, Stone and Company to purchase 1,600 shares of the common stock of Air Associates, Incorporated, by false representations that pursuant to a merger contract with the Borg Warner Corporation, Air Associates' stock would be valued at $6.00 per share over the then current market price, and that financial interests were buying up the stock for the speculative profit. It was alleged that he was not told that Haven B. Page (also named as a defendant but not involved in this review), a director of, and counsel for, Air Associates was then selling his own Air Associates' stock, including some or all that petitioner purchased. Two weeks after the purchase, petitioner disposed of the stock at a loss. Claiming that the loss was due to the firm's misrepresentations and omission of information concerning Mr. Page, he sought damages.

Without answering the complaint, the respondent moved to stay the trial of the action pursuant to §3 of the United States Arbitration Act until an arbitration in accordance with the terms of identical margin agreements was had. An affidavit accompanied the motion stating that the parties' relationship was controlled by the terms of the agreements and that while the firm was willing to arbitrate petitioner had failed to seek or proceed with any arbitration of the controversy.

Finding that the margin agreements provide that arbitration should be the method of settling all future controversies, the District Court held that the agreement to arbitrate deprived petitioner of the advantageous court remedy afforded by the Securities Act, and denied the stay. A divided Court of Appeals concluded that the Act did not prohibit the agreement to refer future controversies to arbitration, and reversed.

The question is whether an agreement to arbitrate a future controversy is a "condition, stipulation, or provision binding any person acquiring any security to waive compliance with any provision" of the Securities Act which §14 declares "void." We granted certiorari to review this important and novel federal question affecting both the Securities Act and the United States Arbitration Act. Cf. *Frost & Co.* v. *Coeur D'Alene Mines Corp., 312 U.S. 38, 40.*

As the margin agreement in the light of the complaint evidenced a transaction in interstate commerce, no issue arises as to the applicability of the provisions of the United States Arbitration Act to this suit, based upon the Securities Act. *9 U. S. C. (Supp. V, 1952) §2.* Cf. *Tejas Development Co.* v. *McGough Bros., 165 F.2d 276, 278,* with *Agostini Bros. Bldg. Corp.* v. *United States, 142 F.2d 854.* See Sturges and Murphy, Some Confusing Matters Relating to Arbitration, 17 Law & Contemp. Prob. 580.

In response to a Presidential message urging that there be added to the ancient rule of *caveat emptor* the further doctrine of "let the seller also beware," Congress passed the Securities Act of 1933. Designed to protect investors, the Act requires issuers, underwriters, and dealers to make full and fair disclosure of the character of securities sold in interstate and foreign commerce and to prevent fraud in their sale. To effectuate this policy, §12 (2) created a special right to recover for misrepresentation which differs substantially from the common-law action in that the seller is made to assume the burden of proving lack of scienter. The Act's special right is enforceable in any court of competent jurisdiction – federal or state – and removal from a state court is prohibited. If suit be brought in a federal court, the purchaser has a wide choice of venue, the privilege of nationwide service of process and the jurisdictional $3,000 requirement of diversity cases is inapplicable.

The United States Arbitration Act establishes by statute the desirability of arbitration as an alternative to the complications of litigation. The reports of both Houses on that Act stress the need for avoiding the delay and expense of litigation, and practice under its terms raises hope for its usefulness both in controversies based on statutes or on standards otherwise created. This hospitable attitude of legislatures and courts toward arbitration, however, does not solve our question as to the validity of petitioner's stipulation by the margin agreements, set out below, to submit to arbitration controversies that might arise from the transactions.

Petitioner argues that §14 shows that the purpose of Congress was to assure that sellers could not maneuver buyers into a position that might weaken their ability to recover under the Securities Act. He contends that arbitration lacks the certainty of a suit at law under the Act to enforce his rights. He reasons that the arbitration paragraph of the margin agreement is a stipulation that waives "compliance with" the provision of the Securities Act, set out in the margin, conferring jurisdiction of suits and special powers.

Respondent asserts that arbitration is merely a form of trial to be used in lieu of a trial at law, and therefore no conflict exists between the Securities Act and the United States Arbitration Act either in their language or in the congressional purposes in their enactment. Each may function within its own scope, the former to protect investors and the latter to simplify recovery for actionable violations of law by issuers or dealers in securities.

Respondent is in agreement with the Court of Appeals that the margin agreement arbitration paragraph does not relieve the seller from either liability or burden of proof imposed by the Securities Act. We agree that in so far as the award in arbitration may be affected by legal requirements, statutes or common law, rather than by considerations of fairness, the provisions of the Securities Act control. This is true even though this proposed agreement has no requirement that the arbitrators follow the law. This agreement of the parties as to the effect of the Securities Act includes also acceptance of the invalidity of the paragraph of the margin agreement that relieves the respondent sellers of liability for all "representation or advice by you or your employees or agents regarding the purchase or sale by me of any property."

The words of §14 void any "stipulation" waiving compliance with any "provision" of the Securities Act. This arrangement to arbitrate is a "stipulation," and we think the right to select the judicial forum is the kind of "provision" that cannot be waived under §14 of the Securities Act. That conclusion is reached for the reasons set out above in the statement of petitioner's contention on this review. While a buyer and seller of securities, under some circumstances, may deal at arm's length on equal terms, it is clear that the Securities Act was drafted with an eye to the disadvantages under which buyers labor. Issuers of and dealers in securities have better opportunities to investigate and appraise the prospective earnings and business plans affecting securities than buyers. It is therefore reasonable for Congress to put buyers of securities covered by that Act on a different basis from other purchasers.

When the security buyer, prior to any violation of the Securities Act, waives his right to sue in courts, he gives up more than would a participant in other business transactions. The security buyer has a wider choice of courts and venue. He thus surrenders one of the advantages the Act gives him and surrenders it at a time when he is less able to judge the weight of the handicap the Securities Act places upon his adversary.

Even though the provisions of the Securities Act, advantageous to the buyer, apply, their effectiveness in application is lessened in arbitration as compared to judicial proceedings. Determination of the quality of a commodity or the amount of money due under a contract is not the type of issue here involved. This case requires subjective findings on the purpose and knowledge of an alleged violator of the Act. They must be not only determined but applied by the arbitrators without judicial instruction on the law. As their award may be made without explanation of their reasons and without a complete record of their proceedings, the arbitrators' conception of the legal meaning of such statutory requirements as "burden of proof," "reasonable care" or "material fact" cannot be examined. Power to vacate an award is limited. While it may be true, as the Court of Appeals thought, that a failure of the arbitrators to decide in accordance with the provisions of the Securities Act would "constitute grounds for vacating the award pursuant to *section 10* of the Federal Arbitration Act," that failure would need to be made clearly to appear. In unrestricted submissions, such as the present margin agreements envisage, the interpretations of the law by the arbitrators in contrast to manifest disregard are not subject, in the federal courts, to judicial review for error in interpretation. The United States Arbitration Act contains no provision for judicial determination of legal issues such as is found in the English law. As the protective provisions of the Securities Act require the exercise of judicial direction to fairly assure their effectiveness, it seems to us that Congress must have intended §14 to apply to waiver of judicial trial and review.

This accords with *Boyd v. Grand Trunk Western R. Co., 338 U.S. 263*. We there held invalid a stipulation restricting an employee's choice of venue in an action under the Federal Employers' Liability Act. Section 6 of that Act permitted suit in any one of several localities and §5 forbade a common carrier's exempting itself from any liability under the Act. Section 5 had been adopted to avoid contracts waiving employers' liability. It is to be noted that in words it forbade exemption only from "liability." We said the right to select the "forum" even after the creation of a liability is a "substantial right" and that the agreement, restricting that choice, would thwart the express purpose of the statute. We need not and do not go so far in this present case. By the terms of the agreement to arbitrate, petitioner is restricted in his choice of forum prior to the existence of a controversy. While the Securities Act does not require petitioner to sue, a waiver in advance of a controversy stands upon a different footing.

Two policies, not easily reconcilable, are involved in this case. Congress has afforded participants in transactions subject to its legislative power an opportunity generally to secure prompt, economical and adequate solution of controversies through arbitration if the parties are willing to accept less certainty of legally correct adjustment. On the other hand, it has enacted the Securities Act to protect the rights of investors and has forbidden a waiver of any of those rights. Recognizing the advantages that prior agreements for arbitration may provide for the solution of commercial controversies, we decide that the intention of Congress concerning the sale of securities is better carried out by holding invalid such an agreement for arbitration of issues arising under the Act.

Reversed.

PRIMA PAINT CORP. v. FLOOD & CONKLIN MFG. CO. SUPREME COURT OF THE UNITED STATES

388 U.S. 395

March 16, 1967, Argued
June 12, 1967, Decided

MR. JUSTICE FORTAS delivered the opinion of the Court.

This case presents the question whether the federal court or an arbitrator is to resolve a claim of "fraud in the inducement," under a contract governed by the United States Arbitration Act of 1925, where there is no evidence that the contracting parties intended to withhold that issue from arbitration.

The question arises from the following set of facts. On October 7, 1964, respondent, Flood & Conklin Manufacturing Company, a New Jersey corporation, entered into what was styled a "Consulting Agreement," with petitioner, Prima Paint Corporation, a Maryland corporation. This agreement followed by less than three weeks the execution of a contract pursuant to which Prima Paint purchased F & C's paint business. The consulting agreement provided that for a six-year period F & C was to furnish advice and consultation "in connection with the formulae, manufacturing operations, sales and servicing of Prima Trade Sales accounts." These services were to be performed personally by F & C's chairman, Jerome K. Jelin, "except in the event of his death or disability." F & C bound itself for the duration of the contractual period to make no "Trade Sales" of paint or paint products in its existing sales territory or to current customers. To the consulting agreement were appended lists of F & C customers, whose patronage was to be taken over by Prima Paint. In return for these lists, the covenant not to compete, and the services of Mr. Jelin, Prima Paint agreed to pay F & C certain percentages of its receipts from the listed customers and from all others, such payments not to exceed $225,000 over the life of the agreement. The agreement took into account the possibility that Prima Paint might encounter financial difficulties, including bankruptcy, but no corresponding reference was made to possible financial problems which might be encountered by F & C. The agreement stated that it "embodies the entire understanding of the parties on the subject matter." Finally, the parties agreed to a broad arbitration clause, which read in part:

"Any controversy or claim arising out of or relating to this Agreement, or the breach thereof, shall be settled by arbitration in the City of New York, in accordance with the rules then obtaining of the American Arbitration Association. . . ."

The first payment by Prima Paint to F & C under the consulting agreement was due on September 1, 1965. None was made on that date. Seventeen days later, Prima Paint did pay the appropriate amount, but into escrow. It notified attorneys for F & C that in various enumerated respects their client had broken both the consulting agreement and the earlier purchase agreement. Prima Paint's principal contention, so far as presently relevant, was that F & C had fraudulently represented that it was solvent and able to perform its contractual obligations, whereas it was in fact insolvent and intended to file a petition under Chapter XI of the Bankruptcy Act, 52 Stat. 905, *11 U. S. C. §701 et seq.*, shortly after execution of the consulting agreement. Prima Paint noted that such a petition was filed by F & C on October 14, 1964, one week after the contract had been signed. F & C's response, on October 25, was to serve a "notice of intention to arbitrate." On November 12, three days before expiration of its time to answer this "notice," Prima Paint filed suit in the United States District Court for the Southern District of New York, seeking rescission of the consulting agreement on the basis of the alleged fraudulent inducement. The complaint asserted that the federal court had diversity jurisdiction.

Contemporaneously with the filing of its complaint, Prima Paint petitioned the District Court for an order enjoining F & C from proceeding with the arbitration. F & C cross-moved to stay the court action pending arbitration. F & C contended that the issue presented – whether there was fraud in the inducement of the consulting agreement – was a question for the arbitrators and not for the District Court. Cross-affidavits were filed on the merits. On behalf of Prima Paint, the charges in the complaint were reiterated. Affiants for F & C attacked the sufficiency of Prima Paint's allegations of fraud, denied that misrepresentations had been made during negotiations, and asserted that Prima Paint had relied exclusively upon delivery of the lists, the promise not to compete, and the availability of Mr. Jelin. They contended that Prima Paint had availed itself of these considerations for nearly a year without claiming "fraud," noting that Prima Paint was in no position to claim ignorance of the bankruptcy proceeding since it had participated therein in February of 1965. They added that F & C was revested with its assets in March of 1965.

The District Court granted F & C's motion to stay the action pending arbitration, holding that a charge of fraud in the inducement of a contract containing an arbitration clause as broad as this one was a question for the arbitrators and not for the court. For this proposition it relied on *Robert Lawrence Co. v. Devonshire Fabrics, Inc., 271 F.2d 402 (C. A. 2d Cir. 1959)*, cert. granted, *362 U.S. 909*, dismissed under Rule 60, 364 U.S. 801 (1960). The Court of Appeals for the Second Circuit dismissed Prima Paint's appeal. It held that the contract in question evidenced a transaction involving interstate commerce; that under the controlling *Robert Lawrence Co.* decision a claim of fraud in the inducement of the contract generally – as opposed to the arbitration clause itself – is for the arbitrators and not for the courts; and that this rule – one of "national substantive law" – governs even in the face of a contrary state rule. We agree, albeit for somewhat different reasons, and we affirm the decision below.

The key statutory provisions are *§§2, 3,* and *4* of the United States Arbitration Act of 1925. *Section 2* provides that a written provision for arbitration "in any maritime transaction or a contract evidencing a transaction involving commerce . . . shall be valid, irrevocable, and enforceable, save upon such grounds as exist at law or in equity for the revocation of any contract." *Section 3* requires a federal court in which suit has been brought "upon any issue referable to arbitration under an agreement in writing for such arbitration" to stay the court action pending arbitration once it is satisfied that the issue is arbitrable under the agreement. *Section 4* provides a federal remedy for a party "aggrieved by the alleged failure, neglect, or refusal of another to arbitrate under a written agreement for arbitration," and directs the federal court to order arbitration once it is satisfied that an agreement for arbitration has been made and has not been honored.

In *Bernhardt v. Polygraphic Co., 350 U.S. 198 (1956)*, this Court held that the stay provisions of *§3*, invoked here by respondent F & C, apply only to the two kinds of contracts specified in *§§1* and *2* of the Act, namely those in admiralty or evidencing transactions in "commerce." Our first question, then, is whether the consulting agreement between F & C and Prima Paint is such a contract. We agree with the Court of Appeals that it is. Prima Paint acquired a New Jersey paint business serving at least 175 wholesale clients in a number of States, and secured F & C's assistance in arranging the transfer of manufacturing and selling operations from New Jersey to Maryland. The consulting agreement was inextricably tied to this interstate transfer and to the continuing operations of an interstate manufacturing and wholesaling business. There could not be a clearer case of a contract evidencing a transaction in interstate commerce.

Having determined that the contract in question is within the coverage of the Arbitration Act, we turn to the central issue in this case: whether a claim of fraud in the inducement of the entire contract is to be resolved by the federal court, or whether the matter is to be referred to the arbitrators. The courts of appeals have differed in their approach to this question. The view of the Court of Appeals for the Second Circuit, as expressed in this case and in others, is that – *except where the parties otherwise intend* – arbitration clauses as a matter of federal law are "separable" from the contracts in which they are embedded, and that where no claim is made that fraud was directed to the arbitration clause itself, a broad arbitration clause will be held to encompass arbitration of the claim that the contract itself was induced by fraud. The Court of Appeals for the First Circuit, on the other hand, has taken the view that the question of "severability" is one of state law, and that where a State regards such a clause as inseparable a claim of fraud in the inducement must be decided by the court. *Lummus Co. v. Commonwealth Oil Ref. Co., 280 F.2d 915, 923–924 (C. A. 1st Cir.)*, cert. denied, *364 U.S. 911 (1960)*.

With respect to cases brought in federal court involving maritime contracts or those evidencing transactions in "commerce," we think that Congress has provided an explicit answer. That answer is to be found in *§4* of the Act, which provides a remedy to a party seeking to compel compliance with an arbitration agreement. Under *§4*, with respect to a matter within the jurisdiction of the federal courts save for the existence of an arbitration clause, the federal court is instructed to order arbitration to proceed once it is satisfied that "the making of the agreement for arbitration or the failure to comply [with the arbitration agreement] is not in issue." Accordingly, if the claim is fraud in the inducement of the arbitration clause itself – an issue which goes to the "making" of the agreement to arbitrate – the federal court may proceed to adjudicate it. But the statutory language does not permit the federal court to consider claims of fraud in the inducement of the contract generally. *Section 4* does not expressly relate to situations like the present in which a stay is sought of a federal action in order that arbitration may proceed. But it is inconceivable that Congress intended the rule to differ depending upon which party to the arbitration agreement first invokes the assistance of a federal court. We hold, therefore, that in passing upon a *§3* application for a stay while the parties arbitrate, a federal court may consider only issues relating to the making and performance of the agreement to arbitrate. In so concluding, we not only honor the plain meaning of the statute but also the unmistakably clear congressional purpose that the arbitration procedure, when selected by the parties to a contract, be speedy and not subject to delay and obstruction in the courts.

There remains the question whether such a rule is constitutionally permissible. The point is made that, whatever the nature of the contract involved here, this case is in federal court solely by reason of diversity of citizenship, and that since the decision in *Erie R. Co. v. Tompkins, 304 U.S. 64 (1938)*, federal courts are bound in diversity cases to follow state rules of decision in matters which are "substantive" rather than "procedural," or where the matter is "outcome determinative." *Guaranty Trust Co. v. York, 326 U.S. 99 (1945)*. The question in this case, however, is not whether Congress may fashion federal substantive rules to govern questions arising in simple diversity cases. See *Bernhardt v. Polygraphic Co., supra, at 202*, and concurring opinion, at 208. Rather, the question is whether Congress may prescribe how federal courts are to conduct themselves with respect to subject matter over which Congress plainly has power to legislate. The answer to that can only be in the affirmative. And it is clear beyond dispute that the federal arbitration statute is based upon and confined to the incontestable federal foundations of "control over interstate commerce and over admiralty." H. R. Rep. No. 96, 68th Cong., 1st Sess., 1 (1924); S. Rep. No. 536, 68th Cong., 1st Sess., 3 (1924).

In the present case no claim has been advanced by Prima Paint that F & C fraudulently induced it to enter into the agreement to arbitrate "any controversy or claim arising out of or relating to this Agreement, or the breach thereof." This contractual language is easily broad enough to encompass Prima Paint's claim that both execution and acceleration of the consulting agreement itself were procured by fraud. Indeed, no claim is made that Prima Paint ever intended that "legal" issues relating to the contract be excluded from arbitration, or that it was not entirely free so to contract. Federal courts are bound to apply rules enacted by Congress with respect to matters – here, a contract involving commerce – over which it has legislative power. The question which Prima Paint requested the District Court to adjudicate preliminarily to allowing arbitration to proceed is one not intended by Congress to delay the granting of a *§3* stay. Accordingly, the decision below dismissing Prima Paint's appeal is

Affirmed.

THE BREMEN ET AL. v. ZAPATA OFF-SHORE CO.
SUPREME COURT OF THE UNITED STATES

407 U.S. 1

March 21, 1972, Argued
June 12, 1972, Decided

MR. CHIEF JUSTICE BURGER delivered the opinion of the Court.

We granted certiorari to review a judgment of the United States Court of Appeals for the Fifth Circuit declining to enforce a forum-selection clause governing disputes arising under an international towage contract between petitioners and respondent. The circuits have differed in their approach to such clauses. For the reasons stated hereafter, we vacate the judgment of the Court of Appeals.

In November 1967, respondent Zapata, a Houston-based American corporation, contracted with petitioner Unterweser, a German corporation, to tow Zapata's ocean-going, self-elevating drilling rig *Chaparral* from Louisiana to a point off Ravenna, Italy, in the Adriatic Sea, where Zapata had agreed to drill certain wells.

Zapata had solicited bids for the towage, and several companies including Unterweser had responded. Unterweser was the low bidder and Zapata requested it to submit a contract, which it did. The contract submitted by Unterweser contained the following provision, which is at issue in this case: "Any dispute arising must be treated before the London Court of Justice."

In addition the contract contained two clauses purporting to exculpate Unterweser from liability for damages to the towed barge.

After reviewing the contract and making several changes, but without any alteration in the forum-selection or exculpatory clauses, a Zapata vice president executed the contract and forwarded it to Unterweser in Germany, where Unterweser accepted the changes, and the contract became effective.

On January 5, 1968, Unterweser's deep sea tug *Bremen* departed Venice, Louisiana, with the *Chaparral* in tow bound for Italy. On January 9, while the flotilla was in international waters in the middle of the Gulf of Mexico, a severe storm arose. The sharp roll of the *Chaparral* in Gulf waters caused its elevator legs, which had been raised for the voyage, to break off and fall into the sea, seriously damaging the *Chaparral*. In this emergency situation Zapata instructed the *Bremen* to tow its damaged rig to Tampa, Florida, the nearest port of refuge.

On January 12, Zapata, ignoring its contract promise to litigate "any dispute arising" in the English courts, commenced a suit in admiralty in the United States District Court at Tampa, seeking $3,500,000 damages against Unterweser *in personam* and the *Bremen in rem*, alleging negligent towage and breach of contract. Unterweser responded by invoking the forum clause of the towage contract, and moved to dismiss for lack of jurisdiction or on *forum non conveniens* grounds, or in the alternative to stay the action pending submission of the dispute to the "London Court of Justice." Shortly thereafter, in February, before the District Court had ruled on its motion to stay or dismiss the United States action, Unterweser commenced an action against Zapata seeking damages for breach of the towage contract in the High Court of Justice in London, as the contract provided. Zapata appeared in that court to contest jurisdiction, but its challenge was rejected, the English courts holding that the contractual forum provision conferred jurisdiction.

In the meantime, Unterweser was faced with a dilemma in the pending action in the United States court at Tampa. The six-month period for filing action to limit its liability to Zapata and other potential claimants was about to expire, but the United States District Court in Tampa had not yet ruled on Unterweser's motion to dismiss or stay Zapata's action. On July 2, 1968, confronted with difficult alternatives, Unterweser filed an action to limit its liability in the District Court in Tampa. That court entered the customary injunction against proceedings outside the limitation court, and Zapata refilled its initial claim in the limitation action.

It was only at this juncture, on July 29, after the six-month period for filing the limitation action had run, that the District Court denied Unterweser's January motion to dismiss or stay Zapata's initial action. In denying the motion, that court relied on the prior decision of the Court of Appeals in *Carbon Black Export, Inc.* v. *The Monrosa, 254 F.2d 297 (CA5 1958)*, cert. dismissed, *359 U.S. 180 (1959)*. In that case the Court of Appeals had held a forum-selection clause unenforceable, reiterating the traditional view of many American courts that "agreements in advance of controversy whose object is to oust the jurisdiction of the courts are contrary to public policy and will not be enforced." *254 F.2d, at 300–301*. Apparently concluding that it was bound by the *Carbon Black* case, the District Court gave the forum-selection clause little, if any, weight. Instead, the court treated the motion to dismiss under normal *forum non conveniens* doctrine applicable in the absence of such a clause, citing *Gulf Oil Corp.* v. *Gilbert, 330 U.S. 501 (1947)*. Under that doctrine "unless the balance is strongly in favor of the defendant, the plaintiff's choice of forum should rarely be disturbed." *Id., at 508*. The District Court concluded: "The balance of conveniences here is not strongly in favor of [Unterweser] and [Zapata's] choice of forum should not be disturbed."

Thereafter, on January 21, 1969, the District Court denied another motion by Unterweser to stay the limitation action pending determination of the controversy in the High Court of Justice in London and granted Zapata's motion to restrain Unterweser from litigating further in the London court. The District Judge ruled that, having taken jurisdiction in the limitation proceeding, he had jurisdiction to determine all matters relating to the controversy. He ruled that Unterweser should be required to "do equity" by refraining from also litigating the controversy in the London court, not only for the reasons he had previously stated for denying Unterweser's first motion to stay Zapata's action, but also because Unterweser had invoked the United States court's jurisdiction to obtain the benefit of the Limitation Act.

On appeal, a divided panel of the Court of Appeals affirmed, and on rehearing *en banc* the panel opinion was adopted, with six of the 14 *en banc* judges dissenting. As had the District Court, the majority rested on the *Carbon Black* decision, concluding that "'at the very least'" that case stood for the proposition that a forum-selection clause "'will not be enforced unless the selected state would provide a more convenient forum than the state in which suit is brought.'" From that premise the Court of Appeals proceeded to conclude that, apart from the forum-selection clause, the District Court did not abuse its discretion in refusing to decline jurisdiction on the basis of *forum non conveniens*. It noted that (1) the flotilla never "escaped the Fifth Circuit's mare nostrum, and the casualty occurred in close proximity to the district court"; (2) a considerable number of potential witnesses, including Zapata crewmen, resided in the Gulf Coast area; (3) preparation for the voyage and inspection and repair work had been performed in the Gulf area; (4) the testimony of the *Bremen* crew was available by way of deposition; (5) England had no interest in or contact with the controversy other than the forum-selection clause. The Court of Appeals majority further noted that Zapata was a United States citizen and "the discretion of the district court to remand the case to a foreign forum was consequently limited" – especially since it appeared likely that the English courts would enforce the exculpatory clauses. In the Court of Appeals' view, enforcement of such clauses would be contrary to public policy in American courts under *Bisso v. Inland Waterways Corp., 349 U.S. 85 (1955)*, and *Dixilyn Drilling Corp.* v. *Crescent Towing & Salvage Co., 372*

U.S. 697 (1963). Therefore, "the district court was entitled to consider that remanding Zapata to a foreign forum, with no practical contact with the controversy, could raise a bar to recovery by a United States citizen which its own convenient courts would not countenance."

We hold, with the six dissenting members of the Court of Appeals, that far too little weight and effect were given to the forum clause in resolving this controversy. For at least two decades we have witnessed an expansion of overseas commercial activities by business enterprises based in the United States. The barrier of distance that once tended to confine a business concern to a modest territory no longer does so. Here we see an American company with special expertise contracting with a foreign company to tow a complex machine thousands of miles across seas and oceans. The expansion of American business and industry will hardly be encouraged if, notwithstanding solemn contracts, we insist on a parochial concept that all disputes must be resolved under our laws and in our courts. Absent a contract forum, the considerations relied on by the Court of Appeals would be persuasive reasons for holding an American forum convenient in the traditional sense, but in an era of expanding world trade and commerce, the absolute aspects of the doctrine of the *Carbon Black* case have little place and would be a heavy hand indeed on the future development of international commercial dealings by Americans. We cannot have trade and commerce in world markets and international waters exclusively on our terms, governed by our laws, and resolved in our courts.

Forum-selection clauses have historically not been favored by American courts. Many courts, federal and state, have declined to enforce such clauses on the ground that they were "contrary to public policy," or that their effect was to "oust the jurisdiction" of the court. Although this view apparently still has considerable acceptance, other courts are tending to adopt a more hospitable attitude toward forum-selection clauses. This view, advanced in the well-reasoned dissenting opinion in the instant case, is that such clauses are prima facie valid and should be enforced unless enforcement is shown by the resisting party to be "unreasonable" under the circumstances. We believe this is the correct doctrine to be followed by federal district courts sitting in admiralty. It is merely the other side of the proposition recognized by this Court in *National Equipment Rental, Ltd.* v. *Szukhent, 375 U.S. 311 (1964)*, holding that in federal courts a party may validly consent to be sued in a jurisdiction where he cannot be found for service of process through contractual designation of an "agent" for receipt of process in that jurisdiction. In so holding, the Court stated:

> "It is settled . . . that parties to a contract may agree in advance to submit to the jurisdiction of a given court, to permit notice to be served by the opposing party, or even to waive notice altogether." *Id., at 315–316.*

This approach is substantially that followed in other common-law countries including England. It is the view advanced by noted scholars and that adopted by the Restatement of the Conflict of Laws. It accords with ancient concepts of freedom of contract and reflects an appreciation of the expanding horizons of American contractors who seek business in all parts of the world. Not surprisingly, foreign businessmen prefer, as do we, to have disputes resolved in their own courts, but if that choice is not available, then in a neutral forum with expertise in the subject matter. Plainly, the courts of England meet the standards of neutrality and long experience in admiralty litigation. The choice of that forum was made in an arm's-length negotiation by experienced and sophisticated businessmen, and absent some compelling and countervailing reason it should be honored by the parties and enforced by the courts.

The argument that such clauses are improper because they tend to "oust" a court of jurisdiction is hardly more than a vestigial legal fiction. It appears to rest at core on historical judicial resistance to any attempt to reduce the power and business of a particular court and has little place in an era when all courts are overloaded and when businesses once essentially local now operate in world markets. It reflects something of a provincial attitude regarding the fairness of other tribunals. No one seriously contends in this case that the forum-selection clause "ousted" the District Court of jurisdiction over Zapata's action. The threshold question is whether that court should have exercised its jurisdiction to do more than give effect to the legitimate expectations of the parties, manifested in their freely negotiated agreement, by specifically enforcing the forum clause.

There are compelling reasons why a freely negotiated private international agreement, unaffected by fraud, undue influence, or overweening bargaining power, such as that involved here, should be given full effect. In this case, for example, we are concerned with a far from routine transaction between companies of two different nations contemplating the tow of an extremely costly piece of equipment from Louisiana across the Gulf of Mexico and the Atlantic Ocean, through the Mediterranean Sea to its final destination in the Adriatic Sea. In the course of its voyage, it was to traverse the waters of many jurisdictions. The *Chaparral* could have been damaged at any point along the route, and there were countless possible ports of refuge. That the accident occurred in the Gulf of Mexico and the barge was towed to Tampa in an emergency were mere fortuities. It cannot be doubted for a moment that the parties sought to provide for a neutral forum for the resolution of any disputes arising during the tow. Manifestly much uncertainty and possibly great inconvenience to both parties could arise if a suit could be maintained in any jurisdiction in which an accident might occur or if jurisdiction were left to any place where the *Bremen* or Unterweser might happen to be found. The elimination of all such uncertainties by agreeing in advance on a forum acceptable to both parties is an indispensable element in international trade, commerce, and contracting. There is strong evidence that the forum clause was a vital part of the agreement, and it would be unrealistic to think that the parties did not conduct their negotiations, including fixing the monetary terms, with the consequences of the forum clause figuring prominently in their calculations. Under these circumstances, as Justice Karminski reasoned in sustaining jurisdiction over Zapata in the High Court of Justice, "the force of an agreement for litigation in this country, freely entered into between two competent parties, seems to me to be very powerful."

Thus, in the light of present-day commercial realities and expanding international trade we conclude that the forum clause should control absent a strong showing that it should be set aside. Although their opinions are not altogether explicit, it seems reasonably clear that the District Court and the Court of Appeals placed the burden on Unterweser to show that London would be a more convenient forum than Tampa, although the contract expressly resolved that issue. The correct approach would have been to enforce the forum clause specifically unless Zapata could clearly show that enforcement would be unreasonable and unjust, or that the clause was invalid for such reasons as fraud or overreaching. Accordingly, the case must be remanded for reconsideration.

We note, however, that there is nothing in the record presently before us that would support a refusal to enforce the forum clause. The Court of Appeals suggested that enforcement would be contrary to the public policy of the forum under *Bisso v. Inland Waterways Corp., 349 U.S. 85 (1955)*, because of the prospect that the English courts would enforce the clauses of the towage contract purporting to exculpate Unterweser from liability for damages to the *Chaparral*. A contractual choice-of-forum clause should be held unenforceable if enforcement would contravene a strong public policy of the forum in which suit is brought, whether declared by statute or by judicial decision. See, *e.g., Boyd v. Grand Trunk W. R. Co., 338 U.S. 263 (1949)*. It is clear, however, that whatever the proper scope of the policy expressed in *Bisso*, it does not reach this case. *Bisso* rested on considerations with respect to the towage business strictly in American waters, and those considerations are not controlling in an international commercial agreement. Speaking for the dissenting judges in the Court of Appeals, Judge Wisdom pointed out:

> "We should be careful not to over-emphasize the strength of the [*Bisso*] policy. . . . Two concerns underlie the rejection of exculpatory agreements: that they may be produced by overweening bargaining power; and that they do not sufficiently discourage negligence. . . . Here the conduct in question is that of a foreign party occurring in international waters outside our jurisdiction. The evidence disputes any notion of overreaching in the contractual agreement. And for all we know, the uncertainties and dangers in the new field of transoceanic towage of oil rigs were so great that the tower was unwilling to take financial responsibility for the risks, and the parties thus allocated responsibility for the voyage to the tow. It is equally possible that the contract price took this factor into account. I conclude that we should not invalidate the forum selection clause here unless we are firmly convinced that we would thereby significantly encourage negligent conduct within the boundaries of the United States." *428 F.2d, at 907–908.*

Courts have also suggested that a forum clause, even though it is freely bargained for and contravenes no important public policy of the forum, may nevertheless be "unreasonable" and unenforceable if the chosen forum is *seriously* inconvenient for the trial of the action. Of course, where it can be said with reasonable assurance that at the time they entered the contract, the parties to a freely negotiated private international commercial agreement contemplated the claimed inconvenience, it is difficult to see why any such claim of inconvenience should be heard to render the forum clause unenforceable. We are not here dealing with an agreement between two Americans to resolve their essentially local disputes in a remote alien forum. In such a case, the serious inconvenience of the contractual forum to one or both of the parties might carry greater weight in determining the reasonableness of the forum clause. The remoteness of the forum might suggest that the agreement was an adhesive one, or that the parties did not have the particular controversy in mind when they made their agreement; yet even there the party claiming should bear a heavy burden of proof. Similarly, selection of a remote forum to apply differing foreign law to an essentially American controversy might contravene an important public policy of the forum. For example, so long as *Bisso* governs American courts with respect to the towage business in American waters, it would quite arguably be improper to permit an American tower to avoid that policy by providing a foreign forum for resolution of his disputes with an American towee.

This case, however, involves a freely negotiated international commercial transaction between a German and an American corporation for towage of a vessel from the Gulf of Mexico to the Adriatic Sea. As noted, selection of a London forum was clearly a reasonable effort to bring vital certainty to this international transaction and to provide a neutral forum experienced and capable in the resolution of admiralty litigation. Whatever "inconvenience" Zapata would suffer by being forced to litigate in the contractual forum as it agreed to do was clearly foreseeable at the time of contracting. In such circumstances it should be incumbent on the party seeking to escape his contract to show that trial in the contractual forum will be so gravely difficult and inconvenient that he will for all practical purposes be deprived of his day in court. Absent that, there is no basis for concluding that it would be unfair, unjust, or unreasonable to hold that party to his bargain.

In the course of its ruling on Unterweser's second motion to stay the proceedings in Tampa, the District Court did make a conclusory finding that the balance of convenience was "strongly" in favor of litigation in Tampa. However, as previously noted, in making that finding the court erroneously placed the burden of proof on Unterweser to show that the balance of convenience was strongly in its favor. Moreover, the finding falls far short of a conclusion that Zapata would be effectively deprived of its day in court should it be forced to litigate in London. Indeed, it cannot even be assumed that it would be placed to the expense of transporting its witnesses to London. It is not unusual for important issues in international admiralty cases to be dealt with by deposition. Both the District Court and the Court of Appeals majority appeared satisfied that Unterweser could receive a fair hearing in Tampa by using deposition testimony of its witnesses from distant places, and there is no reason to conclude that Zapata could not use deposition testimony to equal advantage if forced to litigate in London as it bound itself to do. Nevertheless, to allow Zapata opportunity to carry its heavy burden of showing not only that the balance of convenience is strongly in favor of trial in Tampa (that is, that it will be far more inconvenient for Zapata to litigate in London than it will be for Unterweser to litigate in Tampa), but also that a London trial will be so manifestly and gravely inconvenient to Zapata that it will be effectively deprived of a meaningful day in court, we remand for further proceedings.

Zapata's remaining contentions do not require extended treatment. It is clear that Unterweser's action in filing its limitation complaint in the District Court in Tampa was, so far as Zapata was concerned, solely a defensive measure made necessary as a response to Zapata's breach of the forum clause of the contract. When the six-month statutory period for filing an action to limit its liability had almost run without the District Court's having ruled on Unterweser's initial motion to dismiss or stay Zapata's action pursuant to the forum clause, Unterweser had no other prudent alternative but to protect itself by filing for limitation of its liability. Its action in so doing was a direct consequence of Zapata's failure to abide by the forum clause of the towage contract. There is no basis on which to conclude that this purely necessary defensive action by Unterweser should preclude it from relying on the forum clause it bargained for. For the first time in this litigation, Zapata has suggested to this Court that the forum clause should not be construed to provide for an exclusive forum or to include *in rem* actions. However, the language of the clause is clearly mandatory and all-encompassing; the language of the clause in the *Carbon Black* case was far different.

The judgment of the Court of Appeals is vacated and the case is remanded for further proceedings consistent with this opinion.

Vacated and remanded.

SCHERK v. ALBERTO-CULVER CO.
SUPREME COURT OF THE UNITED STATES

417 U.S. 506

April 29, 1974, Argued
June 17, 1974, Decided

MR. JUSTICE STEWART delivered the opinion of the Court.

Alberto-Culver Co., the respondent, is an American company incorporated in Delaware with its principal office in Illinois. It manufactures and distributes toiletries and hair products in this country and abroad. During the 1960's Alberto-Culver decided to expand its overseas operations, and as part of this program it approached the petitioner Fritz Scherk, a German citizen residing at the time of trial in Switzerland. Scherk was the owner of three interrelated business entities, organized under the laws of Germany and Liechtenstein, that were engaged in the manufacture of toiletries and the licensing of trademarks for such toiletries. An initial contact with Scherk was made by a representative of Alberto-Culver in Germany in June 1967, and negotiations followed at further meetings in both Europe and the United States during 1967 and 1968. In February 1969 a contract was signed in Vienna, Austria, which provided for the transfer of the ownership of Scherk's enterprises to Alberto-Culver, along with all rights held by these enterprises to trademarks in cosmetic goods. The contract contained a number of express warranties whereby Scherk guaranteed the sole and unencumbered ownership of these trademarks. In addition, the contract contained an arbitration clause providing that "any controversy or claim [that] shall arise out of this agreement or the breach thereof" would be referred to arbitration before the International Chamber of Commerce in Paris, France, and that "the laws of the State of Illinois, U.S.A. shall apply to and govern this agreement, its interpretation and performance."

The closing of the transaction took place in Geneva, Switzerland, in June 1969. Nearly one year later Alberto-Culver allegedly discovered that the trademark rights purchased under the contract were subject to substantial encumbrances that threatened to give others superior rights to the trademarks and to restrict or preclude Alberto-Culver's use of them. Alberto-Culver thereupon tendered back to Scherk the property that had been transferred to it and offered to rescind the contract. Upon Scherk's refusal, Alberto-Culver commenced this action for damages and other relief in a Federal District Court in Illinois, contending that Scherk's fraudulent representations concerning the status of the trademark rights constituted violations of §10 (b) of the Securities Exchange Act of 1934, 48 Stat. 891, *15 U. S. C. §78j (b)*, and *Rule 10b-5* promulgated thereunder, *17 CFR §240.10b-5*.

In response, Scherk filed a motion to dismiss the action for want of personal and subject-matter jurisdiction as well as on the basis of *forum non conveniens*, or, alternatively, to stay the action pending arbitration in Paris pursuant to the agreement of the parties. Alberto-Culver, in turn, opposed this motion and sought a preliminary injunction restraining the prosecution of arbitration proceedings. On December 2, 1971, the District Court denied Scherk's motion to dismiss, and, on January 14, 1972, it granted a preliminary order enjoining Scherk from proceeding with arbitration. In taking these actions the court relied entirely on this Court's decision in *Wilko v. Swan, 346 U.S. 427*, which held that an agreement to arbitrate could not preclude a buyer of a security from seeking a judicial remedy under the Securities Act of 1933, in view of the language of §14 of that Act, barring "any condition, stipulation, or provision binding any person acquiring any security to waive compliance with any provision of this subchapter. . . ." 48 Stat. 84, *15 U. S. C. §77n*. The Court of Appeals for the Seventh Circuit, with one judge dissenting, affirmed, upon what it considered the controlling authority of the *Wilko* decision. *484 F.2d 611*. Because of the importance of the question presented we granted Scherk's petition for a writ of certiorari. *414 U.S. 1156*.

I

The United States Arbitration Act, now *9 U. S. C. §1 et seq.*, reversing centuries of judicial hostility to arbitration agreements, [4] was designed to allow parties to avoid "the costliness and delays of litigation," and to place arbitration agreements "upon the same footing as other contracts. . . ." H. R. Rep. No. 96, 68th Cong., 1st Sess., 1, 2 (1924); see also S. Rep. No. 536, 68th Cong., 1st Sess. (1924). Accordingly, the Act provides that an arbitration agreement such as is here involved "shall be valid, irrevocable, and enforceable, save upon such grounds as exist at law or in equity for the revocation of any contract." *9 U. S. C. §2*. The Act also provides in *§3* for a stay of proceedings in a case where a court is satisfied that the issue before it is arbitrable under the agreement, and *§4* of the Act directs a federal court to order parties to proceed to arbitration if there has been a "failure, neglect, or refusal" of any party to honor an agreement to arbitrate.

In *Wilko v. Swan, supra*, this Court acknowledged that the Act reflects a legislative recognition of the "desirability of arbitration as an alternative to the complications of litigation," *346 U.S., at 431*, but nonetheless declined to apply the Act's provisions. That case involved an agreement between Anthony Wilko and Hayden, Stone & Co., a large brokerage firm, under which Wilko agreed to purchase on margin a number of shares of a corporation's common stock. Wilko alleged that his purchase of the stock was induced by false representations on the part of the defendant concerning the value of the shares, and he brought suit for damages under §12 (2) of the Securities Act of 1933, *15 U. S. C. §77l*. The defendant responded that Wilko had agreed to submit all controversies arising out of the purchase to arbitration, and that this agreement, contained in a written margin contract between the parties, should be given full effect under the Arbitration Act.

The Court found that "two policies, not easily reconcilable, are involved in this case." *346 U.S., at 438*. On the one hand, the Arbitration Act stressed "the need for avoiding the delay and expense of litigation," *id., at 431*, and directed that such agreements be "valid, irrevocable, and enforceable" in federal courts. On the other hand, the Securities Act of 1933 was "designed to protect investors" and to require "issuers, underwriters, and dealers to make full and fair disclosure of the character of securities sold in interstate and foreign commerce and to prevent fraud in their sale," by creating "a special right to recover for misrepresentation. . . ." *346 U.S., at 431* (footnote omitted). In particular, the Court noted that §14 of the Securities Act, *15 U. S. C. §77n*, provides:

> "Any condition, stipulation, or provision binding any person acquiring any security to waive compliance with any provision of this subchapter or of the rules and regulations of the Commission shall be void."

The Court ruled that an agreement to arbitrate "is a 'stipulation,' and [that] the right to select the judicial forum is the kind of 'provision' that cannot be waived under §14 of the Securities Act." *346 U.S., at 434–435*. Thus, Wilko's advance agreement to arbitrate any disputes subsequently arising out of his contract to purchase the securities was unenforceable under the terms of §14 of the Securities Act of 1933.

Alberto-Culver, relying on this precedent, contends that the District Court and Court of Appeals were correct in holding that its agreement to arbitrate disputes arising under the contract with Scherk is similarly unenforceable in view of its contentions that Scherk's conduct constituted violations of the Securities Exchange Act of 1934 and rules promulgated thereunder. For the reasons that follow, we reject this contention and hold that the provisions of the Arbitration Act cannot be ignored in this case.

At the outset, a colorable argument could be made that even the semantic reasoning of the *Wilko* opinion does not control the case before us. *Wilko* concerned a suit brought under §12 (2) of the Securities Act of 1933, which provides a defrauded purchaser with the "special right" of a private remedy for civil liability, *346 U.S., at 431*. There is no statutory counterpart of §12 (2) in the Securities Exchange Act of 1934, and neither §10 (b) of that Act nor *Rule 10b-5* speaks of a private remedy to redress violations of the kind alleged here. While federal case law has established that §10 (b) and *Rule 10b-5* create an implied private cause of action, see 6 L. Loss, Securities Regulation 3869–3873 (1969) and cases cited therein; cf. *J. I. Case Co. v. Borak, 377 U.S. 426*, the Act itself does not establish the "special right" that the Court in *Wilko* found significant. Furthermore, while both the Securities Act of 1933 and the Securities Exchange Act of 1934 contain sections barring waiver of compliance with any "provision" of the respective Acts, certain of the "provisions" of the 1933 Act that the Court held could not be waived by Wilko's agreement to arbitrate find no counterpart in the 1934 Act. In particular, the Court in *Wilko* noted that the jurisdictional provision of the 1933 Act, *15 U. S. C. §77v*, allowed a plaintiff to bring suit "in any court of competent jurisdiction – federal or state – and removal from a state court is prohibited." *346 U.S., at 431*. The analogous provision of the 1934 Act, by contrast, provides for suit only in the federal district courts that have "exclusive jurisdiction," *15 U. S. C. §78aa*, thus significantly restricting the plaintiff's choice of forum.

Accepting the premise, however, that the operative portions of the language of the 1933 Act relied upon in *Wilko* are contained in the Securities Exchange Act of 1934, the respondent's reliance on *Wilko* in this case ignores the significant and, we find, crucial differences between the agreement involved in *Wilko* and the one signed by the parties here. Alberto-Culver's contract to purchase the business entities belonging to Scherk was a truly international agreement. Alberto-Culver is an American corporation with its principal place of business and the vast bulk of its activity in this country, while Scherk is a citizen of Germany whose companies were organized under the laws of Germany and Liechtenstein. The negotiations leading to the signing of the contract in Austria and to the closing in Switzerland took place in the United States, England, and Germany, and involved consultations with legal and trademark experts from each of those countries and from Liechtenstein. Finally, and most significantly, the subject matter of the contract concerned the sale of business enterprises organized under the laws of and primarily situated in European countries, whose activities were largely, if not entirely, directed to European markets.

Such a contract involves considerations and policies significantly different from those found controlling in *Wilko*. In *Wilko*, quite apart from the arbitration provision, there was no question but that the laws of the United States generally, and the federal securities laws in particular, would govern disputes arising out of the stock-purchase agreement. The parties, the negotiations, and the subject matter of the contract were all situated in this country, and no credible claim could have been entertained that any international conflict-of-laws problems would arise. In this case, by contrast, in the absence of the arbitration provision considerable uncertainty existed at the time of the agreement, and still exists, concerning the law applicable to the resolution of disputes arising out of the contract.

Such uncertainty will almost inevitably exist with respect to any contract touching two or more countries, each with its own substantive laws and conflict-of-laws rules. A contractual provision specifying in advance the forum in which disputes shall be litigated and the law to be applied is, therefore, an almost indispensable precondition to achievement of the orderliness and predictability essential to any international business transaction. Furthermore, such a provision obviates the danger that a dispute under the agreement might be submitted to a forum hostile to the interests of one of the parties or unfamiliar with the problem area involved.

A parochial refusal by the courts of one country to enforce an international arbitration agreement would not only frustrate these purposes, but would invite unseemly and mutually destructive jockeying by the parties to secure tactical litigation advantages. In the present case, for example, it is not inconceivable that if Scherk had anticipated that Alberto-Culver would be able in this country to enjoin resort to arbitration he might have sought an order in France or some other country enjoining Alberto-Culver from proceeding with its litigation in the United States. Whatever recognition the courts of this country might ultimately have granted to the order of the foreign court, the dicey atmosphere of such a legal no-man's-land would surely damage the fabric of international commerce and trade, and imperil the willingness and ability of businessmen to enter into international commercial agreements.

The exception to the clear provisions of the Arbitration Act carved out by *Wilko* is simply inapposite to a case such as the one before us. In *Wilko* the Court reasoned that "when the security buyer, prior to any violation of the Securities Act, waives his right to sue in courts, he gives up more than would a participant in other business transactions. The security buyer has a wider choice of courts and venue. He thus surrenders one of the advantages the Act gives him. . . ." *346 U.S., at 435*. In the context of an international contract, however, these advantages become chimerical since, as indicated above, an opposing party may by speedy resort to a foreign court block or hinder access to the American court of the purchaser's choice.

Two Terms ago in *The Bremen v. Zapata Off-Shore Co., 407 U.S. 1*, we rejected the doctrine that a forum-selection clause of a contract, although voluntarily adopted by the parties, will not be respected in a suit brought in the United States "'unless the selected state would provide a more convenient forum than the state in which suit is brought.'" *Id., at 7*. Rather, we concluded that a "forum clause should control absent a strong showing that it should be set aside." *Id., at 15*. We noted that "much uncertainty and possibly great inconvenience to both parties could arise if a suit could be maintained in any jurisdiction in which an accident might occur or if jurisdiction were left to any place [where personal or *in rem* jurisdiction might be established]. The elimination of all such uncertainties by agreeing in advance on a forum acceptable to both parties is an indispensable element in international trade, commerce, and contracting." *Id., at 13–14*.

An agreement to arbitrate before a specified tribunal is, in effect, a specialized kind of forum-selection clause that posits not only the situs of suit but also the procedure to be used in resolving the dispute. The invalidation of such an agreement in the case before us would not only allow the respondent to repudiate its solemn promise but would, as well, reflect a "parochial concept that all disputes must be resolved under our laws and in our courts. . . . We cannot have trade and commerce in world markets and international waters exclusively on our terms, governed by our laws, and resolved in our courts." *Id., at 9*.

For all these reasons we hold that the agreement of the parties in this case to arbitrate any dispute arising out of their international commercial transaction is to be respected and enforced by the federal courts in accord with the explicit provisions of the Arbitration Act.

Accordingly, the judgment of the Court of Appeals is reversed and the case is remanded to that court with directions to remand to the District Court for further proceedings consistent with this opinion.

It is so ordered.

CONE MEMORIAL HOSPITAL v. MERCURY CONSTRUCTION CORP. SUPREME COURT OF THE UNITED STATES

460 U.S. 1

November 2, 1982, Argued
February 23, 1983, Decided

JUSTICE BRENNAN delivered the opinion of the Court.

This case, commenced as a petition for an order to compel arbitration under *§4* of the United States Arbitration Act of 1925 (Arbitration Act or Act), *9 U. S. C. §4*, presents the question whether, in light of the policies of the Act and of our decisions in *Colorado River Water Conservation District v. United States, 424 U.S. 800 (1976)*, and *Will v. Calvert Fire Insurance Co., 437 U.S. 655 (1978)*, the District Court for the Middle District of North Carolina properly stayed this diversity action pending resolution of a concurrent state-court suit. The Court of Appeals for the Fourth Circuit reversed the stay. *656 F.2d 933*, rehearing denied, *664 F.2d 936 (1981)*. We granted certiorari. *455 U.S. 937 (1982)*. We affirm.

I

Petitioner Moses H. Cone Memorial Hospital (Hospital) is located in Greensboro, N.C. Respondent Mercury Construction Corp. (Mercury), a construction contractor, has its principal place of business in Alabama. In July 1975, Mercury and the Hospital entered into a contract for the construction of additions to the Hospital building. The contract, drafted by representatives of the Hospital, included provisions for resolving disputes arising out of the contract or its breach. All disputes involving interpretation of the contract or performance of the construction work were to be referred in the first instance to J.N. Pease Associates (Architect), an independent architectural firm hired by the Hospital to design and oversee the construction project. With certain stated exceptions, any dispute decided by the Architect (or not decided by it within a stated time) could be submitted by either party to binding arbitration under a broad arbitration clause in the contract:

> "All claims, disputes and other matters in question arising out of, or relating to, this Contract or the breach thereof, . . . shall be decided by arbitration in accordance with the Construction Industry Arbitration Rules of the American Arbitration Association then obtaining unless the parties mutually agree otherwise. This agreement to arbitrate shall be specifically enforceable under the prevailing arbitration law. The award rendered by the arbitrators shall be final, and judgment may be entered upon it in accordance with applicable law in any court having jurisdiction thereof." App. 29–30.

The contract also specified the time limits for arbitration demands.

Construction on the project began in July 1975. Performance was to be completed by October 1979. In fact, construction was substantially completed in February 1979, and final inspections were made that June.

At a meeting in October 1977 (during construction), attended by representatives of Mercury, the Hospital, and the Architect, Mercury agreed, at the Architect's request, to withhold its claims for delay and impact costs (*i.e.*, claims for extended overhead or increase in construction costs due to delay or inaction by the Hospital) until the work was substantially completed. On this record, the Hospital does not contest the existence of this agreement, although it asserts that the Architect lacked authority to agree to a delay in presentation of claims or to entertain claims after the contract work was completed.

In January 1980, Mercury submitted to the Architect its claims for delay and impact costs. Mercury and the Architect discussed the claims over several months, substantially reducing the amount of the claims. According to the Hospital, it first learned of the existence of Mercury's claims in April 1980; its lawyers assumed active participation in the claim procedure in May. The parties differ in their characterizations of the events of the next few months – whether there were "ongoing negotiations," or merely an "investigation" by the Hospital. In any event, it appears from the record that lawyers for the Hospital requested additional information concerning Mercury's claims. As a result, on August 12, 1980, Mercury gave a detailed presentation of its claims at a meeting attended by Mercury's representatives and lawyers, the Hospital's representatives and lawyers, and representatives of the Architect. Mercury agreed to send copies of its files to an expert hired by the Hospital, and the parties agreed to meet again on October 13.

On October 6, Mercury's counsel telephoned the Hospital's counsel to confirm that the scheduled meeting would go forward. The Hospital's counsel said he would call back the next day. When he did, he informed Mercury's counsel that the Hospital would pay nothing on Mercury's claim. He also said that the Hospital intended to file a declaratory judgment action in North Carolina state court.

True to its word, the Hospital filed an action on the morning of October 8 in the Superior Court of Guilford County, N.C., naming Mercury and the Architect as defendants. The complaint alleged that Mercury's claim was without factual or legal basis and that it was barred by the statute of limitations. It alleged that Mercury had lost any right to arbitration under the contract due to waiver, laches, estoppel, and failure to make a timely demand for arbitration. The complaint also alleged various delinquencies on the part of the Architect. As relief, the Hospital sought a declaration that there was no right to arbitration; a stay of arbitration; a declaration that the Hospital bore no liability to Mercury; and a declaration that if the Hospital should be found liable in any respect to Mercury, it would be entitled to indemnity from the Architect. The complaint was served on Mercury on October 9. On that same day, Mercury's counsel mailed a demand for arbitration.

On October 15, without notice to Mercury, the Hospital obtained an *ex parte* injunction from the state court forbidding Mercury to take any steps directed toward arbitration. Mercury objected, and the stay was dissolved on October 27. As soon as the stay was lifted, Mercury filed the present action in the District Court, seeking an order compelling arbitration under *§4* of the Arbitration Act, *9 U. S. C. §4*. Jurisdiction was based on diversity of citizenship. On the Hospital's motion, the District Court stayed Mercury's federal-court suit pending resolution of the state-court suit because the two suits involved the identical issue of the arbitrability of Mercury's claims. App. to Pet. for Cert. A-38.

Mercury sought review of the District Court's stay by both a notice of appeal and a petition for mandamus. A panel of the Court of Appeals for the Fourth Circuit heard argument in the case, but before the panel issued any decision, the court informed the parties that it would consider the case en banc. After reargument, the en banc court held that it had appellate jurisdiction over the case under *28 U. S. C. §1291*. It reversed the District Court's stay order and remanded the case to the District Court with instructions for entry of an order to arbitrate.

II

Before we address the propriety of the District Judge's stay order, we must first decide whether that order was appealable to the Court of Appeals under *28 U. S. C. §1291*.

Mercury sought appellate review through two alternative routes – a notice of appeal under *§1291*, and a petition for mandamus under the All Writs Act, *28 U. S. C. §1651*. Mercury expressly stated that its appeal was based only on *§1291*, and not on *28 U. S. C. §1292* (relating to interlocutory appeals). The Hospital contends that the order appealed from was not a "final [decision]" within *§1291*. We disagree and hold that the stay order was final for purposes of appellate jurisdiction.

Idlewild Liquor Corp. v. *Epstein, 370 U.S. 713 (1962)*, is instructive in this regard. There the plaintiff brought a federal suit challenging the constitutionality of a state statute. The District Judge declined to convene a three-judge court and stayed the federal suit under the *Pullman* abstention doctrine. We held that the District Court's action was final and therefore reviewable by the Court of Appeals, stating:

> "The Court of Appeals properly rejected the argument that the order of the District Court 'was not final and hence unappealable under *28 U. S. C. §§1291, 1292*,' pointing out that '[appellant] was effectively out of court.'" *370 U.S., at 715, n. 2.*

Here, the argument for finality of the District Court's order is even clearer. A district court stay pursuant to *Pullman* abstention is entered with the expectation that the federal litigation will resume in the event that the plaintiff does not obtain relief in state court on state-law grounds. Here, by contrast, the District Court predicated its stay order on its conclusion that the federal and state actions involved "the identical issue of arbitrability of the claims of Mercury Construction Corp. against the Moses H. Cone Memorial Hospital." App. to Pet. for Cert. A-38. That issue of arbitrability was the only substantive issue present in the federal suit. Hence, a stay of the federal suit pending resolution of the state suit meant that there would be no further litigation in the federal forum; the state court's judgment on the issue would be res judicata. Thus, here, even more surely than in *Idlewild*, Mercury was "effectively out of court." Hence, as the Court of Appeals held, this stay order amounts to a dismissal of the suit.

In any event, if the District Court order were not final for appealability purposes, it would nevertheless be appealable within the exception to the finality rule under *Cohen v. Beneficial Loan Corp., 337 U.S. 541 (1949)*. The factors required to show finality under this exception have been summarized as follows:

> "To come within the 'small class' of decisions excepted from the final-judgment rule by *Cohen*, the order must conclusively determine the disputed question, resolve an important issue completely separate from the merits of the action, and be effectively unreviewable on appeal from a final judgment." *Coopers & Lybrand v. Livesay, 437 U.S. 463, 468 (1978)* (footnote omitted).

There can be no dispute that this order meets the second and third of these criteria. An order that amounts to a refusal to adjudicate the merits plainly presents an important issue separate from the merits. For the same reason, this order would be entirely unreviewable if not appealed now. Once the state court decided the issue of arbitrability, the federal court would be bound to honor that determination as res judicata.

The Hospital contends nevertheless that the District Court's stay order did not meet the first of the criteria, namely that it "conclusively determine the disputed question." But this is true only in the technical sense that every order short of a final decree is subject to reopening at the discretion of the district judge. In this case, however, there is no basis to suppose that the District Judge contemplated any reconsideration of his decision to defer to the parallel state-court suit. He surely would not have made that decision in the first instance unless he had expected the state court to resolve all relevant issues adequately. See Part IV-E, *infra*. It is not clear why the judge chose to stay the case rather than to dismiss it outright; for all that the record shows, there was no reason other than the form of the Hospital's motion. Whatever the reason, however, the practical effect of his order was entirely the same for present purposes, and the order was appealable.

III

We turn now to the principal issue to be addressed, namely, the propriety of the District Court's decision to stay this federal suit out of deference to the parallel litigation brought in state court. *Colorado River Water Conservation District v. United States, 424 U.S. 800 (1976)*, provides persuasive guidance in deciding this question.

A

Colorado River involved the effect of the McCarran Amendment, 66 Stat. 560, *43 U. S. C. §666*, on the existence and exercise of federal-court jurisdiction to adjudicate federal water rights, *28 U. S. C. §1345*. The Amendment waives the Government's sovereign immunity to permit the joinder of the United States in some state-court suits for the adjudication of water rights. In *Colorado River*, however, the Government proceeded in Federal District Court, bringing suit against some 1,000 nonfederal water users, seeking a declaration of the water rights of certain federal entities and Indian tribes. Shortly thereafter, a defendant in that suit sought to join the United States in a state-court proceeding for the comprehensive adjudication and administration of all water rights within the river system that was the subject of the federal-court suit. The District Court dismissed the federal suit, holding that the abstention doctrine required deference to the state-court proceedings. The Court of Appeals for the Tenth Circuit reversed, holding that the suit of the United States was within the District Court's jurisdiction under *28 U. S. C. §1345* and that abstention was inappropriate. We reversed the judgment of the Court of Appeals and affirmed the judgment of the District Court dismissing the complaint.

We began our analysis by examining the abstention doctrine in its various forms. We noted:

> "Abstention from the exercise of federal jurisdiction is the exception, not the rule. 'The doctrine of abstention, under which a District Court may decline to exercise or postpone the exercise of its jurisdiction, is an extraordinary and narrow exception to the duty of a District Court to adjudicate a controversy properly before it. Abdication of the obligation to decide cases can be justified under this doctrine only in the exceptional circumstances where the order to the parties to repair to the State court would clearly serve an important countervailing interest.'"

After canvassing the three categories of abstention, we concluded that none of them applied to the case at hand. *424 U.S., at 813–817*. Nevertheless, we held that the District Court's dismissal was proper on another ground – one resting not on considerations of state-federal comity or on avoidance of constitutional decisions, as does abstention, but on "considerations of '[wise] judicial administration, giving regard to conservation of judicial resources and comprehensive disposition of litigation.'" We noted that "'the pendency of an action in the state court is no bar to proceedings concerning the same matter in the Federal court having jurisdiction,'" and that the federal courts have a "virtually unflagging obligation . . . to exercise the jurisdiction given them." We continued:

> "Given this obligation, and the absence of weightier considerations of constitutional adjudication and state-federal relations, the circumstances permitting the dismissal of a federal suit due to the presence of a concurrent state proceeding for reasons of wise judicial administration are considerably more limited than the circumstances appropriate for abstention. The former circumstances, though exceptional, do nevertheless exist." *Id., at 818.*

We declined to prescribe a hard-and-fast rule for dismissals of this type, but instead described some of the factors relevant to the decision.

> "It has been held, for example, that the court first assuming jurisdiction over property may exercise that jurisdiction to the exclusion of other courts. . . . In assessing the appropriateness of dismissal in the event of an exercise of concurrent jurisdiction, a federal court may also consider such factors as the inconvenience of the federal forum; the desirability of avoiding piecemeal litigation; and the order in which jurisdiction was obtained by the concurrent forums. No one factor is necessarily determinative; a carefully considered judgment taking into account both the obligation to exercise jurisdiction and the combination of factors counselling against that exercise is required. *Only the clearest of justifications will warrant dismissal." Id., at 818–819.*

As this passage makes clear, the decision whether to dismiss a federal action because of parallel state-court litigation does not rest on a mechanical checklist, but on a careful balancing of the important factors as they apply in a given case, with the balance heavily weighted in favor of the exercise of jurisdiction. The weight to be given to any one factor may vary greatly from case to case, depending on the particular setting of the case. *Colorado River* itself illustrates this principle in operation. By far the most important factor in our decision to approve the dismissal there was the "clear federal policy . . . [of] avoidance of piecemeal adjudication of water rights in a river system," *id., at 819*, as evinced in the McCarran Amendment. We recognized that the Amendment represents Congress' judgment that the field of water rights is one peculiarly appropriate for comprehensive treatment in the forums having the greatest experience and expertise, assisted by state administrative officers acting under the state courts. *Id., at 819–820.* In addition, we noted that other factors in the case tended to support dismissal – the absence of any substantial progress in the federal-court litigation; the presence in the suit of extensive rights governed by state law; the geographical inconvenience of the federal forum; and the Government's previous willingness to litigate similar suits in state court. *Id., at 820.*

B

Before discussing the application of *Colorado River's* exceptional-circumstances test, we must address the Hospital's argument that that test was undermined by our subsequent decision in *Will v. Calvert Fire Insurance Co., 437 U.S. 655 (1978)*. We find no merit in this argument for at least two reasons.

The Hospital relies on the opinion of JUSTICE REHNQUIST, announcing the judgment of the Court. The Hospital argues that JUSTICE REHNQUIST's opinion, if not expressly overruling *Colorado River*, at least modifies its holding substantially. But it is clear that a majority of the Court reaffirmed the *Colorado River* test in *Calvert*. JUSTICE REHNQUIST's opinion commanded only four votes. It was opposed by the dissenting opinion, in which four Justices concluded that the *Calvert* District Court's stay was impermissible under *Colorado River. 437 U.S., at 668–669, 672–674* (BRENNAN, J., joined by BURGER, C.J., and MARSHALL and POWELL, J.J., dissenting). JUSTICE BLACKMUN, although concurring in the judgment, agreed with the dissent that *Colorado River's* exceptional-circumstances test was controlling; he voted to remand to permit the District Court to apply the *Colorado River* factors in the first instance. *437 U.S., at 667–668.* On remand, the Court of Appeals correctly recognized that the four dissenting Justices and JUSTICE BLACKMUN formed a majority to require application of the *Colorado River* test. *Calvert Fire Insurance Co.* v. *Will, 586 F.2d 12 (CA7 1978).*

Even on the basis of JUSTICE REHNQUIST's opinion, however, there is an obvious distinction between *Calvert* and this case. The key to *Calvert* was the standard for issuance of a writ of mandamus under *28 U. S. C. §1651.* As JUSTICE REHNQUIST stressed, such extraordinary writs are used in aid of appellate jurisdiction only to confine an inferior court to a lawful exercise of its prescribed authority, or to compel it to exercise its authority when it is its duty to do so. The movant must show that his right to the writ is clear and indisputable. *437 U.S., at 661–662, 664, 665–666* (opinion of REHNQUIST, J.). JUSTICE REHNQUIST concluded that the movant in *Calvert* had failed to meet this burden. At the same time, he noted that the movant might have succeeded on a proper appeal. *Id., at 665.* In this case we have held that the Court of Appeals did have appellate jurisdiction; it properly exercised that jurisdiction to find that the District Court's stay was impermissible under *Colorado River.*

The Hospital further contends that *Calvert* requires reversal here because the opinions of JUSTICE REHNQUIST and JUSTICE BLACKMUN require greater deference to the discretion of the District Court than was given by the Court of Appeals in this case. Under both *Calvert* and *Colorado River*, of course, the decision whether to defer to the state courts is necessarily left to the discretion of the district court in the first instance. Yet to say that the district court has discretion is not to say that its decision is unreviewable; such discretion must be exercised under the relevant standard prescribed by this Court. In this case, the relevant standard is *Colorado River's* exceptional-circumstances test, as elucidated by the factors discussed in that case. As we shall now explain, we agree with the Court of Appeals that the District Court in this case abused its discretion in granting the stay.

IV

Applying the *Colorado River* factors to this case, it is clear that there was no showing of the requisite exceptional circumstances to justify the District Court's stay.

The Hospital concedes that the first two factors mentioned in *Colorado River* are not present here. There was no assumption by either court of jurisdiction over any res or property, nor is there any contention that the federal forum was any less convenient to the parties than the state forum. The remaining factors – avoidance of piecemeal litigation, and the order in which jurisdiction was obtained by the concurrent forums – far from supporting the stay, actually counsel against it.

A

There is no force here to the consideration that was paramount in *Colorado River* itself – the danger of piecemeal litigation.

The Hospital points out that it has two substantive disputes here – one with Mercury, concerning Mercury's claim for delay and impact costs, and the other with the Architect, concerning the Hospital's claim for indemnity for any liability it may have to Mercury. The latter dispute cannot be sent to arbitration without the Architect's consent, since there is no arbitration agreement between the Hospital and the Architect. It is true, therefore, that if Mercury obtains an arbitration order for its dispute, the Hospital will be forced to resolve these related disputes in different forums. That misfortune, however, is not the result of any choice between the federal and state courts; it occurs because the relevant federal law *requires* piecemeal resolution when necessary to give effect to an arbitration agreement. Under the Arbitration Act, an arbitration agreement must be enforced notwithstanding the presence of other persons who are parties to the underlying dispute but not to the arbitration agreement. If the dispute between Mercury and the Hospital *is* arbitrable under the Act, then the Hospital's two disputes will be resolved separately – one in arbitration, and the other (if at all) in state-court litigation. Conversely, if the dispute between Mercury and the Hospital *is not* arbitrable, then both disputes will be resolved in state court. But neither of those two outcomes depends at all on *which court* decides the question of arbitrability. Hence, a decision to allow that issue to be decided in federal rather than state court does not cause piecemeal resolution of the parties' underlying disputes. Although the Hospital will have to litigate the arbitrability issue in federal rather than state court, that dispute is easily severable from the merits of the underlying disputes.

B

The order in which the concurrent tribunals obtained and exercised jurisdiction cuts against, not for, the District Court's stay in this case. The Hospital argues that the stay was proper because the state-court suit was filed some 19 days before the federal suit. In the first place, this argument disregards the obvious reason for the Hospital's priority in filing. An indispensable element of Mercury's cause of action under §4 for an arbitration order is the Hospital's refusal to arbitrate. See n. 27, *infra*. That refusal did not occur until less than a day before the Hospital filed its state suit. Hence, Mercury simply had no reasonable opportunity to file its §4 petition first. Moreover, the Hospital succeeded in obtaining an *ex parte* injunction from the state court forbidding Mercury to take any steps to secure arbitration. Mercury filed its §4 petition the same day that the injunction was dissolved.

That aside, the Hospital's priority argument gives too mechanical a reading to the "priority" element of the *Colorado River* balance. This factor, as with the other *Colorado River* factors, is to be applied in a pragmatic, flexible manner with a view to the realities of the case at hand. Thus, priority should not be measured exclusively by which complaint was filed first, but rather in terms of how much progress has been made in the two actions. *Colorado River* illustrates this point well. There, the federal suit was actually filed first. Nevertheless, we pointed out as a factor favoring dismissal "the apparent absence of any proceedings in the District Court, other than the filing of the complaint, prior to the motion to dismiss." *424 U.S., at 820*. Here, the opposite was true. It was the state-court suit in which no substantial proceedings (excepting only the abortive temporary injunction) had taken place at the time of the decision to stay. In the federal suit, by contrast, the parties had taken most of the steps necessary to a resolution of the arbitrability issue. In realistic terms, the federal suit was running well ahead of the state suit at the very time that the District Court decided to refuse to adjudicate the case.

This refusal to proceed was plainly erroneous in view of Congress' clear intent, in the Arbitration Act, to move the parties to an arbitrable dispute out of court and into arbitration as quickly and easily as possible. The Act provides two parallel devices for enforcing an arbitration agreement: a stay of litigation in any case raising a dispute referable to arbitration, *9 U. S. C. §3*, and an affirmative order to engage in arbitration, *§4*. Both of these sections call for an expeditious and summary hearing, with only restricted inquiry into factual issues. Assuming that the state court would have granted prompt relief to Mercury under the Act, there still would have been an inevitable delay as a result of the District Court's stay. The stay thus frustrated the statutory policy of rapid and unobstructed enforcement of arbitration agreements.

C

Besides the four factors expressly discussed in *Colorado River*, there is another that emerges from *Calvert* – the fact that federal law provides the rule of decision on the merits. The state-versus-federal-law factor was of ambiguous relevance in *Colorado River*. In *Calvert*, however, both the four-vote dissenting opinion and JUSTICE BLACKMUN's opinion concurring in the judgment pointed out that the case involved issues of federal law. *437 U.S., at 667* (BLACKMUN, J., concurring in judgment); *id., at 668–677* (BRENNAN, J., dissenting). See also *Colorado River, 424 U.S., at 815, n. 21*. It is equally apparent that this case involves federal issues.

The basic issue presented in Mercury's federal suit was the arbitrability of the dispute between Mercury and the Hospital. Federal law in the terms of the Arbitration Act governs that issue in either state or federal court. *Section 2* is the primary substantive provision of the Act, declaring that a written agreement to arbitrate "in any maritime transaction or a contract evidencing a transaction involving commerce . . . shall be valid, irrevocable, and enforceable, save upon such grounds as exist at law or in equity for the revocation of any contract." *9 U. S. C. §2*. *Section 2* is a congressional declaration of a liberal federal policy favoring arbitration agreements, notwithstanding any state substantive or procedural policies to the contrary. The effect of the section is to create a body of federal substantive law of arbitrability, applicable to any arbitration agreement within the coverage of the Act. In *Prima Paint Corp.* v. *Flood & Conklin Mfg. Corp., 388 U.S. 395 (1967)*, for example, the parties had signed a contract containing an arbitration clause, but one party alleged that there had been fraud in the inducement of the entire contract (although the alleged fraud did not go to the arbitration clause in particular). The issue before us was whether the issue of fraud in the inducement was itself an arbitrable controversy. We held that the language and policies of the Act required the conclusion that the fraud issue was arbitrable. *Id., at 402–404*. Although our holding in *Prima Paint* extended only to the specific issue presented, the Courts of Appeals have since consistently concluded that questions of arbitrability must be addressed with a healthy regard for the federal policy favoring arbitration. We agree. The Arbitration Act establishes that, as a matter of federal law, any doubts concerning the scope of arbitrable issues should be resolved in favor of arbitration, whether the problem at hand is the construction of the contract language itself or an allegation of waiver, delay, or a like defense to arbitrability.

To be sure, the source-of-law factor has less significance here than in *Calvert*, since the federal courts' jurisdiction to enforce the Arbitration Act is concurrent with that of the state courts. But we emphasize that our task in cases such as this is not to find some substantial reason for the *exercise* of federal jurisdiction by the district court; rather, the task is to ascertain whether there exist "exceptional" circumstances, the "clearest of justifications," that can suffice under *Colorado River* to justify the *surrender* of that jurisdiction. Although in some rare circumstances the presence of state-law issues may weigh in favor of that surrender, see n. 29, *supra*, the presence of federal-law issues must always be a major consideration weighing against surrender.

D

Finally, in this case an important reason against allowing a stay is the probable inadequacy of the state-court proceeding to protect Mercury's rights. We are not to be understood to impeach the competence or procedures of the North Carolina courts. Moreover, state courts, as much as federal courts, are obliged to grant stays of litigation under *§3* of the Arbitration Act. It is less clear, however, whether the same is true of an order to compel arbitration under *§4* of the Act. We need not resolve that question here; it suffices to say that there was, at a minimum, substantial room for doubt that Mercury could obtain from the state court an order compelling the Hospital to arbitrate. In many cases, no doubt, a *§3* stay is quite adequate to protect the right to arbitration. But in a case such as this, where the party opposing arbitration is the one from whom payment or performance is sought, a stay of litigation alone is not enough. It leaves the recalcitrant party free to sit and do nothing – neither to litigate nor to arbitrate. If the state court stayed litigation pending arbitration but declined to compel the Hospital to arbitrate, Mercury would have no sure way to proceed with its claims except to return to federal court to obtain a *§4* order – a pointless and wasteful burden on the supposedly summary and speedy procedures prescribed by the Arbitration Act.

E

The Hospital argues that the *Colorado River* test is somehow inapplicable because in this case the District Court merely stayed the federal litigation rather than dismissing the suit outright, as in *Colorado River*. It contends that Mercury remains free to seek to reopen the federal suit on a showing that the state suit has failed to adjudicate its rights, and that a stay is less onerous than a dismissal. We have already rejected this distinction, for purposes of this case, in discussing appellate jurisdiction. *Supra, at 12–13*. We reject it in this context for the same reasons.

We have no occasion in this case to decide whether a dismissal or a stay should ordinarily be the preferred course of action when a district court properly finds that *Colorado River* counsels in favor of deferring to a parallel state-court suit. We can say, however, that a stay is as much a refusal to exercise federal jurisdiction as a dismissal. When a district court decides to dismiss or stay under *Colorado River*, it presumably concludes that the parallel state-court litigation will be an adequate vehicle for the complete and prompt resolution of the issues between the parties. If there is any substantial doubt as to this, it would be a serious abuse of discretion to grant the stay or dismissal at all. See Part IV-D, *supra; McNeese v. Board of Education, 373 U.S. 668, 674–676 (1963)*. Thus, the decision to invoke *Colorado River* necessarily contemplates that the federal court will have nothing further to do in resolving any substantive part of the case, whether it stays or dismisses. See 17 C. Wright, A. Miller, & E. Cooper, Federal Practice and Procedure §4247, pp. 517–519 (1978).

Moreover, assuming that for some unexpected reason the state forum does turn out to be inadequate in some respect, the Hospital's argument fails to make out any genuine difference between a stay and a dismissal. It is true that Mercury could seek to return to federal court if it proved necessary; but that would be equally true if the District Court had dismissed the case. It is highly questionable whether this Court would have approved a dismissal of a federal suit in *Colorado River* (or in any of the abstention cases, see *supra, at 14*) if the federal courts did not remain open to a dismissed plaintiff who later demonstrated the inadequacy of the state forum.

V

In addition to reversing the District Court's stay, the Court of Appeals decided that the underlying contractual dispute between Mercury and the Hospital is arbitrable under the Arbitration Act and the terms of the parties' arbitration agreement. It reversed the District Court's judgment and remanded the case "with directions to proceed in conformity herewith." *656 F.2d, at 946*. In effect, the Court of Appeals directed the District Court to enter a *§4* order to arbitrate.

In this Court, the Hospital does not contest the substantive correctness of the Court of Appeals' holding on arbitrability. It does raise several objections to the procedures the Court of Appeals used in considering and deciding this case. In particular, it points out that the only issue formally appealed to the Court of Appeals was the propriety of the District Court's stay order. Ordinarily, we would not expect the Court of Appeals to pass on issues not decided in the District Court. In the present case, however, we are not disposed to disturb the court's discretion in its handling of the case in view of the special interests at stake and the apparent lack of any prejudice to the parties. Title *28 U. S. C. §2106* gives a court of appeals some latitude in entering an order to achieve justice in the circumstances. The Arbitration Act calls for a summary and speedy disposition of motions or petitions to enforce arbitration clauses. The Court of Appeals had in the record full briefs and evidentiary submissions from both parties on the merits of arbitrability, and held that there were no disputed issues of fact requiring a jury trial before a §4 order could issue. Under these circumstances, the court acted within its authority in deciding the legal issues presented in order to facilitate the prompt arbitration that Congress envisaged.

Affirmed.

SOUTHLAND CORP. ET AL. v. KEATING ET AL.
SUPREME COURT OF THE UNITED STATES

465 U.S. 1

October 4, 1983, Argued
January 23, 1984, Decided

CHIEF JUSTICE BURGER delivered the opinion of the Court.

This case presents the questions (a) whether the California Franchise Investment Law, which invalidates certain arbitration agreements covered by the Federal Arbitration Act, violates the *Supremacy Clause* and (b) whether arbitration under the federal Act is impaired when a class-action structure is imposed on the process by the state courts.

I

Appellant Southland Corp. is the owner and franchisor of 7-Eleven convenience stores. Southland's standard franchise agreement provides each franchisee with a license to use certain registered trademarks, a lease or sublease of a convenience store owned or leased by Southland, inventory financing, and assistance in advertising and merchandising. The franchisees operate the stores, supply bookkeeping data, and pay Southland a fixed percentage of gross profits. The franchise agreement also contains the following provision requiring arbitration:

> "Any controversy or claim arising out of or relating to this Agreement or the breach hereof shall be settled by arbitration in accordance with the Rules of the American Arbitration Association . . . and judgment upon any award rendered by the arbitrator may be entered in any court having jurisdiction thereof."

Appellees are 7-Eleven franchisees. Between September 1975 and January 1977, several appellees filed individual actions against Southland in California Superior Court alleging, among other things, fraud, oral misrepresentation, breach of contract, breach of fiduciary duty, and violation of the disclosure requirements of the California Franchise Investment Law, *Cal. Corp. Code Ann. §31000 et seq.* (West 1977). Southland's answer, in all but one of the individual actions, included the affirmative defense of failure to arbitrate.

In May 1977, appellee Keating filed a class action against Southland on behalf of a class that assertedly includes approximately 800 California franchisees. Keating's principal claims were substantially the same as those asserted by the other franchisees. After the various actions were consolidated, Southland petitioned to compel arbitration of the claims in all cases, and appellees moved for class certification.

The Superior Court granted Southland's motion to compel arbitration of all claims except those claims based on the Franchise Investment Law. The court did not pass on appellees' request for class certification. Southland appealed from the order insofar as it excluded from arbitration the claims based on the California statute. Appellees filed a petition for a writ of mandamus or prohibition in the California Court of Appeal arguing that the arbitration should proceed as a class action.

The California Court of Appeal reversed the trial court's refusal to compel arbitration of appellees' claims under the Franchise Investment Law. *Keating v. Superior Court, Alameda County, 167 Cal. Rptr. 481 (1980)*. That court interpreted the arbitration clause to require arbitration of all claims asserted under the Franchise Investment Law, and construed the Franchise Investment Law not to invalidate such agreements to arbitrate. Alternatively, the court concluded that if the Franchise Investment Law rendered arbitration agreements involving commerce unenforceable, it would conflict with *§2* of the Federal Arbitration Act, *9 U. S. C. §2*, and therefore be invalid under the *Supremacy Clause. 167 Cal. Rptr., at 493–494*. The Court of Appeal also determined that there was no "insurmountable obstacle" to conducting an arbitration on a classwide basis, and issued a writ of mandate directing the trial court to conduct class-certification proceedings. *Id., at 492*.

The California Supreme Court, by a vote of 4–2, reversed the ruling that claims asserted under the Franchise Investment Law are arbitrable. *Keating v. Superior Court of Alameda County, 31 Cal. 3d 584, 645 P. 2d 1192 (1982)*. The California Supreme Court interpreted the Franchise Investment Law to require judicial consideration of claims brought under that statute and concluded that the California statute did not contravene the federal Act. *Id., at 604, 645 P. 2d, 1203–1204*. The court also remanded the case to the trial court for consideration of appellees' request for classwide arbitration.

We postponed consideration of the question of jurisdiction pending argument on the merits. *459 U.S. 1101 (1983)*. We reverse in part and dismiss in part.

II

A

Jurisdiction of this Court is asserted under *28 U. S. C. §1257(2)*, which provides for an appeal from a final judgment of the highest court of a state when the validity of a challenged state statute is sustained as not in conflict with federal law. Here Southland challenged the California Franchise Investment Law as it was applied to invalidate a contract for arbitration made pursuant to the Federal Arbitration Act. Appellees argue that the action of the California Supreme Court with respect to this claim is not a "final judgment or decree" within the meaning of *§1257(2)*.

Under *Cox Broadcasting Corp. v. Cohn, 420 U.S. 469, 482–483 (1975)*, judgments of state courts that finally decide a federal issue are immediately appealable when "the party seeking review here might prevail [in the state court] on the merits on nonfederal grounds, thus rendering unnecessary review of the federal issue by this Court, and where reversal of the state court on the federal issue would be preclusive of any further litigation on the relevant cause of action. . . ." In these circumstances, we have resolved the federal issue "if a refusal immediately to review the state-court decision might seriously erode federal policy." *Id., at 483*.

The judgment of the California Supreme Court with respect to this claim is reviewable under *Cox Broadcasting, supra.* Without immediate review of the California holding by this Court there may be no opportunity to pass on the federal issue and as a result "there would remain in effect the unreviewed decision of the State Supreme Court" holding that the California statute does not conflict with the Federal Arbitration Act. *Id., at 485.* On the other hand, reversal of a state-court judgment in this setting will terminate litigation of the merits of this dispute.

Finally, the failure to accord immediate review of the decision of the California Supreme Court might "seriously erode federal policy." Plainly the effect of the judgment of the California court is to nullify a valid contract made by private parties under which they agreed to submit all contract disputes to final, binding arbitration. The federal Act permits "parties to an arbitrable dispute [to move] out of court and into arbitration as quickly and easily as possible." *Moses H. Cone Memorial Hospital v. Mercury Construction Corp., 460 U.S. 1, 22 (1983).*

Contracts to arbitrate are not to be avoided by allowing one party to ignore the contract and resort to the courts. Such a course could lead to prolonged litigation, one of the very risks the parties, by contracting for arbitration, sought to eliminate. In *The Bremen v. Zapata Off-Shore Co., 407 U.S. 1, 12 (1972)*, we noted that the contract fixing a particular forum for resolution of all disputes

> "was made in an arm's-length negotiation by experienced and sophisticated businessmen, and absent some compelling and countervailing reason it should be honored by the parties and enforced by the courts."

The *Zapata* Court also noted that

> "the forum clause was a vital part of the agreement, and it would be unrealistic to think that the parties did not conduct their negotiations, including fixing the monetary terms, with the consequences of the forum clause figuring prominently in their calculations." *Id., at 14* (footnote omitted).

For us to delay review of a state judicial decision denying enforcement of the contract to arbitrate until the state-court litigation has run its course would defeat the core purpose of a contract to arbitrate. We hold that the Court has jurisdiction to decide whether the Federal Arbitration Actpre-empts *§31512* of the California Franchise Investment Law.

B

That part of the appeal relating to the propriety of superimposing class-action procedures on a contract arbitration raises other questions. Southland did not contend in the California courts that, and the state courts did not decide whether, state law imposing class-action procedures was pre-empted by federal law. When the California Court of Appeal directed Southland to address the question whether state or federal law controlled the class-action issue, Southland responded that *state law* did not permit arbitrations to proceed as class actions, that the Federal Rules of Civil Procedure were inapplicable, and that requiring arbitrations to proceed as class actions "could well violate the [federal] constitutional guaranty of procedural due process." Southland did not claim in the Court of Appeal that if state law required class-action procedures, it would conflict with the federal Act and thus violate the *Supremacy Clause.*

In the California Supreme Court, Southland argued that California law applied but that neither the contract to arbitrate nor state law authorized class-action procedures to govern arbitrations. Southland also contended that the Federal Rules were inapplicable in state proceedings. Southland pointed out that although California law provided a basis for class-action procedures, the Judicial Council of California acknowledged "the incompatibility of class actions and arbitration." Petition for Hearing 23. It does not appear that Southland opposed class procedures on *federal* grounds in the California Supreme Court. Nor does the record show that the California Supreme Court passed upon the question whether superimposing class-action procedures on a contract arbitration was contrary to the federal Act. Since it does not affirmatively appear that the validity of the state statute was "drawn in question" *on federal grounds* by Southland, this Court is without jurisdiction to resolve this question as a matter of federal law under *28 U. S. C. §1257(2)*. See *Bailey v. Anderson, 326 U.S. 203, 207 (1945).*

III

As previously noted, the California Franchise Investment Law provides:

> "Any condition, stipulation or provision purporting to bind any person acquiring any franchise to waive compliance with any provision of this law or any rule or order hereunder is void." *Cal. Corp. Code Ann. §31512* (West 1977).

The California Supreme Court interpreted this statute to require judicial consideration of claims brought under the state statute and accordingly refused to enforce the parties' contract to arbitrate such claims. So interpreted the California Franchise Investment Law directly conflicts with *§2* of the Federal Arbitration Actand violates the *Supremacy Clause.*

In enacting *§2* of the federal Act, Congress declared a national policy favoring arbitration and withdrew the power of the states to require a judicial forum for the resolution of claims which the contracting parties agreed to resolve by arbitration. The Federal Arbitration Actprovides:

> "A written provision in any maritime transaction or a contract evidencing a transaction involving commerce to settle by arbitration a controversy thereafter arising out of such contract or transaction, or the refusal to perform the whole or any part thereof, or an agreement in writing to submit to arbitration an existing controversy arising out of such a contract, transaction, or refusal, shall be valid, irrevocable, and enforceable, save upon such grounds as exist at law or in equity for the revocation of any contract." *9 U. S. C. §2.*

Congress has thus mandated the enforcement of arbitration agreements.

We discern only two limitations on the enforceability of arbitration provisions governed by the Federal Arbitration Act: they must be part of a written maritime contract or a contract "evidencing a transaction involving commerce" and such clauses may be revoked upon "grounds as exist at law or in equity for the revocation of any contract." We see nothing in the Act indicating that the broad principle of enforceability is subject to any additional limitations under state law.

The Federal ArbitrationAct rests on the authority of Congress to enact substantive rules under the *Commerce Clause*. In *Prima Paint Corp. v. Flood & Conklin Mfg. Co., 388 U.S. 395 (1967)*, the Court examined the legislative history of the Act and concluded that the statute "is based upon . . . the incontestable federal foundations of 'control over interstate commerce and over admiralty.'" *Id., at 405* (quoting H. R. Rep. No. 96, 68th Cong., 1st Sess., 1 (1924)). The contract in *Prima Paint*, as here, contained an arbitration clause. One party in that case alleged that the other had committed fraud in the inducement of the contract, although not of the arbitration clause in particular, and sought to have the claim of fraud adjudicated in federal court. The Court held that, notwithstanding a contrary state rule, consideration of a claim of fraud in the inducement of a contract "is for the arbitrators and not for the courts," *388 U.S., at 400*. The Court relied for this holding on Congress' broad power to fashion substantive rules under the *Commerce Clause*.

At least since 1824 Congress' authority under the *Commerce Clause* has been held plenary. *Gibbons v. Ogden, 9 Wheat. 1, 196 (1824)*. In the words of Chief Justice Marshall, the authority of Congress is "the power to regulate; that is, to prescribe the rule by which commerce is to be governed." *Ibid.* The statements of the Court in *Prima Paint* that the Arbitration Act was an exercise of the *Commerce Clause* power clearly implied that the substantive rules of the Act were to apply in state as well as federal courts. As Justice Black observed in his dissent, when Congress exercises its authority to enact substantive federal law under the *Commerce Clause*, it normally creates rules that are enforceable in state as well as federal courts. *Prima Paint, supra, at 420*.

In *Moses H. Cone Memorial Hospital v. Mercury Construction Corp., 460 U.S., at 1, 25, and n. 32*, we reaffirmed our view that the Arbitration Act "creates a body of federal substantive law" and expressly stated what was implicit in *Prima Paint, i.e.*, the substantive law the Act created was applicable in state and federal courts. *Moses H. Cone* began with a petition for an order to compel arbitration. The District Court stayed the action pending resolution of a concurrent state-court suit. In holding that the District Court had abused its discretion, we found no showing of exceptional circumstances justifying the stay and recognized "the presence of federal-law issues" under the federal Act as "a major consideration weighing against surrender [of federal jurisdiction]." *460 U.S., at 26*. We thus read the underlying issue of arbitrability to be a question of substantive federal law: "Federal law in the terms of the Arbitration Act governs that issue in either state or federal court." *Id., at 24*.

Although the legislative history is not without ambiguities, there are strong indications that Congress had in mind something more than making arbitration agreements enforceable only in the federal courts. The House Report plainly suggests the more comprehensive objectives:

> "The purpose of this bill is to make valid and enforcible *[sic]* agreements for arbitration contained *in contracts involving interstate commerce* or within the jurisdiction or *[sic]* admiralty, *or* which may be the subject of litigation in the Federal courts." H. R. Rep. No. 96, 68th Cong., 1st Sess., 1 (1924) (emphasis added).

This broader purpose can also be inferred from the reality that Congress would be less likely to address a problem whose impact was confined to federal courts than a problem of large significance in the field of commerce. The Arbitration Act sought to "overcome the rule of equity, that equity will not specifically enforce [any] arbitration agreement." Hearing on S. 4213 and S. 4214 before a Subcommittee of the Senate Committee on the Judiciary, 67th Cong., 4th Sess., 6 (1923) (Senate Hearing) (remarks of Sen. Walsh). The House Report accompanying the bill stated:

> "The need for the law arises from . . . the jealousy of the English courts for their own jurisdiction. . . . This jealousy survived for so [long] a period that the principle became firmly embedded in the English common law and was adopted with it by the American courts. The courts have felt that the precedent was too strongly fixed to be overturned without legislative enactment. . . ." H. R. Rep. No. 96, *supra*, at 1–2.

Surely this makes clear that the House Report contemplated a broad reach of the Act, unencumbered by state-law constraints. As was stated in *Metro Industrial Painting Corp. v. Terminal Construction Co., 287 F.2d 382, 387 (CA2 1961)* (Lumbard, C. J., concurring), "the purpose of the act was to assure those who desired arbitration and whose contracts related to interstate commerce that their expectations would not be undermined by federal judges, or . . . by state courts or legislatures." Congress also showed its awareness of the widespread unwillingness of state courts to enforce arbitration agreements, *e.g.*, Senate Hearing, at 8, and that such courts were bound by state laws inadequately providing for

> "technical arbitration by which, if you agree to arbitrate under the method provided by the statute, you have an arbitration by statute but [the statutes] [had] nothing to do with validating the contract to arbitrate." *Ibid.*

The problems Congress faced were therefore twofold: the old common-law hostility toward arbitration, and the failure of state arbitration statutes to mandate enforcement of arbitration agreements. To confine the scope of the Act to arbitrations sought to be enforced in federal courts would frustrate what we believe Congress intended to be a broad enactment appropriate in scope to meet the large problems Congress was addressing.

JUSTICE O'CONNOR argues that Congress viewed the Arbitration Act "as a procedural statute, applicable only in federal courts." *Post*, at 25. If it is correct that Congress sought only to create a procedural remedy in the federal courts, there can be no explanation for the express limitation in the Arbitration Act to contracts "involving commerce." *9 U. S. C. §2*. For example, when Congress has authorized this Court to prescribe the rules of procedure in the federal courts of appeals, district courts, and bankruptcy courts, it has not limited the power of the Court to prescribe rules applicable only to causes of action involving commerce. See, *e.g.*, *28 U. S. C. §§2072, 2075, 2076 (1976 ed. and Supp. V)*. We would expect that if Congress, in enacting the Arbitration Act, was creating what it thought to be a procedural rule applicable only in federal courts, it would not so limit the Act to transactions involving commerce. On the other hand, Congress would need to call on the *Commerce Clause* if it intended the Act to apply in state courts. Yet at the same time, its reach would be limited to transactions involving interstate commerce. We therefore view the "involving commerce" requirement in *§2*, not as an inexplicable limitation on the power of the federal courts, but as a necessary qualification on a statute intended to apply in state and federal courts.

Under the interpretation of the Arbitration Act urged by JUSTICE O'CONNOR, claims brought under the California Franchise Investment Law are not arbitrable when they are raised in state court. Yet it is clear beyond question that if this suit had been brought as a diversity action in a federal district court, the arbitration clause would have been enforceable. *Prima Paint, supra.* The interpretation given to the Arbitration Act by the California Supreme Court would therefore encourage and reward forum shopping. We are unwilling to attribute to Congress the intent, in drawing on the comprehensive powers of the *Commerce Clause*, to create a right to enforce an arbitration contract and yet make the right dependent for its enforcement on the particular forum in which it is asserted. And since the overwhelming proportion of all civil litigation in this country is in the state courts, we cannot believe Congress intended to limit the Arbitration Act to disputes subject only to *federal*-court jurisdiction. Such an interpretation would frustrate congressional intent to place "[an] arbitration agreement . . . upon the same footing as other contracts, where it belongs." H. R. Rep. No. 96, 68th Cong., 1st Sess., 1 (1924).

In creating a substantive rule applicable in state as well as federal courts, Congress intended to foreclose state legislative attempts to undercut the enforceability of arbitration agreements. We hold that *§31512* of the California Franchise Investment Law violates the *Supremacy Clause*.

IV

The judgment of the California Supreme Court denying enforcement of the arbitration agreement is reversed; as to the question whether the Federal Arbitration Actprecludes a class-action arbitration and any other issues not raised in the California courts, no decision by this Court would be appropriate at this time. As to the latter issues, the case is remanded for further proceedings not inconsistent with this opinion.

It is so ordered.

MITSUBISHI MOTORS CORP. v. SOLER CHRYSLER-PLYMOUTH, INC. SUPREME COURT OF THE UNITED STATES

473 U.S. 614

March 18, 1985, Argued
July 2, 1985, Decided*

JUSTICE BLACKMUN delivered the opinion of the Court.

The principal question presented by these cases is the arbitrability, pursuant to the Federal Arbitration Act, *9 U. S. C. §1 et seq.*, and the Convention on the Recognition and Enforcement of Foreign Arbitral Awards (Convention), [1970] 21 U.S.T. 2517, T.I.A.S. No. 6997, of claims arising under the Sherman Act, *15 U. S. C. §1 et seq.*, and encompassed within a valid arbitration clause in an agreement embodying an international commercial transaction.

I

Petitioner-cross-respondent Mitsubishi Motors Corporation (Mitsubishi) is a Japanese corporation which manufactures automobiles and has its principal place of business in Tokyo, Japan. Mitsubishi is the product of a joint venture between, on the one hand, Chrysler International, S.A. (CISA), a Swiss corporation registered in Geneva and wholly owned by Chrysler Corporation, and, on the other, Mitsubishi Heavy Industries, Inc., a Japanese corporation. The aim of the joint venture was the distribution through Chrysler dealers outside the continental United States of vehicles manufactured by Mitsubishi and bearing Chrysler and Mitsubishi trademarks. Respondent-cross-petitioner Soler Chrysler-Plymouth, Inc. (Soler), is a Puerto Rico corporation with its principal place of business in Pueblo Viejo, Guaynabo, Puerto Rico.

On October 31, 1979, Soler entered into a Distributor Agreement with CISA which provided for the sale by Soler of Mitsubishi-manufactured vehicles within a designated area, including metropolitan San Juan. App. 18. On the same date, CISA, Soler, and Mitsubishi entered into a Sales Procedure Agreement (Sales Agreement) which, referring to the Distributor Agreement, provided for the direct sale of Mitsubishi products to Soler and governed the terms and conditions of such sales. *Id.*, at 42. Paragraph VI of the Sales Agreement, labeled "Arbitration of Certain Matters," provides:

> "All disputes, controversies or differences which may arise between [Mitsubishi] and [Soler] out of or in relation to Articles I-B through V of this Agreement or for the breach thereof, shall be finally settled by arbitration in Japan in accordance with the rules and regulations of the Japan Commercial Arbitration Association." *Id.* at 52–53.

Initially, Soler did a brisk business in Mitsubishi-manufactured vehicles. As a result of its strong performance, its minimum sales volume, specified by Mitsubishi and CISA, and agreed to by Soler, for the 1981 model year was substantially increased. *Id., at 179*. In early 1981, however, the new-car market slackened. Soler ran into serious difficulties in meeting the expected sales volume, and by the spring of 1981 it felt itself compelled to request that Mitsubishi delay or cancel shipment of several orders. 1 Record 181, 183. About the same time, Soler attempted to arrange for the transshipment of a quantity of its vehicles for sale in the continental United States and Latin America. Mitsubishi and CISA, however, refused permission for any such diversion, citing a variety of reasons, and no vehicles were transshipped. Attempts to work out these difficulties failed. Mitsubishi eventually withheld shipment of 966 vehicles, apparently representing orders placed for May, June, and July 1981 production, responsibility for which Soler disclaimed in February 1982. App. 131.

The following month, Mitsubishi brought an action against Soler in the United States District Court for the District of Puerto Rico under the Federal Arbitration Actand the Convention. Mitsubishi sought an order, pursuant to *9 U. S. C. §§4* and *201*, to compel arbitration in accord with para. VI of the Sales Agreement. App. 15. Shortly after filing the complaint, Mitsubishi filed a request for arbitration before the Japan Commercial Arbitration Association. *Id.*, at 70.

Soler denied the allegations and counterclaimed against both Mitsubishi and CISA. It alleged numerous breaches by Mitsubishi of the Sales Agreement, raised a pair of defamation claims, and asserted causes of action under the Sherman Act, *15 U. S. C. §1 et seq.*; the federal Automobile Dealers' Day in Court Act, 70 Stat. 1125, *15 U. S. C. §1221 et seq.*; the Puerto Rico competition statute, *P.R. Laws Ann., Tit. 10, §257 et seq.* (1976); and the Puerto Rico Dealers' Contracts Act, *P.R. Laws Ann., Tit. 10, §278 et seq.* (1976 and Supp. 1983). In the counterclaim premised on the Sherman Act, Soler alleged that Mitsubishi and CISA had conspired to divide markets in restraint of trade. To effectuate the plan, according to Soler, Mitsubishi had refused to permit Soler to resell to buyers in North, Central, or South America vehicles it had obligated itself to purchase from Mitsubishi; had refused to ship ordered vehicles or the parts, such as heaters and defoggers, that would be necessary to permit Soler to make its vehicles suitable for resale outside Puerto Rico; and had coercively attempted to replace Soler and its other Puerto Rico distributors with a wholly owned subsidiary which would serve as the exclusive Mitsubishi distributor in Puerto Rico. App. 91–96.

After a hearing, the District Court ordered Mitsubishi and Soler to arbitrate each of the issues raised in the complaint and in all the counterclaims save two and a portion of a third. With regard to the federal antitrust issues, it recognized that the Courts of Appeals, following *American Safety Equipment Corp. v. J. P. Maguire & Co., 391 F.2d 821 (CA2 1968)*, uniformly had held that the rights conferred by the antitrust laws were "'of a character inappropriate for enforcement by arbitration.'" App. to Pet. for Cert. in No. 83–1569, p. B9, quoting *Wilko v. Swan, 201 F.2d 439, 444 (CA2 1953)*, rev'd, *346 U.S. 427 (1953)*. The District Court held, however, that the international character of the Mitsubishi-Soler undertaking required enforcement of the agreement to arbitrate even as to the antitrust claims. It relied on *Scherk v. Alberto-Culver Co., 417 U.S. 506, 515–520 (1974)*, in which this Court ordered arbitration, pursuant to a provision embodied in an international agreement, of a claim arising under the Securities Exchange Act of 1934 notwithstanding its assumption, *arguendo*, that *Wilko, supra*, which held nonarbitrable claims arising under the Securities Act of 1933, also would bar arbitration of a 1934 Act claim arising in a domestic context.

The United States Court of Appeals for the First Circuit affirmed in part and reversed in part. *723 F.2d 155 (1983)*. It first rejected Soler's argument that Puerto Rico law precluded enforcement of an agreement obligating a local dealer to arbitrate controversies outside Puerto Rico. It also rejected Soler's suggestion that it could not have intended to arbitrate statutory claims not mentioned in the arbitration agreement. Assessing arbitrability "on an allegation by allegation basis," *id. at 159*, the court then read the arbitration clause to encompass virtually all the claims arising under the various statutes, including all those arising under the Sherman Act.

Finally, after endorsing the doctrine of *American Safety*, precluding arbitration of antitrust claims, the Court of Appeals concluded that neither this Court's decision in *Scherk* nor the Convention required abandonment of that doctrine in the face of an international transaction. *723 F.2d, at 164–168*. Accordingly, it reversed the judgment of the District Court insofar as it had ordered submission of "Soler's antitrust claims" to arbitration. Affirming the remainder of the judgment, the court directed the District Court to consider in the first instance how the parallel judicial and arbitral proceedings should go forward.

We granted certiorari primarily to consider whether an American court should enforce an agreement to resolve antitrust claims by arbitration when that agreement arises from an international transaction. *469 U.S. 916 (1984).*

II

At the outset, we address the contention raised in Soler's cross-petition that the arbitration clause at issue may not be read to encompass the statutory counterclaims stated in its answer to the complaint. In making this argument, Soler does not question the Court of Appeals' application of para. VI of the Sales Agreement to the disputes involved here as a matter of standard contract interpretation. Instead, it argues that as a matter of law a court may not construe an arbitration agreement to encompass claims arising out of statutes designed to protect a class to which the party resisting arbitration belongs "unless [that party] has expressly agreed" to arbitrate those claims, see Pet. for Cert. in No. 83–1733, pp. 8, i, by which Soler presumably means that the arbitration clause must specifically mention the statute giving rise to the claims that a party to the clause seeks to arbitrate. See *723 F.2d, at 159.* Soler reasons that, because it falls within the class for whose benefit the federal and local antitrust laws and dealers' Acts were passed, but the arbitration clause at issue does not mention these statutes or statutes in general, the clause cannot be read to contemplate arbitration of these statutory claims.

We do not agree, for we find no warrant in the Arbitration Act for implying in every contract within its ken a presumption against arbitration of statutory claims. The Act's centerpiece provision makes a written agreement to arbitrate "in any maritime transaction or a contract evidencing a transaction involving commerce . . . valid, irrevocable, and enforceable, save upon such grounds as exist at law or in equity for the revocation of any contract." *9 U. S. C. §2.* The "liberal federal policy favoring arbitration agreements," *Moses H. Cone Memorial Hospital v. Mercury Construction Corp., 460 U.S. 1, 24 (1983)*, manifested by this provision and the Act as a whole, is at bottom a policy guaranteeing the enforcement of private contractual arrangements: the Act simply "creates a body of federal substantive law establishing and regulating the duty to honor an agreement to arbitrate." *Id. at 25, n. 32.* As this Court recently observed, "[the] preeminent concern of Congress in passing the Act was to enforce private agreements into which parties had entered," a concern which "requires that we rigorously enforce agreements to arbitrate." *Dean Witter Reynolds Inc. v. Byrd, 470 U.S. 213, 221 (1985).*

Accordingly, the first task of a court asked to compel arbitration of a dispute is to determine whether the parties agreed to arbitrate that dispute. The court is to make this determination by applying the "federal substantive law of arbitrability, applicable to any arbitration agreement within the coverage of the Act." *Moses H. Cone Memorial Hospital, 460 U.S., at 24.* See *Prima Paint Corp. v. Flood & Conklin Mfg. Co., 388 U.S. 395, 400–404 (1967)*; *Southland Corp. v. Keating, 465 U.S. 1, 12 (1984).* And that body of law counsels

> "that questions of arbitrability must be addressed with a healthy regard for the federal policy favoring arbitration. . . . The Arbitration Act establishes that, as a matter of federal law, any doubts concerning the scope of arbitrable issues

> should be resolved in favor of arbitration, whether the problem at hand is the construction of the contract language itself or an allegation of waiver, delay, or a like defense to arbitrability." *Moses H. Cone Memorial Hospital, 460 U.S., at 24–25.*

See, *e.g., Steelworkers v. Warrior & Gulf Navigation Co., 363 U.S. 574, 582–583 (1960).* Thus, as with any other contract, the parties' intentions control, but those intentions are generously construed as to issues of arbitrability.

There is no reason to depart from these guidelines where a party bound by an arbitration agreement raises claims founded on statutory rights. Some time ago this Court expressed "hope for [the Act's] usefulness both in controversies based on statutes or on standards otherwise created," *Wilko v. Swan, 346 U.S. 427, 432 (1953)* (footnote omitted); see *Merrill Lynch, Pierce, Fenner & Smith, Inc. v. Ware, 414 U.S. 117, 135, n. 15 (1973)*, and we are well past the time when judicial suspicion of the desirability of arbitration and of the competence of arbitral tribunals inhibited the development of arbitration as an alternative means of dispute resolution. Just last Term in *Southland Corp., supra*, where we held that *§2* of the Act declared a national policy applicable equally in state as well as federal courts, we construed an arbitration clause to encompass the disputes at issue without pausing at the source in a state statute of the rights asserted by the parties resisting arbitration. *465 U.S., at 15*, and n. 7. Of course, courts should remain attuned to well-supported claims that the agreement to arbitrate resulted from the sort of fraud or overwhelming economic power that would provide grounds "for the revocation of any contract." *9 U. S. C. §2*; see *Southland Corp., 465 U.S., at 16, n. 11*; *The Bremen v. Zapata Off-Shore Co., 407 U.S. 1, 15 (1972)*. But, absent such compelling considerations, the Act itself provides no basis for disfavoring agreements to arbitrate statutory claims by skewing the otherwise hospitable inquiry into arbitrability.

That is not to say that all controversies implicating statutory rights are suitable for arbitration. There is no reason to distort the process of contract interpretation, however, in order to ferret out the inappropriate. Just as it is the congressional policy manifested in the Federal Arbitration Actthat requires courts liberally to construe the scope of arbitration agreements covered by that Act, it is the congressional intention expressed in some other statute on which the courts must rely to identify any category of claims as to which agreements to arbitrate will be held unenforceable. See *Wilko v. Swan, 346 U.S., at 434–435*; *Southland Corp., 465 U.S., at 16, n. 11*; *Dean Witter Reynolds Inc., 470 U.S., at 224–225* (concurring opinion). For that reason, Soler's concern for statutorily protected classes provides no reason to color the lens through which the arbitration clause is read. By agreeing to arbitrate a statutory claim, a party does not forgo the substantive rights afforded by the statute; it only submits to their resolution in an arbitral, rather than a judicial, forum. It trades the procedures and opportunity for review of the courtroom for the simplicity, informality, and expedition of arbitration. We must assume that if Congress intended the substantive protection afforded by a given statute to include protection against waiver of the right to a judicial forum, that intention will be deducible from text or legislative history. See *Wilko v. Swan, supra*. Having made the bargain to arbitrate, the party should be held to it unless Congress itself has evinced an intention to preclude a waiver of judicial remedies for the statutory rights at issue. Nothing, in the meantime, prevents a party from excluding statutory claims from the scope of an agreement to arbitrate. See *Prima Paint Corp., 388 U.S., at 406.*

In sum, the Court of Appeals correctly conducted a two-step inquiry, first determining whether the parties' agreement to arbitrate reached the statutory issues, and then, upon finding it did, considering whether legal constraints external to the parties' agreement foreclosed the arbitration of those claims. We endorse its rejection of Soler's proposed rule of arbitration-clause construction.

III

We now turn to consider whether Soler's antitrust claims are nonarbitrable even though it has agreed to arbitrate them. In holding that they are not, the Court of Appeals followed the decision of the Second Circuit in *American Safety Equipment Corp. v. J. P. Maguire & Co., 391 F.2d 821 (1968).* Notwithstanding the absence of any explicit support for such an exception in either the Sherman Act or the Federal Arbitration Act, the Second Circuit there reasoned that "the pervasive public interest in enforcement of the antitrust laws, and the nature of the claims that arise in such cases, combine to make . . . antitrust claims . . . inappropriate for arbitration." *Id., at 827–828.* We find it unnecessary to assess the legitimacy of the *American Safety* doctrine as applied to agreements to arbitrate arising from domestic transactions. As in *Scherk v. Alberto-Culver Co., 417 U.S. 506 (1974),* we conclude that concerns of international comity, respect for the capacities of foreign and transnational tribunals, and sensitivity to the need of the international commercial system for predictability in the resolution of disputes require that we enforce the parties' agreement, even assuming that a contrary result would be forthcoming in a domestic context.

Even before *Scherk*, this Court had recognized the utility of forum-selection clauses in international transactions. In *The Bremen, supra*, an American oil company, seeking to evade a contractual choice of an English forum and, by implication, English law, filed a suit in admiralty in a United States District Court against the German corporation which had contracted to tow its rig to a location in the Adriatic Sea. Notwithstanding the possibility that the English court would enforce provisions in the towage contract exculpating the German party which an American court would refuse to enforce, this Court gave effect to the choice-of-forum clause. It observed:

> "The expansion of American business and industry will hardly be encouraged if, notwithstanding solemn contracts, we insist on a parochial concept that all disputes must be resolved under our laws and in our courts. . . . We cannot have trade and commerce in world markets and international waters exclusively on our terms, governed by our laws, and resolved in our courts." *407 U.S., at 9.*

Recognizing that "agreeing in advance on a forum acceptable to both parties is an indispensable element in international trade, commerce, and contracting," *id., at 13–14*, the decision in *The Bremen* clearly eschewed a provincial solicitude for the jurisdiction of domestic forums.

Identical considerations governed the Court's decision in *Scherk*, which categorized "[an] agreement to arbitrate before a specified tribunal [as], in effect, a specialized kind of forum-selection clause that posits not only the situs of suit but also the procedure to be used in resolving the dispute." *417 U.S., at 519*. In *Scherk*, the American company Alberto-Culver purchased several interrelated business enterprises, organized under the laws of Germany and Liechtenstein, as well as the rights held by those enterprises in certain trademarks, from a German citizen who at the time of trial resided in Switzerland. Although the contract of sale contained a clause providing for arbitration before the International Chamber of Commerce in Paris of "any controversy or claim [arising] out of this agreement or the breach thereof," Alberto-Culver subsequently brought suit against Scherk in a Federal District Court in Illinois, alleging that Scherk had violated *§10(b)* of the Securities Exchange Act of 1934 by fraudulently misrepresenting the status of the trademarks as unencumbered. The District Court denied a motion to stay the proceedings before it and enjoined the parties from going forward before the arbitral tribunal in Paris. The Court of Appeals for the Seventh Circuit affirmed, relying on this Court's holding in *Wilko v. Swan, 346 U.S. 427 (1953)*, that agreements to arbitrate disputes arising under the Securities Act of 1933 are nonarbitrable. This Court reversed, enforcing the arbitration agreement even while assuming for purposes of the decision that the controversy would be nonarbitrable under the holding of *Wilko* had it arisen out of a domestic transaction. Again, the Court emphasized:

> "A contractual provision specifying in advance the forum in which disputes shall be litigated and the law to be applied is . . . an almost indispensable precondition to achievement of the orderliness and predictability essential to any international business transaction. . . .
>
> "A parochial refusal by the courts of one country to enforce an international arbitration agreement would not only frustrate these purposes, but would invite unseemly and mutually destructive jockeying by the parties to secure tactical litigation advantages. . . . [It would] damage the fabric of international commerce and trade, and imperil the willingness and ability of businessmen to enter into international commercial agreements." *417 U.S., at 516–517*.

Accordingly, the Court held Alberto-Culver to its bargain, sending it to the international arbitral tribunal before which it had agreed to seek its remedies.

The Bremen and *Scherk* establish a strong presumption in favor of enforcement of freely negotiated contractual choice-of-forum provisions. Here, as in *Scherk*, that presumption is reinforced by the emphatic federal policy in favor of arbitral dispute resolution. And at least since this Nation's accession in 1970 to the Convention, see [1970] 21 U.S.T. 2517, T.I.A.S. 6997, and the implementation of the Convention in the same year by amendment of the Federal Arbitration Act, that federal policy applies with special force in the field of international commerce. Thus, we must weigh the concerns of *American Safety* against a strong belief in the efficacy of arbitral procedures for the resolution of international commercial disputes and an equal commitment to the enforcement of freely negotiated choice-of-forum clauses.

At the outset, we confess to some skepticism of certain aspects of the *American Safety* doctrine. As distilled by the First Circuit, *723 F.2d, at 162*, the doctrine comprises four ingredients. First, private parties play a pivotal role in aiding governmental enforcement of the antitrust laws by means of the private action for treble damages. Second, "the strong possibility that contracts which generate antitrust disputes may be contracts of adhesion militates against automatic forum determination by contract." Third, antitrust issues, prone to complication, require sophisticated legal and economic analysis, and thus are "ill-adapted to strengths of the arbitral process, *i.e.*, expedition, minimal requirements of written rationale, simplicity, resort to basic concepts of common sense and simple equity." Finally, just as "issues of war and peace are too important to be vested in the generals, . . . decisions as to antitrust regulation of business are too important to be lodged in arbitrators chosen from the business community – particularly those from a foreign community that has had no experience with or exposure to our law and values." See *American Safety, 391 F.2d, at 826–827.*

Initially, we find the second concern unjustified. The mere appearance of an antitrust dispute does not alone warrant invalidation of the selected forum on the undemonstrated assumption that the arbitration clause is tainted. A party resisting arbitration of course may attack directly the validity of the agreement to arbitrate. See *Prima Paint Corp. v. Flood & Conklin Mfg. Co., 388 U.S. 395 (1967).* Moreover, the party may attempt to make a showing that would warrant setting aside the forum-selection clause – that the agreement was "[affected] by fraud, undue influence, or overweening bargaining power"; that "enforcement would be unreasonable and unjust"; or that proceedings "in the contractual forum will be so gravely difficult and inconvenient that [the resisting party] will for all practical purposes be deprived of his day in court." *The Bremen, 407 U.S., at 12, 15, 18.* But absent such a showing – and none was attempted here – there is no basis for assuming the forum inadequate or its selection unfair.

Next, potential complexity should not suffice to ward off arbitration. We might well have some doubt that even the courts following *American Safety* subscribe fully to the view that antitrust matters are inherently insusceptible to resolution by arbitration, as these same courts have agreed that an undertaking to arbitrate antitrust claims entered into *after* the dispute arises is acceptable. See, *e.g., Coenen v. R. W. Pressprich & Co., 453 F.2d 1209, 1215* (CA2), cert. denied, *406 U.S. 949 (1972)*; *Cobb v. Lewis, 488 F.2d 41, 48 (CA5 1974).* See also, in the present cases, *723 F.2d, at 168, n. 12* (leaving question open). And the vertical restraints which most frequently give birth to antitrust claims covered by an arbitration agreement will not often occasion the monstrous proceedings that have given antitrust litigation an image of intractability. In any event, adaptability and access to expertise are hallmarks of arbitration. The anticipated subject matter of the dispute may be taken into account when the arbitrators are appointed, and arbitral rules typically provide for the participation of experts either employed by the parties or appointed by the tribunal. Moreover, it is often a judgment that streamlined proceedings and expeditious results will best serve their needs that causes parties to agree to arbitrate their disputes; it is typically a desire to keep the effort and expense required to resolve a dispute within manageable bounds that prompts them mutually to forgo access to judicial remedies. In sum, the factor of potential complexity alone does not persuade us that an arbitral tribunal could not properly handle an antitrust matter.

For similar reasons, we also reject the proposition that an arbitration panel will pose too great a danger of innate hostility to the constraints on business conduct that antitrust law imposes. International arbitrators frequently are drawn from the legal as well as the business community; where the dispute has an important legal component, the parties and the arbitral body with whose assistance they have agreed to settle their dispute can be expected to select arbitrators accordingly. We decline to indulge the presumption that the parties and arbitral body conducting a proceeding will be unable or unwilling to retain competent, conscientious, and impartial arbitrators.

We are left, then, with the core of the *American Safety* doctrine – the fundamental importance to American democratic capitalism of the regime of the antitrust laws. See, *e.g., United States v. Topco Associates, Inc., 405 U.S. 596, 610 (1972)*; *Northern Pacific R. Co. v. United States, 356 U.S. 1, 4 (1958)*. Without doubt, the private cause of action plays a central role in enforcing this regime. See, *e.g., Hawaii v. Standard Oil Co., 405 U.S. 251, 262 (1972)*. As the Court of Appeals pointed out:

> "'A claim under the antitrust laws is not merely a private matter. The Sherman Act is designed to promote the national interest in a competitive economy; thus, the plaintiff asserting his rights under the Act has been likened to a private attorney-general who protects the public's interest.'" *723 F.2d, at 168*, quoting *American Safety, 391 F.2d, at 826*.

The treble-damages provision wielded by the private litigant is a chief tool in the antitrust enforcement scheme, posing a crucial deterrent to potential violators. See, *e.g., Perma Life Mufflers, Inc. v. International Parts Corp., 392 U.S. 134, 138–139 (1968)*.

The importance of the private damages remedy, however, does not compel the conclusion that it may not be sought outside an American court. Notwithstanding its important incidental policing function, the treble-damages cause of action conferred on private parties by *§4* of the Clayton Act, *15 U. S. C. §15*, and pursued by Soler here by way of its third counterclaim, seeks primarily to enable an injured competitor to gain compensation for that injury.

"*Section 4*... is in essence a remedial provision. It provides treble damages to '[any] person who shall be injured in his business or property by reason of anything forbidden in the antitrust laws....' Of course, treble damages also play an important role in penalizing wrongdoers and deterring wrongdoing, as we also have frequently observed.... It nevertheless is true that the treble-damages provision, which makes awards available only to injured parties, and measures the awards by a multiple of the injury actually proved, is designed primarily as a remedy." *Brunswick Corp. v. Pueblo Bowl-O-Mat, Inc., 429 U.S. 477, 485–486 (1977)*.

After examining the respective legislative histories, the Court in *Brunswick* recognized that when first enacted in 1890 as *§7* of the Sherman Act, 26 Stat. 210, the treble-damages provision "was conceived of primarily as a remedy for '[the] people of the United States as individuals,'" *429 U.S., at 486, n. 10*, quoting 21 Cong. Rec. 1767–1768 (1890) (remarks of Sen. George); when reenacted in 1914 as *§4* of the Clayton Act, 38 Stat. 731, it was still "conceived primarily as '[opening] the door of justice to every man, whenever he may be injured by those who violate the antitrust laws, and [giving] the injured party ample damages for the wrong suffered.'" *429 U.S., at 486, n. 10*, quoting 51 Cong. Rec. 9073 (1914) (remarks of Rep. Webb). And, of course, the antitrust cause of action remains at all times under the control of the individual litigant: no citizen is under an obligation to bring an antitrust suit, see *Illinois Brick Co. v. Illinois, 431 U.S. 720, 746 (1977)*, and the private antitrust plaintiff needs no executive or judicial approval before settling one. It follows that, at least where the international cast of a transaction would otherwise add an element of uncertainty to dispute resolution, the prospective litigant may provide in advance for a mutually agreeable procedure whereby he would seek his antitrust recovery as well as settle other controversies.

There is no reason to assume at the outset of the dispute that international arbitration will not provide an adequate mechanism. To be sure, the international arbitral tribunal owes no prior allegiance to the legal norms of particular states; hence, it has no direct obligation to vindicate their statutory dictates. The tribunal, however, is bound to effectuate the intentions of the parties. Where the parties have agreed that the arbitral body is to decide a defined set of claims which includes, as in these cases, those arising from the application of American antitrust law, the tribunal therefore should be bound to decide that dispute in accord with the national law giving rise to the claim. Cf. *Wilko v. Swan, 346 U.S., at 433–434*. And so long as the prospective litigant effectively may vindicate its statutory cause of action in the arbitral forum, the statute will continue to serve both its remedial and deterrent function.

Having permitted the arbitration to go forward, the national courts of the United States will have the opportunity at the award-enforcement stage to ensure that the legitimate interest in the enforcement of the antitrust laws has been addressed. The Convention reserves to each signatory country the right to refuse enforcement of an award where the "recognition or enforcement of the award would be contrary to the public policy of that country." Art. V(2)(b), 21 U.S.T., at 2520; see *Scherk, 417 U.S., at 519, n. 14*. While the efficacy of the arbitral process requires that substantive review at the award-enforcement stage remain minimal, it would not require intrusive inquiry to ascertain that the tribunal took cognizance of the antitrust claims and actually decided them.

As international trade has expanded in recent decades, so too has the use of international arbitration to resolve disputes arising in the course of that trade. The controversies that international arbitral institutions are called upon to resolve have increased in diversity as well as in complexity. Yet the potential of these tribunals for efficient disposition of legal disagreements arising from commercial relations has not yet been tested. If they are to take a central place in the international legal order, national courts will need to "shake off the old judicial hostility to arbitration," *Kulukundis Shipping Co. v. Amtorg Trading Corp., 126 F.2d 978, 985 (CA2 1942)*, and also their customary and understandable unwillingness to cede jurisdiction of a claim arising under domestic law to a foreign or transnational tribunal. To this extent, at least, it will be necessary for national courts to subordinate domestic notions of arbitrability to the international policy favoring commercial arbitration. See *Scherk, supra*.

Accordingly, we "require this representative of the American business community to honor its bargain," *Alberto-Culver Co. v. Scherk, 484 F.2d 611, 620 (CA7 1973)* (Stevens, J., dissenting), by holding this agreement to arbitrate "[enforceable] . . . in accord with the explicit provisions of the Arbitration Act." *Scherk, 417 U.S., at 520*.

The judgment of the Court of Appeals is affirmed in part and reversed in part, and the cases are remanded for further proceedings consistent with this opinion.

It is so ordered.

RODRIGUEZ DE QUIJAS ET AL. v. SHEARSON/AMERICAN EXPRESS, INC.
SUPREME COURT OF THE UNITED STATES

490 U.S. 477

March 27, 1989, Argued
May 15, 1989, Decided

JUSTICE KENNEDY delivered the opinion of the Court.

The question here is whether a predispute agreement to arbitrate claims under the Securities Act of 1933 is unenforceable, requiring resolution of the claims only in a judicial forum.

I

Petitioners are individuals who invested about $400,000 in securities. They signed a standard customer agreement with the broker, which included a clause stating that the parties agreed to settle any controversies "relating to [the] accounts" through binding arbitration that complies with specified procedures. The agreement to arbitrate these controversies is unqualified, unless it is found to be unenforceable under federal or state law. Customer's Agreement para. 13. The investments turned sour, and petitioners eventually sued respondent and its broker-agent in charge of the accounts, alleging that their money was lost in unauthorized and fraudulent transactions. In their complaint they pleaded various violations of federal and state law, including claims under §12(2) of the Securities Act of 1933, *15 U. S. C. §77l*(2), and claims under three sections of the Securities Exchange Act of 1934.

The District Court ordered all the claims to be submitted to arbitration except for those raised under §12(2) of the Securities Act. It held that the latter claims must proceed in the court action under our clear holding on the point in *Wilko v. Swan, 346 U.S. 427 (1953)*. The District Court reaffirmed its ruling upon reconsideration and also entered a default judgment against the broker, who is no longer in the case. The Court of Appeals reversed, concluding that the arbitration agreement is enforceable because this Court's subsequent decisions have reduced *Wilko* to "obsolescence." *Rodriguez de Quijas v. Shearson/Lehman Bros., Inc., 845 F. 2d 1296, 1299 (CA5 1988)*. We granted certiorari, *488 U.S. 954 (1988)*.

II

The *Wilko* case, decided in 1953, required the Court to determine whether an agreement to arbitrate future controversies constitutes a binding stipulation "to waive compliance with any provision" of the Securities Act, which is nullified by §14 of the Act. *15 U. S. C. §77n*. The Court considered the language, purposes, and legislative history of the Securities Act and concluded that the agreement to arbitrate was void under §14. But the decision was a difficult one in view of the competing legislative policy embodied in the Arbitration Act, which the Court described as "not easily reconcilable," and which strongly favors the enforcement of agreements to arbitrate as a means of securing "prompt, economical and adequate solution of controversies." *346 U.S., at 438.*

It has been recognized that *Wilko* was not obviously correct, for "the language prohibiting waiver of 'compliance with any provision of this title' could easily have been read to relate to substantive provisions of the Act without including the remedy provisions." *Alberto-Culver Co. v. Scherk, 484 F. 2d 611, 618, n. 7 (CA7 1973)* (Stevens, J., dissenting), rev'd, *417 U.S. 506 (1974).* The Court did not read the language this way in *Wilko*, however, and gave two reasons. First, the Court rejected the argument that "arbitration is merely a form of trial to be used in lieu of a trial at law." *346 U.S., at 433.* The Court found instead that §14 does not permit waiver of "the right to select the judicial forum" in favor of arbitration, *id., at 435*, because "arbitration lacks the certainty of a suit at law under the Act to enforce [the buyer's] rights," *id., at 432.* Second, the Court concluded that the Securities Act was intended to protect buyers of securities, who often do not deal at arm's length and on equal terms with sellers, by offering them "a wider choice of courts and venue" than is enjoyed by participants in other business transactions, making "the right to select the judicial forum" a particularly valuable feature of the Securities Act. *Id., at 435.*

We do not think these reasons justify an interpretation of §14 that prohibits agreements to arbitrate future disputes relating to the purchase of securities. The Court's characterization of the arbitration process in *Wilko* is pervaded by what Judge Jerome Frank called "the old judicial hostility to arbitration." *Kulukundis Shipping Co. v. Amtorg Trading Corp., 126 F. 2d 978, 985 (CA2 1942).* That view has been steadily eroded over the years, beginning in the lower courts. See *Scherk, supra, at 616* (Stevens, J., dissenting) (citing cases). The erosion intensified in our most recent decisions upholding agreements to arbitrate federal claims raised under the Securities Exchange Act of 1934, see *Shearson/American Express Inc. v. McMahon, 482 U.S. 220 (1987)*, under the Racketeer Influenced and Corrupt Organizations (RICO) statutes, see *ibid.*, and under the antitrust laws, see *Mitsubishi Motors Corp. v. Soler Chrysler-Plymouth, Inc., 473 U.S. 614 (1985).* See also *Dean Witter Reynolds Inc. v. Byrd, 470 U.S. 213, 221 (1985)* (federal arbitration statute "requires that we rigorously enforce agreements to arbitrate"); *Moses H. Cone Memorial Hospital v. Mercury Construction Corp., 460 U.S. 1, 24 (1983)* ("[Q]uestions of arbitrability must be addressed with a healthy regard for the federal policy favoring arbitration"). The shift in the Court's views on arbitration away from those adopted in *Wilko* is shown by the flat statement in *Mitsubishi:* "By agreeing to arbitrate a statutory claim, a party does not forgo the substantive rights afforded by the statute; it only submits to their resolution in an arbitral, rather than a judicial, forum." *473 U.S., at 628.* To the extent that *Wilko* rested on suspicion of arbitration as a method of weakening the protections afforded in the substantive law to would-be complainants, it has fallen far out of step with our current strong endorsement of the federal statutes favoring this method of resolving disputes.

Once the outmoded presumption of disfavoring arbitration proceedings is set to one side, it becomes clear that the right to select the judicial forum and the wider choice of courts are not such essential features of the Securities Act that §14 is properly construed to bar any waiver of these provisions. Nor are they so critical that they cannot be waived under the rationale that the Securities Act was intended to place buyers of securities on an equal footing with sellers. *Wilko* identified two different kinds of provisions in the Securities Act that would advance this objective. Some are substantive, such as the provision placing on the seller the burden of proving lack of scienter when a buyer alleges fraud. See *346 U.S., at 431*, citing *15 U. S. C. §77l(2)*. Others are procedural. The specific procedural improvements highlighted in *Wilko* are the statute's broad venue provisions in the federal courts; the existence of nationwide service of process in the federal courts; the extinction of the amount-in-controversy requirement that had applied to fraud suits when they were brought in federal courts under diversity jurisdiction rather than as a federal cause of action; and the grant of concurrent jurisdiction in the state and federal courts without possility of removal. See *346 U.S., at 431*, citing *15 U. S. C. §77v(a)*.

There is no sound basis for construing the prohibition in §14 on waiving "compliance with any provision" of the Securities Act to apply to these procedural provisions. Although the first three measures do facilitate suits by buyers of securities, the grant of concurrent jurisdiction constitutes explicit authorization for complainants to waive those protections by filing suit in state court without possibility of removal to federal court. These measures, moreover, are present in other federal statutes which have not been interpreted to prohibit enforcement of predispute agreements to arbitrate. See *Shearson/American Express Inc. v. McMahon, supra* (construing the Securities Exchange Act of 1934; see *15 U. S. C. §78aa*); *ibid.* (construing the RICO statutes; see *18 U. S. C. §1965*); *Mitsubishi Motors Corp. v. Soler Chrysler-Plymouth, Inc., supra* (construing the antitrust laws; see *15 U. S. C. §15*).

Indeed, in *McMahon* the Court declined to read §29(a) of the Securities Exchange Act of 1934, the language of which is in every respect the same as that in §14 of the 1933 Act, compare *15 U. S. C. §77v(a)* with *§78aa*, to prohibit enforcement of predispute agreements to arbitrate. The only conceivable distinction in this regard between the Securities Act and the Securities Exchange Act is that the former statute allows concurrent federal-state jurisdiction over causes of action and the latter statute provides for exclusive federal jurisdiction. But even if this distinction were thought to make any difference at all, it would suggest that arbitration agreements, which are "in effect, a specialized kind of forum-selection clause," *Scherk v. Alberto-Culver Co., 417 U.S. 506, 519 (1974)*, should not be prohibited under the Securities Act, since they, like the provision for concurrent jurisdiction, serve to advance the objective of allowing buyers of securities a broader right to select the forum for resolving disputes, whether it be judicial or otherwise. And in *McMahon* we explained at length why we rejected the *Wilko* Court's aversion to arbitration as a forum for resolving disputes over securities transactions, especially in light of the relatively recent expansion of the Securities and Exchange Commission's authority to oversee and to regulate those arbitration procedures. *482 U.S., at 231–234*. We need not repeat those arguments here.

Finally, in *McMahon* we stressed the strong language of the Arbitration Act, which declares as a matter of federal law that arbitration agreements "shall be valid, irrevocable, and enforceable, save upon such grounds as exist at law or in equity for the revocation of any contract." *9 U. S. C. §2*. Under that statute, the party opposing arbitration carries the burden of showing that Congress intended in a separate statute to preclude a waiver of judicial remedies, or that such a waiver of judicial remedies inherently conflicts with the underlying purposes of that other statute. *482 U.S., at*

226–227. But as Justice Frankfurter said in dissent in *Wilko*, so it is true in this case: "There is nothing in the record before us, nor in the facts of which we can take judicial notice, to indicate that the arbitral system . . . would not afford the plaintiff the rights to which he is entitled." *346 U.S., at 439.* Petitioners have not carried their burden of showing that arbitration agreements are not enforceable under the Securities Act.

The language quoted above from *§2* of the Arbitration Act also allows the courts to give relief where the party opposing arbitration presents "well-supported claims that the agreement to arbitrate resulted from the sort of fraud or overwhelming economic power that would provide grounds 'for the revocation of any contract.'" *Mitsubishi, 473 U.S., at 627.* This avenue of relief is in harmony with the Securities Act's concern to protect buyers of securities by removing "the disadvantages under which buyers labor" in their dealings with sellers. *Wilko, supra, at 435.* Although petitioners suggest that the agreement to arbitrate here was adhesive in nature, the record contains no factual showing sufficient to support that suggestion.

III

We do not suggest that the Court of Appeals on its own authority should have taken the step of renouncing *Wilko*. If a precedent of this Court has direct application in a case, yet appears to rest on reasons rejected in some other line of decisions, the Court of Appeals should follow the case which directly controls, leaving to this Court the prerogative of overruling its own decisions. We now conclude that *Wilko* was incorrectly decided and is inconsistent with the prevailing uniform construction of other federal statutes governing arbitration agreements in the setting of business transactions. Although we are normally and properly reluctant to overturn our decisions construing statutes, we have done so to achieve a uniform interpretation of similar statutory language, *Commissioner v. Estate of Church, 335 U.S. 632, 649–650 (1949)*, and to correct a seriously erroneous interpretation of statutory language that would undermine congressional policy as expressed in other legislation, see, *e.g., Boys Markets, Inc. v. Retail Clerks, 398 U.S. 235, 240–241 (1970)* (overruling *Sinclair Refining Co. v. Atkinson, 370 U.S. 195 (1962))*. Both purposes would be served here by overruling the *Wilko* decision.

It also would be undesirable for the decisions in *Wilko* and *McMahon* to continue to exist side by side. Their inconsistency is at odds with the principle that the 1933 and 1934 Acts should be construed harmoniously because they "constitute interrelated components of the federal regulatory scheme governing transactions in securities." *Ernst & Ernst v. Hochfelder, 425 U.S. 185, 206 (1976).* In this case, for example, petitioners' claims under the 1934 Act were subjected to arbitration, while their claim under the 1933 Act was not permitted to go to arbitration, but was required to proceed in court. That result makes little sense for similar claims, based on similar facts, which are supposed to arise within a single federal regulatory scheme. In addition, the inconsistency between *Wilko* and *McMahon* undermines the essential rationale for a harmonious construction of the two statutes, which is to discourage litigants from manipulating their allegations merely to cast their claims under one of the securities laws rather than another. For all of these reasons, therefore, we overrule the decision in *Wilko*.

Petitioners argue finally that if the Court overrules *Wilko*, it should not apply its ruling retroactively to the facts of this case. We disagree. The general rule of long standing is that the law announced in the Court's decision controls the case at bar. See, *e.g., Saint Francis College v. AlKhazraji, 481 U.S. 604, 608 (1987); United States v. Schooner Peggy, 1 Cranch 103, 109 (1801)*. In some civil cases, the Court has restricted its rulings to have prospective application only, where specific circumstances are present. *Chevron Oil v. Huson, 404 U.S. 97, 106–107 (1971)*. Under the *Chevron* approach, the customary rule of retroactive application is appropriate here. Although our decision to overrule *Wilko* establishes a new principle of law for arbitration agreements under the Securities Act, this ruling furthers the purposes and effect of the Arbitration Act without undermining those of the Securities Act. Today's ruling, moreover, does not produce "substantial inequitable results," *404 U.S., at 107*, for petitioners do not make any serious allegation that they agreed to arbitrate future disputes relating to their investment contracts in reliance on *Wilko*'s holding that such agreements would be held unenforceable by the courts. Our conclusion is reinforced by our assessment that resort to the arbitration process does not inherently undermine any of the substantive rights afforded to petitioners under the Securities Act.

The judgment of the Court of Appeals is

Affirmed.

INTEL CORPORATION, Petitioner v. ADVANCED MICRO DEVICES, INC. SUPREME COURT OF THE UNITED STATES

542 U.S. 241

April 20, 2004, Argued
June 21, 2004, Decided

Justice Ginsburg delivered the opinion of the Court.

This case concerns the authority of federal district courts to assist in the production of evidence for use in a foreign or international tribunal. In the matter before us, respondent Advanced Micro Devices, Inc. (AMD) filed an antitrust complaint against petitioner Intel Corporation (Intel) with the Directorate-General for Competition of the Commission of the European Communities (European Commission or Commission). In pursuit of that complaint, AMD applied to the United States District Court for the Northern District of California, invoking *28 U.S.C. §1782(a)*, for an order requiring Intel to produce potentially relevant documents. *Section 1782(a)* provides that a federal district court "may order" a person "resid[ing]" or "found" in the district to give testimony or produce documents "for use in a proceeding in a foreign or international tribunal . . . upon the application of any interested person."

Concluding that *§1782(a)* did not authorize the requested discovery, the District Court denied AMD's application. The Court of Appeals for the Ninth Circuit reversed that determination and remanded the case, instructing the District Court to rule on the merits of AMD's application. In accord with the Court of Appeals, we hold that the District Court had authority under *§1782(a)* to entertain AMD's discovery request. The statute, we rule, does not categorically bar the assistance AMD seeks: (1) A complainant before the European Commission, such as AMD, qualifies as an "interested person" within *§1782(a)*'s compass; (2) the Commission is a *§1782(a)* "tribunal" when it acts as a first-instance decisionmaker; (3) the "proceeding" for which discovery is sought under *§1782(a)* must be in reasonable contemplation, but need not be "pending" or "imminent"; and (4) *§1782(a)* contains no threshold requirement that evidence sought from a federal district court would be discoverable under the law governing the foreign proceeding. We caution, however, that *§1782(a)* authorizes, but does not require, a federal district court to provide judicial assistance to foreign or international tribunals or to "interested person[s]" in proceedings abroad. Whether such assistance is appropriate in this case is a question yet unresolved. To guide the District Court on remand, we suggest considerations relevant to the disposition of that question.

I

A

Section 1782 is the product of congressional efforts, over the span of nearly 150 years, to provide federal-court assistance in gathering evidence for use in foreign tribunals. Congress first provided for federal-court aid to foreign tribunals in 1855; requests for aid took the form of letters rogatory forwarded through diplomatic channels. See Act of Mar. 2, 1855, ch 140, §2, 10 Stat 630 (circuit court may appoint "a United States commissioner designated . . . to make the examination of witnesses" on receipt of a letter rogatory from a foreign court); Act of Mar. 3, 1863, ch 95, §1, 12 Stat 769 (authorizing district courts to respond to letters rogatory by compelling witnesses here to provide testimony for use abroad in "suit[s] for the recovery of money or property"). In 1948, Congress substantially broadened the scope of assistance federal courts could provide for foreign proceedings. That legislation, codified as *§1782*, eliminated the prior requirement that the government of a foreign country be a party or have an interest in the proceeding. The measure allowed district courts to designate persons to preside at depositions "to be used in *any civil action* pending in any court in a foreign country with which the United States is at peace." Act of June 25, 1948, ch 646, *§1782*, 62 Stat 949 (emphasis added). The next year, Congress deleted "civil action" from *§1782*'s text and inserted "judicial proceeding." Act of May 24, 1949, ch 139, §93, 63 Stat 103. See generally, Jones, International Judicial Assistance: Procedural Chaos and a Program for Reform, 62 Yale L. J. 515 (1953).

In 1958, prompted by the growth of international commerce, Congress created a Commission on International Rules of Judicial Procedure (Rules Commission) to "investigate and study existing practices of judicial assistance and cooperation between the United States and foreign countries with a view to achieving improvements." Act of Sept. 2, Pub L 85–906, §2, 72 Stat 1743; S. Rep. No. 2392, 85th Cong., 2d Sess., p 3 (1958); Smit, International Litigation under the United States Code, 65 Colum. L. Rev. 1015–1016 (1965) (hereinafter Smit, International Litigation). Six years later, in 1964, Congress unanimously adopted legislation recommended by the Rules Commission; the legislation included a complete revision of *§1782*. See Act of Oct. 3, Pub L 88–619, §9, 78 Stat 997; Smit, International Litigation 1026–1035.

As recast in 1964, *§1782* provided for assistance in obtaining documentary and other tangible evidence as well as testimony. Notably, Congress deleted the words "in any judicial proceeding *pending* in any court in a foreign country," and replaced them with the phrase "in a proceeding in a foreign or international tribunal." Brief for United States as *Amicus Curiae* 6, 4a–5a (emphasis added). While the accompanying Senate Report does not account discretely for the deletion of the word "pending," it explains that Congress introduced the word "tribunal" to ensure that "assistance is not confined to proceedings before conventional courts," but extends also to "administrative and quasi-judicial proceedings." S. Rep. No. 1580, 88th Cong., 2d Sess., p 7 (1964); see H. R. Rep. No. 1052, 88th Cong., 1st Sess., p 9 (1963) (same). Congress further amended *§1782(a)* in 1996 to add, after the reference to "foreign or international tribunal," the words "including criminal investigations conducted before formal accusation." National Defense Authorization Act for Fiscal Year 1996, Pub L 104–106, §1342(b), 110 Stat 486. *Section 1782(a)*'s current text reads:

> "The district court of the district in which a person resides or is found may order him to give his testimony or statement or to produce a document or other thing for use in a proceeding in a foreign or international tribunal, including criminal investigations conducted before formal accusation. The order may be made pursuant to a letter rogatory issued, or request made, by a foreign or international tribunal or upon the application of any interested person. . . . The order may prescribe the practice and procedure, which may be in whole or part the practice and procedure of the foreign country or the international tribunal, for taking the testimony or statement or producing the document or other thing . . . [or may be] the Federal Rules of Civil Procedure.
>
> "A person may not be compelled to give his testimony or statement or to produce a document or other thing in violation of any legally applicable privilege."

B

AMD and Intel are "worldwide competitors in the microprocessor industry." *292 F.3d 664, 665 (CA9 2002)*. In October 2000, AMD filed an antitrust complaint with the Directorate-General for Competition (DG-Competition) of the European Commission. *Ibid.;* App. 41. "The European Commission is the executive and administrative organ of the European Communities." Brief for Commission of European Communities as *Amicus Curiae* 1 (hereinafter European Commission *Amicus Curiae*). The Commission exercises responsibility over the wide range of subject areas covered by the European Union treaty; those areas include the treaty provisions, and regulations thereunder, governing competition. See *ibid.;* Consolidated Versions of Treaty on European Union and Treaty Establishing European Community, Arts. 81 and 82, 2002 O. J. (C 325) 33, 64–65, 67 (hereinafter EC Treaty). The DG-Competition, operating under the Commission's aegis, is the European Union's primary antitrust law enforcer. European Commission *Amicus Curiae* 2. Within the DG-Competition's domain are anticompetitive agreements (Art. 81) and abuse of dominant market position (Art. 82). *Ibid.;* EC Treaty 64–65.

AMD's complaint alleged that Intel, in violation of European competition law, had abused its dominant position in the European market through loyalty rebates, exclusive purchasing agreements with manufacturers and retailers, price discrimination, and standard-setting cartels. App. 40–43; Brief for Petitioner 13. AMD recommended that the DG-Competition seek discovery of documents Intel had produced in a private antitrust suit, titled *Intergraph Corp.* v *Intel Corp.*, brought in a Federal District Court in Alabama. *3 F. Supp. 2d 1255 (ND Ala. 1998)*, vacated *195 F.3d 1346 (CA Fed. 1999)*, remanded, *88 F. Supp. 2d 1288 (ND Ala. 2000)*, aff'd *253 F.3d 695 (CA Fed. 2001)*; App. 111; App. to Pet. for Cert. 13a–14a. After the DG-Competition declined to seek judicial assistance in the United States, AMD, pursuant to *§1782(a)*, petitioned the District Court for the Northern District of California for an order directing Intel to produce documents discovered in the *Intergraph* litigation and on file in the federal court in Alabama. App. to Pet. for Cert. 13a–14a. AMD asserted that it sought the materials in connection with the complaint it had filed with the European Commission. *Ibid.*

The District Court denied the application as "[un]supported by applicable authority." *Id.*, at 15a. Reversing that determination, the Court of Appeals for the Ninth Circuit remanded the case for disposition on the merits. *292 F.3d, at 669*. The Court of Appeals noted two points significant to its decision: *§1782(a)* includes matters before "'bodies of a quasi-judicial or administrative nature,'" *id., at 667* (quoting *In re Letters Rogatory from Tokyo District, 539 F.2d 1216, 1218–1219 (CA9 1976))*; and, since 1964, the statute's text has contained "[no] requirement that the proceeding be 'pending,'" *ibid.* (quoting *United States v. Sealed 1, Letter of Request for Legal Assistance, 235 F.3d 1200, 1204 (CA9 2000))*. A proceeding judicial in character, the Ninth Circuit further observed, was a likely sequel to the European Commission's investigation: "[The European Commission is] a body authorized to enforce the EC Treaty with written, binding decisions, enforceable through fines and penalties. [The Commission's] decisions are appealable to the Court of First Instance and then to the [European] Court of Justice. Thus, the proceeding for which discovery is sought is, at minimum, one leading to quasi-judicial proceedings." *292 F.3d at 667, 159 L. Ed. 2d, at 371* (presenting synopsis of Commission proceedings and judicial review of Commission decisions).

The Court of Appeals rejected Intel's argument that *§1782(a)* called for a threshold showing that the documents AMD sought in the California federal court would have been discoverable by AMD in the European Commission investigation had those documents been located within the Union. *292 F.3d, at 668*. Acknowledging that other Courts of Appeals had construed *§1782(a)* to include a "foreign-discoverability" rule, the Ninth Circuit found "nothing in the plain language or legislative history of *Section 1782*, including its 1964 and 1996 amendments, to require a threshold showing [by] the party seeking discovery that what is sought be discoverable in the foreign proceeding," *id., at 669*. A foreign-discoverability threshold, the Court of Appeals added, would disserve *§1782(a)*'s twin aims of "providing efficient assistance to participants in international litigation and encouraging foreign countries by example to provide similar assistance to our courts." *Ibid.*

On remand, a Magistrate Judge found AMD's application "overbroad," and recommended an order directing AMD to submit a more specific discovery request confined to documents directly relevant to the European Commission investigation. App. to Brief in Opposition 1a–6a; Brief for Petitioner 15, n 9. The District Court has stayed further proceedings pending disposition of the questions presented by Intel's petition for certiorari. *Ibid.*; see Order Vacating Hearing Date, No. C 01–7033 MISC JW (ND Cal, Nov. 30, 2003) (stating "Intel may renotice its motion for de novo review of the Magistrate Judge's decision after the Supreme Court issues its ruling").

We granted certiorari, *540 U.S. 1003, 540 U.S. 1003, 157 L. Ed. 2d 408, 124 S. Ct. 531 (2003)*, in view of the division among the Circuits on the question whether *§1782(a)* contains a foreign-discoverability requirement. We now hold that *§1782(a)* does not impose such a requirement. We also granted review on two other questions. First, does *§1782(a)* make discovery available to complainants, such as AMD, who do not have the status of private "litigants" and are not sovereign agents? See Pet. for Cert. (i). Second, must a "proceeding" before a foreign "tribunal" be "pending" or at least "imminent" for an applicant to invoke *§1782(a)* successfully? Compare *In re Letter of Request From Crown Prosecution Service, 870 F.2d 686, 691, 276 U.S. App. D.C. 272 (CADC 1989)* (proceeding must be "within reasonable contemplation"), with *In re Ishihari Chemical Co., 251 F.3d 120, 125 (CA2 2001)* (proceeding must be "imminent – very likely to occur and very soon to occur"); *In re International Judicial Assistance (Letter Rogatory) for Federative Republic of Brazil, 936 F.2d 702, 706 (CA2 1991)* (same). Answering "yes" to the first question and "no" to the second, we affirm the Ninth Circuit's judgment.

II

To place this case in context, we sketch briefly how the European Commission, acting through the DG-Competition, enforces European competition laws and regulations. The DG-Competition's "overriding responsibility" is to conduct investigations into alleged violations of the European Union's competition prescriptions. See European Commission *Amicus Curiae* 6. On receipt of a complaint or *sua sponte*, the DG-Competition conducts a preliminary investigation. *Ibid.* In that investigation, the DG-Competition "may take into account information provided by a complainant, and it may seek information directly from the target of the complaint." *Ibid.* "Ultimately, DG Competition's preliminary investigation results in a formal written decision whether to pursue the complaint. If [the DG-Competition] declines to proceed, that decision is subject to judicial review" by the Court of First Instance and, ultimately, by the court of last resort for European Union matters, the Court of Justice for the European Communities (European Court of Justice). *Id.*, at 7; App. 50; see, *e.g.*, case T-241/97, *Stork Amsterdam BV* v *Commission,* 2000 E. C. R. II-309, [2000] 5 C. M. L. R. 31 (Ct. 1st Instance 2000) (annulling Commission's rejection of a complaint).

If the DG-Competition decides to pursue the complaint, it typically serves the target of the investigation with a formal "statement of objections" and advises the target of its intention to recommend a decision finding that the target has violated European competition law. European Commission *Amicus Curiae* 7. The target is entitled to a hearing before an independent officer, who provides a report to the DG-Competition. *Ibid.*; App. 18 27. Once the DG Competition has made its recommendation, the European Commission may "dismis[s] the complaint, or issu[e] a decision finding infringement and imposing penalties." European Commission *Amicus Curiae* 7. The Commission's final action dismissing the complaint or holding the target liable is subject to review in the Court of First Instance and the European Court of Justice. *Ibid.*; App. 52–53, 89–90.

Although lacking formal "party" or "litigant" status in Commission proceedings, the complainant has significant procedural rights. Most prominently, the complainant may submit to the DG-Competition information in support of its allegations, and may seek judicial review of the Commission's disposition of a complaint. See European Commission *Amicus Curiae* 7–8, and n 5; *Stork Amsterdam*, [2000] E. C. R. II, at 328–329, PP 51–53.

III

As "in all statutory construction cases, we begin [our examination of *§1782*] with the language of the statute." *Barnhart v. Sigmon Coal Co., 534 U.S. 438, 450, 151 L. Ed. 2d 908, 122 S. Ct. 941 (2002)*. The language of *§1782(a)*, confirmed by its context, our examination satisfies us, warrants this conclusion: The statute authorizes, but does not require, a federal district court to provide assistance to a complainant in a European Commission proceeding that leads to a dispositive ruling, *i.e.*, a final administrative action both responsive to the complaint and reviewable in court. Accordingly, we reject the categorical limitations Intel would place on the statute's reach.

A

We turn first to Intel's contention that the catalog of "interested person[s]" authorized to apply for judicial assistance under *§1782(a)* includes only "litigants, foreign sovereigns, and the designated agents of those sovereigns," and excludes AMD, a mere complainant before the Commission, accorded only "limited rights." Brief for Petitioner 10–11, 24, 26–27. Highlighting *§1782*'s caption, "[a]ssistance to foreign and international tribunals and to *litigants* before such tribunals," Intel urges that the statutory phrase "any interested person" should be read, correspondingly, to reach only "litigants." *Id.*, at 24 (internal quotation marks omitted, emphasis in original).

The caption of a statute, this Court has cautioned, "cannot undo or limit that which the [statute's] text makes plain." *Trainmen v. Baltimore & Ohio R. Co., 331 U.S. 519, 529, 91 L. Ed. 1646, 67 S. Ct. 1387 (1947)*. The text of *§1782(a)*, "upon the application of any interested person," plainly reaches beyond the universe of persons designated "litigant." No doubt litigants are included among, and may be the most common example of, the "interested person[s]" who may invoke *§1782*; we read *§1782*'s caption to convey no more. See, *e.g.*, *Whitman v. American Trucking Assns., Inc., 531 U.S. 457, 482–483, 149 L. Ed. 2d 1, 121 S. Ct. 903 (2001)* (rejecting narrow reading of *42 U.S.C. §7511(a)* based on caption in light of "specifically" broader coverage of provision's text).

The complainant who triggers a European Commission investigation has a significant role in the process. As earlier observed, see *159 L. Ed. 2d, at 371*, in addition to prompting an investigation, the complainant has the right to submit information for the DG-Competition's consideration, and may proceed to court if the Commission discontinues the investigation or dismisses the complaint. App. 52–53. Given these participation rights, a complainant "possess[es] a reasonable interest in obtaining [judicial] assistance," and therefore qualifies as an "interested person" within any fair construction of that term. See Smit, International Litigation 1027 ("any interested person" is "intended to include not only litigants before foreign or international tribunals, but also foreign and international officials as well as any other person whether he be designated by foreign law or international convention or merely possess a reasonable interest in obtaining the assistance").

B

We next consider whether the assistance in obtaining documents here sought by an "interested person" meets the specification "for use in a foreign or international tribunal." Beyond question the reviewing authorities, both the Court of First Instance and the European Court of Justice, qualify as tribunals. But those courts are not proof-taking instances. Their review is limited to the record before the Commission. See Tr. of Oral Arg. 17. Hence, AMD could "use" evidence in the reviewing courts only by submitting it to the Commission in the current, investigative stage.

Moreover, when Congress established the Commission on International Rules of Judicial Procedure in 1958, see *159 L. Ed. 2d, at 367*, it instructed the Rules Commission to recommend procedural revisions "for the rendering of assistance to foreign courts *and quasi-judicial agencies.*" §2, 72 Stat 1743 (emphasis added). *Section 1782* had previously referred to "any judicial proceeding." The Rules Commission's draft, which Congress adopted, replaced that term with "a proceeding in a foreign or international tribunal." See *159 L. Ed. 2d, at 368*. Congress understood that change to "provid[e] the possibility of U. S. judicial assistance in connection with [administrative and quasi-judicial proceedings abroad]." S. Rep. No. 1580, at 7–8; see Smit, International Litigation 1026–1027, and nn 71, 73 ("[t]he term 'tribunal' . . . includes investigating magistrates, administrative and arbitral tribunals, and quasi-judicial agencies, as well as conventional civil, commercial, criminal, and administrative courts"; in addition to affording assistance in cases before the European Court of Justice, *§1782*, as revised in 1964, "permits the rendition of proper aid in proceedings before the [European] Commission in which the Commission exercises quasi-judicial powers"). See also European Commission *Amicus Curiae* 9 ("[W]hen the Commission acts on DG Competition's final recommendation . . . the investigative function blur[s] into decisionmaking."). We have no warrant to exclude the European Commission, to the extent that it acts as a first-instance decisionmaker, from *§1782(a)*'s ambit. See *292 F.3d at 667*.

C

Intel also urges that AMD's complaint has not progressed beyond the investigative stage; therefore, no adjudicative action is currently or even imminently on the Commission's agenda. Brief for Petitioner 27–29.

Section 1782(a) does not limit the provision of judicial assistance to "pending" adjudicative proceedings. In 1964, when Congress eliminated the requirement that a proceeding be "judicial," Congress also deleted the requirement that a proceeding be "pending." See *159 L. Ed. 2d, at 368*. "When Congress acts to amend a statute, we presume it intends its amendment to have real and substantial effect." *Stone v. INS, 514 U.S. 386, 397, 131 L. Ed. 2d 465, 115 S. Ct. 1537 (1995)*. The legislative history of the 1964 revision is in sync; it reflects Congress' recognition that judicial assistance would be available "whether the foreign or international proceeding *or investigation* is of a criminal, civil, administrative, or other nature." S. Rep. No. 1580, at 9 (emphasis added).

In 1996, Congress amended *§1782(a)* to clarify that the statute covers "criminal investigations conducted before formal accusation." See §1342(b), 110 Stat 486; *159 L. Ed. 2d, at 368.* Nothing suggests that this amendment was an endeavor to rein in, rather than to confirm, by way of example, the broad range of discovery authorized in 1964. See S. Rep. No. 1580, at 7 ("[T]he [district] court[s] have discretion to grant assistance when proceedings are pending before investigating magistrates in foreign countries.").

In short, we reject the view, expressed in *In re Ishihara Chemical Co.*, that *§1782* comes into play only when adjudicative proceedings are "pending" or "imminent." See *251 F.3d, at 125* (proceeding must be "imminent – very likely to occur and very soon to occur" (internal quotation marks omitted)). Instead, we hold that *§1782(a)* requires only that a dispositive ruling by the Commission, reviewable by the European courts, be within reasonable contemplation. See *Crown Prosecution Service, 870 F.2d at 691*; *In re Request for Assistance from Ministry of Legal Affairs, 848 F.2d 1151, 1155, and n 9 (CA11 1988)*; Smit, International Litigation 1026 ("It is not necessary . . . for the [adjudicative] proceeding to be pending at the time the evidence is sought, but only that the evidence is eventually to be used in such a proceeding.").

D

We take up next the foreign-discoverability rule on which lower courts have divided: Does *§1782(a)* categorically bar a district court from ordering production of documents when the foreign tribunal or the "interested person" would not be able to obtain the documents if they were located in the foreign jurisdiction? See *159 L. Ed. 2d, at 369–370*, and n 7.

We note at the outset, and count it significant, that *§1782(a)* expressly shields privileged material: "A person may not be compelled to give his testimony or statement or to produce a document or other thing in violation of any legally applicable privilege." See S. Rep. No. 1580, at 9 ("[N]o person shall be required under the provisions of *[§1782]* to produce any evidence in violation of an applicable privilege."). Beyond shielding material safeguarded by an applicable privilege, however, nothing in the text of *§1782* limits a district court's production-order authority to materials that could be discovered in the foreign jurisdiction if the materials were located there. "If Congress had intended to impose such a sweeping restriction on the district court's discretion, at a time when it was enacting liberalizing amendments to the statute, it would have included statutory language to that effect." *In re Application of Gianoli Aldunate, 3 F.3d 54, 59 (CA2 1993)*; accord *Four Pillars Enters. Co. v. Avery Dennison Corp., 308 F.3d 1075, 1080 (CA9 2002)*; *292 F.3d, at 669* (case below); *In re Bayer AG, 146 F.3d 188, 193–194 (CA3 1998).*

Nor does *§1782(a)*'s legislative history suggest that Congress intended to impose a blanket foreign-discoverability rule on the provision of assistance under *§1782(a)*. The Senate Report observes in this regard that *§1782(a)* "leaves the issuance of an appropriate order to the discretion of the court which, in proper cases, may refuse to issue an order or may impose conditions it deems desirable." S. Rep. No. 1580, at 7.

Intel raises two policy concerns in support of a foreign-discoverability limitation on *§1782(a)* aid – avoiding offense to foreign governments, and maintaining parity between litigants. Brief for Petitioner 23–24; Reply Brief 5, 13–14; see *In re Application of Asta Medica, S. A., 981 F.2d 1, 6 (CA1 1992)* ("Congress did not seek to place itself on a collision course with foreign tribunals and legislatures, which have carefully chosen the procedures and laws best suited to their concepts of litigation."). While comity and parity concerns may be important as touchstones for a district court's exercise of discretion in particular cases, they do not permit our insertion of a generally applicable foreign-discoverability rule into the text of *§1782(a)*.

We question whether foreign governments would in fact be offended by a domestic prescription permitting, but not requiring, judicial assistance. A foreign nation may limit discovery within its domain for reasons peculiar to its own legal practices, culture, or traditions – reasons that do not necessarily signal objection to aid from United States federal courts. See *Bayer, 146 F.3d, at 194* ("[T]here is no reason to assume that because a country has not adopted a particular discovery procedure, it would take offense at its use."); Smit, Recent Developments in International Litigation, *35 S. Tex. L. Rev. 215, 235–236 (1994)* (hereinafter Smit, Recent Developments) (same). A foreign tribunal's reluctance to order production of materials present in the United States similarly may signal no resistance to the receipt of evidence gathered pursuant to *§1782(a)*. See *South Carolina Ins. Co.* v *Assurantie Maatschappij "De Zeven Provincien" N. V., [1987] 1 App. Cas. 24* (House of Lords ruled that nondiscoverability under English law did not stand in the way of a litigant in English proceedings seeking assistance in the United States under *§1782*). When the foreign tribunal would readily accept relevant information discovered in the United States, application of a foreign-discoverability rule would be senseless. The rule in that situation would serve only to thwart *§1782(a)*'s objective to assist foreign tribunals in obtaining relevant information that the tribunals may find useful but, for reasons having no bearing on international comity, they cannot obtain under their own laws.

Concerns about maintaining parity among adversaries in litigation likewise do not provide a sound basis for a cross-the-board foreign-discoverability rule. When information is sought by an "interested person," a district court could condition relief upon that person's reciprocal exchange of information. See *Euromepa, S. A. v. R. Esmerian, Inc., 51 F.3d 1095, 1102 (CA2 1995)*; Smit, Recent Developments 237. Moreover, the foreign tribunal can place conditions on its acceptance of the information to maintain whatever measure of parity it concludes is appropriate. See *Euromepa, 51 F.3d, at 1101*.

We also reject Intel's suggestion that a *§1782(a)* applicant must show that United States law would allow discovery in domestic litigation analogous to the foreign proceeding. Brief for Petitioner 19–20 ("[I]f AMD were pursuing this matter in the United States, U. S. law would preclude it from obtaining discovery of Intel's documents."). *Section 1782* is a provision for assistance to tribunals abroad. It does not direct United States courts to engage in comparative analysis to determine whether analogous proceedings exist here. Comparisons of that order can be fraught with danger. For example, we have in the United States no close analogue to the European

Commission regime under which AMD is not free to mount its own case in the Court of First Instance or the European Court of Justice, but can participate only as complainant, an "interested person," in Commission-steered proceedings. See L. Ritter, W. Braun, & F. Rawlinson, European Competition Law: A Practitioner's Guide 824–826 (2d ed. 2000) (describing a complaint as a potentially "more certain (and cheaper) alternative to private enforcement through the [European Union's member states'] courts").

IV

As earlier emphasized, see *159 L. Ed. 2d, at 375*, a district court is not required to grant a *§1782(a)* discovery application simply because it has the authority to do so. See *United Kingdom v. United States, 238 F.3d 1312, 1319 (CA11 2001)* ("a district court's compliance with a *§1782* request is not mandatory"). We note below factors that bear consideration in ruling on a *§1782(a)* request.

First, when the person from whom discovery is sought is a participant in the foreign proceeding (as Intel is here), the need for *§1782(a)* aid generally is not as apparent as it ordinarily is when evidence is sought from a nonparticipant in the matter arising abroad. A foreign tribunal has jurisdiction over those appearing before it, and can itself order them to produce evidence. App. to Reply Brief 4a ("When th[e] person [who is to produce the evidence] is a party to the foreign proceedings, the foreign or international tribunal can exercise its own jurisdiction to order production of the evidence." (quoting Decl. of H. Smit in *In re: Application of Ishihara Chemical Co., Ltd., For order to take discovery of Shipley Company, L.L.C., Pursuant to 28 USC §1782,* Misc. 99–232 (FB) (EDNY, May 18, 2000)). In contrast, nonparticipants in the foreign proceeding may be outside the foreign tribunal's jurisdictional reach; hence, their evidence, available in the United States, may be unobtainable absent *§1782(a)* aid. See App. to Reply Brief 4a.

Second, as the 1964 Senate Report suggests, a court presented with a *§1782(a)* request may take into account the nature of the foreign tribunal, the character of the proceedings underway abroad, and the receptivity of the foreign government or the court or agency abroad to U.S. federal-court judicial assistance. See S. Rep. No. 1580, at 7. Further, the grounds Intel urged for categorical limitations on *§1782(a)*'s scope may be relevant in determining whether a discovery order should be granted in a particular case. See Brief for United States as *Amicus Curiae* 23. Specifically, a district court could consider whether the *§1782(a)* request conceals an attempt to circumvent foreign proof-gathering restrictions or other policies of a foreign country or the United States. See *id.*, at 27. Also, unduly intrusive or burdensome requests may be rejected or trimmed. See *Bayer, 146 F.3d at 196* (remanding for district-court consideration of "appropriate measures, if needed, to protect the confidentiality of materials"); *Esses v. Hanania (In re Esses), 101 F.3d 873, 876 (CA2 1996)* (affirming limited discovery that is neither "burdensome [n]or duplicative").

Intel maintains that, if we do not accept the categorical limitations it proposes, then, at least, we should exercise our supervisory authority to adopt rules barring *§1782(a)* discovery here. Brief for Petitioner 34–36; cf. *Thomas v. Arn, 474 U.S. 140, 146–147, 88 L. Ed. 2d 435, 106 S. Ct. 466 (1985)* (this Court can establish rules of "sound judicial practice" (internal quotation marks omitted)). We decline, at this juncture, to adopt supervisory rules. Any such endeavor at least should await further experience with *§1782(a)* applications in the lower courts. The European Commission has stated in *amicus curiae* briefs to this Court that it does not need or want the District Court's assistance. See European Commission *Amicus Curiae* 11–16; Brief for European Commission as *Amicus Curiae* in Support of Pet. for Cert. 4–8. It is not altogether clear, however, whether the Commission, which may itself invoke *§1782(a)* aid, means to say "never" or "hardly ever" to judicial assistance from United States courts. Nor do we know whether the European Commission's views on *§1782(a)*'s utility are widely shared in the international community by entities with similarly blended adjudicative and prosecutorial functions.

Several facets of this case remain largely unexplored. Intel and its *amici* have expressed concerns that AMD's application, if granted in any part, may yield disclosure of confidential information, encourage "fishing expeditions," and undermine the European Commission's Leniency Program. See Brief for Petitioner 37; European Commission *Amicus Curiae* 11–16.[18] Yet no one has suggested that AMD's complaint to the Commission is pretextual. Nor has it been shown that *§1782(a)*'s preservation of legally applicable privileges, see *159 L. Ed. 2d, at 374–375*, and the controls on discovery available to the District Court, see, *e.g.*, *Fed. Rule Civ. Proc. 26(b)(2) and (c)*, would be ineffective to prevent discovery of Intel's business secrets and other confidential information.

On the merits, this case bears closer scrutiny than it has received to date. Having held that *§1782(a)* authorizes, but does not require, discovery assistance, we leave it to the courts below to assure an airing adequate to determine what, if any, assistance is appropriate.

For the reasons stated, the judgment of the Court of Appeals for the Ninth Circuit is affirmed.

BUCKEYE CHECK CASHING, INC. v. JOHN CARDEGNA ET AL.
SUPREME COURT OF THE UNITED STATES

546 U.S. 440

November 29, 2005, Argued
February 21, 2006, Decided

JUSTICE SCALIA delivered the opinion of the Court.

We decide whether a court or an arbitrator should consider the claim that a contract containing an arbitration provision is void for illegality.

I

Respondents John Cardegna and Donna Reuter entered into various deferred-payment transactions with petitioner Buckeye Check Cashing (Buckeye), in which they received cash in exchange for a personal check in the amount of the cash plus a finance charge. For each separate transaction they signed a "Deferred Deposit and Disclosure Agreement" (Agreement), which included the following arbitration provisions:

1. "*Arbitration Disclosure* By signing this Agreement, you agree that if a dispute of any kind arises out of this Agreement or your application therefore or any instrument relating thereto, then either you or we or third-parties involved can choose to have that dispute resolved by binding arbitration as set forth in Paragraph 2 below. . . .
2. *Arbitration Provisions* Any claim, dispute, or controversy . . . arising from or relating to this Agreement . . . or the validity, enforceability, or scope of this Arbitration Provision or the entire Agreement (collectively 'Claim'), shall be resolved, upon the election of you or us or said third-parties, by binding arbitration. . . . This arbitration Agreement is made pursuant to a transaction involving interstate commerce, and shall be governed by the Federal Arbitration Act ('FAA'), *9 U.S.C. Sections 1–16*. The arbitrator shall apply applicable substantive law constraint *[sic]* with the FAA and applicable statutes of limitations and shall honor claims of privilege recognized by law. . . ."

Respondents brought this putative class action in Florida state court, alleging that Buckeye charged usurious interest rates and that the Agreement violated various Florida lending and consumer-protection laws, rendering it criminal on its face. Buckeye moved to compel arbitration. The trial court denied the motion, holding that a court rather than an arbitrator should resolve a claim that a contract is illegal and void *ab initio*. The District Court of Appeal of Florida for the Fourth District reversed, holding that because respondents did not challenge the arbitration provision itself, but instead claimed that the entire contract was void, the agreement to arbitrate was enforceable, and the question of the contract's legality should go to the arbitrator.

Respondents appealed, and the Florida Supreme Court reversed, reasoning that to enforce an agreement to arbitrate in a contract challenged as unlawful "'could breathe life into a contract that not only violates state law, but also is criminal in nature. . . .'" *894 So. 2d 860, 862 (2005)* (quoting *Party Yards, Inc. v. Templeton, 751 So. 2d 121, 123 (Fla. App. 2000))*. We granted certiorari. *545 U.S. 1127, 125 S. Ct. 2937, 162 L. Ed. 2d 864 (2005)*.

II

A

To overcome judicial resistance to arbitration, Congress enacted the Federal Arbitration Act(FAA), *9 U.S.C. §§1–16*. *Section 2* embodies the national policy favoring arbitration and places arbitration agreements on equal footing with all other contracts:

> "A written provision in . . . a contract . . . to settle by arbitration a controversy thereafter arising out of such contract . . . or an agreement in writing to submit to arbitration an existing controversy arising out of such a contract . . . shall be

valid, irrevocable, and enforceable, save upon such grounds as exist at law or in equity for the revocation of any contract."

Challenges to the validity of arbitration agreements "upon such grounds as exist at law or in equity for the revocation of any contract" can be divided into two types. One type challenges specifically the validity of the agreement to arbitrate. See, *e.g., Southland Corp. v. Keating, 465 U.S. 1, 4–5, 104 S. Ct. 852, 79 L. Ed. 2d 1 (1984)* (challenging the agreement to arbitrate as void under California law insofar as it purported to cover claims brought under the state Franchise Investment Law). The other challenges the contract as a whole, either on a ground that directly affects the entire agreement (*e.g.*, the agreement was fraudulently induced), or on the ground that the illegality of one of the contract's provisions renders the whole contract invalid. Respondents' claim is of this second type. The crux of the complaint is that the contract as a whole (including its arbitration provision) is rendered invalid by the usurious finance charge.

In *Prima Paint Corp. v. Flood & Conklin Mfg. Co., 388 U.S. 395, 87 S. Ct. 1801, 18 L. Ed. 2d 1270 (1967)*, we addressed the question of who – court or arbitrator – decides these two types of challenges. The issue in the case was "whether a claim of fraud in the inducement of the entire contract is to be resolved by the federal court, or whether the matter is to be referred to the arbitrators." *Id., at 402, 87 S. Ct. 1801, 18 L. Ed. 2d 1270.* Guided by *§4 of the FAA*, we held that "if the claim is fraud in the inducement of the arbitration clause itself – an issue which goes to the making of the agreement to arbitrate – the federal court may proceed to adjudicate it. But the statutory language does not permit the federal court to consider claims of fraud in the inducement of the contract generally." *Id., at 403–404, 87 S. Ct. 1801, 18 L. Ed. 2d 1270* (internal quotation marks and footnote omitted). We rejected the view that the question of "severability" was one of state law, so that if state law held the arbitration provision not to be severable a challenge to the contract as a whole would be decided by the court. See *id., at 400, 402–403, 87 S. Ct. 1801, 18 L. Ed. 2d 1270.*

Subsequently, in *Southland Corp.*, we held that the FAA "created a body of federal substantive law," which was "applicable in state and federal court." *465 U.S., at 12, 104 S. Ct. 852, 79 L. Ed. 2d 1* (internal quotation marks omitted). We rejected the view that state law could bar enforcement of §2, even in the context of state-law claims brought in state court. See *id., at 10–14, 104 S. Ct. 852, 79 L. Ed. 2d 1*; see also *Allied-Bruce Terminix Cos. v. Dobson, 513 U.S. 265, 270–273, 115 S. Ct. 834, 130 L. Ed. 2d 753 (1995).*

B

Prima Paint and *Southland* answer the question presented here by establishing three propositions. First, as a matter of substantive federal arbitration law, an arbitration provision is severable from the remainder of the contract. Second, unless the challenge is to the arbitration clause itself, the issue of the contract's validity is considered by the arbitrator in the first instance. Third, this arbitration law applies in state as well as federal courts. The parties have not requested, and we do not undertake, reconsideration of those holdings. Applying them to this case, we conclude that because respondents challenge the Agreement, but not specifically its arbitration provisions, those provisions are enforceable apart from the remainder of the contract. The challenge should therefore be considered by an arbitrator, not a court.

In declining to apply *Prima Paint*'s rule of severability, the Florida Supreme Court relied on the distinction between void and voidable contracts. "Florida public policy and contract law," it concluded, permit "no severable, or salvageable, parts of a contract found illegal and void under Florida law." *894 So. 2d, at 864*. *Prima Paint* makes this conclusion irrelevant. That case rejected application of state severability rules to the arbitration agreement *without discussing* whether the challenge at issue would have rendered the contract void or voidable. See *388 U.S., at 400–404, 87 S. Ct. 1801, 18 L. Ed. 2d 1270*. Indeed, the opinion expressly disclaimed any need to decide what state-law remedy was available, *id., at 400, n. 3, 87 S. Ct. 1801, 18 L. Ed. 2d 1270*, (though Justice Black's dissent *asserted* that state law rendered the contract void, *id., at 407, 87 S. Ct. 1801, 18 L. Ed. 2d 1270*). Likewise in *Southland*, which arose in state court, we did not ask whether the several challenges made there – fraud, misrepresentation, breach of contract, breach of fiduciary duty, and violation of the California Franchise Investment Law – would render the contract void or voidable. We simply rejected the proposition that the enforceability of the arbitration agreement turned on the state legislature's judgment concerning the forum for enforcement of the state-law cause of action. See *465 U.S., at 10, 104 S. Ct. 852, 79 L. Ed. 2d 1*. So also here, we cannot accept the Florida Supreme Court's conclusion that enforceability of the arbitration agreement should turn on "Florida public policy and contract law," *894 So. 2d, at 864*.

C

Respondents assert that *Prima Paint*'s rule of severability does not apply in state court. They argue that *Prima Paint* interpreted only *§§3* and *4* – two of the FAA's procedural provisions, which appear to apply by their terms only in federal court – but not *§2*, the only provision that we have applied in state court. This does not accurately describe *Prima Paint*. Although *§4*, in particular, had much to do with *Prima Paint*'s understanding of the rule of severability, see *388 U.S., at 403–404, 87 S. Ct. 1801, 18 L. Ed. 2d 1270*, this rule ultimately arises out of *§2, the FAA*'s substantive command that arbitration agreements be treated like all other contracts. The rule of severability establishes how this equal-footing guarantee for "a written [arbitration] provision" is to be implemented. Respondents' reading of *Prima Paint* as establishing nothing more than a federal-court rule of procedure also runs contrary to *Southland*'s understanding of that case. One of the bases for *Southland*'s application of *§2* in state court was precisely *Prima Paint*'s "reliance for [its] holding on Congress' broad power to fashion substantive rules under the *Commerce Clause*." *465 U.S., at 11, 104 S. Ct. 852, 79 L. Ed. 2d 1*; see also *Prima Paint, supra, at 407, 87 S. Ct. 1801, 18 L. Ed. 2d 1270* (Black, J., dissenting) ("the Court here holds that the [FAA], as a matter of *federal substantive law* . . ." (emphasis added)). *Southland* itself refused to "believe Congress intended to limit the Arbitration Act to disputes subject only to *federal*-court jurisdiction." *465 U.S., at 15, 104 S. Ct. 852, 79 L. Ed. 2d 1*.

Respondents point to the language of *§2*, which renders "valid, irrevocable, and enforceable" "a written provision in" or "an agreement in writing to submit to arbitration an existing controversy arising out of" a "contract." Since, respondents argue, the only arbitration agreements to which §2 applies are those involving a "contract," and since an agreement void *ab initio* under state law is not a "contract," there is no "written provision" in or "controversy arising out of" a "contract," to which §2 can apply. This argument echoes Justice Black's dissent in *Prima Paint:* "*Sections 2* and *3* of the Act assume the existence of a valid contract. They merely provide for enforcement where such a valid contract exists." *388 U.S., at 412–413, 87 S. Ct. 1801, 18 L. Ed. 2d 1270.* We do not read "contract" so narrowly. The word appears four times in §2. Its last appearance is in the final clause, which allows a challenge to an arbitration provision "upon such grounds as exist at law or in equity for the revocation of any *contract.*" (Emphasis added.) There can be no doubt that "contract" as used this last time must include contracts that later prove to be void. Otherwise, the grounds for revocation would be limited to those that rendered a contract voidable – which would mean (implausibly) that an arbitration agreement could be challenged as voidable but not as void. Because the sentence's final use of "contract" so obviously includes putative contracts, we will not read the same word earlier in the same sentence to have a more narrow meaning. We note that neither *Prima Paint* nor *Southland* lends support to respondents' reading; as we have discussed, neither case turned on whether the challenge at issue would render the contract voidable or void.

It is true, as respondents assert, that the *Prima Paint* rule permits a court to enforce an arbitration agreement in a contract that the arbitrator later finds to be void. But it is equally true that respondents' approach permits a court to deny effect to an arbitration provision in a contract that the court later finds to be perfectly enforceable. *Prima Paint* resolved this conundrum – and resolved it in favor of the separate enforceability of arbitration provisions. We reaffirm today that, regardless of whether the challenge is brought in federal or state court, a challenge to the validity of the contract as a whole, and not specifically to the arbitration clause, must go to the arbitrator.

The judgment of the Florida Supreme Court is reversed, and the case is remanded for further proceedings not inconsistent with this opinion.

It is so ordered.

THOMSON-CSF, S.A., Plaintiff-Appellant, v. AMERICAN ARBITRATION ASSOCIATION, Defendant, EVANS & SUTHERLAND COMPUTER CORPORATION, Defendant-Appellee.

UNITED STATES COURT OF APPEALS FOR THE SECOND CIRCUIT

64 F.3d 773

April 18, 1995, Argued
August 24, 1995, Decided

ALTIMARI, Circuit Judge:

Plaintiff-appellant Thomson-CSF, S.A. ("Thomson") appeals from a judgment entered in the United States District Court for the Southern District of New York (Keenan, J.), denying its request for declaratory and injunctive relief and granting defendant-appellee Evans & Sutherland Computer Corporation's ("E & S") cross-motion to compel arbitration. Thomson asserts that the district court improvidently compelled it to arbitrate against E & S based upon an arbitration agreement between E & S and Thomson's subsidiary, to which Thomson was not a signatory. Because, under ordinary principles of contract and agency law, Thomson cannot be said to have voluntarily submitted to arbitrate its disputes with E & S, we reverse the judgment of the district court and remand for proceedings consistent with this opinion.

BACKGROUND

Rediffusion Simulation Limited ("Rediffusion") was a British company engaged in the business of building flight simulators for the training of pilots. In 1986, Rediffusion entered into a "Working Agreement" with E & S, located in Salt Lake City, Utah. Under the Working Agreement, Rediffusion agreed to purchase computer-generated image equipment (the computer "brain" of the flight simulator) exclusively from E & S and to use its best efforts to market those systems containing E & S equipment; in return, E & S agreed to supply its imaging equipment only to Rediffusion.

Subsequent to entering into the Working Agreement, Rediffusion was sold to Hughes Aircraft Company. Hughes amended and extended the Working Agreement between Rediffusion and E & S. On December 31, 1993, Hughes sold Rediffusion to Thomson, which renamed it Thomson Training and Simulation Limited. Prior to purchasing Rediffusion, Thompson maintained a division engaged in the business of building flight simulation equipment (the Training and Simulation Systems Division) into which it began integrating Rediffusion.

At the time Thomson began publicly contemplating the acquisition of Rediffusion, E & S informed Thomson that, if it purchased Rediffusion, E & S intended to bind Thomson and its flight simulation division to the Working Agreement. Specifically, E & S told Thomson that upon purchasing Rediffusion both Rediffusion and Thomson's Training and Simulation Systems Division would be required to purchase all needed computer-generated image equipment from E & S. In response, Thomson wrote to E & S seeking to have it waive those provisions of the Working Agreement that E & S believed to be binding upon Thomson. Thomson did not, however, concede that it would be bound by Rediffusion's Working Agreement. In fact, when it became clear that Thomson and E & S could reach no agreement prior to Thomson's acquisition of Rediffusion, Thomson explicitly informed E & S that it was not adopting the Working Agreement and did not consider itself bound by Rediffusion's Agreement which it had neither negotiated nor signed.

The Working Agreement

Section 6.1 of the Working Agreement provides for the arbitration of all disputes between the "parties" to the Agreement. While the Agreement provides no explicit definition of "parties," it does define "E & S" and "Rediffusion":

> 1.14 the term "E & S," wherever used in this Working Agreement, shall include the affiliates of E & S. The term "Rediffusion" wherever used in this Working Agreement, shall . . . mean Rediffusion and each of its affiliates.

1.6 An "affiliate" of a party hereto shall mean any person, firm or corporation that, directly or indirectly, through one or more intermediaries, controls, or is controlled by, or is under common control with, such party.

Despite the lack of definition for "parties" in the Working Agreement, the district court found that the term "parties" was intended to mean "E & S and Rediffusion" and, therefore, was also intended to include the affiliates of the parties. Accordingly, the arbitration clause in the Working Agreement purported to bind not only Rediffusion, but also its affiliates – namely, Thomson (given that Thomson indisputably controlled Rediffusion).

Injunctive Relief

While under Thomson's ownership, Rediffusion's share of the flight simulator market drastically decreased. On August 8, 1994, E & S filed a demand for arbitration under the Working Agreement against both Rediffusion and its parent-company Thomson, asserting a breach of their obligations arising out of the Working Agreement. Despite Thomson's insistence that it was not bound by the Working Agreement (and the arbitration clause contained therein), E & S filed a demand for arbitration against both Rediffusion and Thomson on August 8, 1994. While Rediffusion did not contest the applicability of the arbitration clause to it, Thomson refused to answer E & S's demand for arbitration. On August 29, 1994, Thomson commenced this action in the Southern District of New York, seeking 1) a declaration that it was not bound by the arbitration clause of the Working Agreement and 2) an injunction prohibiting further proceedings against it under the Working Agreement. E & S cross-moved to compel Thomson to arbitrate.

The district court granted E & S's cross-motion to compel arbitration. In doing so, the district court stated that while E & S's claims did not fall under any of the traditional categories for binding a nonsignatory to an arbitration clause, Thomson was bound nonetheless. Adopting a hybrid approach to binding a nonsignatory to an arbitration agreement, the district court accepted E & S's assertion that "the Court may bind Thomson based on its conduct in voluntarily becoming . . . an affiliate, on the degree of control Thomson exercises over [Rediffusion], and on the interrelatedness of the issues."

DISCUSSION

Arbitration is contractual by nature – "a party cannot be required to submit to arbitration any dispute which he has not agreed so to submit." *United Steelworkers of America v. Warrior & Gulf Navigation Co., 363 U.S. 574, 582, 4 L. Ed. 2d 1409, 80 S. Ct. 1347 (1960)*. Thus, while there is a strong and "liberal federal policy favoring arbitration agreements," *Mitsubishi Motors Corp. v. Soler Chrysler-Plymouth, Inc., 473 U.S. 614, 625, 87 L. Ed. 2d 444, 105 S. Ct. 3346 (1985)* (quotations omitted), such agreements must not be so broadly construed as to encompass claims and parties that were not intended by the original contract. "It does not follow, however, that under the [Federal Arbitration] Act an obligation to arbitrate attaches only to one who has personally signed the written arbitration provision." *Fisser v. International Bank, 282*

F.2d 231, 233 (2d Cir. 1960); see also *Deloitte Noraudit A/S v. Deloitte Haskins & Sells, U.S., 9 F.3d 1060, 1064 (2d Cir. 1993)*. This Court has made clear that a nonsignatory party may be bound to an arbitration agreement if so dictated by the "ordinary principles of contract and agency." *McAllister Bros., Inc. v. A & S Transp. Co., 621 F.2d 519, 524 (2d Cir. 1980)*; see also *A/S Custodia v. Lessin Int'l, Inc., 503 F.2d 318, 320 (2d Cir. 1974)*.

I. Traditional Bases for Binding Nonsignatories

This Court has recognized a number of theories under which nonsignatories may be bound to the arbitration agreements of others. Those theories arise out of common law principles of contract and agency law. Accordingly, we have recognized five theories for binding nonsignatories to arbitration agreements: 1) incorporation by reference; 2) assumption; 3) agency; 4) veil-piercing/alter ego; and 5) estoppel. The district court properly rejected each of these traditional theories as sufficient justification for binding Thomson to the arbitration agreement of its subsidiary.

A. Incorporation by Reference

A nonsignatory may compel arbitration against a party to an arbitration agreement when that party has entered into a separate contractual relationship with the nonsignatory which incorporates the existing arbitration clause. See *Import Export Steel Corp. v. Mississippi Valley Barge Line Co., 351 F.2d 503, 505–506 (2d Cir. 1965)* (separate agreement with nonsignatory expressly "assuming all the obligations and privileges of [signatory party] under the subcharter" constitutes grounds for enforcement of arbitration clause by nonsignatory); *Matter of Arbitration Between Keystone Shipping Co. and Texport Oil Co., 782 F. Supp. 28, 31 (S.D.N.Y. 1992)*; *Continental U.K. Ltd. v. Anagel Confidence Compania Naviera, S.A., 658 F. Supp. 809, 813 (S.D.N.Y. 1987)* (if a "party's arbitration clause is expressly incorporated into a bill of lading, nonsignatories who are linked to that bill through general principles of contract law or agency law may be bound"). As the district court noted, E & S has not attempted to show that the Working Agreement was incorporated into any document which Thomson adopted. Thus, Thomson cannot be bound under an incorporation theory.

B. Assumption

In the absence of a signature, a party may be bound by an arbitration clause if its subsequent conduct indicates that it is assuming the obligation to arbitrate. See *Gvozdenovic v. United Air Lines, Inc., 933 F.2d 1100, 1105* (2d Cir.) (flight attendants manifested a clear intention to arbitrate by sending a representative to act on their behalf in arbitration process), cert. denied, *502 U.S. 910, 116 L. Ed. 2d 248, 112 S. Ct. 305 (1991)*; *Keystone Shipping, 782 F. Supp. at 31*; *In re Transrol Navegacao S.A., 782 F. Supp. 848, 851 (S.D.N.Y. 1991)*. While Thomson was aware that the Working Agreement purported to bind it as an "affiliate" of Rediffusion, at no time did Thomson manifest an intention to be bound by that Agreement. In fact, Thomson explicitly disavowed any obligations arising out of the Working Agreement and filed this action seeking a declaration of non-liability under the Agreement. Accordingly, it cannot be said that Thomson assumed the obligation to arbitrate.

C. Agency

Traditional principles of agency law may bind a nonsignatory to an arbitration agreement. See *Interbras Cayman Co. v. Orient Victory Shipping Co., S.A., 663 F.2d 4, 6–7 (2d Cir. 1981)*; *A/S Custodia, 503 F.2d at 320*; *Fisser, 282 F.2d at 233–38*; *Keystone Shipping, 782 F. Supp. at 31–32*. Because the Working Agreement was entered into well before Thomson purchased Rediffusion, Thomson could not possibly be bound under an agency theory.

D. Veil Piercing/Alter Ego

In some instances, the corporate relationship between a parent and its subsidiary are sufficiently close as to justify piercing the corporate veil and holding one corporation legally accountable for the actions of the other. As a general matter, however, a corporate relationship alone is not sufficient to bind a nonsignatory to an arbitration agreement. See *Keystone Shipping, 782 F. Supp. at 30–31*. Nonetheless, the courts will pierce the corporate veil "in two broad situations: to prevent fraud or other wrong, or where a parent dominates and controls a subsidiary." Carte Blanche (Singapore) *Pte., Ltd. v. Diners Club Int'l, Inc., 2 F.3d 24, 26 (2d Cir. 1993)*; see also *Wm. Passalacqua Builders, Inc. v. Resnick Developers S., Inc., 933 F.2d 131, 138–39 (2d Cir. 1991)* ("Liability may be predicated either upon a showing of fraud or upon complete control by the dominating corporation that leads to a wrong against third parties."). While the district court below noted that, "counsel for E & S also denied at oral-argument that its claim was properly articulated as veil-piercing," E & S now asserts that an alter ego relationship between Thomson and Rediffusion may exist. While E & S concedes that it can make no showing of fraud, it argues that Thomson sufficiently dominated Rediffusion as to justify veil piercing.

Veil piercing determinations are fact specific and "differ with the circumstances of each case." *American Protein Corp. v. AB Volvo, 844 F.2d 56, 60* (2d Cir.), cert. denied, *488 U.S. 852, 102 L. Ed. 2d 109, 109 S. Ct. 136 (1988)*. This Court has determined that a parent corporation and its subsidiary lose their distinct corporate identities when their conduct demonstrates a virtual abandonment of separateness. See Carte Blanche, 2 F.3d at 29 ("No bank accounts, offices, stationery, transactions, or any other activities were maintained or carried on in the name of [the subsidiary]."); *Wm. Passalacqua, 933 F.2d at 139* (corporate veil is pierced where, among other things, parent and subsidiary 1) share common office and staff; 2) are run by common officers; 3) intermingle funds; 4) do not deal at arms length with each other; and 5) are not treated as separate profit centers); see also *Walter E. Heller & Co. v. Video Innovations, Inc., 730 F.2d 50, 53 (2d Cir. 1984)* (absence of corporate formalities relevant factor in piercing corporate veil). "The factors that determine the question of control and domination are less subjective than 'good faith'; they relate to how the corporation was actually operated." Carte Blanche, 2 F.3d at 28–29.

E & S has not demonstrated that Thomson exerted the degree of control over Rediffusion necessary to justify piercing the corporate veil. While the district court found that "Thomson has common ownership with [Rediffusion]; that Thomson actually controls [Rediffusion]; [and] that Thomson incorporated [Rediffusion] into its own organizational and decision-making structure," the district court did not find an abandonment of the corporate structure. E & S has not shown an absence of corporate formalities, nor has it shown an intermingling of corporate finances and directorship. Rather, as the district court found, Rediffusion continued to function as a distinct entity closely incorporated into the existing corporate structure of its parent company, Thomson. Accordingly, in light of the totality of the circumstances, Thomson cannot be bound by Rediffusion's arbitration agreement under a veil piercing/alter ego theory.

E. Estoppel

This Court has also bound nonsignatories to arbitration agreements under an estoppel theory. In *Deloitte Noraudit A/S v. Deloitte Haskins & Sells, U.S., 9 F.3d 1060, 1064 (2d Cir. 1993)*, a foreign accounting firm received a settlement agreement concerning the use of the trade name "Deloitte" in association with accounting practices. Under the agreement – containing an arbitration clause – local affiliates of the international accounting association Deloitte Haskins & Sells International were entitled to use the trade name "Deloitte" in exchange for compliance with the dictates of the agreement. A Norwegian accounting firm received the agreement, made no objection to the terms of the agreement, and proceeded to utilize the trade name. This Court held that by knowingly exploiting the agreement, the accounting firm was estopped from avoiding arbitration despite having never signed the agreement. See *9 F.3d at 1064* ("Noraudit failed to object to the Agreement when it received it.... In addition, Noraudit knowingly accepted the benefits of the Agreement.... Thus, Noraudit is estopped from denying its obligation to arbitrate under the 1990 Agreement.").

Although the district court did not analyze the case at hand under an estoppel theory, the court specifically found that:

> Thomson had notice of the Working Agreement prior to ... completing the purchase of Rediffusion, that E & S expressed the intention to bind Thomson to the Agreement prior to the completion of the purchase of Rediffusion, that Thomson incorporated [Rediffusion] into its own organizational and decision-making structure, and that Thomson benefitted from that incorporation.

On their face, these factual findings appear sufficient to bind Thomson to the arbitration clause of its subsidiary under Deloitte. Upon closer inspection, however, the district court's determination that Thomson derived direct benefit from the Working Agreement is erroneous.

As Thomson points out, the Working Agreement provided that Rediffusion would purchase computer-generated image equipment exclusively from E & S and, in return, E & S would supply its imaging equipment only to Rediffusion. E & S concedes that Thomson has never acquired, nor sought to acquire, imaging equipment from E & S. Rather, E & S asserts a theory of benefit under the Working Agreement which in essence amounts to an anti-trust violation – according to E & S, Thomson purchased Rediffusion (its only serious competitor in the flight simulation industry) so that it could keep Rediffusion from competing; by incorporating Rediffusion into its own structure, Thomson was able to eliminate all simulators utilizing E & S imaging equipment from the market; because E & S was contractually bound to supply only Rediffusion with imaging equipment, it was effectively shut out of the market; thus, E & S contends that Thomson benefitted from the Working Agreement by eliminating E & S as a competitor.

This indirect benefit which E & S asserts – and the district court implicitly adopts – is not the sort of benefit which this Court envisioned as the basis for estopping a nonsignatory from avoiding arbitration. Had Thomson *directly* benefitted from the Working Agreement by seeking to purchase equipment from E & S or enforcing the exclusivity provisions of the Agreement, it would be estopped from avoiding arbitration. The benefit which E & S asserts, however, derives directly from Thomson's purchase of Rediffusion, and not from the Working Agreement itself; Thomson received no benefit at all from the Working Agreement (as opposed to the acquisition). Thus, Thomson is not bound by its subsidiary's arbitration agreement under Deloitte.

Several courts of appeal have recognized an alternative estoppel theory requiring arbitration between a signatory and nonsignatory. See *Sunkist Soft Drinks, Inc. v. Sunkist Growers, Inc., 10 F.3d 753, 757–58 (11th Cir. 1993)*, cert. denied, *115 S. Ct. 190 (1994)*; *J.J. Ryan & Sons, Inc. v. Rhone Poulenc Textile, S.A., 863 F.2d 315, 320–21 (4th Cir. 1988)*; *McBro Planning & Dev. Co. v. Triangle Elec. Constr. Co., 741 F.2d 342, 344 (7th Cir. 1984)*. In these cases, a signatory was bound to arbitrate with a nonsignatory at the nonsignatory's insistence because of "the close relationship between the entities involved, as well as the relationship of the alleged wrongs to the nonsignatory's obligations and duties in the contract . . . and [the fact that] the claims were 'intimately founded in and intertwined with the underlying contract obligations.'" *Sunkist, 10 F.3d at 757* (quoting *McBro Planning, 741 F.2d at 344*). It is clear that an arbitration clause bound Thomson's subsidiary, Rediffusion. The district court also found that the management of Rediffusion and Thomson were closely related. Moreover, E & S argues that the claims against Thomson are "intimately founded in and intertwined with" the Working Agreement. Nonetheless, Thomson can not be bound to arbitrate under this line of cases.

As these cases indicate, the circuits have been willing to estop a *signatory* from avoiding arbitration with a nonsignatory when the issues the nonsignatory is seeking to resolve in arbitration are intertwined with the agreement that the estopped party has signed. As the district court pointed out, however, "the situation here is inverse: E & S, as signatory, seeks to compel Thomson, a non-signatory." While E & S suggests that this is a non-distinction, the nature of arbitration makes it important. Arbitration is strictly a matter of contract; if the parties have not agreed to arbitrate, the courts have no authority to mandate that they do so. See *United Steelworkers, 363 U.S. at 582*. In the line of cases discussed above, the courts held that the parties were estopped from avoiding arbitration because they had entered into written arbitration agreements, albeit with the affiliates of those parties asserting the arbitration and not the parties themselves. Thomson, however, cannot be estopped from denying the existence of an arbitration clause to which it is a signatory because no such clause exists. At no point did Thomson indicate a willingness to arbitrate with E & S. Therefore, the district court properly determined these estoppel cases to be inapposite and insufficient justification for binding Thomson to an agreement that it never signed.

Moreover, these estoppel cases all involve claims which are integrally related to the contract containing the arbitration clause. The same cannot be said of the case at hand. As discussed above, E & S's claims against Thomson amount to the assertion that Thomson purchased Rediffusion in order to eliminate it as a competitor. While a cause of action may lie against Thomson for such alleged predatory business practices, the violation can hardly be characterized as arising out of or being integrally related to the Working Agreement between E & S and Rediffusion. Thus, the analogy to this line of estoppel cases again must fail.

II. The District Court's Hybrid Approach

Despite properly determining that E & S's claims did not fall within any of the traditional theories for binding a nonsignatory, the district court stated, "nevertheless, E & S asserts that the Court may bind Thomson based on its conduct in 'voluntarily becoming an affiliate,' on the degree of control Thomson exercises over [Rediffusion], and on the interrelatedness of the issues. This Court agrees." (citations omitted). In so doing, the district court improperly extended the law of this Circuit and diluted the protections afforded nonsignatories by the "ordinary principles of contract and agency." *McAllister, 621 F.2d at 524*. A nonsignatory may not be bound to arbitrate except as dictated by some accepted theory under agency or contract law.

The district court's opinion relies principally upon two decisions of this Court, McAllister and Deloitte. According to the district court, these cases in combination provide sufficient support to bind Thomson to the arbitration clause despite Thomson having never signed the Agreement. The district court found that many of the elements present in McAllister and Deloitte were also present in the case at hand: 1) Thomson's common ownership of Rediffusion; 2) Thomson's actual control of Rediffusion; 3) Thomson's notice of the Working Agreement prior to purchasing Rediffusion; 4) E & S's express intention to bind Thomson to the Working Agreement; 5) Thomson's incorporation of Rediffusion into its own organizational and decision-making structure; and 6) Thomson's benefit from that incorporation. Based upon the totality of these factors, the district court held that McAllister and Deloitte bound Thomson to Rediffusion's arbitration clause.

The district court's reliance upon McAllister and Deloitte is misplaced. Both McAllister and Deloitte fall squarely within traditional theories for binding nonsignatories to an arbitration agreement. In McAllister, this Court remanded the case to the district court for an evidentiary hearing in light of indications (on a "scant record") of a close affiliation between the signatory and nonsignatory. This Court, however, specifically instructed the district court to apply "ordinary principles of contract and agency," and clearly pointed to the traditional theories of agency and piercing the corporate veil when directing the district court to reconsider its determination. *621 F.2d at 524*. The district court's reliance on Deloitte is equally misplaced. As in McAllister, this Court in Deloitte stated that the district court should apply "ordinary principles of contract and agency." *9 F.3d at 1064*. This Court again pointed to traditional theories for binding nonsignatories, specifically estoppel and agency. Id. ("We believe that appellants have . . . strong arguments, particularly those based upon estoppel."). Neither McAllister or Deloitte indicate that a nonsignatory can be bound to an arbitration agreement with a less than full showing of some articulable theory under contract or agency law.

The district court below improperly extended the limited theories upon which this Court is willing to enforce an arbitration agreement against a nonsignatory. The district court's hybrid approach dilutes the safeguards afforded to a nonsignatory by the "ordinary principles of contract and agency" and fails to adequately protect parent companies, the subsidiaries of which have entered into arbitration agreements. Anything short of requiring a *full* showing of some accepted theory under agency or contract law imperils a vast number of parent corporations. This Court did not intend such an outcome in Deloitte or McAllister and does not adopt such an approach here.

CONCLUSION

Accordingly, the judgment of the district court is reversed and remanded for proceedings consistent with the foregoing.

BAKER MARINE (NIG.) LTD., Petitioner-Appellant, v. CHEVRON (NIG.) LTD. and CHEVRON CORP., INC., Respondents-Appellees. BAKER MARINE (NIG.) LTD., Petitioner-Appellant, v. DANOS AND CUROLE MARINE CONTRACTORS, INC., Respondent-Appellee.

UNITED STATES COURT OF APPEALS FOR THE SECOND CIRCUIT

191 F.3d 194

September 23, 1998, Argued
August 12, 1999, Decided

LEVAL, Circuit Judge:

Baker Marine (Nig.) Ltd. ("Baker Marine") appeals from two judgments of the United States District Court for the Northern District of New York (Thomas J. McAvoy, *District Judge*), in favor of appellees Chevron-Nigeria and Chevron Corporation ("Chevron") and Danos and Curole Marine Contractors, Inc. ("Danos").

BACKGROUND

Baker Marine, Danos, and Chevron are corporations involved in Nigeria's oil industry. In September 1992, Baker Marine and Danos entered a contract to bid to provide barge services for Chevron. Baker Marine agreed it would provide local support, while Danos agreed it would provide management and technical equipment. The bid by Baker Marine and Danos was successful, and in October 1992, the two companies jointly entered a contract with Chevron to provide barge services.

The contract with Chevron included provisions for the arbitration of disputes which the contract between Baker Marine and Danos incorporated by reference. These provisions stated that "any dispute, controversy or claim arising out of this

Contract, or the breach, termination or validity thereof, shall be finally and conclusively settled by arbitration in accordance with the Arbitration Rules of the United Nations Commission on International Trade Law (UNCITRAL)." Two different clauses further specified that the arbitration "procedure (insofar as not governed by said UNCITRAL rules . . .) shall be governed by the substantive laws of the Federal Republic of Nigeria" and that the contracts "shall be interpreted in accordance with the laws of the Federal Republic of Nigeria." The contracts also provided that "judgment upon the award of the arbitrators may be entered in any court having jurisdiction thereof," and that the contract and awards under it "shall be governed by the 1958 United Nations Convention on Recognition and Enforcement of Foreign Arbitration Awards ['Convention' or 'New York Convention']." The United States and Nigeria are parties to the Convention.

Baker Marine charged Chevron and Danos with violating the contracts. Pursuant to those contracts, the parties submitted to arbitration before panels of arbitrators in Lagos, Nigeria. By written decisions of early 1996, one panel of arbitrators awarded Baker Marine $2.23 million in damages against Danos a second panel awarded Baker Marine $750,000 in damages against Chevron.

Baker Marine promptly sought enforcement of both awards in the Nigerian Federal High Court. Danos and Chevron appealed to the same court to vacate the awards on various grounds. By written opinions of November 1996 and May 1997, the Nigerian court set aside the two arbitration awards. In the Chevron action, the court concluded that the arbitrators had improperly awarded punitive damages, gone beyond the scope of the submissions, incorrectly admitted parole evidence, and made inconsistent awards, among other things. The court found that the Danos award was unsupported by the evidence.

In August 1997, Baker Marine brought these actions in the Northern District of New York seeking confirmation of the awards under the United States law implementing the Convention, chapter 2 of the Federal Arbitration Act("FAA"), *9 U.S.C. §§201–09.*

The district court denied Baker Marine's petitions to enforce the arbitral awards, concluding that under the Convention and principles of comity, "it would not be proper to enforce a foreign arbitral award under the Convention when such an award has been set aside by the Nigerian courts." Baker Marine appeals.

This dispute falls under the Convention because Baker Marine is seeking enforcement of arbitration awards in a nation other than the nation where the awards were made. *See* Convention, art. I ("This Convention shall apply to the recognition and enforcement of arbitral awards made in the territory of a State other than the State where the recognition and enforcement of such awards are sought"). Under American law, when a party brings an action to confirm an arbitration award falling under the Convention, a court "shall confirm the award unless it finds one of the grounds for refusal or deferral of recognition or enforcement of the award specified in the said Convention." *9 U.S.C. §207.* Article V of the Convention provides that a court may refuse to enforce an arbitration award "only" upon proof of the conditions specified therein. Convention, art. V; *see also Yusuf Ahmed Alghanim & Sons v. Toys "R" Us, Inc., 126 F.3d 15, 20 (2d Cir. 1997)* (Article V provides exclusive grounds for setting aside an arbitral award), *cert. denied, 522 U.S. 1111, 118 S. Ct. 1042, 140 L. Ed. 2d 107 (1998).* Article V(1)(e) provides that a court may refuse enforcement of an award that "has been set aside or suspended by a competent authority of the country in which, or under the law of which, the award was made." Convention, art. V(1)(e). Baker Marine does not contest that the Nigerian High Court is a competent authority in the country in which, and under the law of which, the award was made. The district court relied on the decision of the Nigerian court and Article V(1)(e) in declining to enforce the award.

Baker Marine argues that the district court's ruling failed to give effect to Article VII of the Convention, which provides that the Convention shall not "deprive any interested party of any right he may have to avail himself of an arbitral award in the manner and to the extent allowed by the law or the treaties of the country where such award is sought to be relied upon." Art. VII(1). Baker Marine contends that the awards were set aside by the Nigerian courts for reasons that would not be recognized under U.S. law as valid grounds for vacating an arbitration award, and that under Article VII, it may invoke this country's national arbitration law, notwithstanding the action of the Nigerian court.

We reject Baker Marine's argument. It is sufficient answer that the parties contracted in Nigeria that their disputes would be arbitrated under the laws of Nigeria. The governing agreements make no reference whatever to United States law. Nothing suggests that the parties intended United States domestic arbitral law to govern their disputes. The "primary purpose" of the FAA is "ensuring that private agreements to arbitrate are enforced according to their terms." *Volt Information Sciences, Inc. v. Board of Trustees, 489 U.S. 468, 479, 103 L. Ed. 2d 488, 109 S. Ct. 1248 (1989)*; *see also Prima Paint Corp. v. Flood & Conklin Mfg. Co., 388 U.S. 395, 404 n.12, 18 L. Ed. 2d 1270, 87 S. Ct. 1801 (1967)* (the FAA aimed "to make arbitration agreements as enforceable as other contracts, but not more so"). Furthermore Baker Marine has made no contention that the Nigerian courts acted contrary to Nigerian law. *See Yusuf*, 126 F.3d at 21 ("[A] court in the country under whose law the arbitration was conducted [may] apply domestic arbitral law . . . to a motion to set aside or vacate that arbitral award.").

Baker Marine makes a further argument premised on the language of Article V(1)(e) of the Convention. Article V(1)(e) provides that when a party seeks confirmation of an award, "recognition and enforcement of the award *may* be refused" if the award has been set aside by a competent authority of the country in which the award was made. Baker Marine argues that this use of the permissive "may," rather than a mandatory term, implies that the court might have enforced the awards, notwithstanding the Nigerian judgments vacating them. It is sufficient answer that Baker Marine has shown no adequate reason for refusing to recognize the judgments of the Nigerian court.

Baker Marine also contends that the district court improperly imposed sanctions on it for failing to reveal in its petitions for enforcement of the awards that they had been vacated by the court of Nigeria. The contention is moot.

It is true the court expressed its intention at oral argument to impose sanctions under *Rule 11(b), Fed. R. Civ. P.*, requiring the payment of expenses (not including attorneys fees). However, the judgment ultimately rendered awarded only statutory costs to be taxed by the Clerk, and made no mention of sanctions or of expenses. Accordingly, we have no reason to consider whether the court might properly have imposed sanctions.

CONCLUSION

The judgments of the district court declining to enforce the arbitration awards are affirmed. The applications for sanctions are denied.

DUFERCO INTERNATIONAL STEEL TRADING, Petitioner-Appellant, v. T. KLAVENESS SHIPPING A/S, Respondent-Appellee.

UNITED STATES COURT OF APPEALS FOR THE SECOND CIRCUIT

333 F.3d 383

November 1, 2002, Argued
June 24, 2003, Decided

CARDAMONE, Circuit Judge:

This appeal stems from arbitration proceedings arising under a shipping contract between Duferco International Steel Trading Co. (Duferco or appellant) and T. Klaveness Shipping A/S (Klaveness). Duferco appeals from an order of the United States District Court for the Southern District of New York (Swain, J.), entered February 20, 2002, denying its petition to vacate, in part, an arbitration award and granting Klaveness' cross-petition for confirmation of the award.

In its petition to vacate the arbitral award, Duferco relies on the doctrine of manifest disregard of the law. For us to vacate an arbitral award on the grounds of manifest disregard of the law – a step we very seldom take – we must be persuaded that the arbitrators understood but chose to disregard a clearly defined law or legal principle applicable to the case before them. The error must be so palpably evident as to be readily perceived as such by the average person qualified to serve as an arbitrator. Any plausible reading of an award that fits within the law will sustain it. Here we believe there is such a plausible reading. Hence, we affirm.

BACKGROUND

A. *Facts*

On November 30, 1993, Duferco contracted with Klaveness to charter a seagoing vessel to carry a cargo of steel slabs from Taranto, Italy, to New Orleans, Louisiana. Duferco's contract with Klaveness was in the form of a voyage charter that covered only the specific voyage set out in the document. The voyage charter provided that the steel would be loaded onto Klaveness' vessel at "one(1) safe port/safe berth Taranto."

To fulfill its charter with Duferco, Klaveness in turn chartered the M.V. ARISTIDIS from its owner, Lifedream Shipping Company, Ltd. (Lifedream). Klaveness chartered the ARISTIDIS on January 3, 1994 by means of a time charter, a type of shipping agreement that allows a party to use an owner's vessel for a specified period of time. Klaveness' time charter with Lifedream allowed use of the ARISTIDIS for two to four months, plus or minus ten days at Klaveness' option. In addition, the time charter contained a safe-berth warranty, which required that the vessel trade via "safe port(s), safe berth(s), [and] safe anchorage(s)." In January and

February 1994, while the ARISTIDIS was moored at the port of Taranto, its crew loaded aboard her the steel slabs for shipment to New Orleans. Due to seasonal swells and back waves at Taranto, the crew of the ARISTIDIS experienced major difficulties in the loading operation resulting in damage to the mooring equipment and extra costs from measures taken to keep the vessel stable.

B. *London Arbitration*

Lifedream, as a result of the difficulties encountered in Taranto, sought arbitration against Klaveness in London to recover for the damages and extra costs incurred (London arbitration). The London arbitrators found Klaveness liable for these damages because it had breached the safe-berth warranty by mooring the ARISTIDIS where sea conditions made the port unsafe.

Klaveness moved to vouch Duferco into the London arbitration to obtain indemnification. Vouching-in is a common law procedural device that allows a party to arbitration to join a nonparty alleged indemnitor, referred to as the vouchee, by notifying the nonparty of the pendency of an arbitration that might obligate the vouchee to indemnify the defendant. *See SCAC Transp. (USA), Inc. v. S.S. Danaos, 845 F.2d 1157, 1161–62 (2d Cir. 1988)*; *see also Washington Gas Light Co. v. Dist. of Columbia, 161 U.S. 316, 329–30, 40 L. Ed. 712, 16 S. Ct. 564 (1896)*; *Universal Am. Barge Corp. v. J-Chem, Inc., 946 F.2d 1131, 1138 (5th Cir. 1991)*. Vouching-in is used where the vouchee cannot be impleaded because of defects in personal jurisdiction. The purpose of this legal device is to avoid duplicative litigation and the attendant possibility of inconsistent results. *SCAC Transp. (USA), Inc., 845 F.2d at 1162.*

Once notified, the vouchee has the option of joining the arbitration to defend the action. If the vouchee refuses to join, it may nonetheless be bound by the result in any subsequent litigation by principles analogous to collateral estoppel. *Washington Gas Light, 161 U.S. at 329–30.* For the vouchee to be bound, the party seeking to join the vouchee must be able to represent that party's interests fully and fairly in the arbitration. *Universal, 946 F.2d at 1139–40.*

Duferco declined to be vouched into the London arbitration, and on June 24, 1997 the arbitration panel found against Klaveness for all expenses and damages incurred at the port of Taranto. The award amounted to $150,000 in damages plus $37,900.50 in interest (London award).

C. *New York Arbitration*

Klaveness thereafter began arbitration in New York seeking, *inter alia*, full indemnification from Duferco for the London award to Lifedream that it was obligated to pay, as well as for attorneys' and arbitrators' fees from both arbitrations. At the arbitration hearing, Klaveness maintained that the warranty in its charter with Duferco – stating that it would load at "one(1) safe port/safe berth Taranto" – was similar to the one included in the charter between Klaveness and Lifedream, which provided that the vessel trade "via safe port(s), safe berth(s), [and] safe anchorage(s)," and therefore declared that vouching-in had been appropriate and that Duferco could thus be bound by the London award based on collateral estoppel principles.

Duferco did not challenge the findings of the London arbitrators, but it countered that collateral estoppel could not apply because significant differences between the time and voyage charters made the sweep of Klaveness' liability under its time charter with Lifedream far greater than Duferco's liability under its voyage charter with Klaveness. Essentially, Duferco asserted the Klaveness-Duferco voyage charter specifically waived any safe-berth warranty. Under settled principles of maritime law, a voyage charter that names a specific port relieves the charterer of liability for damage arising from conditions at that port so long as those conditions were reasonably foreseeable. *See Tweedie Trading Co. v. N.Y. & B. Dyewood Co., 127 F. 278, 280–81 (2d Cir. 1903)*; *see also* 2A *Benedict on Admiralty* §175, at 17–26 (7th ed. 2002). Since the named port of Taranto had predictable seasonal swell conditions, Duferco insisted the safe-berth warranty had been waived, and it therefore had no liability for damages occurring there.

Duferco further averred that it should not be bound by any findings of the London arbitrators because its interests could not have been fully and fairly represented in the London arbitration. It argued that since Klaveness could not advance the named-port argument, as Duferco could have, to relieve itself of liability, Klaveness could not have fully and fairly represented its interests in the London arbitration.

A divided panel of the New York arbitrators found for Klaveness in an arbitration decision and award entered on April 18, 2001 (New York award). The majority found that Klaveness did not waive the safe-berth warranty by agreeing with Duferco to load the ship at Taranto, and that the safe-berth warranties of both charters were sufficiently identical for vouching-in. The panel therefore found Duferco to be bound by the outcome of the London arbitration with respect to the damage portion of the London award and ordered it to indemnify Klaveness for the amount Klaveness paid Lifedream in satisfaction of the London award.

The panel went on to rule nonetheless that collateral estoppel principles prevented Klaveness from collecting attorneys' and arbitrators' fees from Duferco for the London arbitration. The majority reasoned, somewhat confusingly, that "inasmuch as the London arbitrators did not consider the safe-berth warranties of the voyage charter, as properly not before them, no 'previous determination' had been made, and therefore, Klaveness must not be permitted to now use the London award against Duferco offensively for vouching-in or collateral estoppel purposes." On its own motion, the arbitration panel awarded Klaveness $120,000 as an allowance toward attorneys' fees and expenses for the New York arbitration. The panel majority made several other determinations of liability related to events at the port of New Orleans. Neither party contests these additional determinations and, in any event, they are not relevant to this appeal.

D. *District Court Proceedings*

Following the conclusion of the New York arbitration, Duferco, as noted, petitioned the Southern District to vacate that portion of the arbitration award compelling it to indemnify Klaveness for the London arbitration. The district court denied the petition and confirmed the award. *See Duferco Int'l Steel Trading v. T. Klaveness Shipping A/S, 184 F. Supp. 2d 271, 272 (S.D.N.Y. 2002)*. Duferco appeals.

DISCUSSION

I. Standard of Review

We review a district court's decision to confirm an arbitration award *de novo* to the extent it turns on legal questions, and we review any findings of fact for clear error. *Westerbeke Corp. v. Daihatsu Motor Co., Ltd., 304 F.3d 200, 208 (2d Cir. 2002).*

It is well established that courts must grant an arbitration panel's decision great deference. A party petitioning a federal court to vacate an arbitral award bears the heavy burden of showing that the award falls within a very narrow set of circumstances delineated by statute and case law. The Federal Arbitration Act(FAA), *9 U.S.C. §1, et seq.*, which defines federal policy on arbitration proceedings, permits vacatur of an arbitration award in only four specifically enumerated situations, all of which involve corruption, fraud, or some other impropriety on the part of the arbitrators.

In addition to the grounds afforded by statute, we permit vacatur of an arbitral award that exhibits a "manifest disregard of law." *See, e.g., Goldman v. Architectural Iron. Co., 306 F.3d 1214, 1216 (2d Cir. 2002)*; *Westerbeke, 304 F.3d at 208.* Appellant Duferco does not advance statutory grounds for vacating the New York arbitration award. It argues instead that the New York arbitrators manifestly disregarded the law.

II. Manifest Disregard of the Law

A. *An Overview*

The manifest disregard standard finds its origins in dicta from Wilko v. Swan, 346 U.S.427, 98 L. Ed. 168, 74 S. Ct. 182 (1953), overruled on other grounds, Rodriguez de Quijas v. Shearson/Am. Express, Inc., 490 U.S. 477, 485, 104 L. Ed. 2d 526, 109 S. Ct. 1917 (1989). The Supreme Court there stated that "the interpretations of the law by the arbitrators in contrast to manifest disregard are not subject, in the federal courts, to judicial review for error in interpretation." 346 U.S. at 436–37 (emphasis added). From this statement we have inferred that in addition to the statutory grounds set forth in the FAA, an arbitral award may be vacated if manifest disregard of the law is plainly evident from the arbitration record.

Our review under the doctrine of manifest disregard is "severely limited." *Gov't of India v. Cargill Inc., 867 F.2d 130, 133 (2d Cir. 1989).* It is highly deferential to the arbitral award and obtaining judicial relief for arbitrators' manifest disregard of the law is rare.

We first mentioned this standard in Amicizia Societa Navegazione v. Chilean Nitrate & Iodine Sales Corp., 274 F.2d 805, 808 (2d Cir.), cert. denied, 363 U.S. 843, 4 L. Ed. 2d 1727, 80 S. Ct. 1612 (1960). And, since 1960 we have vacated some part or all of an arbitral award for manifest disregard in the following four out of at least 48 cases where we applied the standard: Halligan v. Piper Jaffray, Inc., 148 F.3d 197, 204 (2d Cir. 1998) (finding manifest disregard of law, evidence, or both because of great weight of evidence of age discrimination under ADA); New York Telephone Co. v. Communication Workers of America, 256 F.3d 89, 92–93 (2d Cir. 2001) (per curiam) (vacating portion of award ordering payments found to be illegal and contrary to public policy under Circuit precedent); Fahnestock & Co., Inc. v. Waltman, 935 F.2d 512, 519 (2d Cir. 1991) (vacating portion of arbitral award mandating punitive damages as contrary to New York law prohibiting arbitrators from ordering punitive damages); Perma-Line Corp. of America v. Sign Pictorial & Display Union, 639 F.2d 890, 894–96 (2d Cir. 1981) (remanding arbitration award based on an illegal contract provision, with possibility of confirmation if arbitrators could justify illegal provision).

All of the four cases finding manifest disregard, except *Halligan*, involved an arbitral decision that exceeded the legal powers of the arbitrators. In those cases, it is arguable that manifest disregard need not have been the basis for vacating the award, since vacatur would have been warranted under the FAA. Our reluctance over the years to find manifest disregard is a reflection of the fact that it is a doctrine of last resort – its use is limited only to those exceedingly rare instances where some egregious impropriety on the part of the arbitrators is apparent, but where none of the provisions of the FAA apply. It should be remembered that arbitrators are hired by parties to reach a result that conforms to industry norms and to the arbitrator's notions of fairness. To interfere with this process would frustrate the intent of the parties, and thwart the usefulness of arbitration, making it "the commencement, not the end, of litigation." *Burchell v. Marsh, 58 U.S. (17 How.) 344, 349, 15 L. Ed. 96 (1854).*

B. *Application of the Doctrine*

Perhaps because we so infrequently find manifest disregard, its precise boundaries are ill defined, although its rough contours are well known. *See Merrill Lynch, Pierce, Fenner & Smith, Inc. v. Bobker, 808 F.2d 930, 933 (2d Cir. 1986).* We know that it is more than a simple error in law or a failure by the arbitrators to understand or apply it; and, it is more than an erroneous interpretation of the law. *See Westerbeke, 304 F.3d at 208; see also Folkways Music Publishers., Inc. v. Weiss, 989 F.2d 108, 111 (2d Cir. 1993).* A party seeking vacatur bears the burden of proving that the arbitrators were fully aware of the existence of a clearly defined governing legal principle, but refused to apply it, in effect, ignoring it. *Merrill Lynch, 808 F.2d at 933; see also Greenberg v. Bear, Stearns & Co., 220 F.3d 22, 28 (2d Cir. 2000), cert. denied, 531 U.S. 1075, 148 L. Ed. 2d 669, 121 S. Ct. 770 (2001).*

The above principles, by extension, lead us to infer that the application of the manifest disregard standard involves at least three inquiries. First, we must consider whether the law that was allegedly ignored was clear, and in fact explicitly applicable to the matter before the arbitrators. *See Westerbeke, 304 F.3d at 209; Merrill Lynch, 808 F.2d at 934.* An arbitrator obviously cannot be said to disregard a law that is unclear or not clearly applicable. Thus, misapplication of an ambiguous law does not constitute manifest disregard.

Second, once it is determined that the law is clear and plainly applicable, we must find that the law was in fact improperly applied, leading to an erroneous outcome. We will, of course, not vacate an arbitral award for an erroneous application of the law if a proper application of law would have yielded the same result. In the same vein, where an arbitral award contains more than one plausible reading, manifest disregard cannot be found if at least one of the readings yields a legally correct justification for the outcome. *See Willemijn Houdstermaatschappij, BV v. Standard Microsystems Corp., 103 F.3d 9, 13 (2d Cir. 1997)* (citing *Matter of Andros Compania Maritima, S.A. of Kissavos, 579 F.2d 691, 704 (2d Cir. 1978))*. Even where explanation for an award is deficient or non-existent, we will confirm it if a justifiable ground for the decision can be inferred from the facts of the case. *Sobel v. Hertz, Warner & Co., 469 F.2d 1211, 1216 (2d Cir. 1972); see also Siegel v. Titan Indus. Corp., 779 F.2d 891, 893–95 (2d Cir. 1985)* (per curiam).

Third, once the first two inquiries are satisfied, we look to a subjective element, that is, the knowledge actually possessed by the arbitrators. In order to intentionally disregard the law, the arbitrator must have known of its existence, and its applicability to the problem before him. *Merrill Lynch, 808 F.2d at 933*. In determining an arbitrator's awareness of the law, we impute only knowledge of governing law identified by the parties to the arbitration. *DiRussa v. Dean Witter Reynolds Inc., 121 F.3d 818, 823 (2d Cir. 1997), cert. denied, 522 U.S. 1049, 139 L. Ed. 2d 639, 118 S. Ct. 695 (1998)*. Absent this, we will infer knowledge and intentionality on the part of the arbitrator only if we find an error that is so obvious that it would be instantly perceived as such by the average person qualified to serve as an arbitrator. *Merrill Lynch, 808 F.2d at 933*. We undertake such a lenient subjective inquiry in recognition of the reality that arbitrators often are chosen for reasons other than their knowledge of applicable law, and that it is often more important to the parties to have trustworthy arbitrators with expertise regarding the commercial aspects of the dispute before them. *See Goldman, 306 F.3d at 1216*.

III. Analysis of the Doctrine in the Present Case

A. *Clear Applicability of Law Under Manifest Disregard Test*

Examining the first prong of the manifest disregard inquiry, we conclude that the significant principles of law relevant to the case at hand are clearly defined and plainly applicable. Neither party contests that a party vouched into an arbitration may be bound by any determination made in the arbitration, even if the vouchee elects not to participate and defend. *See SCAC Transp. (USA), Inc., 845 F.2d at 1162–63; Universal, 946 F.2d at 1136*. The principle allowing a vouchee to be bound by an arbitration in which it does not participate is analogous to collateral estoppel. Accordingly, the same due process and fairness considerations that govern the application of collateral estoppel in court proceedings govern it in arbitration as well. *See Universal, 946 F.2d at 1136*. This means that collateral estoppel cannot be used offensively against a party with respect to issues not fully and fairly litigated or issues which are not necessary to a final disposition. *Parklane Hosiery Co. v. Shore, 439 U.S. 322, 332–33, 58 L. Ed. 2d 552, 99 S. Ct. 645, (1979); Blonder-Tongue Lab., Inc. v. University of Illinois Foundation, 402 U.S. 313, 329, 28 L. Ed. 2d 788, 91 S. Ct. 1434 (1971)*. This principle is well recognized in our law, and was plainly known both by appellants and the New York arbitrators as evidenced by the arbitrators' written decision.

In the context of this case, offensive collateral estoppel could not be used by Klaveness against Duferco for preclusion purposes unless the issue involving the safe-berth warranties under consideration in the New York proceeding was identical to the corresponding issue fully and vigorously litigated in London. The London arbitrators' conclusions about the safe-berth warranty must also have been necessary to its judgment. In addition, there must have existed no special circumstances that would render preclusion inappropriate or unfair. *Parklane Hosiery, 439 U.S. at 326–32; Universal, 946 F.2d at 1136.*

Yet, the fact that the applicable rules of law here were clear and recognized by the arbitrators does not end the inquiry. We must also examine whether the principles were misapplied, yielding an improper result. In doing so, we bear in mind that even a "barely colorable" justification for the outcome reached will save an arbitral award. *See Willemijn Houdstermaatschappij, 103 F.3d at 13.*

B. *Application of Law by New York Arbitrators*

The precise rationale employed by the New York arbitrators is difficult for us to discern. The panel majority found first that the vouching-in procedure was proper, and then went on to rule that because the safe-port/safe-berth warranties in both the time and voyage charters were sufficiently identical, appellant is bound by the outcome of the London arbitration. The panel then continued to make what appears to be a separate finding that appellant warranted the safety of the berth and Klaveness had waived that warranty when it agreed to Taranto. The opinion goes on to recount the London arbitrators' finding that the conditions at the unsafe berth caused the damage, and that Klaveness' ordering of the vessel to that berth caused its breach with Lifedream. The arbitrators then state that "having declined to assume the defense in the original action, Duferco is bound by that decision and is liable to indemnify Klaveness."

But later, when discussing legal fees and costs sought by Klaveness, the arbitrators take a different tack and state that the London arbitrators "did not consider the safe-berth warranties of the voyage charter" and made no "previous determination" as to them, hence, concluding that "Klaveness must not be permitted to now use the London award against Duferco offensively for vouching-in or collateral estoppel purposes."

Such reasoning appears to contradict what the panel had just held on the damage issue. On that issue collateral estoppel based on "sufficiently identical" charter provisions, barred appellant's arguments. But the panel thereafter refused to apply collateral estoppel to Klaveness' request for attorney fees, concluding that the voyage charter had not even been before the London arbitrators, thereby finding the voyage charter not identical to the time charter. The dissenting arbitrator lends support to this reading, resting his analysis on the fact that the vouching-in procedure was inappropriate because, in his opinion, the time and voyage charters were significantly different.

Reading the arbitral award in this way would imply a misapplication of the law, as Duferco asserts, because if the warranties were identical, collateral estoppel should be applied to both liability and attorneys' fees; if the charter provisions were different, then collateral estoppel could not be applied to either, because Klaveness could not in such case have presented a defense of waiver of the safe-berth warranty, and therefore Klaveness in the London arbitration could not have fully and fairly represented Duferco's interest. Either way, appellant insists the arbitrators' split decision indicates a misapplication of laws that the arbitrators seem to have understood.

C. *Plausible Reading of Award*

Notwithstanding the foregoing interpretation, another reading of the New York arbitral award, one advanced by the district court, makes sense of the arbitral opinion. That court believed the arbitrators' opinion could be read to include an independent finding that the two charters were so "substantially identical" as to their damage liability provisions that Duferco could be made to indemnify Klaveness. This is supported by the arbitrators' statement that they "do not find Klaveness to have waived the safe berth warranty." Once this determination was made, the New York arbitrators could then properly have used collateral estoppel to import the London arbitrators' findings of *fact* regarding liability against Klaveness, which were certainly fully and fairly litigated in London. These findings of fact could in turn be applied to Duferco's "substantially identical" safe-berth warranty, so determined independently in New York, to impute liability as Klaveness' indemnitor.

The New York arbitrators could have found that the time and voyage charters were *not* "sufficiently identical" for purposes of finding an obligation to pay attorneys' and arbitrators' fees, and that no finding of the London arbitrators could be imported to support such an award. Since collateral estoppel is issue specific, it is not inconsistent to find it applicable to one issue, but not to another in the same proceeding. This plausible reading of the award resolves its apparent contradiction. *See Willemijn Houdstermaatschappij, 103 F.3d at 13.*

Duferco contests the foregoing reading of the award, stating that it does not reflect the arguments originally made by appellees before the panel. However, whether appellees actually raised the issues reflected in the district court's reading of the award is immaterial. In construing an arbitral award we look only to plausible readings of the award, and not to probable readings of it. Even absent a plausible reading free of error, we would confirm the award if we independently found legal grounds to do so.

Finally, the arbitrators' award was not irrational or inexplicable, as appellant contends. Although it only arguably conforms to legal standards, the award evinces the arbitrators' desire not to saddle Klaveness with the burden of Duferco's decision to order the ARISTIDIS into unsafe waters. In any event, it is not our role to substitute our judgment for those of arbitrators hired by the parties – this is why our standard for vacatur is so very high. We review only for a clear demonstration that the panel intentionally defied the law. We find no such evidence here and hence must confirm the award.

CONCLUSION

Accordingly, having found no manifest disregard of the law, the judgment of the district court confirming the arbitral award is affirmed.

IN RE: PATRICIO CLERICI, Appellant.
UNITED STATES COURT OF APPEALS FOR THE ELEVENTH CIRCUIT

481 F.3d 1324

March 21, 2007, Decided
March 21, 2007, Filed

HULL, Circuit Judge:

This case involves the authority of federal district courts to assist in the production of evidence – here, sworn answers to written questions – for use in a foreign court. Appellant Patricio Clerici ("Clerici") appeals the district court's January 27, 2006 order denying his motion to vacate the district court's October 12, 2005 order granting the government's application, filed pursuant to *28 U.S.C. §1782*, for judicial assistance to foreign tribunals. In its January 27, 2006 order, the district court appointed an Assistant United States Attorney to obtain sworn answers from Clerici to the questions posed in the Panamanian Court's letter rogatory. After review and oral argument, we affirm.

I. BACKGROUND

A. Clerici's Lawsuit in Panama

Clerici is a Panamanian citizen and merchant who also resides in Miami, Florida. In 1998 in Panama, Clerici initiated a civil lawsuit against NoName Corporation ("NoName") and others in the Second Court of the Circuit of Colon, Civil Branch, Republic of Panama ("Panamanian Court"). As part of these proceedings, Clerici requested the attachment of NoName's property, which the Panamanian Court granted by judicial decree. As a result, certain property of NoName was seized.

Thereafter, on August 27, 1999, NoName filed a motion to dismiss Clerici's Panama lawsuit, alleging that Clerici had failed to prosecute his civil lawsuit. On February 11, 2000, the Panamanian Court granted NoName's motion to dismiss Clerici's lawsuit, and the attachment of NoName's property was vacated. The resolution of Clerici's civil lawsuit was appealed and affirmed by Panama's First Superior Court of Justice on November 13, 2000.

B. NoName's Proceedings in Panama

On April 27, 2001, NoName filed an incidental proceeding in the Panamanian Court claiming damages arising from Clerici's civil lawsuit and the attachment proceeding. Specifically, NoName alleged that it was a new business in Panama and in the process of expanding, but that Clerici's lawsuit "changed the commercial image of the company." NoName alleged that Clerici's lawsuit negatively impacted NoName's credit with various banks and its image in the community, resulted in the denial of its request for an increase in credit, and led to lost sales and profits. On September 27, 2002, the Panamanian Court entered Judicial Decree No. 1166, in which Clerici was "condemn[ed] . . . to pay" NoName, in balboas, 1,996,598.00

in damages and 294,589.70 in costs. Thus, NoName obtained a sizable foreign judgment against Clerici in Panama.

It is undisputed that NoName's foreign judgment against Clerici has not been domesticated and is not currently enforceable in Florida. While NoName filed a domestication action, NoName never pursued it.

Subsequently, on January 27, 2005, NoName filed a post-judgment petition in the same Panamanian Court where NoName had obtained the sizable judgment against Clerici. NoName's post-judgment petition was entitled "Ordinary Proceeding Involving More Than a Certain Amount (Incident of Damages) Petition (Complementary Execution)."

In its petition, NoName requested that the Panamanian Court "begin the procedure complementary to the execution" of its judgment "pursuant to the provisions of Article 1049 and 1050 of the Judicial Code" of Panama. NoName's petition identified the following questions to be asked to Clerici regarding his assets and other financial matters "in the Republic of Panama or in any other part of the world":

1. What properties (real or personal), credits, sustenance means or any other source of income did he [have] on April 27, 2001 in the Republic of Panama or in any other part of the world?
2. What properties (real or personal), credits, sustenance means or any other source of income did he [have] on September 27, 2002 in the Republic of Panama or in any other part of the world?
3. What transfers, conveyances or donations has he made after April 27, 2001 and September 27, 2002 in the Republic of Panama or in any other part of the world? Please explain the reasons for these conveyances.
4. What is the amount of your patrimony to the date of this proceeding?
5. How and by what means are you going to fulfill the obligations acquired by means of Resolution No. 1166 of September 27, 2002, announced by the Second Court of the Civil Circuit of Colon (Republic of Panama), wherein you are condemned to pay an amount greater than TWO MILLION BALBOAS (B/2,000,000.00) (legal currency of the Republic of Panama) to the corporation NONAME CORP.?
6. Are you in bankruptcy? Please explain the reasons.
7. How many nationalities or citizenships do you have up to date?
8. In what countries do you file income-tax returns?
9. With what financial entities (banks, investment houses, to mention some) in the world have you had or have business relations or a relation as a client?

Because Clerici resided in the United States, NoName's petition suggested that the Panamanian Court obtain this evidence through the issuance of a letter rogatory.

The Panamanian Court granted NoName's petition, finding that

> the petition is based in the provisions of Article 1049 of the Judicial Code, allowing the executant, when the obligation is not paid within the respective term, to interrogate the debtor, or request the judge to do it, in order that under oath he may answer the questions made in relation to his properties, rights, credits, sustenance means, source of income, as from the date of this claimed obligation.

Because Clerici resided in Florida, the Panamanian Court issued a letter rogatory to the "Judicial Authorities of the City of Miami" requesting assistance with obtaining answers from Clerici, while under oath, to NoName's proposed questions. The Panamanian Court's letter rogatory stated that the evidence obtained "will be used in the civil process before this court," and the Panamanian Court cited as authority for its request the Inter-American Convention Regarding Letters Rogatory ("the Convention"). The questions listed in the Panamanian Court's letter rogatory were substantially similar to the questions proposed by NoName.

C. *Section 1782* Application in District Court

On October 11, 2005, the United States filed an *ex parte* application in the United States District Court for the Southern District of Florida, pursuant to *28 U.S.C. §1782*, for an order appointing an Assistant United States Attorney as a commissioner for the purpose of obtaining the evidence requested by the Panamanian Court in its letter rogatory. *Section 1782(a)* provides that the district court where Clerici resides "may order him to give his testimony or statement . . . for use in a proceeding in a foreign . . . tribunal." *28 U.S.C. §1782(a)*. On October 12, 2005, the district court granted the government's *§1782* application and appointed a commissioner "to take such steps as are necessary to obtain the evidence in conformity with the Letters Rogatory." The court-appointed commissioner then sent a letter to Clerici requesting that he sit for a deposition to answer the Panamanian Court's questions.

On December 27, 2005, Clerici filed a memorandum in opposition to the government's application. The district court construed Clerici's memorandum as a motion to vacate its previous order granting the *§1782* application and appointing a commissioner. In the motion, Clerici asserted that NoName's judgment against him is invalid, is being challenged in Panama, and in any event, is unenforceable in Florida because it has not been domesticated. Clerici argued that the application should be denied because (1) the Panamanian Court's letter rogatory does not contain the necessary documentation under the terms of the Convention; and (2) *§1782* cannot be used to enforce a foreign judgment pursuant to a letter rogatory. Clerici also argued that, even if *§1782* authorized the requested assistance, the district court should, in its discretion, decline to grant judicial assistance because (1) the letter rogatory is an attempt to enforce a foreign judgment that has not been domesticated, and therefore, is unenforceable; and (2) the application is "unduly intrusive."

In response, the government argued that its application for judicial assistance was properly made pursuant to *§1782* despite the content of the Panamanian Court's letter rogatory. The government explained that, although the letter rogatory claimed to be sent under the terms of the Convention, "[a]s a matter of comity and assistance to foreign litigants," it generally treated such "mislabel[ed]" requests for assistance as requests made pursuant to *§1782*.

The government also emphasized that the Panamanian Court was not requesting that the district court enforce the foreign judgment. Rather, the government pointed out that the Panamanian Court was seeking only assistance in obtaining evidence and that this was a proper use of *§1782*.

The district court denied Clerici's motion to vacate. First, the district court found that, "[n]otwithstanding the form used to draft the Panamanian [C]ourt's request," the application for judicial assistance was filed pursuant to *§1782*, and therefore, did not have to comply with the requirements of the Convention. Next, the district court rejected Clerici's argument that *§1782* was being used to enforce a foreign judgment through a letter rogatory. Instead, the district court found that the *§1782* application and exhibits "demonstrate clearly that the Panamanian [C]ourt is seeking assistance in obtaining 'a sworn statement' from [Clerici]: it is not requesting that [the district court] enforce the judgment NoName received against him." The district court concluded that this was a proper request under *§1782* for assistance in procuring evidence. Finally, the district court declined to exercise its discretion to deny the requested assistance, noting that Clerici still was "free to argue against a domestication of the Panamanian judgment in Florida state court and to proceed with his appeal of the foreign judgment in Panama."

As to the scope of the evidence requested, the district court noted that Clerici had argued, in the alternative, that it was "unduly intrusive" but had "failed to identify specifically the terms of the request which he contends are overly broad, a legal basis for these contentions, and how the scope of the request should be narrowed." The district court then denied Clerici's "'unduly intrusive' argument without prejudice." The district court indicated that if Clerici wished to pursue this argument, Clerici "shall file a motion to limit the scope of the request on or before Monday, February 6, 2006."

Clerici did not file a motion to limit the scope of the request. Rather, on February 9, 2006, Clerici timely appealed the district court's order denying his motion to vacate the district court's earlier order granting the government's *§1782* application for judicial assistance. Clerici also moved for a stay pending appeal, which the district court granted.

II. STANDARD OF REVIEW

Beginning in 1948, "Congress substantially broadened the scope of assistance federal courts could provide for foreign proceedings," pursuant to *28 U.S.C. §1782*. *Intel Corp. v. Advanced Micro Devices, Inc., 542 U.S. 241, 247–48, 124 S. Ct. 2466, 2473, 159 L. Ed. 2d 355 (2004)* (reviewing at length the 150-year history of congressional efforts to provide judicial assistance to foreign tribunals and amendments designed to broaden the scope of *§1782*). "The history of *Section 1782* reveals Congress' wish to strengthen the power of district courts to respond to requests for international assistance." *Lo Ka Chun v. Lo To, 858 F.2d 1564, 1565 (11th Cir. 1988)*.

Because "Congress has given the district courts such broad discretion in granting judicial assistance to foreign countries, this court may overturn the district court's decision only for abuse of discretion." *United Kingdom v. United States, 238 F.3d 1312, 1319 (11th Cir. 2001)* (quotation marks omitted). This review is "extremely limited and highly deferential." *Id.* Further, "[t]his deferential standard is identical to that used in reviewing the district court's ordinary discovery rulings." *Id.*

However, "to the extent the district court's decision is based on an interpretation of law, our review is de novo." *Id. at 1319 n.8*. Thus, this Court reviews *de novo* the district court's interpretation of a treaty or a federal statute such as *§1782*. *In re Commissioner's Subpoenas, 325 F.3d 1287, 1292 (11th Cir. 2003)*.

III. DISCUSSION

A. *Section 1782*

A district court has the authority to grant an application for judicial assistance if the following statutory requirements in *§1782(a)* are met: (1) the request must be made "by a foreign or international tribunal," or by "any interested person"; (2) the request must seek evidence, whether it be the "testimony or statement" of a person or the production of "a document or other thing"; (3) the evidence must be "for use in a proceeding in a foreign or international tribunal"; and (4) the person from whom discovery is sought must reside or be found in the district of the district court ruling on the application for assistance. *28 U.S.C. §1782(a)*. If these requirements are met, then *§1782* "authorizes, but does not require, a federal district court to provide assistance. . . ." *Intel, 542 U.S. at 255, 124 S. Ct. at 2478*; *see also United Kingdom, 238 F.3d at 1319* ("[A] district court's compliance with a *§1782* request is not mandatory.").

Here, Clerici does not dispute that the Panamanian Court is a foreign tribunal or that he resides within the Southern District of Florida. Therefore, the first and fourth requirements for a proper request under *§1782* are met.

As to the second statutory requirement – that the request must seek evidence – Clerici argues that the Panamanian Court is not seeking evidence, but rather is attempting to enforce its judgment through a *§1782* request. We disagree because the Panamanian Court asked for assistance in obtaining only Clerici's sworn answers to questions regarding his assets and other financial matters. The district court recognized this key distinction and properly concluded that the request for assistance was limited to seeking evidence from Clerici, and therefore, was proper under *§1782*. Unlike the requests for judicial assistance in the cases cited in Clerici's brief, *see, e.g., In re Letter Rogatory Issued by the Second Part of the III Civil Reg'l Court of Jabaquara/Saude, Sao Paulo, Braz., No. 01-M C-212, 2002 U.S. Dist. LEXIS 2702, 2002 WL 257822 (E.D.N.Y. Feb. 6, 2002)* (denying request to order judgment-debtor to deposit $ 8,642,802.94 into an account with the court); *Tacul, S.A. v. Hartford Nat'l Bank & Trust Co., 693 F. Supp. 1399, 1399–1400 (D. Conn. 1988)* (quashing writ of execution against the assets of judgment-debtor issued by the clerk based on a letter rogatory), the Panamanian Court never requested that the district court sequester, levy on, or seize control of Clerici's assets or otherwise help enforce NoName's judgment. The Panamanian Court requested only assistance in obtaining evidence – sworn answers from Clerici to written questions – and this is the primary purpose of *§1782*. Therefore, the second requirement for a proper request under *§1782* is met.

As to the third statutory requirement, we reject Clerici's contention that the requested evidence was not "for use in a proceeding" before the Panamanian Court. Here, there is a proceeding currently pending before the Panamanian Court that allows NoName or the Panamanian Court to question Clerici under oath about his properties, rights, credits, sustenance means, and other sources of income from the date of his court-ordered obligation. Had Clerici been residing in Panama, NoName or the Panamanian Court would have been able to interrogate Clerici directly with the questions proposed by NoName. Because Clerici was residing in Florida, however, the Panamanian Court issued a letter rogatory seeking international assistance in order to obtain this evidence. The Panamanian Court's letter rogatory itself stated that this evidence "will be used in the civil process before this court." Such a request is clearly within the range of discovery authorized under *§1782* and comports with the purpose of the statute to provide assistance to foreign tribunals.

Given the pending proceeding before the Panamanian Court, Clerici is reduced to arguing that a "proceeding" means an adjudicative proceeding, and thus, NoName's post-judgment petition regarding a judgment that already has been rendered is not a "proceeding" within the meaning of the statute. This argument is also without merit for several reasons. First, *§1782* only states that the evidence must be "for use in a proceeding," and nothing in the plain language of *§1782* requires that the proceeding be adjudicative in nature. *See 28 U.S.C. §1782(a).* In fact, the statute specifically provides that the evidence obtained through *§1782* can be used in "criminal investigations conducted *before* formal accusation," even though such investigations are not adjudicative proceedings. *Id.*

Second, the Supreme Court has recognized the "broad range of discovery" authorized under *§1782* and has held that *§1782* is not limited to proceedings that are pending or imminent. *Intel, 542 U.S. at 259, 124 S. Ct. at 2480; see also* Hans Smit, *American Assistance to Litigation in Foreign and International Tribunals: Section 1782 of Title 28 of the U.S.C. Revisited, 25 Syracuse J. Int'l L. & Com. 1, 9 (1998)* ("The purpose of *Section 1782* is to liberalize the assistance given to foreign and international tribunals."). Rather, the proceeding for which discovery is sought need only be "within reasonable contemplation." *Intel, 542 U.S. at 259, 124 S. Ct. at 2480.* Here, the proceeding actually was filed before the letter rogatory was even issued, and the third statutory requirement for a proper request under *§1782* is satisfied.

Because all four statutory requirements are met, the Panamanian Court's request for assistance in obtaining Clerici's sworn answers for use in the proceeding in Panama was proper under *§1782*. Accordingly, the district court had authority to grant the *§1782* discovery application.

Even so, "a district court is not required to grant a *§1782(a)* discovery application simply because it has the authority to do so." *Intel, 542 U.S. at 264, 124 S. Ct. at 2482–83* ("[A] district court's compliance with a *§1782* request is not mandatory." (quoting *United Kingdom, 238 F.3d at 1319*)). Once the prima facie requirements are satisfied, the Supreme Court in *Intel* noted these factors to be considered in exercising the discretion granted under *§1782(a)*: (1) whether "the person from whom discovery is sought is a participant in the foreign proceeding," because "the need for *§1782(a)* aid generally is not as apparent as it ordinarily is when evidence is sought from a nonparticipant"; (2) "the nature of the foreign tribunal, the character of the proceedings underway abroad, and the receptivity of the foreign government or the court or agency abroad to U.S. federal-court judicial assistance"; (3) "whether the *§1782(a)* request conceals an attempt to circumvent foreign proof-gathering restrictions or other policies of a foreign country or the United States"; and (4) whether the request is otherwise "unduly intrusive or burdensome." *Id. at 264–65, 124 S. Ct. at 2483.* The Supreme Court in *Intel* added that "unduly intrusive or burdensome requests may be rejected or trimmed." *Id. at 265, 124 S. Ct. at 2483.*

Our review of the *Intel* factors reveals that none of the factors favors Clerici, and that the district court did not abuse its discretion in granting the *§1782* application.

As to the first *Intel* factor, because Clerici is a party in the foreign proceeding, this factor normally would favor Clerici and suggest that *§1782* assistance is not necessary. *See Intel, 542 U.S. at 264, 124 S. Ct. at 2483* ("A foreign tribunal has jurisdiction over those appearing before it, and can itself order them to produce evidence."). [14] In this case, however, the first factor does not favor Clerici because Clerici has left Panama and the Panamanian Court cannot enforce its order against Clerici directly while Clerici is in the United States. Given the particular factual circumstances in this case, the first *Intel* factor does not favor Clerici.

As to the second and third *Intel* factors, there is nothing in the record to suggest that the district court should have declined to grant the *§1782* application based on the nature of the foreign tribunal or the character of the proceedings in Panama, or that the Panamanian Court's request is merely an attempt to circumvent Clerici had failed to identify any "proof-gathering restrictions" in the Panamanian Court case that would be circumvented if the *§1782* request were granted. Finally, as to the fourth factor, the district court noted that foreign proof-gathering restrictions. Rather, these factors all support the district court's decision to grant the *§1782* application given that the foreign tribunal here is the Panamanian Court and the Panamanian Court itself issued the letter rogatory requesting assistance due to Clerici's presence in the United States.

Finally, as to the fourth *Intel* factor – whether the *§1782* request is unduly intrusive – the district court's order granting the *§1782* application specifically indicated that if Clerici wished to pursue his "unduly intrusive" argument, Clerici should file a motion to limit discovery. Clerici never did so and instead chose to appeal the grant of *any* discovery whatsoever. On appeal, as in the district court, Clerici does not identify the terms of the written request that are overly broad or assert how the scope of the request should be narrowed. Thus, we, like the district court, have no occasion to address the scope of the Panamanian Court's discovery request.

In sum, the district court had authority to grant the *§1782* application, and Clerici has not shown that the district court abused its discretion in doing so.

B. Federal Rules of Civil Procedure

Clerici alternatively asserts that, even if the district court had authority to grant the discovery application under *§1782*, *Rule 69(a) of the Federal Rules of Civil Procedure* bars any *§1782* discovery in this case. More specifically, Clerici contends that (1) any evidence must be obtained in accordance with the Federal Rules of Civil Procedure; (2) Federal *Rule 69(a)* is applicable because the Panamanian Court is seeking discovery to aid NoName in the execution of its judgment; and (3) no discovery is authorized under *Rule 69(a)* until NoName obtains a valid, domesticated judgment in this country. We agree that the discovery rules in the Federal Rules of Civil Procedure apply here but conclude that *Rule 69(a)* does not. We explain why.

The district court's authority to order Clerici to give testimony "for use in a proceeding in a foreign . . . tribunal" stems from *§1782. 28 U.S.C. §1782(a). Section 1782(a)* then provides that, in its order granting *§1782* assistance, the district court "may prescribe the *practice and procedure* . . . for taking the testimony or statement or producing the document or other thing." *Id.* (emphasis added). This "practice and procedure" may be "in whole or part the practice and procedure of the foreign country or the international tribunal." *Id.* To the extent that the district court does not otherwise prescribe the practice and procedure, *§1782(a)* provides that "the testimony or statement shall be taken, and the document or other thing produced, in accordance with the Federal Rules of Civil Procedure." *Id.*

Here, the district court's order did not prescribe the "practice and procedure" for taking Clerici's testimony. Thus, under *§1782*, this testimony must be taken "in accordance with the Federal Rules of Civil Procedure." *Section 1782(a)* refers to the Federal Rules, not for whether the district court can order Clerici to give any testimony, but only for the procedures or manner in which that testimony is to be taken.

Once discovery is authorized under *§1782*, the federal discovery rules, *Fed. R. Civ. P. 26–36*, contain the relevant practices and procedures for the taking of testimony and the production of documents. For example, *Rule 26(a)(5)* authorizes the taking of testimony by deposition upon written questions, and *Rule 31* provides the specific practices and procedures for taking depositions upon written questions. *See Fed. R. Civ. P. 26(a)(5), 31.*

In contrast, *Rule 69(a)* provides the process by which a judgment creditor can enforce a money judgment and authorizes post-judgment discovery in aid of execution of that judgment. *Fed. R. Civ. P. 69(a). Rule 69(a)* itself does not prescribe a practice and procedure for gathering evidence, but gives the judgment creditor the choice of federal or state discovery rules. *Rule 69(a)* simply authorizes a setting, post-judgment execution, in which discovery may take place, not the specific manner or procedures in which testimony should be taken or documents should be produced. *Id.* Because *§1782(a)* refers to the Federal Rules only for the manner or procedure in which evidence is to be obtained, and *Rule 69(a)* prescribes no such manner or procedure, *Rule 69(a)* is inapplicable to *§1782* orders.

Even assuming *arguendo* that the discovery authorized by the district court's *§1782* order had to comply with *Rule 69(a)*, Clerici's testimony still could be taken in this case as long as it was taken in accordance with the federal discovery rules. *Rule 69(a)* itself expressly permits a "judgment creditor" to obtain discovery "[i]n aid of the judgment or execution," and gives the "judgment creditor" the choice of federal or state discovery procedures to conduct post-judgment discovery. *Fed. R. Civ. P. 69(a); see also F.D.I.C. v. LeGrand, 43 F.3d 163, 171 (5th Cir. 1995)* (rejecting judgment debtor's argument that "state procedural rules apply to the determination of the post-judgment discovery issue"). Thus, similar to *§1782, Rule 69(a)* gives a judgment creditor the option of taking a judgment debtor's testimony in accordance with the federal discovery rules. Nothing in *Rule 69(a)* conflicts with *§1782*. In any event, the *§1782* request for judicial assistance here was made by the Panamanian Court *after* NoName had obtained a judgment against Clerici. At a minimum, nothing in *Rule 69(a)* requires domestication of a foreign judgment before discovery is permitted under *§1782* for use in a proceeding in a foreign tribunal.

Moreover, imposing a requirement that a foreign judgment first must be domesticated in the United States before a *§1782* application for assistance can be granted by the district court to a foreign court would render *§1782* unnecessary in many circumstances. For example, in this case after Clerici's testimony is taken regarding his assets in Panama (if he has assets in Panama), NoName may be able to execute on its judgment in Panama and have no need to domesticate its judgment in this country.

In sum, *Rule 69(a)* does not bar the discovery authorized in this case by the district court's *§1782* order just because NoName's foreign judgment has not been domesticated in the United States. However, we do agree that until NoName's foreign judgment has been domesticated in this country, NoName cannot sequester, levy on, or seize control of, any assets of Clerici in this country. Further, although we affirm the district court's order granting the *§1782* application, Clerici remains free to argue against domestication of the Panamanian Court's judgment in this country when and if NoName pursues domestication.

IV. CONCLUSION

For all of these reasons, we affirm the district court's January 27, 2006 order denying Clerici's motion to vacate the district court's October 12, 2005 order granting the government's *§1782* application.

AFFIRMED.

TERMORIO S.A. E.S.P. AND LEASECO GROUP, LLC, APPELLANTS v. ELECTRANTA S.P., ET AL., APPELLEES UNITED STATES COURT OF APPEALS FOR THE DISTRICT OF COLUMBIA CIRCUIT

487 F.3d 928

February 12, 2007, Argued
May 25, 2007, Decided

EDWARDS, Senior Circuit Judge:

Appellant TermoRio S.A. E.S.P. ("TermoRio") and appellee Electrificadora del Atlantico S.A. E.S.P. ("Electranta"), a state-owned public utility, entered into a Power Purchase Agreement ("Agreement") pursuant to which TermoRio agreed to generate energy and Electranta agreed to buy it. When appellee allegedly failed to meet its obligations under the Agreement, the parties submitted their dispute to an arbitration Tribunal in Colombia in accordance with their Agreement. The Tribunal issued an award in excess of $60 million dollars in favor of TermoRio. Shortly after the Tribunal issued its award, Electranta filed an "extraordinary writ" in a Colombia court seeking to overturn the award. In due course, the Consejo de Estado ("Council of State"), Colombia's highest administrative court, nullified the arbitration award on the ground that the arbitration clause contained in the parties' Agreement violated Colombian law.

Following the judgment by the Consejo de Estado, TermoRio and co-appellant LeaseCo Group, LLC ("LeaseCo"), an investor in TermoRio, filed suit in the District Court against Electranta and the Republic of Colombia seeking enforcement of the Tribunal's arbitration award. Appellants contended that enforcement of the award is required under the Federal Arbitration Act, *9 U.S.C. §201* ("FAA"), which implements the Convention on the Recognition and Enforcement of Foreign Arbitral Awards, *opened for signature* June 10, 1958, 21 U.S.T. 2517, *reprinted in 9 U.S.C. §201* (historical and statutory notes) ("New York Convention"). The District Court dismissed LeaseCo as a party for want of standing, dismissed appellants' enforcement action for failure to state a claim upon which relief could be granted, and, in the alternative, dismissed appellants' action on the ground of *forum non conveniens*. *TermoRio S.A. E.S.P. v. Electrificadora del Atlantico S.A. E.S.P., 421 F. Supp. 2d 87 (D.D.C. 2006).*

We affirm the judgment of the District Court. The arbitration award was made in Colombia and the Consejo de Estado was a competent authority in that country to set aside the award as contrary to the law of Colombia. *See* New York Convention art. V(1)(e) ("Recognition and enforcement of the award may be refused, at the request of the party against whom it is invoked . . . if that party furnishes . . . proof that: . . . [t]he award . . . has been set aside . . . by a competent authority of the country in which, or under the law of which, that award was made."). Because there is nothing in the record here indicating that the proceedings before the Consejo de Estado were tainted or that the judgment of that court is other than authentic, the District Court was, as it held, obliged to respect it. *See Baker Marine (Nig.) Ltd. v. Chevron (Nig.) Ltd., 191 F.3d 194 (2d Cir. 1999).* Accordingly, we hold that, because the arbitration award was lawfully nullified by the country in which the award was made, appellants have no cause of action in the United States to seek enforcement of the award under the FAA or the New York Convention.

I. BACKGROUND

The facts in this case are carefully set forth in the District Court's published Memorandum opinion. *See TermoRio, 421 F. Supp. 2d at 89–91.* Because the facts relevant to this appeal are undisputed, we have incorporated significant portions of the District Court's statement as a part of our Background section.

> Defendant Republic of Colombia is a foreign state. Defendant [Electranta], incorporated in 1957 to provide electricity services in and around Barranquilla, Colombia, was 87% owned and controlled by Colombia. Consequently, it is an agency or instrumentality of Colombia within the meaning of the Foreign Sovereign Immunities Act (*28 U.S.C. §1603(b)*).
>
> In the mid-1990s, Colombia's Atlantic coast experienced significant electricity shortages. In 1995 LeaseCo entered into discussions with Electranta to modernize Electranta's operations and build a new power plant in Colombia. A year later, LeaseCo and Electranta formed two Colombian entities seriatim: first, Coenergia, and then TermoRio. Coenergia owned 99.9% of all shares of TermoRio. Initially, LeaseCo and Electranta owned roughly equal shares of Coenergia, so that they accordingly owned roughly equal shares of TermoRio. However, at the time of Electranta's complaint (in June 2004), LeaseCo and Electranta were transferring sole ownership of 99.9% of the shares of TermoRio to LeaseCo.
>
> At the heart of this lawsuit is [the Agreement] between TermoRio and Electranta [executed] in June 1997. Under this Agreement, TermoRio agreed to generate energy and Electranta agreed to buy it. In reliance on this Agreement, TermoRio invested more than $7 million to construct a power plant. The Agreement also provided that any dispute between the parties would be resolved by binding arbitration in Colombia.

However, in March 1998, Colombia announced a plan to sell the assets of all its Atlantic Coast utilities, including Electranta, to private owners and other Colombian utilities. On April 16, 1998, Colombia began to privatize by creating a new company, Electrocaribe, to receive and hold Electranta's assets and liabilities. However, at the behest of Colombia, Electranta did not transfer its duties under the Agreement to buy power from TermoRio. Electranta was left with obligations under the Agreement to buy power, but no resources to do so. As a result, Electranta failed to buy power from TermoRio and breached the Agreement. This breach of the Agreement, plaintiffs allege, had a direct effect in the United States affecting the extensive marketing of [Electrocaribe's] assets in the United States, by affecting the price of these assets, by causing United States purchasers to acquire a substantial interest in these assets, and by eliminating any obligation for Electrocaribe . . . to fulfill the [Agreement].

The Agreement's arbitration clause provides (as translated):

Any dispute or controversy arising between the Parties in connection to the execution, interpretation, performance or liquidation of the Contract shall be settled through mechanisms of conciliation, amiable composition or settlement, within a term no longer than three weeks. If no agreement is reached, either party may have recourse to an arbitral tribunal that *shall be governed in accordance with the Rules of Conciliation and Arbitration of the International Chamber of Commerce.* The tribunal shall be made up of three (3) members appointed by the Chamber, and shall be seated in the city of Barranquilla, Colombia]. The award, which shall be binding on the parties, must be rendered within a maximum term of three months.

Pursuant to this provision, after defendants failed to meet their obligations under the Agreement, the parties entered into a long arbitration process. On December 21, 2000, a Tribunal of three arbitrators, applying ICC procedural rules, determined that Electranta breached the Agreement at the direction of Colombia. The Tribunal ordered Electranta to pay TermoRio an award of $60.3 million USD.

Neither the Republic of Colombia nor Electranta has complied with the $60 million arbitral award, and both have refused to pay any portion of it. Plaintiffs allege that Colombia and Electranta have also sought to undermine the award in several other respects.

[O]n December 23, 2000 (right after the Tribunal issued the award), Electranta filed an "extraordinary writ" with a court in Barranquilla, seeking to overturn the award. In response the Council of State vacated it. The Council of State reasoned that the arbitration had to be conducted in accordance with Colombian law, and Colombian law in effect as of the date of the Agreement did not expressly permit the use of ICC procedural rules in arbitration.

In another action, plaintiff TermoRio filed two lawsuits in Colombian courts to rescind the transfer of Electranta's assets and to hold Colombia liable for breach of the Agreement. A Colombian court dismissed the first action on procedural grounds. The second count [was] still pending in the Colombian court system [as of March 17, 2006]. *Id. at 89–90.*

In the District Court, appellants TermoRio and LeaseCo filed an Amended Complaint and Application for Confirmation and Enforcement of Arbitral Award and for Other Relief. The appellants initially alleged four causes of action: fraudulent conveyance, expropriation, an action to enforce the arbitration award, and breach of contract. By stipulation, however, the first two claims were dropped, leaving only the action to enforce the arbitration award and the breach of contract claim before the District Court. Appellees filed a motion to dismiss in which they raised numerous defenses, including, *inter alia*, that the award was properly vacated by a Colombian court; that the District Court lacked subject matter jurisdiction by operation of the Foreign Sovereign Immunities Act and because the statute of limitations barred the suit; that the complaint should be dismissed under the doctrine of *forum non conveniens*; and that LeaseCo, an American corporation not party to the Agreement, lacked standing to enforce the arbitral award.

The District Court, after hearing arguments on the motion and reviewing the submissions of the parties – which included supporting memoranda, affidavits, sworn declarations, and the decisions of the Colombian courts – granted appellees' motion to dismiss. The trial court ruled as follows:

> [A]n accompanying Order dismisses LeaseCo for lack of standing. The court lacks subject matter jurisdiction over plaintiffs' breach of contract claim both under the Foreign Sovereign Immunities Act and by operation of the applicable statute of limitations. Although the court has subject matter jurisdiction over the remaining arbitral award enforcement claim, it is dismissed for failure to state a claim, the Colombian courts have vacated the award. In the alternative, the order dismisses the complaint on the ground of forum non conveniens. In this light, defendants' remaining arguments regarding abstention, dismissal of Colombia as a party, and service of process on defendants need not be addressed.
> *Id. at 92.*

Because it is clear and undisputed that TermoRio has standing to bring this lawsuit, we need not address the standing of LeaseCo. *Military Toxics Project v. EPA, 331 U.S. App. D.C. 7, 146 F.3d 948, 954 (D.C. Cir. 1998)* ("If one party has standing in an action, a court need not reach the issue of standing of other parties when it makes no difference to the merits of the case." (quoting *Ry. Labor Executives' Ass'n v. United States, 300 U.S. App. D.C. 142, 987 F.2d 806, 810 (D.C. Cir. 1993)*). In addition, because we hold that the District Court properly dismissed appellants' enforcement action under Article V(1)(e) of the New York Convention, we find it unnecessary to determine whether the case might have been dismissed on the ground of *forum non conveniens*, the alternative basis announced by the District Court. Likewise, we find it unnecessary to address any presumptive veil-piercing claim asserted by appellants to allow suit against the Republic of Colombia or whether such a claim is barred by the relevant statute of limitations. The only issue of consequence before this court is whether the District Court erred in dismissing appellants' claim to enforce the disputed arbitration award.

II. ANALYSIS

B. The Applicable International Agreement

As the District Court noted,

> [t]he United States has ratified and codified two Conventions that allow courts in one country to enforce arbitral awards rendered in other signatory countries.

> *See* Inter-American Convention on International Commercial Arbitration, *opened for signature* Jan. 30, 1975, O.A.S.T.S. No. 42, 1438 U.N.T.S. 245,] (the "Panama Convention") (reprinted after *9 U.S.C. §301*), and The Convention on the Recognition and Enforcement of Arbitral Awards (the "New York Convention") (reprinted after *9 U.S.C. §201*). Colombia is a signatory to both of these Conventions. The New York Convention provides that signatory nations are to recognize and enforce arbitral awards rendered in other nations. *See* New York Convention Art. III. However, enforcement of awards "may be refused" if, *inter alia*, they were set aside by a competent authority in the country in which the award was made. *See* New York Convention Art. V(1)(e).

TermoRio, 421 F. Supp. 2d at 91 & n.4. We need not decide whether *9 U.S.C. §302* incorporates the New York Convention, as opposed to other provisions of law related to the New York Convention, because the relevant provisions of the Panama Convention and the New York Convention are substantively identical for purposes of this case and neither party challenges the District Court's analysis. We therefore resolve this matter with reference to and using the language of the New York Convention.

C. *The Validity of a Foreign Judgment Vacating an Arbitration Award*

The Supreme Court has recognized an "emphatic federal policy in favor of arbitral dispute resolution." Mitsubishi Motors Corp. v. Soler Chrysler-Plymouth, Inc., 473 U.S.614, 631, 105 S. Ct. 3346, 87 L. Ed. 2d 444 (1985); see also Dean Witter Reynolds Inc. v. Byrd, 470 U.S. 213, 217, 105 S. Ct. 1238, 84 L. Ed. 2d 158 (1985) (noting that where parties have seen fit to adopt arbitration clauses in their agreements, there is a "strong federal policy in favor of enforcing [them]"). "And at least since this Nation's accession in 1970 to the [New York] Convention, and the implementation of the Convention in the same year by amendment of the Federal Arbitration Act, [9 U.S.C. §§201–208], that federal policy applies with special force in the field of international commerce." Mitsubishi, 473 U.S. at 631 (internal citation omitted). "As international trade has expanded in recent decades, so too has the use of international arbitration to resolve disputes arising in the course of that trade." Id. at 638. The Convention's purpose was to "encourage the recognition and enforcement of commercial arbitration agreements in international contracts and to unify the standards by which agreements to arbitrate are observed and arbitral awards are enforced in the signatory countries." Scherk v. Alberto-Culver Co., 417 U.S.506, 520 n.15, 94 S. Ct. 2449, 41 L. Ed. 2d 270 (1974). And, as the Court has noted, "[t]he utility of the [New York] Convention in promoting the process of international commercial arbitration depends upon the willingness of national courts to let go of matters they normally would think of as their own." Mitsubishi, 473 U.S. at 639 n.21.

The basic understanding of the New York Conventionis that "[e]ach Contracting State shall recognize arbitral awards as binding and enforce them in accordance with the rules of procedure of the territory where the award is relied upon, under the conditions laid down in the . . . articles [of the Convention]." New York Convention, art. III. Under the Convention, "the critical element is the place of the award: if that place is in the territory of a party to the Convention, all other Convention states are required to recognize and enforce the award, regardless of the citizenship or domicile of the parties to the arbitration." *Creighton Ltd. v. Gov't of the State of Qatar, 337 U.S. App. D.C. 7, 181 F.3d 118, 121 (D.C. Cir. 1999)* (quoting *RESTATEMENT (THIRD) OF FOREIGN RELATIONS LAW §487 cmt. b* (1987)).

Although its purpose is to encourage the recognition and enforcement of commercial arbitration agreements in international contracts, the New York Conventionenumerates specific grounds upon which a court may refuse recognition and enforcement of an arbitration award. These provisions of the Convention have been implemented by the FAA. *See 9 U.S.C. §207* ("The court shall confirm the award unless it finds one of the grounds for refusal or deferral of recognition or enforcement of the award specified in the said Convention.").

The Convention provides a carefully crafted framework for the enforcement of international arbitral awards. Under the Convention, "[o]nly a court in a country with primary jurisdiction over an arbitral award may annul that award." *Karaha Bodas Co. v. Perusahaan Pertambangan Minyak Dan Gas Bumi Negara, 364 F.3d 274, 287 (5th Cir. 2004)* ("*Karaha Bodas II*"). As the Second Circuit has noted:

> the Convention mandates very different regimes for the review of arbitral awards (1) in the state in which, or under the law of which, the award was made, and (2) in other states where recognition and enforcement are sought. The Convention specifically contemplates that the state in which, or under the law of which, the award is made, will be free to set aside or modify an award in accordance with its domestic arbitral law and its full panoply of express and implied grounds for relief. *See* Convention art. V(1)(e). However, the Convention is equally clear that when an action for enforcement is brought in a foreign state, the state may refuse to enforce the award only on the grounds explicitly set forth in Article V of the Convention. *Yusuf Ahmed Alghanim & Sons v. Toys "R" Us, Inc., 126 F.3d 15, 23 (2d Cir. 1997).*

In this case, appellees point out that, because the arbitration award was made by a Colombian Tribunal convened in that country, pursuant to an agreement between Colombian companies to buy and sell electrical power in that country, Colombia is the nation with primary jurisdiction over this dispute. Appellees argue further that, under the clear terms of the Convention, appellants' action to enforce the arbitration award fails to state a cause of action. On this latter point, appellees point to Article V(1)(e) of the Convention, which provides that

> [r]ecognition and enforcement of [an] award may be refused, at the request of the party against whom it is invoked, . . . if that party furnishes . . . proof that: . . . [t]he award . . . has been set aside . . . by a competent authority of the country in which, or under the law of which, that award was made.

New York Conventionart. V(1)(e). Pursuant to this provision of the Convention, a secondary Contracting State normally may not enforce an arbitration award that has been lawfully set aside by a "competent authority" in the primary Contracting State. Because the Consejo de Estado is undisputedly a "competent authority" in Colombia (the primary State), and because there is nothing in the record here indicating that the proceedings before the Consejo de Estado were tainted or that the judgment of that court is other than authentic, appellees contend that appellants have no cause of action under the FAA or the New York Convention to enforce the award in a Contracting State outside of Colombia. On the record at hand, we agree.

In reaching this conclusion, we generally subscribe to the reasoning of the Second Circuit in *Baker Marine, 191 F.3d 194*. In that case, Baker Marine, a barge company, executed a services contract with Danos, a shipping concern. The contract contained a clause requiring the parties to arbitrate disputes or controversies arising under their agreement. Following such a dispute, the parties "submitted to arbitration before panels of arbitrators in Lagos, Nigeria." *Id. at 195*. The panels awarded Baker Marine nearly $3 million in damages, but the award was subsequently set aside by a Nigerian court. Baker Marine then sought enforcement of the award in the United States District Court for the Northern District of New York. The trial court refused to recognize the award, citing Article V(1)(e) of the New York Convention, as well as principles of comity. On appeal, Baker Marine argued that the trial court erred in refusing to enforce the award, because it had been set aside by the Nigerian court on grounds that would have been invalid under U.S. law if presented in an American court. The appellate court rejected this argument and affirmed the trial court's decision not to recognize the award, noting that the parties "contracted in Nigeria that their disputes would be arbitrated under the laws of Nigeria." *Id. at 197*. The court also remarked on the undesirable consequences that would likely follow from adoption of Baker Marine's argument:

> [A]s a practical matter, mechanical application of domestic arbitral law to foreign awards under the Convention would seriously undermine finality and regularly produce conflicting judgments. If a party whose arbitration award has been vacated at the site of the award can automatically obtain enforcement of the awards under the domestic laws of other nations, a losing party will have every reason to pursue its adversary "with enforcement actions from country to country until a court is found, if any, which grants the enforcement."

Id. at 197 n.2 (quoting ALBERT JAN VAN DEN BERG, THE NEW YORK ARBITRATION CONVENTION OF 1958: TOWARDS A UNIFORM JUDICIAL INTERPRETATION 355 (1981)). The same principles and concerns govern here, where appellants seek to enforce an arbitration award that has been vacated by Colombia's Consejo de Estado. For us to endorse what appellants seek would seriously undermine a principal precept of the New York Convention: an arbitration award does not exist to be enforced in other Contracting States if it has been lawfully "set aside" by a competent authority in the State in which the award was made. This principle controls the disposition of this case.

D. Considerations of "Public Policy"

Appellants argue that courts in the United States "have discretion under the Convention to enforce an award despite annulment in another country," *Karaha Bodas Co. v. Perusahaan Pertambangan Minyak Dan Gas, 335 F.3d 357, 369 (5th Cir. 2003)*, because Article V(1)(e) merely says that "[r]ecognition and enforcement *may* be refused" if the award has been set aside by a competent authority in the primary state, New York Conventionart. V(1)(e) (emphasis added). More particularly, appellants contend that "a state is not required to give effect to foreign judicial proceedings grounded on policies which do violence to its own fundamental interests." Appellants' Br. at 22 (quoting *Laker Airways Ltd. v. Sabena, Belgian World Airlines, 235 U.S. App. D.C. 207, 731 F.2d 909, 931 (D.C. Cir. 1984))*. Appellants' characterizations of the applicable law are understated and thus misguided.

Appellants concede that *Baker Marine* is not incorrect in its holding that "it is insufficient to enforce an award solely because a foreign court's grounds for nullifying the award would not be recognized under domestic United States law." Appellants' Br. at 24. Rather, appellants allege that the District Court should have exercised its discretion to enforce the arbitration award in this case, because, *inter alia*, "the Council of State's decision was contrary to both domestic Colombian and international law; recognition of that decision would frustrate clearly expressed international and United States policy; and the process leading to the nullification decision demonstrated the Colombian government's determination to deny Plaintiffs fair process." *Id.*

In advancing their claims, appellants rely heavily on *In re Chromalloy Aeroservices, 939 F. Supp. 907 (D.D.C. 1996)*. In that case, the District Court addressed an arbitration agreement between the Egyptian Air Force and an American in which the parties provided that the losing party would not seek review of the arbitration award. While the American company's petition for enforcement of its award was pending before the District Court, Egypt filed an appeal with the Egyptian Court of Appeal to nullify the award. The District Court refused to recognize the decision of the Egyptian court to nullify the award, finding that to do so would violate clear United States public policy in favor of arbitration and would reward Egypt's breach of the express contractual agreement not to take any appeal from the arbitration award. We need not decide whether the holding in *Chromalloy* is correct, because, as appellees point out, "the present case is plainly distinguishable from *Chromalloy* where an express contract provision was violated by pursuing an appeal to vacate the award. Here, Electranta preserved its objection that the panel was not proper or authorized by law, promptly raised it in the Colombian courts, and received a definitive ruling by the highest court on this question of law." Appellees' Br. at 13 (internal citation omitted).

Furthermore, appellants are simply mistaken in suggesting that the Convention policy in favor of enforcement of arbitration awards effectively swallows the command of Article V(1)(e). A judgment whether to recognize or enforce an award that has not been set aside in the State in which it was made is quite different from a judgment whether to disregard the action of a court of competent authority in another State. "The Convention specifically contemplates that the state in which, or under the law of which, the award is made, will be free to set aside or modify an award in accordance with its domestic arbitral law and its full panoply of express and implied grounds for relief." *Yusuf Ahmed Alghanim & Sons, 126 F.3d at 23; see also Karaha Bodas II, 364 F.3d at 287–88*. This means that a primary State necessarily may set aside an award on grounds that are not consistent with the laws and policies of a secondary Contracting State. The Convention does not endorse a regime in which secondary States (in determining whether to enforce an award) routinely second-guess the judgment of a court in a primary State, when the court in the primary State has lawfully acted pursuant to "competent authority" to "set aside" an arbitration award made in its country. Appellants go much too far in suggesting that a court in a secondary State is free as it sees fit to ignore the judgment of a court of competent authority in a primary State vacating an arbitration award. It takes much more than a mere assertion that the judgment of the primary State "offends the public policy" of the secondary State to overcome a defense raised under Article V(1)(e).

The decision in *Baker Marine* notes that the "[r]ecognition of the [foreign court's] judgment in [that] case d[id] not conflict with United States public policy," *191 F.3d at 197 n.3*, thus at least implicitly endorsing a "public policy" gloss on Article V(1)(e). However, the decision does not say that a court in the United States has unfettered discretion to impose its own considerations of public policy in reviewing the judgment of a court in a primary State vacating an arbitration award based upon the foreign court's construction of the law of the primary State. Rather, as appellees argue, *Baker Marine* is consistent with the view that, "[w]hen a competent foreign court has nullified a foreign arbitration award, United States courts should not go behind that decision absent extraordinary circumstances not present in this case." Appellees' Br. at 12.

In applying Article V(1)(e) of the New York Convention, we must be very careful in weighing notions of "public policy" in determining whether to credit the judgment of a court in the primary State vacating an arbitration award. The test of public policy cannot be simply whether the courts of a secondary State would set aside an arbitration award if the award had been made and enforcement had been sought within its jurisdiction. As noted above, the Convention contemplates that different Contracting States may have different grounds for setting aside arbitration awards. Therefore, it is unsurprising that the courts have carefully limited the occasions when a foreign judgment is ignored on grounds of public policy.

> A judgment is unenforceable as against public policy to the extent that it is "repugnant to fundamental notions of what is decent and just in the State where enforcement is sought." *Tahan v. Hodgson, 213 U.S. App. D.C. 306, 662 F.2d 862, 864 (D.C. Cir. 1981)* (quoting *Rest.2d Conflict of Laws §117, comment c* (1971)). The standard is high, and infrequently met. As one court wrote, "[o]nly in clear-cut cases ought it to avail defendant." *Tahan, 662 F.2d at 866 n.17* (citing von Mehren & Trautman, *Recognition of Foreign Adjudications: A Survey and a Suggested Approach*, 81 HARV. L. REV. 1601, 1670 (1968); Paulsen & Sovern, *"Public Policy" in the Conflict of Laws*, 56 COLUM.L.REV. 969, 980–81, 1015–16 (1956)). In the classic formulation, a judgment that "tends clearly" to undermine the public interest, the public confidence in the administration of the law, or security for individual rights of personal liberty or of private property is against public policy. *Ackermann v. Levine, 788 F.2d 830, 841 (2d Cir. 1986)*.

Article V(2)(b) of the Convention, unlike Article V(1)(e), incorporates an express public policy exception. Article V(2)(b) provides:

> Recognition and enforcement of an arbitral award may also be refused if the competent authority in the country where recognition and enforcement is sought finds that . . . [t]he recognition or enforcement of the award would be contrary to the public policy of that country.

New York Convention, art. V(2)(b). It is noteworthy that in construing this provision the courts have been very careful not to stretch the compass of "public policy." As one court has noted:

> Under Article V(2)(b) of the New York Convention, a court may refuse to recognize or enforce an arbitral award if it would be contrary to the public policy of that country. The public policy defense is to be construed narrowly to be applied only where enforcement would violate the forum state's most basic notions of morality and justice.

Karaha Bodas II, 364 F.3d at 305–06 (internal citations and quotation marks omitted). Given that Article V(1)(e) contains no exception for public policy, it would be strange indeed to recognize such an implicit limitation in Article V(1)(e) that is broader than the express limitation in Article V(2)(b).

Accepting that there is a narrow public policy gloss on Article V(1)(e) of the Convention and that a foreign judgment is unenforceable as against public policy to the extent that it is "repugnant to fundamental notions of what is decent and just in the United States," *Tahan, 662 F.2d at 864* (internal quotation marks omitted), appellants' claims still fail. Appellants have neither alleged nor provided any evidence to suggest that the parties' proceedings before Colombia's Consejo de Estado or the judgment of that court violated any basic notions of justice to which we subscribe.

Appellants contend that the Consejo de Estado's ruling conflicts with Colombia's obligation under the New York Convention, but that bare allegation surely provides no basis for us to ignore Article V(1)(e) on grounds of public policy. As the court noted in *Yusuf Ahmed Alghanim & Sons*:

> [U]nder the Convention, the power and authority of the local courts of the rendering state remain of paramount importance. "What the Convention did not do . . . was provide any international mechanism to insure the validity of the award where rendered. This was left to the provisions of local law. The Convention provides no restraint whatsoever on the control functions of local courts at the seat of arbitration." [W. Laurence Craig, *Some Trends and Developments in the Laws and Practice of International Commercial Arbitration, 30 TEX. INT'L L.J. 1, 11 (1995).*]. Another commentator explained:
>
> Significantly, [Article V(1)(e)] fails to specify the grounds upon which the rendering State may set aside or suspend the award. While it would have provided greater reliability to the enforcement of awards under the Convention had the available grounds been defined in some way, such action would have constituted meddling with national procedure for handling domestic awards, a subject beyond the competence of the Conference.
>
> Leonard V. Quigley, *Accession by the United States to the United Nations Convention on the Recognition and Enforcement of Foreign Arbitral Awards*, 70 YALE L.J. 1049, 1070 (1961). From the plain language and history of the Convention, it is thus apparent that a party may seek to vacate or set aside an award in the state in which, or under the law of which, the award is rendered. Moreover, the language and history of the Convention make it clear that such a motion is to be governed by domestic law of the rendering state. *126 F.3d at 22–23.*

The District Court correctly observed that "[t]his matter is a peculiarly Colombian affair," concerning, as it does, "a dispute involving Colombian parties over a contract to perform services in Colombia which led to a Colombian arbitration decision and Colombian litigation." *TermoRio, 421 F. Supp. 2d at 101, 103*. To this, we would add that the parties also agreed to be bound by Colombian law. The Consejo de Estado, Colombia's highest administrative court, is the final expositor of Colombian law, and we are in no position to pronounce the decision of that court wrong.

E. *The District Court's Grant of Appellees' Motion to Dismiss*

Appellants have raised one final issue that warrants our attention. The District Court dismissed appellants' action under *Federal Rule of Civil Procedure 12(b)(6)*, which provides that a suit may be dismissed on the pleadings for "failure to state a claim upon which relief can be granted." *FED. R. CIV. P. 12(b)(6)*. Normally, dismissal is appropriate under *Rule 12(b)(6)* only if it is "clear that no relief could be granted under any set of facts that could be proved consistent with the allegations." *Broudy v. Mather, 373 U.S. App. D.C. 170, 460 F.3d 106, 116–17 (D.C. Cir. 2006)* (internal quotation marks omitted) (discussing dismissal under *FED. R. CIV. P. 12(b)(6)*). Appellants claim that the District Court erred in granting the motion to dismiss under *Rule 12(b)(6)*, because an affirmative defense only supports dismissal if that defense is unavoidably established by the facts alleged on the face of the complaint. Appellants argue that Colombia's nullification of the arbitration award is only grounds for a *Rule 12(b)(6)* dismissal if the nullification conclusively defeats appellants' claim. Application of Article V(1)(e) cannot be conclusive, appellants say, because, in their view, the New York Conventionand United States law provide that an arbitration award can be enforced despite having been nullified in the country in which it was issued. Thus, according to appellants, the District Court erred in dismissing their action under *Rule 12(b)(6)* solely on the basis of a foreign nullification.

The short answer to appellants' claim is that their reference to the requirements of *Rule 12(b)(6)* is misplaced. Chapter 2 of the FAA incorporates and codifies the New York Convention. *9 U.S.C. §201*. However, the statute makes clear that "[Chapter 1 of the FAA] applies to actions and proceedings brought under [Chapter 2] to the extent [Chapter 1] is not in conflict with [Chapter 2] or the Convention as ratified by the United States." *Id. §208*. Chapter 1, in turn, states that "[a]ny application to the court hereunder shall be made and heard in the manner provided by law for the making and hearing of motions, except as otherwise herein expressly provided." *Id. §6*. Therefore, it appears that motions to enforce arbitral awards should proceed under motions practice, not notice pleading. Indeed,

> [o]ne of the clearest examples of the operation of *Section 208* is its making motion practice under *Section 6* applicable to proceedings under the [New York Convention]. Thus, an arbitration award under the Convention may be enforced by filing a petition or application for an order confirming the award supported by an affidavit. The hearing on such a petition or application will

take the form of a summary procedure in the nature of federal motion practice.
3 FED. PROC., L. ED. §4:183 (1999).

In light of the foregoing, it is clear that the District Court properly addressed appellants' application for enforcement of the arbitration award. The District Court reviewed appellants' application and appellees' response, reviewed the affidavits submitted by the parties in support of their respective positions, and, on the basis of that review, arrived at its judgment. This satisfied the District Court's obligation under the New York Conventionand squared with the approach that has been endorsed by some of our sister circuits. *See, e.g., Productos Mercantiles E Industriales, S.A. v. Faberge USA, Inc., 23 F.3d 41, 46 (2d Cir. 1994)* ("Since [appellee] appropriately sought relief in the form of a motion, the court was not required to comply with the pleading requirements of *FED. R. CIV. P. 12(b).*"); *O.R. Sec., Inc. v. Prof'l Planning Assocs., 857 F.2d 742, 745–46 (11th Cir. 1988)* (same); *Imperial Ethiopian Gov't v. Baruch-Foster Corp., 535 F.2d 334, 335 & n.2 (5th Cir. 1976)* (same).

Furthermore, we note that, even if we were to assess the District Court's action by reference to the rules of notice pleading, we would find no error. Where, as here, both parties had sufficient opportunity to present evidence beyond the pleadings, this court has the authority to convert a motion to dismiss under *Rule 12(b)(6)* to a grant of summary judgment under *Federal Rule of Civil Procedure 56* and affirm the judgment of the District Court. *Ctr. for Auto Safety v. Nat'l Highway Traffic Safety Admin., 371 U.S. App. D.C. 422, 452 F.3d 798, 805 (D.C. Cir. 2006).* Summary judgment under *Rule 56* is appropriate where the pleadings and the record "show that there is no genuine issue as to any material fact and that the moving party is entitled to judgment as a matter of law." *Kingman Park Civic Ass'n v. Williams, 358 U.S. App. D.C. 295, 348 F.3d 1033, 1041 (D.C. Cir. 2003)* (quoting *FED. R. CIV. P. 56(c)*). Such is the case here.

Both parties had ample time to submit documents outside of the pleadings and did, in fact, submit such evidence. However, as noted by the District Court, appellants did not so much as allege that the proceedings in Colombia were repugnant to the public policy of the United States. *TermoRio, 421 F. Supp. 2d at 102.* And during oral argument before this court, appellants conceded that they were in no way foreclosed from introducing additional evidence or materials to the District Court to support a challenge to the validity or integrity of the proceedings that took place in Colombia. On this record, given the undisputed facts and the command of Article V(1)(e) of the New York Convention, summary judgment is appropriate. We must honor the judgment of the Colombia court vacating the disputed arbitration award, because there is nothing in the record here indicating that the proceedings before the Consejo de Estado were fatally flawed or that the judgment of that court is other than authentic.

III. CONCLUSION

For the foregoing reasons, the judgment of the District Court dismissing appellants' application for enforcement of the arbitration award is affirmed.

So ordered.

IN THE MATTER OF THE ARBITRATION OF CERTAIN CONTROVERSIES BETWEEN CHROMALLOY AEROSERVICES, a Division of Chromalloy Gas Turbine Corporation, Petitioner, and THE ARAB REPUBLIC OF EGYPT, Respondent.

UNITED STATES DISTRICT COURT FOR THE DISTRICT OF COLUMBIA

939 F. Supp. 907

July 31, 1996, Decided
July 31, 1996, FILED

UNITED STATES DISTRICT JUDGE JUNE L. GREEN

MEMORANDUM

I. Introduction

This matter is before the Court on the Petition of Chromalloy Aeroservices, Inc., ("CAS") to Confirm an Arbitral Award, and a Motion to Dismiss that Petition filed by the Arab Republic of Egypt ("Egypt"), the defendant in the arbitration. This is a case of first impression. The Court **GRANTS** Chromalloy Aeroservices' Petition to Recognize and Enforce the Arbitral Award, and **DENIES** Egypt's Motion to Dismiss, because the arbitral award in question is valid, and because Egypt's arguments against enforcement are insufficient to allow this Court to disturb the award.

II. Background

This case involves a military procurement contract between a U.S. corporation, Chromalloy Aeroservices, Inc., and the Air Force of the Arab Republic of Egypt.

On June 16, 1988, Egypt and CAS entered into a contract under which CAS agreed to provide parts, maintenance, and repair for helicopters belonging to the Egyptian Air Force. (Arbitration Award ("Award") at 3.) On December 2, 1991, Egypt terminated the contract by notifying CAS representatives in Egypt. (Award at 5.) On December 4, 1991, Egypt notified CAS headquarters in Texas of the termination. (*Id.*) On December 15, 1991, CAS notified Egypt that it rejected the cancellation of the contract "and commenced arbitration proceedings on the basis of the arbitration clause contained in Article XII and Appendix E of the Contract." (*Id.*) Egypt then drew down CAS' letters of guarantee in an amount totaling some $11,475,968. (*Id.*)

On February 23, 1992, the parties began appointing arbitrators, and shortly thereafter, commenced a lengthy arbitration. (*Id.*) On August 24, 1994, the arbitral panel ordered Egypt to pay to CAS the sums of $272,900 plus 5 percent interest from July 15, 1991, (interest accruing until the date of payment) and $16,940,958 plus 5 percent interest from December 15, 1991 (interest accruing until the date of payment). (*Id.* at 65–66.) The panel also ordered CAS to pay to Egypt the sum of 606,920 pounds sterling, plus 5 percent interest from December 15, 1991 (interest accruing until the date of payment). (*Id.*)

On October 28, 1994, CAS applied to this Court for enforcement of the award. On November 13, 1994, Egypt filed an appeal with the Egyptian Court of Appeal, seeking nullification of the award. On March 1, 1995, Egypt filed a motion with this Court to adjourn CAS's Petition to enforce the award. On April 4, 1995, the Egyptian Court of Appeal suspended the award, and on May 5, 1995, Egypt filed a Motion in this Court to Dismiss CAS's petition to enforce the award. On December 5, 1995, Egypt's Court of Appeal at Cairo issued an order nullifying the award. (Decision of Egyptian Court of Appeal ("Egypt Ct.") at 11.) This Court held a hearing in the matter on December 12, 1995.

Egypt argues that this Court should deny CAS' Petition to Recognize and Enforce the Arbitral Award out of deference to its court. (Response to Petitioner's Post-Hearing Brief at 2.) CAS argues that this Court should confirm the award because Egypt "does not present any serious argument that its court's nullification decision is consistent with the New York Conventionor United States arbitration law." (Petitioner's Rejoinder at 1.)

III. Discussion

A. Jurisdiction

This Court has original jurisdiction under the Foreign Sovereign Immunities Act, *28 U.S.C. §1330, et. seq. (1976)*, which provides in relevant part that:

> The district courts shall have original jurisdiction without regard to amount in controversy of any non-jury civil action against a foreign state as defined in *section 1603(a)* of this title as to any claim for relief in personam with respect to which the foreign state is not entitled to immunity . . . under sections 1605–1607 of this title.

28 U.S.C. §1330(a). Both the Arab Republic of Egypt and the Egyptian Air Force are foreign states under 28 U.S.C. §1603(a)&(b). See Republic of Argentina v. Weltover, 504 U.S. 607, 612, n.1, 119 L. Ed. 2d 394, 112 S. Ct. 2160. (1992).

> (a) A foreign state shall not be immune from the jurisdiction of courts of the United States . . . in any case
>
> * * *
>
> (6) *in which the action is brought*, either to enforce an agreement made by the foreign state with or for the benefit of a private party to submit to arbitration all or any differences which have arisen or which may arise between the parties with respect to a defined legal relationship, whether contractual or not, concerning a subject matter capable of settlement by arbitration under the laws of the United States, or *to confirm an award made pursuant to such an agreement*, if
>
> (B) the agreement or award is . . . governed by a treaty or other international agreement in force for the United States calling for the recognition and enforcement of arbitral awards.

28 U.S.C. §1605(a) & (a)(6) & (a)(6)(B)(emphasis added).

CAS brings this action to confirm an arbitral award made pursuant to an agreement to arbitrate any and all disputes arising under a contract between itself and Egypt, a foreign state, concerning a subject matter capable of settlement by arbitration under U.S. law. *See 9 U.S.C. §§1–14*. Enforcement of the award falls under the Convention on Recognition and Enforcement of Foreign Arbitral Awards, ("Convention"), *9 U.S.C. §202*, which grants "the district courts of the United States . . . original jurisdiction over such an action or proceeding, regardless of the amount in controversy." *9 U.S.C. §203*.

B. Chromalloy's Petition for Enforcement

A party seeking enforcement of a foreign arbitral award must apply for an order confirming the award within three years after the award is made. *9 U.S.C. §207*. The award in question was made on August 14, 1994. CAS filed a Petition to confirm the award with this Court on October 28, 1994, less than three months after the arbitral panel made the award. CAS's Petition includes a "duly certified copy" of the original award as required by Article IV(1)(a) of the Convention, translated by a duly sworn translator, as required by Article IV(2) of the Convention, as well as a duly certified copy of the original contract and arbitration clause, as required by Article IV(1)(b) of the Convention. *9 U.S.C. §201*. CAS's Petition is properly before this Court.

1. The Standard under the Convention

This Court *must* grant CAS's Petition to Recognize and Enforce the arbitral "award unless it finds one of the grounds for refusal . . . of recognition or enforcement of the award specified in the . . . Convention." *9 U.S.C. §207*. Under the Convention, "Recognition and enforcement of the award *may* be refused" if Egypt furnishes to this Court "proof that . . . the award has . . . been set aside . . . by a competent authority of the country in which, or under the law of which, that award was made." Convention, Article V(1) & V(1)(e) (emphasis added), *9 U.S.C. §201*. In the present case, the award was made in Egypt, under the laws of Egypt, and has been nullified by the court designated by Egypt to review arbitral awards. Thus, the Court *may*, at its discretion, decline to enforce the award.

While Article V provides a discretionary standard, Article VII of the Convention *requires* that, "The provisions of the present Convention *shall not* . . . deprive any interested party of any right he may have to avail himself of an arbitral award in the manner and to the extent allowed by the law . . . of the country where such award is sought to be relied upon." *9 U.S.C. §201* (emphasis added). In other words, under the Convention, CAS maintains all rights to the enforcement of this Arbitral Award that it would have in the absence of the Convention. Accordingly, the Court finds that, if the Convention did not exist, the Federal Arbitration Act("FAA") would provide CAS with a legitimate claim to enforcement of this arbitral award. *See 9 U.S.C. §§1–14*. Jurisdiction over Egypt in such a suit would be available under *28 U.S.C. §§1330* (granting jurisdiction over foreign states "as to any claim for relief in personam with respect to which the foreign state is not entitled to immunity . . . under sections 1605–1607 of this title) and 1605(a)(2) (withholding immunity of foreign states for "an act outside the United States in connection with a commercial activity of the foreign state elsewhere and that act causes a direct effect in the United States"). *See Weltover, 504 U.S. at 607.* Venue for the action would lie with this Court under *28 U.S.C. §1391(f)* & *(f)(4)* (granting venue in civil cases against foreign governments to the United States District Court for the District of Columbia).

2. Examination of the Award under *9 U.S.C. §10*

Under the laws of the United States, arbitration awards are presumed to be binding, and may only be vacated by a court under very limited circumstances:

(a) In any of the following cases the United States court in and for the district wherein the award was made may make an order vacating the award upon the application of any party to the arbitration
   (1) Where the award was procured by corruption, fraud, or undue means.
   (2) Where there was evident partiality or corruption in the arbitrators, or either of them.
   (3) Where the arbitrators were guilty of misconduct in refusing to postpone the hearing, upon sufficient cause shown, or in refusing to hear evidence pertinent and material to the controversy; or of any other misbehavior by which the rights of any party have been prejudiced.
   (4) Where the arbitrators exceeded their powers, or so imperfectly executed them that a mutual, final, and definite award upon the subject matter submitted was not made. *9 U.S.C. §10.*

An arbitral award will also be set aside if the award was made in "'manifest disregard' of the law." *First Options of Chicago v. Kaplan, 131 L. Ed. 2d 985, 115 S. Ct. 1920, 1923 (1995).* "Manifest disregard of the law may be found if [the] arbitrator[s] understood and correctly stated the law but proceeded to ignore it." *Kanuth v. Prescott, Ball, & Turben, Inc., 292 U.S. App. D.C. 319, 949 F.2d 1175, 1179 (D.C. Cir. 1991).*

> Plainly, this non-statutory theory of vacatur cannot empower a District Court to conduct the same de novo review of questions of law that an appellate court exercises over lower court decisions. Indeed, we have in the past held that it is clear that [manifest disregard] means more than error or misunderstanding with respect to the law. *Al-Harbi v. Citibank, 85 F.3d 680, 683 (D.C. Cir. 1996).*

In *Al-Harbi*, "The submission agreement under which the arbitrator decided the controversy mandated that the arbitrator apply 'the procedural and substantive laws of the Southern District of New York, U.S.A.'" *Id. at 684.* The arbitrator in *Al-Harbi* ruled that a court applying the laws of New York would dismiss the case on *forum non conveniens* grounds. *Id.* Appellant argued on appeal that the arbitrator had manifestly disregarded the substantive laws of New York by disposing of the case on procedural grounds. *Id.* The D.C. Circuit emphatically rejected this argument, stating that:

> Appellant's argument then depends upon the proposition that where a tribunal is to render [a] decision based on procedural and substantive law that tribunal has not only erred, but acted in manifest disregard of the law if it finds that procedural factors are dispositive of the case without then going on to consider substantive law rendered apparently moot by that procedural decision. To state that proposition is to reject it. We find no basis for vacatur. *Id.*

In the present case, the language of the arbitral award that Egypt complains of reads:

> The Arbitral tribunal considers that it does not need to decide the legal nature of the contract. It appears that the Parties rely principally for their claims and defences, on the interpretation of the contract itself and on the facts presented. Furthermore, the Arbitral tribunal holds that the legal issues in dispute are not affected by the characterization of the contract. (*Award* at 30.)

Like the arbitrator in *Al-Harbi*, the arbitrators in the present case made a procedural decision that allegedly led to a misapplication of substantive law. After considering Egypt's arguments that Egyptian administrative law should govern the contract, the majority of the arbitral panel held that it did not matter which substantive law they applied – civil or administrative. *Id.* At worst, this decision constitutes a mistake of law, and thus is not subject to review by this Court. *See Al-Harbi, 85 F.3d at 684.*

In the United States, "We are well past the time when judicial suspicion of the desirability of arbitration and of the competence of arbitral tribunals inhibited the development of arbitration as an alternative means of dispute resolution." *Mitsubishi Motors Corp. v. Soler Chrysler Plymouth, Inc., 473 U.S. 614, 626, 87 L. Ed. 2d 444, 105 S. Ct. 3346 (1985).* In Egypt, however, "It is established that arbitration is an exceptional means for resolving disputes, requiring departure from the normal means of litigation before the courts, and the guarantees they afford." (Nullification Decision at 8.) Egypt's complaint that, "The Arbitral Award is null under Arbitration Law, . . . because it is not properly 'grounded' under Egyptian law," reflects this suspicious view of arbitration, and is precisely the type of technical argument that U.S. courts are not to entertain when reviewing an arbitral award. *See Montana Power Company v. Federal Power Commission, 144 U.S. App. D.C. 263, 445 F.2d 739, 755 (D.C. Cir. 1971) (cert. den. 400 U.S. 1013, 27 L. Ed. 2d 627, 91 S. Ct. 566 (1971))* (holding that, "Arbitrators do not have to give reasons") (*citing United Steelworkers v. Enterprise Wheel & Car Corp., 363 U.S. 593, 598, 4 L. Ed. 2d 1424, 80 S. Ct. 1358 (1960)).*

The Court's analysis thus far has addressed the arbitral award, and, as a matter of U.S. law, the award is proper. *See Sanders v. Washington Metro, Area Transit Auth., 260 U.S. App. D.C. 359, 819 F.2d 1151, 1157,* (D.C. Cir. 1988)(holding that, "When the parties have had a full and fair opportunity to present their evidence, the decisions of the arbitrator should be viewed as conclusive as to subsequent proceedings, absent some abuse of discretion by the arbitrator") (*citing* the *Restatement (Second) of Judgments §84(3)* (1982), *Greenblatt v. Drexel Burnham Lambert, Inc., 763 F.2d 1352 (11th Cir. 1985)).* The Court now considers the question of whether the decision of the Egyptian court should be recognized as a valid foreign judgment.

As the Court stated earlier, this is a case of first impression. There are no reported cases in which a court of the United States has faced a situation, under the Convention, in which the court of a foreign nation has nullified an otherwise valid arbitral award. This does not mean, however, that the Court is without guidance in this case. To the contrary, more than twenty years ago, in a case involving the enforcement of an arbitration clause under the FAA, the Supreme Court held that:

> An agreement to arbitrate before a specified tribunal is, in effect, a specialized kind of forum-selection clause. . . . The invalidation of such an agreement . . . would not only allow the respondent to repudiate its solemn promise but would, as well, reflect a parochial concept that all disputes must be resolved

under our laws and in our courts. *Scherk v. Alberto-Culver Co., 417 U.S. 506, 518 (1974).*

In *Scherck*, the Court forced a U.S. corporation to arbitrate a dispute arising under an international contract containing an arbitration clause. *Id. at 518.* In so doing, the Court relied upon the FAA, but took the opportunity to comment upon the purposes of the newly acceded-to Convention:

> The delegates to the Convention voiced frequent concern that courts of signatory countries in which an agreement to arbitrate is sought to be enforced should not be permitted to decline enforcement of such agreements on the basis of parochial views of their desirability or in a manner that would diminish the mutually binding nature of the agreements.... We think that this country's adoption and ratification of the Convention and the passage of Chapter 2 of the United States Arbitration Act provide strongly persuasive evidence of congressional policy consistent with the decision we reach today.

Id. at n.15. The Court finds this argument equally persuasive in the present case, where Egypt seeks to repudiate its solemn promise to abide by the results of the arbitration.

C. The Decision of Egypt's Court of Appeal

1. The Contract

"The arbitration agreement is a contract and the court will not rewrite it for the parties." Williams V. E.F. Hutton & Co., Inc., 753 F.2d 117, 119, 243 U.S. App. D.C. 299, (D.C. Cir. 1985) (citing Davis v. Chevy Chase Financial Ltd., 215 U.S. App. D.C. 117, 667 F.2d 160, 167 (D.C. Cir. 1981)). The Court "begin[s] with the 'cardinal principle of contract construction: that a document should be read to give effect to all its provisions and to render them consistent with each other.'" United States v. Insurance Co. of North America, 317 U.S. App. D.C. 459, 83 F.3d 1507, 1511 (D.C. Cir. 1996) (quoting Mastrobuono v. Shearson Lehman Hutton, Inc., 514 U.S. 52, 131 L. Ed. 2d 76, 115 S. Ct. 1212, 1219 (1995)). Article XII of the contract requires that the parties arbitrate all disputes that arise between them under the contract. Appendix E, which defines the terms of any arbitration, forms an integral part of the contract. The contract is unitary. Appendix E to the contract defines the "Applicable Law Court of Arbitration." The clause reads, in relevant part:

> It is... understood that both parties have irrevocably agreed to apply Egypt (sic) Laws and to choose Cairo as seat of the court of arbitration.
>
> The decision of the said court shall be final and binding and cannot be made subject to any appeal or other recourse. (Appendix E ("Appendix") to the Contract.)

This Court may not assume that the parties intended these two sentences to contradict one another, and must preserve the meaning of both if possible. *Insurance Co., 317 U.S. App. D.C. 459, 83 F.3d 1507, 1511 (D.C. Cir. 1996).* Egypt argues that the first quoted sentence supersedes the second, and allows an appeal to an Egyptian court. Such an interpretation, however, would vitiate the second sentence, and would ignore the plain language on the face of the contract. The Court concludes that the first sentence defines choice of law and choice of forum for the hearings of the arbitral panel. The Court further concludes that the second quoted sentence indicates the clear intent of the parties that any arbitration of a dispute arising under the contract is not to be appealed to any court. This interpretation, unlike that offered by Egypt, preserves the meaning of both sentences in a manner that is consistent with the plain language of the contract. The position of the latter sentence as the seventh and final paragraph, just before the signatures, lends credence to the view that this sentence is the final word on the arbitration question. In other words, the parties agreed to apply Egyptian Law to the arbitration, but, more important, they agreed that the arbitration ends with the decision of the arbitral panel.

2. The Decision of the Egyptian Court of Appeal

The Court has already found that the arbitral award is proper as a matter of U.S. law, and that the arbitration agreement between Egypt and CAS precluded an appeal in Egyptian courts. The Egyptian court has acted, however, and Egypt asks this Court to grant *res judicata* effect to that action.

The "requirements for enforcement of a foreign judgment . . . are that there be 'due citation' [*i.e.*, proper service of process] and that the original claim not violate U.S. public policy." *Tahan v. Hodgson, 213 U.S. App. D.C. 306, 662 F.2d 862, 864 (D.C. Cir. 1981)* (*citing Hilton v. Guyot, 159 U.S. 113, 202, 40 L. Ed. 95, 16 S. Ct. 139 (1895)*). The Court uses the term "public policy" advisedly, with a full understanding that, "Judges have no license to impose their own brand of justice in determining applicable public policy." *Northwest Airlines Inc. v. Airline Pilots Association, Int'l, 257 U.S. App. D.C. 181, 808 F.2d 76, 78 (D.C. Cir. 1987)*. Correctly understood, "Public policy emanates [only] from clear statutory or case law, 'not from general considerations of supposed public interest.'" *Id.* (*quoting U.S. Postal Workers Union v. United States Postal Service, 252 U.S. App. D.C. 169, 789 F.2d 1 (D.C. Cir. 1986)*).

The U.S. public policy in favor of final and binding arbitration of commercial disputes is unmistakable, and supported by treaty, by statute, and by case law. The Federal Arbitration Act"and the implementation of the Convention in the same year by amendment of the Federal Arbitration Act," demonstrate that there is an "emphatic federal policy in favor of arbitral dispute resolution," particularly "in the field of international commerce." *Mitsubishi v. Soler Chrysler Plymouth, 473 U.S. 614, 631, 87 L. Ed. 2d 444, 105 S. Ct. 3346 (1985)* (internal citation omitted); *cf. Revere Copper & Brass, Inc., v. Overseas Private Investment Corporation, 202 U.S. App. D.C. 81, 628 F.2d 81, 82 (D.C. Cir. 1980)* (holding that, "There is a strong public policy behind judicial enforcement of binding arbitration clauses"). A decision by this Court to recognize the decision of the Egyptian court would violate this clear U.S. public policy.

3. International Comity

"No nation is under an unremitting obligation to enforce foreign interests which are fundamentally prejudicial to those of the domestic forum." *Laker Airways Ltd. v. Sabena, Belgian World Airlines, 235 U.S. App. D.C. 207, 731 F.2d 909, 937 (D.C. Cir. 1984)*. "Comity *never* obligates a national forum to ignore 'the rights of its own citizens or of other persons who are under the protection of its laws.'" *731 F.2d at 942*, (emphasis added) (quoting *Hilton v. Guyot, 159 U.S. 113, 164, 40 L. Ed. 95, 16 S. Ct. 139 (1895)*. Egypt alleges that, "Comity is the chief doctrine of international law *requiring* U.S. courts to respect the decisions of competent foreign tribunals." However, comity does not and may not have the preclusive effect upon U.S. law that Egypt wishes this Court to create for it.

The Supreme Court's unanimous opinion in W.S. Kirkpatrick & Co., Inc. v. Environmental Tectonics Corp., Int'l, 493 U.S. 400, 408, 107 L. Ed. 2d 816, 110 S. Ct. 701 (1990), defines the proper limitations of the "act of state doctrine" and, by implication, judicial comity as well. Kirkpatrick arose out of a dispute between two U.S. companies over a government construction project in Nigeria. Kirkpatrick, the losing bidder, sued Environmental Techtonics, ("ETC"), the winning bidder, alleging that ETC acquired the contract by bribing Nigerian officials in violation of U.S. law. Id. ETC argued that the act of state doctrine precluded U.S. courts from hearing the case because to do so "would impugn or question the nobility of a foreign nation's motivations," and would "result in embarrassment to the sovereign or constitute interference in the conduct of [the] foreign policy of the United States." Id. at 408. The Supreme Court rejected this argument:

> The short of the matter is this: Courts in the United States have the power, and ordinarily the obligation, to decide cases and controversies properly presented to them. The act of state doctrine does not establish an exception for cases and controversies that may embarrass foreign governments, but merely requires that, in the process of deciding, the acts of foreign sovereigns taken within their own jurisdictions shall be deemed valid. *That doctrine has no application to the present case because the validity of no foreign sovereign act is at issue. Id. at 409* (emphasis added).

Similarly, in the present case, the question is whether this Court should give *res judicata* effect to the decision of the Egyptian Court of Appeal, not whether that court properly decided the matter under Egyptian law. Since the "act of state doctrine," as a whole, does not require U.S. courts to defer to a foreign sovereign on these facts, comity, which is but one of several "policies" that underlie the act of state "doctrine," *id. at 409*, does not require such deference either.

4. Choice of Law

Egypt argues that by choosing Egyptian law, and by choosing Cairo as the sight of the arbitration, CAS has for all time signed away its rights under the Convention and U.S. law. This argument is specious. When CAS agreed to the choice of law and choice of forum provisions, it waived its right to sue Egypt for breach of contract in the courts of the United States in favor of final and binding arbitration of such a dispute under the Convention. Having prevailed in the chosen forum, under the chosen law, CAS comes to this Court seeking recognition and enforcement of the award. The Convention was created for just this purpose. It is untenable to argue that by choosing arbitration under the Convention, CAS has waived rights specifically guaranteed by that same Convention.

5. Conflict between the Convention & the FAA

As a final matter, Egypt argues that, "Chromalloy's use of Article VII [to invoke the Federal Arbitration Act] contradicts the clear language of the Convention and would create an impermissible conflict under *9 U.S.C. §208*," by eliminating all consideration of Article V of the Convention. *See Vimar Seguros Y Reaseguros, S.A. v. M/V Sky Reefer, 132 L. Ed. 2d 462, 115 S. Ct. 2322, 2325 (1995)* (holding that, "When two statutes are capable of coexistence . . . it is the duty of the courts, absent a clearly expressed congressional intention to the contrary, to regard each as effective"). As the Court has explained, however, Article V provides a permissive standard, under which this Court *may* refuse to enforce an award. Article VII, on the other hand, mandates that this Court *must* consider CAS' claims under applicable U.S. law.

Article VII of the Convention provides that:

> The provisions of the present Convention shall not . . . deprive any interested party of any right he may have to avail himself of an arbitral award in the manner and to the extent allowed by the law . . . of the country where such award is sought to be relied upon.

9 U.S.C. §201. Article VII does not eliminate all consideration of Article V; it merely requires that this Court protect any rights that CAS has under the domestic laws of the United States. There is no conflict between CAS' use of Article VII to invoke the FAA and the language of the Convention.

IV. Conclusion

The Court concludes that the award of the arbitral panel is valid as a matter of U.S. law. The Court further concludes that it need not grant *res judicata* effect to the decision of the Egyptian Court of Appeal at Cairo. Accordingly, the Court **GRANTS** Chromalloy Aeroservices' Petition to Recognize and Enforce the Arbitral Award, and **DENIES** Egypt's Motion to Dismiss that Petition.

JUNE L. GREEN
UNITED STATES DISTRICT JUDGE
Dated: July 31, 1996

In re Application of: ROZ TRADING LTD., Elizabeth Square, P.O. Box 847, Grand Cayman, Grand Cayman Islands, British West Indies, Applicant.
UNITED STATES DISTRICT COURT FOR THE NORTHERN DISTRICT OF GEORGIA, ATLANTA DIVISION

469 F. Supp. 2d 1221

December 19, 2006, Decided
December 19, 2006, Filed

UNITED STATES DISTRICT JUDGE WILLIAM S. DUFFEY, JR.

This matter is before the Court on the Application of Roz Trading, Ltd. for an Order Directing The Coca-Cola Company to Produce Documents Pursuant to *28 U.S.C. §1782* For Use in A Proceeding Before a Foreign Tribunal ("Application"), Respondent The Coca-Cola Company's Opposition to Petitioner's Application for

Discovery Pursuant to *28 U.S.C §1782* ("Response,"), and Roz Trading's Reply in Support of Its Application for Discovery Under *28 U.S.C. §1782* ("Reply").

I. BACKGROUND

This dispute concerns Roz Trading, Ltd.'s ("Petitioner's") request that the Court compel The Coca-Cola Company ("Respondent") to produce documents for use in arbitration proceedings ("foreign arbitration") before an arbitral panel of the International Arbitral Centre of the Austrian Federal Economic Chamber in Vienna (the "Centre"), in which Petitioner, Respondent's subsidiary The Coca-Cola Export Company ("CCEC"), and others are involved. The foreign arbitration concerns an alleged breach of contract between Petitioner and CCEC. The contract was entered into in connection with a joint venture between Petitioner, CCEC, and the government of Uzbekistan (the "joint venture"). Petitioner alleges the government of Uzbekistan violently seized Petitioner's interest in the joint venture. Petitioner alleges that its employees, fearful for their lives, left Uzbekistan. Under the circumstances of their departure, Petitioner claims its employees were unable to take any corporate documents with them, and that they have been to this day unable to return to Uzbekistan to retrieve them. Petitioner alleges that CCEC and the Respondent assisted the Uzbek government in eliminating Petitioner from the joint venture.

Petitioner has filed a claim before an arbitral panel of the Centre, pursuant to the contract governing the joint venture. Petitioner requests this Court to exercise its discretion under *28 U.S.C. §1782(a)* to compel Respondent to produce documents for those arbitration proceedings.

In this case, two issues determine whether the Court will grant Petitioner's Application: i) whether the Court has the authority to entertain the Application, specifically, whether the scope of *28 U.S.C. §1782(a)* includes proceedings before an arbitral panel of the Centre; and ii) whether the factors listed in *Intel Corp. v. Advanced Micro Devices, Inc., 542 U.S. 241, 124 S. Ct. 2466, 159 L. Ed. 2d 355 (2004)* favor granting the Application.

II. DISCUSSION

A. *Authority to Entertain the Application*

The Court first considers whether *§1782(a)* authorizes it to entertain the Application. *Section 1782(a)* provides:

> The district court of the district in which a person resides or is found may order him to give his testimony or statement or to produce a document or other thing for use in a proceeding in a foreign or international tribunal, including criminal investigations conducted before formal accusation. The order may be made pursuant to a letter rogatory issued, or request made, by a foreign or international tribunal or upon the application of any interested person and may direct that the testimony or statement be given, or the document or other thing be produced, before a person appointed by the court. By virtue of his appointment, the person appointed has power to administer any necessary oath and take the testimony or statement. The order may prescribe the practice

> and procedure, which may be in whole or part the practice and procedure of the foreign country or the international tribunal, for taking the testimony or statement or producing the document or other thing. To the extent that the order does not prescribe otherwise, the testimony or statement shall be taken, and the document or other thing produced, in accordance with the Federal Rules of Civil Procedure. *28 U.S.C. §1782(a) (2006).*

Section 1782(a) allows the Court to entertain Petitioner's request if: i) the target of the discovery "resides or is found" within this District; ii) the requesting party is a foreign or international tribunal or an "interested person" in the foreign proceeding; and iii) the discovery is requested "for use in a proceeding in a foreign or international tribunal."

Respondent does not dispute that the first two conditions have been met. Respondent's corporate headquarters are located in this judicial district, and Petitioner is a party to the arbitration for which the discovery is requested. Respondent also does not dispute that Petitioner requests discovery for use in a foreign proceeding.

Respondent argues, however, that the Centre is not a "tribunal" within the meaning of the statute. Respondent contends that, because the Centre is a private institution whose proceedings are voluntary and arbitral, an arbitral panel convened by the Centre is not a "tribunal" within the meaning of *§1782(a)*.

This issue is both interesting and one of first impression in this Circuit. The seminal Supreme Court case interpreting §1782(a) is Intel Corp. v. Advanced Micro Devices, Inc., 542 U.S.241, 124 S. Ct. 2466, 159 L. Ed. 2d 355 (2004). Although the Supreme Court in Intel did not address the precise issue of whether private arbitral panels are "tribunals" within the meaning of the statute, it provided sufficient guidance for this Court to determine that arbitral panels convened by the Centre are "tribunals" within the statute's scope.

In *Intel*, the Supreme Court held that the Directorate-General of Competition for the Commission of the European Communities ("DG-Competition") was a "tribunal" within the meaning of *§1782(a)*. This body "is the European Union's primary antitrust law enforcer." *Id. at 250*. The DG-Competition accepts antitrust complaints and conducts preliminary investigations. *Id. at 254*. The DG-Competition's decisions are "subject to review in the Court of First Instance and the European Court of Justice." *Id. at 255*.

The Supreme Court's reasons for finding the DG-Competition to constitute a "tribunal" in that case are instructive. The Supreme Court began by restating its firmly held principle that "in all statutory construction cases, we begin . . . with the language of the statute." *Id. quoting Barnhart v. Sigmon Coal Co., 534 U.S. 438, 450, 122 S. Ct. 941, 151 L. Ed. 2d 908 (2002)*. The Supreme Court began its statutory construction by noting that, in a 1964 amendment to *§1782*, "Congress deleted the words 'in any judicial proceeding pending in any court in a foreign country,' and replaced them with the phrase 'in a proceeding in a foreign or international tribunal.'" *Intel, 542 U.S. at 248–49* (citations omitted). The Supreme Court also observed: "Congress understood that change to provide the possibility of U.S. judicial assistance in connection with administrative and quasi-judicial proceedings."

Id. at 258 (internal quotation omitted). The Supreme Court stated expressly, albeit in dicta: "[T]he term 'tribunal' . . . includes investigating magistrates, administrative and *arbitral* tribunals, and quasi-judicial agencies, as well as conventional . . . courts." *Id., quoting* Hans Smit, *Int'l Lit. Under the United States Code*, 65 Colum. L. Rev. at 1026–27 (1965) (emphasis added).

In considering the status of the DG-Competition, the Supreme Court found that *§1782(a)* "authorizes, but does not require, a federal district court to provide assistance to a complainant in a European Commission proceeding that leads to a dispositive ruling, i.e., a final administrative action both responsive to the complaint and reviewable in court." *Id. at 255*. The Court also reasoned that the DG-Competition "is a *§1782(a)* 'tribunal' when it acts as a first-instance decisionmaker." *Id. at 247*. That is, the Supreme Court found the DG-Competition to constitute a *§1782(a)* tribunal to the extent that it acted as a first-instance decisionmaker, capable of rendering a decision on the merits, and as part of the process that could ultimately lead to final resolution of the dispute.

A finding that an arbitral panel of the Centre is a "tribunal" within the meaning of *§1782(a)* is consistent with the reasoning in *Intel*. Although *Intel* did not expressly hold arbitral bodies to be "tribunals," it quoted approvingly language that included "arbitral tribunals" within the term's meaning in *§1782(a)*. The Supreme Court also determined the DG-Competition to constitute a "tribunal" when it acted as a first-instance decisionmaker in a proceeding "that leads to a dispositive ruling, i.e., a final administrative action both responsive to the complaint and reviewable in court." *Id. at 255*. The Centre's arbitral panels are similarly "first-instance decisionmaker[s]" that issue decisions "both responsive to the complaint and reviewable in court." Respondent does not dispute that the Centre "is constituted to hear disputes, weigh evidence, and issue rulings that will finally bind the parties in accordance with its Rules . . ." (Memorandum of Law in Support of Pet. App. at 11.) Respondent also does not dispute that the Centre's orders "are enforceable in Austrian courts . . ." (*Id.*) The Centre, when examined under the same functional lens with which the Supreme Court in *Intel* examined the DG-Competition, must necessarily be considered a "tribunal" under *§1782(a)*.

Statutory construction of *§1782(a)* confirms this conclusion. The first step of statutory construction is to start "with the words of the statutory provision." *CBS Inc. v. PrimeTime 24 Joint Venture, 245 F.3d 1217, 1222 (11th Cir. 2001)*. When "the words of a statute are unambiguous . . . this first canon is also the last: judicial inquiry is complete." *Merritt v. Dillard Paper Co., 120 F.3d 1181, 1186 (11th Cir. 1997). See also United States v. Turkette, 452 U.S. 576, 580, 101 S. Ct. 2524, 69 L. Ed. 2d 246 (1981)*. When examining the words of a statute, "[i]n the absence of a statutory definition of a term, we look to the common usage of words for their meaning." *CBS, 245 F.3d at 1222*. When the words used are terms of art, a "cardinal" rule of statutory construction is that:

> [W]here Congress borrows terms of art in which are accumulated the legal tradition and meaning of centuries of practice, it presumably knows and adopts the cluster of ideas that were attached to each borrowed word in the body of learning from which it was taken and the meaning its use will convey to

> the judicial mind unless otherwise instructed. In such case, absence of contrary direction may be taken as satisfaction with widely accepted definitions, not as a departure from them. *Morissette v. United States, 342 U.S. 246, 263 (1952).*

When the language of a statute is unambiguous, courts are not entitled to impose their own limitations upon it. *See e.g., Turkette, 452 U.S. at 587* (reversing the First Circuit's construction of RICO because the limitations imposed were mandated by "neither the language nor structure of RICO . . ."). Unless there is a "clearly expressed legislative intent to the contrary, [unambiguous] language must ordinarily be regarded as conclusive." *Id. at 580* (quotation omitted).

Both the "common usage" and "widely accepted definition" of "tribunal" include arbitral bodies. *See, e.g., Scherk v. Alberto-Culver Co., 417 U.S. 506, 519–25, 94 S. Ct. 2449, 41 L. Ed. 2d 270 (1974)* (referring to the International Chamber of Commerce of Paris as a "tribunal"); *Mitsubishi Motors Corp. v. Soler Chrysler-Plymouth, Inc., 473 U.S. 614, 627, 105 S. Ct. 3346, 87 L. Ed. 2d 444 (1985)* (referring to arbitral bodies generally as "tribunals"); *Baltin v. Alaron Trading Corp, 128 F.3d 1466, 1468 (11th Cir. 1997)* (referring to an arbitral body as a "tribunal"). *See also* Smit, *International Litigation* at 1026–1027 ("the term 'tribunal' . . . includes investigating magistrates, administrative and *arbitral* tribunals, and quasi-judicial agencies, as well as conventional . . . courts."); *Black's Law Dictionary*, "tribunal" (8th ed. 2004) (defining "tribunal" as a "court or *other* adjudicatory body.") (emphasis added); William Blackstone, 3 *Commentaries* 17 (London, Strahan, Cadell, and Prince 1787) (10th ed.) (referring to arbitral bodies as "tribunals"); Joseph Story, *Commentaries on Equity Jurisprudence* §1457 at 686 (Boston, Little Brown and Co. 1866) (9th ed.) (referring to private arbitration proceedings as "tribunals").

The history of amendment to the statute supports a plain reading of the term "tribunal." In 1964, Congress by amendment deleted language that previously limited the type of adjudicatory body for which *§1782(a)* could be invoked. Congress expressly struck the phrase "judicial proceeding," and replaced it with "international or foreign tribunal." The clear import of the change is to broaden the scope of the statute to include non-judicial proceedings. The Supreme Court in *Intel* noted, "The legislative history of the 1964 revision . . . reflects Congress' recognition that judicial assistance would be available whether the foreign or international proceeding or investigation is of a criminal, civil, administrative, or other nature." *542 U.S. at 259* (internal quotation omitted). That is, the type of proceeding that Congress intended to benefit from judicial assistance under *§1782* is broad.

The language of *§1782(a)* is unambiguous. The common usage and widely accepted definition of "tribunal" are consistent with the structure of the statute. Reading the statute as a "consistent whole," *Burlison v. McDonald's Corp., 455 F.3d 1242, 1245–46 (11th Cir. 2006)*, the Court finds that "tribunal" should be construed consistent with its common usage and widely accepted definition. There is no clearly expressed legislative intent that the term "tribunal" does not include arbitral panels such as those convened by the Centre or that the term should be construed other than as it is commonly defined. In the absence of ambiguity, it would be improper for the Court to consider legislative history or impose its own limitations upon the meaning of the statute's terms. *Turkette, 542 U.S. at 587.*

The Centre is an arbitral body whose panels function in accordance with the widely accepted definition of the term "tribunal." The Court holds that the Centre is a "foreign or international tribunal" within the meaning of *§1782(a)*.

Respondent argues that Intel does not apply and that the Court should instead be guided by the decisions in Nat'l Broad. Co., Inc. v. Bear Stearns & Co., Inc., 165 F.3d 184 (2d. Cir. 1999) and Republic of Kazakhstan v. Beidermann Int'l, 168 F.3d 880 (5th Cir. 1999). These decisions are cited to support Respondent's contention that only governmental bodies qualify as "tribunals" under §1782(a). Both of these cases were decided five years before Intel. Their reasoning, and particularly that of Nat'l Broad. Co., is materially impacted by Intel. The reasoning in Intel demonstrates the structural and analytical flaws in the Second and Fifth Circuits' interpretations of §1782(a).

The Second Circuit in *Nat'l Broad. Co.* found *§1782(a)* to be ambiguous with respect to whether the term "tribunal" includes private arbitral bodies. The Second Circuit acknowledged that legal and conventional authorities, including cases, treaties, congressional statements, and academic writings including the works of Blackstone and Story, define the term "tribunal" to include private arbitral panels. Despite acknowledging this uniformly understood definition of "tribunal," the court reached the inconsistent conclusion that the term is ambiguous. *165 F.3d at 188*. It summarily concluded that "the fact that the term 'foreign or international tribunals' is broad enough to include both state-sponsored and private tribunals fails to mandate a conclusion that the term, as used in *§1782*, does include both." *Id.* The court then concluded that "the term 'foreign or international tribunal' is sufficiently ambiguous that it does not necessarily include or exclude the arbitral panel at issue here." *Id.* The court turned to the legislative history of *§1782(a)* to resolve this "ambiguity," and held ultimately that the legislative history suggested that the term "tribunal" does not include private arbitral panels. *Id.*

The Supreme Court's decision in *Intel* undermines the reasoning of *Nat'l Broad. Co.* The *Intel* court reviewed the legislative history of *§1782*, and found a legislative intent to broaden the scope of the term "tribunal." It noted specifically that "[t]he legislative history of the 1964 revision . . . reflects Congress' recognition that judicial assistance would be available whether the foreign or international proceeding or investigation is of a criminal, civil, administrative, or *other nature*." *Intel, 542 U.S. at 259* (emphasis added) (internal quotation omitted). The Supreme Court's interpretation and application of the legislative history contradicts the interpretations and applications of the Second and Fifth Circuits, which incorrectly concluded that Congress intended to limit the availability of judicial assistance under *§1782* to governmental – that is criminal, civil, or administrative – proceedings.

The definition of the term tribunal is, in basic terms, a body that performs a specific adjudicatory function. By rejecting "categorical limitations" on the scope of *§1782(a)*, *id. at 256*, and instead determining whether the DG-Competition constituted a "tribunal" within the meaning of the statute by analyzing its function, the Supreme Court elected to treat the term "tribunal" in accordance with the term's widely accepted definition. That is, it is the function of the body that makes it a "tribunal," not its formal identity as a "governmental" or "private" institution. Where a body makes adjudicative decisions responsive to a complaint and reviewable in court, it falls within the widely accepted definition of "tribunal," the reasoning of *Intel*, and the scope of *§1782(a)*, regardless of whether the body is governmental or private. The Supreme Court's approach recognizes this reality, and thus undermines the formalistic approach taken by the Second and Fifth Circuits.

For these reasons, this Court declines to follow the Second and Fifth Circuits because, in light of *Intel*, they are not persuasive authority. The Court instead relies instead on the statutory construction above and the reasoning in *Intel*.

B. The §1782(a) Petition

It is within the Court's discretion to grant or deny an application under *28 U.S.C. §1782(a)*. *Intel, 542 U.S. at 246*. Several factors guide the Court's consideration of an application under *§1782(a)*:

> First, when the person from whom discovery is being sought is a participant in the foreign proceeding . . . the need for *§1782(a)* aid is generally not as apparent as it ordinarily is when evidence is sought from a nonparticipant in the matter arising abroad. A foreign tribunal has jurisdiction over those appearing before it, and can itself order them to produce evidence. . . . Second, as the 1964 Senate report suggests, a court presented with a *§1782(a)* request may take into account the nature of the foreign tribunal, the character of the proceedings underway abroad, and the receptivity of the foreign government or the court or agency abroad to U.S. federal-court judicial assistance.

Id. at 244. See also Lopes v. Lopes, 180 Fed. Appx. 874, 877 (11th Cir. 2006). In exercising its informed discretion, the Court will, in addition to these factors, consider the scope of the information requested and its relation to the proceedings abroad. *Cf. Intel, 542 U.S. at 245* (noting that "unduly intrusive or burdensome requests may be rejected or trimmed.").

Respondent does not dispute that it is not a participant in the foreign proceeding, and notes that the agreement governing the joint venture was entered into between Petitioner and CCEC. Because Respondent was not a named party to that agreement, it appears that Petitioner cannot compel Respondent to the arbitral proceeding, and that the Centre does not have jurisdiction to compel discovery from Respondent. These circumstances weigh in favor of ordering discovery, because the foreign tribunal cannot "itself order [Respondent] to produce evidence." *Id.* "[T]he person from whom discovery is sought *must* . . . be a person or entity outside of the jurisdiction of the foreign tribunal . . ." *Lopes, 180 Fed. Appx. at 877* (emphasis added) (internal quotation omitted). Respondent meets this criteria.

The nature of the Centre, its character as a place for formal dispute resolution between international parties, and its likely receptivity of the aid of this Court, all weigh in favor of providing judicial assistance. The Centre is an international commercial arbitral body located in Vienna. According to Article 1 of the Centre's Rules of Arbitration, the purpose of the Centre is "to make arrangements for the settlement by arbitration of disputes in which not all contracting parties . . . had their place of business or their normal residence in Austria . . ." The Centre is fundamentally international in nature. It must rely on the aid of courts beyond its jurisdiction – such as United States District Courts acting pursuant to *§1782(a)* – to enforce its demands and to aid its inquiries, both within and without Austria.

The Centre is receptive to aid from courts such as this one. Article 589 of the Centre's Rules of Civil Procedure effective at the time Petitioner filed its Statement of Claims reads:

1. Those judicial acts considered necessary by the arbitrators but which they have no jurisdiction to undertake will be carried out by the State Court which has jurisdiction on the application of the arbitrators. In case of doubt the application is to be made to the District Court in whose district the act is to be carried out or the evidence to be taken.
2. The Court to which the application is made shall accede to it insofar as it is not legally inadmissable. In particular the Court shall also take those decisions regarding taking of evidence which are reserved by the present statute in the case of taking of evidence on commission to the Court hearing the case.

The Centre's Rules embrace discovery sought through mechanisms such as *§1782(a)*. This circumstance also weighs in favor of the Court granting Petitioner's request.

Petitioner claims, and Respondent does not dispute, that many of the documents previously in its possession were seized or made unavailable to it by the Uzbek government, and are now in the possession of Respondent. Thus, Respondent may be the only source for at least some of the documents requested. Petitioner claims further that Respondent, although not a formal party to the foreign proceeding, participated in the events that made these documents unavailable.

Respondent suggests that Petitioner should first seek discovery from CCEC through the arbitration proceedings. Respondent argues, "If the arbitration panel orders Coca-Cola Export to produce documents that are found only in the possession, custody, or control of The Coca-Cola Company, The Coca-Cola Company will have a strong incentive to cooperate with its subsidiary." (Resp. Brief in Opp. at 15.) This argument is not persuasive. *Section 1782(a)* does not contain an exhaustion requirement. The Petitioner meets the requirements of the statute, and is thus entitled under the present circumstances to seek judicial assistance for use in the foreign proceeding, regardless of other discovery means that may be available. Discovery is particularly appropriate where, as here, the practical availability of documents requested through other means of discovery is uncertain.

This case presents a unique set of facts. Petitioner suggests, and Respondent does not deny, that Respondent was in some measure involved in the events underlying the arbitration. Petitioner suggests, and Respondent does not deny, that some of the documents at issue in the arbitration may be in Respondent's exclusive possession, custody, and control. Petitioner also argues, and Respondent also does not deny, that many of the purportedly "public" documents on Petitioner's discovery list are closely held by the government of Uzbekistan, and cannot be accessed by Petitioner without great risk to its personnel. Respondent, as the CCEC's parent company, may have superior or exclusive access to many of the documents relevant to this dispute. In light of Petitioner's allegations that Respondent was involved to some degree in the underlying dispute, and in view of the likelihood that Respondent has unique access to relevant documents, the Court will exercise its discretion under *§1782(a)*.

Under *§1782(a)*, the Court is entitled to order discovery "in accordance with the Federal Rules of Civil Procedure." "[U]nduly intrusive or burdensome requests may be rejected or trimmed." *Intel, 542 U.S. at 245*. This Court will aid Petitioner to obtain discovery consistent with the scope imposed by *Federal Rule of Civil Procedure 26(b)(1)*:

> Parties may obtain discovery regarding any matter, not privileged, that is relevant to the claim or defense of any party. . . . For good cause, the court may order discovery of any matter relevant to the subject matter involved in the action. Relevant information need not be admissible at the trial if the discovery appears reasonably calculated to lead to the discovery of admissible evidence.

Petitioner first requests "an order directing [Respondent] to produce all documents relating to [Petitioner], the government of Uzbekistan, the Maqsudi family, the Karimov family, and [the joint venture], including its newest partner . . . Zeromax." (Memorandum of Law in Support of Peti. App. at 29.) This request is overbroad on its face. Petitioner demands information in several wide categories without limitation as to time, or place, and virtually without limitation as to subject matter.

Alternately, Petitioner presents a list of fifty-four (54) specific documents or document categories that it seeks from Respondent ("Documents to Be Produced") (Pet. App., Exh. A). The Court has considered each of these requests, and they appear to the Court generally relevant to the dispute, as described in the Statement of Claims filed by Petitioner in the proceedings before the Centre.

The Court will grant the petition with respect to Petitioner's "Documents to be Produced," with the following limitations:

1. All requests shall be limited to the period of January 1, 2000 to the date of this Order ("Order Date"), with the exception that requests for documents embodying communications to or from the Uzbek government or its officials. Requests for documents embodying communications to or from the Uzbek government or its officials shall be limited to the period of January 1, 1992 to the Order date.
2. The requests are limited to the extent that documents concerning private third parties such as Zeromax need only be produced if they pertain to the joint venture, communications with the Respondent or members of the joint venture from January 1, 2000 to the Order Date, inclusive, or the circumstances of Petitioner's expulsion from Uzbekistan.

In accordance with the *Rule 37(a)(2)(A)*, the parties are directed to work in good faith toward resolving any disputes regarding the production of this discovery prior to seeking the aid of this Court. If the parties are unable to resolve any disputes in good faith, they are directed to contact the Court to discuss the method for addressing any disputes they are unable to resolve between themselves.

Accordingly,

IT IS HEREBY ORDERED that the Application of Roz Trading, Ltd. for an Order Directing The Coca-Cola Company to Produce Documents Pursuant to *28 U.S.C. §1782* For Use in A Proceeding Before a Foreign Tribunal is **GRANTED**. Pursuant to this Order, Respondent is ordered to produce all documents responsive to the numbered requests in Petitioner's "Documents to be Produced" within its possession, custody, or control. These requests are limited as discussed above. Respondent is directed to produce the materials required by this Order on or before 5:00 p.m., EST, on January 20, 2007.

SO ORDERED, this 19th day of December, 2006.
WILLIAM S. DUFFEY, JR.
UNITED STATES DISTRICT JUDGE

APPENDIX C

The New York Convention, The Federal Arbitration Act, and 28 U.S.C. §1782

Convention on the Recognition and Enforcement of Foreign Arbitral Awards The "New York Convention"

Done at New York, on 10 June 1958

Article I

1. This Convention shall apply to the recognition and enforcement of arbitral awards made in the territory of a State other than the State where the recognition and enforcement of such awards are sought, and arising out of differences between persons, whether physical or legal. It shall also apply to arbitral awards not considered as domestic awards in the State where their recognition and enforcement are sought.
2. The term "arbitral awards" shall include not only awards made by arbitrators appointed for each case but also those made by permanent arbitral bodies to which the parties have submitted.
3. When signing, ratifying or acceding to this Convention, or notifying extension under article X thereof, any State may on the basis of reciprocity declare that it will apply the Convention to the recognition and enforcement of awards made only in the territory of another Contracting State. It may also declare that it will apply the Convention only to differences arising out of legal relationships, whether contractual or not, which are considered as commercial under the national law of the State making such declaration.

Article II

1. Each Contracting State shall recognize an agreement in writing under which the parties undertake to submit to arbitration all or any differences which have arisen or which may arise between them in respect of a defined legal relationship, whether contractual or not, concerning a subject matter capable of settlement by arbitration.
2. The term "agreement in writing" shall include an arbitral clause in a contract or an arbitration agreement, signed by the parties or contained in an exchange of letters or telegrams.

3. The court of a Contracting State, when seized of an action in a matter in respect of which the parties have made an agreement within the meaning of this article, shall, at the request of one of the parties, refer the parties to arbitration, unless it finds that the said agreement is null and void, inoperative or incapable of being performed.

Article III

Each Contracting State shall recognize arbitral awards as binding and enforce them in accordance with the rules of procedure of the territory where the award is relied upon, under the conditions laid down in the following articles. There shall not be imposed substantially more onerous conditions or higher fees or charges on the recognition or enforcement of arbitral awards to which this Convention applies than are imposed on the recognition or enforcement of domestic arbitral awards.

Article IV

1. To obtain the recognition and enforcement mentioned in the preceding article, the party applying for recognition and enforcement shall, at the time of the application, supply:
   (a) The duly authenticated original award or a duly certified copy thereof;
   (b) The original agreement referred to in article II or a duly certified copy thereof.
2. If the said award or agreement is not made in an official language of the country in which the award is relied upon, the party applying for recognition and enforcement of the award shall produce a translation of these documents into such language. The translation shall be certified by an official or sworn translator or by a diplomatic or consular agent.

Article V

1. Recognition and enforcement of the award may be refused, at the request of the party against whom it is invoked, only if that party furnishes to the competent authority where the recognition and enforcement is sought, proof that:
   (a) The parties to the agreement referred to in article II were, under the law applicable to them, under some incapacity, or the said agreement is not valid under the law to which the parties have subjected it or, failing any indication thereon, under the law of the country where the award was made; or
   (b) The party against whom the award is invoked was not given proper notice of the appointment of the arbitrator or of the arbitration proceedings or was otherwise unable to present his case; or
   (c) The award deals with a difference not contemplated by or not falling within the terms of the submission to arbitration, or it contains decisions on matters beyond the scope of the submission to arbitration, provided that, if the decisions on matters submitted to arbitration can be separated from those

not so submitted, that part of the award which contains decisions on matters submitted to arbitration may be recognized and enforced; or

(d) The composition of the arbitral authority or the arbitral procedure was not in accordance with the agreement of the parties, or, failing such agreement, was not in accordance with the law of the country where the arbitration took place; or

(e) The award has not yet become binding on the parties, or has been set aside or suspended by a competent authority of the country in which, or under the law of which, that award was made.

2. Recognition and enforcement of an arbitral award may also be refused if the competent authority in the country where recognition and enforcement is sought finds that:

(a) The subject matter of the difference is not capable of settlement by arbitration under the law of that country; or

(b) The recognition or enforcement of the award would be contrary to the public policy of that country.

Article VI

If an application for the setting aside or suspension of the award has been made to a competent authority referred to in article V(1)(e), the authority before which the award is sought to be relied upon may, if it considers it proper, adjourn the decision on the enforcement of the award and may also, on the application of the party claiming enforcement of the award, order the other party to give suitable security.

Article VII

1. The provisions of the present Convention shall not affect the validity of multilateral or bilateral agreements concerning the recognition and enforcement of arbitral awards entered into by the Contracting States nor deprive any interested party of any right he may have to avail himself of an arbitral award in the manner and to the extent allowed by the law or the treaties of the country where such award is sought to be relied upon.
2. The Geneva Protocol on Arbitration Clauses of 1923 [2] and the Geneva Convention on the Execution of Foreign Arbitral Awards of 1927 [3] shall cease to have effect between Contracting States on their becoming bound and to the extent that they become bound, by this Convention.

Article VIII

1. This Convention shall be open until 31 December 1958 for signature on behalf of any Member of the United Nations and also on behalf of any other State which is or hereafter becomes a member of any specialized agency of the United Nations, or which is or hereafter becomes a party to the Statute of the International Court of Justice, or any other State to which an invitation has been addressed by the General Assembly of the United Nations.

2. This Convention shall be ratified and the instrument of ratification shall be deposited with the Secretary-General of the United Nations.

Article IX

1. This Convention shall be open for accession to all States referred to in article VIII.
2. Accession shall be effected by the deposit of an instrument of accession with the Secretary-General of the United Nations.

Article X

1. Any State may, at the time of signature, ratification or accession, declare that this Convention shall extend to all or any of the territories for the international relations of which it is responsible. Such a declaration shall take effect when the Convention enters into force for the State concerned.
2. At any time thereafter any such extension shall be made by notification addressed to the Secretary-General of the United Nations and shall take effect as from the ninetieth day after the day of receipt by the Secretary-General of the United Nations of this notification, or as from the date of entry into force of the Convention for the State concerned, whichever is the later.
3. With respect to those territories to which this Convention is not extended at the time of signature, ratification or accession, each State concerned shall consider the possibility of taking the necessary steps in order to extend the application of this Convention to such territories, subject, where necessary for constitutional reasons, to the consent of the Governments of such territories.

Article XI

In the case of a federal or non-unitary State, the following provisions shall apply:

(a) With respect to those articles of this Convention that come within the legislative jurisdiction of the federal authority, the obligations of the federal Government shall to this extent be the same as those of Contracting States which are not federal States;

(b) With respect to those articles of this Convention that come within the legislative jurisdiction of constituent states or provinces which are not, under the constitutional system of the federation, bound to take legislative action, the federal Government shall bring such articles with a favourable recommendation to the notice of the appropriate authorities of constituent states or provinces at the earliest possible moment;

(c) A federal State Party to this Convention shall, at the request of any other Contracting State transmitted through the Secretary-General of the United Nations, supply a statement of the law and practice of the federation and its constituent units in regard to any particular provision of this Convention, showing the extent to which effect has been given to that provision by legislative or other action.

Article XII

1. This Convention shall come into force on the ninetieth day following the date of deposit of the third instrument of ratification or accession.
2. For each State ratifying or acceding to this Convention after the deposit of the third instrument of ratification or accession, this Convention shall enter into force on the ninetieth day after deposit by such State of its instrument of ratification or accession.

Article XIII

1. Any Contracting State may denounce this Convention by a written notification to the Secretary-General of the United Nations. Denunciation shall take effect one year after the date of receipt of the notification by the Secretary-General.
2. Any State which has made a declaration or notification under article X may, at any time thereafter, by notification to the Secretary-General of the United Nations, declare that this Convention shall cease to extend to the territory concerned one year after the date of the receipt of the notification by the Secretary-General.
3. This Convention shall continue to be applicable to arbitral awards in respect of which recognition or enforcement proceedings have been instituted before the denunciation takes effect.

Article XIV

A Contracting State shall not be entitled to avail itself of the present Convention against other Contracting States except to the extent that it is itself bound to apply the Convention.

Article XV

The Secretary-General of the United Nations shall notify the States contemplated in article VIII of the following:

(a) Signatures and ratifications in accordance with article VIII;
(b) Accessions in accordance with article IX;
(c) Declarations and notifications under articles I, X and XI;
(d) The date upon which this Convention enters into force in accordance with article XII;
(e) Denunciations and notifications in accordance with article XIII.

Article XVI

1. This Convention, of which the Chinese, English, French, Russian and Spanish texts shall be equally authentic, shall be deposited in the archives of the United Nations.
2. The Secretary-General of the United Nations shall transmit a certified copy of this Convention to the States contemplated in article VIII.

The Federal Arbitration Act

Chapter 1. GENERAL PROVISIONS

Section 1. "Maritime transactions" and "commerce" defined; exceptions to operation of title

"Maritime transaction," as herein defined, means charter parties, bills of lading of water carriers, agreements relating to wharfage, supplies furnished vessels or repairs to vessels, collisions, or any other matters in foreign commerce which, if the subject of controversy, would be embraced within admiralty jurisdiction; "commerce," as herein defined, means commerce among the several States or with foreign nations, or in any Territory of the United States or in the District of Columbia, or between any such Territory and another, or between any such Territory and any State or foreign nation, or between the District of Columbia and any State or Territory or foreign nation, but nothing herein contained shall apply to contracts of employment of seamen, railroad employees, or any other class of workers engaged in foreign or interstate commerce.

Section 2. Validity, irrevocability, and enforcement of agreements to arbitrate

A written provision in any maritime transaction or a contract evidencing a transaction involving commerce to settle by arbitration a controversy thereafter arising out of such contract or transaction, or the refusal to perform the whole or any part thereof, or an agreement in writing to submit to arbitration an existing controversy arising out of such a contract, transaction, or refusal, shall be valid, irrevocable, and enforceable, save upon such grounds as exist at law or in equity for the revocation of any contract.

Section 3. Stay of proceedings where issue therein referable to arbitration

If any suit or proceeding be brought in any of the courts of the United States upon any issue referable to arbitration under an agreement in writing for such arbitration, the court in which such suit is pending, upon being satisfied that the issue involved in such suit or proceeding is referable to arbitration under such an agreement, shall on application of one of the parties stay the trial of the action until such arbitration has been had in accordance with the terms of the agreement, providing the applicant for the stay is not in default in proceeding with such arbitration.

Section 4. Failure to arbitrate under agreement; petition to United States court having jurisdiction for order to compel arbitration; notice and service thereof; hearing and determination

A party aggrieved by the alleged failure, neglect, or refusal of another to arbitrate under a written agreement for arbitration may petition any United States district court which, save for such agreement, would have jurisdiction under Title 28, in a civil action or in admiralty of the subject matter of a suit arising out of the controversy between the parties, for an order directing that such arbitration proceed in the manner provided for in such agreement. Five days' notice in writing of such application shall be served upon the party in default. Service thereof shall be made in the manner provided by the Federal Rules of Civil Procedure. The court shall hear the parties, and upon being satisfied that the making of the agreement for arbitration or the failure to comply therewith is not in issue, the court shall make an order directing the parties to proceed to arbitration in accordance with the terms of the agreement. The hearing and proceedings, under such agreement, shall be within the district in which the petition for an order directing such arbitration is filed. If the making of the arbitration agreement or the failure, neglect, or refusal to perform the same be in issue, the court shall proceed summarily to the trial thereof. If no jury trial be demanded by the party alleged to be in default, or if the matter in dispute is within admiralty jurisdiction, the court shall hear and determine such issue. Where such an issue is raised, the party alleged to be in default may, except in cases of admiralty, on or before the return day of the notice of application, demand a jury trial of such issue, and upon such demand the court shall make an order referring the issue or issues to a jury in the manner provided by the Federal Rules of Civil Procedure, or may specially call a jury for that purpose. If the jury find that no agreement in writing for arbitration was made or that there is no default in proceeding thereunder, the proceeding shall be dismissed. If the jury find that an agreement for arbitration was made in writing and that there is a default in proceeding thereunder, the court shall make an order summarily directing the parties to proceed with the arbitration in accordance with the terms thereof.

Section 5. Appointment of arbitrators or umpire

If in the agreement provision be made for a method of naming or appointing an arbitrator or arbitrators or an umpire, such method shall be followed; but if no method be provided therein, or if a method be provided and any party thereto shall fail to avail himself of such method, or if for any other reason there shall be a lapse in the naming of an arbitrator or arbitrators or umpire, or in filling a vacancy, then upon the application of either party to the controversy the court shall designate and appoint an arbitrator or arbitrators or umpire, as the case may require, who shall act under the said agreement with the same force and effect as if he or they had been specifically named therein; and unless otherwise provided in the agreement the arbitration shall be by a single arbitrator.

Section 6. Application heard as motion

Any application to the court hereunder shall be made and heard in the manner provided by law for the making and hearing of motions, except as otherwise herein expressly provided.

Section 7. Witnesses before arbitrators; fees; compelling attendance

The arbitrators selected either as prescribed in this title or otherwise, or a majority of them, may summon in writing any person to attend before them or any of them as a witness and in a proper case to bring with him or them any book, record, document, or paper which may be deemed material as evidence in the case. The fees for such attendance shall be the same as the fees of witnesses before masters of the United States courts. Said summons shall issue in the name of the arbitrator or arbitrators, or a majority of them, and shall be signed by the arbitrators, or a majority of them, and shall be directed to the said person and shall be served in the same manner as subpoenas to appear and testify before the court; if any person or persons so summoned to testify shall refuse or neglect to obey said summons, upon petition the United States district court for the district in which such arbitrators, or a majority of them, are sitting may compel the attendance of such person or persons before said arbitrator or arbitrators, or punish said person or persons for contempt in the same manner provided by law for securing the attendance of witnesses or their punishment for neglect or refusal to attend in the courts of the United States.

Section 8. Proceedings begun by libel in admiralty and seizure of vessel or property

If the basis of jurisdiction be a cause of action otherwise justiciable in admiralty, then, notwithstanding anything herein to the contrary, the party claiming to be aggrieved may begin his proceeding hereunder by seizure of the vessel or other property of the other party according to the usual course of admiralty proceedings, and the court shall then have jurisdiction to direct the parties to proceed with the arbitration and shall retain jurisdiction to enter its decree upon the award.

Section 9. Award of arbitrators; confirmation; jurisdiction; procedure

If the parties in their agreement have agreed that a judgment of the court shall be entered upon the award made pursuant to the arbitration, and shall specify the court, then at any time within one year after the award is made any party to the arbitration may apply to the court so specified for an order confirming the award, and thereupon the court must grant such an order unless the award is vacated, modified, or corrected as prescribed in sections 10 and 11 of this title. If no court is specified in the agreement of the parties, then such application may be made to the United States court in and for the district within which such award was made. Notice of the application shall be served upon the adverse party, and thereupon the court shall have jurisdiction of such party as though he had appeared generally in the proceeding. If the adverse party is a resident of the district within which the award was made, such service shall be made upon the adverse party or his attorney as prescribed by law for service of notice of motion in an action in the same court. If the adverse party shall be a nonresident, then the notice of the application shall be served by the marshal of any district within which the adverse party may be found in like manner as other process of the court.

Section 10. Same; vacation; grounds; rehearing

a. In any of the following cases the United States court in and for the district wherein the award was made may make an order vacating the award upon the application of any party to the arbitration
   1. Where the award was procured by corruption, fraud, or undue means.

2. Where there was evident partiality or corruption in the arbitrators, or either of them.
3. Where the arbitrators were guilty of misconduct in refusing to postpone the hearing, upon sufficient cause shown, or in refusing to hear evidence pertinent and material to the controversy; or of any other misbehavior by which the rights of any party have been prejudiced.
4. Where the arbitrators exceeded their powers, or so imperfectly executed them that a mutual, final, and definite award upon the subject matter submitted was not made.
5. Where an award is vacated and the time within which the agreement required the award to be made has not expired the court may, in its discretion, direct a rehearing by the arbitrators.

b. The United States district court for the district wherein an award was made that was issued pursuant to section 590 of title 5 may make an order vacating the award upon the application of a person, other than a party to the arbitration, who is adversely affected or aggrieved by the award, if the use of arbitration or the award is clearly inconsistent with the factors set forth in section 582 of title 5.

Section 11. Same; modification or correction; grounds; order

In either of the following cases the United States court in and for the district wherein the award was made may make an order modifying or correcting the award upon the application of any party to the arbitration –

a. Where there was an evident material miscalculation of figures or an evident material mistake in the description of any person, thing, or property referred to in the award.
b. Where the arbitrators have awarded upon a matter not submitted to them, unless it is a matter not affecting the merits of the decision upon the matter submitted.
c. Where the award is imperfect in matter of form not affecting the merits of the controversy.

The order may modify and correct the award, so as to effect the intent thereof and promote justice between the parties.

Section 12. Notice of motions to vacate or modify; service; stay of proceedings

Notice of a motion to vacate, modify, or correct an award must be served upon the adverse party or his attorney within three months after the award is filed or delivered. If the adverse party is a resident of the district within which the award was made, such service shall be made upon the adverse party or his attorney as prescribed by law for service of notice of motion in an action in the same court. If the adverse party shall be a nonresident then the notice of the application shall be served by the marshal of any district within which the adverse party may be found in like manner as other process of the court. For the purposes of the motion any judge who might make an order to stay the proceedings in an action brought in the same court may make an order, to be served with the notice of motion, staying the proceedings of the adverse party to enforce the award.

Section 13. Papers filed with order on motions; judgment; docketing; force and effect; enforcement

The party moving for an order confirming, modifying, or correcting an award shall, at the time such order is filed with the clerk for the entry of judgment thereon, also file the following papers with the clerk:

a. The agreement; the selection or appointment, if any, of an additional arbitrator or umpire; and each written extension of the time, if any, within which to make the award.
b. The award.
c. Each notice, affidavit, or other paper used upon an application to confirm, modify, or correct the award, and a copy of each order of the court upon such an application

The judgment shall be docketed as if it was rendered in an action.

The judgment so entered shall have the same force and effect, in all respects, as, and be subject to all the provisions of law relating to, a judgment in an action; and it may be enforced as if it had been rendered in an action in the court in which it is entered.

Section 14. Contracts not affected

This title shall not apply to contracts made prior to January 1, 1926.

Section 15. Inapplicability of the Act of State doctrine

Enforcement of arbitral agreements, confirmation of arbitral awards, and execution upon judgments based on orders confirming such awards shall not be refused on the basis of the Act of State doctrine.

Section 16. Appeals

a. An appeal may be taken from
    1. an order –
        A. refusing a stay of any action under section 3 of this title,
        B. denying a petition under section 4 of this title to order arbitration to proceed,
        C. denying an application under section 206 of this title to compel arbitration,
        D. confirming or denying confirmation of an award or partial award, or
        E. modifying, correcting, or vacating an award;
    2. an interlocutory order granting, continuing, or modifying an injunction against an arbitration that is subject to this title; or
    3. a final decision with respect to an arbitration that is subject to this title.

b. Except as otherwise provided in section 1292(b) of title 28, an appeal may not be taken from an interlocutory order –
   1. granting a stay of any action under section 3 of this title;
   2. directing arbitration to proceed under section 4 of this title;
   3. compelling arbitration under section 206 of this title; or
   4. refusing to enjoin an arbitration that is subject to this title.

Chapter 2. CONVENTION ON THE RECOGNITION AND ENFORCEMENT OF FOREIGN ARBITRAL AWARDS

Section 201. Enforcement of Convention

The Convention on the Recognition and Enforcement of Foreign Arbitral Awards of June 10, 1958, shall be enforced in United States courts in accordance with this chapter.

Section 202. Agreement or award falling under the Convention

An arbitration agreement or arbitral award arising out of a legal relationship, whether contractual or not, which is considered as commercial, including a transaction, contract, or agreement described in section 2 of this title, falls under the Convention. An agreement or award arising out of such a relationship which is entirely between citizens of the United States shall be deemed not to fall under the Convention unless that relationship involves property located abroad, envisages performance or enforcement abroad, or has some other reasonable relation with one or more foreign states. For the purpose of this section a corporation is a citizen of the United States if it is incorporated or has its principal place of business in the United States.

Section 203. Jurisdiction; amount in controversy

An action or proceeding falling under the Convention shall be deemed to arise under the laws and treaties of the United States. The district courts of the United States (including the courts enumerated in section 460 of title 28) shall have original jurisdiction over such an action or proceeding, regardless of the amount in controversy.

Section 204. Venue

An action or proceeding over which the district courts have jurisdiction pursuant to section 203 of this title may be brought in any such court in which save for the arbitration agreement an action or proceeding with respect to the controversy between the parties could be brought, or in such court for the district and division which embraces the place designated in the agreement as the place of arbitration if such place is within the United States.

Section 205. Removal of cases from State courts

Where the subject matter of an action or proceeding pending in a State court relates to an arbitration agreement or award falling under the Convention, the defendant or the defendants may, at any time before the trial thereof, remove such action or proceeding to the district court of the United States for the district and division embracing the place where the action or proceeding is pending. The procedure for removal of causes otherwise provided by law shall apply, except that the ground for removal provided in this section need not appear on the face of the complaint but may be shown in the petition for removal. For the purposes of Chapter 1 of this title any action or proceeding removed under this section shall be deemed to have been brought in the district court to which it is removed.

Section 206. Order to compel arbitration; appointment of arbitrators

A court having jurisdiction under this chapter may direct that arbitration be held in accordance with the agreement at any place therein provided for, whether that place is within or without the United States. Such court may also appoint arbitrators in accordance with the provisions of the agreement.

Section 207. Award of arbitrators; confirmation; jurisdiction; proceeding

Within three years after an arbitral award falling under the Convention is made, any party to the arbitration may apply to any court having jurisdiction under this chapter for an order confirming the award as against any other party to the arbitration. The court shall confirm the award unless it finds one of the grounds for refusal or deferral of recognition or enforcement of the award specified in the said Convention.

Section 208. Chapter 1; residual application

Chapter 1 applies to actions and proceedings brought under this chapter to the extent that chapter is not in conflict with this chapter or the Convention as ratified by the United States.

Chapter 3. INTER-AMERICAN CONVENTION ON INTERNATIONAL COMMERCIAL ARBITRATION

Section 301. Enforcement of Convention

The Inter-American Convention on International Commercial Arbitration of January 30, 1975, shall be enforced in United States courts in accordance with this chapter.

Section 302. Incorporation by reference

Sections 202, 203, 204, 205, and 207 of this title shall apply to this chapter as if specifically set forth herein, except that for the purposes of this chapter "the Convention" shall mean the Inter-American Convention.

Section 303. Order to compel arbitration; appointment of arbitrators; locale

(a) A court having jurisdiction under this chapter may direct that arbitration be held in accordance with the agreement at any place therein provided for, whether that place is within or without the United States. The court may also appoint arbitrators in accordance with the provisions of the agreement.

(b) In the event the agreement does not make provision for the place of arbitration or the appointment of arbitrators, the court shall direct that the arbitration shall be held and the arbitrators be appointed in accordance with Article 3 of the Inter-American Convention.

Section 304. Recognition and enforcement of foreign arbitral decisions and awards; reciprocity

Arbitral decisions or awards made in the territory of a foreign State shall, on the basis of reciprocity, be recognized and enforced under this chapter only if that State has ratified or acceded to the Inter-American Convention.

Section 305. Relationship between the Inter-American Convention and the Convention on the Recognition and Enforcement of Foreign Arbitral Awards of June 10, 1958

When the requirements for application of both the Inter-American Convention and the Convention on the Recognition and Enforcement of Foreign Arbitral Awards of June 10, 1958, are met, determination as to which Convention applies shall, unless otherwise expressly agreed, be made as follows:

1. If a majority of the parties to the arbitration agreement are citizens of a State or States that have ratified or acceded to the Inter-American Convention and are member States of the Organization of American States, the Inter-American Convention shall apply.
2. In all other cases the Convention on the Recognition and Enforcement of Foreign Arbitral Awards of June 10, 1958, shall apply.

Section 306. Applicable rules of Inter-American Commercial Arbitration Commission

a. For the purposes of this chapter the rules of procedure of the Inter-American Commercial Arbitration Commission referred to in Article 3 of the Inter-American Convention shall, subject to subsection (b) of this section, be those rules as promulgated by the Commission on July 1, 1988.
b. In the event the rules of procedure of the Inter-American Commercial Arbitration Commission are modified or amended in accordance with the procedures for amendment of the rules of that Commission, the Secretary of State, by regulation in accordance with section 553 of title 5, consistent with the aims and purposes of this Convention, may prescribe that such modifications or amendments shall be effective for purposes of this chapter.

Section 307. Chapter 1; residual application

Chapter 1 applies to actions and proceedings brought under this chapter to the extent chapter 1 is not in conflict with this chapter or the Inter-American Convention as ratified by the United States.

§1782. Assistance to foreign and international tribunals and to litigants before such tribunals

(a) The district court of the district in which a person resides or is found may order him to give his testimony or statement or to produce a document or other thing for use in a proceeding in a foreign or international tribunal, including criminal investigations conducted before formal accusation. The order may be made pursuant to a letter rogatory issued, or request made, by a foreign or international tribunal or upon the application of any interested person and may direct that the testimony or statement be given, or the document or other thing be produced, before a person appointed by the court. By virtue of his appointment, the person appointed has power to administer any necessary oath and take the testimony or statement. The order may prescribe the practice and procedure, which may be in whole or part the practice and procedure of the foreign country or the international tribunal, for taking the testimony or statement or producing the document or other thing. To the extent that the order does not prescribe otherwise, the testimony or statement shall be taken, and the document or other thing produced, in accordance with the Federal Rules of Civil Procedure.

A person may not be compelled to give his testimony or statement or to produce a document or other thing in violation of any legally applicable privilege.

(b) This chapter [*28 USCS §§1781* et seq.] does not preclude a person within the United States from voluntarily giving his testimony or statement, or producing a document or other thing, for use in a proceeding in a foreign or international tribunal before any person and in any manner acceptable to him.

APPENDIX D

Amendments to 28 U.S.C. §1782

1949. Act May 24, 1949, in the first para. deleted "residing" following "witness" and substituted "judicial proceeding" for "civil action."

1964. Act Oct. 3, 1964 substituted this heading and section for ones which read:

"Testimony for use in foreign country.

'The deposition of any witness within the United States to be used in any judicial proceeding pending in any court in a foreign country with which the United States is at peace may be taken before a person authorized to administer oaths designated by the district court of any district where the witness resides or may be found.

"The practice and procedure in taking such depositions shall conform generally to the practice and procedure for taking depositions to be used in courts of the United States."

1996. Act Feb. 10, 1996, in subsec. (a), inserted "including criminal investigations conducted before formal accusation."

APPENDIX E

Selected Rules of Civil Procedure

Rule 3. Commencement of Action

A civil action is commenced by filing a complaint with the court.

Rule 26. General Provisions Governing Discovery; Duty of Disclosure

(a) Required Disclosures; Methods to Discover Additional Matter.
  (1) Initial Disclosures.

Except in categories of proceedings specified in Rule 26(a)(1)(E), or to the extent otherwise stipulated or directed by order, a party must, without awaiting a discovery request, provide to other parties:

- (A) the name and, if known, the address and telephone number of each individual likely to have discoverable information that the disclosing party may use to support its claims or defenses, unless solely for impeachment, identifying the subjects of the information;
- (B) a copy of, or a description by category and location of, all documents, electronically stored information, and tangible things that are in the possession, custody, or control of the party and that the disclosing party may use to support its claims or defenses, unless solely for impeachment;
- (C) a computation of any category of damages claimed by the disclosing party, making available for inspection and copying as under Rule 34 the documents or other evidentiary material, not privileged or protected from disclosure, on which such computation is based, including materials bearing on the nature and extent of injuries suffered; and
- (D) for inspection and copying as under Rule 34 any insurance agreement under which any person carrying on an insurance business may be liable to satisfy part or all of a judgment which may be entered in the action or to indemnify or reimburse for payments made to satisfy the judgment.
- (E) The following categories of proceedings are exempt from initial disclosure under Rule 26(a)(1):
  - (i) an action for review on an administrative record;
  - (ii) a forfeiture action in rem arising from a federal statute;
  - (iii) a petition for habeas corpus or other proceeding to challenge a criminal conviction or sentence;

(iv) an action brought without counsel by a person in custody of the United States, a state, or a state subdivision;
(v) an action to enforce or quash an administrative summons or subpoena;
(vi) an action by the United States to recover benefit payments;
(vii) an action by the United States to collect on a student loan guaranteed by the United States;
(viii) a proceeding ancillary to proceedings in other courts; and
(ix) an action to enforce an arbitration award.

These disclosures must be made at or within 14 days after the Rule 26(f) conference unless a different time is set by stipulation or court order, or unless a party objects during the conference that initial disclosures are not appropriate in the circumstances of the action and states the objection in the Rule 26(f) discovery plan. In ruling on the objection, the court must determine what disclosures – if any – are to be made, and set the time for disclosure. Any party first served or otherwise joined after the Rule 26(f) conference must make these disclosures within 30 days after being served or joined unless a different time is set by stipulation or court order. A party must make its initial disclosures based on the information then reasonably available to it and is not excused from making its disclosures because it has not fully completed its investigation of the case or because it challenges the sufficiency of another party's disclosures or because another party has not made its disclosures.

(2) Disclosure of Expert Testimony.
(A) In addition to the disclosures required by paragraph (1), a party shall disclose to other parties the identity of any person who may be used at trial to present evidence under Rules 702, 703, or 705 of the Federal Rules of Evidence.
(B) Except as otherwise stipulated or directed by the court, this disclosure shall, with respect to a witness who is retained or specially employed to provide expert testimony in the case or whose duties as an employee of the party regularly involve giving expert testimony, be accompanied by a written report prepared and signed by the witness. The report shall contain a complete statement of all opinions to be expressed and the basis and reasons therefore; the data or other information considered by the witness in forming the opinions; any exhibits to be used as a summary of or support for the opinions; the qualifications of the witness, including a list of all publications authored by the witness within the preceding ten years; the compensation to be paid for the study and testimony; and a listing of any other cases in which the witness has testified as an expert at trial or by deposition within the preceding four years.
(C) These disclosures shall be made at the times and in the sequence directed by the court. In the absence of other directions from the court or stipulation by the parties, the disclosures shall be made at least 90 days before the trial date or the date the case is to be ready for trial or, if the evidence is intended solely to contradict or rebut evidence on the same subject matter identified by another party under paragraph

(2)(B), within 30 days after the disclosure made by the other party. The parties shall supplement these disclosures when required under subdivision (e)(1).

(3) Pretrial Disclosures.

In addition to the disclosures required by Rule 26(a)(1) and (2), a party must provide to other parties and promptly file with the court the following information regarding the evidence that it may present at trial other than solely for impeachment:

(A) the name and, if not previously provided, the address and telephone number of each witness, separately identifying those whom the party expects to present and those whom the party may call if the need arises;
(B) the designation of those witnesses whose testimony is expected to be presented by means of a deposition and, if not taken stenographically, a transcript of the pertinent portions of the deposition testimony; and
(C) an appropriate identification of each document or other exhibit, including summaries of other evidence, separately identifying those which the party expects to offer and those which the party may offer if the need arises.

Unless otherwise directed by the court, these disclosures must be made at least 30 days before trial. Within 14 days thereafter, unless a different time is specified by the court, a party may serve and promptly file a list disclosing (i) any objections to the use under Rule 32(a) of a deposition designated by another party under Rule 26(a)(3)(B), and (ii) any objection, together with the grounds therefor, that may be made to the admissibility of materials identified under Rule 26(a)(3)(C). Objections not so disclosed, other than objections under Rules 402 and 403 of the Federal Rules of Evidence, are waived unless excused by the court for good cause.

(4) Form of Disclosures; Filing.

Unless the court orders otherwise, all disclosures under Rules 26(a)(1) through (3) must be made in writing, signed, and served.

(5) Methods to Discover Additional Matter.

Parties may obtain discovery by one or more of the following methods: depositions upon oral examination or written questions; written interrogatories; production of documents or things or permission to enter upon land or other property under Rule 34 or 45(a)(1)(C), for inspection and other purposes; physical and mental examinations; and requests for admission.

(b) Discovery Scope and Limits.

Unless otherwise limited by order of the court in accordance with these rules, the scope of discovery is as follows:

(1) In General.

Parties may obtain discovery regarding any matter, not privileged, that is relevant to the claim or defense of any party, including the existence, description, nature, custody, condition, and location of any books, documents, or other tangible things and the identity and location of persons having knowledge of any discoverable matter. For good cause, the court may order discovery of any matter relevant to the subject matter involved in the action. Relevant information need not be admissible at the trial if the discovery appears reasonably calculated to lead to the discovery of admissible evidence. All discovery is subject to the limitations imposed by Rule 26(b)(2)(i), (ii), and (iii).

(2) Limitations.
   (A) By order, the court may alter the limits in these rules on the number of depositions and interrogatories or the length of depositions under Rule 30. By order or local rule, the court may also limit the number of requests under Rule 36.
   (B) A party need not provide discovery of electronically stored information from sources that the party identifies as not reasonably accessible because of undue burden or cost. On motion to compel discovery or for a protective order, the party from whom discovery is sought must show that the information is not reasonably accessible because of undue burden or cost. If that showing is made, the court may nonetheless order discovery from such sources if the requesting party shows good cause, considering the limitations of Rule 26(b)(2)(C). The court may specify conditions for the discovery.
   (C) The frequency or extent of use of the discovery methods otherwise permitted under these rules and by any local rule shall be limited by the court if it determines that: (i) the discovery sought is unreasonably cumulative or duplicative, or is obtainable from some other source that is more convenient, less burdensome, or less expensive; (ii) the party seeking discovery has had ample opportunity by discovery in the action to obtain the information sought; or (iii) the burden or expense of the proposed discovery outweighs its likely benefit, taking into account the needs of the case, the amount in controversy, the parties' resources, the importance of the issues at stake in the litigation, and the importance of the proposed discovery in resolving the issues. The court may act upon its own initiative after reasonable notice or pursuant to a motion under Rule 26(c).
(3) Trial Preparation: Materials.

Subject to the provisions of subdivision (b)(4) of this rule, a party may obtain discovery of documents and tangible things otherwise discoverable under subdivision (b)(1) of this rule and prepared in anticipation of litigation or for trial by or for another party or by or for that other party's representative (including the other party's attorney, consultant, surety, indemnitor, insurer, or agent) only upon a showing that the party seeking discovery has substantial need of the materials in the preparation of the party's case and that the party is unable without undue hardship to obtain the substantial equivalent of the materials by other means. In ordering discovery of such materials when the required showing has been made, the court shall protect against disclosure of the mental impressions, conclusions, opinions, or legal theories of an attorney or other representative of a party concerning the litigation.

A party may obtain without the required showing a statement concerning the action or its subject matter previously made by that party. Upon request, a person not a party may obtain without the required showing a statement concerning the action or its subject matter previously made by that person. If the request is refused, the person may move for a court order. The provisions of Rule 37(a)(4) apply to the award of expenses incurred in relation to the motion. For purposes of this paragraph, a statement previously made is (A) a written statement signed or otherwise adopted or approved by the person making it, or (B) a stenographic, mechanical, electrical, or other recording, or a transcription thereof, which is a substantially verbatim recital of an oral statement by the person making it and contemporaneously recorded.

(4) Trial Preparation: Experts.
(A) A party may depose any person who has been identified as an expert whose opinions may be presented at trial. If a report from the expert is required under subdivision (a)(2)(B), the deposition shall not be conducted until after the report is provided.
(B) A party may, through interrogatories or by deposition, discover facts known or opinions held by an expert who has been retained or specially employed by another party in anticipation of litigation or preparation for trial and who is not expected to be called as a witness at trial, only as provided in Rule 35(b) or upon a showing of exceptional circumstances under which it is impracticable for the party seeking discovery to obtain facts or opinions on the same subject by other means.
(C) Unless manifest injustice would result, (i) the court shall require that the party seeking discovery pay the expert a reasonable fee for time spent in responding to discovery under this subdivision; and (ii) with respect to discovery obtained under subdivision (b)(4)(B) of this rule the court shall require the party seeking discovery to pay the other party a fair portion of the fees and expenses reasonably incurred by the latter party in obtaining facts and opinions from the expert.

(5) Claims of Privilege or Protection of Trial Preparation Materials.
(A) Information Withheld.

When a party withholds information otherwise discoverable under these rules by claiming that it is privileged or subject to protection as trial-preparation material, the party shall make the claim expressly and shall describe the nature of the documents, communications, or things not produced or disclosed in a manner that, without revealing information itself privileged or protected, will enable other parties to assess the applicability of the privilege or protection.

(B) Information Produced.

If information is produced in discovery that is subject to a claim of privilege or of protection as trial-preparation material, the party making the claim may notify any party that received the information of the claim and the basis for it. After being notified, a party must promptly return, sequester, or destroy the specified information and any copies it has and may not use or disclose the information until the claim is resolved. A receiving party may promptly present the information to the court under seal for a determination of the claim. If the receiving party disclosed the information before being notified, it must take reasonable steps to retrieve it. The producing party must preserve the information until the claim is resolved.

(c) Protective Orders.

Upon motion by a party or by the person from whom discovery is sought, accompanied by a certification that the movant has in good faith conferred or attempted to confer with other affected parties in an effort to resolve the dispute without court action, and for good cause shown, the court in which the action is pending or alternatively, on matters relating to a deposition, the court in the district where the deposition is to be taken may make any order which justice requires to protect a party or person from annoyance, embarrassment, oppression, or undue burden or expense, including one or more of the following:

(1) that the disclosure or discovery not be had;
(2) that the disclosure or discovery may be had only on specified terms and conditions, including a designation of the time or place;
(3) that the discovery may be had only by a method of discovery other than that selected by the party seeking discovery;
(4) that certain matters not be inquired into, or that the scope of the disclosure or discovery be limited to certain matters;
(5) that discovery be conducted with no one present except persons designated by the court;
(6) that a deposition, after being sealed, be opened only by order of the court;
(7) that a trade secret or other confidential research, development, or commercial information not be revealed or be revealed only in a designated way; and
(8) that the parties simultaneously file specified documents or information enclosed in sealed envelopes to be opened as directed by the court.

If the motion for a protective order is denied in whole or in part, the court may, on such terms and conditions as are just, order that any party or other person provide or permit discovery. The provisions of Rule 37(a)(4) apply to the award of expenses incurred in relation to the motion.

(d) Timing and Sequence of Discovery.

Except in categories of proceedings exempted from initial disclosure under Rule 26(a)(1)(E), or when authorized under these rules or by order or agreement of the parties, a party may not seek discovery from any source before the parties have conferred as required by Rule 26(f). Unless the court upon motion, for the convenience of parties and witnesses and in the interests of justice, orders otherwise, methods of discovery may be used in any sequence, and the fact that a party is conducting discovery, whether by deposition or otherwise, does not operate to delay any other party's discovery.

(e) Supplementation of Disclosures and Responses.

A party who has made a disclosure under subdivision (a) or responded to a request for discovery with a disclosure or response is under a duty to supplement or correct the disclosure or response to include information thereafter acquired if ordered by the court or in the following circumstances:

(1) A party is under a duty to supplement at appropriate intervals its disclosures under subdivision (a) if the party learns that in some material respect the information disclosed is incomplete or incorrect and if the additional or corrective information has not otherwise been made known to the other parties during the discovery process or in writing. With respect to testimony of an expert from whom a report is required under subdivision (a)(2)(B) the duty extends both to information contained in the report and to information provided through a deposition of the expert, and any additions or other changes to this information shall be disclosed by the time the party's disclosures under Rule 26(a)(3) are due.
(2) A party is under a duty seasonably to amend a prior response to an interrogatory, request for production, or request for admission if the party learns that the response is in some material respect incomplete or incorrect and if the additional or corrective information has not otherwise been made known to the other parties during the discovery process or in writing.

(f) Conference of Parties; Planning for Discovery.

Except in categories of proceedings exempted from initial disclosure under Rule 26(a)(1)(E) or when otherwise ordered, the parties must, as soon as practicable and in any event at least 21 days before a scheduling conference is held or a scheduling order is due under Rule 16(b), confer to consider the nature and basis of their claims and defenses and the possibilities for a prompt settlement or resolution of the case, to make or arrange for the disclosures required by Rule 26(a)(1), to discuss any issues relating to preserving discoverable information, and to develop a proposed discovery plan that indicates the parties' views and proposals concerning:

(1) what changes should be made in the timing, form, or requirement for disclosures under Rule 26(a), including a statement as to when disclosures under Rule 26(a)(1) were made or will be made;
(2) the subjects on which discovery may be needed, when discovery should be completed, and whether discovery should be conducted in phases or be limited to or focused upon particular issues;
(3) any issues relating to disclosure or discovery of electronically stored information, including the form or forms in which it should be produced;
(4) any issues relating to claims of privilege or of protection as trial-preparation material, including – if the parties agree on a procedure to assert such claims after production – whether to ask the court to include their agreement in an order;
(5) what changes should be made in the limitations on discovery imposed under these rules or by local rule, and what other limitations should be imposed; and
(6) any other orders that should be entered by the court under Rule 26(c) or under Rule 16(b) and (c).

The attorneys of record and all unrepresented parties that have appeared in the case are jointly responsible for arranging the conference, for attempting in good faith to agree on the proposed discovery plan, and for submitting to the court within 14 days after the conference a written report outlining the plan. A court may order that the parties or attorneys attend the conference in person. If necessary to comply with its expedited schedule for Rule 16(b) conferences, a court may by local rule (i) require that the conference between the parties occur fewer than 21 days before the scheduling conference is held or a scheduling order is due under Rule 16(b), and (ii) require that the written report outlining the discovery plan be filed fewer than 14 days after the conference between the parties, or excuse the parties from submitting a written report and permit them to report orally on their discovery plan at the Rule 16(b) conference.

(g) Signing of Disclosures, Discovery Requests, Responses, and Objections.
   (1) Every disclosure made pursuant to subdivision (a)(1) or subdivision (a)(3) shall be signed by at least one attorney of record in the attorney's individual name, whose address shall be stated. An unrepresented party shall sign the disclosure and state the party's address. The signature of the attorney or party constitutes a certification that to the best of the signer's knowledge, information, and belief, formed after a reasonable inquiry, the disclosure is complete and correct as of the time it is made.
   (2) Every discovery request, response, or objection made by a party represented by an attorney shall be signed by at least one attorney of record in the attorney's individual name, whose address shall be stated. An unrepresented party shall sign the request, response, or objection and state the party's address. The signature of the attorney or party constitutes a certification that to the best of the signer's knowledge, information, and belief, formed after a reasonable inquiry, the request, response, or objection is:
      (A) consistent with these rules and warranted by existing law or a good faith argument for the extension, modification, or reversal of existing law;
      (B) not interposed for any improper purpose, such as to harass or to cause unnecessary delay or needless increase in the cost of litigation; and
      (C) not unreasonable or unduly burdensome or expensive, given the needs of the case, the discovery already had in the case, the amount in controversy, and the importance of the issues at stake in the litigation.

If a request, response, or objection is not signed, it shall be stricken unless it is signed promptly after the omission is called to the attention of the party making the request, response, or objection, and a party shall not be obligated to take any action with respect to it until it is signed.

   (3) If without substantial justification a certification is made in violation of the rule, the court, upon motion or upon its own initiative, shall impose upon the person who made the certification, the party on whose behalf the disclosure, request, response, or objection is made, or both, an appropriate sanction, which may include an order to pay the amount of the reasonable expenses incurred because of the violation, including a reasonable attorney's fee.

Rule 27. Depositions Before Action or Pending Appeal

(a) Before Action.

(1) Petition.

A person who desires to perpetuate testimony regarding any matter that may be cognizable in any court of the United States may file a verified petition in the United States district court in the district of the residence of any expected adverse party. The petition shall be entitled in the name of the petitioner and shall show: (1) that the petitioner expects to be a party to an action cognizable in a court of the United States but is presently unable to bring it or cause it to be brought, (2) the subject matter of the expected action and the petitioner's interest therein, (3) the facts which the petitioner desires to establish by the proposed testimony and the reasons for desiring to perpetuate it, (4) the names or a description of the persons the petitioner expects will be adverse parties and their addresses so far as known, and (5) the names and addresses of the persons to be examined and the substance of the testimony which the petitioner expects to elicit from each, and shall ask for an order authorizing the petitioner to take the depositions of the persons to be examined named in the petition, for the purpose of perpetuating their testimony.

(2) Notice and Service.

At least 20 days before the hearing date, the petitioner must serve each expected adverse party with a copy of the petition and a notice stating the time and place of the hearing on the petition. The notice may be served either inside or outside the district or state in the manner provided in Rule 4. If service cannot be made with due diligence on an expected adverse party, the court may order service by publication or otherwise. The court must appoint an attorney to represent persons not served in the manner provided by Rule 4 and to cross-examine the deponent on behalf of persons not served and not otherwise represented. Rule 17(c) applies if any expected adverse party is a minor or is incompetent.

(3) Order and Examination.

If the court is satisfied that the perpetuation of the testimony may prevent a failure or delay of justice, it shall make an order designating or describing the persons whose depositions may be taken and specifying the subject matter of the examination and whether the depositions shall be taken upon oral examination or written interrogatories. The depositions may then be taken in accordance with these rules; and the court may make orders of the character provided for by Rules 34 and 35. For the purpose of applying these rules to depositions for perpetuating testimony, each reference therein to the court in which the action is pending shall be deemed to refer to the court in which the petition for such deposition was filed.

(4) Use of Deposition.

If a deposition to perpetuate testimony is taken under these rules or if, although not so taken, it would be admissible in evidence in the courts of the state in which it is taken, it may be used in any action involving the same subject matter subsequently brought in a United States district court, in accordance with the provisions of Rule 32(a).

(b) Pending Appeal.

If an appeal has been taken from a judgment of a district court or before the taking of an appeal if the time therefor has not expired, the district court in which the judgment was rendered may allow the taking of the depositions of witnesses to perpetuate their testimony for use in the event of further proceedings in the district court. In such case the party who desires to perpetuate the testimony may make a motion in the district court for leave to take the depositions, upon the same notice and service thereof as if the action was pending in the district court. The motion shall show (1) the names and addresses of persons to be examined and the substance of the testimony which the party expects to elicit from each; (2) the reasons for perpetuating their testimony. If the court finds that the perpetuation of the testimony is proper to avoid a failure or delay of justice, it may make an order allowing the depositions to be taken and may make orders of the character provided for by Rules 34 and 35, and thereupon the depositions may be taken and used in the same manner and under the same conditions as are prescribed in these rules for depositions taken in actions pending in the district court.

(c) Perpetuation by Action.

This rule does not limit the power of a court to entertain an action to perpetuate testimony.

Rule 30. Deposition Upon Oral Examination

(a) When Depositions May Be Taken; When Leave Required.
- (1) A party may take the testimony of any person, including a party, by deposition upon oral examination without leave of court except as provided in paragraph (2). The attendance of witnesses may be compelled by subpoena as provided in Rule 45.
- (2) A party must obtain leave of court, which shall be granted to the extent consistent with the principles stated in Rule 26(b)(2), if the person to be examined is confined in prison or if, without the written stipulation of the parties.
  - (A) A proposed deposition would result in more than ten depositions being taken under this rule or Rule 31 by the plaintiffs, or by the defendants, or by third-party defendants.
  - (B) The person to be examined already has been deposed in the case.
  - (C) A party seeks to take a deposition before the time specified in Rule 26(d) unless the notice contains a certification, with supporting facts, that the person to be examined is expected to leave the United States and be unavailable for examination in this country unless deposed before that time.

(b) Notice of Examination: General Requirements; Method of Recording; Production of Documents and Things; Deposition of Organization; Deposition by Telephone.
- (1) A party desiring to take the deposition of any person upon oral examination shall give reasonable notice in writing to every other party to the action.

The notice shall state the time and place for taking the deposition and the name and address of each person to be examined, if known, and, if the name is not known, a general description sufficient to identify the person or the particular class or group to which the person belongs. If a subpoena duces tecum is to be served on the person to be examined, the designation of the materials to be produced as set forth in the subpoena shall be attached to, or included in, the notice.

(2) The party taking the deposition shall state in the notice the method by which the testimony shall be recorded. Unless the court orders otherwise, it may be recorded by sound, sound-and-visual, or stenographic means, and the party taking the deposition shall bear the cost of the recording. Any party may arrange for a transcription to be made from the recording of a deposition taken by nonstenographic means.

(3) With prior notice to the deponent and other parties, any party may designate another method to record the deponent's testimony in addition to the method specified by the person taking the deposition. The additional record or transcript shall be made at that party's expense unless the court otherwise orders.

(4) Unless otherwise agreed by the parties, a deposition shall be conducted before an officer appointed or designated under Rule 28 and shall begin with a statement on the record by the officer that includes (A) the officer's name and business address; (B) the date, time and place of the deposition; (C) the name of the deponent; (D) the administration of the oath or affirmation to the deponent; and (E) an identification of all persons present. If the deposition is recorded other than stenographically, the officer shall repeat items (A) through (C) at the beginning of each unit of recorded tape or other recording medium. The appearance or demeanor of deponents or attorneys shall not be distorted through camera or sound-recording techniques. At the end of the deposition, the officer shall state on the record that the deposition is complete and shall set forth any stipulations made by counsel concerning the custody of the transcript or recording and the exhibits, or concerning other pertinent matters.

(5) The notice to a party deponent may be accompanied by a request made in compliance with Rule 34 for the production of documents and tangible things at the taking of the deposition. The procedure of Rule 34 shall apply to the request.

(6) A party may in the party's notice and in a subpoena name as the deponent a public or private corporation or a partnership or association or governmental agency and describe with reasonable particularity the matters on which examination is requested. In that event, the organization so named shall designate one or more officers, directors, or managing agents, or other persons who consent to testify on its behalf, and may set forth, for each person designated, the matters on which the person will testify. A subpoena shall advise a non-party organization of its duty to make such a designation. The persons so designated shall testify as to matters known or reasonably available to the organization. This subdivision (b)(6) does not preclude taking a deposition by any other procedure authorized in these rules.

(7) The parties may stipulate in writing or the court may upon motion order that a deposition be taken by telephone or other remote electronic means. For the purposes of this rule and Rules 28(a), 37(a)(1), and 37(b)(1), a deposition taken by such means is taken in the district and at the place where the deponent is to answer questions.

(c) Examination and Cross-Examination; Record of Examination; Oath; Objections

Examination and cross-examination of witnesses may proceed as permitted at the trial under the provisions of the Federal Rules of Evidence except Rules 103 and 615. The officer before whom the deposition is to be taken shall put the witness on oath or affirmation and shall personally, or by someone acting under the officer's direction and in the officer's presence, record the testimony of the witness. The testimony shall be taken stenographically or recorded by any other method authorized by subdivision (b)(2) of this rule. All objections made at the time of the examination to the qualifications of the officer taking the deposition, to the manner of taking it, to the evidence presented, to the conduct of any party, or to any other aspect of the proceedings shall be noted by the officer upon the record of the deposition; but the examination shall proceed, with the testimony being taken subject to the objections. In lieu of participating in the oral examination, parties may serve written questions in a sealed envelope on the party taking the deposition and the party taking the deposition shall transmit them to the officer, who shall propound them to the witness and record the answers verbatim.

(d) Schedule and Duration; Motion to Terminate or Limit Examination.

(1) Any objection during a deposition must be stated concisely and in a non-argumentative and non-suggestive manner. A person may instruct a deponent not to answer only when necessary to preserve a privilege, to enforce a limitation directed by the court, or to present a motion under Rule 30(d)(4).

(2) Unless otherwise authorized by the court or stipulated by the parties, a deposition is limited to one day of seven hours. The court must allow additional time consistent with Rule 26(b)(2) if needed for a fair examination of the deponent or if the deponent or another person, or other circumstance, impedes or delays the examination.

(3) If the court finds that any impediment, delay, or other conduct has frustrated the fair examination of the deponent, it may impose upon the persons responsible an appropriate sanction, including the reasonable costs and attorney's fees incurred by any parties as a result thereof.

(4) At any time during a deposition, on motion of a party or of the deponent and upon a showing that the examination is being conducted in bad faith or in such manner as unreasonably to annoy, embarrass, or oppress the deponent or party, the court in which the action is pending or the court in the district where the deposition is being taken may order the officer conducting the examination to cease forthwith from taking the deposition, or may limit the scope and manner of the taking of the deposition as provided in Rule 26(c). If the order made terminates the examination, it may be resumed thereafter only upon the order of the court in which the action is pending. Upon demand of the objecting party or deponent, the taking of the deposition

must be suspended for the time necessary to make a motion for an order. The provisions of Rule 37(a)(4) apply to the award of expenses incurred in relation to the motion.

(e) Review by Witness; Changes; Signing.

If requested by the deponent or a party before completion of the deposition, the deponent shall have 30 days after being notified by the officer that the transcript or recording is available in which to review the transcript or recording and, if there are changes in form or substance, to sign a statement reciting such changes and the reasons given by the deponent for making them. The officer shall indicate in the certificate prescribed by subdivision (f)(1) whether any review was requested and, if so, shall append any changes made by the deponent during the period allowed.

(f) Certification and Filing by Officer; Exhibits; Copies; Notices of Filing.
  (1) The officer must certify that the witness was duly sworn by the officer and that the deposition is a true record of the testimony given by the witness. This certificate must be in writing and accompany the record of the deposition. Unless otherwise ordered by the court, the officer must securely seal the deposition in an envelope or package endorsed with the title of the action and marked "Deposition of [here insert name of witness]" and must promptly send it to the attorney who arranged for the transcript or recording, who must store it under conditions that will protect it against loss, destruction, tampering, or deterioration. Documents and things produced for inspection during the examination of the witness must, upon the request of a party, be marked for identification and annexed to the deposition and may be inspected and copied by any party, except that if the person producing the materials desires to retain them the person may (A) offer copies to be marked for identification and annexed to the deposition and to serve thereafter as originals if the person affords to all parties fair opportunity to verify the copies by comparison with the originals, or (B) offer the originals to be marked for identification, after giving to each party an opportunity to inspect and copy them, in which event the materials may then be used in the same manner as if annexed to the deposition. Any party may move for an order that the original be annexed to and returned with the deposition to the court, pending final disposition of the case.
  (2) Unless otherwise ordered by the court or agreed by the parties, the officer shall retain stenographic notes of any deposition taken stenographically or a copy of the recording of any deposition taken by another method. Upon payment of reasonable charges therefor, the officer shall furnish a copy of the transcript or other recording of the deposition to any party or to the deponent.
  (3) The party taking the deposition shall give prompt notice of its filing to all other parties.

(g) Failure to Attend or to Serve Subpoena; Expenses.
  (1) If the party giving the notice of the taking of a deposition fails to attend and proceed therewith and another party attends in person or by attorney pursuant to the notice, the court may order the party giving the notice to

pay to such other party the reasonable expenses incurred by that party and that party's attorney in attending, including reasonable attorney's fees.

(2) If the party giving the notice of the taking of a deposition of a witness fails to serve a subpoena upon the witness and the witness because of such failure does not attend, and if another party attends in person or by attorney because that party expects the deposition of that witness to be taken, the court may order the party giving the notice to pay to such other party the reasonable expenses incurred by that party and that party's attorney in attending, including reasonable attorney's fees.

Rule 33. Interrogatories to Parties

(a) Availability.

Without leave of court or written stipulation, any party may serve upon any other party written interrogatories, not exceeding 25 in number including all discrete subparts, to be answered by the party served or, if the party served is a public or private corporation or a partnership or association or governmental agency, by any officer or agent, who shall furnish such information as is available to the party. Leave to serve additional interrogatories shall be granted to the extent consistent with the principles of Rule 26(b)(2). Without leave of court or written stipulation, interrogatories may not be served before the time specified in Rule 26(d).

(b) Answers and Objections.

(1) Each interrogatory shall be answered separately and fully in writing under oath, unless it is objected to, in which event the objecting party shall state the reasons for objection and shall answer to the extent the interrogatory is not objectionable.

(2) The answers are to be signed by the person making them, and the objections signed by the attorney making them.

(3) The party upon whom the interrogatories have been served shall serve a copy of the answers, and objections if any, within 30 days after the service of the interrogatories. A shorter or longer time may be directed by the court or, in the absence of such an order, agreed to in writing by the parties subject to Rule 29.

(4) All grounds for an objection to an interrogatory shall be stated with specificity. Any ground not stated in a timely objection is waived unless the party's failure to object is excused by the court for good cause shown.

(5) The party submitting the interrogatories may move for an order under Rule 37(a) with respect to any objection to or other failure to answer an interrogatory.

(c) Scope; Use at Trial.

Interrogatories may relate to any matters which can be inquired into under Rule 26(b)(1), and the answers may be used to the extent permitted by the rules of evidence.

An interrogatory otherwise proper is not necessarily objectionable merely because an answer to the interrogatory involves an opinion or contention that relates to fact or the application of law to fact, but the court may order that such an interrogatory need not be answered until after designated discovery has been completed or until a pre-trial conference or other later time.

(d) Option to Produce Business Records.

Where the answer to an interrogatory may be derived or ascertained from the business records, including electronically stored information, of the party upon whom the interrogatory has been served or from an examination, audit or inspection of such business records, including a compilation, abstract or summary thereof, and the burden of deriving or ascertaining the answer is substantially the same for the party serving the interrogatory as for the party served, it is a sufficient answer to such interrogatory to specify the records from which the answer may be derived or ascertained and to afford to the party serving the interrogatory reasonable opportunity to examine, audit or inspect such records and to make copies, compilations, abstracts, or summaries. A specification shall be in sufficient detail to permit the interrogating party to locate and to identify, as readily as can the party served, the records from which the answer may be ascertained.

Rule 34. Production of Documents and Things and Entry Upon Land for Inspection and Other Purposes

(a) Scope.

Any party may serve on any other party a request (1) to produce and permit the party making the request, or someone acting on the requestor's behalf, to inspect, copy, test, or sample any designated documents or electronically stored information – including writings, drawings, graphs, charts, photographs, sound recordings, images, and other data or data compilations stored in any medium from which information can be obtained – translated, if necessary, by the respondent into reasonably usable form, or to inspect, copy, test, or sample any designated tangible things which constitute or contain matters within the scope of Rule 26(b) and which are in the possession, custody or control of the party upon whom the request is served; or (2) to permit entry upon designated land or other property in the possession or control of the party upon whom the request is served for the purpose of inspection and measuring, surveying, photographing, testing, or sampling the property or any designated object or operation thereon, within the scope of Rule 26(b).

(b) Procedure.

The request shall set forth, either by individual item or by category, the items to be inspected, and describe each with reasonable particularity. The request shall specify a reasonable time, place, and manner of making the inspection and performing the related acts. The request may specify the form or forms in which electronically stored information is to be produced. Without leave of court or written stipulation, a request may not be served before the time specified in Rule 26(d).

The party upon whom the request is served shall serve a written response within 30 days after the service of the request. A shorter or longer time may be directed by the court or, in the absence of such an order, agreed to in writing by the parties, subject to Rule 29. The response shall state, with respect to each item or category, that inspection and related activities will be permitted as requested, unless the request is objected to, including an objection to the requested form or forms for producing electronically stored information, stating the reasons for the objection. If objection is made to part of an item or category, the part shall be specified and inspection permitted of the remaining parts. If objection is made to the requested form or forms for producing electronically stored information – or if no form was specified in the request – the responding party must state the form or forms it intends to use. The party submitting the request may move for an order under Rule 37(a) with respect to any objection to or other failure to respond to the request or any part thereof, or any failure to permit inspection as requested.

Unless the parties otherwise agree, or the court otherwise orders:

(i) a party who produces documents for inspection shall produce them as they are kept in the usual course of business or shall organize and label them to correspond with the categories in the request;

(ii) if a request does not specify the form or forms for producing electronically stored information, a responding party must produce the information in a form or forms in which it is ordinarily maintained or in a form or forms that are reasonably usable; and

(iii) a party need not produce the same electronically stored information in more than one form.

(c) Persons Not Parties.

A person not a party to the action may be compelled to produce documents and things or to submit to an inspection as provided in Rule 45.

Rule 36. Requests for Admission

(a) Request for Admission.

A party may serve upon any other party a written request for the admission, for purposes of the pending action only, of the truth of any matters within the scope of Rule 26(b)(1) set forth in the request that relate to statements or opinions of fact or of the application of law to fact, including the genuineness of any documents described in the request. Copies of documents shall be served with the request unless they have been or are otherwise furnished or made available for inspection and copying. Without leave of court or written stipulation, requests for admission may not be served before the time specified in Rule 26(d).

Each matter of which an admission is requested shall be separately set forth. The matter is admitted unless, within 30 days after service of the request, or within such shorter or longer time as the court may allow or as the parties may agree to in writing, subject to Rule 29, the party to whom the request is directed serves upon the party requesting the admission a written answer or objection addressed to the matter, signed by the party or by the party's attorney. If objection is made, the reasons therefor shall be stated. The answer shall specifically deny the matter or set forth in detail the reasons why the answering party cannot truthfully admit or deny the matter. A denial shall fairly meet the substance of the requested admission, and when good faith requires that a party qualify an answer or deny only a part of the matter of which an admission is requested, the party shall specify so much of it as is true and qualify or deny the remainder. An answering party may not give lack of information or knowledge as a reason for failure to admit or deny unless the party states that the party has made reasonable inquiry and that the information known or readily obtainable by the party is insufficient to enable the party to admit or deny. A party who considers that a matter of which an admission has been requested presents a genuine issue for trial may not, on that ground alone, object to the request; the party may, subject to the provisions of Rule 37(c), deny the matter or set forth reasons why the party cannot admit or deny it.

The party who has requested the admissions may move to determine the sufficiency of the answers or objections. Unless the court determines that an objection is justified, it shall order that an answer be served. If the court determines that an answer does not comply with the requirements of this rule, it may order either that the matter is admitted or that an amended answer be served. The court may, in lieu of these orders, determine that final disposition of the request be made at a pre-trial conference or at a designated time prior to trial. The provisions of Rule 37(a)(4) apply to the award of expenses incurred in relation to the motion.

(b) Effect of Admission.

Any matter admitted under this rule is conclusively established unless the court on motion permits withdrawal or amendment of the admission. Subject to the provision of Rule 16 governing amendment of a pre-trial order, the court may permit withdrawal or amendment when the presentation of the merits of the action will be subserved thereby and the party who obtained the admission fails to satisfy the court that withdrawal or amendment will prejudice that party in maintaining the action or defense on the merits. Any admission made by a party under this rule is for the purpose of the pending action only and is not an admission for any other purpose nor may it be used against the party in any other proceeding.

Rule 37. Failure to Make or Cooperate in Discovery; Sanctions

(a) Motion for Order Compelling Disclosure or Discovery.

A party, upon reasonable notice to other parties and all persons affected thereby, may apply for an order compelling disclosure or discovery as follows:

(1) Appropriate Court.

An application for an order to a party shall be made to the court in which the action is pending. An application for an order to a person who is not a party shall be made to the court in the district where the discovery is being, or is to be, taken.

(2) Motion.

(A) If a party fails to make a disclosure required by Rule 26(a), any other party may move to compel disclosure and for appropriate sanctions. The motion must include a certification that the movant has in good faith conferred or attempted to confer with the party not making the disclosure in an effort to secure the disclosure without court action.

(B) If a deponent fails to answer a question propounded or submitted under Rules 30 or 31, or a corporation or other entity fails to make a designation under Rule 30(b)(6) or 31(a), or a party fails to answer an interrogatory submitted under Rule 33, or if a party, in response to a request for inspection submitted under Rule 34, fails to respond that inspection will be permitted as requested or fails to permit inspection as requested, the discovering party may move for an order compelling answer, or a designation, or an order compelling inspection in accordance with the request. The motion must include a certification that the movant has in good faith conferred or attempted to confer with the person or party failing to make the discovery in an effort to secure the information or material without court action. When taking a deposition on oral examination, the proponent of the question may complete or adjourn the examination before applying for an order.

(3) Evasive or Incomplete Disclosure, Answer, or Response.

For purposes of this subdivision an evasive or incomplete disclosure, answer, or response is to be treated as a failure to disclose, answer, or respond.

(4) Expenses and Sanctions.

(A) If the motion is granted or if the disclosure or requested discovery is provided after the motion was filed, the court shall, after affording an opportunity to be heard, require the party or deponent whose conduct necessitated the motion or the party or attorney advising such conduct or both of them to pay to the moving party the reasonable expenses incurred in making the motion, including attorney's fees, unless the court finds that the motion was filed without the movant's first making a good faith effort to obtain the disclosure or discovery without court action, or that the opposing party's nondisclosure, response, or objection was substantially justified, or that other circumstances make an award of expenses unjust.

(B) If the motion is denied, the court may enter any protective order authorized under Rule 26(c) and shall, after affording an opportunity to be heard, require the moving party or the attorney filing the motion or both of them to pay to the party or deponent who opposed the motion the reasonable expenses incurred in opposing the motion, including attorney's fees, unless the court finds that the making of the motion was substantially justified or that other circumstances make an award of expenses unjust.

(C) If the motion is granted in part and denied in part, the court may enter any protective order authorized under Rule 26(c) and may, after affording an opportunity to be heard, apportion the reasonable expenses incurred in relation to the motion among the parties and persons in a just manner.

(b) Failure to comply with order.

(1) Sanctions by Court in District Where Deposition is Taken.

If a deponent fails to be sworn or to answer a question after being directed to do so by the court in the district in which the deposition is being taken, the failure may be considered a contempt of that court.

(2) Sanctions by Court in Which Action Is Pending.

If a party or an officer, director, or managing agent of a party or a person designated under Rule 30(b)(6) or 31(a) to testify on behalf of a party fails to obey an order to provide or permit discovery, including an order made under subdivision (a) of this rule or Rule 35, or if a party fails to obey an order entered under Rule 26(f), the court in which the action is pending may make such orders in regard to the failure as are just, and among others the following:

(A) An order that the matters regarding which the order was made or any other designated facts shall be taken to be established for the purposes of the action in accordance with the claim of the party obtaining the order;
(B) An order refusing to allow the disobedient party to support or oppose designated claims or defenses, or prohibiting that party from introducing designated matters in evidence;
(C) An order striking out pleadings or parts thereof, or staying further proceedings until the order is obeyed, or dismissing the action or proceeding or any part thereof, or rendering a judgment by default against the disobedient party;
(D) In lieu of any of the foregoing orders or in addition thereto, an order treating as a contempt of court the failure to obey any orders except an order to submit to a physical or mental examination;
(E) Where a party has failed to comply with an order under Rule 35(a) requiring that party to produce another for examination, such orders as are listed in paragraphs (A), (B), and (C) of this subdivision, unless the party failing to comply shows that that party is unable to produce such person for examination.

In lieu of any of the foregoing orders or in addition thereto, the court shall require the party failing to obey the order or the attorney advising that party or both to pay the reasonable expenses, including attorney's fees, caused by the failure, unless the court finds that the failure was substantially justified or that other circumstances make an award of expenses unjust.

(c) Failure to Disclose; False or Misleading Disclosure; Refusal to Admit.
(1) A party that without substantial justification fails to disclose information required by Rule 26(a) or 26(e)(1), or to amend a prior response to discovery as required by Rule 26(e)(2), is not, unless such failure is harmless, permitted to use as evidence at a trial, at a hearing, or on a motion any witness or information not so disclosed. In addition to or in lieu of this sanction, the court, on motion and after affording an opportunity to be heard, may impose other appropriate sanctions. In addition to requiring payment of reasonable expenses, including attorney's fees, caused by the failure, these sanctions may include any of the actions authorized under Rule 37(b)(2)(A),

(B), and (C) and may include informing the jury of the failure to make the disclosure.

(2) If a party fails to admit the genuineness of any document or the truth of any matter as requested under Rule 36, and if the party requesting the admissions thereafter proves the genuineness of the document or the truth of the matter, the requesting party may apply to the court for an order requiring the other party to pay the reasonable expenses incurred in making that proof, including reasonable attorney's fees. The court shall make the order unless it finds that (A) the request was held objectionable pursuant to Rule 36(a), or (B) the admission sought was of no substantial importance, or (C) the party failing to admit had reasonable ground to believe that the party might prevail on the matter, or (D) there was other good reason for the failure to admit.

(d) Failure of Party to Attend at Own Deposition or Serve Answers to Interrogatories or Respond to Request for Inspection.

If a party or an officer, director, or managing agent of a party or a person designated under Rule 30(b)(6) or 31(a) to testify on behalf of a party fails (1) to appear before the officer who is to take the deposition, after being served with a proper notice, or (2) to serve answers or objections to interrogatories submitted under Rule 33, after proper service of the interrogatories, or (3) to serve a written response to a request for inspection submitted under Rule 34, after proper service of the request, the court in which the action is pending on motion may make such orders in regard to the failure as are just, and among others it may take any action authorized under subparagraphs (A), (B), and (C) of subdivision (b)(2) of this rule. Any motion specifying a failure under clause (2) or (3) of this subdivision shall include a certification that the movant has in good faith conferred or attempted to confer with the party failing to answer or respond in an effort to obtain such answer or response without court action. In lieu of any order or in addition thereto, the court shall require the party failing to act or the attorney advising that party or both to pay the reasonable expenses, including attorney's fees, caused by the failure unless the court finds that the failure was substantially justified or that other circumstances make an award of expenses unjust.

The failure to act described in this subdivision may not be excused on the ground that the discovery sought is objectionable unless the party failing to act has a pending motion for a protective order as provided by Rule 26(c).

(e) [Abrogated]

(f) Electronically Stored Information.

Absent exceptional circumstances, a court may not impose sanctions under these rules on a party for failing to provide electronically stored information lost as a result of the routine, good-faith operation of an electronic information system.

(g) Failure to Participate in the Framing of a Discovery Plan.

If a party or a party's attorney fails to participate in the development and submission of a proposed discovery plan as required by Rule 26(f), the court may, after opportunity for hearing, require such party or attorney to pay to any other party the reasonable expenses, including attorney's fees, caused by the failure.

Rule 60. Relief from Judgment or Order

(a) Clerical Mistakes.

Clerical mistakes in judgments, orders or other parts of the record and errors therein arising from oversight or omission may be corrected by the court at any time of its own initiative or on the motion of any party and after such notice, if any, as the court orders. During the pendency of an appeal, such mistakes may be so corrected before the appeal is docketed in the appellate court, and thereafter while the appeal is pending may be so corrected with leave of the appellate court.

(b) Mistakes; Inadvertence; Excusable Neglect; Newly Discovered Evidence; Fraud, Etc.

On motion and upon such terms as are just, the court may relieve a party or a party's legal representative from a final judgment, order, or proceeding for the following reasons: (1) mistake, inadvertence, surprise, or excusable neglect; (2) newly discovered evidence which by due diligence could not have been discovered in time to move for a new trial under Rule 59(b); (3) fraud (whether heretofore denominated intrinsic or extrinsic), misrepresentation, or other misconduct of an adverse party; (4) the judgment is void; (5) the judgment has been satisfied, released, or discharged, or a prior judgment upon which it is based has been reversed or otherwise vacated, or it is no longer equitable that the judgment should have prospective application; or (6) any other reason justifying relief from the operation of the judgment. The motion shall be made within a reasonable time, and for reasons (1), (2), and (3) not more than one year after the judgment, order, or proceeding was entered or taken. A motion under this subdivision (b) does not affect the finality of a judgment or suspend its operation. This rule does not limit the power of a court to entertain an independent action to relieve a party from a judgment, order, or proceeding, or to grant relief to a defendant not actually personally notified as provided in Title 28, U.S.C., §1655, or to set aside a judgment for fraud upon the court. Writs of coram nobis, coram vobis, audita querela, and bills of review and bills in the nature of a bill of review, are abolished, and the procedure for obtaining any relief from a judgment shall be by motion as prescribed in these rules or by an independent action.

APPENDIX F

Geneva Convention of 1927

Geneva Convention, 1927

CONVENTION ON THE EXECUTION OF FOREIGN ARBITRAL AWARDS SIGNED AT GENEVA ON THE TWENTY-SIXTH DAY OF SEPTEMBER, NINETEEN HUNDRED AND TWENTY-SEVEN

ARTICLE 1

In the territories of any High Contracting Party to which the present Convention applies, an arbitral award made in pursuance of an agreement, whether relating to existing or future differences (hereinafter called "a submission to arbitration") covered by the Protocol on Arbitration Clauses, opened at Geneva on September 24, 1923, shall be recognized as binding and shall be enforced in accordance with the rules of the procedure of the territory where the award is relied upon, provided that the said award has been made in a territory of one of the High Contracting Parties to which the present Convention applies and between persons who are subject to the jurisdiction of one of the High Contracting Parties.

To obtain such recognition or enforcement, it shall, further, be necessary:

(a) That the award has been made in pursuance of a submission to arbitration which is valid under the law applicable thereto;
(b) That the subject-matter of the award is capable of settlement by arbitration under the law of the country in which the award is sought to be relied upon;
(c) That the award has been made by the Arbitral Tribunal provided for in the submission to arbitration or constituted in the manner agreed upon by the parties and in conformity with the law governing the arbitration procedure;
(d) That the award has become final in the country in which it has been made, in the sense that it will not be considered as such if it is open to opposition, appel or pourvoi en cassation (in the countries where such forms of procedure exist) or if it is proved that any proceedings for the purpose of contesting the validity of the award are pending;
(e) That the recognition or enforcement of the award is not contrary to the public policy or to the principles of the law of the country in which it is sought to be relied upon.

ARTICLE 2

Even if the conditions laid down in Article 1 hereof are fulfilled, recognition and enforcement of the award shall be refused if the Court is satisfied:

(a) That the award has been annulled in the country in which it was made;
(b) That the party against whom it is sought to use the award was not given notice of the arbitration proceedings in sufficient time to enable him to present his case; or that, being under a legal incapacity, he was not properly represented;
(c) That the award does not deal with the differences contemplated by or fading within the terms of the submission to arbitration or that it contains decisions on matters beyond the scope of the submission to arbitration.

If the award has not covered all the questions submitted to the arbitral tribunal, the competent authority of the country where recognition or enforcement of the award is sought can, if it think fit, postpone such recognition or enforcement or grant it subject to such guarantee as that authority may decide.

ARTICLE 3

If the party against whom the award has been made proves that, under the law governing the arbitration procedure, there is a ground, other than the grounds referred to in Article 1 (*a*) and (*c*), and Article 2 (*b*) and (*c*), entitling him to contest the validity of the award in a Court of Law, the Court may, if it thinks fit, either refuse recognition or enforcement of the award or adjourn the consideration thereof, giving such party a reasonable time within which to have the award annulled by the competent tribunal.

ARTICLE 4

The party relying upon an award or claiming its enforcement must supply, in particular:

(1) The original award or a copy thereof duly authenticated, according to the requirements of the law of the country in which it was made;
(2) Documentary or other evidence to prove that the award has become final, in the sense defined in Article 1 (*d*), in the country in which it was made;
(3) When necessary, documentary or other evidence to prove that the conditions laid down in Article 1, paragraph 1 and paragraph 2 (*a*) and (*c*), have been fulfilled.

A translation of the award and of the other documents mentioned in this Article into the official language of the country where the award is sought to be relied upon may be demanded. Such translation must be certified correct by a diplomatic or consular agent of the country to which the party who seeks to rely upon the award belongs or by a sworn translator of the country where the award is sought to be relied upon.

ARTICLE 5

The provisions of the above Articles shall not deprive any interested party of the right of availing himself of an arbitral award in the manner and to the extent allowed by the law or the treaties of the country where such award is sought to be relied upon.

ARTICLE 6

The present Convention applies only to arbitral awards made after the coming into force of the Protocol on Arbitration Clauses, opened at Geneva on September 24th, 1923.

ARTICLE 7

The present Convention, which will remain open to the signature of all the signatories of the Protocol of 1923 on Arbitration Clauses, shall be ratified.

It may be ratified only on behalf of those Members of the League of Nations and non-Member States on whose behalf the Protocol of 1923 shall have been ratified.

Ratifications shall be deposited as soon as possible with the Secretary-General of the League of Nations, who will notify such deposit to all the signatories.

ARTICLE 8

The present Convention shall come into force three months after it shall have been ratified on behalf of two High Contracting Parties. Thereafter, it shall take effects in the case of each High Contracting Party, three months after the deposit of the ratifications on its behalf with the Secretary-General of the League of Nations.

ARTICLE 9

The present Convention may be denounced on behalf of any Member of the League or Non-Member State. Denunciation shall be notified in writing to the Secretary-General of the League of Nations, who will immediately send a copy thereof, certified to be in conformity with the notification, to all the other Contracting Parties, at the same time informing them of the date on which he received it.

The denunciation shall come into force only in respect of the High Contracting Party which shall have notified it and one year after such notification shall have reached the Secretary-General of the League of Nations.

The denunciation of the Protocol on Arbitration Clauses shall entail, ipso facto, the denunciation of the present Convention.

ARTICLE 10

The present Convention does not apply to the Colonies, Protectorates or territories under suzerainty or mandate of any High Contracting Party unless they are specially mentioned.

The application of this Convention to one or more of such Colonies, Protectorates or territories to which the Protocol on Arbitration Clauses, opened at Geneva on September 24th, 1923, applies, can be effected at any time by means of a declaration addressed to the Secretary-General of the League of Nations by one of the High Contracting Parties.

Such declaration shall take effect three months after the deposit thereof.

The High Contracting Parties can at any time denounce the Convention for all or any of the Colonies, Protectorates or territories referred to above. Article 9 hereof applies to such denunciation.

ARTICLE 11

A certified copy of the present Convention shall be transmitted by the Secretary-General of the League of Nations to every Member of the League of Nations and to every Non-Member State which signs the same.

APPENDIX G

Selections from the Legislative History of the Federal Arbitration Act

HOUSE REPORT NO. 91-1181
JUNE 11, 1970

THE COMMITTEE ON THE JUDICIARY, TO WHOM WAS REFERRED THE BILL (S.3274) TO IMPLEMENT THE CONVENTION ON THE RECOGNITION AND ENFORCEMENT OF FOREIGN ARBITRAL AWARDS, HAVING CONSIDERED THE SAME, REPORT FAVORABLY THEREON WITH AMENDMENT AND RECOMMEND

THAT THE BILL DO PASS.

THE AMENDMENT IS AS FOLLOWS:

ON THE FIRST PAGE, LINE 4, STRIKE OUT 'OF' AND INSERT 'ON THE'.

PURPOSE OF THE AMENDMENT

THE AMENDMENT CORRECTS A TYPOGRAPHICAL ERROR IN THE BILL.

STATEMENT

THE PURPOSE OF S. 3274 IS TO IMPLEMENT THE CONVENTION OF THE RECOGNITION AND ENFORCEMENT OF FOREIGN ARBITRAL AWARDS WHICH WAS APPROVED BY THE SENATE ON OCTOBER 4, 1968. THE BILL WOULD CREATE A NEW CHAPTER UNDER TITLE 9 OF THE U.S.C. (THE FEDERAL ARBITRATION ACT) DEALING EXCLUSIVELY WITH THE RECOGNITION AND ENFORCEMENT OF AWARDS PURSUANT TO THE PROVISIONS OF THE CONVENTION.

THE CONVENTION ON THE RECOGNITION AND ENFORCEMENT OF FOREIGN

ARBITRAL AWARDS WAS ADOPTED AT THE CONCLUSION OF A UNITED NATIONS CONFERENCE WHICH WAS HELD IN NEW YORK FROM MAY 20 TO JUNE 10, 1958. THE CONVENTION ENTERED INTO FORCE ON JUNE 7, 1959, AND AT THE PRESENT IT IS IN EFFECT FOR 34 COUNTRIES. ALTHOUGH THE UNITED STATES PARTICIPATED IN THE CONFERENCE, THE CONVENTION WAS NOT SIGNED

ON BEHALF OF OUR GOVERNMENT AT THAT TIME BECAUSE THE AMERICAN DELEGATION FELT THAT CERTAIN PROVISIONS WERE IN CONFLICT WITH SOME OF OUR DOMESTIC LAWS. ACCORDING TO THE ADMINISTRATION, HOWEVER, AS A RESULT OF INCREASING SUPPORT FOR THE CONVENTION (BOTH WITHIN AND WITHOUT THE GOVERNMENT), THE UNITED STATES DECIDED IN FAVOR OF ACCESSION AND IT WAS TRANSMITTED TO THE SENATE FOR ADVICE AND CONSENT ON APRIL 24, 1968. EVEN THOUGH THE CONVENTION WAS APPROVED IN OCTOBER 1968, THE INSTRUMENT OF ACCESSION WILL NOT BE DEPOSITED UNTIL S. 3274 IS ENACTED INTO LAW.

YOUR COMMITTEE HAS RECEIVED A NUMBER OF COMMUNICATIONS FROM LAWYERS AND BUSINESSMEN URGING EARLY AND FAVORABLE ACTION ON S. 3274, AND SO FAR AS IS KNOWN, THERE IS NO OPPOSITION TO THE BILL. IT HAS THE SUPPORT OF THE AMERICAN BAR ASSOCIATION, THE ASSOCIATION OF THE BAR OF THE CITY OF NEW YORK, THE AMERICAN ARBITRATION ASSOCIATION, THE INTER-AMERICAN COMMERCIAL ARBITRATION COMMISSION, THE INTERNATIONAL CHAMBER OF COMMERCE, OFFICE AND PROFESSIONAL EMPLOYEES INTERNATIONAL UNION, THE DEPARTMENT OF STATE, THE DEPARTMENT OF JUSTICE, AND THE BUREAU OF THE BUDGET.

IN THE COMMITTEE'S VIEW, THE PROVISIONS OF S. 3274 WILL SERVE THE BEST INTERESTS OF AMERICANS DOING BUSINESS ABROAD BY ENCOURAGING THEM TO SUBMIT THEIR COMMERCIAL DISPUTES TO IMPARTIAL ARBITRATION FOR AWARDS WHICH CAN BE ENFORCED IN BOTH U.S. AND FOREIGN COURTS. THE COMMITTEE RECOMMENDS, THEREFORE, THAT THE HOUSE APPROVE S.3274 AT AN EARLY DATE.

SECTION-BY-SECTION ANALYSIS

A SUMMARY OF THE PROPOSED PROVISIONS OF THE NEW CHAPTER 2 WHICH WOULD BE ADDED TO THE FEDERAL ARBITRATION ACT (TITLE 9, U.S.C.) IS SET FORTH BELOW:

SECTION 201 PROVIDES THAT THE CONVENTION SHALL BE ENFORCED IN U.S. COURTS IN ACCORDANCE WITH THE PROVISIONS OF THE NEW CHAPTER.

SECTION 2.2 DEFINES THE AGREEMENTS OR AWARDS THAT FALL UNDER THE CONVENTION. THE SECOND SENTENCE OF SECTION 202 IS INTENDED TO MAKE IT CLEAR THAT AN AGREEMENT OR AWARD ARISING OUT OF A LEGAL

RELATIONSHIP EXCLUSIVELY BETWEEN CITIZENS OF THE UNITED STATES IS

NOT ENFORCEABLE UNDER THE CONVENTION IN U.S. COURTS UNLESS IT HAS A REASONABLE RELATION WITH A FOREIGN STATE.

SECTION 203 GIVES ORIGINAL JURISDICTION OVER ANY ACTION OR PROCEEDING FALLING UNDER THE CONVENTION TO THE DISTRICT COURTS OF THE UNITED STATES REGARDLESS OF THE AMOUNT IN CONTROVERSY.

SECTION 204 CONTAINS PROVISIONS RELATING TO VENUE WITH RESPECT TO SUCH ACTION OR PROCEEDING.

SECTION 605 PERMITS REMOVAL OF AN ACTION OR PROCEEDING RELATING TO AN AGREEMENT OR AWARD FALLING UNDER THE CONVENTION FROM A STATE COURT TO A DISTRICT COURT OF THE UNITED STATES.

SECTION 206 PERMITS A COURT TO DIRECT THAT ARBITRATION BE HELD AT THE PLACE PROVIDED FOR IN THE ARBITRATION AGREEMENT 'WHETHER THAT PLACE IS WITHIN OR WITHOUT THE UNITED STATES.' IT ALSO PERMITS THE COURT TO APPOINT ARBITRATORS IN ACCORDANCE WITH THE PROVISIONS OF THE AGREEMENT.

SECTION 207 PROVIDES THAT WITHIN 3 YEARS AFTER AN ARBITRAL AWARD IS MADE, ANY PARTY TO THE ARBITRATION MAY APPLY TO ANY COURT HAVING JURISDICTION FOR AN ORDER CONFIRMING THE AWARD AGAINST ANY PARTY TO THE ARBITRATION.

SECTION 208 MAKES THE PROVISIONS OF THE FEDERAL ARBITRATION ACT APPLICABLE TO ACTIONS BROUGHT UNDER THE CONVENTION TO THE EXTENT THAT SUCH PROVISIONS ARE NOT IN CONFLICT WITH THE IMPLEMENTING LEGISLATION OR THE CONVENTION AS RATIFIED BY THE UNITED STATES.

EXECUTIVE COMMUNICATIONS

ATTACHED AND MADE A PART OF THIS REPORT IS A LETTER DATED DECEMBER 3, 1969, FROM MR. H. G. TORBERT, JR., ACTING ASSISTANT SECRETARY FOR CONGRESSIONAL RELATIONS, DEPARTMENT OF STATE, TO THE SPEAKER, HOUSE OF REPRESENTATIVES, REQUESTING THE ENACTMENT OF THE SUBJECT LEGISLATION.

DEPARTMENT OF STATE,

WASHINGTON, D.C., DECEMBER 3, 1969.
HON. JOHN W. MCCORMACK,
SPEAKER OF THE HOUSE OF REPRESENTATIVES.

DEAR MR. SPEAKER: ON BEHALF OF THE DEPARTMENT OF STATE I AM FORWARDING DRAFT LEGISLATION TO IMPLEMENT THE CONVENTION ON THE RECOGNITION AND ENFORCEMENT OF FOREIGN ARBITRAL AWARDS. THE SENATE GAVE ITS ADVICE AND CONSENT TO U.S. ACCESSION TO THE CONVENTION ON OCTOBER 4, 1968. AT THE HEARINGS ON THE CONVENTION,

THE WITNESS FROM THE DEPARTMENT INFORMED THE FOREIGN RELATIONS COMMITTEE THAT DEPOSIT OF THE U.S. INSTRUMENT OF ACCESSION WOULD BE DEFERRED UNTIL THE CONGRESS ENACTED THE NECESSARY IMPLEMENTING LEGISLATION (SENATE EXECUTIVE REPT. 10, 90TH CONG., SECOND SESS.).

THE FEDERAL ARBITRATION ACT, WHICH HAS BEEN CODIFIED IN TITLE 9 OF THE U.S.C. EMBODIES BASIC NATIONAL POLICY CONCERNING ARBITRATION. THE SECRETARY OF STATE'S ADVISORY COMMITTEE ON PRIVATE INTERNATIONAL LAW, WHICH INCLUDES REPRESENTATIVES OF THE AMERICAN BAR ASSOCIATION, THE CONFERENCE OF CHIEF JUSTICES, AND THE CONFERENCE OF COMMISSIONERS ON UNIFORM STATE LAWS, SUGGESTED THAT THE DEPARTMENT DISCUSS WITH A SMALL GROUP OF REPRESENTATIVES OF THE AMERICAN ARBITRATION ASSOCIATION, MEMBERS OF THE ARBITRATION BAR, AND LAW SCHOOL PROFESSORS, THE MOST EFFECTIVE APPROACH TO THE IMPLEMENTING LEGISLATION. THE CONSENSUS OF THE GROUP, WITH WHICH THE DEPARTMENT OF JUSTICE CONCURS, WAS THAT RATHER THAN AMENDING A SERIES OF SECTIONS OF THE FEDERAL ARBITRATION ACT IT WOULD BE PREFERABLE TO ENACT A NEW CHAPTER DEALING EXCLUSIVELY WITH RECOGNITION AND ENFORCEMENT OF AWARDS FALLING UNDER THE CONVENTION. THIS APPROACH WOULD LEAVE UNCHANGED THE LARGELY SETTLED INTERPRETATION OF THE FEDERAL ARBITRATION ACT BUT NOT UNDER THE CONVENTION.

THE PROPOSED NEW CHAPTER HAS EIGHT SECTIONS.

SECTION 201 PROVIDES THAT THE CONVENTION SHALL BE ENFORCED IN U.S.

COURTS IN ACCORDANCE WITH THE PROVISIONS OF THE PROPOSED NEW CHAPTER.

SECTION 202 DEFINES THE AGREEMENTS OR AWARDS THAT FALL UNDER THE CONVENTION. THE SECOND SENTENCE OF SECTION 202 IS INTENDED TO MAKE IT CLEAR THAT AN AGREEMENT OR AWARD ARISING OUT OF A LEGAL RELATIONSHIP EXCLUSIVELY BETWEEN CITIZENS OF THE UNITED STATES IS NOT ENFORCEABLE UNDER THE CONVENTION IN U.S. COURTS UNLESS IT HAS A REASONABLE RELATION WITH A FOREIGN STATE.

SECTION 203 GIVES ORIGINAL JURISDICTION OVER ANY ACTION OR PROCEEDING FALLING UNDER THE CONVENTION TO THE DISTRICT COURTS OF THE UNTIED STATES REGARDLESS OF THE AMOUNT IN CONTROVERSY. SECTION 204 ESTABLISHES VENUE WITH RESPECT TO SUCH ACTION OR PROCEEDING.

SECTION 205 PERMITS REMOVAL OF AN ACTION OR PROCEEDING RELATING TO AN AGREEMENT OR AWARD FALLING UNDER THE CONVENTION FROM A STATE COURT TO A DISTRICT COURT OF THE UNTIED STATES.

SECTION 106 PERMITS A COURT TO DIRECT THAT ARBITRATION BE HELD AT THE PLACE PROVIDED FOR IN THE ARBITRATION AGREEMENT. SINCE THERE MAY BE CIRCUMSTANCES IN WHICH IT WOULD BE HIGHLY DESIRABLE TO DIRECT ARBITRATION WITHIN THE DISTRICT IN WHICH THE ACTION IS BROUGHT AND INAPPROPRIATE TO DIRECT ARBITRATION ABROAD, SECTION 206 IS PERMISSIVE RATHER THAN MANDATORY.

SECTION 207 DEALS WITH CONFIRMATION OF AN AWARD MADE UNDER THE CONVENTION. A SIMILAR PROVISION IS INCLUDED IN SECTION 9 OF THE FEDERAL ARBITRATION ACT.

THE PURPOSE OF SECTION 208 IS TO MAKE THE PROVISIONS OF THE FEDERAL ARBITRATION ACT APPLICABLE TO ACTIONS BROUGHT UNDER THE CONVENTION TO THE EXTENT THAT SUCH PROVISIONS ARE NOT IN CONFLICT WITH THE IMPLEMENTING LEGISLATION OR THE CONVENTION AS RATIFIED BY THE UNITED STATES.

THE DEPARTMENT OF STATE HAS BEEN INFORMED BY THE BUREAU OF THE BUDGET THAT THERE IS NO OBJECTION FROM THE STANDPOINT OF THE ADMINISTRATION'S PROGRAM TO THE SUBMISSION OF THIS PROPOSAL TO THE CONGRESS FOR ITS CONSIDERATION.

SINCERELY YOURS,

H. G. TORBERT, JR.,
ACTING ASSISTANT SECRETARY,
FOR CONGRESSIONAL RELATIONS.

675 P.L. 101-369, INTER-AMERICAN CONVENTION ON INTERNATIONAL

COMMERCIAL ARBITRATION

DATES OF CONSIDERATION AND PASSAGE

House: June 5, 1990
Senate: August 4, 1990
House Report (Judiciary Committee) No. 101-501,
May 31, 1990 (To accompany H.R. 4314)
Cong. Record Vol. 136 (1990)
No Senate Report was submitted with this legislation.

HOUSE REPORT NO. 101-501
May 31, 1990

The Committee on the Judiciary, to whom was referred the bill (H.R. 4314) to implement the Inter-American Convention on International Commercial Arbitration, having considered the same, report favorably thereon with an amendment and recommend that the bill as amended do pass.

PURPOSE OF LEGISLATION

The purpose of H.R. 4314, as amended, is to implement the Inter-American Convention on International Commercial Arbitration, and thereby provide a dependable mechanism for Latin American and U.S. business entities to compel arbitration and enforce awards where the underlying contract contemplated such arbitration. Inasmuch as H.R. 4314 was ordered reported with an amendment in the nature of a substitute, the contents of this report constitute an explanation of the amendment.

HISTORY OF LEGISLATION

In the 99th Congress legislation to implement the Inter-American Convention on International Commercial Arbitration ("Inter-American Convention") was introduced in the House by Judiciary Committee Chairman Peter W. Rodino, Jr. on September 22, 1986. A similar bill was introduced in the Senate by Senator Richard G. Lugar on November 5, 1985, and passed by voice vote in the Senate on October 18, 1986. No action was taken on the Senate bill in the House.

In the 100th Congress Senator Claiborne Pell introduced implementing legislation (S. 2204) in the Senate, which passed on October 1, 1988. On October 21, 1988, the House passed S. 2204 with an amendment striking all of the relevant provisions and substituting the provisions of another, unrelated bill.

Judiciary Committee Chairman Jack Brooks introduced H.R. 4314 on March 20, 1990, at the request of the Administration. A similar bill (S. 1941) was introduced in the Senate by Senator Claiborne Pell on November 20, 1989.

The House Subcommittee on Immigration, Refugees, and International Law, held a hearing on H.R. 4314 on May 1, 1990. The witnesses testifying on the bill were (1) Harold Burman of the Office of Legal Adviser of the State Department; (2) Garylee Cox, Regional Vice President of the American Arbitration Association; and (3) Houston Putnam Lowry, Chairman of the Connecticut Bar Association's Section on International Law and World Peace.

The Subcommittee also received, and included in the hearing record, written statements from (1) the American Bar Association; (2) Mr. Peter Trooboff, a Washington attorney active in the fields of international trade and investment law; and (3) Professor Richard J. Graving, Director of the Institute for Transnational Arbitration.

The Subcommittee marked up H.R. 4314 immediately following the hearing. One technical amendment was passed clarifying that the rules of procedure of the Inter-American Convention referred to in Article 3 of the Inter-American Convention are the rules promulgated on July 1, 1988, not January 1, 1978. The bill, as amended, was then favorably reported to the full Judiciary Committee by a recorded vote of 8 to 0.

COMMITTEE VOTE

H.R. 4314, as amended, was considered by the full Judiciary Committee on May 22, 1990, and was ordered favorably reported, as amended, by voice vote.

NEED FOR LEGISLATION

The Inter-American Convention on International Commercial Arbitration ("Inter-American Convention") was adopted in 1975 at a diplomatic conference under the auspices of the Organization of American States ("OAS"), with the strong support of the United States. The Inter-American Convention is modeled after an earlier United Nations Convention on the Recognition and Enforcement of Foreign Arbitral Awards, to which the United States became a party in 1970 ("New York Convention").

The Senate gave its advice and consent to ratification of the Inter-American Convention on October 9, 1986, with the understanding that ratification would not be effected until implementing legislation was enacted. H.R. 4314 would accomplish that and extend the benefits of arbitration to parties engaging in commerce between the United States and other OAS countries that are also parties to the Convention.

Essential to the smooth flow of international commerce is an efficient and flexible method for settling disputes. As the volume of international commerce accelerates, business parties have increasingly looked to arbitration for settlement of international commercial disputes. Parties who enter into an arbitration agreement can choose the forum, the rules of procedure, and the applicable law. This flexibility can reduce the need for any party to subject itself to the unfamiliar laws and procedures of the courts of other countries, allows disputes to be settled more expeditiously and enables parties to seek arbitrators with specialized knowledge in appropriate cases. For arbitration agreements to be effective, however, national courts of law must be able to enforce agreements to arbitrate and the ensuing arbitral awards. The New York Convention and the Inter-American Convention both seek to do that. This is consistent with U.S. domestic policy as spelled out in the Federal Arbitration Act, set out in Title IX, United States Code.

Furthermore, enactment of this legislation and ratification of the Inter-American Convention would serve American hemispheric interests. Ratification would be a significant adjunct to other U.S. policies in relation to our neighbors in the region. Those policies emphasize the encouragement of expanded trade and increased foreign investment as a spur to economic development, as well as to the peaceful settlement of disputes. Developing an international framework for the settlement of commercial disputes through arbitration under this OAS-sponsored Convention is consistent with this policy.

The Inter-American Convention has drawn widespread support from U.S. business and legal communities. Ratification has been recommended by the Secretary of State's Advisory Committee on Private International Law, the American Law Institute, the American Association for the Comparative Study of Law, the American Bar Association, the American Arbitration Association, the United States Chamber of Commerce and numerous bar associations and private commentators.

H.R. 4314 addresses a fundamental problem that has plagued the resolution of disputes arising in inter-American commercial transactions, namely the traditional wariness of Latin American nations to international conventions. These countries have shown less resistance to joining regionally based conventions. For example, of the thirteen nations[1] which have become parties to the Inter-American Convention, El Salvador, Honduras, Paraguay, and Venezuela are not parties to the New York Convention. U.S. ratification, predicated on this implementing legislation, should encourage more Latin American nations to join the Inter-American Convention.

Enactment of H.R. 4314, and consequent ratification of the Inter-American Convention, are important because these acts will encourage inter-American trade and commerce by providing a dependable mechanism for businesses to compel arbitration under contracts that call for such arbitration. The Inter-American Convention provisions and the implementing legislation will assure transacting businesses that arbitration clauses and arbitral awards will be enforced, and that rules of procedural fairness will be observed. With the prospect of Europe uniting economically and the ever greater economic influence of Japan in Asia, the Committee believes it becomes particularly important for the United States to promote economic cooperation in its own hemisphere. [See appendix for text of the Inter-American Convention.]

ANALYSIS OF THE LEGISLATION, AS AMENDED

H.R. 4314, as amended, creates a new Chapter 3 to the Federal Arbitration Act specifically to implement the provisions of the Inter-American Convention. It does so mainly by incorporation existing provisions of law already enacted as Chapter 2 which were adopted to implement the earlier New York Convention. It draws on years of tested legal and commercial ideas and provisions. Thus, the bill incorporates all of the existing provisions of the Federal Arbitration Act except where necessary to reflect changes under the Inter-American Convention. The principle change is a reference in the OAS Convention and in this legislation to the Rules of Arbitration of the Inter-American Commercial Arbitration Commission, which would be used in those cases where the parties to an arbitration agreement have failed to specify applicable rules.

In addition to incorporating existing laws, several provisions of H.R. 4314, as amended, carry out the three reservations added by the Senate when granting advice and consent to ratification in 1986. Two provisions relate to the use of the Inter-American Commission's arbitration rules. Another provision applies the same rule followed under the earlier New York Convention, that foreign arbitral awards, on the basis of reciprocity, will only be recognized from countries that have also ratified the Convention. Finally, a provision of the bill spells out, in those cases where both the Inter-American and New York Conventions could be applicable, which Convention would apply.

The New York Conventionand the Inter-American Convention are intended to achieve the same results, and their key provisions adopt the same standards, phrased in the legal style appropriate for each organization. It is the Committee's expectation,

[1] The are the United States, Chile, Colombia, Costa Rica, El Salvador, Guatemala, Honduras, Mexico, Panama, Paraguay, Peru, Uruguay, and Venezuela.

in view of that fact and the parallel legislation under the Federal Arbitration Act that would be applied to the Conventions, that courts in the United States would achieve a general uniformity of results under the two conventions.

ADMINISTRATION POSITION

The Administration supports the enactment of this legislation.

OVERSIGHT STATEMENT

Pursuant to clause 2(1)(3)(A) of rule XI of the Rules of the House of Representatives, the Committee states that it has exercised close oversight with regard to the operation of laws designed to implement treaties and conventions of the United States and will continue to do so.

Clause 2(1)(3)(D) of rule XI of the Rules of the House of Representatives is inapplicable since no oversight findings and recommendation have been received from the Committee on Government Operations.

INFLATIONARY IMPACT STATEMENT

Pursuant to clause 2(1)(4) of rule XI of the Rules of the House of Representatives, the Committee estimates that this bill will not have an inflationary effect on prices and costs in the operation of the national economy.

ESTIMATE OF COST

Pursuant to clause 7, rule XIII of the Rules of the House of Representatives, the Committee concurs with the cost estimates set forth below by the Congressional Budget Office.

BUDGETARY INFORMATION

Clause 2(1)(3)(B) of rule XI of the Rules of the House of Representatives is inapplicable because the instant legislation does not provide new budget authority. Pursuant to Clause 2(1)(3)(C) of rule XI, the following estimate was prepared by the Congressional Budget Office and submitted to the Committee:

U.S. CONGRESS,
CONGRESSIONAL BUDGET OFFICE,

Washington, DC, May 24, 1990.
Hon. JACK BROOKS,
Chairman, Committee on the Judiciary,
House of Representatives, Washington, DC.

DEAR MR. CHAIRMAN: The Congressional Budget Office has reviewed H.R. 4314, a bill to Implement the Inter-American Convention on International

Commercial Arbitration, as ordered reported by the House Committee on the Judiciary on May 22, 1990.

The Inter-American Convention on International Commercial Arbitration is patterned after the New York Conventionon the Recognition and Enforcement of Arbitral Awards, to which the United States became a party in 1970. Both are designed to facilitate the settlement of international commercial disputes through the use of arbitration. Supporters of the Inter-American Convention are hopeful that its adoption by the United States and other member states of the Organization of American States will increase the use of arbitration in international commercial disputes in this hemisphere.

Implementation of the Inter-American Convention would not create any new organizations or commissions, nor would its implementation require any funding from government entities. Enactment of H.R. 4314 is therefore not expected to affect the budgets of federal, state or local governments.

The CBO staff contact for questions about this estimate is Kent R. Christensen, who may be reached at 226-2840.

Sincerely,
ROBERT D. REISCHAUER.

COMMITTEE RECOMMENDATION

After careful consideration of this legislation, the Committee is of the opinion that this bill should be enacted and accordingly recommends that H.R. 4314, as amended, do pass.

3931 P.L. 101-552, ADMINISTRATIVE DISPUTE RESOLUTION ACT

SENATE REPORT NO. 101-543
October 19, 1990

The Committee on Governmental Affairs, to which was referred the bill (S. 971) to authorize and encourage Federal agencies to use mediation, conciliation, arbitration, and other techniques for the prompt and informal resolution of disputes, and for other purposes, having considered the same, reports favorably thereon with an amendment in the nature of a substitute and recommends that the bill as amended do pass.

CONTENTS

I. PURPOSE

Alternative dispute resolution (ADR) procedures are informal, consensual procedures which can be used by parties in a dispute to obtain a resolution in lieu of formal litigation. These procedures include settlement negotiations, conciliation, facilitation, mediation, fact-finding, mini-trials and arbitration or any combination of these. Often, the use of ADR procedures can result in more effective, fair, timely and less costly dispute resolution.

Agencies are currently able to, and several do, take advantage of ADR methods without express authorization by statute or regulation. The purpose of S. 971 is to place government-wide emphasis on the use of innovative ADR procedures by agencies and to put in place a statutory framework to foster the effective and sound use of these flexible alternatives to litigation. The goal of the bill is to send a clean message to agencies and private parties that the use of ADR to resolve disputes involving the federal government is an accepted practice and to provide support for agency efforts to develop and/or enhance individual ADR programs.

S. 971 encourages agencies to consider potential ADR uses and requires them to develop a specific policy to implement such uses. The bill calls for each agency to appoint a dispute resolution specialist and to establish an appropriate personnel training program in the use of negotiation and other dispute resolution methods. It provides a new Subchapter within Title 5 of the United States Code on use of ADR techniques and resolves issues related to such matters as confidentiality and use of neutrals. Specific provisions on arbitration are included to resolve questions and constitutional concerns about the use of this technique to resolve disputes involving the United States.

Participation in the ADR techniques authorized by the Act is predicated on the voluntary, informed agreement of all parties to a dispute. These techniques are intended to supplement – not replace or limit – existing dispute resolution practices and procedures.

II. BACKGROUND

The number of lawsuits filed in the United States is enormous. The number of civil cases alone is substantial. According to the Administrative Office of the U.S. Courts, in the year ending December 31, 1989, the total number of civil cases commenced in the United States was over 220,000. The Federal government was a party in over 55,000 of these cases, and there were over 100,000 private civil cases involving a federal question.

In response to this situation, the private sector has increasingly turned to alternative methods to litigation such as those promoted by S. 971. An increasing number of lawyers are being trained in ADR methods. According to an article entitled, "Congress, The Executive Branch, and The Dispute Resolution Process," written by Senator Charles Grassley and Charles Pou, Jr. of the Administrative Conference of the United States, over half the law schools in the nation now offer courses in dispute resolution. Also, there are over 360 non-profit community resolution programs in operation. Moreover, states have also recognized ADR methods as valuable tools. According to this article, over 20 state legislatures have enacted laws establishing statewide mediation centers or other dispute resolution procedures, and there are as many as 275 operational court-related ADR programs of various types in over 40 states.

In recent years, interested individuals have argued that federal agencies should take greater advantage of ADR methods to allow them enhanced flexibility in resolving disputes. Federal agencies are currently authorized to engage in many ADR techniques such as mediation, conciliation, and minitrials. In fact, agencies such as the Environmental Protection Agency (EPA), the Army Corps of Engineers, the Merit System Protection Board, and the Department of Justice have individual programs which utilize ADR methods. However, up to now, there has been no government-wide emphasis on the use of ADR techniques and, therefore, there is little knowledge on the part of many agencies as to what ADR methods exist and what the accepted procedures are for their use.

The Administrative Conference of the United States (ACUS), with its responsibility to promote the efficiency, adequacy and fairness of federal administrative procedures, has performed a great deal of work in the last several years regarding federal agency use of ADR techniques.

In the early 1980's ACUS formally recommended that agencies consider using negotiation in formulating rules – a procedure now known as negotiated rulemaking. Negotiated rulemaking is a process by which an agency invites the parties that will be affected by a rule to join the agency in forming an ad hoc committee to develop a consensus draft of the rule. If consensus on the draft rule is reached, that draft become the base document for the proposed rule which is then published for public comment. ACUS Recommendation 82-4 Procedures for Negotiating Proposed Regulations (1 CFR 305.82-4) encouraged and provided guidance to agencies on the use of this technique.

The goal was to arrive at more effective, timely, and fair rulemaking through these informal, voluntary proceedings. By including affected parties in the rulemaking process at an early stage and in a nonadversarial setting, the resulting rule has proven itself to have a better chance of acceptance and, most importantly, of being a more sound, realistic and effective rule. Agencies such as the Federal Aviation Administration and the Environmental Protection Agency have used – and continue to use – this technique in the development of their rules. Due to the positive experience of these and other agencies, legislation has now passed both Houses of Congress to establish a statutory framework for conducting negotiated rulemaking in order to encourage federal agencies to use the procedure when it enhances conventional rulemaking.

While negotiated rulemaking was proving itself to be a successful alternative means of rulemaking, relying on informality and nonadversarial relationships, ACUS began to explore the broader topic of ADR techniques, which take a similar informal and nonadversarial approach to resolving disputes.

In 1986, the ACUS issued Recommendation 86-3 on Agencies' Use of Alternative Means of Dispute Resolution (1 CFR 305.86-3). This recommendation, like the earlier one regarding negotiated rulemaking, encouraged agency use of ADR methods and provided guidance on how and when to use them. Once again, the goal was to promote more efficient, effective administrative procedures through the use of voluntary, informal procedures.

Recommendation 86-3 urges agencies to make use of ADR techniques, within their existing statutory authority, to settle disputes. Although ACUS believes federal agencies already possess the authority to use most ADR procedures, it discovered that agencies often avoid ADR techniques due to confusion over agency authority to use them and the acceptability of such techniques within the Executive Branch. As a result, ACUS recommended legislation to clarify and expand agency authority with regard to the appropriate use of ADR methods to resolve disputes involving the federal government.

During the 100th Congress, legislation was introduced by Senator Charles Grassley and Representative Donald Pease to accomplish that goal. The two bills, S. 2274 in the Senate and H.R. 5101 in the House of Representatives, were modeled after the 1986 ACUS recommendation. Hearings were held on the bills in the Senate Subcommittee on Courts and Administrative Practice and the House Subcommittee on Administrative Law and Governmental Relations. No further action was taken subsequent to those hearings.

Senator Grassley reintroduced his bill in the 101st Congress on May 11, 1989. That bill, S. 971, was referred to the Senate Committee on Governmental Affairs and, subsequently, to the Subcommittee on Oversight of Government Management.

Hearings were held on S. 971 in the Oversight Subcommittee on September 19, 1989. The hearing focused on the appropriateness of utilizing ADR techniques with regard to various federal disputes and the ability of the framework created by S. 971 to accomplish the effective and responsible use of ADR in the federal government.

Additional issues that were addressed at the hearing included: (1) Constitutional concerns regarding the expansion of the use of arbitration by federal agencies; and (2) the qualification and training of neutrals to be used in ADR proceedings.

The witnesses at the September 19 hearing were: Senator Grassley; an agency panel consisting of the Environmental Protection Agency, the Department of Justice, and the Merit Systems Protection Board (MSPB); and a panel of private sector individuals experienced in the use of ADR techniques consisting of the Director of Environmental Dispute Resolution for the Conservation Foundation, a senior partner with Crowell and Mooring, a Washington D.C. law firm, and a representative of the American Bar Association.

Each of the agencies that testified had some experience using some form of ADR. For example, as a result of the enactment of the Civil Service Reform Act of 1978, the MSPB is allowed to arbitrate cases and also has a Voluntary Expedited Appeals Procedure (VEAP) which makes use of various forms of ADR. EPA has recently initiated an ADR program and is authorized by statute to arbitrate specific cases arising under Superfund. EPA expressed interest at the hearing in expanding its ADR program, and it is an agency that could greatly benefit from such an expansion. The Department of Justice has utilized and experimented with various ADR techniques, such as minitrials, within its own agency.

The representative from the Conservation Foundation, Ms. Gail Bingham, and the representative from Crowell and Mooring, Mr. Eldon Crowell, were both in favor of expanding the use of ADR in the federal government, and both were familiar with its use in the private sector. Ms. Bingham is a practicing mediator, and Mr. Crowell is an expert in contract law and the use of ADR methods in this area.

EPA and the MSPB both testified in support of S. 971. The MSPB testified that in their five-year history of using ADR methods, "the ADR techniques used by the board have resulted in faster, less expensive case processing." The MSPB went on to state that in 1988, cases using ADR were disposed to in 65 days, and cases which progressed through the usual Board procedure took 99 days.

In August 1987, EPA Administrator Lee M. Thomas wrote in a memo to Assistant Administrators and Regional Administrators of the EPA the "ADR holds the promise of lowering the transaction costs to both the agency and the regulated community of resolving applicable disputes." He closed the cover memorandum by stating, "I challenge each of you to help in our efforts to apply ADR to the enforcement process. I ask the Regional Administrators to review the enforcement actions now under development and those cases which have already been filed to find cases which could be resolved by ADR." Both agencies stressed the need for flexibility in ADR programs and the importance of sending a clear signal to agencies regarding the use of ADR as an accepted alternative to formal litigation.

The Department of Justice, as mentioned before, has also experimented with the use of ADR and is supportive of its expansion in the federal government. However, the Justice Department objected to the inclusion of binding arbitration in the methods available to agencies to resolve disputes. The Justice Department argued that the use of binding arbitration by agencies which do not already have specific statutory authorization to do so raises serious constitutional concerns.

The Department listed these constitutional concerns:

(1) that the appointment of individuals to be arbitrators may interfere with the Article II Appointments Clause, since arbitrators will oftentimes not be federal employees;

(2) that a separation-of-powers question would arise due to the fact that Congress, under S. 971, would be authorizing private parties to perform agency decision-making powers;

(3) that judicial responsibility and authority would be removed from constitutionally established Article III Courts; and

(4) that arbitration may interfere with due process.

The Department also described two statutory barriers to the use of arbitration by federal agencies:

(1) 31 U.S.C. Sec. 1346 prohibits the use of federal funds to pay, "the pay or expenses of a commission, council, board, or similar group, or a member of that group, or expenses related to the work or results of work or action of that group" unless authorized by law.

(2) 31 U.S.C. Sec. 3702 provides that "the Comptroller General shall settle all claims of or against the United States Government."

The General Accounting Office has traditionally interpreted these two statutes to prohibit the use of arbitration by federal agencies unless such use is specifically authorized by Congress such as under the Federal Arbitration Act or the Civil Service Reform Act or in other very specific instances.

Supporters of agency use of ADR argue that these prohibitions have been too expansively interpreted and that S. 971's explicit authorization would solve any existing problem.

Supporters of S. 971 also argue that the specific provisions of the bill guard against any constitutional problems, because the decision to arbitrate is voluntary on the part of all parties and is subject to the guidelines in section 582 of the bill which outline instances in which an alternative dispute proceeding would be inappropriate. Individuals who do not believe binding arbitration by federal agencies, absent specific statutory authority, violates the Constitution often point to an article by Harold Bruff, a noted constitutional scholar and University of Texas law professor, defending the constitutionality of arbitration in federal programs. This article entitled, "Public Programs, Private Deciders: The Constitutionality of Arbitration in Federal Programs," from the 1989 Texas Law Review is included in the Senate Subcommittee's September 19, 1989, hearing record (S.Hrg. 101–494). The article traces the case history of arbitration programs within the federal government and defends the use of arbitration in federal programs as long as certain specific protections are taken against the misuse of this authority. Supporters of S. 971 point to the inclusion of many of these protections in S. 971 such as those mentioned above.

In order to further clarify this issue, the Subcommittee on Oversight requested that the American Law Division of CRS identify any constitutional problems with S. 971. The CRS brief, dated August 17, 1989, and included in the September 19, 1989, hearing report, concludes that S. 971 could meet a constitutional challenge:

It appears that S. 971 could withstand constitutional challenge under Article II, Article III, and the Due Process Clause. Under Article II, it does not appear that arbitrators would have to be appointed by the President, or that the use of private parties as arbitrators would be an impermissible delegation of governmental power. Under Article III, arbitrators would not have to be judges with life tenure subject to good behavior. Finally, under the Due Process Clause, S. 971's providing for unbiased arbitrators and for limited judicial review would appear adequate.

Despite this analysis, the constitutionality of binding arbitration remains an issue over which there is much debate. During the course of the hearing, the Department of Justice stated that true binding arbitration is not in use in the federal government except, perhaps, in the Federal Labor Relations Authority. The Justice witness argued that the arbitration currently authorized by statute for federal agencies is reviewable by the agency head before the resultant award becomes final and, therefore, is not truly "binding" arbitration. The arbitration procedure currently used by the EPA to resolve cases in the Superfund Program includes a provision which calls for public review and comment of arbitral decisions before such decisions become final.

Similar concerns had been raised by the Justice Department during hearings held on the House counterpart to S. 971, H.R. 2497 introduced by Congressman Glickman. In the weeks following the September 19, 1989 hearing, the Justice Department worked with other interested parties to develop a procedure which would put to rest these constitutional concerns. A provision was agreed upon, and H.R. 2497 was amended to provide that an arbitral award would be reviewable and reversible by the agency head for a period of 30 days before becoming final. This solution ensures that an officer of the United States is ultimately responsible for the decision reached as the result of an arbitration proceeding, not an outside party. The arbitration proceeding is, in effect, "non-binding" for a period of 30 days. This same provision has been included in S. 971, as amended, and thus addresses any remaining constitutional concerns with regard to the Act.

On September 25, 1990, the Senate Subcommittee on Oversight of Government Management reported S. 971 to the full Committee on Governmental Affairs, with an amendment in the nature of a substitute. On October -, 1990, the Committee voted unanimously in favor of the substitute and several technical amendments and ordered the bill as amended reported to the full Senate for passage.

III. SUMMARY

S. 971 amends the Administrative Procedure Act to authorize parties involved in disputes arising under federal administrative programs to agree to use ADR methods. The use of such methods is subject to certain specific guidelines regarding cases which may be inappropriate for resolution through ADR methods. Voluntary, binding arbitration is authorized when all parties consent, subject to safeguards of judicial review and agency review of the appropriateness of arbitral awards. The bill establishes standards of confidentiality in ADR proceedings, facilitates agency use of ADR techniques, and lays out judicial review procedures.

The bill makes certain necessary modifications to the Federal Acquisition Regulation, Contract Disputes Act and Federal Tort Claims Act to facilitate the use of ADR in these areas.

S. 971 draws on the experience and expertise of the Administrative Conference (ACUS) and the Federal Mediation and Conciliation Service (FMCS) to further aid agency use of ARD. Agencies are instructed to seek guidance from these two entities. ACUS is required to support, assist, and monitor agency use of ADR. ACUS is also charged with reporting to Congress periodically on agency implementation of the law and with establishing a roster (with the assistance of FMCS) of qualified neutrals for optional use by parties in a dispute. This bill increases the scope of duties for the FMCS to include mediation, training, and other ADR assistance.

IV. SECTION-BY-SECTION ANALYSIS

The Committee on Governmental Affairs reported S. 971 with a single amendment in the nature of a substitute. This section-by-section analysis is based upon the substitute.

Section 1. Short title

The section states the title of the bill as the "Administrative Dispute Resolution Act."

Section 2. Findings

Section 2 contains the findings on administrative dispute resolution (ADR) techniques. It states that the Administrative Procedure Act was intended to offer prompt resolution of disputes as an alternative to litigation, but that administrative proceedings have become formal and lengthy.

The section finds that ADR techniques can provide decisions which are faster, less expensive and less contentious as well as outcomes which are more creative, efficient and sensible. It encourages agency use of ADR, and states that explicit authorization of agency use of ADR techniques will eliminate any ambiguity about an agency's power to engage in such procedures.

Section 3. Promotion of Alternative Means of Dispute Resolution

To encourage agency use of ADR, Section 3 requires federal agencies to adopt policies on the use of ADR techniques, to designate a senior official as the dispute resolution specialist for the agency, and to provide training for this specialist.

The section also requires agencies to review any standard language for the agency's contracts, grants or other agreements to determine whether to include provisions on the use of ADR. The section also requires to amendment of the Federal Acquisition Regulation to provide standard contract language on the use of ADR techniques to resolve disputes and to carry out other provisions in this Act affecting federal contracts, grants and other agreements.

Section 4. Administrative procedures

Section 4 amends Title 5 of the United States Code, in the chapter on administrative procedures, to include a new subchapter on the use of ADR techniques.

The new subchapter would be entitled, "Alternative Means of Dispute Resolution in the Administrative Process." Its provisions are described in the following section numbers as they would appear in Title 5, Chapter 5.

"Section 581. Definitions"

A new Section 581 lists the following definitions that would apply to the subchapter:

"Agency" has the same meaning as in Section 551(1) of Title 5.

"Administrative program" is a federal function which involves the protection of the public interest and the determination of rights, privileges, and obligations of private persons through rulemakings, formal or informal adjudications, licensing procedures, or investigations.

"Alternative means of dispute resolution" means any procedure used in lieu of a formal, adjudicative agency proceeding to resolve a controversy. Such alternative means typically make use of a neutral to facilitate dispute resolution between an agency and other parties, and include such techniques as negotiation, conciliation, facilitation, mediation, fact finding, minitrials, and arbitration.

"Award" means the written decision issued by an arbitrator to resolve a dispute.

"Dispute resolution communication" means any oral communication during a dispute resolution proceeding – whether by a party, neutral or nonparty participant – which was made in confidence.

"Dispute resolution document" means any written material which was prepared or provided in confidence during a dispute resolution proceeding by a party, neutral or nonparty participant.

The definition specifically excludes "agreements" to enter into arbitration and documents setting forth arbitration "awards," because such documents describe the status of disputes involving the federal government, should be made available to the public in the vast majority of cases, and do not create reasonable expectations of confidentiality since they involve United States policy and actions. Such agreements and awards can be considered "dispute resolution documents" only when the government and other parties to the dispute explicitly agree in writing to this status, and the law otherwise permits such documents to be kept out of the public domain.

"Dispute resolution proceeding" means any proceeding in which ADR is being used to resolve a dispute between the federal government and specific parties.

"In confidence" means, with respect to information, dispute resolution communications and dispute resolution documents, that the information, communication or document was provided with an explicit request by the source for nondisclosure or under circumstances which created a reasonable expectation in the source that disclosure outside the ADR proceeding would not take place.

"Issue in controversy" means an issue which is material to a decision in an administrative program and with which there is a disagreement between the agency responsible for making that decision and a party or parties who would be substantially affected by that decision.

"Neutral" means an individual who functions to aid federal agencies and other parties to resolve an issue in controversy using ADR techniques.

"Party" has the same meaning as in Section 551(3) of Title 5 or, for a proceeding without named parties, a person who will be significantly affected by the decision in the proceeding and who participates in that proceeding.

"Person" has the same meaning as in Section 551(2) of Title 5.

"Roster" means a list of persons qualified to provide services as neutrals.

"Section 582. General authority"

A new Section 582 provides an explicit statutory authorization allowing federal agencies to use ADR techniques to resolve a dispute regarding the agency's administrative programs when all the parties to the dispute voluntarily agree to its use.

The section also provides guidelines on when ADR techniques should not be used. The section lists six factors which, if one or more is present, make use of ADR techniques inappropriate. If one or more of these factors is present, an agency can still use ADR, but only if it has first carefully analyzed the situation and made a specific decision that the ADR proceeding can be structured to avoid the identified problem or because other concerns significantly outweigh the factors that normally make ADR inappropriate.

The six factors present a number of considerations. For example, they require an agency to consider the importance of using the dispute to establish an authoritative precedent or resolve significant policy questions. Dispute resolutions reached through ADR procedures normally cannot fulfill such functions, since they may utilize a nongovernmental decision-maker, will bypass normal levels of agency review and consultation, may not include consideration of similar disputes or related policy questions, and may be subject to confidentiality requirements.

Another factor is the importance of the agency's maintaining an established policy and minimizing variations among individual decisions in a particular subject area. ADR techniques have few mechanisms to achieve such objectives. Special care must also be taken by the agency to weigh the effect of a dispute resolution on persons and organizations not party to the proceeding and to consider the agency's ability to provide a public record of the proceeding if necessary. ADR techniques vary in the extent to which they can take into account such concerns. Finally, the agency must consider the need for it to maintain continuing jurisdiction over a matter and alter the disposition of a dispute if circumstances change, and whether use of ADR techniques would interfere with such agency obligations. Where such continuing obligations exist, ADR may be an inappropriate means of dispute resolution.

These factors play an especially important role in decisions on the use of arbitration, due to the more formal and binding nature of arbitration procedures. As established in Section 5 of S. 971, they are also part of a new legal standard for judicial review of arbitral awards by persons who were not parties to the arbitration but were adversely affected by the award and want to overturn or modify it.

In addition to encouraging use of ADR techniques, this section contains a provision to make clear that the intent of the Act is to promote ADR methods as a supplement to already existing agency dispute resolution procedures. The provisions of the Act are not meant to interfere with or limit any procedures or practices already in use. The Tennessee Valley Authority (TVA) contacted the Subcommittee to express their concern that certain provisions of the Act, particularly those concerning arbitration, would limit TVA's existing authority to arbitrate. This language in the Act is intended to allay that concern.

"Section 583. Neutrals"

A new Section 583 of Title 5 establishes guidelines for the selection and use of neutrals in ADR proceedings.

The section permits neutrals to be full or part-time officers or employees of any federal agency, or any other individual, upon which the parties agree. It establishes that neutrals other than arbitrators serve at the will of the parties. It states that a neutral is not allowed to have a conflict of interest relating to the issues in the ADR proceeding, unless there is written disclosure of the conflict to all parties in the proceeding and the parties, upon receipt of such disclosure, agree the neutral may serve.

The section outlines the responsibilities of ACUS with regard to agency use of neutrals. It requires ACUS, after consulting with FMCS and other agencies and organizations, to publish recommended professional standards for neutrals, to maintain a roster of individuals who meet these standards and are qualified to serve as neutrals in agency ADR proceedings, and to make this roster available to agencies considering use of ADR techniques. Because ACUS is to assist but not control agency use of ADR techniques, agencies are encouraged but not required to select neutrals who meet the ACUS standards and are included in the ACUS roster.

The section also authorizes ACUS to enter into contracts with neutrals who may be used by agencies on an elective basis. It also directs ACUS to develop other procedures which will allow agencies to obtain the services of a neutral on an expedited basis.

On the issue of compensation, the section requires all parties to an ADR proceeding, including the federal government, to reach agreement on payment for the neutral's services. This provision replaces language in the House bill which would have required the federal government alone to pay this cost. Allocating this expense solely to the government would be not only an unfair burden on taxpayers, but also an unwholesome influence over neutrals who would have a single source for their paychecks. A better and more common practice is to have the government and all other parties to the dispute pay an equal share of the neutral's services.

The section explicitly authorizes agencies to enter into contracts and interagency agreements to obtain the services of a neutral. It authorizes them to design contracts and interagency agreements which will implement the agreed – to compensation scheme. It also explicitly authorizes agencies to enter into contracts and interagency agreements to obtain training in ADR techniques.

The section requires the government and other parties to the dispute to agree on a rate of compensation for the neutral that "is fair and reasonable to the Government." This language is intended to prohibit excessive fees, but also to make it clear that an agency is not necessarily required to demand that the group select the lowest bid of those seeking to serve as the neutral in the ADR proceeding.

"Section 584. Confidentiality"

A new Section 584 of Title 5 establishes rules to protect the confidentiality of ADR proceedings.

These protections are created to enable parties to ADR proceedings to be forthcoming and candid, without fear that frank statements may later be used against them. Thus, documents produced during an ADR proceeding, such as a proposal to resolve the dispute, are immune to discovery unless certain specific conditions are met. At the same time, these confidentiality provisions are not intended to frustrate normal discovery in legal proceedings. Thus, the section provides that ADR documents which are otherwise discoverable, such as those which existed prior to the ADR proceeding, remain subject to discovery. In this way, the section attempts to balance the need for confidentiality in ADR proceedings with the right to discovery in other legal settings.

The section treats neutrals and parties separately. It protects communications and documents in the possession of neutrals from discovery or voluntary disclosure unless: the parties consent in writing; the communication or document is already in the public domain; disclosure is required by statute; or a court, using a balancing test which weighs the need for confidentiality in ADR proceedings, determines disclosure is necessary to prevent injustice, reveal a violation of law, or prevent harm to the public health or safety.

The section protects communications and documents in the possession of the parties to ADR proceedings unless: they agree to disclosure in writing; the communication or document is already in the public domain; disclosure is required by statute; a court, using a balance test which weighs the need for confidentiality in ADR proceedings, determines disclosure is necessary to prevent injustice, reveal a violation of law, or prevent harm to the public health or safety; or the communication or document is needed to establish, clarify, or enforce an agreement or award resulting from the ADR proceeding.

The section imposes a sanction for violating the Act's confidentiality requirements by disallowing the subsequent use in a related legal proceeding of the communication or document that was improperly disclosed.

The section allows the parties to agree to alternative confidentiality procedures if the neutral is informed of the agreement prior to the commencement of the ADR proceeding. If the parties reach agreement after the ADR proceeding has begun, their agreement can bind only themselves. Disclosure requests to the neutral will have to comply with the other provisions in the Act.

The section provides that, in the event a demand for disclosure, pursuant to legal process, is made upon a neutral, the neutral must make reasonable efforts to notify all parties and any affected nonparty participant. Any such person who receives such notice must, within 15 calendar days of receiving it, either defend the right of the neutral to refuse disclosure or waive any right to prevent the neutral from complying with the disclosure request.

The section explicitly preserves the discovery and admissibility of any information, communication or document which is otherwise discoverable under federal or other rules of evidence.

The section provides that the confidentiality procedures do not preclude the use of documents or communications from an ADR proceeding to prove the existence of an agreement, award or order issued pursuant to an ADR proceeding or to resolve an internal dispute between the neutral and the parties. The confidentiality procedures also do not preclude the gathering of non-specific data from ADR proceedings for research or educational purposes.

"Section 585. Authorization of Arbitration"

The rest of the new sections within Title 5, from Section 585 to 591, focus on arbitration. These sections are intended to be read in tandem with The Arbitration Act, which is codified in Title 9 of the United States Code and which provides the statutory framework for binding arbitration in the private sector and, in many respects, in ongoing federal arbitration programs.

A new Section 585 authorizes the use of arbitration whenever all parties consent in writing. It prohibits a federal agency from requiring any person to consent to arbitration as a condition of receiving a contract or benefit. This prohibition is intended to help ensure that the use of arbitration is truly voluntary on all sides.

"Section 586. Enforcement of Arbitration Agreements"

A new Section 586 provides that an agreement to arbitrate a matter is enforceable against the United States under Title 9, Section 4 of the United States Code (the Arbitration Act). The purpose of this provision is to coordinate and clarify the relationship between the subchapter and the existing Arbitration Act, and to stress that existing law applies to the enforcement of arbitration agreements reached pursuant to the subchapter.

"Section 587. Arbitrators"

A new Section 587 provides that the parties to an arbitration – which includes the United States and all other parties – are entitled to participate in the selection of the arbitrator. The particular procedure to be used is left to the discretion of the agencies and parties involved. The section requires the arbitrator to be a neutral who meets the requirements of Section 583.

"Section 588. Authority of the Arbitrator"

A new Section 588 enumerates the powers of arbitrators selected under the subchapter. It authorizes them to conduct hearings, administer oaths, and issue subpoenas for witnesses and evidence in order to resolve the disputes that have been referred to them. The section also explicitly authorizes arbitrators to issue decisions, called "awards," to resolve referred disputes.

This section is intended to provide arbitrators with the appropriate authority and flexibility to conduct arbitral proceedings in an informal and efficient manner and to keep the arbitral proceedings from becoming, in essence, full-blown litigation proceedings. An arbitrator should not use the authority granted in this section to indulge in or permit excessive discovery. Instead, the arbitrator should make appropriate use of the authority provided in this section to gather the necessary materials and information to conduct a fair, effective and expeditious inquiry.

The section also limits arbitrators to the subpoena authority granted by the Arbitration Act and to the agency sponsoring the arbitral proceeding. This language is intended to ensure that the same practices and body of law apply to all arbitrations of disputes with federal agencies, whether initiated under the ADR subchapter in Title 5 or the Arbitration Act in Title 9. It is also intended to ensure that federal agencies do not gain, as a consequence of this Act, any subpoena powers that they do not already possess.

"Section 589. Arbitration Proceedings"

A new Section 589 establishes basic rules for the conduct of arbitration proceedings, including a hearing. It authorizes the arbitrator to set the time and place for the hearing and notify the parties. It provides basic due process rights and declares that the hearing "shall be conducted expeditiously and in an informal manner." It requires the arbitrator to issue the award within 30 days of the close of the hearing, unless the relevant agency has a different rule or the parties reach agreement otherwise.

The section allows arbitrators to exclude evidence that is "irrelevant, immaterial, unduly repetitious, or privileged." This common standard for evidence in arbitral hearings is again designed to insure proceedings which are informal and expeditious.

The section authorizes a record of the proceeding to be kept where one or more parties agree to pay for the cost. It prohibits ex parte communications and allows the arbitrator to impose sanctions for violations of this rule.

"Section 590. Arbitration awards"

A new Section 590 provides standards for the issuance and finalization of arbitral awards. The section requires written awards, with a brief, informal discussion of the factual and legal basis for the decision made, unless an agency rule provides otherwise.

The section provides that awards become final 30 days after they are served on all parties unless an agency extends the 30-day period by serving notice before the end of the initial 30-day period. The section authorizes the head of an agency, at any time before an award becomes final, to terminate the arbitration proceeding or vacate the issued award by serving written notice on all other parties. This provision, which was added to resolve Constitutional concerns about an arbitrator's making decisions for the federal government, clearly places ultimate decision-making authority will the agency head.

The section prohibits any agency employee or agent who was an investigator or prosecutor in the matter from advising the agency head on a decision to terminate proceedings or vacate an award, except in a public setting. The purpose of this provision is to prevent a situation in which, for example, the agency counsel who presented the case to the arbitrator and lost, then meets with the agency head privately and argues for reversal of the arbitrator. The Act disallows such ex parte sessions, because the decision to terminate arbitration or vacate an arbitral award is a grave one and should be reached without showing favoritism to the agency's own personnel. Agency personnel are allowed, under the section, to participate in exchanges in which opponents can hear and respond to the arguments used. The section also allows the agency's investigators and prosecutors to testify or argue in such related public proceedings as a hearing on a motion to recover attorney fees.

Once an award becomes final, the section provides that it is binding and enforceable against the United States pursuant to the Arbitration Act. Arbitral awards which are vacated, on the other hand, are inadmissible in any related proceeding.

The section provides that, in the event an agency vacates an award or terminates an arbitration, any party to the arbitration other than the United States, may petition for attorney fees and expenses pursuant to the Equal Access to Justice Act (EAJA). This petition may be filed with a court or administrative law judge using the standards for recovery articulated in the EAJA. The section references the EAJA in order to make use of the complex body of law already developed under that statute and to ensure that persons using ADR procedures have the same rights as persons who engage in litigation.

The section also provides that, if ordered by a court or administrative law judge, payment for such attorney fees and expenses must be taken from the funds of the agency that vacated the arbitration award or terminated the arbitration proceedings. The purpose of this provision is twofold: (1) to reimburse parties who engaged in the arbitration process for their out-of-pocket expenses, and (2) to provide an incentive for agencies to abide by an arbitration by making them otherwise liable for the other parties' costs.

"Section 591. Judicial review"

A new Section 591 authorizes judicial review of arbitral awards pursuant to the Arbitration Act, except that it prohibits judicial review of any agency decision, under Section 590, to terminate an arbitral proceeding or vacate an arbitral award. The section also prohibits judicial review of an agency decision to use – or not to use – ADR proceedings (other than arbitration) to resolve a particular dispute. That decision is left to the discretion of the agency.

Section 592. Compilation of information"

A new section 592 authorizes the Administrative Conference of the United States to collect data on agency ADR proceedings and requires agencies to provide to ACUS requested data on their ADR proceedings.

"Section 593. Support services"

A new section 595 of Title 5 authorizes agencies to use the services of the agencies and private organizations and individuals for ADR proceedings, with or without compensation, and without regard to restrictions in Section 1342 of Title 31.

The final portion of Section 4 of the Act amends the table of contents in Title 5, to include the new subchapter and its sections.

Section 5. Judicial review of arbitration awards

Section 5 amends Section 10 of the Arbitration Act to provide a right of judicial review to nonparties affected by arbitration awards. A new subsection (b) provides that a person who was not party to an arbitration proceeding may obtain judicial review of the arbitral award, if that person was adversely affected and if agency use of arbitration was clearly inconsistent with the factors in Section 582 of Title 5, as established by this Act.

Section 6. Government contract claims

Section 6 amends the Contract Disputes Act of 1978 (CDA) to encourage contracting officers to resolve claims consensually through the use of ADR techniques.

The section amends the CDA by: (1) explicitly authorizing the use of ADR proceedings pursuant to the new subchapter in Title 5; (2) requiring the contractor to certify that a contract claim submitted for resolution using ADR techniques is made in good faith, with accurate supporting information and with an accurate request for a contract adjustment; and (3) authorizing judicial review of arbitral awards on CDA contract claims pursuant to the Arbitration Act and subject to any amount limitations in the CDA or other laws. The section imposes the same five-year sunset provision on the CDA amendments as apply to the rest of the Act.

Section 7. Federal Mediation and Conciliation Service

Section 7 authorizes the Federal Mediation and Conciliation Service (FMCS) to make its services available to Federal agencies using ADR proceedings under the new subchapter in Title 5. The section authorizes FMCS to provide such services as training, furnishing neutrals, and maintaining rosters of neutrals, including arbitrators.

Section 8. Government tort claims

Section 8 amends the Federal Tort Claims Act to authorize federal agencies to use ADR techniques, pursuant to the new subchapter in Title 5, to resolve tort claims against the United States. The section authorizes agencies to settle such claims to the same extent that the Attorney General has delegated settlement authority to the agency head. However, the section also imposes a ceiling on the agencies' settlement authority, indicating that it may not exceed the settlement authority delegated by the Attorney General to the U.S. Attorneys to settle claims for money damages against the United States.

Section 9. Use of nonattorneys

Section 9 requires each agency to consider whether to allow nonattorney representation in its ADR proceedings. It also requires agencies, if nonattorneys are permitted, to develop an agency policy on the disqualification of such nonattorney representatives when warranted.

Section 10. Definitions

Section 10 defines certain terms used in this Act including: "agency," "administrative program," and "alternative means of dispute resolution." The terms have the same meaning as they do in the new Section 581 of Title 5, as provided in this Act.

Section 11. Sunset provision

Section 11 imposes a five-year sunset (until October 1, 1995) on the Act.

V. ESTIMATED COST OF LEGISLATION

U.S. Congress,
Congressional Budget Office,
Washington, DC, October 17, 1990.

Hon. John Glenn,
Chairman, Committee on Governmental Affairs,
U.S. Senate, Washington, DC.

Dear Mr. Chairman: The Congressional Budget Office has prepared the attached cost estimate for S. 971, the Administrative Dispute Resolution Act.

If you wish further details on this estimate, we will be pleased to provide them.

Sincerely,
Robert D. Reischauer, Director.

CONGRESSIONAL BUDGET OFFICE–COST ESTIMATE

1. Bill number: S. 971.
2. Bill title: The Administrative Dispute Resolution Act.
3. Bill status: As ordered reported by the Senate Committee on Governmental Affairs, October 17, 1990.
4. Bill purpose: S. 971 would authorize and encourage federal agencies to use alternative methods of dispute resolution – such as mediation, conciliation, and

arbitration – instead of conventional adjudication to resolve disputes. The bill would require the Administrative Conference of the United States (ACUS) and the Federal Mediation and Conciliation Service (FMCS) to assist agencies in adopting these alternative methods.

5. Estimated cost to the Federal Government.

TABULAR OR GRAPHIC MATERIAL SET FORTH AT THIS POINT IS NOT DISPLAYABLE

The costs of this bill would be in budget function 750.

This table does not include possible budgetary savings from increased use of alternative methods of dispute resolution, which we cannot estimate. These alternative methods are generally less expensive than conventional proceedings, such as hearings before administrative law judges, because they take less time and usually result in less litigation.

Basis of estimate: Although S. 971 would not authorize the appropriation of any funds, CBO expects that the ACUS and the FMCS would require additional resources to implement the bill effectively. Based on information provided by the ACUS and the FMCS, we estimate that these agencies would incur additional costs of about $1 million annually for the two years after enactment of the bill; this amount is shown in the table above. These costs would be for securing the services of neutral facilitators, training programs, and other general support for agencies seeking to use alternative methods of dispute resolution. The estimate outlays are based on historical spending patterns and assume appropriations of the necessary amounts.

6. Estimated cost to State and local governments: None.
7. Estimate comparison: None.
8. Previous CBO estimate: On May 24, 1990, CBO prepared an estimate for H.R. 2497, the Administrative Dispute Resolution Act, as ordered reported by the House Committee on the Judiciary, May 22, 1990. The estimated costs of S. 971 are the same as for H.R. 2497.
9. Estimate prepared by: Michael Sieverts (226-2860) and Cory Leach (226-2820).
10. Estimate approved by: C.G. Nuckols for James L. Blum, Assistant Director for Budget Analysis.

VI. REGULATORY IMPACT STATEMENT

The purpose of S. 971 is to encourage federal agencies to use alternative dispute resolution (ADR) techniques. The only regulatory change required by the Act is amendment of the Federal Acquisition Regulation (FAR) to include standard language permitting use of ADR techniques, on a voluntary basis, to resolve disputes arising in connection with federal contracts, grants and other agreements. The Act also requires agencies to issue policies, but not necessarily regulations, regarding the use of ADR techniques and ADR case management. Finally, the bill requires the Administrative Conference of the United States to issue recommended professional standards for persons qualified to serve as neutrals in agency ADR proceedings. The Committee expects that some agencies will issue regulations to implement some of the provisions of the Act – for example, agency use of arbitration. Such regulations are not expected, however, to impose any burden on potential ADR participants, but rather would provide public informaton on how the agency's ADR procedures work.

VII. CHANGES IN EXISTING LAW

TITLE 5, UNITED STATES CODE
PART I-THE AGENCIES GENERALLY

CHAPTER 5-ADMINISTRATIVE PROCEDURE

SUBCHAPTER I-GENERAL PROVISIONS

Sec. 500. Administrative practice: general provisions.

SUBCHAPTER IV-ALTERNATIVE MEANS OF DISPUTE RESOLUTION IN THE ADMINISTRATIVE PROCESS

581. Definitions.
582. General authority.
583. Neutrals.
584. Confidentiality.
585. Authorization of arbitration.
586. Enforcement of arbitration agreements.
587. Arbitrators.
588. Authority of the arbitrator.
589. Arbitration proceedings.
590. Arbitration awards.
591. Judicial review.
592. Authorization to use services of employees of other agencies.
593. Qualifications and roster of neutrals: procurement.
594. Compilation of information.
595. Support services.

SUBCHAPTER II-ADMINISTRATIVE PROCEDURE

S. 556. Hearings; presiding employees; powers and duties; burden of proof; evidence; record as basis of decision

(a)

(c) Subject to published rules of the agency and within its powers, employees presiding at hearings may-

(1)

(6) hold conferences for the settlement or simplification of the issues by consent of the parties or by the use of alternative means of dispute resolution as provided in subchapter IV of this chapter;

(7) inform the parties as to the availability of one or more alternative means of dispute resolution, and encourage use of such methods;

(8) require the attendance at any conference held pursuant to paragraph (6) of at least one representative of each party who has authority to negotiate concerning resolution of issues in controversy;

[(7)] (9) dispose of procedural requests or similar matters;

[(8)] (10) make or recommend decisions in accordance with section 557 of this title; and

[(9)] (11) take other action authorized by agency rule consistent with this subchapter.

SUBCHAPTER IV-ALTERNATIVE MEANS OF DISPUTE RESOLUTION IN THE ADMINISTRATIVE PROCESS

S. 581. Definitions

For the purposes of this subchapter, the term-

(1) "agency" has the same meaning as in section 551(1) of this title;
(2) "administrative program" includes a Federal function which involves protection of the public interest and the determination of rights, privileges, and obligations of private persons through rule making, adjudication, licsening, or investigation, as those terms are used in subchapter II of this chapter;
(3) "alternative means of dispute resolution" means any procedure that is used, in lieu of an adjudication as defined in section 551(7) of this title, to resolve issues in controversy, including but not limited to, settlement negotiations, conciliation, facilitation, mediation, factfinding, minitrials, and arbitration, or any combination thereof;
(4) "award" means any decision by an arbitrator resolving the issues in controversy;
(5) "dispute resolution communication" means any oral or written communication made in confidence in connection with a dispute resolution proceeding by any party, neutral, or nonparty participant;
(6) "dispute resolution document" means any written material that is-
    (A) prepared for the purpose of, in the course of, or pursuant to a dispute resolution proceeding, including any memoranda, notes, or work product of the neutral or the parties; or
    (B) provided in confidence to the neutral or other parties in a dispute resolution proceeding for purposes of that dispute resolution proceeding;

    except that an agreement or arbitral award reached as a result of a dispute resolution proceeding is not a dispute resolution document unless the parties so agree in writing and the law otherwise allows that it shall be regarded as such a document;
(7) "dispute resolution proceeding" means any process in which an alternative means of dispute resolution is used to resolve an issue in controversy in which a neutral is appointed and specified parties participate;

(8) "in confidence" means, with respect to information, that the information is provided–
   (A) with the expressed intent of the source that it not be disclosed; or
   (B) under circumstances that would create the reasonable expectation on behalf of the source that the information will not be disclosed;
(9) "issue in controversy" means an issue which is material to a decision concerning an administrative program of an agency, and with which there is disagreement between the agency and persons who would be substantially affected by the decision;
(10) "neutral" means an individual who, with respect to an issue in controversy, functions specifically to aid the parties in resolving the controversy;
(11) "party" means–
   (A) for a proceeding with named parties, the same as in section 551(3) of this title; and
   (B) for a proceeding without named parties, a person who will be significantly affected by the decision in the proceeding and who participates in the proceeding;
(12) "person" has the same meaning as in section 551(2) of this title; and
(13) "roster" means a list of persons qualified to provide services as neutrals.

S 582. General authority

(a) An agency may use a dispute resolution proceeding for the resolution of an issue in controversy that relates to an administrative program, if the parties agree to such proceeding.
(b) An agency shall consider not using a dispute resolution proceeding if–
   (1) a definitive or authoritative resolution of the matter is required for precedential value, and such a proceeding is not likely to be accepted generally as an authoritative precedent;
   (2) the matter involves or may bear upon significant questions of Government policy that require additional procedures before a final resolution may be made, and such a proceeding would not likely serve to develop a recommended policy for the agency;
   (3) maintaining established policies is of special importance, so that variations among individual decisions are not increased and such a proceeding would not likely reach consistent results among individual decisions;
   (4) the matter significantly affects persons or organizations who are not parties to the proceeding;
   (5) a full public record of the proceeding is important, and a dispute resolution proceeding cannot provide such a record; and
   (6) the agency must maintain continuing jurisdiction over the matter with authority to alter the disposition of the matter in the light of changed circumstances, and a dispute resolution proceeding would interfere with the agency's fulfilling that requirement.
(c) Alternative means of dispute resolution authorized under this subchapter are voluntary procedures which supplement rather than limit other available agency dispute resolution techniques.

S 583. Neutrals

(a) A neutral may be a permanent or temporary officer or employee of the Federal Government or any other individual who is acceptable to the parties to a dispute resolution proceeding. A neutral shall have no official, financial, or personal conflict of interest with respect to the issues in controversy, unless such interest is fully disclosed in writing to all parties and all parties agree that the neutral may serve.

(b) A neutral who serves as a conciliator, facilitator, or mediator serves at the will of the parties.

(c) In consultation with the Federal Mediation and Conciliation Service, other appropriate Federal agencies, and professional organizations experienced in matters concerning dispute resolution, the Administrative Conference of the United States shall-

 (1) establish standards for neutrals (including experience, training, affiliations, diligence, actual or potential conflicts of interest, and other qualifications) to which agencies may refer;

 (2) maintain a roster of individuals who meet such standards and are otherwise qualified to act as neutrals, which shall be made available upon request;

 (3) enter into contracts for the services of neutrals that may be used by agencies on an elective basis in dispute resolution proceedings; and

 (4) develop procedures that permit agencies to obtain the services of neutrals on an expedited basis.

(d) An agency may use the services of one or more employees of other agencies to serve as neutrals in dispute resolution proceedings. The agencies may enter into an interagency agreement that provides for the reimbursement by the user agency or the parties of the full or partial cost of the services of such an employee.

(e) Any agency may enter into a contract with any person on a roster established under subsection (c)(2) or a roster maintained by other public or private organizations, or individuals for services as a neutral, or for training in connection with alternative means of dispute resolution. The parties in a dispute resolution proceeding shall agree on compensation for the neutral that is fair and reasonable to the Government.

S 584. Confidentiality

(a) Except as provided in subsections (d) and (e), a neutral in a dispute resolution proceeding shall not voluntarily or through discovery or compulsory process be required to disclose any information concerning any dispute resolution document or any dispute resolution communication, unless-

 (1) all parties to the dispute resolution proceeding and the neutral consent in writing, and, if the dispute resolution communication or dispute resolution document was provided by a nonparty participant, that participant also consents in writing;

 (2) the dispute resolution document has already been made public;

(3) the dispute resolution communication or dispute resolution document is required by statute to be made public, but a neutral should make such communication or document public only if no other person is reasonably available to provide the document or disclose the communication; or
(4) a court determines that such testimony or disclosure is necessary to–
(A) prevent a manifest injustice;
(B) help establish a violation of law; or
(C) prevent harm to the public health or safety, of sufficent magnitude in the particular case to outweigh the integrity of dispute resolution proceedings in general by reducing the confidence of parties in future cases that their communications will remain confidential.

(b) Except as provided in subsection (d), a party to a dispute resolution proceeding shall not voluntarily or through discovery or compulsory process be required to disclose any information concerning any dispute resolution document or any dispute resolution communication, unless–
(1) all parties to the dispute resolution proceeding consent in writing;
(2) the dispute resolution document has already been made public;
(3) the dispute resolution communication or dispute resolution document is required by statute to be made public;
(4) such testimony or disclosure is necessary to–
(A) prevent a manifest injustice;
(B) help establish a violation of law; or
(C) prevent harm to the public health and safety, of sufficient magnitude in the particular case to outweigh the integrity of dispute resolution proceedings in general by reducing the confidence of parties in future cases that their communications will remain confidential; or
(5) the dispute resolution document or dispute resolution communication is relevant to determining the existence or meaning of an agreement or award that resulted from the dispute resolution proceeding or to the enforcement of such an agreement or award.

(c) Any dispute resolution communication or dispute resolution document that is disclosed in violation of subsection (a) or (b), shall not be admissible in any proceeding relating to the issues in controversy with respect to which the communication or document was made.

(d) The parties may agree to alternative confidential procedures. Upon such agreement the parties shall inform the neutral before the commencement of the dispute resolution proceeding of any modifications to the provisions of subsection (a) that will govern the confidentiality of the dispute resolution proceeding. If the parties do not so inform the neutral, subsection (a) shall apply.

(e) If a demand for disclosure, by way of discovery request or other legal process, is made upon a neutral regarding a dispute resolution document or communication, the neutral shall make reasonable efforts to notify the parties and any affected nonparty participants of the demand. Any party or affected nonparty participant who receives such notice and within 15 calendar days does not offer to defend a refusal of the neutral to disclose the requested information shall have waived any objection to such disclosure.

(f) Nothing in this section shall prevent the discovery or admissibility of any evidence that is otherwise discoverable, merely because the evidence was presented in the course of a dispute resolution proceeding.
(g) Subsections (a) and (b) shall have no effect on the information and data that are necessary to document an agreement reached or order issued pursuant to a dispute resolution proceeding.
(h) Subsections (a) and (b) shall not prevent the gathering of information for research of educational purposes, in connection with other agencies, governmental entities, or dispute resolution programs, so long as the parties and the specific issues in controversy are not identifiable.
(i) Subsections (a) and (b) shall not prevent use of a dispute resolution document to resolve a dispute between the neutral in a dispute resolution proceeding and a party to or participant in such proceeding, so long as such dispute resolution document is disclosed only to the extent necessary to resolve such dispute.

S 585. AUTHORIZATION OF ARBITRATION

(a) (1) Arbitration may be used as an alternative means of dispute resolution whenever all parties consent. Consent may be obtained either before or after an issue in controversy has arisen. A party may agree to-
(A) submit only certain issues in controversy to arbitration; or
(B) arbitration on the condition that the award must be within a range of possible outcomes.
(2) Any arbitration agreement that sets forth the subject matter submitted to the arbitrator shall be in writing.
(3) An agency may not require any person to consent to arbitration as a condition of entering into a contract or obtaining a benefit.
(b) An officer or employee of an agency may offer to use arbitration for the resolution of issues in controversy, if such officer or employee-
(1) has authority to enter into a settlement concerning the matter; or
(2) is otherwise specifically authorized by the agency to consent to the use of arbitration.

S 586. ENFORCEMENT OF ARBITRATION AGREEMENTS

An agreement to arbitrate a matter to which this subchapter applies is enforceable pursuant to section 4 of title 9, and no action brought to enforce such an agreement shall be dismissed nor shall relief therein be denied on the grounds that it is against the United States or that the United States is an indispensable party.

S 587. ARBITRATORS

(a) The parties to an arbitration proceeding shall be entitled to participate in the selection of the arbitrator.
(b) The arbitrator shall be a neutral who meets the criteria of section 583 of this title.

S 588. AUTHORITY OF THE ARBITRATOR

An arbitrator to whom a dispute is referred under this subchapter may-

(1) regulate the course of and conduct arbitral hearings:
(2) administer oaths and affirmations;
(3) complete the attendance of witnesses and production of evidence at the hearing under the provisions of section 7 of title 9 only to the extent the agency involved is otherwise authorized by law to do so; and
(4) make awards.

S 589. Arbitration proceedings

(a) The arbitrator shall set a time and place for the hearing on the dispute and shall notify the parties not less than 5 days before the hearing.
(b) Any party wishing a record of the hearing shall-
  (1) be responsible for the preparation of such record;
  (2) notify the other parties and the arbitrator of the preparation of such record;
  (3) furnish copies to all identified parties and the arbitrator; and
  (4) pay all costs for such record, unless the parties agree otherwise or the arbitrator determines that the costs should be apportioned.
(c) (1) The parties to the arbitration are entitled to be heard, to present evidence material to the controversy, and to cross-examine witnesses appearing at the hearing.
  (2) The arbitrator may, with the consent of the parties, conduct all or part of the hearing by telephone, television, computer, or other electronic means, if each party has an opportunity to participate.
  (3) The hearing shall be conducted expeditiously and in an informal manner.
  (4) The arbitrator may receive any oral or documentary evidence, except that irrelevant, immaterial, unduly repetitious, or privileged evidence may be excluded by the arbitrator.
  (5) The arbitrator shall interpret and apply relevant statutory and regulatory requirements, legal precedents, and policy directives.
(d) No interested person shall make or knowingly cause to be made to the arbitrator an unauthorized ex parte communication relevant to the merits of the proceeding, unless the parties agree otherwise. If a communication is made in violation of this subsection, the arbitrator shall ensure that a memorandum of the communication is prepared and made a part of the record, and that an opportunity for rebuttal is allowed. Upon receipt of a communication made in violation of this subsection, the arbitrator may, to the extent consistent with the interests of justice and the policies underlying this subchapter, require the offending party to show cause why the claim of such party should not be resolved against such party as a result of the improper conduct.
(e) The arbitrator shall make the award within 30 days after the close of the hearing, or the date of the filing of any briefs authorized by the arbitrator, whichever date is later, unless-
  (1) the parties agree to some other time limit; or
  (2) the agency provides by rule for some other time limit.

S 590. Arbitration awards

(a) (1) Unless the agency provides otherwise by rule, the award in an arbitration proceeding under this subchapter shall include a brief, informal discussion of the factual and legal basis for the award, but formal findings of fact or conclusions of law shall not be required.

(2) The prevailing parties shall file the award with all relevant agencies, along with proof of service on all parties.

(b) The award in an arbitration proceeding shall become final 30 days after it is served on all parties. Any agency that is a party to the proceeding may extend this 30-day period for an additional 30-day period by serving a notice of such extension on all other parties before the end of the first 30-day period.

(c) The head of any agency that is a party to an arbitration proceeding conducted under this subchapter is authorized to terminate the arbitration proceeding or vacate any award issued pursuant to the proceeding before the award becomes final by serving on all other parties a written notice to that effect, in which case the award shall be null and void. Notice shall be provided to all parties to the arbitration proceeding of any request by a party, nonparty participant or other person that the agency head terminate the arbitration proceeding or vacate the award. An employee or agent engaged in the performance of investigative or prosecuting functions for an agency may not, in that or a factually related case, advise in a decision under this subsection to terminate an arbitration proceeding or to vacate an arbitral award, except as witness or counsel in public proceedings.

(d) A final award is binding on the parties to the arbitration proceeding, and may be enforced pursuant to sections 9 through 13 of title 9. No action brought to enforce such an award shall be dismissed nor shall relief therein be denied on the grounds that it is against the United States or that the United States is an indispensable party.

(e) An award entered under this subchapter in an arbitration proceeding may not serve as an estoppel in any other proceeding for any issue that was resolved in the proceeding. Such an award also may not be used as precedent or otherwise be considered in any factually unrelated proceeding, whether conducted under this subchapter, by an agency, or in a court, or in any other arbitration proceeding.

(f) An arbitral award that is vacated under subsection (c) shall not be admissible in any proceeding relating to the issues in controversy with respect to which the award was made.

(g) If an agency vacates an award under subsection (c), a party to the arbitration other than the United States may petition for an award of attorney fees and expenses pursuant to the Equal Access to Justice Act. Such fees and expenses shall be paid from the funds of the agency that vacated the award.

S 591. Judicial Review

(a) Notwithstanding any other provision of law, any person adversely affected or aggrieved by an award made in an arbitration proceeding conducted under this subchapter may bring an action for review of such award only pursuant to the provisions of sections 9 through 13 of title 9.

(b) (1) A decision by an agency to use or not to use a dispute resolution proceeding under this subchapter shall be committed to the discretion of the agency and shall not be subject to judicial review, except that arbitration shall be subject to judicial review under section 10(b) of title 9.

(2) A decision by the head of an agency under section 590 to terminate an arbitration proceeding or vacate an arbitral award shall be committed to the discretion of the agency and shall not be subject to judicial review.

S 592. Compilation of information

"The Chairman of the Administrative Conference of the United States shall compile and maintain data on the use of alternative means of dispute resolution in conducting agency proceedings. Agencies shall, upon the request of the Chairman of the Administrative Conference of the United States, supply such information as is required to enable the Chairman to comply with this section.

S 593. Support services

For the purposes of this subchapter, an agency may use (with or without reimbursement) the services and facilities of other Federal agencies, public and private organizations and agencies, and individuals, with the consent of such agencies, organizations, and individuals. An agency may accept voluntary and uncompensated services for purposes of this subchapter without regard to the provisions of section 1342 of title 31.

SECTION 10 of Title 9, United States Code

S 10. Same: vacation; grounds; rehearing

[In either] (a) In any of the following cases the United States court in and for the district wherein the award was made may make an order vacating the award upon the application of any party to the arbitration–

[(a)] (1) Where the award was procured by corruption, fraud, or undue means.

[(b)] (2) Where there was evident partiality or corruption in the arbitrators, or either of them.

[(c)] (3) Where the arbitrators were guilty of misconduct in refusing to postpone the hearing, upon sufficient cause shown, or in refusing to hear evidence pertinent and material to the controversy; or of any other misbehavior by which the rights of any party have been prejudiced.

[(d)] (4) Where the arbitrators exceeded their powers, or so imperfectly executed them that a mutual, final, and definite award upon the subject matter submitted was not made.

[(e)] (5) Where an award is vacated and the time within which the agreement required the award to be made has not expired the court may, in its discretion, direct a rehearing by the arbitrators.

(b) The United States district court for the district wherein an award was made that was issued pursuant to section 590 of title 5 may make an order vacating the award upon the application of a person, other than a party to the arbitration, who is adversely affected or aggrieved by the award, if the use of arbitration or the award is clearly inconsistent with the factors set forth in section 582 of title 5.

THE CONTRACT DISPUTES ACT OF 1978

DECISION BY THE CONTRACTING OFFICER

Sec. 6.

(a)

(d) Notwithstanding any other provision of this Act, a contractor and a contracting officer may use any alternative means of dispute resolution under subchapter IV of chapter 5 of title 5, United States Code, or other mutually agreeable procedures, for resolving claims. In a case in which such alternative means of dispute resolution or other mutually agreeable procedures are used, the contractor shall certify that the claim is made in good faith, that the supporting data are accurate and complete to the best of his or her knowledge and belief, and that the amount requested accurately reflects the contract adjustment for which the contractor believes the Government is liable. All provisions of subchapter IV of chapter 5 of title 5, United States Code, shall apply to such alternative means of dispute resolution.

(e) The authority of agencies to use dispute resolution proceedings under section (d) shall cease to be effective on October 1, 1995, except that such authority shall continue in effect with respect to then pending proceedings which, in the judgment of the agencies that are parties to such proceedings, require such continuation, until such proceedings terminate.

AGENCY BOARDS OF CONTRACT APPEALS

Sec. 8.

(a)

(g)(1)

(3) An award by an arbitrator under this Act shall be reviewed pursuant to sections 9 through 13 of title 9, United States Code, except that the court may set aside or limit any award that is found to violate limitations imposed by Federal statute.

Section 203 of the Labor Management Relations Act, 1947

FUNCTIONS OF THE SERVICE

Sec. 203. (a)

(f) The Service may make its services available to Federal agencies to aid in the resolution of disputes under the provisions of subchapter IV of chapter 5 of title 5, United States Code. Functions performed by the Service may include assisting parties to disputes relating to administrative programs, training persons in skills and procedures employed in alternative means of dispute resolution, and furnishing officers and employees of the Service to act as neutrals. Only officers and employees who are qualified in accordance with section 583 of title 5, United States Code, may be assigned to act as neutrals. The Service may consult and cooperate with the Administrative Conference of the United States and other agencies in maintaining rosters of neutrals and arbitrators, and to adopt such procedures and rules as are necessary to carry out the services authorized in this subsection.

Section 2672 of Title 28, United States Code

S 2672. Administrative adjustment of claims

The head of each Federal agency or his designee, in accordance with regulations prescribed by the Attorney General, may consider, ascertain, adjust, determine, compromise, and settle any claim for money damages against the United States for injury or loss of property or personal injury or death caused by the negligent or wrongful act or omission of any employee of the agency while acting within the scope of his office or employment, under circumstances where the United States, if a private person, would be liable to the claimant in accordance with the law of the place where the act or omission occurred: Provided, that any award, compromise, or settlement in excess of $25,000 shall be effected only with the prior written approval of the Attorney General or his designee. Notwithstanding the proviso contained in the preceding sentence, any award, compromise, or settlement may be effected without the prior written approval of the Attorney General or his or her designee, to the extent that the Attorney General delegates to the head of the agency the authority to make such award, compromise, or settlement. Such delegations may not exceed the authority delegated by the Attorney General to the United States attorneys to settle claims for money damages against the United States. Each Federal agency may use arbitration, or other alternative means of dispute resolution under the provisions of subchapter IV of chapter 5 of title 5, to settle any tort claim against the United States, to the extent of the agency's authority to award, compromise, or settle such claim without the prior written approval of the Attorney General or his or her designee.

Subject to the provisions of this title relating to civil actions on tort claims against the United States, any such award, compromise, settlement, or determination shall be final and conclusive on all offices of the Government, except when procured by means of fraud.

Any award, compromise, or settlement in an amount of $2,500 or less made pursuant to this section shall be paid by the head of the Federal agency concerned out of appropriations available to that agency. Payment of any award, compromise, or settlement in an amount in excess of $2,500 made pursuant to this section or made by the Attorney General in any amount pursuant to section 2677 of this title shall be paid in a manner similar to judgments and compromises in like causes and appropriations or funds available for the payment of such judgments and compromises are hereby made available for the payment of awards, compromises, or settlements under this chapter.

The acceptance by the claimant of any such award, compromise, or settlement shall be final and conclusive on the claimant, and shall constitute a complete release of any claim against the United States and against the employee of the government whose act or omission gave rise to the claim, by reason of the same subject matter.

PROVIDING FOR CONSIDERATION OF H.R. 3425 HOUSE REPORT NO. 103-372

November 17, 1993
[To accompany H. Res. 312]

The Committee on Rules, having had under consideration House Resolution 312 by record vote of 5 to 2 report the same to the House with the recommendation that the resolution do pass.

The following are the amendments made in order under House Resolution 312.

1. The Amendment To Be Offered by Representative Traficant of Ohio or His Designee, Debatable for Not To Exceed 10 Minutes

At the end of title I, add the following:

SEC.. SENSE OF THE CONGRESS REGARDING COMPLIANCE WITH BUY AMERICAN ACT.

It is the sense of the Congress that the Secretary should comply with title III of the Act of March 3, 1933 (41 U.S.C. 10a et seq.; popularly known as the "Buy American Act").

2. The Amendment To Be Offered by Representative Pryce of Ohio or Her Designee, Debatable for Not To Exceed 10 Minutes

In section 106(c), strike "periodically" and insert "at least annually".
In section 106(c), strike "2 years" and insert "1 year".

3. The Amendment To Be Offered by Representative Delay of Texas or His Designee, Debatable for Not To Exceed 10 Minutes

In section 105, insert "(a) In General.-" before "The Office".

At the end of section 105 add the following:

(b) Task Force.-The Inspector General of the Department may enter into an interdepartmental investigatory task force with the Department of Justice to identify waste, fraud, and criminal misconduct within the Department of Environmental Protection.

4. The Amendment To Be Offered by Representative Thomas of Wyoming or His Designee, Debatable for Not To Exceed 10 Minutes

At the end of title I, add the following (and amend the table of contents accordingly):

SEC.. SMALL BUSINESS COMPLIANCE TECHNICAL ASSISTANCE.

The Secretary shall establish within the Department a Small Business Ombudsman Office. The Office shall be headed by a Director designated by the Secretary, who shall report directly to the Secretary. The Secretary, acting through the Director, shall provide technical assistance to small business concerns (as that term is defined in section 3 of the Small Business Act), including family farms, in complying with laws administered by the Department.

SEC.. SMALL GOVERNMENTAL JURISDICTION COMPLIANCE ASSISTANCE.

The Secretary shall establish within the Department a Small Governmental Jurisdiction Ombudsman Office. The Office shall be headed by a Director designated by the Secretary, who shall report directly to the Secretary. The Secretary, acting through the Director, shall provide technical assistance to small governmental jurisdictions (as that term is defined in section 601(5) of title 5, United States Code) in complying with laws administered by the Department.

5. The Amendment To Be Offered by Representative DeLay of Texas or His Designee, Debatable for Not To Exceed 10 Minutes

In section 102(a), in the matter preceding paragraph (1), strike "10" and insert "7".

6. The Amendment To Be Offered by Representative DeLay of Texas or His Designee, Debatable for Not To Exceed 10 Minutes

In section 103(a), strike "20" and insert "14".

7. The Amendment To Be Offered by Representative DeLay of Texas or His Designee, Debatable for Not To Exceed 10 Minutes

In section 106(a)(1), strike "10" and insert "8".

8. The Amendment To Be Offered by Representative Clinger of Pennsylvania or His Designee, Debatable for Not To Exceed 20 Minutes

At the end of section 102 add the following:

(d) Assistant Secretary Assigned Functions for Intergovernmental Affairs.-

(1) In general.-The Assistant Secretary of the Department who is assigned functions for intergovernmental affairs pursuant to subsection (b)(1)(W) shall develop and, with the approval of the Secretary, implement a strategy to promote, to the greatest extent practicable and consistent with laws applicable to the Department (including regulations under those laws), easing of unfunded environmental mandates imposed on State and local governments.

(2) Report.-Not later than 1 year after the date of the enactment of this Act, the Secretary shall submit a report to the Congress on the implementation of the strategy developed under paragraph (1), including recommendations for easing burdens referred to in paragraph (1).

9. The Amendment in the Nature of a Substitute To Be Offered by Representative Clinger of Pennsylvania or His Designee, Debatable for Not To Exceed 30 Minutes

Strike all after the enacting clause and insert the following:

SECTION 1. SHORT TITLE.

This Act may be cited as the "Department of Environmental Protection Act".

TITLE I-REDESIGNATION OF ENVIRONMENTAL PROTECTION AGENCY AS DEPARTMENT OF ENVIRONMENTAL PROTECTION

SEC. 101. REDESIGNATION OF ENVIRONMENTAL PROTECTION AGENCY AS DEPARTMENT OF ENVIRONMENTAL PROTECTION.

(a) Redesignation.-The Environmental Protection Agency is redesignated as the Department of Environmental Protection (hereinafter in this Act referred to as the "Department"), and shall be an executive department in the executive branch of the Government. The Department shall be headquartered at the seat of Government. The official acronym of the Department shall be "D.E.P.".

(b) Secretary of the Environment.-(1) There shall be at the head of the Department a Secretary of Environmental Protection (hereinafter in this Act referred to as the "Secretary") who shall be appointed by the President, by and with the advice and consent of the Senate.

    (2) Office of the Secretary.-The Office of the Secretary shall consist of the Secretary and the Deputy Secretary appointed under subsection (d), and may include an Executive Secretary.

(c) Transfer.-The functions, powers, and duties of the Administrator, other officers and employees of the Environmental Protection Agency, and the various offices and agencies of the Environmental Protection Agency are transferred to and vested in the Secretary.

(d) Deputy Secretary.-There shall be in the Department a Deputy Secretary of Environmental Protection, who shall be appointed by the President, by and with the advice and consent of the Senate. The Deputy Secretary shall perform such functions as the Secretary shall prescribe, and shall act as the Secretary during the absence or disability of the Secretary or in the event of a vacancy in the Office of the Secretary.

(e) Delegation of Authority.-Except as provided in this Act and other existing laws, the Secretary may delegate any functions, including the making of regulations, to such officers and employees of the Department as the Secretary may designate, and may authorize such successive redelegations of such functions within the Department as the Secretary considers to be necessary or appropriate.

SEC. 102. ASSISTANT SECRETARIES.

(a) Establishment of Positions.-There shall be in the Department such number of Assistant Secretaries, not to exceed 10, as the Secretary shall determine, each of whom-

    (1) shall be appointed by the President, by and with the advice and consent of the Senate; and

    (2) shall perform such functions as the Secretary shall prescribe.

(b) Functions.-The Secretary shall assign to each Assistant Secretary of the Department such functions as the Secretary considers appropriate.

(c) Designation of Functions Prior to Confirmation.-Whenever the President submits the name of an individual to the Senate for confirmation as an Assistant Secretary under this section, the President shall state the particular functions of the Department (as assigned by the Secretary under subsection (b)) such individual will exercise upon taking office.

SEC. 103. DEPUTY ASSISTANT SECRETARIES.

(a) Establishment of Positions.-There shall be in the Department 20 Deputy Assistant Secretaries, or such number as the Secretary determines is appropriate.
(b) Appointments.-Each Deputy Assistant Secretary-
   (1) shall be appointed by the Secretary; and
   (2) shall perform such functions as the Secretary shall prescribe.
(c) Career Senior Executive Service.-At least one-half of positions established under subsection (a) and filled by subsection (b) shall be in the career Senior Executive Service.
(d) Functions.-Functions assigned to an Assistant Secretary under section 102(b) may be performed by one or more Deputy Assistant Secretaries appointed to assist such Assistant Secretary.

SEC. 104. OFFICE OF THE GENERAL COUNSEL.

(a) General Counsel.-There shall be in the Department the Office of the General Counsel. There shall be at the head of such office a General Counsel who shall be appointed by the President, by and with the advice and consent of the Senate. The General Counsel shall be the chief legal officer of the Department and shall provide legal assistance to the Secretary concerning the programs and policies of the Department.
(b) Deputy General Counsel.-There shall be in the Office of the General Counsel at least one Deputy General Counsel, who-
   (1) shall be appointed by the General Counsel; and
   (2) shall perform such functions as the Secretary shall prescribe.

SEC. 105. OFFICE OF INSPECTOR GENERAL.

The Office of Inspector General of the Environmental Protection Agency, established in accordance with the Inspector General Act of 1978 (5 U.S.C. App.), is redesignated as the Office of Inspector General of the Department of Environmental Protection.

SEC. 106. REGIONAL ADMINISTRATORS.

There shall be in the Department not more than 11 regional administrators, each of whom shall be appointed by the Secretary. Political affiliation or political qualification may not be the primary factor taken into account in connection with the appointment of any person to a position as a regional administrator of the Department. Each regional administrator shall-

(1) perform in accordance with applicable law such of the functions transferred or delegated to or vested in the Secretary as the Secretary shall prescribe in accordance with the provisions of this Act and other applicable law; and
(2) implement program policies and priorities as established by the Secretary, Assistant Secretaries, and Deputy Secretaries.

SEC. 107. CONTINUING PERFORMANCE OF FUNCTIONS.

(a) Redesignation of Positions.-(1) The Administrator of the Environmental Protection Agency is redesignated as the Secretary of the Department of Environmental Protection.
  (2) The Deputy Administrator of such agency is redesignated as the Deputy Secretary of the Department of Environmental Protection.
  (3) Each Assistant Administrator of such agency is redesignated as an Assistant Secretary of the Department.
  (4) The General Counsel of such agency is redesignated as the General Counsel of the Department.
  (5) The Inspector General of such agency is redesignated as the Inspector General of the Department.
(b) Not Subject to Renomination or Reconfirmation.-An individual serving at the pleasure of the President in a position that is redesignated by subsection (a) may continue to serve in and perform functions of that position after the date of the enactment of this Act without renomination by the President or reconfirmation by the Senate.

SEC. 108. REFERENCES.

Reference in any other Federal law, Executive order, rule, regulation, reorganization plan, or delegation of authority, or in any document-

(1) to the Environmental Protection Agency is deemed to refer to the Department of Environmental Protection;
(2) to the Administrator of the Environmental Protection Agency is deemed to refer to the Secretary of Environmental Protection;
(3) to the Deputy Administrator of the Environmental Protection Agency is deemed to refer to the Deputy Secretary of Environmental Protection; and
(4) to an Assistant Administrator of the Environmental Protection Agency is deemed to refer to the corresponding Assistant Secretary of the Department of Environmental Protection who is assigned the functions of that Assistant Administrator.

SEC. 109. SAVINGS PROVISIONS.

(a) Continuing Effect of Legal Documents.-All orders, determinations, rules, regulations, permits, grants, contracts, certificates, licenses, privileges, and other administrative actions-
  (1) which have been issued, made, granted or allowed to become effective by the President, the Administrator or other authorized official of the Environmental Protection Agency, or by a court of competent jurisdiction, which relate to functions of the Administrator or any other officer or agent of the Environmental Protection Agency actions; and
  (2) which are in effect at the time this Act takes effect;

  shall continue in effect according to their terms until modified, terminated, superseded, set aside, or revoked in accordance with law by the President, the Secretary, or other authorized official, by a court of competent jurisdiction, or by operation of law.

(b) Proceedings Not Affected.-This Act shall not affect any proceeding, proposed rule, or application for any license, permit, certificate, or financial assistance pending before the Environmental Protection Agency at the time this Act takes effect, and such proceedings and applications shall be continued. Orders shall be issued in such proceedings, appeals shall be taken therefrom, and payments shall be made pursuant to such orders, as if this Act had not been enacted, and orders issued in any such proceedings shall continue in effect until modified, terminated, superseded, or revoked by a duly authorized official, by a court of competent jurisdiction, or by operation of law. Nothing in this subsection prohibits the discontinuance or modification of any such proceeding under the same terms and conditions and to the same extent that such proceeding could have been discontinued or modified if this Act had not been enacted.

(c) Suits Not Affected.-This Act shall not affect suits commenced before the effective date of this Act, and in all such suits proceedings shall be had, appeals taken, and judgments rendered in the same manner and with the same effect as if this Act had not been enacted.

(d) Nonabatement of Actions.-No suit, action, or other proceeding commenced by or against the Environmental Protection Agency, or by or against any individual in the official capacity of such individual as an officer of the Environmental Protection Agency, shall be abated by reason of the enactment of this Act.

(e) Property and Resources.-The contracts, liabilities, records, property, and other assets and interests of the Environmental Protection Agency shall, after the effective date of this Act, be considered to be contracts, liabilities, records, property, and other assets and interests of the Department.

SEC. 110. CONFORMING AMENDMENTS.

(a) Presidential Succession.-Section 19(d)(1) of title 3, United States Code, is amended by inserting before the period at the end thereof the following: ", Secretary of Environmental Protection."

(b) Definition of Department in Civil Service Laws.-Section 101 of title 5, United States Code, is amended by adding at the end thereof the following:

"The Department of Environmental Protection."

(c) Compensation, Level I.-Section 5312 of title 5, United States Code, is amended by adding at the end thereof the following:

"Secretary of Environmental Protection."

(d) Compensation, Level II.-Section 5313 of title 5, United States Code, is amended by striking "Administrator of Environmental Protection Agency" and inserting in lieu thereof "Deputy Secretary of Environmental Protection."

(e) Compensation, Level IV.-Section 5315 of title 5, United States Code, is amended-

(1) by striking "Inspector General, Environmental Protection Agency" and inserting in lieu thereof "Inspector General, Department of Environmental Protection";

(2) by striking each reference to an Assistant Administrator, or Assistant Administrators, of the Environmental Protection Agency; and

(3) by adding at the end thereof the following:

"Assistant Secretaries, Department of Environmental Protection.

"General Counsel, Department of Environmental Protection."

(f) Inspector General Act.-The Inspector General Act of 1978 is amended-
  (1) in section 11(1)-
    (A) by inserting "Environmental Protection," after "Energy,"; and
    (B) by striking "Environmental Protection,"; and
  (2) in section 11(2)-
    (A) by inserting "Environmental Protection," after "Energy,"; and
    (B) by striking "the Environmental Protection Agency,".

SEC. 111. ADDITIONAL CONFORMING AMENDMENTS.

After consultation with the Committee on Government Operations of the House of Representatives, the Committee on Governmental Affairs of the Senate, and other appropriate committees of the Congress, the Secretary shall prepare and submit to the Congress proposed legislation containing technical and conforming amendments to the laws of the United States, to reflect the changes made by this Act. Such proposed legislation shall be submitted not later than 1 year after the effective date of this Act.

TITLE II-ADMINISTRATIVE PROVISIONS

SEC. 201. ACQUISITION OF COPYRIGHTS AND PATENTS.

The Secretary may acquire any of the following rights if the property acquired thereby is for use by or for, or useful to, the Department:

(1) Copyrights, patents, and applications for patents, designs, processes, and manufacturing data.
(2) Licenses under copyrights, patents, and applications for patents.
(3) Releases, before suit is brought, for past infringement of patents or copyrights.

SEC. 202. GIFTS AND BEQUESTS.

The Secretary may accept, hold, administer, and utilize gifts, bequests, and devices of real or personal property for the purpose of aiding or facilitating the work of the Department. Gifts, bequests, and devises of money and proceeds from sales of other property received as gifts, bequests, or devises shall be deposited in the Treasury and shall be available for disbursement upon the order of the Secretary.

SEC. 203. OFFICIAL SEAL OF DEPARTMENT.

On and after the effective date of this Act, the seal of the Environmental Protection Agency, with appropriate changes, shall be the official seal of the Department, until such time as the Secretary may cause an official seal to be made for the Department of such design as the Secretary shall approve.

SEC. 204. USE OF LIKENESS OF OFFICIAL SEAL OF DEPARTMENT.

(a) Display of Seal.-Whoever knowingly displays any printed or other likeness of the official seal of the Department, or any facsimile thereof, in or in connection with, any advertisement, poster, circular, book, pamphlet, or other publication, public meeting, play, motion picture, telecast, or other production, or on any building, monument, or stationery, for the purpose of conveying, or in a manner reasonably calculated to convey, a false impression of sponsorship or approval by the Government of the United States or by any department, agency, or instrumentality thereof, shall be fined not more than $250 or imprisoned not more than 6 months, or both.

(b) Manufacture, Reproduction, Sale, or Purchases for Resale.-Except as authorized under regulations promulgated by the Secretary and published in the Federal Register, whoever knowingly manufactures, reproduces, sells, or purchases for resale, either separately or appended to any article manufactured or sold, any likeness of the official seal of the Department or any substantial part thereof (except for manufacture or sale of the article for the official use of the Government of the United States), shall be fined not more than $250 or imprisoned not more than 6 months, or both.

(c) Injunctions.-A violation of subsection (a) or (b) may be enjoined by an action brought by the Attorney General in the appropriate district court of the United States. The Attorney General shall file such an action upon request of the Secretary or any authorized representative of the Secretary.

SEC. 205. USE OF STATIONERY, PRINTED FORMS, AND SUPPLIES OF ENVIRONMENTAL PROTECTION AGENCY.

The Secretary shall ensure that, to the extent practicable, existing stationery, printed forms, and other supplies of the Environmental Protection Agency are used to carry out functions of the Department before procuring new stationery, printed forms, and other supplies for the Department.

138 P.L. 107-169, 1 ARBITRATION-TECHNICAL AMENDMENTS

DATES OF CONSIDERATION AND PASSAGE

House: March 14, 2001
Senate: April 18, 2002
Cong. Record Vol. 148 (2002)

House Report (Judiciary Committee)
No. 107-16, March 12, 2001
[To accompany H.R. 861]

HOUSE REPORT NO. 107-16
March 12, 2001
Mr. Sensenbrenner, from the Committee on the Judiciary,
submitted the following
REPORT

The Committee on the Judiciary, to whom was referred the bill (H.R. 861) to make technical amendments to section 10 of title 9, United States Code, having considered the same, report favorably thereon without amendment and recommend that the bill do pass.

PURPOSE AND SUMMARY

H.R. 861 makes technical corrections to subsection 10(a) of title 9 of the United States Code.

BACKGROUND AND NEED FOR THE LEGISLATION

On March 6, 2001, Representative George Gekas (R-Pa.) introduced H.R. 861 for the purpose of making certain technical amendments to subsection 10(a) of title 9 of the United States Code.

Title 9 of the United States Code pertains to domestic and international arbitration law. Chapter 1 of title 9 contains the title's general provisions, including section 10. Subsection 10(a) enumerates the grounds for which a Federal district court may vacate an arbitration award. It also authorizes the court to order a rehearing, under certain circumstances.

As drafted, subsection 10(a) consists of five paragraphs, four of which enumerate the grounds for vacating an arbitration award. The fifth paragraph, however, is clearly intended to be a separate provision of subsection 10(a) as it specifies the basis of the court's authority to direct a rehearing by the arbitrator.

H.R. 861 simply corrects this drafting error, which has existed from the legislation's original enactment in 1925. The bill simply converts the fifth paragraph into a separate subsection of section 10, namely, subsection 10(b), and makes conforming grammatical and technical revisions to section 10.

H.R. 861 is identical to H.R. 916, which was introduced by Representative George W. Gekas on March 2, 1999. After the Committee reported H.R. 916 on June 10, 1999, the House passed the bill under suspension of the rules by voice vote on July 13, 1999 with an unrelated amendment. The Senate did not act upon the House measure. H.R. 2440, legislation identical to H.R. 861, was passed by the House in the 105th Congress. On the last day of the 105th Congress, the Senate passed H.R. 2440 with an unrelated amendment by unanimous consent. The House did not act on the Senate-passed measure.

HEARINGS

No hearings were held on H.R. 861.

COMMITTEE CONSIDERATION

On March 8, 2001, the Committee met in open session and ordered favorably reported the bill H.R. 861 without amendment by voice vote, a quorum being present.

COMMITTEE OVERSIGHT FINDINGS

In compliance with clause 3(c)(1) of rule XIII of the Rules of the House of Representatives, the Committee reports that the findings and recommendations of the Committee, based on oversight activities under clause 2(b)(1) of rule X of the

Rules of the House of Representatives, are incorporated in the descriptive portions of this report.

PERFORMANCE GOALS AND OBJECTIVES

H.R. 861 does not authorize funding. Therefore, clause 3(c) of rule XIII of the Rules of the House is inapplicable.

NEW BUDGET AUTHORITY AND TAX EXPENDITURES

Clause 3(c)(2) of rule XIII of the Rules of the House is inapplicable because this legislation does not provide new budgetary authority or increased tax expenditures.

CONGRESSIONAL BUDGET OFFICE COST ESTIMATE

In compliance with clause 3(c)(3) of rule XIII of the Rules of the House, the Committee sets forth, with respect to the bill, H.R. 861, the following estimate and comparison prepared by the Director of the Congressional Budget Office under section 402 of the Congressional Budget Act of 1974:

U.S. Congress,
Congressional Budget Office,
Washington, DC, March 9, 2001.

Hon. F. James Sensenbrenner Jr., Chairman
Committee on the Judiciary,
U.S. House of Representatives, Washington, DC.

Dear Mr. Chairman: The Congressional Budget Office has prepared the enclosed cost estimate for H.R. 861, a bill to make technical amendments to section 10 of title 9, United States Code.

If you wish further details on this estimate, we will be pleased to provide them. The CBO staff contact is Lanette J. Walker, who can be reached at 226-2860.

Sincerely,
Dan L. Crippen, Director.
Enclosure.

H.R. 861-A bill to make technical amendments to section 10 of title 9, United States Code.

CBO estimates that enacting H.R. 861 would not have any impact on the federal budget. Because enactment of the bill would not affect direct spending or receipts, pay-as-you-go procedures would not apply. H.R. 861 contains no intergovernmental or private-sector mandates as defined in the Unfunded Mandates Reform Act and would not affect the budgets of state, local, and tribal governments.

H.R. 861 would correct punctuation errors and make other minor wording changes to section 10 of title 9, United States Code, which specifies the grounds under which a federal judge can vacate an arbitrator's award. Because these changes are technical and would make no substantive changes to the laws affecting arbitration, CBO estimates that enacting H.R. 861 would not have any budgetary impact.

The CBO staff contact for this estimate is Lanette J. Walker, who can be reached at 226-2860. This estimate was approved by Robert A. Sunshine, Assistant Director for Budget Analysis.

CONSTITUTIONAL AUTHORITY STATEMENT

Pursuant to clause 3(d)(1) of rule XIII of the Rules of the House, the Committee finds the authority for this legislation in Article I, section 8, of the Constitution.

SECTION-BY-SECTION ANALYSIS AND DISCUSSION

SECTION 1.

Vacation of Awards. Section 1 of the bill redesignates paragraph (5) of subsection 10(a) as subsection 10(b) and replaces the word "Where" with "If" in that provision. It also makes a conforming change by redesignating subsection (b) of section 10 as subsection (c). In addition, section 1 adjusts the indentation margins for paragraphs (1) through (4) of subsection (a); corrects punctuation and capitalization errors; and makes other minor conforming corrections.

CHANGES IN EXISTING LAW MADE BY THE BILL, AS REPORTED

In compliance with clause 3(e) of rule XIII of the Rules of the House of Representatives, changes in existing law made by the bill, as reported, are shown as follows (existing law proposed to be omitted is enclosed in black brackets, new matter is printed in italic, existing law in which no change is proposed is shown in roman):

SECTION 10 OF TITLE 9, UNITED STATES CODE

S 10. Same; vacation; grounds; rehearing

(a) In any of the following cases the United States court in and for the district wherein the award was made may make an order vacating the award upon the application of any party to the arbitration-
  (1) [Where] the award was procured by corruption, fraud, or undue means[.];
  (2) [Where] there was evident partiality or corruption in the arbitrators, or either of them[.];
  (3) [Where] the arbitrators were guilty of misconduct in refusing to postpone the hearing, upon sufficient cause shown, or in refusing to hear evidence pertinent and material to the controversy; or of any other misbehavior by which the rights of any party have been prejudiced[.]; or
  (4) [Where] the arbitrators exceeded their powers, or so imperfectly executed them that a mutual, final, and definite award upon the subject matter submitted was not made.
  (5) [Where] (b) If an award is vacated and the time within which the agreement required the award to be made has not expired, the court may, in its discretion, direct a rehearing by the arbitrators.

[(b)] (c) The United States district court for the district wherein an award was made that was issued pursuant to section 580 of title 5 may make an order vacating the award upon the application of a person, other than a party to the arbitration, who is adversely affected or aggrieved by the award, if the use of arbitration or the award is clearly inconsistent with the factors set forth in section 572 of title 5.

BUSINESS MEETING

The committee met, pursuant to notice, at 10 a.m., in Room 2141, Rayburn House Office Building, Hon. F. James Sensenbrenner (chairman of the committee) presiding.

Pursuant to Notice, I call up the bill H.R. 861, a bill making technical corrections to Section 10 of Title 9 of the United States Code for purposes of markup, and move its favorable recommendation to the House.

Index